TARGET
TOKYO

★

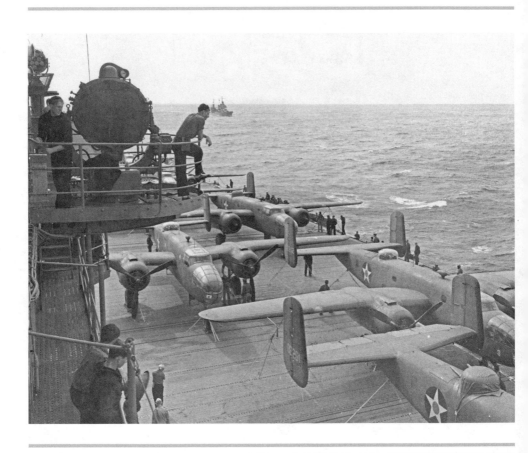

TARGET TOKYO

Jimmy Doolittle and the Raid That Avenged Pearl Harbor

JAMES M. SCOTT

W. W. NORTON & COMPANY

New York • London

For information about permission to reproduce selections from this book, write to
Permissions, W. W. Norton & Company, Inc., 500 Fifth Avenue, New York, NY 10110

For information about special discounts for bulk purchases, please contact
W. W. Norton Special Sales at specialsales@wwnorton.com or 800-233-4830

Manufacturing by Quad Graphics Fairfield
Book design by Ellen Cipriano Design
Production manager: Julia Druskin

Library of Congress Cataloging-in-Publication Data

Scott, James (James M.)
Target Tokyo : Jimmy Doolittle and the raid that avenged
Pearl Harbor / James M. Scott.
— First edition.
pages cm
Includes bibliographical references and index.
ISBN 978-0-393-08962-2 (hardcover)
1. Tokyo (Japan)—History—Bombardment, 1942. 2. Doolittle,
James Harold, 1896–1993.
3. World War, 1939–1945—Aerial operations, American. I. Title.
D767.25.T6S37 2015
940.54′252135—dc23
2014043257

W. W. Norton & Company, Inc., 500 Fifth Avenue, New York, N.Y. 10110
www.wwnorton.com

W. W. Norton & Company Ltd., Castle House, 75/76 Wells Street, London W1T 3QT

1 2 3 4 5 6 7 8 9 0

FOR THE MEN
FROM SHANGRI-LA

His deeds are in sharp contrast to his name.

—*MIAMI DAILY NEWS*,
OCTOBER 4, 1929

CONTENTS

★

INTRODUCTION

★

THE DOOLITTLE RAID IS one of the most iconic stories of World War II. Even before rescuers could pluck all the dead from the oily Hawaiian waters following Japan's December 7, 1941, surprise attack on Pearl Harbor, American war planners started work on an ambitious counterassault, a strike not against an outlying enemy base in the far-flung Pacific islands but against the heart of the Japanese Empire: Tokyo. That April 1942 raid led by famed stunt and racing pilot Jimmy Doolittle would test American ingenuity, gamble the precious few flattops and warships left in the Pacific Fleet's battered arsenal, and jump-start Japan on the road to ruin.

Sixteen Army bombers crewed by eighty volunteers specially trained in carrier takeoffs would thunder into the skies over the enemy's capital and key industrial cities, pummel factories, refineries, and dockyards and then escape to Free China. At home in the United States the mission would derail questions over the government's failure to guard against Japanese aggression in the Pacific and buoy the morale of a shell-shocked nation. The forty-five-year-old Doolittle would come to personify the raid's success, his grinning image would be plastered around the nation on war bond posters, and strangers would write him poems and songs. A Missouri town would even take his name.

Postwar interviews and records would reveal that Doolittle's brazen raid had accomplished far more, convincing Japan's reluctant military leaders of the need to extend the nation's defensive perimeter and annihilate America's aircraft carriers to prevent possible future strikes. That plan would center on the capture of a tiny wind-ravaged atoll in the middle of the Pacific, one Japanese war planners knew America would risk its prized few flattops to protect. The June 1942 Battle of Midway would end in crushing defeat for Japan—America would sink four of its best aircraft carriers—and prove the pivotal turning point of the war, setting the stage for the Navy's offensive drive across the Pacific that would ravage Emperor Hirohito's empire.

But declassified records in both nations coupled with long-forgotten missionary files reveal a more nuanced story. Japanese documents show that the raiders—albeit unintentionally—destroyed private homes and killed civilians, including women and children. One of the bombers mistakenly strafed a school. Records likewise illustrate how the Roosevelt administration, desperate for positive press, deliberately deceived the American people about the mission's actual losses and even the capture of some of the airmen to elevate the public relations value of the raid, sparking a propaganda battle between the United States and Japan. In one of the story's uglier chapters, General Douglas MacArthur's chief of intelligence secretly protected the Japanese general who allegedly signed the death order of some of the captured raiders, believing him too valuable a postwar asset to be prosecuted in the war crimes trials.

More importantly, the audacious raid that had so humiliated Japan's leaders triggered a retaliatory campaign of rape and murder against the Chinese that reduced villages, towns, and cities to rubble. Enemy troops cut the ears and noses off of villagers, set others on fire, and drowned entire families in wells. The Japanese not only used incendiary squads to systematically torch entire towns but unleashed bacteriological warfare in the form of plague, anthrax, cholera, and typhoid. The brutal campaign that killed as many as a quarter million Chinese—and prompted comparisons to the "Rape of Nanking"—was a slaughter senior American leaders anticipated and judged a worthwhile risk long before Doolittle's bombers ever lifted off from the flight deck.

None of these facts undermine the bravery of the eighty volunteers at the heart of this story who climbed inside those bombers that cold wet morning of April 18, 1942. Those young men from small towns and cities across America, knowing that the odds of survival were against them, suppressed their own personal fears and set out to accomplish the impossible—and did. Rather, these important new elements of the story help frame the political and wartime context of an embattled America, a nation fighting for its very survival. Senior leaders calculated that victory would carry consequences and chose to deemphasize or cover up the negative aspects of Doolittle's campaign in order to enhance the rightful accounts of the heroism of American airmen.

TARGET TOKYO

★

PROLOGUE

★

Hawaii is just like a rat in a trap. Enjoy your
dream of peace just one more day!

—REAR ADMIRAL MATOME UGAKI,
DECEMBER 6, 1941, DIARY ENTRY

VICE ADMIRAL CHUICHI NAGUMO stared at the dark sea that spread out before him from the bridge of the aircraft carrier *Akagi* as it steamed north of Hawaii in the predawn hours of December 7, 1941. The fifty-four-year-old admiral, whose bald head, furrowed brow, and square jaw gave him the appearance of a bulldog, brooded over his mission. The sullen humor that had haunted him for months was in stark contrast to the otherwise arrogant demeanor of a man who, with a puffed chest and a peacock's swagger, had once disrupted a royal garden party by threatening to gut a fellow officer with a dagger. Months of stress had robbed Nagumo of his trademark bravado, prompting some senior leaders to question whether he might fail. "I hope he will not fall into nervous prostration beforehand," Rear Admiral Matome Ugaki, the Combined Fleet's chief of staff, confided in his diary. "Life and death are according to the will of heaven. If only he can obtain a glorious result in the coming fight, he may rest in peace."

Nagumo's anxiety had not abated once he had put to sea. If anything, his fears increased. He seemed to draw little comfort from the fact that he commanded the most powerful carrier task force the world had ever seen. More than fifteen thousand officers and enlisted men stoked boilers, manned guns, and stood lookout across some thirty-one ships, from submarines and oilers to battlewagons and flattops. The nineteen-day-old moon occasionally punched through the storm clouds to silhouette this forbidding armada. The last of the strike force's eight oilers had turned back only hours earlier, leaving the combatants to make the final charge south through the swells toward Oahu at twenty-four knots. An arrow formation of battleships, cruisers, and destroyers shielded Nagumo's flagship, the *Akagi*, and five other first-line carriers that steamed in two parallel columns. Some 350 fighters and dive and torpedo bombers crowded the flattops, ready to roar down the wooden flight decks at dawn.

Nagumo's fears were not wholly unfounded. His orders stipulated he execute the dramatic opening act of war against the United States, a surgical strike that would mortally wound America's powerful Pacific Fleet, anchored in the cool waters of Pearl Harbor. Even if he could make it 3,500 miles across the Pacific without running into a submarine, merchant ship, or patrol plane, Nagumo understood that an attack on Pearl Harbor was like kicking a hornet's nest. Shore batteries along with battleships, cruisers, and destroyers boasted 993 antiaircraft guns that could shred Japanese pilots. Army and Navy airfields scattered around Oahu could throw up another four hundred fighters and bombers. Those planes could devastate Nagumo's carriers and doom Japan before the sun set on the first day of war. The incredible risks of the mission were reflected in Nagumo's final message from the Combined Fleet commander. "The fate of our empire," Admiral Isoroku Yamamoto warned, "depends upon this expedition."

These worries had kept the husky admiral awake at night, even though he knew strategists had perfected the plan down to the wooden torpedo fins needed to run in Pearl Harbor's shallow waters. On the eve of the task force's departure sailors had stripped the warships of all flammable and unnecessary equipment, from gangways and practice weapons to the paintings and flower vases that enlivened the destroyer *Akigumo*'s wardroom. To increase the task force's range, workers had pumped extra fuel into trimming tanks, while sailors bedded down next to oil drums. Fuel conservation demanded that the ships dim lights, forgo heat, and limit bathing for the duration of the mission. One by one the warships had slipped port, rendezvousing in Hitokappu Bay off Etorofu Island, a desolate outpost a thousand miles north of Tokyo in the Kuril Islands that was home only to a handful of fishermen. A gunboat had arrived in advance of the force, shutting down the town's wireless station and post office.

To throw off American eavesdroppers, the task force operated in radio silence. The chief communications officer went so far as to pluck out an essential component of his transmitter, hiding it in a wooden box that doubled as his pillow. The Japanese flooded the airwaves with dummy messages to disguise the task force's departure, while busloads of sailors from the Yokosuka naval barracks arrived daily in Tokyo, paraded around the city on sightseeing tours for American diplomats to see. This charade had allowed Nagumo's task force to depart undetected from Hitokappu Bay soon after daybreak on November 26. War planners had consulted a decade of weather data before setting a course across the stormy northern Pacific, one that promised a December average of just seven days of clear weather. Few ships would risk such turbulent seas. Those that did, orders demanded, should be destroyed: "Sink anything flying any flag."

Those orders had so far proven unnecessary. Despite the task force's good fortune, Nagumo couldn't shake his fears, refusing to change out of his uniform even as he lay awake at night in bed. The graduate of Japan's prestigious Eta Jima Naval Academy summoned subordinates at all hours to hash over trivial matters. Was his staff certain that the American ships would be in Pearl Harbor and not at the Lahaina anchorage off Maui? He dragged his flight commander from bed one night distressed over his unfounded suspicion that an American submarine was shadowing the force. To his chief of staff, Rear Admiral Ryunosuke Kusaka, the nervous Nagumo confided his true concerns. He felt he had overreached, taking on a mission that was too risky. If only he had been strong enough to refuse the operation. Now that the task force was at sea—each day steaming closer and closer to Hawaii—the admiral droned on about the mission's chances for success. "I wonder if it will go well."

"*Daijobu*," his patient chief of staff repeated. "Don't worry."

But Nagumo did.

★

THE JAPANESE ADMIRAL wasn't the only anxious one. The break-down in relations between America and Japan had left little doubt that the two nations were marching toward war. The questions seemed more about when and where the conflict would begin. The Navy only nine days earlier had ordered Pacific Fleet commander Admiral Husband Kimmel to take defensive measures. "This despatch is to be considered a war warning," cabled Admiral Harold Stark, the chief of naval opera-tions in Washington. "Negotiations with Japan looking toward stabiliza-tion of conditions in the Pacific have ceased and an aggressive move by Japan is expected within the next few days." His Army counterpart Lieu-tenant General Walter Short, who commanded a garrison of 42,959 offi-cers and men trusted to protect Pearl Harbor, had received a similar alert that same day from Army chief of staff General George Marshall. "Japa-nese future action unpredictable," Marshall warned, "but hostile action possible at any moment."

Most expected the first punch to land in the Far East—Thailand, Malaysia, or perhaps the Philippines or Guam—but not Hawaii. Not the Paradise of the Pacific. That Saturday night as Nagumo's carriers charged through the swells toward Oahu, Admiral Kimmel dined at the Haleku-lani Hotel while General Short attended a charity dance at Schofield Bar-racks officers club. Off-duty troops cruised down Honolulu's famous Hotel Street, lined with tattoo parlors, pinball joints, and shooting gal-leries. Others laughed through the variety show "Tantalizing Tootsies" at the Princess Theater or danced to jukebox tunes at favorite watering holes, like Two Jacks, New Emma Café, and the Mint. Airmen over at Hickam could catch Clark Gable as a frontier conman in *Honky Tonk*, while the new Bloch Recreation Center at Pearl Harbor hosted the finals in a battle of the bands that pitted the ships in the fleet against one another. The battleship *Pennsylvania*'s band claimed victory that night before everyone sang "God Bless America."

The waters of Pearl Harbor that Saturday night resembled a parking lot. The bustling port just a short drive from Oahu's famed Waikiki Beach counted ninety-four ships, almost half of the entire Pacific Fleet. Eight of the fleet's nine battleships were in port along with eight heavy and light cruisers, twenty-nine destroyers, and five submarines. The Pacific Fleet's three carriers, which the Japanese so hungered to destroy, were absent. The *Lexington* steamed to Midway to deliver a squadron of scout bombers, while the *Enterprise* sliced trough the swells a few hundred miles west of Oahu after ferrying fighters to Wake. The *Saratoga* had returned to the West Coast for repairs. General Short on his drive home that evening at nine thirty looked down upon the lit-up battlewagons, most moored side by side along the southeast shore of Ford Island, the view interrupted only by the occasional searchlight. "Isn't that a beautiful sight?" the general said, "and what a target they would make."

Pacific Fleet intelligence officer Lieutenant Commander Edwin Layton tried to shake his fears that Saturday night as he dined and danced on the terrace of the Royal Hawaiian Hotel, just down from where Admiral Kimmel finished his dinner. When the evening ended at midnight with the familiar refrain of "The Star-Spangled Banner," Layton stood at attention and fought the urge to shout, "Wake up, America!" Earlier that day the veteran intelligence officer learned that the Japanese consulate had begun torching official records and codes; this came on top of the sudden increased radio security. The Japanese used multiple addresses and blanket coverage—messages sent from nobody to nobody, but that copied everyone—that seemed designed to muddy the waters, measures Layton feared masked an offensive operation. His concerns deepened when the Japanese changed naval call signs on November 1 and then again one month later. Analysts realized in the shuffle that Japan's main carriers had vanished.

Where were Japan's flattops?

Layton had struggled to answer that question a few days earlier when he prepared the December 2 intelligence sheet. Trusted to keep Admiral Kimmel informed of when, where, and how the Japanese might strike, Layton could only guess the location of the Imperial Navy's carriers, writing simply, "Unknown—home waters?"

"What?" Kimmel had erupted. "You don't know where the carriers are?"

"No, sir," Layton had answered, pointing out that he had only guessed homeland waters.

"You mean to say that you, the intelligence officer, don't know where the carriers are?" the admiral pressed.

"No, sir," Layton replied. "I don't."

"You mean they could be coming around Diamond Head, and you wouldn't know it?"

"Yes, sir," Layton answered, "but I hope they'd have been sighted before now."

But no one had spotted Nagumo's forces.

NOW AFTER MONTHS of worry—and just hours before his planes would lift off—a calm washed over Nagumo. No patrol plane had appeared overhead, nor an enemy armada on the horizon. The gentle Hawaiian tunes from Honolulu's KGMB radio station that emanated from the *Akagi*'s receivers only confirmed that the Americans on that volcanic archipelago a few hundred miles south had no clue of the steel typhoon that bore down on them; pilots would go so far as to dance clumsy hulas that mocked America's ignorance.

Aircrews on the Japanese task force's six carriers rose as early as three thirty this first Sunday morning in December. Many had spent the journey east across the Pacific studying silhouettes of American carriers, battleships, and cruisers along with detailed maps, including a six-square-foot scale model of Oahu and one of Pearl Harbor. Others had climbed into the cockpit to grip the controls or peered through the bombardier's sight so as not to forget the feel of combat. Fighter pilot Yoshio Shiga had painted eight watercolors of a temple. Certain he would not survive the attack, Shiga arranged a private showing for his fellow officers on the carrier *Kaga*. That same fear no doubt triggered the destroyer *Akigumo*'s executive officer to close his eyes night after night and to dream about his wife, Fumiko, and the couple's children. Many of the airmen spent the final hours before the dawn attack penning letters home to wives and parents, enclosing fingernail trimmings and clips of hair.

The airmen dressed in clean loincloths, pressed uniforms, and special thousand-stitch belts, a traditional bellyband in which wives, mothers, and sisters stood on corners to solicit passersby to contribute a stitch, each one considered a prayer for good luck. The thirty-nine-year-old Commander Mitsuo Fuchida, who would lead the air attack on Pearl Harbor, slipped on long red underwear and a red shirt. He felt that if he were wounded in the raid the color would camouflage his blood and not demoralize his troops. The aircrews paused alongside portable Shinto shrines to pray for victory and sip sake before sitting down to a special breakfast of red rice with *okashiratsuki*, sea bream cooked with the head and tail, and so-called victory chestnuts known as *kachiguri*. The apprehension that flooded the carriers resonated back home in Japan, a sentiment captured in Ugaki's diary. "We await the day with our necks craned," he wrote. "What a big drama it is, risking the fate of a nation and so many lives!"

Nagumo's carriers battled angry waves some 230 miles north of Oahu, pitching as much as fifteen degrees, while sea spray soaked the flight decks crowded with planes parked wingtip to wingtip. One hundred and eighty-three fighters, bombers, and torpedo planes would lift off in the first wave, followed by a second strike of 167. Across one of the bombs someone scribbled a message in chalk: "First bomb in the war on America." The propellers roared to life—audible even on the decks of the escort ships—spewing blue exhaust. The faint light of dawn punctured the clouds and illuminated the eastern horizon as the carriers increased speed and swung into the wind. Sailors waved hats and erupted in cheers as the first plane roared down the flight deck, followed seconds later by another then another. The same scene played out across all six carriers as one after the other the planes swarmed into the skies. The moment Nagumo and his superiors had long awaited had finally arrived. There was no retreat.

War had come.

CHAPTER 1

★

Air raid on Pearl Harbor. This is not drill.

—U.S. NAVY RADIO MESSAGE, DECEMBER 7, 1941

PRESIDENT FRANKLIN ROOSEVELT WAS enjoying a late lunch in his White House study Sunday afternoon, December 7, 1941. The fifty-nine-year-old three-term president had transformed the parlor off his second-floor bedroom—a room where Thomas Jefferson played his violin and Abraham Lincoln read the Bible—into a cluttered study that reflected his lifelong love of the sea. Model ships ranging from river packets and square riggers to a modern destroyer adorned tables and the fireplace mantel, while Currier and Ives lithographs crowded the ivory walls, depicting life along the Hudson River, whose muddy banks formed the western boundary of Roosevelt's native Hyde Park. A portrait of Revolutionary War naval hero John Paul Jones—rescued from a second-hand shop for twenty-five dollars—kept watch over the president as he worked at his oak desk, crafted from timbers salvaged from the ill-fated Arctic explorer HMS *Resolute*, an 1880 gift from Queen Victoria to the then president Rutherford Hayes.

With its commanding views of the White House's south lawn and the Washington Monument in the distance, the oval study had become the center of Roosevelt's presidency during his nine years in power. The wheelchair-bound leader, who had battled polio two decades earlier, often preferred the study's convenience to his more formal office down-stairs in the executive wing. He not only conducted the nation's business from the comfort of the study's worn leather sofa and chairs—hand-me-downs from Theodore Roosevelt's old presidential yacht *Mayflower*—but hosted a 7:15 p.m. cocktail hour for his senior aides, pouring bourbon old-fashioneds and martinis on a tray atop his desk, often flavoring them with a dash of absinthe. "He mixed the ingredients with the deliberation of an alchemist," recalled his speechwriter Robert Sherwood, "but with what appeared to be a certain lack of precision since he carried on a steady conversation while doing it."

Roosevelt's Sunday lunch capped a week made stressful by the deteri-orating situation in the Pacific, so much so that the president decided to pass on a luncheon hosted by his wife, Eleanor, for thirty-one people, including his own cousin Frederick Adams. Instead, he chose to dine in his study at 1:15 p.m. with his longtime friend and trusted aide Harry Hopkins before he planned to settle in for a quiet afternoon of work on his treasured stamp collection. Despite the demands he faced as the nation's commander in chief, Roosevelt carved out time each week to sort, clip, and affix stamps into more than one hundred hand-tooled leather albums. The collection would grow over his lifetime to number 1.2 million stamps, including ones from countries as far-flung as Haiti and Hong Kong and even a few of the last twenty-cent Confederate stamps believed ever sold at a postal station. Roosevelt's boyhood hobby had over the years evolved into a form of occupational therapy, which the president needed now more than ever.

Roosevelt had long struggled to prepare the American public and lawmakers for war, many of whom argued that the vast Atlantic and Pacific Oceans served as natural barriers against foreign aggressors. He focused much of his attention on Europe. Adolf Hitler's Germany had invaded Poland in September 1939. Denmark and Norway soon fell, fol-lowed by the Netherlands, Belgium, Luxembourg, and France. Hitler unleashed his bombers on Great Britain in September 1940, in an eight-month assault known as the blitz that killed 43,000 and left another 1.4 million homeless. Roosevelt had watched the destruction with horror—and an eye toward the future. The broad expanse of the oceans, he warned, was not the same as in the days of clipper ships. America's best hope to remain on the sidelines was to arm friendly nations now at war. "No man can tame a tiger into a kitten by stroking it," he declared in a December 1940 fireside chat. "We must be the great arsenal of democracy."

Much to the frustration of the president, who hoped to forestall a fight in the Pacific, Japan had continued on a collision course with the United States, triggered in part by unique social and geographical challenges. The island nation, whose population had tripled to seventy-three million in less than a century, was materially bankrupt, forced to import even its most basic food source—rice. The military only increased Japan's dependence on foreign resources, from the bauxite needed to build fighters down to the cotton to sew uniforms. But the oil that powered battleships at sea and bombers through the skies topped Japan's list of critical imports. Japan could produce a mere two million barrels a year, a figure equal to just 0.1 percent of the world's oil output. The United States by comparison—the world's largest producer—delivered seven hundred times that amount. "Napoleon's armies moved on their stomachs," observed a *New York Times* writer. "Modern motorized armies move on gasoline."

The hunger for natural resources had led Japan to invade Manchuria in 1931 and push into northern China six years later. Roosevelt had watched Japan's aggression with alarm, but just as in Europe he found his options limited. He sent bombers and fighters to the Chinese, hoping to bog down Japanese forces. In an effort to better project American power in the region—and over the fierce objections of some of the Navy's top admirals—Roosevelt ordered the Pacific Fleet redeployed from California to Hawaii. These token measures, however, failed to dissuade the Japanese, who sided with Germany and Italy to form what the president called an "unholy alliance." Japan invaded southern French Indochina in July 1941, a clear prelude to the capture of Hong Kong, Singapore, and the Dutch East Indies. Roosevelt felt he had no choice but to retaliate. He ordered Japan's assets frozen and shut off oil exports, a devastating blow since America supplied more than 80 percent of the empire's oil.

Roosevelt knew Japan promised a formidable fight even though the four-year war with China had proven costly. Japan had stockpiled raw materials, from iron ore and rubber to a two-year supply of oil. To stretch supplies it had ordered gas rationed and later halted all civilian traffic, including buses and taxis. Essential vehicles burned charcoal or wood. Workers punched out more than 550 planes a month, boosting Japan's air forces to some 7,500 aircraft; a figure that counted some 2,675 Imperial Army and Navy tactical planes, like fighters and bombers. But Japan's muscle spread beyond the skies. Aggressive recruitment would soon swell the Army's 1,700,000 soldiers to 5,000,000, while the Navy's register listed 381 warships, including 10 battleships, 10 aircraft carriers, 18 heavy cruisers, and 112 destroyers. The Japanese Navy not only outgunned American forces in the Pacific but proved more powerful in that ocean than the combined navies of the United States, Great Britain, and the Netherlands.

These issues weighed upon the president this first weekend in December. Treasury Secretary Henry Morgenthau Jr. had asked Roosevelt only a week earlier, as his office prepared a $1.5 billion bond offering, whether he foresaw a crisis that would disrupt the financial markets. "I cannot guarantee anything," Roosevelt had replied. "It is all in the laps of the Gods." But the president still clung to the hope that he might avert war. In a move just the night before that reflected his sense of urgency, he had ignored Japan's political protocol and fired off at nine a message directly to Emperor Hirohito. "Only in situations of extraordinary importance to our two countries need I address to Your Majesty messages on matters of state," Roosevelt began. "Developments are occurring in the Pacific area which threaten to deprive each of our Nations and all humanity of the beneficial influence of the long peace between our two countries. Those developments contain tragic possibilities."

Roosevelt's message would be too late.

THE BLACK PHONE ON the president's *Resolute* desk rang at 1:40 p.m. on Sunday, interrupting his lunchtime conversation with Hopkins, Roosevelt's closet adviser, whose chronic ill health and shriveled stature led others to describe him as resembling "a strange, gnomelike creature" and even "a cadaver." Dressed in an old gray sweater given to him by his eldest son, James, Roosevelt polished off the last few bites of an apple as he took the call from Navy Secretary Frank Knox.

"Mr. President," Knox began. "It looks like the Japanese have attacked Pearl Harbor."

"No!" Roosevelt exclaimed.

"It's true," Knox replied. "I'll read you the message."

Knox had no formal report yet of the attack, just a nine-word radio message from the Pacific Fleet's headquarters alerting all stations of an air raid and warning that the assault was no drill. Hopkins protested that the message must be a mistake, arguing that surely Japan would not attack Hawaii, but Roosevelt was more pragmatic. His long wait for when and where Japan might strike was now over; the empire's elusive carriers had been found. "It was just the kind of unexpected thing the Japanese would do," Hopkins wrote, summarizing the president's views. "At the very time they were discussing peace in the Pacific they were plotting to overthrow it."

Roosevelt called Secretary of War Henry Stimson. The seventy-four-year-old New York native, who had begun his career as a Wall Street lawyer and federal prosecutor, had served as war secretary for President Howard Taft and later as Herbert Hoover's secretary of state. The tensions with Japan had prompted Stimson to spend the morning with Knox and Secretary of State Cordell Hull. When the trio broke, Stimson hustled home for a late lunch at Woodley, the twenty-acre Rock Creek Valley estate that he had purchased for the princely sum of $800,000 and that had once been home to Presidents Martin Van Buren and Grover Cleveland as well as General George Patton.

"Have you heard the news?" the president asked.

"Well," Stimson replied. "I have heard the telegrams which have been coming in about the Japanese advances in the Gulf of Siam."

"Oh, no," Roosevelt stated. "I don't mean that. They have attacked Hawaii. They are now bombing Hawaii."

Chief of naval operations Admiral Harold Stark phoned at 2:28 p.m. to confirm the attack. The four-star admiral had spent the morning downtown at the Navy Department on Constitution Avenue. Soon after news of the raid reached Washington, Stark had jumped on the phone with Rear Admiral Claude Bloch in Hawaii, demanding a damage report. Even though he used the conversation scrambler, Bloch feared the call might not be secure. His vague assessment had only irritated his boss.

"Claude," Stark finally barked. "How about it?"

"Well, Betty," Bloch said, referring to Stark by his nickname. "It's pretty bad. I don't know how secure this telephone is."

"Go ahead," Stark demanded. "Tell me."

Bloch did as ordered.

The attack by Japanese fighters and bombers, Stark informed the president, had caused severe loss of life and damage to the Pacific Fleet. Though the precise details would emerge only in the days and weeks ahead—once crews could extinguish the flames and tally the dead—the raid had destroyed or damaged eighteen ships, including eight battlewagons, three cruisers, and several destroyers. Attackers also wiped out 188 planes. The human toll would prove horrific. Casualties among soldiers, sailors, marines, and civilians would soar to 3,581, a figure that counted 2,403 killed. Roosevelt directed the bespectacled admiral to execute the Army's and Navy's agreed-upon orders in the event of an outbreak of hostilities in the Pacific.

The president hung up the phone with Stark and called Press Secretary Steve Early on the private line that connected his Morningside Drive home in northeast Washington to the White House. Early had hosted an uneventful news conference the day before with reporters, assuring them that there was no exciting news to anticipate this weekend.

"I think the President decided you fellows have been so busy lately and Christmas is coming so close that he would give you a day off to do some shopping."

"I suppose he is over at the House writing a declaration of war, isn't he?" one of the reporters had joked.

Other than a meeting with his budget director to sign routine papers, Early promised, the president had nothing newsworthy planned. "No appointments for today and none tomorrow," he had told them, "and I don't assume there will be."

That was about to change.

"Have you got a pencil handy?" Roosevelt asked.

"Do I need it?" Early replied, suspecting a joke.

"Yes," the president said. "I have a very important statement. It ought to go out verbatim."

Early knew nothing yet of the attack, but sensed a crisis from Roosevelt's serious tone. The press secretary summoned his wife, who retrieved a pencil and a few scraps of lined notebook paper. Early instructed her to write as he repeated the president's twenty-eight-word message. Within minutes Early placed a three-way call via the White House switchboard to the Associated Press, United Press, and International News Service, preparing to deliver the first news of the attack to the wire services.

"All on?" he asked, making a quick roll call. "This is Steve Early. I am calling from home. I have a statement here which the president has asked me to read."

The quiet Sunday afternoon was over.

America was at war.

Secret Service agent Mike Reilly was swapping fishing stories with chief usher Wilson Searles when news of the attack reached the White House. The second-in-command of the president's nine-member security team—and senior agent on duty this Sunday afternoon—Reilly darted from the usher's office down to the switchboard. "Start calling in all the Secret Service men who are off duty," he ordered the operator. "Don't tell 'em why, just call 'em in. All the White House police, too."

Secret Service chief Frank Wilson, who had attended church and enjoyed a nice drive through Rock Creek Park, had just sat down to dinner of roast pork, mashed potatoes, and hubbard squash when the phone rang.

"Why don't they let us eat in peace!" Wilson griped.

His wife returned moments later with a grim look on her face; the White House operator was on the phone.

"Chief!" Reilly blurted out when Wilson finally picked up. "The Japs have bombarded Pearl Harbor."

The news left Wilson speechless. "I'll be down," he finally muttered, "as soon as my Lincoln will get there."

Reilly phoned Washington police chief Ed Kelley, requesting that sixteen uniformed officers report to the White House immediately. Treasury Secretary Morgenthau rang moments later. He ordered Reilly to double the guard. Ten seconds later he called back and demanded that Reilly quadruple it—and issue machine guns.

Roosevelt likewise summoned his advisers and senior staff to the White House for a 3 p.m. conference. His trusted personal secretary, Grace Tully, was relaxing with the newspaper at her Connecticut Avenue apartment, trying to ignore the troubling message she had typed the night before to Emperor Hirohito, just as her phone rang. "The president wants you right away," the White House chief telephone operator told her.

"There's a car on the way to pick up you. The Japs just bombed Pearl Harbor!" Tully didn't waste time dressing, but "jumped to like a fireman going down the pole."

The president phoned his eldest son, a captain in the Marine Corps Reserve who lived in the suburbs. Just a few weeks shy of his thirty-fourth birthday, James Roosevelt often served as an aide and surrogate, dubbed by the press the "Crown Prince."

"Hi, Old Man," James Roosevelt answered, rustled from an afternoon nap by the White House operator. "What can I do for you?"

"I don't have time to talk right now," the president replied, "but could you come right away?"

"Pa," the younger Roosevelt protested. "It's Sunday afternoon."

The president insisted.

James Roosevelt arrived in the oval study, proud to see his father wearing his old sweater, but he sensed trouble when his father did not even look up. "I became aware of his extreme calmness—almost a sad, fatalistic, but courageous acceptance of something he had tried to avert but which he feared might be inevitable."

"Hello, Jimmy," the president said when he finally acknowledged his son's arrival. "It's happened."

Roosevelt's advisers crowded into the study at 3:05 p.m. Stimson, Knox, and naval adviser Admiral John Beardall joined Hopkins, Early, appointments secretary Marvin McIntyre, and Tully. Fifteen minutes later Army chief of staff General George Marshall and Secretary of State Hull arrived. The president discussed the disposition of troops and the air force with Marshall and stressed to Hull the importance of keeping the South American nations on the side of the United States. Roosevelt ordered the Justice Department to protect the Japanese embassy and all the consulates and instructed Stimson and Knox to guard all arsenals as well as private munitions factories and bridges. "Many of the moves required the President to sign an executive order," Hopkins wrote. "The President instructed the person to whom he talked to go ahead and execute the order and he would sign it later."

Admiral Stark continued to phone in updates from the Navy Department, at first to the president and then to Tully, who took the admiral's calls in the second-floor hallway until the confusion and noise forced her to retreat to Roosevelt's bedroom. Tully jotted down the details in shorthand, typed them up as several of the president's men hovered over her, and then handed the reports to Roosevelt, each more horrendous than the one before. "The news was shattering," Tully would later write. "I could hear the shocked unbelief in Admiral Stark's voice as he talked to me. At first the men around the President were incredulous; that changed to angry acceptance as new messages supported and amplified the previous ones. The Boss maintained greater outward calm than anybody else but there was rage in his very calmness. With each new message he shook his head grimly and tightened the expression of his mouth."

The president continued to field calls, even as he met with his advisers. The White House switchboard connected Roosevelt at one point that afternoon with Joseph Poindexter, the governor of the territory of Hawaii. Poindexter told the president that the attack had killed at least fifty civilians and that Hawaii desperately needed food and planes. He asked permission to approve martial law, which Roosevelt granted. Poindexter interrupted his update with a sudden shriek, spooked by what was likely American planes in the skies over Oahu. "My God," the president announced to his aides. "There's another wave of Jap planes over Hawaii right this minute."

Roosevelt took another call, from Winston Churchill. The British prime minister had dined with American ambassador John Winant and special envoy Averell Harriman at Chequers, his country residence fifty miles northwest of London in Buckinghamshire. The beleaguered leader had moped through dinner—his head often in his hands—until news of the attack crackled over the portable radio. The shock revived Churchill, who slammed down the top of the radio.

"We shall declare war on Japan," the prime minister said.

"Good God," Winant said. "You can't declare war on a radio announcement."

Churchill darted out the door to his office. Within three minutes he placed a call to Roosevelt. "Mr. President," Churchill exclaimed. "What's this about Japan?"

"It's quite true," Roosevelt replied. "They have attacked us at Pearl Harbor. We are all in the same boat now."

The confirmation thrilled Churchill, who had struggled through seventeen months of war as German submarines ravaged British merchant ships on the high seas and bombers reduced docks, power plants, and factories to rubble. America would now join the fight, promising England's salvation and total Allied victory. "To have the United States at our side was to me the greatest joy," Churchill later wrote. "Hitler's fate was sealed. Mussolini's fate was sealed. As for the Japanese, they would be ground to powder."

"This certainly simplifies things," Churchill told Roosevelt. "God be with you."

Reports continued to arrive in Washington, framing a portrait of the destruction in the Pacific that would take shape in the hours and days ahead.

"The *Oklahoma* has capsized in Pearl Harbor," stated one. "The *Tennessee* is on fire with a bad list."

"Three battleships sunk," read another. "All others variously damaged."

"Heavy losses sustained Hawaii."

With each update, Roosevelt sank farther. "My God, how did it happen," he muttered at one point. "I will go down in disgrace."

Still unaware of the war's outbreak, many Americans were enjoying a few final moments of peace that Sunday afternoon, including 27,102 football fans crowded into the stands at Griffith Stadium to watch the Washington Redskins battle the Philadelphia Eagles.

Up in the press box a Morse telegrapher passed Associated Press reporter Pat O'Brien a message from his office late in the first quarter.

"Keep it short," the note read.

A second message followed minutes later, explaining why the wire service didn't need much game coverage: "The Japanese have kicked off. War now!"

The stadium loudspeaker began paging important military and civilian officials. "Admiral W. H. P. Bland is asked to report to his office at once!" demanded one announcement, summoning the chief of the Navy's Bureau of Ordnance.

"The Resident Commissioner of the Philippines, Mr. Joaquim Elizalde, is urged to report to his office immediately."

Other announcements followed, summoning federal agents, army officers, and newspaper reporters and editors. Fans began to buzz, though no general announcement of the war's outbreak was made, because it would have violated the Redskins' policy against broadcasting nonsports news over the address system. The mass exodus left only a single news photographer to cover the Redskins' 20–14 victory.

Similar scenes played out around the country. Crowds in Times Square read the bulletins in shock while the New York Philharmonic Symphony Orchestra burst into "The Star-Spangled Banner" as the audience of 2,200 sang. A man showed up at a recruiting station in Norfolk, Virginia. "I want to beat them Japs," he declared, "with my own bare hands." At the Majestic Theater in Dallas, when *Sergeant York* ended and news of the attack was announced, the crowd fell silent then broke out in a roaring applause. A steelworker captured the sentiment: "We'll stamp their front teeth in."

Inside the White House, Roosevelt adjourned the conference with his advisers around 4:30 p.m. and summoned Tully. The secretary entered to find the president seated alone at his desk, the telephone close at hand and with several piles of afternoon notes stacked before him. Roosevelt lit a cigarette and inhaled deeply.

"Sit down, Grace," he said. "I'm going before Congress tomorrow. I'd like to dictate my message. It will be short."

Tully took a seat. Roosevelt normally depended on a team of several writers to help him draft major speeches, a process that could typically take up to ten days. Not only were two of those writers now in New York, but the president could spare at best just a few hours—if that—to craft what would prove to be one of the most important speeches of his career. Secretary of State Hull had pressed Roosevelt to deliver a long and detailed speech, examining the history of American and Japanese relations, but the president disagreed. The American people did not need a history lesson, but a rundown of the facts. Roosevelt took another long drag of his cigarette and began.

"Yesterday, December seventh, 1941, a date which will live in world history," he dictated, "the United States was simultaneously and deliberately attacked by naval and air forces of the Empire of Japan."

Tully jotted down each word, noting that the president's voice was just as calm as when he dictated the mail, though he took care to pronounce each word and specify the precise punctuation and paragraph breaks. While the address lacked the "eloquent defiance" of Churchill's and Hitler's "hysterical bombast," speechwriter Robert Sherwood later observed, it "represented Roosevelt at his simplest and most direct."

When the president finished his dictation, Tully typed a draft and returned it to Roosevelt to edit. Armed with a pencil, the president attacked the opening sentence, scratching out "world history" and writing above it "infamy," the one word that his son James later noted "would forever describe what happened that day." He likewise marked out "simultaneously" and substituted "suddenly." The president made other tweaks as the speech went through two more drafts that evening and the next morning, including the insertion of news of Japan's attacks elsewhere in the Pacific against Hong Kong, Guam, the Philippines, Wake, and Midway. His trusted aide Hopkins would make the only other major addition to the six-and-a-half-minute speech, adding a sentence to the closing. "With confidence in our armed forces—with the unbounding determination of our people—we will gain the inevitable triumph—so help us God."

Reporters who had abandoned the Press Club bar and the afternoon Redskins game now flooded the downstairs press room, clamoring for information and littering the floor with cigarette butts. "No story at the White House ever brought out the crowd of reporters that Pearl Harbor did," Merriman Smith, a reporter with United Press, later wrote. "There must have been one hundred reporters, radio men, newsreel and still photographers, assorted secretaries and Washington big shots trying to crowd into the press room where normally about a dozen men work."

At the same time the president dictated his speech, Press Secretary Steve Early stood up for another briefing with reporters. Early had met with the press and issued bulletins with the latest details on the attack throughout the afternoon, but America's wartime reality meant new restrictions would now apply.

"I want to ask you before you leave if there is any one of you reporting for Japanese agencies," he said. "If there are, I am giving you no information and I have asked the Secret Service to take up the credentials of Japanese correspondents."

"Will they be put under arrest?" a reporter asked.

"That is an activity of the Department of Justice."

People poured out of area movie houses—like the Metropolitan, where Errol Flynn starred in the western *They Died with Their Boots On*—and flocked toward the White House. Cars were backed up on

Pennsylvania Avenue. As many as one thousand bystanders, according to press estimates, crowded inside Lafayette Park just across the street, braving a frigid Potomac wind. The shouts of newsboys crying "Extra" were soon overcome by the masses singing "My Country, 'Tis of Thee" and "God Bless America." "Folks wanted to be together," a reporter for the *Evening Star* newspaper observed. "Strangers spoke to strangers. A sense of comradeship of all the people was apparent."

Vice President Henry Wallace and members of the cabinet filed into the oval study at 8:30 p.m., many of whom had caught afternoon flights to Washington. Maps dangled from easels, and extra chairs ringed the president's desk. Secretary of State Hull sulked up front in a Chippendale armchair, his fingers together amid an air of gloom. Navy Secretary Knox and Press Secretary Early continued to rush in and out with more updates. Roosevelt sat behind his desk, where he had been most of the day, a cigarette perched between his lips, nodding at each member who entered. "There was none of the usual cordial, personal greeting," recalled Labor Secretary Frances Perkins, who had just arrived on a flight from New York City with the postmaster general and vice president. "This was one of the few occasions he couldn't muster a smile."

"I'm thankful you all got here," Roosevelt began, noting that this was the most important session of the cabinet since Abraham Lincoln met with his at the outbreak of the Civil War. "Of course, you all know what's happened."

"Mr. President, several of us have just arrived by plane. We don't know anything except a scare headline," interrupted Attorney General Francis Biddle, who had rushed back to Washington from Detroit. "Could you tell us?"

Roosevelt turned to Knox, who related the day's events with occasional additions by Stimson, Hull, and the president. News that eight of the Pacific Fleet's nine battleships had been damaged or destroyed shocked the cabinet. "The Secretary of the Navy had lost his air of bravado," Agriculture Secretary Claude Wickard noted in his diary. "Secretary Stimson was very sober." Even Roosevelt, who had a few hours to adjust to the devastating news, struggled to comprehend how the Pacific Fleet had been caught so off guard. "His pride in the Navy was so terrific that he was having actual physical difficulty in getting out the words that bombs dropped on ships that were not in fighting shape and prepared to move, just tied up," observed Perkins. Twice the president barked at Knox, "Find out, for God's sake, why the ships were tied up in rows."

"That's the way they berth them," the Navy secretary replied.

Roosevelt informed the cabinet that he planned to go before a joint session of Congress at noon the next day to deliver a speech and request a declaration of war. The president then read his remarks aloud. Afterward Hull interjected that the brief message was inadequate and again urged Roosevelt to deliver a more in-depth report. "The President disagreed," Wickard recorded in his diary, "but Hull said he thought the most important war in 500 years deserved more than a short statement."

Speaker of the House Sam Rayburn of Texas accompanied by four congressmen and five senators joined the meeting at 9:45 p.m. Roosevelt again reviewed the latest damage reports. "The effect on the Congressmen was tremendous," Stimson wrote in his diary. "They sat in dead silence and even after the recital was over they had very few words." When the shock of the news faded, the search for blame began. While a few red-faced congressmen muttered profanities, Senate Foreign Relations Committee Chairman Tom Connally of Texas exploded. "How did it happen that our warships were caught like tame ducks in Pearl Harbor?" Connally demanded, his face turning purple as he banged his fist on the desk. "I am amazed at the attack by Japan, but I am still more astounded at what happened to our Navy. They were all asleep."

"I don't know, Tom," the president answered, his head bowed. "I just don't know."

CHAPTER 2

★

To the enemy we answer—you have unsheathed
the sword, and by it you shall die.
—SENATOR ARTHUR VANDENBERG,
DECEMBER 8, 1941

PRESIDENT ROOSEVELT GATHERED IN the oval study with his
advisers on the frigid afternoon of December 21, 1941, two weeks to the
day after the Japanese pounded Pearl Harbor. The president had
addressed Congress at 12:30 p.m. the day after the attack. Sixty-two
million listeners—almost one out of every two Americans—tuned in to
hear his 518-word speech, the largest daytime audience ever for a radio
broadcast. Roosevelt followed those remarks a day later with a fireside
chat designed to prepare the public for life at war, from the need for
troops to fight on foreign shores to the material shortages, increased
taxes, and long hours Americans would battle on the home front. "We
are now in this war. We are all in it—all the way," Roosevelt warned in
the twenty-six-minute speech. "Every single man, woman, and child is a
partner in the most tremendous undertaking of our American history.
We must share together the bad news and the good news, the defeats
and the victories—the changing fortunes of war."

Only days earlier Navy Secretary Frank Knox, who had flown to
Pearl Harbor to survey the damage sustained in the 110-minute assault,

submitted his nineteen-page report to the president. Of the eight battle-ships at Pearl Harbor that Sunday morning, the *Maryland*, *Pennsylva-nia*, and *Tennessee* had escaped serious damage. Knox estimated that the *Nevada* and the *California*—hit by a combined three torpedoes and six bombs—could both be refloated in a few months. The *West Virginia* in contrast had taken a much bigger beating, pounded by as many as nine torpedoes that ripped open the entire port side. Knox reported that the ship could be raised but would require two years to overhaul. The cap-sized *Oklahoma* likewise could be righted, but the Navy secretary ques-tioned whether the aged battleship even warranted salvage. The worst damage centered on the *Arizona*, hit by aerial bombs that blew out the sides. Some eleven hundred sailors remained entombed inside. "The *Ari-zona*," Knox reported, "is a total wreck."

The surprise attack had outraged the American public, a reaction reflected in newspaper editorials nationwide. "The battle is on," declared the *New York Herald Tribune*, while the *Los Angeles Times* denounced the raid as the "act of a mad dog." "Japan has asked for it," the paper wrote. "Now she is going to get it." "Do the war-mad officials of the Jap-anese Government honestly believe they can get away with a crime like this," asked the *Philadelphia Inquirer.* "Or are they intent upon commit-ting national hara-kiri?" Beneath the bluster and bravado many papers underlined the importance of national unity. "If we have not forgotten our differences before, we will forget them now," observed the *Palm Beach Post*, while the *Chicago Sun* wrote that "the nation is one or it is nothing." " 'Politics is adjourned,' whether between parties, factions, or economics," argued the *San Francisco Chronicle*. "From now on Amer-ica is an army with every man, woman, and child a solider in it, all joined to the one end of victory."

The president didn't need the papers to read the nation's mood. Thousands of telegrams and letters arrived daily at the White House, including messages of support from nearly three dozen of the nation's forty-eight governors, many echoing New Mexico's governor, John Miles. "This is the home of the Rough Riders," Miles wrote. "You can depend on us." Even Roosevelt's former foe in the 1936 election, Gover-nor Alf Landon of Kansas, vowed his support: "Please command me in any way I can be of service." Dozens of mayors likewise wrote in support, from large cities such San Francisco, Atlanta, and New Orleans to small towns like Minnesota's Anoka, home to just seven thousand residents. Diverse groups, from the Crow Indians of Montana to African Americans and even the Ku Klux Klan, cabled support. Many more letters and telegrams arrived from regular citizens, including a taxicab driver in Washington who had just paid off his car and offered to chauffeur government officials for free. Others offered up their children and husbands. Even four-year-old Ivor Ollivier of California vowed to fight: "I would like to kick every Jap into the middle of the Pacific and watch them sink."

Roosevelt knew he needed all the support he could muster as the news worsened. The Japanese had not stopped at Pearl Harbor, but targeted American forces across the Pacific. Guam fell soon after the raid on Hawaii, and forces on Wake stood just hours before surrender. The enemy likewise had wiped out much of America's airpower in the Philippines and would soon seize the capital of Manila. The British had suffered similar defeats. Hirohito's forces sank the battleship *Prince of Wales* and the battle cruiser *Repulse*—important symbols of British naval power in the Pacific—and would soon capture Malaya. The Japanese onslaught appeared unstoppable. "I never wanted to have to fight this war on two fronts. We haven't got the Navy to fight in both the Atlantic and the Pacific," the president had confessed to his wife, Eleanor, soon after Pearl Harbor. "We will have to build up the Navy and the Air Force, and that will mean that we will have to take a good many defeats before we can have a victory."

The president understood that continued defeats would only demoralize the American public, already anxious now that sandbags crowded West Coast windows and blackout curtains dangled in the White House. Polls showed that one out of every two Americans now feared the enemy would bomb American cities. Those worries had even infected some of the president's top advisers. "You are not only the most important man to the United States today, but to the world," chief of naval operations Admiral Harold Stark warned in a letter five days after the attack. "If anything should happen to you, it would be a catastrophe." The Secret Service aimed to prevent such a crisis, converting a vault under the Treasury Department into a bomb shelter. The president had bristled at the increased security, but consented to at least strap a gas mask to his wheelchair. "Henry," he told Treasury Secretary Morgenthau, "I will not go down into the shelter unless you allow me to play poker with all the gold in your vaults."

Victory on the battlefield and at sea was the only way to allay the nation's fears and nurture the vital patriotism that had arisen from the ashes of Pearl Harbor. Once that unity faded, the blame would begin. Already those resentments festered beneath the surface, as evidenced by a White House report days after the attack that had analyzed editorial opinions. "The shock and awareness of loss occasioned by the attack gave rise to the expression of certain resentments in the press," warned the December 15 memo. "There was guarded criticism of the military and naval command in the Pacific." Many Americans no doubt shared the private outrage Roosevelt's close friend Assistant Secretary of State Breckinridge Long captured in his diary the day after the attack. "Sick at heart," Long wrote. "I am so damned mad at the Navy for being asleep at the switch at Honolulu. It is the worst day in American history. They spent their lives in preparation for a supreme moment—and then were asleep when it came."

These challenges confronted Roosevelt as he welcomed his military advisers into his cluttered study at 2:55 p.m. Despite the troubles in the Pacific, he had enjoyed a quiet Sunday. Eleanor had hopped the train to New York for the weekend, where she had seen the Cole Porter play *Let's Face It!* on Broadway before traveling up to the family's home in Hyde Park. Snow flurries fell and the pond showed signs of freezing as she marveled at the foothills of the Catskills, a welcome reprieve from the war that now dominated her husband's life. "I wish I could tell you how clear and beautiful the stars were that twinkled through the windows of my porch Saturday night. I almost felt I could touch them," she wrote. "They made the world of war and sorrow seem so very far away and unreal." The president had eaten lunch with Harry Hopkins before meeting for twenty-five minutes with Ambassador Lord Halifax of Britain. Roosevelt had seen the diplomat out the door as he ushered in his war council.

Around the study sat Hopkins, War Secretary Stimson, Knox, Admiral Stark, newly appointed U.S. Fleet commander Admiral Ernest King, Army chief of staff General Marshall, and Lieutenant General Henry "Hap" Arnold, chief of the U.S. Army Air Forces. Roosevelt opened with news that Prime Minister Churchill and his team of more than eighty advisers would arrive the next day in Washington. Marshall gave the president an estimate of the situation, before Roosevelt zeroed in on the Far East, demanding America build up forces in Australia, the East Indies, and the Philippines. The president, like most Americans, felt anxious to fight. He planned to press Churchill about sending American troops into battle in the Atlantic theater, a move he felt would not only deliver a blow to German morale but buoy domestic spirits. Roosevelt wanted to achieve the same goal in the Pacific, where a White House analysis of editorial opinion revealed "almost unanimous endorsement of forceful action against Japan."

The challenge Roosevelt faced was that America was in no position to go on the offensive. The president's long struggle against isolationist lawmakers had handicapped America's war preparation at the same time Japan had stockpiled raw materials and hammered out thousands of new tanks, planes, and warships. Roosevelt had witnessed firsthand the struggle of the Army when he inspected maneuvers in August 1940 in upstate New York, only to discover soldiers drilling with drainpipes in place of mortars and broomsticks for machine guns. Some had never even fired a rifle. The Air Forces suffered similar shortages. Of America's three thousand combat planes, only about one-third were ready for war. So desperate was the Navy to recruit new sailors that it slashed standards for eyesight, height, and teeth; applicants needed as few as eighteen teeth, including just two molars. Even the president's war council appeared to suffer from such disorganization—no one bothered to take formal meeting minutes—that it would only infuriate British military leaders scheduled to arrive within hours. "The whole organization," one later griped, "belongs to the days of George Washington."

Roosevelt looked past these challenges and pressed his advisers: When could America operate from airfields in China? China appeared America's only real option to take the fight to Japan. The fall of Guam coupled with the siege of Wake and the attack on the Philippines had robbed America of strategic air and naval bases in the region. The Russian port city of Vladivostok would have been preferable—it was only 675 miles from Tokyo—but the Soviet-Japanese Neutrality Pact of April 1941 meant Premier Joseph Stalin would likely refuse such a request. Allowing American bombers to operate from Russia would only risk Japanese retaliation, a threat the beleaguered Soviets could not afford, given the war in the west against Germany. Marshall briefed Roosevelt on militarizing ex-Army officers who had volunteered to fly missions in China under Colonel Claire Chennault, a former fighter instructor who had passed on a quiet Louisiana retirement to advise the Chinese. The morning papers reported that Chennault's fliers had shot down four Japanese planes only the day before.

Though pleased with the news, the president wanted more. It was not enough to pick off a handful of enemy planes over the distant skies of China. Such a scuffle would hardly dent Japan's powerful war machine, much less spark fear among the empire's military leaders or civilian population. Likewise, such a small victory set against the continued defeats would have no real effect on the shell-shocked American public, particularly when compared with the spectacular raid on Pearl Harbor that had killed and injured thousands and crippled an entire fleet. The Japanese needed to experience the same shock, humiliation, and destruction that America had suffered. Roosevelt understood there was only one way to accomplish that lofty goal, a demand he would repeatedly press upon his advisers in the days and weeks to come. "The president was insistent," Arnold recalled, "that we find ways and means of carrying home to Japan proper, in the form of a bombing raid, the real meaning of war."

ADMIRAL ERNEST KING RETIRED to his cabin after dinner on the evening of Saturday, January 10, 1942. Much to the frustration of the sixty-three-year-old Ohioan, who served as commander in chief of the U.S. Fleet, Christmas and New Year's had passed without any reprieve from the bad news that dominated the Pacific. The admiral had spent the afternoon at a conference of two dozen senior American and British military leaders at the Federal Reserve Building, downtown on Constitution Avenue, the eighth of twelve such war strategy sessions that would later be known as the Arcadia Conference. The two-and-a-half-hour meeting, which had focused on topics ranging from how to blunt Japan's southward advance to immediate assistance for China, had adjourned with plans to meet again the following afternoon. King had hurried back to the Washington Navy Yard in time for dinner and an evening of work aboard his flagship, the *Vixen*, a 333-foot steel-hulled yacht moored in the frigid Anacostia River.

King was no stranger to long hours. The six-foot-tall admiral, who always wore a hat to hide his baldness, had graduated fourth in the class of 1901 at the Naval Academy, where his rosy cheeks had earned him the nickname Dolly, which he despised, favoring instead the name Rey, the Spanish word for king. He had served aboard destroyers and battleships and later commanded submarine divisions and even the sub base in New London, Connecticut. Recognizing the importance of naval aviation, King had earned his wings at forty-eight and later commanded the carrier *Lexington*. But the admiral wasn't without his flaws, from his wandering hands, which left women afraid to sit next to him at dinner parties, to the thirst for booze that had prompted him to invent his own cocktail, a mix of brandy and champagne that he dubbed "the King's Peg." The admiral's biggest fault, however, was his volcanic wrath, best described by one of his daughters: "He is the most even-tempered man in the Navy. He is always in a rage."

Despite his personal failings King had passion for military history and proved a brilliant strategist. A crossword puzzle addict, he admired Napoleon and walked the Civil War battlefields of Antietam and Gettysburg. His appreciation of history had led King—appointed by the president on December 20—to try to stall the official date he would take command until January 1, a move he felt would prevent the calamitous losses of 1941 from staining the legacy he hoped to create. Though America's war plan called largely for playing defense in the Pacific until the defeat of Hitler, King planned to seize every opportunity to go after the Japanese. That was the best way to keep the enemy off guard and unable to strike, a philosophy he outlined in a memo to fellow senior military leaders. "No fighter ever won his fight by covering up—by merely fending off the other fellow's blows," King wrote. "The winner hits and keeps on hitting even though he has to take some stiff blows in order to be able to keep on hitting."

Captain Francis Low appeared at the admiral's door on the *Vixen*. The forty-seven-year-old New York native, who served as King's operations officer, had graduated in 1915 from the Naval Academy. The son of a retired Navy commander, Low captained the academy's swim team, setting the school's 220-yard record and earning the nickname Frog. He had spent much of his career in the submarine service, commanding five boats and later a squadron before he landed on the admiral's staff. If anyone was used to King's tirades it was Low, who viewed his boss at times as both "rather cruel and unusual" and a "little understood and immensely complicated individual." "He was difficult to work for," Low later wrote in his unpublished memoir, "but serving with him was a liberal education—if one survived." Low had suffered one such blowup a year earlier on the battleship *Texas* when he was executing a routine course change in the middle of the night. The admiral appeared on the bridge within minutes.

"Who made that signal?" King barked.

"I did," Low answered.

King exploded, accusing Low of usurping power and undermining his authority. The shocked subordinate escaped to a wing of the bridge, his pride wounded. King cooled down and tried to apologize. "Low," the admiral began, putting his hand on his shoulder. "Don't feel too badly about this."

But Low turned on his boss.

"Admiral," he fired back, "aside from asking for my immediate detachment, there is not one goddamn thing that you can do to me that I can't take."

That bold move had earned King's respect.

"What is it, Low?" the admiral asked this January evening.

Low had what he later described as a "foolish idea," but given the dark early days of the war felt it was at least worth a mention.

"I've been to the Norfolk yard, as you know sir, to see the progress made on the *Hornet*," the captain began. "At the airfield they have marked out a strip about the size of a carrier deck, and they practice take-offs constantly."

"Well," King replied, baffled by the direction of Low's comments. "That's a routine operation for training carrier-based pilots."

"If the Army has some plane that could take off in that short distance," Low continued. "I mean a plane capable of carrying a bomb load, why couldn't we put a few of them on a carrier and bomb the mainland of Japan? Might even bomb Tokyo."

Low waited for the irascible admiral to brush him off—or worse—but to his surprise King leaned back in his chair. This was precisely the bold concept that appealed to the admiral's desire to go on the offensive.

"Low," King answered, "that might be a good idea. Discuss it with Duncan and tell him to report to me."

Low phoned Captain Donald Duncan, King's air operations officer. The forty-five-year-old Michigan native, who still answered to his Naval Academy nickname Wu, had graduated just two years behind Low. A trained naval aviator with a master's degree from Harvard, Duncan had served as navigator on the carrier *Saratoga*, as the executive officer of the Pensacola Naval Air Station, and later as commander of the first aircraft carrier escort, *Long Island*. He was also politically connected. His sister Barbara, before her 1937 death of cancer, was married to Harry Hopkins. "One thing I'll say about you," King once told Duncan, "you're no yes-man." Duncan would never forget that comment: "I always thought that, coming from Admiral King, was a very great compliment."

"This better be important," Duncan warned Low when the two met that Sunday morning at the Navy Department on Constitution Avenue.

"How would you like to plan a carrier-based strike against Tokyo?"

Low had piqued Duncan's interest.

"As I see it," Low explained, "there are two big questions that have to be answered first: Can an Army medium bomber land aboard a carrier? Can a land-based bomber loaded down with bombs, gas, and crew take off from a carrier deck?"

Duncan considered the questions, explaining that a carrier deck was too short for a bomber to land on. Even if it could, the fragile tail would never handle the shock of the arresting gear. Furthermore, a bomber would not fit in the aircraft elevator, making it impossible to stow the plane below to allow others to land.

"And my second question?" Low pressed.

"I'll have to get back to you."

Duncan started right away, drafting a preliminary plan. The main question was what, if any, plane could handle such a mission. Low had initially suggested the bombers might return to the carrier and ditch in the water, though Duncan's study showed it would be better if the planes could fly on to airfields in China. Since intelligence indicated that Japanese patrol planes flew as far as three hundred miles offshore, America would need a bomber that could launch well outside that range, strike Tokyo, and still have enough fuel to reach the mainland. Duncan reviewed the performance data of various Army planes. The Martin B-26 could cover the distance and carry a large bomb load, but it was questionable whether the bomber could lift off from a carrier's deck. Likewise, the B-23 could handle the demands of the mission, but the plane's larger wingspan risked a collision with the carrier's superstructure and limited how many bombers would fit on deck. Duncan realized that the twin-engine North American B-25 appeared best suited for the mission. Not only would its wings likely clear the island, but with modified fuel tanks the B-25 could handle the range and still carry a large bomb load.

Duncan next turned to ships. The Pacific Fleet had just four flattops, the *Saratoga*, *Enterprise*, *Lexington*, and *Yorktown*, the latter reassigned from the Atlantic after the attack on Pearl Harbor. But Duncan had another carrier in mind—the new 19,800-ton *Hornet*, undergoing shakedown in Virginia. Duncan knew the *Hornet* would report to the Pacific about the time it would take to finalize such an operation. Low had recommended the use of a single carrier, but Duncan realized the mission would require two. With the cumbersome bombers crowding the *Hornet*'s flight deck, a second flattop would have to accompany the task force to provide fighter coverage along with more than a dozen other cruisers, destroyers, and oilers. Lastly, a check of historical data revealed a likely window of favorable weather over Tokyo from mid-April to mid-May.

When Duncan concluded his preliminary study, he and Low presented the results to King. The aggressive admiral liked what he heard.

"Go see General Arnold about it, and if he agrees with you, ask him to get in touch with me," King ordered. "And don't you two mention this to another soul!"

The men agreed.

King then turned to Duncan. "If this plan gets the green light from General Arnold," he said, "I want you to handle the Navy end of it."

GENERAL ARNOLD HAD FOR weeks mulled over the president's demand that America bomb Japan, struggling to determine how the Army Air Forces might best execute such a bold mission. Few people in the nation could top the airpower expertise of the fifty-five-year-old Arnold, whose trademark grin had long ago earned him the nickname Hap, short for "happy." A 1907 graduate of the U.S. Military Academy, he had learned to fly from none other than Orville and Wilbur Wright, taking to the skies in a primitive biplane that lacked safety belts and whose sole instrumentation consisted of a simple string that fluttered in the wind to indicate the aircraft's skid. Only after a bug hit Arnold in the eye one day while landing did pilots adopt the trademark goggles. The six-foot-tall Arnold had completed his aviation course in just ten days in May 1911—his total flight time amounted to less than four hours—to become one of only two qualified pilots in the Army.

An avid prankster who once rolled cannonballs down a dormitory stairwell at West Point, Arnold was one of aviation's leading pioneers. He not only earned the distinction of being the first military man to fly more than a mile high, but he was the first pilot to carry the mail and even buzz the nation's Capitol, a stunt he joked in a letter to his mother prompted lawmakers "to adjourn." But the two-time recipient of aviation's prestigious Mackay Trophy nearly suffered tragedy in the fall of 1912 on an experimental flight in Kansas designed to observe artillery fire. Arnold's plane suddenly spun around, stalled, and dove. Only seconds before his plane would have hit, Arnold pulled the aircraft out of the dive and landed. The near crash so rattled him that he refused to fly. "At the present time," Arnold wrote to his commanding officer, "my nervous system is in such a condition that I will not get in any machine." To a fellow flier he was more blunt. "That's it," he confessed. "A man doesn't face death twice."

A sense of failure haunted Arnold for the next four years until he finally conquered his fear and climbed back into a cockpit. Over the years, Arnold advanced up the ranks, often in spite of himself. The maverick spirit that propelled him to risk his life in flimsy early airplanes made Arnold bristle at authority, drawing the frequent wrath of his superior officers, one of whom went so far as to hurl a paperweight at him. Arnold even clashed with Roosevelt in the spring of 1940 over Allied aircraft sales, resulting in the president's threatening to send him to Guam and exiling him from the White House for nine months. Despite his bull-headed personality—as well as his notoriously poor administrative skills—few could help admiring the tenacious general. The zealous advocate of American airpower, who had learned to fly in an Ohio cow pasture under the watchful eye of the local undertaker, had over three decades helped shape aviation's fundamental mission of bombardment. "The best defense," Arnold wrote, "is attack."

Arnold had walked out of Roosevelt's December 21 meeting with an order to bomb Japan but no clear path on how to execute such a mission. The general knew from experience that that was Roosevelt's style. "Once the President of the United States agreed upon the general principles," Arnold once observed, "he relied upon his Chiefs of Staff to carry them out—to make plans for the consummation of these general ideas." But the challenge Arnold faced was that his forces in the Pacific had been decimated in the opening hours of the war. Of the 231 planes assigned to the Hawaiian air force, only 79 still worked. The Japanese likewise had wiped out half the Far East air force in the Philippines. The immediate demands for airplanes had reached a climax, as Americans feared further attacks on Hawaii, Alaska, and even the West Coast. "Every commanding officer everywhere needed airplanes to stop the Japs from attacking his particular bailiwick," Arnold later wrote. "They all wanted heavy bombers and light bombers; they wanted patrol planes and fighters."

Arnold struggled to balance his limited resources with the increased pressure to take the fight to Japan. Ideas for how to avenge Pearl Harbor flooded Washington—a California tire dealer had even offered a $1,000 reward to the first flier to hit Tokyo. Though well-intentioned, most of the proposals showed little understanding of the logistics involved, from the great distances to the fuel and range limitations of American aircraft. Some of the ideas bordered on the absurd, including the recommendation that America drop bombs into volcanoes to trigger eruptions that might "convince the mass of Japanese that their gods were angry with them." The *Fort Worth Star-Telegram*'s president, Amon Carter, a close friend of Roosevelt's aide Edwin "Pa" Watson, suggested one of the more novel ideas: tap commercial airline pilots to fly four-engine bombers to Tokyo via Alaska. "It could, with proper secrecy and press censorship, be made in the nature of a surprise, the same as they gave our men in Pearl Harbor," Carter wrote. "Five hundred planes carrying from two to four thousands pounds of bombs could blow Tokio off the map."

Other ideas emerged from discussions between senior British and American officers. In a Christmas Eve conference with chief of air staff Sir Charles Portal, the British officer outlined his vision for an attack. "In his opinion," Arnold wrote, "attacking Japan was a Navy job, that the carriers, even at this early date, could sneak up to the vicinity of Japan and make the same kind of attack that the Japanese had made on Pearl

Harbor." The mission would involve no more risk than the Japanese took at Hawaii, Portal argued, yet it would force the Japanese Navy to return to home island waters, relieving pressure on the Philippines and Singapore. Arnold dismissed the idea. He not only felt reluctant to risk the Navy's few aircraft carriers but also questioned Portal's motives, given the British hunger for American planes. "I always thought that Portal mixed wishful thinking in with his reasoning concerning the Pacific aerial strategy," Arnold wrote. "I thought he was afraid if our Air Force planned to use heavy bombers against Japan it would cut down the number he would receive."

In another conference that same day, Admiral Stark followed up on the possibility of launching attacks from Chinese airfields. Arnold pointed out that America did not yet have enough bombers in China and warned against launching a raid until the Air Forces could send enough planes to create significant damage. "The minimum number of bombers should be 50," Arnold advised Stark. "Unsustained attacks would only tend to solidify the Japanese people." With Russia out and China short on planes, America's options appeared to dwindle, unless Arnold followed Portal's advice and ceded the operation to the Navy. At a January 4 White House conference about the possible invasion of North Africa, Admiral King suggested shipping Army bombers aboard carriers. The idea piqued Arnold's curiosity, as evidenced by the notes he scribbled. "By transporting these Army bombers on a carrier, it will be necessary for us to take off from the carrier," he wrote. "We will have to try bomber takeoff from carriers. It has never been done before but we must try out and check on how long it takes."

Arnold's staff started to examine the idea immediately, though focusing on the limited concept of using Army cargo planes aboard a carrier to transport fuel for an expeditionary force of naval fighters. An informal agreement between Arnold and King—described in a January 5 memo—even proposed testing various transports off a flattop. In response, analysts pulled together data on planes with wingspans under ninety feet, including true air speed, flap settings, and ground run required for takeoff as well as the height of each plane and feasibility of removing the wings to allow storage in a hangar deck. Analysts ruled out the DC-3 and DC-2 because neither plane's wingspan would clear a carrier's superstructure and because the fuselages were too long to ride down the aircraft elevator. The C-63 was another option, but the Army simply didn't have enough of them available yet. In a January 13 memo Arnold's staff leveled with the general: cargo planes wouldn't work. "It is not believed that any plane now available, which can operate from a carrier, would justify the test under consideration."

About this time Low and Duncan appeared in the general's office. Rather than launch cargo planes in support of the Navy, why not use B-25s and make them raiders? The greater range of the twin-engine Army bombers would mean the carriers would not have to approach so close to Japan. If the bombers flew on to China as proposed, then the carriers could immediately turn back, further limiting the risk to America's precious flattops. Arnold enthusiastically embraced the concept, but he wanted to run it by his staff troubleshooter, Lieutenant Colonel Jimmy Doolittle. The forty-five-year-old Doolittle had grabbed national headlines over the years as a stunt and racing pilot who Arnold knew also happened to boast master's and doctoral degrees from the prestigious Massachusetts Institute of Technology. If anyone could evaluate this plan's chance of success, Doolittle could. Arnold summoned him to his office.

"Jim, what airplane do we have that can take off in 500 feet, carry a 2,000-pound bomb load, and fly 2,000 miles with a full crew?"

Doolittle conducted a mental inventory of America's arsenal, deducing that only a medium bomber would be able to lift off in that short distance. Of the four bombers he considered, three might be able to handle the job.

"General," he answered, "give me a little time and I'll give you an answer."

Doolittle researched each plane's performance data before reporting the next day that either the B-23 or the B-25 would work. Both would require extra fuel tanks.

Arnold added another demand: the plane must have a narrow enough wingspan to lift off in an area less than seventy-five feet wide.

"Then there's only plane that can do it," Doolittle replied. "The B-25 is the answer to your question."

Arnold thanked Doolittle, who exited the office.

Doolittle had hit on the exact plane as Duncan. Arnold picked up the phone to Admiral King. The plan was a go. The *Hornet* would depart the West Coast around April 1, a date that would allow the carrier time to finish its shakedown and transit the Panama Canal. Duncan would handle logistics for the Navy. That would include overseeing trial take-offs from the *Hornet* as well as a visit to Pearl Harbor to organize the task force. Arnold would need to pick someone on his side to direct the modification of the bombers and to train the aircrews. The general summoned Doolittle again the next day.

"Jim, I need someone take this job over—"

"And I know where you can get that someone," Doolittle interrupted.

"Okay, it's your baby," Arnold told him. "You'll have first priority on anything you need to get the job done. Get in touch with me directly if anybody gets in your way."

CHAPTER 3

★

Doolittle is as gifted with brains as he is with courage.
—*NEW YORK TIMES*,
SEPTEMBER 23, 1927

THE PLAN LAID OUT by General Arnold was the perfect operation for Jimmy Doolittle, a man who on first glimpse did not appear to be such a formidable fighter. The gray-eyed Doolittle stood just five feet four—two inches shorter than Napoleon—though he frequently upped his height a couple of inches on official records. His short stature had shaped his personality from his childhood days along the Alaskan frontier, where his father, Frank Doolittle, had relocated the family from California during the gold rush at the turn of the twentieth century. The rugged town of Nome looked to Doolittle as he disembarked the ship like a sea of tents, shacks, and cabins. Mud paths served as roads, and public sanitation consisted of toilets built atop pilings along the waterfront to let the daily tides flush away the waste. Dysentery and typhoid fever flourished, as did crime in a town that boasted two dozen saloons and liquor stores. Doolittle even watched one day as half a dozen wild dogs tore apart his best friend in the streets.

Doolittle's small size was a disadvantage among his peers. Students picked on him in school, and as punishment one time his teacher made him write twenty-five times on the chalkboard, "Jimmy Doolittle is the smallest boy in the school." Doolittle raised his fists for the first time at the age of five when he battled a native Alaskan child. "One of my punches caught him on the nose and blood spurted all over his parka. It scared us both," Doolittle later recalled. "I ran home to my mother, certain that I had killed an Eskimo." He soon proved he was a capable fighter despite his small size. Word spread, and bigger children lined up for the chance to battle the scrappy youth. Doolittle, in turn, found that he actually enjoyed the challenge of a good fight. "Since my size was against me, I decided my survival could be insured only by a speedy attack right from the start," he later wrote. "I found it was easy to draw blood if you were nimble on your feet, aimed at a fellow's nose, and got your licks in early."

Doolittle's father never found much gold, but instead worked mostly as a carpenter. Tools fascinated the younger Doolittle so much that his father gave him his own set and encouraged him to learn to work with his hands. Doolittle helped his father build furniture and even houses, developing important mechanical skills that would prove vital years later when he worked on engines and airplanes. Doolittle joined his father in the summer of 1904 on a six-week trip to Seattle, San Francisco, and Los Angeles that turned out to be transformative. "The sights and sounds in the three big cities were strange and exciting to me at age seven, since I had forgotten everything of what I had seen before we went to Nome," Doolittle later wrote. "I saw my first automobile, train, and trolley car. There were modern houses and stores with paint on them. My values changed right then and there. I saw everything in a new perspective and I wanted very much to be a part of the exciting life I saw all too briefly during that trip."

His mother, Rosa, agreed and packed up and returned to California in 1908 with her then eleven-year-old son, leaving his quixotic father behind in Alaska. Rather than return to Doolittle's native Alameda, she settled near family in Los Angeles. The schoolyard brawls that had helped shape Doolittle's time in Alaska continued. One such fight caught the attention of an English teacher and boxing instructor, Forest Bailey. "You're going to get hurt badly fighting the way you do," Bailey told Doolittle. "You get mad when you fight. If you lose your temper, you're eventually going to lose a fight because you let your emotions instead of your head rule your body." Bailey stripped Doolittle of his rough street-fighting form and coached him instead on how to bob and weave as well as target his blows with greater power to compensate for his short arms. These skills helped the fifteen-year-old Doolittle, fighting as a 105-pound flyweight, win the Amateur Boxing Championship of the Pacific Coast in 1912.

But the teenage hothead continued to battle outside the ring as well, landing in jail one Saturday night on a charge of disturbing the peace. The police phoned Doolittle's mother to come retrieve him. Never a fan of his boxing, she had finally had enough. "She wants you to stay here until Monday morning," the officer told Doolittle. "She'll drop by then and get you out in time for school." The adolescent was stunned that his mother would leave him in jail for the weekend, but the experience taught him an invaluable lesson. "Being incarcerated in a cold, unheated cell for two nights and being totally deprived of the right to leave was a shocking experience for me," Doolittle later wrote. "I vowed never again to let my emotions overcome reason." His mother tried to bribe him with a motorcycle to quit boxing, but the crafty teen instead adopted the pseudonym Jim Pierce and used his new bike to motor up and down the West Coast, earning as much as thirty dollars a bout boxing professionally in various clubs.

Doolittle let his emotions overcome him again when he met Josephine Daniels, a classmate at Los Angeles Manual Arts High School who went by the nickname Joe. The pretty young woman with long dark hair rebuffed her cocky suitor for several years until, like a boxer, he finally wore her down. The two of them could not have been more different. "She was a very good little girl. I was a very naughty little boy," Doolittle recalled. "She got all A's; I had a hard time getting C's." Joe came from a cultured family, who had moved to California from Louisiana. Her parents frowned on Doolittle, a roughneck who cared little for academics and often sported bruises and a split lip from his battles in the ring. Even Doolittle's own mother warned Joe that she could do better than her troublesome son. "There's no doubt that Joe changed my life," he later said. "I began to comb my hair, wear a tie, look after my clothes, and watch my language around her." During his senior year of high school he asked her to marry him.

"You must think I am out of my mind," she answered. "I could never marry a man who wants to fight all the time."

"I'll give up fighting," he argued, telling her of his plans to return to Alaska and hunt for gold. "As soon as I have some money, I'll send for you."

"My mother would never approve."

"I am going to marry you," he countered, "not your mother."

When he graduated from high school in spring of 1914, Doolittle accepted his father's invitation to return to Alaska. Doolittle and his father had never been close, and the reunion failed to remedy the pair's strained relationship. The younger Doolittle soon set off on his own, living in a tent and eating nothing but salmon as he panned unsuccessfully for gold. Doolittle realized after several weeks that he had had enough. He hitchhiked back to the coastal town of Seward and bade his father farewell, not knowing that it would be the last time he ever saw him. Doolittle hired on as a steward aboard a Seattle-bound ship and then stowed away on a freighter to Los Angeles, his dream of striking it rich now over. He planned instead to enroll in college and earn a degree. "Alaska was not the land of opportunity I thought it might be," he later wrote, adding, "It was a far wiser Jim Doolittle who entered college."

Doolittle studied at Los Angeles Junior College for two years, then enrolled at the University of California School of Mines at Berkeley, where he boxed on the varsity team and professionally to help pay the bills. He resurrected the alias Jim Pierce to hide his bouts from his mother and Joe. He slugged his way through a string of weak opponents before he climbed into the ring with a nimble pro. Doolittle knew right away he was in trouble. "He made a monkey out of me," he later recalled. "That was the end of my boxing career." Doolittle decided instead to focus on his education, though his battles in the ring had taught him an invaluable lesson in life, one he would articulate years later in a letter to his wife after the couple's youngest son lost a college boxing match. "Luckiest thing in the world that John was whipped by the Syracuse boy. Some time in life we have to learn how to lose and the sooner the better," Doolittle wrote. "Every boy should learn how to win graciously and lose courageously."

The United States entered World War I in 1917, prompting many of Doolittle's classmates to enlist. Never one to miss out on a good fight, Doolittle decided to skip his senior year and join the Army. He had no desire to serve in the infantry or coastal artillery, but saw potential in the fledgling air force after a recruiter told him the Army planned to train as many as five thousand new pilots. Flight had long fascinated Doolittle, who as a teenager had attempted to build both a glider and a monoplane on the basis of plans he found in the magazine *Popular Mechanics*, neither of which ever flew. He attended ground school for eight weeks at the University of California, using his holiday break to persuade Joe to marry him. Doolittle had no money, so Joe paid for the license with cash her mother had given her as a Christmas gift. The couple wed Christmas Eve at Los Angeles City Hall. Joe's remaining twenty dollars paid for the honeymoon in San Diego, where the couple survived off cafeterias that offered service members free meals.

Doolittle finished ground school and then reported for pilot training at Rockwell Field near San Diego. He had never before been up in a plane and was excited for the experience when he climbed into a Curtis JN-4 for his first flight, on January 28, 1918. The two-seater biplane commonly known as a Jenny was America's first mass-produced aircraft. Made from little more than wood, fabric, and wires, the trainer had a maximum speed of just seventy-five miles per hour. Doolittle and instructor Charles Todd taxied out for takeoff when two planes collided in the skies over the airfield and crashed. Doolittle jumped from the cockpit and darted to the wreckage of the closest plane, occupied by a student pilot who had flown solo. To Doolittle's horror, the student was dead. In the second plane Doolittle found an instructor and student, both badly injured but still alive. Doolittle and Todd helped pull the two injured aviators from the wreckage as the fire truck and ambulance roared up.

"You all right?" Todd asked Doolittle.

The crash had rattled him, but he confirmed he was fine.

"Okay," Todd replied. "Let's go."

Doolittle climbed back into the Jenny, and Todd fired up the engine. The biplane roared down the runway and lifted off into the sky. Doolittle quickly forgot the tragedy on the ground below as Todd guided the plane up to twelve hundred feet. Doolittle's logbook shows that the flight lasted just twenty-two minutes, time enough to hook Doolittle on aviation. "My love for flying," he later wrote, "began on that day during that hour." The eager student soaked up his time in the cockpit, soloing after just seven hours and four minutes of instruction. Doolittle graduated from flight school and earned his commission as a second lieutenant on March 11, 1918. He knew exactly what type of pilot he wanted to be. "I naturally went into fighter pilot aviation, because there is a basic difference between the fighter pilot and the bomber pilot," he later recalled. "The fighter pilot is almost always a rugged individualist. The bomber pilot, in that he works with a team, in the airplane, is much more inclined to be a team player."

Much to his frustration, Doolittle sat out World War I, bouncing around from various posts before landing as an aviation instructor at Ream Field near San Diego. "I was pretty upset," he later recalled. "My students were going overseas and becoming heroes. My job was to make more heroes." The experience was not without tragedy. When Doolittle came in one day on his final approach, a student pilot in another plane cut beneath him. Neither Doolittle nor the student with him saw the other plane. The collision damaged Doolittle's propeller and took off his landing gear, forcing him to put the plane down on its belly. He then learned the gruesome news that his propeller had decapitated the other flyer. Another time as Doolittle and a student took off, a solo pilot drifted across his flight path. Doolittle's propeller cut off the tail of the other plane. To his horror the other plane crashed and burned, killing the student. In each case Doolittle applied the same approach Todd had taken with him.

"Who's next?" he called out after one mishap.

"What in the hell have you got in your veins—ice water?" one of the other instructors demanded of Doolittle. "Doesn't that kid's death mean a thing to you?"

"I'll think of that kid tonight," he fired back. "Meanwhile my job is to make flyers out of these men. So is yours."

When World War I ended, on November 11, 1918, Doolittle faced a difficult decision: return to the University of California to finish his mining degree or remain in the Army. Many aviators who left the military bought up some of the more than eight thousand Jennys built during the war that the military now sold as surplus for as little as a few hundred dollars. These pilots traveled the nation barnstorming, performing aerial stunts like wing walking, barrel rolls, and loops. Others offered rides to curious passengers for a couple of dollars apiece. Doolittle knew not only that barnstorming was dangerous and nomadic work but that the pay was abysmal. He now had a wife to support. "I was making about $140 a month and the money was there on payday without fail," Doolittle later wrote. "The security of the military life was very appealing to me as hundreds of men were demobilized and had to look for jobs while the nation tried to rebuild a peacetime economy. But it was the flying that made up my mind."

"What future is there in being a pilot?" one of Doolittle's friends asked.

"Someday aviation is going to be real big business," he replied. "I'm going to stay in the Army and let the government teach me everything there is to be learned about airplanes."

The military air show late that November in San Diego convinced Doolittle he had made the right decision when he and other pilots dazzled the crowd with aerial acrobatics. "So close to one another that they seemed almost to touch, they formed a ceiling over the sky that almost blotted out the struggling rays of the sun," gushed the *Los Angeles Times*. "With majestic solemnity they patrolled the air, magnificent in the perfection of their formation, and while they framed a perfect background at 5,000 feet, the five acrobats below swooped, dived, looped and spun in as perfect unison as though they had been operated by a single hand." The air service looked to increase the public's enthusiasm for aviation, encouraging aviators to perform stunts at county fairs as well as attempt record-setting flights, anything to garner headlines. The adventurous Doolittle jumped at the opportunity. "I tried to invent new stunts and realized there was a similarity between aerobatics in the air and acrobatics on the ground in that you mentally previewed a maneuver," he wrote. "If you failed, you tried it again and again until you mastered it."

Doolittle pushed himself and his airplane to the limit, much to the frustration of his commanding officers, a reaction captured in an early efficiency report. "He is energetic mentally and physically and possesses but one serious drawback," the report noted. "That is his inclination occasionally to use poor judgment; i.e., take exceptional and unnecessary risks in flying." That recklessness was on display one afternoon when he spotted two soldiers walking on a road and decided to give them a fright. He buzzed the soldiers, only to look back and find them waving at him. The indignant Doolittle circled back and flew even lower. This time he felt a bump. A glance over his shoulder horrified him: one of the soldiers lay face down. Doolittle felt certain he had killed the soldier and in his shock failed to spot a fence. He snagged his landing gear on the barbed wire and crashed a $10,000 taxpayer-funded plane. Much to Doolittle's relief, he had only grazed the soldier. "Gee, Lieutenant," the gracious soldier offered, "I'm glad you weren't hurt."

Another time Doolittle bet friends five dollars he could sit on the wheel axle while landing, a stunt that happened to be caught on film by movie director Cecil B. DeMille, who was shooting at the field that day. When Doolittle's commanding officer saw the grainy footage, he knew exactly who it was. "It has to be Doolittle," he erupted. "No one else would be that crazy!" News of his antics rose up the chain of command. Hap Arnold at the time commanded nearby Rockwell Field when one of his subordinates barged into his office. "Colonel," he said, "there's a man down at Ream Field whose conduct has been so bad it requires your personal attention." Arnold grounded him for a month. Though many of Doolittle's antics were no doubt reckless, each time he pushed himself he did so in an effort to learn the boundaries of his ability. "The only really dangerous pilot is the one that flies beyond his limitation," Doolittle later said. "A poor pilot is not necessarily a dangerous pilot, as long as he remains within his limitations."

Despite Doolittle's exploits that at times drove his superiors to distraction—from flying through a hangar in order to sweep it out to severing phone lines when he flew under a bridge—there was little doubt the young aviator possessed unique skill. His early efficiency reports often glowed about him, predicting a bright future.

"Doolittle is more valuable to the Air Service than any officer I know," stated one such report.

"Dynamic personality," argued another. "An exceptional combination of very capable engineer and superior pilot."

"One of the most daring and skillful young aviators in the Air Service accomplished in the highest form of combat training."

Doolittle used his daring in 1922 to attempt to make the first cross-country flight in less than twenty-four hours, from Florida's Pablo Beach to San Diego. Doolittle had organized a similar transcontinental flight from California to Washington several years earlier; it had ended in failure after two of the three Jennys had run out of fuel or crashed just a few hundred miles into the flight. Doolittle returned to San Diego, only to bang up his own plane after he put it down on a soft and freshly plowed field, having battled heavy winds. The veteran aviator was determined to avoid the same mistakes that had plagued him before. Doolittle spent two months mapping his route, studying decades of weather data, and overseeing each day adjustments to his plane. "The preparations for this flight were mainly personal," Doolittle wrote in his report. "Physical, in order to stand the severe strain of the trip, and mental to obviate all chance of worry which, I believe is the factor most apt to cause mental fatigue and bad judgment."

On the evening of August 6 Doolittle climbed into the cockpit of a specially built De Havilland DH-4, a biplane with a maximum speed of 128 miles per hour. The confident aviator had publicized his planned feat, and thousands turned out to see him off. He throttled up the engine at 9:40 p.m. and roared down the beach. Several hundred yards into the takeoff, the plane hit a patch of soft sand and veered toward the surf. The plane crashed into the waves and flipped over, crushing the nose and ramming the motor back four inches. Doolittle's elbow smashed the tachometer. He unbuckled his safety belt and dropped out, landing on his head and knocking his helmet and goggles down over his face. Disoriented and convinced he was underwater, he grabbed the fuselage to pull himself up. "I was shocked to find how heavy I was because I thought I would be more buoyant in the water," he later wrote. "When I pushed the helmet and goggles off my eyes and put my feet down, I found I was standing in only about 10 inches of water!"

The crowd erupted in laughter at the sight of the dazed airman struggling to save himself from drowning in the shallow surf.

One woman asked whether he was hurt.

"No," a humiliated Doolittle replied, "but my feelings are."

The young aviator refused to give up. He oversaw the plane's repairs, ranging from a new motor and propeller to tail section and wings. Armed with thermoses of ice water and hot coffee—each equipped with special drinking straws—Doolittle climbed back into his repaired De Havilland a month later. This time he made no advance publicity of his trip. Eighteen lanterns lined the edge of the surf as he raced down the beach and lifted off at 9:52 p.m. on September 4. A few hours into the trip Doolittle ran into a massive electrical storm. The lightning crashed so close that he could smell the ozone while the cold rains stung his face. "I realized the storm area was too extensive to dodge, and plunged directly into it, trusting my compass to steer a straight course," Doolittle later wrote. "At each flash of lightning I peeked over the side of the cockpit, saw familiar landmarks, and, after consulting the Rand-McNally road maps spread out before me, knew that I was flying high and free and true."

Doolittle flew a straight course, passing just west of New Orleans and on to San Antonio, where he landed just past daybreak. He stayed on the ground only long enough to take on fuel before he charged back into the skies. The empty desert below coupled with the roar of the engine forced Doolittle to fight his body's hunger for sleep as the hours droned past. Two fellow pilots intercepted the exhausted airman as he approached Rockwell, guiding Doolittle down to the field after twenty-two hours and thirty minutes. The 2,163-mile trip across eight states, which demonstrated how the Army could deploy planes from one coast to another in a single day, earned Doolittle both the Distinguished Flying Cross and the prestigious Mackay Trophy. Major General Mason Patrick, commander of the air service, sent Doolittle a letter of personal thanks. "I have read with a great deal of interest the report of your transcontinental flight," Patrick wrote, "and desire to extend my most hearty congratulations for your fine work."

Doolittle applied the next year for one of the Army's six slots for postgraduate students at MIT. His failure to finish college would have rendered him ineligible, but colleagues persuaded officials at the University of California to award Doolittle his degree on the basis of his work with the Army. The new college graduate and now father of two young sons moved his family to Massachusetts in September 1923. Doolittle set out to solve the mystery of how much punishment a pilot could withstand, as well as a plane before it broke apart, hoping to shed important new light on unexplained crashes. Doolittle married his classroom work with almost one hundred hours of experimentation in the skies, putting a Dutch Fokker PW-7 fighter through a series of intense loops, rolls, and spirals at various speeds. He pushed himself and his plane so hard that he nearly ripped the wings off during a dive at two hundred miles per hour. "I was glad I wore my parachute that day," he later said. "I almost needed it."

Doolittle's experiments helped define the limits of plane endurance and revealed important effects of gravitational forces on pilots. Though fliers could handle short spikes in g-forces, Doolittle found, sustained acceleration led pilots to black out. The key was blood pressure. The higher a pilot's blood pressure, the higher acceleration the flier could endure. Doolittle published his findings in a paper that was translated into a dozen languages and led the Army to later award him a second Distinguished Flying Cross. The humble aviator who earned both a master's and a doctorate of science from MIT later confessed that his academic success came down to the dedication of his wife, Joe, who each day typed up his class notes and drilled him on them. "We would often study together far into the night," Doolittle recalled. "She would ask me questions, and her technique served to refresh my memory and reinforce what I had heard that day. She often put into words the thoughts I was trying to express."

Doolittle applied his newfound expertise when the Army tapped him to compete in the 1925 Pulitzer and Schneider Cup races. A coin toss determined that his fellow Army pilot Lieutenant Cyrus Bettis would fly the Pulitzer Race at Long Island's Mitchel Field, while Doolittle stood by as his alternate. The aviators would rotate roles two weeks later near Baltimore for the Schneider Cup. To drum up interest the pilots took to the skies over Manhattan, buzzing down Broadway and over Times Square. Doolittle soaked it up. "We performed aerobatics all over downtown New York City," he later recalled. "It was a rare thrill to fly down the city streets and look up at the tall buildings. It was also interesting to do it inverted." Doolittle cheered Bettis to victory on October 12 in the Pulitzer, studying how he and other pilots rounded the course pylons. Doolittle calculated that he could shave them even closer with sharper banks, moves that would guarantee his victory when he climbed into the cockpit to compete for the coveted Schneider Cup.

Unlike the Pulitzer, the Schneider Cup was a seaplane race—and Doolittle had never before flown one. The race required pilots to fly seven laps around a 31-mile triangular course for a total of 217 miles. The gun fired at 2:30 p.m. that sunny October 26, and Doolittle roared into the skies over the Chesapeake Bay. He charged around the course at an average speed of 232 miles per hour; 55 miles an hour faster than the preceding year's record. Determined he could fly even faster, he took off the next day and set the world seaplane record over a straightaway course with an average speed of 245 miles per hour, smashing the previous record of 228 miles per hour. The self-taught seaplane newbie infuriated his vanquished Navy competitors. "The flying of Doolittle was masterly," observed the *New York Times*. "When Doolittle banked around the home pylon he held his plane in so tightly that he passed over the heads of those on the judges' stand so closely that they felt the wind from his propeller."

The audience erupted in cheers when Doolittle taxied to the pier, prompting the gracious aviator to slip off his leather hat and offer a humble bow. Air force commander General Patrick greeted him at the pier's end with congratulations. "This was one of the most able demonstrations I have ever witnessed," he wrote in a commendation letter, "one of which I am extremely proud." Even Secretary of War Dwight Davis telegrammed his congratulations. "Your splendid accomplishment in winning the Jacques Schneider once more proves America's position among the nations of the world. The victory was won through your superior knowledge of aeronautics," Davis cabled. "The War Department is proud of you." Doolittle's friends planned a proper celebration upon his return to Ohio's McCook Field, forcing the victor into a naval uniform and then into a lifeboat mounted atop a truck bed. The gang then drove him through Dayton with signs attached to the boat that read, "Admiral James H. Doolittle."

Doolittle's fame grew so much that the Curtis Aeroplane and Motor Company asked the Army in 1926 to allow him to travel to Chile and Argentina to demonstrate the company's P-1 Hawk fighter. "I believe it very desirable that this should be permitted," Patrick advised the chief of staff. "We are trying hard here to keep aircraft manufacturers in being. Any foreign business they can secure is advantageous alike to them and to the United States." Doolittle saw the opportunity differently. "It was a dream assignment," he recalled. "I would get paid for stunting and there would be no rules about how low I could get or what maneuvers I could perform." At a May 23 cocktail party at the Santiago officers club, conversation turned to famed silent picture actor Douglas Fairbanks, known for his swashbuckling roles. Under the influence of a few pisco sours—a popular South American cocktail—Doolittle boasted that all Americans could perform like Fairbanks. He walked across the room on his hands to prove it.

The Chilean pilots cheered his feat, which only encouraged the intoxicated airman. Someone volunteered that Fairbanks could do a handstand on a window ledge. Not to be outdone Doolittle climbed out an open window onto a two-foot ledge. He rose up on his hands to the eager applause of his audience. The ledge crumbled seconds later, and Doolittle plunged fifteen feet to the walkway below. The excruciating pain that shot through his legs when he hit alerted him that he was in serious trouble. X-rays revealed that Doolittle had broken both of his ankles. The injured aviator spent fifteen days in bed at San Vincente de Paul Hospital, followed by another forty-five days on his back at the Union Club of Santiago. Doolittle sank into despair. His recklessness meant Curtis had no one to demonstrate the company's prized fighter. "Embarrassment overcame pain," Doolittle later wrote. "There was no way I was going to stay in that hospital while my competitors were touting their wares at El Bosque."

Doolittle summoned Curtis mechanic Boyd Sherman and instructed him to bring a hacksaw. Sherman cut his casts down below the knee and made clips to attach Doolittle's flying boots to the pedals. The first time he went up he put so much pressure on his right leg in a snap roll that he cracked the cast. Doolittle's furious doctors refused to treat him again, so Sherman helped him remove the casts. He then hired a German prostheses maker to fashion special casts reinforced with flexible metal corset stays. Doolittle took to the skies, buzzing his competition and dazzling the crowd on the ground below with his aerial acrobatics. His tenaciousness not only helped Curtis score its biggest military contract since World War I but wowed the military attaché, who sent a report to General Patrick, informing him that Doolittle left his room a total of four times to make aerial demonstrations. "These flights," Colonel James Hanson wrote, "were made with legs in plaster casts, and he was carried to and from the aeroplane."

Doolittle returned home to the United States at the completion of the trip and checked into Walter Reed Army Medical Center in Washington. Four months had passed since his fall, yet Doolittle still required crutches to walk. He had grown alarmed while still in Chile over his slow recovery and had a second set of x-rays taken, only to learn that the treating doctors had mistakenly reversed his casts, causing his ankles to heal improperly. By the time Doolittle reached Walter Reed, his prognosis did not look good, as revealed by the chief of the orthopedic service's testimony before a board of medical officers. "His injury may result in a permanent disability," the doctor told the board, "which will unfit him for the duties of an officer." Rather than rebreak Doolittle's ankles, doctors chose instead to set them in new casts and ordered him back to bed. This time he stayed put. When his treatment finally ended, in April 1927, Doolittle was relieved that a medical board found him fit for duty.

The restless Doolittle was itching to return to flying. He and other pilots at Walter Reed had discussed the challenge of flying an outside loop, a never-before-accomplished feat. Unlike a common aerial loop in which a pilot flies up and over backward, the outside loop required a pilot to fly first down and then loop underneath. Many aviators wondered whether the reverse forces would prove too much for the plane and the pilot. Doolittle decided to find out. He practiced the stunt until he felt confident he could pull it off. He summoned half a dozen fellow fliers to serve as witnesses and took off in a Curtis Hawk on May 25, 1927. He climbed up to eight thousand feet then turned the plane over and dove. From 150 miles per hour, his speed shot up to 280 as he turned the Hawk over on its back, remembering despite his disorientation to keep the stick pressed forward. He shot out of the loop and landed in the nation's headlines. "Nothing to it," Doolittle later told the press. "Why, it's just an uncomfortable feeling that's all."

The famed aviator returned to South America in 1928 to demonstrate airplanes for Curtis, this time with a stern warning from Joe to avoid officers clubs that served pisco sours. Doolittle's voyage home that summer by ship offered the thirty-one-year-old a chance to consider his future. With a wife and two growing boys to support, he started to contemplate a career outside the Army. "What would I do?" he wondered. "Who would want me? If I got a nonflying civilian job, would I miss flying and regret my decision to resign my regular commission?" Doolittle reached McCook Field without any resolution on his future, when an offer arrived from the Daniel Guggenheim Fund for the Promotion of Aeronautics, one that would allow him to remain in the Army yet tackle an important new project that promised once again to push the limits of aviation. Doolittle would head up a laboratory at Mitchel Field, overseeing a one-year experiment on blind flight. The analytical airman jumped at the opportunity.

Aviation had greatly evolved over the years, but foul weather still handicapped even the most experienced pilots. "Fog is one of the greatest enemies of modern transportation," famed pilot Charles Lindbergh wrote in a January 1929 editorial. "It often brings shipping to a standstill and seriously delays ground travel, but the greatest effect of low visibility and bad weather is in aviation." Blind flight presented three major challenges: takeoff, navigation, and landing, the last the most difficult. Overcoming those challenges called for new instrumentation to help orient a blind pilot. Doolittle recruited inventor Paul Kollsman, who had just devised a new barometric altimeter accurate to within a few feet. He worked with engineer Elmer Sperry and his son to simulate an artificial horizon that revealed the bank and pitch of a plane as well as a directional gyroscope that would provide a pilot with a more accurate heading than a compass. A radio beacon would help a flier navigate.

For more than ten months the team worked to develop the necessary equipment as well as devise proper flying techniques to master blind flight. Doolittle had personally made hundreds of blind and simulated blind landings. The time to finally test those strategies arrived on the morning of September 24, 1929. A heavy fog blanketed Mitchel Field. The impatient Doolittle had made an unofficial test flight shortly past daybreak as he waited on his team to assemble. That flight had revealed a dense fog up to five hundred feet, perfect conditions for the feat. Harry Guggenheim, the fund's president, arrived to witness the official test. Even Joe turned out to watch. Doolittle climbed inside the rear cockpit of a Consolidated NY-2 Husky, zipping a canvas hood over the top. His only view would be the lighted dials that lined his instrument panel. Guggenheim insisted pilot Ben Kelsey accompany Doolittle as a precaution, though he would keep his hands above his head so ground observers could see he was not flying.

Doolittle throttled up his plane and took off into the morning wind, leveling off at about a thousand feet. He flew five miles west of the airfield before he banked and circled back. The radio beacon that consisted of two reeds that vibrated as he neared the signal alerted him as he passed directly over the airfield. Doolittle shot a glance at his air speed indicator as he clicked his stopwatch. He flew another two miles east before he turned back and began a gradual descent. Anxious witnesses on the ground watched as Doolittle cleared the edge of the field by fifty feet. The plane slowed to a glide, then dropped down to fifteen feet above the runway, when Doolittle pulled the nose up, touching down just a few feet from where he had lifted off only fifteen minutes earlier. "This entire flight was made under the hood in a completely covered cockpit which had been carefully sealed to keep out all light," Doolittle later said. "It was the first time an airplane had been taken off, flown over a set course and landed by instruments alone."

News of Doolittle's achievement landed him again on the nation's front pages and would forever change aviation. "On Tuesday a brilliant victory was recorded," heralded the *New York Times*. "No more versatile aviator than Lieutenant James H. Doolittle of the army could have been chosen." One of those most impressed was Hap Arnold, who a decade earlier had grounded Doolittle over his flying antics at Ream Field. "That took real courage," Arnold would write in a 1941 letter. "There was no cheering crowd. No Audience. Just Jim Doolittle, risking one life that many others might live." Doolittle celebrated with his team that night over dinner, each member autographing Joe's white damask tablecloth. She later embroidered each signature with black thread to preserve them in what would become a Doolittle family tradition. "Over the years, everyone who broke bread at our table was asked to do the same," he later wrote. "Joe painstakingly stitched over 500 signatures on the tablecloth."

Doolittle's concerns over his future returned after he completed his tenure with the blind-flight laboratory; this time he made the difficult decision to jump to the Shell Petroleum Corporation as head of the aviation department. "I left the Air Force in 1930 for one reason and one reason only and that was because my wife's mother was ill, my mother was ill, her father was gone, my father was gone, it had come upon us to take care of them," Doolittle later said. "We couldn't do it properly on my military pay. When I went to the Shell Oil Company my pay was triple." For Shell that was a bargain. The famed aviator, who remained in the Army as reservist, continued to race. He won the Bendix Trophy in 1931, setting a new transcontinental record of just eleven hours and fifteen minutes. The next year he cinched the Thompson Trophy. Doolittle had not only won three of air racing's leading prizes but managed at 293 miles per hour to unofficially best the world's land plane speed record by 15 miles per hour.

Doolittle had in the past promised to give up racing, but kept returning to the sport. "Air racing is like hay fever," he liked to say. "It crops up when the season is ripe." When Doolittle learned that newspaper photographers had shadowed Joe and his two sons during the Thompson race, hoping to record their horror if he was killed, he finally decided to quit. A wiser Doolittle acknowledged the danger in a speech the next year: "I have yet to hear of the first case of anyone engaged in this work dying of old age." Racing had helped advance aviation, arousing public interest, sparking new ideas for wing and fuselage designs as well as increased engine power and improved fuels, but it had come at a great cost in the lives of pilots. Doolittle went on to shock many in aviation circles when he emerged as a vocal critic of the sport. "Aviation has become a necessity in our daily lives," he told reporters in 1934. "It has long since passed the point where it can, or should be, used as a spectacle or as an entertaining medium."

Doolittle instead focused his energy again on how best to advance aviation. He had grown alarmed as the air forces of other nations surpassed that of America, his beloved Army air service reduced to flying the mail. To remain strong, Doolittle believed, the United States needed to develop more powerful engines so that future warplanes could carry heavier loads. The only way to build a more powerful engine, he knew, was to develop a better fuel—and he worked for a fuel company. Aviation gas at the time varied widely, with some eighteen different leaded and unleaded fuels. Those ranged from the 65-octane gasoline used by the Army up to the 95-octane needed for special test work by the Wright Corporation. Doolittle felt the time had arrived to standardize and reduce fuel specifications. He pitched the idea to Shell to develop a 100-octane fuel, persuading the company to invest millions in a product that at that time had no market. Many of his colleagues dubbed the venture "Doolittle's folly."

But Doolittle had to do more than persuade just Shell; he had to convince the Army. He knew from his contacts in the military that the future fighters and bombers then on the design boards would never fly without stronger engines, but he was up against a reluctant brass that failed to grasp that motorcycles and fighters demanded different fuels. Shell delivered the first 1,000 gallons of the new fuel to the Army in 1934. Tests immediately confirmed Doolittle's predictions, showing that even existing engines could produce as much as 30 percent more power with it than with regular fuel. Officials at Wright Field leaked the test results to the press, triggering a wave of interest from engine manufacturers. The

Army held hearings and eventually ordered all planes manufactured to use 100-octane fuel after January 1, 1938. "Shell had taken a big commercial gamble," Doolittle later wrote. "The venture paid off handsomely when the company was later asked to supply 20 million gallons of 100-octane fuel to the military services *daily*."

Doolittle traveled extensively with Shell over the years and grew alarmed at the increased militarization he found in the Far East and Germany. He had developed a close friendship with German World War I flying ace Ernst Udet, visiting his home, where the two men drank French champagne and shot pistols into a steel box filled with sand atop the fireplace mantel. Doolittle's friendship with the German aviator served as a barometer for the worsening relations between the two countries. As Germany marched down the path to war, Doolittle noted that Udet grew increasingly distant, even though he abhorred Adolf Hitler. Doolittle returned to Germany in 1939. This time his old friend seemed embarrassed to be seen with Doolittle. War was coming. Doolittle spotted great piles of wood and timber, which he recognized as potential fortifications, despite German protestations that the materials were bound for pulp mills. "On the streets, uniforms were everywhere," he observed. "People went about their daily business with a grimness that was distressing."

Doolittle returned home and sought out General Arnold. The two men had grown close over the years; Doolittle even asked Arnold in 1941 to write a recommendation letter for his youngest son to attend West Point. "This thing is very close to my heart," Doolittle wrote, "or I should not take the liberty of inviting it to your attention." Arnold was glad to help—and his muscle worked. "Don't think for a moment that your commendation of John Doolittle wasn't a real factor," Senator Prentiss Brown of Michigan wrote Arnold. "While I cannot always oblige, the views of the Service officers on these appointments mean much to me." Even though many in the air service felt Arnold favored Doolittle, the latter said he never sensed any special treatment. "General Arnold supported me in everything I did where he felt I was right," Doolittle once said. "And he chewed my ears off whenever he felt I was wrong. The thought that personal friendship entered into his military decisions is contrary to his nature."

Doolittle relayed to Arnold what he had seen in Germany, warning his boss that war was inevitable and that the United States would no doubt have to fight. Doolittle still felt bitter at having had to sit out World War I. He didn't plan to let that happen again. He told Arnold he wanted to go back on active duty. "I am entirely and immediately at the disposal of the Air Corps for whatever use they care to make of me," he wrote in 1940. "The only suggestion that I would like to make is to recommend that I be given such duty or duties as will best take advantage of my particular experience, associations and abilities." Shell granted Doolittle indefinite leave, and Arnold was thrilled to see him again in uniform. "When he resigned from the Air Corps in 1931 to become aviation director of the Shell Petroleum Corporation, the Air Corps lost a real pilot and a real man. But not for long, because we have him back now," Arnold wrote in a 1941 letter. "Jim Doolittle is a spectacular person, without meaning to be one."

Arnold dispatched Doolittle to Indianapolis and later Detroit to help prep American businesses for the increased demands of war. "My job was to marry the aviation industry and the automobile industry," Doolittle later said, "neither of whom wanted to get married." He suffered a restless night after the Japanese attack on Pearl Harbor. As long as the United States had remained on the war's sidelines, he had felt content to solve the problems of production. Not anymore. He fired off a one-page letter to Arnold, noting that he had 7,730 hours of flying time, much of it in fighters. "I respectfully request that I be relieved of my present duties and re-assigned to a tactical unit," Doolittle wrote on December 8. "The reason for making this request is a sincere belief that, due to recent developments, production problems will in future be simplified and operational problems aggravated. I consequently feel that my training and experience will be of greater value in operations than production."

Arnold read the letter and picked up the phone.

"How quickly can you be here?" he asked. "I want you on my immediate staff."

"Will tomorrow be all right?" Doolittle answered.

Doolittle landed in Washington with a promotion to lieutenant colonel. His unique background as an aeronautical engineer, stunt pilot, and businessman made him a perfect candidate to serve as Arnold's troubleshooter. His first job was to examine the Martin B-26, an unforgiving medium bomber involved in a series of fatal training flights. Pilots quipped that the plane's name Marauder should be changed to Murderer.

Arnold wanted Doolittle to investigate the problem and determine whether the Army Air Forces should cancel contracts for future B-26s. He visited the factory near Baltimore and spent hours in the skies testing the bomber, even demonstrating it before skeptical pilots. Doolittle realized that the problem was not the bomber but inadequate pilot training. He recommended continued production and devised an amended training program. "The B-26 was a good airplane, but it had some tricks," Doolittle later said. "There wasn't anything about its flying characteristics that good piloting skill couldn't overcome."

Doolittle was ready in late January for his next project.

That's when Arnold summoned him for what Doolittle later described as "the most important military assignment of my life thus far."

CHAPTER 4

★

If you have one plane available use it to bomb Tokio.

—ALLAN JOHNSON, CONSTITUENT TELEGRAM
TO ROOSEVELT

DOOLITTLE IMMEDIATELY STARTED to plan what he dubbed "Special Aviation Project No. 1." To meet the tentative April departure date, he knew he would have to hustle to map out logistics, modify bombers, and pick and train his aircrews. But Arnold had given him what he needed most: top priority. If anyone gives you flak, Arnold instructed Doolittle, tell him to call the general. That fear would motivate others. "Anything that I wanted I got," Doolittle recalled, "ahead of every one else." The first task was to map out basic logistics of the operation. The veteran aviator envisioned that his bombers would take off as much as 500 miles east of Tokyo. The flight to China would add at least another 1,200 miles. Doolittle estimated that the greatest nonstop flight would be 2,000 miles, though to be safe he set a necessary cruising range of 2,400 miles with a bomb load of 2,000 pounds. He knew those demands would require engineers to modify the twin-engine B-25s, whose maximum range topped out at just 1,300 miles.

Named for airpower pioneer General William "Billy" Mitchell, the B-25 was one of the newest planes in America's arsenal. It was developed by the North American Aviation Company in 1939 in response to the needs in Europe. The initial design proposal took just forty days. The Mitchell bomber made its first test flight in August 1940, forgoing the luxury of prototypes or even wind tunnel tests. The 53-foot-long bomber consisted of no fewer than 165,000 parts, excluding the engines, instrumentation, and some 150,000 rivets. Powered by twin 1,700-horsepower Wright Cyclone engines, the B-25 could fly at 300 miles per hour and up to 23,500 feet. The Army's initial order of 184 bombers—made just nineteen days after Hitler's forces marched into Poland—would prove only a fraction of the 9,816 planes workers would manufacture over the course of the war, hitting a peak rate of almost 10 a day. "It is a good, stable ship," proclaimed the *New York Times* in 1941, "not spectacular but reliable."

The $180,031 bomber was far from perfect. It lacked the power and speed of Martin's rival B-26 Marauder, and its three machine guns fell short of the thirteen that guarded Boeing's larger, four-engine B-17 Flying Fortress. The B-25's 3,500-pound payload likewise could not compete with the ten tons that Boeing's B-29 Superfortress would deliver later in the war. But the Mitchell bomber was chosen for the Tokyo raid for one reason—its sixty-seven-foot wingspan would clear the superstructure of an aircraft carrier. The size and versatility that made the B-25 a natural fit for Doolittle's mission would propel the rugged bomber into combat in every major theater of the war, from Europe and North Africa to the remote islands of the Pacific. Engineers along the way would improve the bomber's firepower and armor, increase the fuel capacity, and add torpedo and wing bomb racks, allowing this aerial workhorse to tackle missions ranging from reconnaissance to antisubmarine patrols.

Another feature that made the B-25 an optimal plane for Doolittle's mission was that it required a small crew of just five airmen to operate, half of those needed to fly a B-17. The pilot and copilot sat shoulder to shoulder in the tight cockpit, while the navigator occupied a tiny compartment just behind the flight deck. The bombardier reached the bubbled nose via a crawlway beneath the navigator's compartment. A similar passage above the bomb bay connected the fore and aft sections where the gunner sat. The austere aircraft offered few frills, though regulations at least allowed airmen to smoke above one thousand feet. "The B-26 was a Lincoln Town Car," joked one former navigator. "The B-25 was a Model-A Ford." What the Mitchell bomber lacked in comfort, it made up for in ease of flying, a fact aircrews loved. "It is so much more than an inanimate mass of material, intricately geared and wired and riveted into a tight package," recalled Ted Lawson, one of the mission's pilots. "It's a good, trustworthy friend."

To help modify the B-25s for the mission, Doolittle turned to the engineers at Ohio's Wright Field, the main experimental and development center for the U.S. Army Air Forces. Opened in 1927 on more than five thousand acres near Dayton, Wright Field held a special significance for Doolittle, who performed in the aerial circus before fifteen thousand awed spectators at the center's dedication that October. Wright Field had since developed into one of the world's top aeronautical research hubs, with a staggering $150 million in laboratories and scientific equipment. Engineers labored each day in various workshops, wind tunnels, and pressure chambers designed to simulate high altitudes and subzero temperatures. Others tested new parachutes and body armor and pushed airplanes to the breaking point to determine structural strength. A reporter with the *Milwaukee Sentinel* described it all best: "Wright Field is the place where miracles are performed so that American airmen can kill their enemies and stay alive themselves."

Those miracle workers drew up the necessary plans as Doolittle hurried to round up the planes. The size of the *Hornet*'s flight deck would limit how many bombers he could take on the mission, but until Captain Duncan could put a few B-25s aboard a flattop to conduct test trials, Doolittle would not have a precise number. Regardless, he did not have time to wait. "It is requested that one B-25B airplane be made available to the Mid-Continent Airlines at Minneapolis, Minnesota on January 23, 1942, or at the earliest possible moment thereafter," Doolittle wrote to the chief of the air staff. "It is further requested that 17 more B-25B's be diverted to the Mid-Continent Airlines for alteration as required." Doolittle upped his request a week later to twenty-four planes, a move designed to guarantee that he would have at least eighteen bombers in excellent shape for the mission. Orders called for the bombers to arrive on a staggered schedule every four days throughout the first half of February.

The most critical modification centered on fuel. The B-25 boasted two wing tanks that held a total of 646 gallons. Adding another thousand miles to the bomber's range meant Doolittle would need to almost double the B-25's fuel capacity, increasing the bomber's weight six pounds per gallon and therefore the distance needed to take off. The aircraft's tight space meant a single added fuel tank was not an option. Creative engineers instead would have to develop several tanks of various capacities that could be shoehorned into unused compartments. Workers with the McQuay Company initially constructed a 265-gallon steel tank, but Doolittle later ordered it replaced with a smaller yet malleable 225-gallon bulletproof bladder made by the United States Rubber Company out of Mishawaka, Indiana. Engineers planned to squeeze the rubber bladder into the top of the bomb bay, though allowing enough room for the plane to still carry up to four 500-pound demolition bombs or four 500-pound incendiary clusters.

The rubber tank, however, proved problematic, often developing leaks in the connections. After constructing a single satisfactory tank, engineers reduced the size of the outer cover to facilitate installation but failed to shrink the inner container, causing the tank to develop wrinkles that reduced capacity and increased the likelihood of leaks or even failure. Time would prohibit workers from making new covers for all the tanks, but putting air pressure on them increased the capacity by as much as 15 gallons. Engineers meanwhile devised a 160-gallon rubber bladder that would fit in the crawlway above the bomb bay. Once the fuel was used, a crew member could flatten the empty bladder to allow the engineer-gunner to crawl forward. A third 60-gallon leakproof tank would replace the bomber's faulty lower gun turret. Lastly, each plane would carry ten 5-gallon cans of gasoline in the radio operator's rear compartment, giving the bombers a total of 1,141 gallons, of which 1,100 were available.

Doolittle needed more than gas tanks. He ordered the pyrotechnics removed from the bombers to reduce the fire hazard and free up weight, while workers installed two conventional landing flares just forward of the rear-armored bulkhead to protect against enemy fire. Doolittle demanded the installation of deicers and anti-icers, reducing the cruising speed, though a necessary precaution in the off chance that the Russians allowed the bombers to land in Vladivostok. To document the mission workers installed automatic cameras in the tail of the lead ship and each flight leader's plane. Capable of snapping sixty pictures at half-second intervals, the cameras were designed to start filming automatically when the first bomb dropped. Doolittle likewise requested that technicians install 16-millimeter movie cameras in the other ten bombers. Since he planned to maintain radio silence throughout the flight, Doolittle ordered the 230-pound liaison radios removed to free up weight. To further guard against unintentional broadcasts with the interphone, crews later plucked out the coils from the command transmitters.

Doolittle began to outline the actual raid, drafting a handwritten memo on lined notebook paper. "The purpose of this special project is to bomb and fire the industrial center of Japan," he wrote. "It is anticipated that this will not only cause confusion and impede production but will undoubtedly facilitate operation against Japan in other theaters due to their probable withdrawal of troops for the purpose of defending the home country. An action of this kind is most desirable now due to the psychological effect on the American public, our allies, and our enemies." The plan called for the bombers to concentrate on Tokyo, though a few would hit the cities of Yokohama, Nagoya, Osaka, and Kobe. Doolittle ordered target maps of the area's iron, steel, and aluminum industries as well as aircraft plants, shipyards, and oil refineries, while the Chemical Warfare Services began preparing forty-eight special incendiary bomb clusters ready for shipment from Edgewood Arsenal in Maryland no later than March 15.

Arnold helped shoulder some of the burden, reaching out to Brigadier General Carl Spaatz, the chief of the air staff. "It is desired that you select for me the objectives in Japan you consider most desirable to be attacked in case we find it possible to send bombardment airplanes over Japan sometime in the near future," Arnold wrote in a January 22 memo. "The bombing mission should be able to cover any part of Japan from Tokyo south." Spaatz's office sent a detailed three-page analysis back just nine days later, citing Nakajima's and Tokyo Gas' aircraft and engine plants in the nation's capital, along with Kawasaki's factories in Kobe and Mitsubishi's and Aichi's plants in Nagoya. "The above aircraft factories represent approximately 75% of the aircraft productive capacity of Japan," the memo stated. "These are considered vital targets because Japan is dependent alone upon what they can manufacture."

The report further identified important targets in the iron, steel, aluminum, and magnesium industries as well as in critical petroleum refineries. The study concluded with a calculation of the total volume of potential targets for each major city. Tokyo and its suburbs of Kawasaki and Tsurumi contained thirteen power plants, six oil refineries, four aircraft factories, two steel plants, and an arsenal. One of the principal cities of Japan's aircraft industry, Nagoya was home to four such factories, including one of the largest airframe plants in the world, a more than four-million-square-foot facility owned by Mitsubishi. Kobe offered up another four aircraft factories, plus two steel plants, two dockyards, and two power plants. "Many of these objectives," the January 31 report noted, "are concentrated in fairly small areas so that by careful selection several individual objectives might well be grouped into excellent area targets."

Doolittle envisioned that his bombers would take off at night and arrive over Japan at dawn. An attack at first light would guarantee greater accuracy as well as allow crews time to fly to China, refuel at airfields near the coast, and push another eight hundred miles inland to Chungking and beyond the reach of Japanese forces fighting on the mainland, all before nightfall. If enemy forces discovered the task force or if intelligence for any reason demanded that his bombers attack at night, Doolittle believed it would need to be a moonlit night in case Japanese cities observed blackout restrictions. Otherwise a moonless evening would be best. Doolittle studied up on the weather, hoping to avoid morning fog over Tokyo, low overcast skies over China, strong westerly winds, and icing. He suggested daily weather updates from China be sent in special code. "An initial study of meteorological conditions indicates that the sooner the raid is made the better," he wrote. "The weather will become increasingly unfavorable after the end of April."

China remained one of Doolittle's biggest logistical challenges, because Japanese forces occupied strategic positions along the coast. He selected several airfields around Chuchow—seventy miles inland and some two hundred miles south of Shanghai—and estimated that crews would need at least 20,000 gallons of 100-octane aviation fuel and another 600 gallons of lubricating oil. Doolittle recommended that First Lieutenant Harry Howze with the Air Service Command, formerly with Standard Oil Company of New Jersey, help make arrangements in China. Colonel Claire Chennault, aviation adviser to the Chinese, should then assign a responsible American or English-speaking native to physically check that supplies were in place. Doolittle suggested that work start at once and cautioned that secrecy was vital. Even the Chinese should not be informed until the planes were airborne, for fear that news of the operation would leak to the Japanese. "Premature notification," Doolittle warned, "would be fatal to the project."

ON THE FRIGID SUNDAY afternoon of February 1, 1942, Captain Duncan reported to the aircraft carrier *Hornet*, moored alongside Pier 7 at Norfolk Naval Operating Base. The $32 million flattop had returned to Virginia just forty-eight hours earlier, concluding a thirty-five-day shakedown cruise in the Gulf of Mexico. Duncan had raced in recent weeks to map out the Navy's preliminary plan for the mission to bomb Tokyo, an operation that until now had been largely theoretical, involving an analysis of aircraft wingspans, takeoff speeds, and carrier deck space. The time to test the ambitious plan had finally arrived. If Duncan had erred in his calculations, or if the bombers for any reason proved unable to take off from the carrier's short flight deck, the mission in all likelihood was dead in the water. These concerns hung over Duncan as he climbed the carrier's gangway at 4:50 p.m. and hurried to the in-port cabin of Captain Marc Mitscher, the *Hornet*'s fifty-five-year-old skipper.

Mitscher was one of the Navy's more colorful captains, an officer whose undisciplined youth hardly foreshadowed that he might one day earn the prized command of America's newest carrier. The wiry officer who stood barely five feet six and weighed 135 pounds grew up in Oklahoma during the land rush, a time when Indian raid alarms still terrified residents. He learned to count by playing cards and once watched a deputy marshal dump a dead outlaw on the street. Mitscher's feral manner clashed with the rigidity of the Naval Academy, where he struggled in the classroom, racked up 280 demerits—30 more than the maximum allowed—and was caught up in a hazing scandal after the death of a classmate. The academy finally kicked him out in his second year. Though his politically connected father secured him reappointment, Mitscher had to start over. Even then he continued to struggle, but managed to graduate in 1910. "I was a 2.5 man," he later joked. "That was good enough for me."

This unlikely leader found his passion in the skies, earning his wings in June 1916 to become naval aviator no. 33. Mitscher received the Navy

Cross three years later for his participation in the service's first transatlantic flight, from Newfoundland to Portugal. He later served as the executive officer of the carriers *Langley* and *Saratoga* and skippered the seaplane tender *Wright* before the Navy offered him command of the *Hornet*, commissioned in October. The humble skipper still sewed his own buttons on his shirt and loved trout fishing, though his lack of time off forced him to derive most of his pleasure swapping fish tales on the bridge, dressed as always with an open collar and a long-billed cap to protect his bald head from the tropical sun that scorched his hands and freckled his nose and cheeks. Long cruises would dry his skin like parchment, forcing him to scratch incessantly as he perched in his swivel chair, always facing aft. "I'm an old man now," he liked to say. "I spent my youth looking ahead."

Those closest to Mitscher marveled at his modesty. When he learned of his recent selection for rear admiral, he worried about his fellow officers who had been passed over. "In being selected for promotion over so many of my classmates and others whom I consider good friends and much better Naval officers than myself," he wrote a colleague, "I have a feeling of regret about the whole business." Not only did Mitscher shun self-promotion, but he proved a surprisingly reserved and quiet leader in a military filled with oversize personalities. "He wasted no words," recalled George Murray, skipper of the *Enterprise*. "One short little expression or the lifting of an eyebrow or just a word conveyed more meaning in so far as he was concerned than somebody else talking for fifteen minutes." The few words he spoke came out like a whisper. "Even when he shakes with laughter, he somehow manages to do it silently," observed the *Saturday Evening Post*. "And when he swears, he does it as softly as most men pray."

Though Mitscher did not yet know it, Duncan had him and his carrier in mind to transport Doolittle to Japan—if the test proved successful.

"Can you put a loaded B-25 in the air on a normal deck run?" Duncan asked when he met Mitscher that afternoon.

"How many B-25's on deck?"

"Fifteen."

Mitscher consulted a scale replica of the *Hornet*'s flight deck known as the spotting board. "Yes," he finally answered, "it can be done."

"Good," Duncan answered, "I'm putting two aboard for a test launching tomorrow."

Arnold's staff had ordered three B-25s with the "best combat crews available" to report to Norfolk no later than January 20: "Airplanes will have combat equipment installed, less bombs." The plan called for the first B-25 to take off carrying only a full load of gas. The second bomber would then roar down the flight deck with a medium load, followed lastly by a fully loaded plane: "Successive take-offs will, of course, be gauged by the preceding ones." A burned-out engine on the eve of the test had sidelined one of the bombers. The carrier's boat- and airplane-hoisting crane lifted the other two aboard, using a special sling manufactured for the operation by the Norfolk Naval Air Station. Mitscher ordered one bomber spotted forward where the first of fifteen B-25s would go; he ordered the other aft. In following Admiral King's strict order for secrecy, the *Hornet*'s deck log contains no record of the bombers.

Sailors lit a fire under boiler no. 6 at 5:30 a.m. on February 2, followed forty-five minutes later by boilers no. 3 and no. 5. A harbor pilot climbed aboard at 9:15 a.m., and the *Hornet* got underway seventeen minutes later. Winds blew out of the northwest at four miles per hour this winter morning as temperatures hovered around freezing. A light snow began to fall. Sailors lit fires under five more boilers moments before Mitscher took the conn at 9:52 a.m. An hour and a half later the 809-foot flattop glided past the floating lighthouse *Chesapeake*. The destroyers *Ludlow* and *Hilary P. Jones* patrolled ahead as the *Hornet* increased speed to twenty-two knots.

The zero hour finally arrived. The deck log shows that the *Hornet* went to flight quarters at 12:55 p.m. and turned into the wind twenty-three minutes later. First up was Lieutenant John Fitzgerald Jr., who had earned his wings in 1940. The Army aviator had so far logged some fifteen hundred hours in the skies with more than four hundred of those in B-25s. Fitzgerald's current assignment as a B-25 test officer at Ohio's Wright Field made him a perfect candidate for the afternoon's test. "Since flying a B-25 off a carrier simply had never been done there was no kind of previous instruction available," he recalled. "All we could do was practice extremely short takeoffs on land."

That uncertainty was evident in the response one of the bomber pilots gave communication officer Lieutenant Commander Oscar Dodson when he wished the airman good luck. "If we go into the water, don't run over us."

Duncan dressed in foul-weather gear and stood on the port wing of the bridge alongside Mitscher. One deck down below, Fitzgerald throttled up his B-25. His cockpit windshield revealed five hundred feet of deck space. During the more than two dozen short-field takeoffs he had practiced, Fitzgerald had managed to get his bomber up in as little as three hundred feet. The plane's air speed indicator revealed that the carrier's speed combined with the wind across the deck gave him forty-five miles per hour before he even released the brakes. He needed to accelerate only twenty-three miles per hour more and he would be airborne. Fitzgerald's biggest concern centered on the proximity of the carrier's island as the B-25's 67-foot wingspan left him perilously little room for error.

The launching officer flashed Fitzgerald the signal at 1:27 p.m., and he released the brakes. The bomber charged down the flight deck. Duncan watched as the B-25 stubbornly remained on deck. Just a few feet before the edge of the deck the bomber climbed into the skies. The experience felt much different for Fitzgerald in the cockpit. "When I got the signal to go, I let the brakes off and was airborne almost immediately," Fitzgerald later recalled. "The wing of my plane rose so fast I was afraid I'd strike the ship's 'island' over the flight deck. But I missed it."

Mitscher flashed a smile at Duncan.

Lieutenant James McCarthy went next. The Army aviator throttled up the B-25's engines, released the brakes, and the second bomber roared into the skies, this time in just 275 feet. The *Hornet*'s deck log shows the carrier completed the launches at 1:47 p.m. The two bombers, unable to land back on the *Hornet*, returned to the airfield.

Duncan had little time to celebrate. The ship's general quarters alarm sounded at 2 p.m. The *Hornet*'s air patrol reported a submarine periscope. The destroyers charged through the waves, dropping depth charges as the air patrol zeroed in on the target. The *Hornet* changed course as the carrier's five-inch batteries opened fire. Mitscher watched the action unfold. "Frank, it's a nice oil slick," he said to Commander Frank Akers, the ship's navigator. "But I can still see a foot or so of what appears to be a periscope sticking up. This is the first blasted submarine that I've ever seen like that."

The *Ludlow* made a closer inspection and reported the alleged submarine periscope was actually the mast of a sunken ship, news that drew a laugh from Mitscher. "Very realistic drill," he said to Akers. "Send them a 'well done.'"

The *Hornet* returned to port, anchoring at 5:27 p.m. in Berth 27 at Hampton Roads. Duncan hurried back to Washington, thrilled his calculations were correct. "There was a six foot clearance between the wing tip and the island," he wrote in a two-page memo to Admiral King. "This did not seem to bother the pilots as both airplanes maintained perfectly straight courses on the take-off run and appeared to be under excellent control." Duncan reported that the *Hornet* could carry between fifteen and twenty bombers, depending on whether the Navy wanted to leave enough deck space to operate a possible squadron of fighters. King reviewed the memo, scrawling a single word of approval across the bottom in pencil: "Excellent."

Mitscher gathered that evening with his executive officer, air officer, and navigator to discuss the operation. Duncan had told Mitscher only that the afternoon's operation was designed to test the B-25's takeoff capabilities, tests the skipper knew could just as easily be performed at an airfield on shore. He likewise knew that if the Navy planned to use the *Hornet* to transport Army bombers to a remote base a crane would more easily facilitate the off-loading of the planes. Mitscher could draw only one conclusion: his flattop was about to go into battle, but he felt miffed that his old friend Duncan had not told him about the mission. So did his men, but the skipper counseled them to remain patient. "The less you know," he cautioned, "the better."

DOOLITTLE STILL NEEDED AIRCREWS—enough pilots, bombardiers, and gunners to operate two dozen planes. The B-25 was such a new bomber that only a few outfits in the country flew them. Doolittle had asked for bombers and learned that the Air Forces could spare planes most easily from the Seventeenth Bombardment Group, comprising the Thirty-Fourth, Thirty-Seventh, and Ninety-Fifth Squadrons and the associated Eighty-Ninth Reconnaissance Squadron, all based in Pendleton, Oregon. Rather than leave aircrews idle without planes, Doolittle decided to recruit his fliers from the same group. Given the danger of the mission, he wanted only volunteers. Not a single airman in Seventeenth Bombardment Group had flown in combat, and few if any of the gunners had ever fired a machine gun from a plane. The navigators likewise had little practical experience, particularly over open water. Orders rolled off the Teletype on February 3, transferring all planes, aircrews, and ground personnel to the Columbia Army Air Base in South Carolina.

The first outfit in the nation to receive the B-25, the Seventeenth's crews had marveled at the twin-tail bomber with a tricycle landing gear. "When I saw it for the first time, I was in awe. It looked so huge. It was so sleek and powerful," remembered pilot Edgar McElroy. "Reminded me of a big old scorpion, just ready to sting!" "I couldn't eat until I had a crack at mine," noted Ted Lawson, another pilot. "You just had to stand there and look at them, and breathe heavily." Compared with the lumbering Douglas B-18s the crews had flown, the Mitchell bombers felt like a real upgrade, earning the nickname "rocket plane." New bombers arrived every few days throughout the spring of 1941 as pilots pilgrimaged down to North American's Los Angeles headquarters to retrieve the planes right off the line, spending several days test-flying them. "Not only did we have a good time in that area down there for a week, but it was all at North American's expense," recalled fellow pilot Bob Emmens. "We signed chits for everything—the bar, the dining room—and then flew our airplane back to the unit."

The bombardment group had served as aerial guinea pigs, testing the B-25's speed, firepower, and gas consumption, even flying the planes cross-country to Virginia's Langley Field. Many participated that summer and fall in Army training maneuvers across the Southeast. "It was the first time that I got a good, close look at tanks, fighters and other Army bombers," recalled pilot Jack Sims. "I'm sure that ground personnel got their first view of our B-25s." The bomber crews simulated combat, practicing night formation flying as well as targeting infantry forces and fending off fighter attacks. Even on the ground the men slept in steel helmets. "The maneuvers were close to the real McCoy," remembered Lawson. "We were on alert twenty-four hours a day. Other bombing squadrons would come over, night or day, and litter our hangars with sacks of flour, while our fighting planes buzzed around them. We tried to bomb Shreveport before the P 38's and P-39's could intercept us."

The men of the Seventeenth Bombardment Group represented a

cross section of American life. The airmen had come from big cities and small towns, from frigid Alaska in the north to the dusty southern plains of Texas. Some had grown up the sons of white-collar workers—doctors, dentists, engineers, and accountants—while others shared Doolittle's blue-collar roots, the offspring of farmers and ranchers, grocers and oil field workers. A few of the men, like Captain Edward "Ski" York and Second Lieutenant Charles Ozuk Jr., came from new immigrant families, while First Lieutenant Harry McCool's father was born on a wagon train rolling west from Missouri to California. Despite the varied backgrounds, the crews had all jelled. "It was the greatest, wildest bunch of men that I have ever been associated with. There was just something about that 17th Group, about the collection of people that were in it, that I have never experienced since," remembered pilot Bill Bower. "We played hard, we worked hard."

The attack on Pearl Harbor had brought the airmen back to the Pacific Northwest to fly antisubmarine patrols off the Oregon and Washington coasts, but the missions proved anticlimactic compared with the stories out of the Pacific. America was a long way from the fight, and many of the airmen felt restless and frustrated. "There was no tangible enemy. It was like being slugged with a single punch in a dark room, and having no way of knowing where to slug back," Lawson later wrote. "There was a helpless, filled-up, want-to-do-something feeling that they *weren't* coming—that we'd have to go all the way over there to punch back and get even." That was fine by most. "Everybody was interested in getting to the scene of the action," recalled Bower, "going to war, volunteering for some mission." Furious over the attack on Pearl Harbor, bombardier Sergeant Robert Bourgeois captured the feelings of his fellow fliers with his daily mantra: "I sure would give anything to drop a bomb on Tokyo."

Doolittle planned to offer the men that chance.

The pilots flew the B-25s cross-country, with some directed to divert to Minneapolis for fuel tank modifications. Others in the bomb group took the train from Oregon to South Carolina, a roughly five-day journey east through Denver. "We played poker all day and in the evening," Sergeant Joseph Manske, an engineer-gunner, wrote in his diary. "We got some whiskey and I got sick on it." The airmen arrived that February at the Columbia Army Air Base, camping outdoors as the winter rains soon turned the fields to mud. "We lived in tents on the field—ours leaked like a sieve," Second Lieutenant Billy Farrow, a South Carolina native and pilot, wrote to his mother. "Sure took a ragging about the 'sunny South'—we nearly froze getting up in the mornings. Sometimes, the temperature was below freezing. You know how that temperature numbs you down there. Oregon weather is a summer zephyr in comparison."

Many assumed that the transfer to South Carolina meant the group would fly similar missions off the East Coast, hunting German submarines that menaced American convoys. Others speculated that the planes might soon deploy to England and execute bomber missions over Europe. Doolittle flew to Columbia soon thereafter to help organize the crews. Captain Ross Greening and Major Jack Hilger watched his bomber circle down with the nimble air of a fighter plane.

"Damn it," Hilger exclaimed. "With all our experience none of us can fly a B-25 like that."

The men watched the bomber taxi to the control tower and stop before the pilot climbed down.

"For God's sake," exclaimed Greening. "It's Doolittle."

"What in hell is The Little Man doing here?" Hilger asked.

Doolittle assembled group commander Lieutenant Colonel William Mills and squadron leaders Hilger and Captains Ski York, Al Rutherford, and Karl Baumeister. He told the men that he was in charge of a dangerous mission, one that would require the bombers to take off in just five hundred feet.

The officers blinked.

"That's about all I can tell you," Doolittle concluded. "It's strictly a volunteer operation. And the men must volunteer in the dark. It'll take us away about six weeks, but that's all you can tell your men."

Doolittle trusted Mills and his squadron leaders to select the two dozen crews. The only person Doolittle was certain he didn't want was Mills, who would soon swap his oak leaf insignia for the silver eagle of a full-bird colonel, outranking Doolittle. "The group commander was a colonel. I was a light colonel," he recalled. "He was the last guy I wanted because I had not yet been given permission to lead the flight."

Doolittle would have to divide his time between Washington and Minneapolis. He asked Mills to recommend an experienced deputy, who could oversee mission training at Eglin Field, a secluded airbase Doolittle arranged in Florida, where crews could practice short-field takeoffs, gunnery, and open-ocean navigation. Mills recommended Hilger. The three captains all volunteered, but Mills would only permit York to go.

The squadron leaders put the word out, but not everyone jumped at the opportunity. "Some of you fellows are going to get killed," one of the captains warned his men. "How many of you will volunteer?"

"Boy," thought Corporal Jacob DeShazer, a bombardier from Oregon, "I don't want to do that."

"Would you go?" the captain asked the first man in the line.

"Yes."

He moved on to the next airman.

"Would you go?"

Affirmative.

"Would you go?"

"Yes."

The captain reached the end of the line and stood before DeShazer. He heard his fellow fliers answer affirmative. When it came to him, he muttered the same: "I was too big a coward," he recalled, "to say no."

For many others, there was no hesitation when asked for a show of hands.

"The entire group stood," remembered Bob Emmens of Oregon. "Every man in every squadron volunteered for this mission."

"Hands just kept going up," added Charles Ozuk Jr., a Pennsylvania native. "There was no time to think about it. No second thoughts."

Few dared miss out on the chance to fly with legendary stunt and racing pilot Jimmy Doolittle, who had inspired many to join the Army Air Forces. "The name 'Doolittle' meant so much to aviators that man, we just volunteered like crazy," remembered Bobby Hite, a pilot. "He was a real leader. The men loved him and respected him."

Edgar McElroy's copilot was shocked to see his hand in the air. "You can't volunteer, Mac!" he exclaimed. "You're married, and you and Aggie are expecting a baby soon. Don't do it!"

"I got into the Air Force to do what I can," McElroy answered. "Aggie understands how I feel. The war won't be easy for any of us."

Oklahoma native Corporal Bert Jordan had been on guard duty all night. He arrived late to morning formation and found his fellow fliers with hands raised.

"What are you holding your hand up for?" he asked.

"Well," one answered, "they want somebody to go someplace."

Jordan was already tired of South Carolina, living in tents in the cold and mud. His feet itched; he felt eager to travel.

"I just wanted to get out of Columbia so I held up my hand," he recalled. "I was one of the fortunate or unfortunate, whichever the case may be, to be selected."

Bill Birch felt the same way. "It was disgusting," he recalled of the rain and mud. "So I figured whatever came up, I'd volunteer for it."

Herb Macia knew for sure he wanted to go when he knocked on the door of Jack Hilger's office, unaware that the major already had plans for him.

"Herb, what do you want?" he asked.

"I'm ready to volunteer for that mission."

"You are already a volunteer," Hilger informed him. "You are on my mission and you are on my crew and you are going to be a navigator and bombardier."

Most of the officers in York's squadron were in Minneapolis for fuel tank installation. He phoned his deputy Captain Davy Jones, directing him to meet him at Wright Field, where the aviators climbed up into the catwalk of a hanger.

"Doolittle has been here looking for volunteers. It's a dangerous mission," York told him. "You go back and tell the troops that much."

Jones returned to Minneapolis and summoned his fellow airmen to his hotel suite. Two dozen men crammed inside, some stretched out on the beds, others in chairs. Cigarette smoke clouded the air.

"There's been a change," Jones told them. "We're not going to work out of Columbia. Captain York wanted me to talk to you and see how many of you would volunteer for a special mission. It's dangerous, important and interesting."

"Well," one of the others prodded. "What is it?"

"I can't tell you. I don't even know myself," Jones said. "All I can tell you is that it's dangerous and that it'll take you out of the country for maybe two or three months."

"Where?" someone asked.

"I'm sorry I can't tell you any more," Jones said. "You've heard all the particulars I can give you. Now, who'll volunteer?"

All did.

Not everyone would be so lucky.

"Don't go denuding the outfit because I have to go to Europe," Mills warned York. "I need some good people, too."

The flood of volunteers exceeded the two dozen crews Doolittle needed. "We had so many," remembered York. "We had to pick and choose."

One of those unable to go was Robert Emmens.

"You have to stay behind—you are the oldest guy in the squadron now—and run the squadron," Hilger told him.

Richard Knobloch returned to base after visiting his girlfriend to learn the news of the mission. "Knobby, you should have been here," one of his friends told him. "They want volunteers to fly with Jimmy Doolittle."

The opportunity to fly with such a famous aviator thrilled Knobloch. "Boy, here's a chance for a great adventure," the pilot thought. "I'm going to be a hero."

"How about me?" Knobloch asked. "Didn't anybody put my name in?"

"No," someone told him. "Too late now."

Knobloch went to his boss, the squadron ops officer, and begged to go. "It's too late," he told him.

So Knobloch hurried to see Captain Baumeister, the squadron commander. "Sir," he pleaded. "I want to go on this operation."

"It's too late," Baumeister said.

Knobloch pleaded his case all the way up to group commander Mills, who only echoed the others.

"Will you at least put me on the alternate list? I want to go," he begged. "Here's an opportunity to fly with a great aviator, Doolittle."

JAPAN'S RAMPAGE ACROSS ASIA and the Pacific had left Roosevelt exhausted and irritable with Congress, the media, and even the American public. The news had grown so bad in recent weeks that Secretary of State Hull had begun cleaning out his desk and the perennially sick Hopkins landed in the hospital. Isolationist newspapers, from the *New York Daily News* and the *Washington Times Herald* to the *Chicago Tribune*, once critical of the president's foreign policy now targeted his handling of the war. Editorials argued that Japan was the real menace and that America should concentrate its strength in the Pacific, not in Europe, while others even criticized military sales and loans to Allies as weakening American power. "There is a prevailing desire in the press for offensive warfare," noted one White House analysis of the editorial opinion. "It appears to be motivated, not merely by an eagerness for revenge against the Japanese, but also by a recognition that only offensive strategy can bring the war to a successful conclusion."

America's efforts to rebuff the Japanese had met disaster in December when the Navy attempted to relieve Wake, a remote outpost built on the 2.5-square-mile rim of a submerged volcano. More than five hundred marines and sailors—aided by about twelve hundred civilian construction workers—repelled the Japanese for fifteen days, a story that gripped the American public. The carriers *Saratoga* and *Lexington* rushed toward Wake as the Japanese charged ashore. "The enemy is on the island," Commander Winfield Scott Cunningham, the garrison's senior officer, signaled on December 23. "The issue is in doubt." With the *Saratoga* just 425 miles away, the Navy aborted the operation, afraid to risk the loss of a carrier or trigger another attack on Hawaii. Wake fell that afternoon. Some on board the *Saratoga* wept, while *Enterprise* aviators vented in an unofficial log: "Everyone seems to feel that it's the war between the two yellow races." Even Roosevelt felt Wake's loss "a worse blow than Pearl Harbor."

The British had proven equally impotent seven weeks later to stop the fall of Singapore, a far greater strategic loss than Wake. Constructed atop a mangrove swamp over some two decades—and at a price of some $400,000,000—the equatorial fortress had served to check Japanese expansion into the Indian Ocean. Singapore's fall opened the doors for the Japanese to cut off lifelines to Russia and China, target India, and possibly link up with German forces in the Middle East. The loss put the oil-rich Dutch East Indies and even Australia in the Japanese crosshairs. Lieutenant General Joseph Stilwell, whom Roosevelt tapped to serve as chief of staff to Generalissimo Chiang Kai-shek in China, captured his shock over Singapore's loss in his diary. "Christ," he wrote. "What the hell is the matter?" For the first time the press speculated that the United States might lose the war. "There can now be no doubt," observed a reporter in the *New York Times*, "that we are facing perhaps the blackest period in our history."

Attention next focused on the Philippines, where some 110,000 American and Filipino troops under the command of General Douglas MacArthur had retreated to the Bataan Peninsula and the fortified island of Corregidor. The Japanese had entered Manila on January 2 and cut off any hope of reinforcement. Despite the media's lionized coverage of the gallant stand, Roosevelt knew MacArthur's forces were doomed. During a February news conference, when pressed about America's inability to supply more planes, Roosevelt barked at a reporter, "If you will tell me how to get a bomber in there, they can have a bomber." The Germans and Japanese mocked MacArthur in shortwave broadcasts, paying tribute to his struggle as a way to embarrass the United States. "In the name of fair play and chivalry," one broadcast trumpeted, "the Japanese nation demands that the United States give General MacArthur the reinforcements he needs, so he will be able to wage a war that would be to his satisfaction, win or lose."

The unity that had enveloped the nation in the wake of Pearl Harbor had now vanished, replaced by fear, hostility, and racism directed at many of Japanese descent. Long-simmering jealousy along the West Coast over the economic success of many immigrants fueled public pressure to relocate families to internment camps in the nation's interior; the proponents of such action ranged from the governor of California to the entire West Coast congressional delegation. "A viper is nonetheless a viper wherever the egg is hatched," declared an editorial in the *Los Angeles Times*. "Herd 'em up, pack 'em off and give 'em the inside room of the badlands," wrote syndicated columnist Henry McLemore. "Personally, I hate the Japanese. And that goes for all of them." Some senior military leaders also championed the idea. "A Jap's a Jap—it makes no difference whether he is an American citizen or not," announced Lieutenant General John DeWitt, head of the Army's Western Defense Force. "I don't want any of them."

Roosevelt felt pressure even from members of his own cabinet. "It looks to me like it will explode any day now," warned Assistant to the Attorney General James Rowe Jr. in early February, one of the few who argued against such a move. "If it happens, it will be one of the great mass exoduses of history." Roosevelt viewed the issue as one of military necessity, a step that had to be taken to protect the country. He signed Executive Order 9066 on February 19, relocating more than 100,000 citizens and aliens to internment camps. "I do not think he was much concerned with the gravity or implications of this step," Attorney General Francis Biddle later wrote. "Nor do I think that the constitutional difficulty plagued him—the Constitution has never greatly bothered any wartime president." But the decision bothered Eleanor. "These people were not convicted of any crime, but emotions ran too high," she wrote in *Collier's* in 1943. "Too many people wanted to wreak vengeance on Oriental-looking people."

Social tensions spread beyond those of Japanese descent. A White House public opinion analysis revealed how in the black community the war had triggered a "deep undercurrent of bitterness and resentment." Many begrudged the Marine Corps' refusal to admit blacks and the Army's policy of segregation. Others complained that the Navy accepted blacks only for menial jobs, such as that of mess attendants. "The Navy has a woeful need of men, but it doesn't need us," wrote *Pittsburgh Courier* columnist Marjorie McKenzie. "Can we honestly feel like strong, courageous, loyal Americans in the face of that?" Another flashpoint of tension centered on the refusal of the American Red Cross at the war's outbreak to accept blood from blacks. The organization agreed under pressure to reverse the policy, though it still segregated blood by race. "It is a matter of the deepest resentment," noted an administration report, "that White men who ask Negroes to sacrifice their lives refuse to have Negro blood mingled with their own."

Roosevelt understood that the continued defeats and the growing social tensions threatened the war effort. As the news deteriorated, his demands for an attack on Japan increased. Roosevelt hammered that point home in a January 28 White House conference, questioning whether the United States could even set up bomber bases in Mongolia, a discussion Arnold captured in his notes: "The president stated that, from a psychological standpoint, both of Japan and the United States, it was most important to bomb Japan as soon as possible." Arnold cautioned Roosevelt afterward in a memo that Mongolia—far outside the control of the Chinese government—was not a safe option. Roosevelt needed to be patient. "For this reason I feel that the plan, which is now in progress, for carrying out an attack upon the Japanese enemy's center of gravity, by making use of facilities for which the Chinese Government can guarantee us a reasonable degree of security on the Eastern Asiatic mainland, is the logical and most effective plan."

The president in the short term would have to look elsewhere for ways to distract the American public. Eleanor used her daily newspaper column to try to buoy public morale after the fall of Singapore. "Perhaps it is good for us to have to face disaster, because we have been so optimistic and almost arrogant in our expectation of constant success," she wrote. "Now we shall have to find within us the courage to meet defeat and fight right on to victory." The president took to the airwaves in a fireside chat on February 23, echoing his wife in an effort to dispel growing public apathy. What America needed, he knew, was a victory. "Let me say once and for all to the people of the world: We Americans have been compelled to yield ground, but we will regain it," Roosevelt told an estimated audience of sixty-two million. "We are daily increasing our strength. Soon, we and not our enemies will have the offensive; we, not they, will win the final battles; and we, not they, will make the final peace."

CHAPTER 5

★

For a while we'll have everything our own way, stretching
out in every direction like an octopus spreading its tentacles.
But it'll last for a year and a half at the most.

—ADMIRAL ISOROKU YAMAMOTO,
SEPTEMBER 1941

ADMIRAL ISOROKU YAMAMOTO STEWED aboard his flagship, the
Yamato, safely anchored off the island of Hashirajima in Japan's Inland
Sea. The fifty-seven-year-old commander of the Combined Fleet—and
architect of the surprise attack on Hawaii—understood the danger the
United States still posed to Japan, even as much of the Pacific Fleet now
rusted on the muddy bottom of Pearl Harbor. Yamamoto had long warned
his superiors about the industrial power of the United States. The victories
Japan now enjoyed, he knew, were merely the prelude to the war's main
act. "Britain and America may have underestimated Japan somewhat, but
from their point of view it's like having one's hand bitten rather badly by a
dog one was feeding. It seems that America in particular is determined
before long to embark on full-scale operations against Japan," he wrote a
colleague. "The mindless rejoicing at home is really deplorable; it makes
me fear that the first blow at Tokyo will make them wilt on the spot."

Yamamoto was unique among the empire's senior leaders. The son of
a former samurai warrior, he stood just five feet three inches tall, one

inch shorter than Jimmy Doolittle. A graduate of Japan's renowned Eta Jima Naval Academy, he shunned alcohol even as he nursed a lifelong love of gambling. Yamamoto had fought as a young ensign in the Russo-Japanese War. A gun explosion aboard the armored cruiser *Nisshin* in the 1905 Battle of Tsushima Strait robbed him of the index and middle finger of his left hand, earning him the nickname "eighty sen" from the geishas in Tokyo's Shimbashi district who charged one yen for a ten-finger manicure. The explosion had peppered Yamamoto's lower body with more than a hundred pieces of shrapnel, leaving the paunchy admiral forever scarred and self-conscious. "Whenever I go into a public bath," he used to quip, "people think I'm a gangster."

Yamamoto twice lived in the United States, where he studied at Harvard and later served as naval attaché at the embassy in Washington. An avid admirer of Abraham Lincoln, he devoured biographies of America's sixteenth president, demanding that his subordinates read them. Visits to the Detroit auto plants and the oil fields of Texas convinced him that the world was moving away from a dependency on iron and coal and more toward oil, gasoline, and light metals better suited for planes. When his superiors shot down his request for cash to tour Mexico, the dedicated officer opted to pay for the trip on his own meager salary, ultimately drawing the scrutiny of Mexican authorities. "A man who claims to be Yamamoto Isoroku, a commander in the Japanese navy, is traveling around the country inspecting oil fields. He stays in the meanest attics in third-rate hotels and never eats the hotel food, subsisting instead on bread, water, and bananas," Mexican authorities cabled the embassy. "Please confirm his identity."

These experiences had convinced Yamamoto of the United States' raw industrial might, even as isolationist policies in the wake of World War I had stunted America's military growth. Yamamoto opposed Japan's alliance with Germany and Italy and long resisted war with the United States, arguing that his nation's limited resources would run out in eighteen months. His dissent had led some in Japan's militaristic right wing to threaten to assassinate him, forcing the military police to guard him. One of Yamamoto's top aides even slept each night with a sword. But the admiral refused to back down, voicing his concerns in 1940 to the then prime minister, Fumimaro Konoye, when pressed on Japan's chances of success. "If we are ordered to do it," Yamamoto had answered, "then I can guarantee to put up a tough fight for the first six months, but I have absolutely no confidence as to what would happen if it went on for two or three years."

Despite Yamamoto's protestations, Japan had continued the march toward war, leaving the admiral in the awkward position of planning an operation he opposed, a predicament he captured in an October 1941 letter to a friend. "My present situation is very strange. Because I have been assigned the mission, entirely against my private opinion, and also I am expected to do my best," he wrote. "Alas, maybe, this is my fate." In past war games the Japanese Navy had never won an overwhelming victory against the United States, leading to the maneuvers' suspension for fear the Navy would be dragged into gradual defeat. The best way to improve Japan's chances, Yamamoto realized, was a surprise strike against American forces in Hawaii. "The most important thing we have to do first of all in a war with the U.S., I firmly believe, is to fiercely attack and destroy the U.S. main fleet at the outset of the war," he wrote. "Only then shall we be able to secure an invincible stand in key positions in East Asia."

The success of the attack on Pearl Harbor had made Yamamoto a national celebrity, a status he despised even as a stack of new fan mail nearly a foot high landed daily on his desk. A request by famed painter Yasuda Yukihiko to paint his portrait only outraged the admiral, who remained troubled by Japan's failure to sink any of America's powerful aircraft carriers in the raid on Hawaii. "As I see it," Yamamoto wrote a friend, "portraits are vulgarities to be shunned only less rigorously than bronze statues." Likewise, he rejected an offer to write the original calligraphy for a new monument in central Tokyo's Hibiya Park. When presented with two military decorations, he refused to accept them, burdened by a sense of guilt that, even though he commanded sailors, he had yet to see an enemy warship or plane. "I could never wear them," Yamamoto said. "I'd be ashamed." In a personal letter he was more blunt: "I wonder how the men who've seen action in the front line would feel about it?"

Underlying Yamamoto's unease was his fear that Japan's euphoria over the attack on Pearl Harbor was premature. After more than four years of war with China—and with Japan already devouring its stockpiles of raw materials—Yamamoto knew the nation now lived on borrowed time. In his first wartime State of the Union address only weeks earlier, President Roosevelt had demanded that America produce 60,000 bombers, fighters, and cargo planes, 45,000 tanks, and 20,000 antiaircraft guns that year, along with eight million tons of ships. The Pearl Harbor attack was only the opening salvo of what promised to be a long and hard war, a view Yamamoto captured best in a letter to a colleague. "A military man can scarcely pride himself on having 'smitten a sleeping enemy'; it is more a matter of shame, simply, for the one smitten," he wrote. "I would rather you made your appraisal after seeing what the enemy does, since it is certain that, angered and outraged, he will soon launch a determined counterattack."

Yamamoto's fears ran counter to the views of his fellow military leaders, the press, and general public. In the weeks after the attack on Pearl Harbor, newspapers printed photos and dramatic accounts of the raid, described by the *Osaka Mainichi* newspaper as "the brilliant curtain raiser for the destruction of the United States and Britain." Other papers published poems celebrating the attack, while a motion picture compiled of edited assault footage played for packed theaters nationwide. With each passing day—and as Japan's victories mounted—the national ego swelled. The press began to refer to Japanese forces as "superhuman" and even celebrated them as gods. One newspaper article went so far as to proclaim that Japan's conquest of the oil-rich Dutch East Indies fulfilled a centuries-old prophecy of the deity Boyo Moyo. "As our country was founded by God," declared planning board president Lieutenant General Teiichi Suzuki, "so our men in the fighting forces are God's troops."

Yamamoto watched as this national fervor reached a climax with the February fall of Singapore. Members of the House of Representatives erupted in shouts of "Banzai." Schools suspended class, while newspapers published special "Victory Supplements." Despite rationing, the government announced each family would be given two bottles of beer, rubber goods, and red beans; children under thirteen would receive caramel drops. Even Emperor Hirohito put in a special public appearance—dressed in his military uniform and mounted on his favorite horse, White Snow—to accept the banzais of the adoring crowd of thousands gathered in front of the Imperial Palace. "The downfall of Singapore," the *Osaka Mainichi* wrote, "has definitely decided the history of the world." The *Japan Times & Advertiser* compared the victory to Hannibal's legendary crossing of the Alps and Genghis Khan's passage through the Hindu Kush. "Our men," the paper declared, "are now among the world's immortals."

The press went so far as to boast that it would be easy for Japanese soldiers to storm the beaches of California. "Once a landing is made on the American continent, it will be a simple matter for a well-trained, courageous army to sweep everything before it," argued an editorial in the *Japan Times & Advertiser.* "The contention that the United States cannot be invaded is a myth." At the same time the possibility that America might actually strike back at Japan was viewed as impossible, if not laughable. "Japan Raid by U.S. Is Out of Question," declared one headline; another stated, "No Fear of America Attacking Empire." Most pointed out that Japan, after seizing American bases across the Pacific, now controlled much of the seas and the skies. "As for aerial attacks from aircraft-carriers," argued a correspondent for the *Asahi* newspaper, "any such attempt is believed suicidal because, unlike Hawaii, a very vigorous vigil is kept along the Japanese coasts and American raids will be nipped in the bud."

Yamamoto wasn't so cocky, particularly since he knew how few the resources were to protect Japan's crowded cities from attack. Most of the nation's fighters had deployed to the front lines, leaving behind just three hundred planes to safeguard the homeland—two hundred Navy and one hundred Army. Only fifty of those were dedicated to the defense of Tokyo and the industrial suburb of Yokohama. The Osaka and Kobe regions were equally ill equipped, with just twenty defensive fighters, while Nagoya counted only ten. Many of the planes were older Nakajima Type 97, code-named Nate by the Allies, a single-seat fighter with a fixed-landing gear. Yamamoto knew that antiaircraft defense was likewise inadequate. Tokyo had just 150 of the nation's 700 antiaircraft guns—most 75 millimeter—while Kobe and Osaka had a combined 70 and Nagoya a mere 20. "Compared with the Japanese forces in the overseas areas," one postwar Japanese report noted, "the air defense units in the home islands were poorly equipped and trained."

Many of Japan's senior leaders, however, did not share Yamamoto's fears. During a meeting with his military councillors on November 4, 1941, Prime Minister Hideki Tojo dismissed the threat of an air raid against Japan, insisting that the nation dedicate its forces to overseas operations. "I do not think the enemy could raid Japan proper from the air immediately after the outbreak of hostilities," Tojo said. "Some time would elapse before the enemy could attempt such raids." That same confidence led him to reject the first comprehensive air defense measures proposed by the War Ministry in mid-January, which called for dispersing factories, protecting utilities, communication and transportation systems, and even evacuating major urban centers. Tojo likewise shot down a proposal in February to at least evacuate women and children, claiming that such action would merely threaten Japan's important family structure. Only cowards, he argued, evacuated.

Yamamoto disagreed. The veteran admiral had set a precedent with the surprise attack on Pearl Harbor. He understood that America's strong national character—coupled with Japan's failure to sink the nation's flat-tops at Pearl Harbor—would no doubt lead to a retaliatory carrier strike against the Japanese homeland. Yamamoto recalled that during the Russo-Japanese War when a Russian naval force arrived off Tokyo's shores, many terrified residents fled to the mountains while others stoned the home of Vice Admiral Kamimura, the officer trusted to protect the homeland from attack. Yamamoto vowed never to let that happen again, and his determination to protect the seat of the emperor, aides remembered, grew into an obsession. "He never failed, before giving his attention to any thing else, to ask for the latest Tokyo weather report," recalled Mitsuo Fuchida, the pilot who led the air attack on Pearl Harbor. "If the reports were bad, he felt relieved because they gave added assurance that the capital was safe."

Yamamoto ordered daily long-range air patrols in the waters east of Japan, along with the creation of a fleet of picket boats, a force that would eventually count 171 such vessels, most small fishing boats requisitioned from private owners that ranged in size from 50 to 250 tons. Armed with radios to flash reports of any approaching enemy fleet, the boats operated anywhere from eighty to a thousand miles off shore, anchoring during the day and patrolling at night. Despite these precautions Yamamoto remained so concerned he even advised a geisha friend to move her property outside the city. "A lot of people are feeling relieved, or saying they're 'grateful to Admiral Yamamoto' because there hasn't been a single air raid," he wrote. "They're very wrong: the fact that the enemy hasn't come is no thanks to Admiral Yamamoto, but to the enemy himself. So if they want to express gratitude to somebody, I wish they'd express it to America. If the latter really made up its mind to wade in on us, there'd be no way of defending a city like Tokyo."

LIEUTENANT HENRY MILLER CLIMBED down from his Vought SBU Corsair biplane at Eglin Field on the Sunday morning of March 1, 1942. The twenty-nine-year-old Alaska native, who answered to the nickname Hank, clutched orders directing him to temporary duty at the Army airfield. A 1934 graduate of the Naval Academy, where he had boxed under famed coach Spike Webb, Miller had begun his career on the battleship *Texas*. He went on to earn his wings in June 1938 and later served on the carrier *Saratoga*. Since November 1940 he had worked as a flight instructor and personnel officer at the naval air station Ellyson Field, in the Florida Panhandle near Pensacola; a flight from there to Eglin he had made that morning in just fifty minutes. Miller's orders made no mention of what he would do for the Army, though the assistant training officer at Pensacola told him that the assignment was to assist a Lieutenant Colonel Doolittle.

"Is that the Great Jimmy Doolittle?" Miller asked.

Doolittle had requested a secure place to train near the coast that would allow his crews to practice overwater navigation, an imperative skill the men would need for the raid. The Army Air Forces had assigned him Eglin Field. Though founded in 1933 near the town of Valparaiso in the panhandle, Eglin was still very much a work in progress. The year before had seen the completion of a 1,000-seat mess hall, and workers now hustled to complete the base chapel by May. The first on-base movie theater would open in July. The day Miller first stepped onto the tarmac, Eglin counted 1,526 airmen living in barracks, another 1,872 in tents, and 632 off base. It would soon become obvious to Doolittle's fliers why the Army chose Eglin and its various satellite fields. "It was out in the boonies; there wasn't anybody around," recalled pilot Everett "Brick" Holstrom, then a young first lieutenant. "It was completely isolated."

The Army had sent orders to Eglin's commanding officer to be ready to house upwards of twenty combat crews as well as to service as many bombers as early as February 21. That included guaranteeing the base enough bombs in its arsenal, along with .50-caliber and .30-caliber machine-gun rounds to aid in the airmen's training. "Inasmuch as this is an extremely confidential project," orders stated, "it is directed that no information be permitted to get out regarding the arrival, departure or activities of these airplanes and crews." In advance of the airmen's transfer to Eglin, the Army had likewise reached out to the Navy's Bureau of Aeronautics: "It is requested that a Naval aviator, experienced in the art of taking heavily loaded airplanes off from the deck of a carrier, be available at Eglin Field, Valparaiso, Florida, from March 1 to March 15, for the purpose of instructing Army pilots in this art." The Navy had answered with Miller.

The young lieutenant reported to the base commander. "Do you know what I'm down here for?" Miller asked.

"No," the colonel replied.

Miller explained he was a carrier pilot and instructor over at Pensacola and was supposed to teach some Army pilots how to take off from a flattop.

The colonel said he still had no idea.

Convinced his orders must be a mistake, Miller rose to leave when he happened to mention Doolittle's detachment.

The colonel then closed the doors, his voice dropped to a whisper.

Miller had come to the right place.

The colonel drove the lieutenant over to the barracks and allowed him to drop off his gear before shuttling him over to the building where Doolittle's detachment was set up. Neither Doolittle nor the squadron's executive officer, Jack Hilger, was there, but Miller met Captains Ski York, Davy Jones, and Ross Greening. The aircrews had begun to arrive in the modified B-25s, though official training would not start for a few days. Miller introduced himself to the three pilots, informing them that he was there to teach them how to take off from a carrier.

"Have you ever flown a B-25?" one of the men asked.

Miller confessed he had never even seen one.

"Well, that's all right," the Army airmen assured him. "Because none of us know anything about the Navy either."

The four men headed down to the line and climbed inside a B-25. With Jones as the pilot and Miller his copilot, the airmen throttled up the engines and flew over to the auxiliary runway set aside for the crews to train. The brief flight gave Miller a feel for the medium bomber, while the airmen explained that a typical takeoff required a speed of about 110 miles per hour, a figure Miller told them he could cut in half. The Navy lieutenant gave his first lesson: hold both feet on the brakes, put the stabilizer back three-fourths, and throttle up the engine. With the engine roaring at full throttle, release the brakes and pull back on the yoke until the plane lifts off. Miller demonstrated, charging into the skies with an air speed of around 65 miles per hour.

"That is impossible," one of the airmen said. "You can't do that."

"Okay," he answered. "Come on back and we'll land and try it again."

Miller charged into the skies again, this time at a speed of about seventy miles per hour. The three Army airmen were convinced.

THE TWO DOZEN AIRCREWS had all arrived by March 3, when Doolittle touched down at Eglin. He had mapped out a fifty-five-hour training program, the bare essentials of what it would take to get his men in shape for the mission. That regime included a six-hour preliminary period in which each aircraft commander would calibrate his airspeed indicators, compass, and automatic flight control equipment. Doolittle planned for his crews to then spend five hours each working with Lieutenant Miller on short-field takeoffs: four with an empty plane, four with a bomber weighing about 28,000 pounds, and finally two takeoffs with a fully loaded plane of 31,000 pounds. Crews would spend another fifteen hours practicing daytime and nighttime bombing on ground targets and oil slicks in the Gulf of Mexico, followed by another fifteen hours of gunnery practice that included making dry practice runs against attacking pursuits.

Doolittle lastly wanted each crew to perform fourteen hours of overwater navigation. He planned for the airmen to fly from Eglin to Fort Meyer, Florida. From there, crews would fly across the gulf to Houston before returning to Eglin; the outgoing flight would be made during the day, the return at night. The training in the skies would be complemented by ground lectures on pursuit and antiaircraft evasion tactics. The airmen had come from four different squadrons, so Doolittle organized the fliers into a cohesive single unit, which he deemed important since he would be gone much of the time. In addition to his executive officer,

Hilger, Doolittle picked York to serve as operations officer. Jones would handle navigation and intelligence, while Greening would serve as gunnery officer. He tapped Bill Bower as the squadron's engineering officer and Travis Hoover to oversee supplies. Doolittle wanted Hoover, York, Jones, Greening, and Hilger also to serve as the mission's five flight commanders.

With this in mind Doolittle summoned the roughly 140 officers and enlisted men to the Operations Office, where the fliers crowded onto benches and windowsills. This was the first time many had ever seen the famous flier in the flesh.

"I was a little awestruck," remembered Bill Bower. "This was my idol."

"He was a legend," added navigator and bombardier Herb Macia. "He was a person that you never expected to see or have any personal contact with."

A few were surprised by his small stature. "I'd built him up as quite a giant," recalled Harry McCool, another navigator. "He was such a short little duck."

Doolittle's charisma overshadowed his size. "We were immediately captivated," Jones said. "It didn't take but two minutes and you were under his spell."

More than anything else the famed aviator's presence communicated the importance of the mission. "As soon as we heard his name we knew we could depend on real action," remembered navigator Charles McClure. "Something really big was in prospect."

"My name's Doolittle," he announced to the airmen, his voice calm and measured. "If you men have any idea that this isn't the most dangerous thing you've ever been on, don't even start this training period. You can drop out now. There isn't much sense wasting time and money training men who aren't going through with this thing. It's perfectly all right for any of you to drop out."

The room fell quiet, then several hands shot up.

"Sir," a young officer asked, "can you give us any more information about the mission?"

"No, I can't—just now," Doolittle answered. "But you'll begin to get an idea of what it's all about the longer we're down here training for it. Now, there's one important thing I want to stress. This whole thing must be kept secret. I don't even want you to tell your wives, no matter what you see, or are asked to do, down here. If you've guessed where we're going, don't even talk about your guess. That means every one of you. Don't even talk among yourselves about this thing."

Doolittle fell silent, letting his message register.

"The lives of many men are going to depend on how well you keep this project to yourselves," he continued. "Not only your lives but the lives of hundreds of others."

He warned the men to avoid rumors and report any curious strangers to him; he would contact the Federal Bureau of Investigation.

"Our training here will stress teamwork," he said. "I want every man to do his assigned job. We've got a lot of work to do on those planes to get them in shape."

Beyond the planes, every airman, from the bombardiers and navigators to the gunners and pilots, would have to train for the mission.

"We've got about three weeks—maybe less," Doolittle concluded. "Remember, if anyone wants to drop out, he can. No questions asked."

None did.

MILLER STARTED WORK IMMEDIATELY, formulating a takeoff procedure based on a study of the characteristics and performance data of the B-25 and its engines. He assumed that the maximum number of bombers would be placed aboard the carrier, slashing takeoff space to as little as 350 feet. The naval aviator calculated that the combined wind and carrier speed would create a forty-knot wind across the flight deck to help each fully loaded bomber lift off. Miller ordered crews to paint a yellow stripe down the runway so that pilots could practice holding the left wheel on the line, an imperative skill since pilots would have just 7 feet of clearance between the bomber's wingtip and the carrier's island. In addition, he requested flags planted at 250 feet and 400 feet and then every 50 feet after that, up to 700 feet, to help pilots mark takeoff distances.

Miller first trained Jones, who managed to lift off with an airspeed of just fifty-miles per hour, then recruited the captain to serve as his assistant. Each pilot reported to the runway in his bomber. Jones would make one takeoff in the pilot's seat, explaining the procedure, while the aircraft commander flew as his copilot. Jones would then trade seats with the pilot, allowing the other flier a chance. Miller assigned an airman to time the plane when it reached the 250-foot mark as well as on takeoff. Another measured the plane's distance when it left the runway. Miller stood behind the pilot and recorded the airspeed and offered advice. The concept proved alien to the Army pilots, who were accustomed to using every inch of a runway that stretched for thousands of feet. Travis Hoover's response was typical of many after hearing Miller's lesson.

"We can't do that," the pilot protested.

"Oh, yes," Miller said, "you can."

Most of the airmen proved fast learners. During preliminary training in a bomber weighing around 26,000 pounds, Harold Watson managed to get airborne at just sixty-two miles per hour, better even than Miller. Donald Smith topped everyone for the record for shortest distance, lifting off in as little as 294 feet. "Excellent," Miller scribbled in his notes. "This pilot has the news!" Once the aviators mastered takeoffs with a lightly loaded plane, Miller ordered them to report with a full load of gas, ammunition, and equipment that brought the bomber's weight up to around 29,000 pounds. Each pilot again made several takeoffs while Jones and Miller watched, the brakes at times heating up so much that pilots had to fly around with the landing gear down to cool them off. "After a little practice," one report later noted, "the observers on the ground could tell almost exactly what the pilot was doing in the cockpit."

For the final round crews loaded the B-25s with practice bombs and even stacked boxes of extra .50-caliber machine-gun rounds in the navigator's compartment, upping the weight to 31,000 pounds. That was how much Doolittle predicted each plane would weigh as it charged down the *Hornet*'s flight deck filled with bombs and extra fuel needed to reach China. Watson again bested everyone for the low-speed record, lifting off at just fifty-five miles per hour. "It became an intense competition to see who could take off in the shortest distance with the greatest load," Bower recalled. "The only weight we had for the airplane was .50 caliber ammunition in boxes, and people, so one man would make his attempt and record the distance, and then we'd all climb in the next airplane and load it up a little more, and see whether we could best that distance."

Though most of the fliers had no trouble—Miller rated Doolittle,

Jones, and Robert Gray the best—the naval aviator struggled with James Bates, a first lieutenant who had almost five hundred hours in the cockpit, including two hundred in a B-25. Those problems came to a head on the morning of March 23 in the final round of training.

"Bates, you have to try it again," an exasperated Miller instructed him. "You fly the plane. Don't let it fly you. Once more around."

The lieutenant throttled up the engine and released the brakes at 10:03 a.m. To Miller's horror the bomber lifted off in a skid. Bates pushed it harder and the right engine stalled out at about twenty-five feet. The bomber crashed to ground, crushing the landing gear and propellers and tearing up the fuselage. The other crew members, afraid the plane would explode, started to climb out the windows.

"Sit down and wait until those props stop," Miller ordered. "Turn off all your switches."

Miller reached into the back to grab his papers and notebook, only to turn around and find the others had all jumped out. "No one was hurt," Bates would later tell investigators, "but the airplane was totally washed out."

The loss of the bomber created a problem. York picked up the phone and called Columbia. His close friend and fellow pilot Bob Emmens answered. Ordered to remain behind in South Carolina by Hilger, Emmens had listened in awe to the stories that drifted back of short takeoffs and long overwater flights the crews practiced.

"We just lost an airplane," York told him. "We need another airplane right away down here."

"Ski," he said, spotting his opportunity, "I will see you about 3:30 or 4:00."

Emmens was thrilled. The pilot hurried back to his tent and grabbed a few uniforms, underwear, and toiletries. He packed the rest of his gear in his footlocker, ordering it sent to his home at 1443 East Main Street in Medford, Oregon. On heading out to his plane, he collided with Colonel Mills, the group commander.

"Emmens," Mills said, "where are you off to?"

"Sir," he said, "York just called from Eglin, and they had some bad luck with an airplane. They need another airplane down there. So I told him I would be down there about 3:30 or 4:00."

"I don't know whether I trust you or not. You had better find somebody else to take that airplane down. If you take it down there, I'm afraid you won't come back."

"Colonel, sir," Emmens protested. "I promise I will be back this evening."

Mills considered it. "Well, since you are all ready, okay," he said, reluctantly. "But if you don't come back, I am going to have your you know what."

"Oh, sir," he replied. "I will be back."

MAINTENANCE PROBLEMS SOON CUT into the aircrew's training time. The B-25's meager armament consisted of twin .50-caliber machine guns mounted in top and bottom turrets along with a single .30-caliber machine gun in the nose, a setup the aviators described as "woefully deficient." Exacerbating the airmen's concerns, the few guns the bombers did have often failed to work. The blast from the machine-gun muzzle when fired close to the fuselage popped rivets and tore the plane's thin skin, forcing workers to install steel blast plates. Neither the lower gun turret's activating or extending and retracting mechanisms functioned properly, and the complicated gun sight proved impossible for the men to learn in the few weeks before the mission. "A man could learn to play the violin well enough for Carnegie Hall," Doolittle griped, "before he could learn to fire that thing."

Greening worked to remedy these problems. He recommended that workers remove the belly guns—the low-altitude mission made them worthless anyway—which would reduce weight and free up space for the extra sixty-gallon gas tank. To shore up the unprotected tail, Greening devised a ruse. Crews cut holes in the bomber's tail and installed two black wooden poles reminiscent of broomsticks designed to resemble .50-caliber machine guns, exaggerating the barrel size to make them more visible to a pursuing fighter. Many of the real guns either failed to fire or easily jammed, forcing the gunner to waste valuable time stripping them. With the help of an armaments expert from Wright Field, crews either replaced defective guns or swapped out faulty parts. Though the men practiced with .50-caliber machine guns at a ground range, all this added work meant that none of the gunners ever fired on a moving target in the skies.

Greening zeroed in as well on the B-25's classified Norden bomb-sight, a seventy-five-pound analog computer consisting of more than two thousand parts. The sophisticated instrument named for Dutch designer Carl Norden carried a hefty price tag of almost $10,000—enough cash to buy ten new Studebaker Commanders. Not only would the Japanese pos-sibly capture the bombsight if a plane was shot down, but Greening knew the Norden worked best at altitudes of at least four thousand feet, a much higher bombing altitude than Doolittle had planned for the mission. Greening with the help of Staff Sergeant Edwin Bain fashioned a simpli-fied replacement made from scrap Dural aluminum that he dubbed the Mark Twain in honor of the primitive lead-line depth finders once used along the Mississippi River. Tests would later show that Greening's twenty-cent sight worked far better at the proposed bombing height of fifteen hundred feet than the more complicated and pricey Norden. "It was fine for the things we had in mind," recalled pilot Ted Lawson. "It was as simple as pointing a rifle at the object to be bombed and letting the bomb go when you had a bead."

Crews focused on more than just armament. The mission would require bombers to fly a minimum of 1,900 miles nonstop from the moment the wheels left the carrier's flight deck until touchdown more than twelve hours later in eastern China. Even with the three added gaso-line tanks, the distance demanded that crews maximize fuel efficiency. North American developed cruise control charts that demonstrated how pilots could increase manifold pressure and lower propeller rpm settings to squeeze more miles out of each gallon. Swapping out scratched props likewise allowed pilots without any added power to increase speed from 220 miles per hour to 275. Though these measures improved efficiency, tests revealed that no two bombers burned fuel at the same rate. Doolit-tle requested the help of a civilian carburetor expert from the Bendix fac-tory. Much to his frustration, the company sent a cocky blowhard.

"I understand you want some carburetors pressure checked," the fac-tory representative told Doolittle. "I can tell you now they have been checked before they left the factory. As a matter of fact we just don't send out equipment that is not in perfect condition. Furthermore—"

"Hold it, son," Doolittle interrupted, clearly irritated. "What did the factory send? An expert or a salesman? If you're a salesman, go home, we have plenty of carburetors. If you're an expert, stick around, we need you."

The man stayed put.

Pilots flew under simulated mission conditions to calculate fuel consumption, determining that the bombers burned on average sixty-five gallons per hour with a light load and up to seventy-eight gallons with a full one. Doolittle demanded his crews fly out over the Gulf of Mexico so pilots and navigators could learn to operate without landmarks or radio references. Greening's copilot Second Lieutenant Ken Reddy of Texas described in his diary a near tragedy that occurred on one such flight over the gulf when the inside plate that covered the hole left by the lower turret started to jump up and down. The rattle irritated the crew's engineer-gunner, Sergeant Melvin Gardner, who attempted to weight down the plate with two full toolboxes. "This did not do the trick," Reddy wrote, "so he sat on the tool boxes." Greening called Gardner, instructing him to take a headset to navigator Second Lieutenant Frank Kappeler. "It was while he was doing this that both plates and the boxes dropped out of the ship. They are all in Davey Jones' Locker," Reddy continued. "Gardner was wearing no chute so he was lucky."

Doolittle likewise demanded that his crews drill on low-altitude target approaches followed by rapid bombing and evasive measures. Much of the training involved sand-loaded bombs, though each crew practiced once with a 100-pound live weapon. Sandbags weighted down the tails of parked bombers so machine gunners could fire the .50 calibers at temporary targets set up on Eglin's auxiliary fields. Other times the gunners strafed sea slicks in the gulf or practiced tracking pursuit planes. Doolittle had hoped his crews might fire on towed targets, but time did not allow it. "Many Florida coast towns were subjected to vigorous low altitude dry run attacks," noted one report. "The numerous complaining telephone calls to the commander at Eglin Field gave evidence to the enthusiasm displayed by the pilots during this particular practice."

The aviators would have to look after not just the bombers but themselves as well, a job that fell to First Lieutenant Thomas White, the mission's thirty-two-year-old flight surgeon, known simply as Doc. A Maui native and 1937 graduate of Harvard Medical School, White had volunteered for the mission, only to have Jack Hilger dash his hopes. There was no slot for a doctor. If White wanted to go, the major told him, he would have to learn how to shoot the .50-caliber machine guns. "To his great credit, he did," Doolittle later wrote. "He scored second highest of all the gunners on the firing range with the twin .50s and thus earned his way onto a crew."

Mindful of weight limits, White planned to pack only a medical officer's field kit, plus a few added supplies, including a thousand sulfathiazole tablets, two metal catheters, and a pocket surgical kit. He overhauled the two first aid kits in each plane, checking to make sure each contained morphine syrettes and sulfanilamide tablets. "Difficulty was experienced in obtaining foot powder for the men," White later noted. "The supposition being, apparently, that Air Corps troops never walk but always fly." The doctor checked blood types and made sure the information was recorded on each airman's dog tags. Only after Doolittle flew to Washington and intervened was White able to obtain the necessary vaccines. He administered updated shots for typhoid, tetanus, smallpox, and yellow fever and started the men on injections against pneumonia, typhus, cholera, and bubonic plague. "No marked reactions were observed," White noted, "even to the plague vaccine, which enjoys a bad reputation."

In addition to teaching carrier takeoffs, Miller gave the airmen a crash course on naval etiquette, instructing them when boarding a ship to salute the national ensign on the stern and the officer of the deck. He told them how to take a shower without wasting water and gave them a rundown of naval terminology, from the difference between port and starboard to floor versus deck. The rest of the time the airmen relaxed, taking in a performance of the Alabama College Glee Club and spending an afternoon deep-sea fishing in the gulf. "We caught a good mess of fish," Reddy wrote in his diary. "I caught about six; one was a triggerfish. Most of them were red and white snappers."

Others used the downtime to write letters home, including Richard Cole. "Our commanding officer is none other than 'Jimmie Doolittle' the famous speed demon—he flies a B-25 the same way," he wrote to his parents in Ohio. "We have learned a lot of new data about our ships and from the looks of things we will be needing all of it." Pilot Billy Farrow's mother worked as a stenographer for the Board of Economic Warfare in Washington, where she battled long food lines and crowded buses. He implored her in a letter to remain strong. "You're helping in national defense too, remember, so if things get tough, know that you're doing it for your country, and there's nothing too good to do for our country," Farrow wrote. "*Remember that—nothing!*"

Lawson came out to his plane one morning to discover that someone had chalked the name *Ruptured Duck* on the fuselage. He liked the name so much he recruited a gunner to paint an accompanying caricature of Donald Duck, complete with his headphone cords twisted around his head and a set of crossed crutches. Other crews followed Lawson's lead, and soon many of the B-25s had been christened with names such as *Whiskey Pete, Whirling Dervish, Bat out of Hell, Avenger, Green Hornet, TNT, Fickle Finger of Fate*, and, of course, *Hari Kari-er.*

Throughout the training the airmen respected Doolittle's warning not to talk about the mission, though the secrecy at times proved fodder for humor.

"Doolittle has got some kind of horrible disease," pilot Travis Hoover joked. "He's going on a one-way mission and taking us with him."

Miller's lessons on Navy life alerted many that the mission would likely involve a carrier, though the airmen wondered whether that might mean a trip to Europe or Japan. "It was sort of obvious, but we weren't permitted to talk about it," Knobloch recalled. "We weren't permitted to guess about it. If one of us would open his mouth and get out of line, the other guys would jump on him." The final destination, the men realized, had little bearing on the training. "We could do what we had to do and have our fun," Bower recalled, "without talking about what was going to come tomorrow."

Fog and foul weather limited flying for days at a time, but Doolittle felt his crews had learned a lot, though he didn't fool himself. Three weeks was not much time to prepare for a strike against the Japanese homeland. The more than four-year war with China had transformed the empire's aviators into some of the world's best. American pilots in contrast had no real combat experience. Operating a bomber was a team effort. It wasn't enough to have a good pilot or gunner. Each man had to be the best. The weeks at Elgin had revealed to the pragmatic Doolittle the varying gaps in crew skills, though at this late stage there was little more he could do to remedy them. "The first pilots were all excellent," he noted in his report. "The co-pilots were all good for co-pilots. The bombardiers were fair but needed brushing up. The navigators had had good training but very little practical experience. The gunners, almost without exception, had never fired a machine gun from an airplane at either a moving or stationary target."

AS THE CREWS FINISHED training at Eglin, Doolittle returned to Washington to make a final pitch to Arnold. The veteran airman who had sat out World War I didn't want to just plan and organize the mission. Doolittle wanted to lead it.

"General, it occurred to me that I'm the one guy on this project who knows more about it than anyone else," he began. "You asked me to get the planes modified and the crews trained and this is being done. They're the finest bunch of boys I've ever worked with. I'd like your authorization to lead this mission myself."

Arnold's trademark grin vanished. Though he appreciated Doolittle's enthusiasm—and understood his desire to see combat—Arnold needed his troubleshooter in Washington. "I'm sorry, Jim," the general answered. "I need you right here on my staff. I can't afford to let you go on every mission you might help to plan."

The calculating Doolittle had assumed Arnold would put up such resistance. He countered with a sales pitch, wearing the general down.

"All right, Jim," Arnold finally answered. "It's all right with me provided it's all right with Miff Harmon."

Arnold had referred to Brigadier General Millard Harmon Jr., his chief of staff. Doolittle suspected a ruse. He saluted and exited Arnold's office, sprinting down the passageway to Harmon's office. He knocked and entered.

"Miff," a winded Doolittle began. "I've just been to see Hap about that project I've been working on and said I wanted to lead the mission. Hap said it was okay with him if it's okay with you."

"Well," Harmon stammered, clearly blindsided, "whatever is all right with Hap is certainly all right with me."

Doolittle thanked him and left. Just as he closed the door, he heard Arnold over the squawk box. He didn't want to wait to be summoned back. As he disappeared, he heard Harmon protest, "But Hap, I told him he could go."

CHAPTER 6

═══════════

★

These brutal and inexcusable attacks on civilian populations
have created a hatred of the Japanese in China which
it will take centuries to eradicate.

—OFFICE OF STRATEGIC SERVICES,
FEBRUARY 3, 1942

DONALD DUNCAN STEPPED OFF the plane on Thursday, March 19, in
Hawaii after two straight days of travel from Washington. The Navy captain was no doubt tired from the trip across five time zones, one made all
the more stressful by a snafu in his orders that nearly left him stranded on
the tarmac in New Mexico. Duncan had failed to make sure his orders
stated that he had top priority, an error he didn't realize until the stewardess woke him up in the middle of the night near Albuquerque. She
informed him that Army pilots, traveling under top-priority orders,
waited to board at the next stop, en route back to San Francisco after
delivering airplanes. There wasn't room on board the commercial flight
for everyone. Duncan would have to get off.

The naval officer protested that he was under orders to connect in
San Francisco for Hawaii and that he simply could not get off.

The stewardess protested.

"Well," Duncan countered, "I'm not getting off."

The commotion drew the attention of the pilot, who came back and told Duncan that he had to go along with established priority.

Duncan showed the pilot his orders, which, in an effort to maintain total secrecy, mentioned only that he had to attend a conference in Hawaii.

The pilot appeared sympathetic, but said someone would have to direct him to allow Duncan to remain on board.

Duncan suggested he call General Arnold in Washington.

The pilot said he would discuss the situation with the Army aviators about to board. If he couldn't work something out, the pilot would call Washington.

"Well, that's fine, but if I leave the airplane, you will have to carry me off," Duncan told him. "I'm not going to get out of this bunk and off the airplane."

The Navy captain went back to bed only to awake the next morning as his plane approached San Francisco.

Duncan put the experience behind him as he hastened to see Pacific Fleet commander Admiral Chester Nimitz. The wreckage of Japan's December 7 surprise attack still crowded the cool waters of Pearl Harbor, the entire bay rimmed by a two-foot-thick film of oil. The burned-out battleship *Arizona* rested on the muddy bottom with eleven hundred sailors entombed inside while, as *Time* magazine noted, the Hawaiian sun reflected off the rusty keels of the capsized battleship *Oklahoma* and the former battleship turned target ship *Utah*. Thousands of divers, welders, and engineers now risked poison gas and unexploded ordnance to untangle the destruction even as grim reminders of the awful tragedy still surfaced. Workers only the month before had salvaged thousands of waterlogged and rust-stained Christmas cards from one vessel, while the marked-out dates on a calendar discovered in a storeroom of the sunken battleship *West Virginia* revealed that three men had survived until December 23 before the oxygen ran out.

A fifty-seven-year-old Texas native—and 1905 graduate of the Naval Academy—Nimitz had spent much of his career in the undersea service. The laconic four-star admiral had assumed command of the battered Pacific Fleet just three weeks after the Japanese attack. "May the good Lord help and advise me," he had written to his wife that day, "and may I have all the support I can get for I will need it!" The deteriorating situation in the Pacific depressed Nimitz, who lay awake long hours each night. The Pacific Fleet had so far executed several carrier raids against outlying Japanese bases, hoping to relieve the pressure on forces fighting in the southwest Pacific, but without any real luck. "The Japs didn't mind them," one officer quipped, "any more than a dog minds fleas." The lack of success made Nimitz doubt he would survive long in his new job. "I will be lucky to last six months," he wrote to his wife that month. "The public may demand action and results faster than I can produce."

Duncan only promised to increase Nimitz's stress. The sole record of the captain's secret visit was the terse notation in Nimitz's unofficial war diary: "arrived for conference." Nimitz summoned Vice Admiral William "Bull" Halsey Jr. and his chief of staff, Captain Miles Browning. The audacious operation to raid the Japanese capital existed only in the form of a handwritten plan, one so secretive that Duncan refused to allow even his trusted secretary to type it. The roughly thirty-page outline boasted a weather annex, a breakdown of the proposed ships, and the route across the Pacific, all the logistical details Duncan believed he needed to share with Nimitz. "I had been told by Admiral King to tell Admiral Nimitz that this was not a proposal made for him to consider but a plan to be carried out by him," Duncan recalled. "So that cleared up any matter of whether we should do it or not; it was on the books by then."

Nimitz listened as Duncan outlined his proposal. The admiral was guarded in how he chose to commit his forces, a caution that had led him to clash with Admiral King after barely a month on the job. King had pressed Nimitz to execute aggressive carrier raids that would rattle the Japanese and inspire the American public. Nimitz had felt more reluctant, afraid to risk his precious carriers. "Pacific Fleet markedly inferior in all types to enemy," Nimitz had cabled King in early February. "Cannot conduct aggressive action Pacific except raids of hit-and-run character." Nimitz's message had drawn a stern rebuke. "Pacific Fleet not repeat not markedly inferior in all types to forces enemy can bring to bear within operating radius of Hawaii," King countered. "Your forces will however be markedly inferior from Australia to Alaska when the enemy has gained objectives in Southwest Pacific unless every effort is continuously made to damage his ships and bases."

A raid against Tokyo certainly qualified as aggressive.

Nimitz's orders were to guard Hawaii and Midway and protect the sea-lanes to Australia. The Pacific Fleet commander understood the incredible risk involved in a raid against Tokyo—his own staff had even proposed and then nixed just such an idea in February. The Japanese attacks on Pearl Harbor and the Philippines had wrecked two of America's three fleets. Even with the addition of the *Hornet* the backbone of America's Pacific defense rested on just five aircraft carriers, half the number of flattops Japan counted. The cumbersome B-25s were too large to fit inside a carrier's aircraft elevator, forcing the Navy to crowd the bombers on the deck of the *Hornet*, a move that would render the carrier unable to launch fighters in an emergency. To protect the *Hornet* from surprise attack Nimitz would have to dispatch the carrier *Enterprise*. Two of America's five Pacific carriers—the flattops Yamamoto so hungered to destroy in his quest for Pacific dominance—would steam to within four hundred miles of the enemy's homeland.

The opportunities for disaster were numerous. Not only would America risk two of its prized carriers, but fourteen support ships, including four cruisers, eight destroyers, and two oilers as well as the lives of some ten thousand sailors. This strike force would have to thread its ways across the Pacific in complete radio silence, avoiding the constellations of Japanese bases that stretched from the Marianas to New Guinea. Enemy fighters, bombers, and reconnaissance planes crowded the skies, while warships, patrol craft, and submarines plowed the Pacific waters, any one of which could jeopardize the mission. Beyond the operation's logistics loomed the larger question of what the Japanese would do in retaliation. Would such a raid invite a second attack against Pearl Harbor or possibly Midway? What about the West Coast? Would an outraged Yamamoto order his forces to attack Seattle, San Francisco, or Los Angeles?

But as Duncan had made clear, Nimitz had no choice.

The mission was a go.

Duncan fired off a prearranged dispatch to Captain Francis Low, directing him to alert Doolittle that it was time to move his men west from Eglin Field to California. The coded message simply read, "Tell Jimmy to get on his horse."

Nimitz conferred with Halsey.

"Do you believe it would work, Bill?" he asked.

"They'll need a lot of luck," Halsey answered.

"Are you willing to take them out there?" Nimitz pressed.

"Yes, I am."

"Good," Nimitz replied. "It's all yours!"

PLANS PROGRESSED IN CHINA to prepare for the raiders. Doolittle in his initial handwritten outline of the mission had suggested coordinating with Colonel Claire Chennault, aviation adviser to the Chinese government and the commander of the American Volunteer Group, better known as the Flying Tigers. Chennault, however, was widely disliked; Arnold deemed him a mercenary and a "crackpot." The chief of the Army Air Forces instead turned to Lieutenant General Joseph Stilwell, whom Roosevelt had recently tapped to serve as commander of American Army Forces in China, Burma, and India as well as chief of staff to Generalissimo Chiang Kai-shek. Few military leaders had as much experience in China as the fifty-nine-year-old Stilwell, a Florida native and 1904 graduate of the U.S. Military Academy. Able to speak Chinese as well as French and Spanish—he taught the latter two languages at West Point—Stilwell had served three tours in China between the wars, in posts ranging from language officer to military attaché.

Stilwell's slender physique, gray hair, and wire-frame glasses—more befitting a college professor than a warrior—masked an acerbic personality that earned him the nickname Vinegar Joe. "Dour, belligerent, and weather beaten," is how his colleague Lewis Brereton once characterized him in his diary. In an essay written for his own family even Stilwell described himself as "unreasonable, impatient, sour-balled, sullen, mad, hard, profane, vulgar." The brilliant tactician had little use for social diplomacy. He referred to blacks as "niggers" or "coons," Chinese as "chinks" or "chinos," and the Germans as either "huns" or "squareheads." Stilwell targeted the Japanese with special disdain. "When I think of how these bowlegged cockroaches have ruined our calm lives," he once wrote, "it makes me want to wrap Jap guts around every lamppost in Asia." Stilwell even disparaged his commander in chief, whom he viewed as a "rank amateur in all military matters," after a meeting on the eve of his February departure. "Very unimpressive," he wrote in his diary. "Just a lot of wind."

Stilwell had the unenviable job of fighting a war in what amounted to a political, military, and economic backwater made all the more challenging by years of conflict and bloodshed. Spread across more than 4.2 million square miles, China had a population of almost 500 million people, 80 percent of them rural farmers. In addition to Manchuria and portions of Mongolia, Japan had wrestled away another 800,000 square miles, including coastal ports, railways, and industrial and commercial centers, effectively cutting China off from the outside world. One of Stilwell's top aides, Frank "Pinkie" Dorn, would later summarize it best. "Our ally, China, was a place rather than a nation; a makeshift affair whose economy was wrecked and whose currency was bolstered by the simple expedient of printing more unbacked paper money," Dorn wrote. "Tens of millions of its people had died from bullet, disease, or starvation, been forced to flee their homes, or deserted to the ministrations of a ruthless enemy."

Further complicating Stilwell's job was his disgust with Generalissimo Chiang Kai-shek, the fifty-four-year-old head of the National People's Party. The bespectacled Chinese leader spent most of his time battling the communists under Mao Zedong, while he populated his own government with cronies and family; his wife even served at one point as deputy chief of the air force. Stilwell viewed him as mentally unstable and arrogant. "He thinks he knows psychology," he wrote in his diary. "In fact, he thinks he knows everything." Stilwell often referred to the generalissimo by the diminutive name "Peanut" after an aide once described him as "a peanut perched on top of a dung heap." Relations soured further because of Stilwell's refusal to keep his views private. "The trouble in China is simple," he once told a reporter for *Time* magazine. "We are allied to an ignorant, illiterate, superstitious, peasant son of a bitch." When Roosevelt asked for his views of the generalissimo, Stilwell was equally crass and impolitic: "He's a vacillating, tricky, undependable old scoundrel, who never keeps his word."

Stilwell's views stood in contrast to those of most Americans, thanks in part to the herculean public relations efforts of Henry Luce, the *Time* and *Life* magazine publisher. Luce had been born in China to missionary parents and lionized Chiang Kai-shek, whose Christianity made him popular in the religious community. In 1937 *Time* named Chiang and his attractive spouse as the "Man & Wife of the Year." The Chinese leader's image over the years would appear on the cover of *Time* no fewer than ten times—two more than either Roosevelt or Winston Churchill and three more than Adolf Hitler. The press proved equally adoring of his wife, describing her as a cross between Joan of Arc and Florence Nightingale, a carefully crafted image that infuriated Stilwell and his aides. Those views even percolated inside the White House, where presidential aide Laughlin Currie remarked after one visit, "Each night it was like being tucked into bed by an *empress*!" Such undeserving adoration only made Stilwell's already tough task more unpalatable, a sentiment best captured by a reporter for *Harper's Magazine* in 1944: "If St. Francis of Assisi were put in charge of the CBI theater, he would be known as 'Vinegar Frank' before his brass buttons had time to tarnish."

American leaders had done little in recent years to earn Chinese goodwill, watching from the sidelines as Japan burned villages and slaughtered hundreds of thousands of men, women, and children. The United States instead had focused on defeating Germany, directing nine-tenths of its $13 billion lend-lease program to Britain, while China's share of American ordnance, aircraft, and tanks amounted to $618 million, just 4.6 percent. Leaders often claimed that the United States' meager war production meant it had little to offer, but an American intelligence report more accurately fingered the cause. "The true explanation for our ironic failure to give China more extensive support against our present enemy, Japan, seems rather to lie in an American attitude of mind," the report noted. "We have feared Germany and have been contemptuous of Japan. We have indulged the persistent hope that we could patch things up with Japan, a fallacy which has had its roots in our intellectual absorption in the familiar problems of Europe rather than in the exotic far-off conflicts of Eastern Asia."

Chiang Kai-shek may have been the son of a merchant, but he was savvy enough to understand that the attack on Pearl Harbor had transformed China's strategic value. With American bases in Guam and Wake gone and the Philippines under siege, the United States had no toehold in Asia from which to attack Japan. Furthermore, if Chinese forces could tie down the Japanese, it would slow the empire's progress elsewhere. But

Stilwell feared that Chiang Kai-shek was more concerned with his own political self-interest and the struggle against Mao Zedong. That left the Chinese leader all too eager to exploit America's weakened position. "The probabilities are that the CKS regime is playing the USA for a sucker; that it will stall and promise, but not do anything; that it is looking for an allied victory without making any further effort on its part to secure it; and that it expects to have piled up at the end of the war a supply of munitions that will allow it to perpetuate itself indefinitely," Stilwell wrote in a 1942 memo. "They think we are dumb, easily fooled, and gullible, and that all they have to do to bring us to heel is to threaten to make a separate peace."

This was the contemptuous political backdrop Hap Arnold and Jimmy Doolittle faced in planning the raid's terminus. The war may have elevated China's importance, but it did not eradicate America's focus on its own self-interest. Preservation of those interests demanded the mission remain a secret from Chiang Kai-shek. On one level American officials knew that the generalissimo's staff could not be trusted. General Marshall reminded Arnold of that in a February memo. "With relation to the highly confidential project you and King have on," he wrote, "please read Magruder's telegram of yesterday regarding lack of secrecy in all discussions at Chungking." Marshall referred to Brigadier General John Magruder, the outgoing chief of the American military mission to China, who had shared an alarming personal experience. "Despite my request for confidential treatment of matter at height of interview an unexpectedly drawn curtain disclosed four servants absorbing the facts," he wrote. "This is characteristic and indicates futility of efforts to maintain secrecy regarding any military matters."

Beyond the fear of leaks American leaders had other more important reasons for keeping the mission a secret from Chiang Kai-shek. A raid against Tokyo—home of the emperor and the nerve center of the Japanese empire—promised to invite retaliation against the Chinese. That probability would likely trigger Chiang Kai-shek's refusal to allow the bombers to land at Chinese airfields. American leaders, of course, knew all of this. Japanese atrocities against the Chinese had grown so notorious throughout the years that the State Department dedicated an entire report to them in February 1942. "Inhuman acts have been committed by Japanese armies on the civilian populations in varying degrees in every city or town captured by them, from one end of China to the other," the report stated. "The entry of Japanese troops has repeatedly been accompanied by wholesale robbing, raping and butchery of innocent civilians."

The thirteen-page, single-spaced report—later circulated at the highest levels of the government and military—offered American policy makers a horrific window into what Japanese forces might do to any captured airmen or local villagers who assisted them. In previous campaigns Japanese troops had used prisoners for bayonet practice, buried others alive, and set some on fire, forcing villagers to watch as a means to extract information. Soldiers formed rings around entire villages, torched them, and then machine-gunned the residents who tried to escape. Following the fall of Shanghai in 1937, Japanese newspapers chronicled a "murder race" between two junior officers, competing to see who would be the first to kill 100 Chinese with a sword. "There came a day when each of the men passed the 100 mark, but as there was some dispute as to who had first reached the number, it was decided to extend the contest to a new goal, variously reported as 150 to 250," the report stated. "One of the officers interviewed in the field by a Japanese correspondent declared that the contest had been 'fun.'"

These atrocities reached a climax when troops entered the Chinese capital of Nanking in December 1937. The Japanese coaxed many of the Chinese soldiers into surrender, luring them outside the city and slaughtering them by the thousands. Inside the city's walls gangs of soldiers brutalized civilians. So vast was the slaughter that dead bodies piled along the banks of the Yangtze turned the mighty river red. As many as one thousand rapes occurred each night, many of the women killed afterwards to cover up the crime. "Perhaps when we were raping her, we looked at her as a woman," one soldier wrote after the war, "but when we killed her, we just thought of her as something like a pig." The war crimes tribunal would later estimate that the Rape of Nanking—as it became known—claimed more than 260,000 noncombatants, while some experts would later push the total as high 350,000, horrors America knew of long before the war's end. "The actions of the Japanese soldiery," the State Department report concluded, "constitute the blackest, most shameful page in the military annals of modern times."

With the Navy's task force slated for departure, Arnold demanded an update from Stilwell on the raid's preparations in China. The general had briefed Stilwell shortly before he left the United States, informing him only of the operation's basic logistics while omitting that the planes would in fact bomb Tokyo en route to China. The plan demanded the use of five airfields at Chuchow, Kweilin, Lishui, Kian, and Yushan. Signal flares and radio beacons would guide the bombers in to these primitive airfields, where the crews could then take on fuel and oil before pressing on to Chungking, the new capital of China, some eight hundred miles farther inland. There the bombers would form a new squadron to attack the Japanese in China. Arnold had heard nothing from Stilwell since his departure, and time now ran short. "What progress is being made on laying down gasoline supplies and bomb supplies on airports in eastern China?" Arnold's staff messaged Stilwell on March 16. "What progress on airports?" Stilwell failed to respond, prompting a follow-up message two days later. "Time is getting short for spotting gas at agreed points."

Stilwell had only recently arrived in China after a twenty-three-day voyage that covered some twenty thousand miles. His touchdown had coincided with the Japanese assault on southern Burma, a vital fulcrum on which the direction of the war balanced. The capital and principal seaport of Rangoon—the start of the Burma Road—had fallen to the Japanese in early March. This thin jungle membrane stood as a final barrier, blocking the Japanese from pushing through India and joining forces with the Germans in the Middle East. Much to Stilwell's frustration Chinese forces proved far outmatched. Although China boasted almost three million uniformed men, a lack of resources forced most to bed down beneath shared blankets and to fight in straw sandals. Disease and malnutrition compounded China's woes, robbing the nation of as much 40 percent of its forces each year. Officer desertions likewise were frequent. "You will know long before you get this what I'm up against," Stilwell wrote to his wife. "It's not a pretty picture."

Because he was not briefed about the raid, Stilwell failed to appreciate Arnold's urgency in finalizing the plans. He at last cabled Arnold on March 22 that Standard Oil of Calcutta had 30,000 gallons of 100-octane gasoline plus another 500 gallons of 120-oil in 5-gallon tins. "Please advise purpose for which it is being held," Stilwell asked. "For use in American Army Aircraft, request authority to move this fuel to China." Arnold ordered the fuel moved to Kweilin immediately; he would provide ten transports to help. He further ordered twelve men stationed at each airfield, including one who spoke English. All men and supplies had to be in place by midnight on April 9–10. To illuminate the runways, five flares would line either side, plus an additional five on the windward end of each runway. "The success of a vital project which I discussed with you prior to your departure depends upon this movement being accomplished by air without delay and in using every possible precaution to preserve its secrecy."

Rather than import fuel from India, Stilwell in a March 29 message recommended using Chinese gasoline. Only the airfields at Chuchow and Kweilin, the Chinese advised, were safe for heavy bombers. If America wanted to use the others, a qualified officer would first have to inspect them. "Other than fuel, no ammunition, bombs, or supplies are required," Arnold cabled. "To meet date of April 10, use Chinese 100 octane or any other gasoline available. One take-off and landing only by medium bombers contemplated by operation. Only those airdromes for this operation should be marked. To insure availability, oil and gasoline supplies at these airdromes must be checked, and as soon as possible this information forwarded here. Means for rapid servicing from drums must be furnished servicing details." The date for the task force's departure loomed: time was up. "On April 20th, special project will arrive destination. An attempt will be made to notify you should a change in arrival date arise," Arnold cabled. "For variation without notice you must however be prepared."

DOOLITTLE HAD GOTTEN the message from Arnold that the time had come to depart Eglin for the West Coast. He summoned his men at 3 a.m. on March 24. For Brick Holstrom the news arrived with a bang on his hotel wall from York in the next room. "Hey, come on," York shouted. "We've got to go!"

Doolittle informed his men that twenty-two aircrews would fly cross-country to the air depot at McClellan Field in Sacramento for final modifications and tune-ups. From there crews would continue on to Alameda Naval Air Station and load the *Hornet*. Any extra aircrews would return to Columbia.

"Get your financial affairs in shape—all of you," Doolittle warned. "And don't, in your letters to the folks or to your wives, give any hint where you are going."

The stress of the operation finally caught up with the pilot Vernon Stintzi, who developed severe gastric symptoms—an ulcer. Thomas White, the mission doctor, diagnosed the lieutenant with anxiety neurosis and relieved him from flying duty. Doolittle saw Stintzi's departure as an opportunity. "Rather than bump somebody else out of a position," he said, "I will take this crew that doesn't have a pilot."

The aircrews hustled that Tuesday morning to prepare to depart, a scene captured by Ken Reddy in his diary. "Operations was like a mad house," he wrote, "everyone trying to get off on a very short notice."

Miller watched the hurrying fliers with envy just as Doolittle approached. "I hear you had an accident," Doolittle said, referring to Bates's crash the day before.

"Yes, Sir," the Navy lieutenant replied. "But there's nothing wrong with the technique or anything else of the airplane. What was wrong was Bates. He just wasn't flying the airplane. The airplane was flying him."

Doolittle understood. He told Miller that the crews were headed to the West Coast and would finish up final instruction at a California airfield.

"Well, you know, Colonel," Miller said, "it's a matter of professional pride with me. I don't want anybody on the West Coast telling you, 'No, let's start all over again with this technique.' If it's possible I'd like to go with you, if we're going to have time to do more of this practice out there."

"If it's all right with Washington," Doolittle answered, "you can fly out with me this afternoon."

Doolittle wanted to keep York as well, who had been given permission by Colonel Mills to help train the fliers in Florida, but not actually go on the mission. He phoned Mills up in South Carolina.

"Newt, old boy," Doolittle said, "I am going to need York out in Sacramento for a few days. You don't mind if he comes out there and then he comes right back afterwards?"

Mills hesitated, no doubt suspicious, before he relented: "All right."

When Robert Emmens landed that afternoon in Florida with the bomber to replace the one Bates had crashed, he discovered that most of the other aircrews had all cleared out, leaving York to sweep out the operations building.

"Where is everybody?" Emmens asked.

"They have all left for the West Coast," York answered. "Do you want to go on this thing?"

"More than anything."

"We could be that substitute crew," York said. "They got pretty shook up in their accident, and they need another crew as well as the airplane."

Doolittle wanted to use the cross-country flight as another training exercise, instructing his pilots to hedgehop west and test gas consumption, buzzing the rural countryside just as the men would Japan. The aircrews, who flew in formations of up to half a dozen bombers, decided to have some fun.

"We kept so low we could look up at the telegraph wires," Lawson later wrote. "All of us seemed to figure we might not be around very long, so we might as well do things we always wanted to do. It was the craziest flying I had ever done, and I had done some kid-stuff tricks, like banking a B-25 through a low, open drawbridge."

Lawson's navigator Second Lieutenant Charles McClure described how the pilots terrorized some of the locals on the ground below. "When we departed Eglin, going across Alabama we were flying below many trees and in general, were chasing farmers, particularly Negroes, as they plowed. One old colored boy was dragged across the field by his scared mule because he had the reins wrapped under his arms," McClure later wrote. "One Negro man grabbed two colored children and ran for a shack which I am sure would have blown over had the prop wash hit it."

The pilots did more than scare the locals. "The trip to the West Coast was an enjoyable legal cross country buzz job which would probably give me a screaming class A nervous breakdown now," recalled Aden Jones. "I pulled some sagebrush off of the bottom of that airplane," remembered Jacob DeShazer. "I'd see the cattle stick their tails up in the air and run. We'd just go over their backs."

Bad weather forced many of the crews to break up the trip in Texas, spending a night in San Antonio before flying on the next day to Phoenix, Riverside, and ultimately Sacramento. Doolittle, however, pushed onward, flying across the Rocky Mountains on instruments.

Navigator George Barr used his downtime in Texas to call the family he lived with after the death of his mother. "I am going on a special mission with Jimmy Doolittle," Barr exclaimed. "Wish me luck."

The airmen pressed on the next day. "We flew to Sacramento nonstop in the longest flight I have made, being nine hrs. and 25 minutes," Reddy wrote in his diary. "I rode most of the way in the nose and I really got a good look at the country."

Hilger flew across southern Arizona, following Highway 10 through the Dragoon Mountains and Texas Canyon.

"Can you see that little spot over there of a town?" Macia asked the major. "That is where I was raised."

"What in the hell is the name of that place?" Hilger asked.

"Tombstone."

Lawson and McClure's mischief continued on the final day of the flight. "Over Texas, we chased cattle for hours. Near El Paso we were chasing automobiles off of the highways and at one point, a bus skidded to a stop and as we pulled up, we saw passengers heading for the open country," McClure wrote. "Going up the valley to Sacramento, we were right on the deck and noticed when we passed over farmers, each of them waved to us which was not at all like the colored people in the South."

Doolittle landed at McClellan and met with air depot commander Colonel John Clark and his senior engineering and maintenance personnel. Doolittle still had a list of modifications and equipment he needed before the task force's April departure.

"I would like to have a complete inspection of each airplane including airplane engine, equipment, and accessories," Doolittle began, according to a transcript of the meeting. "We don't want the airplanes taken to pieces. Just inspected insofar as they can be inspected—cowling, doors opened, etc. Also a pair of propellers installed on each plane. Forty-four have been ordered."

"We did not get any teletype on it," one of the men protested.

"They were ordered three weeks ago."

Doolittle felt the now familiar pushback to his demands, even though the depot's instructions to cooperate were clear. "Services and supplies requested by Colonel Doolittle," orders stated, "will be given the highest priority."

He pressed on with the briefing, alerting the officers that the planes had been modified with several added gas tanks. The sixty-gallon rubber bag that would go in place of the lower gun turret would arrive in Sacramento either that day or the next along with new covers to replace the larger ones for the added bomb bay tanks.

"My ship is complete," Doolittle told them. "Use it as a model."

He instructed the officers to remove the liaison radio sets from each bomber and the tracing antenna and asked for parachutes.

"How many were you supposed to have, sir?"

"About 60 pack type and about 40 detachable. When they come in we want to have them fitted to the pilots and labeled," Doolittle continued. "There will be a man here from Wright Field to install six still cameras in six of the airplanes and 16 movie cameras in the other airplanes."

Doolittle again warned them not to tamper with the planes unless maintenance crews found a major issue. "If you find something definitely wrong, we want that fixed," he said. "We are anxious to give them the last finishing touch and take them away."

Since the plan was to turn the bombers over to China, Doolittle instructed them that the original Norden bombsights, radios, and instrument accessories would all be collected in Sacramento and then shipped to the final destination.

"I am particularly interested in propellers," Doolittle said, returning to his earlier topic. "They should be painted. Don't want shiny ones. They should have been here two weeks ago."

"What about ammunition?"

"We'll get that from Benicia Arsenal."

Doolittle requested that any burned-out instrumentation lights be replaced. "Wherever there are places for spares I would like to have spares put in," he added. "Also spare fuses. All we are going to have for these ships are what is on them."

If any problems came up, Doolittle instructed the depot officials to contact Captain York.

"This project is a highly confidential one," he concluded. "As a matter of fact, I am having to notify General Arnold in code that I arrived."

Doolittle's meeting translated into serious orders—at least on paper. "Under no circumstances is any equipment to be removed or tampered with on these airplanes," orders stated. "This will be strictly complied with at all times on this Project. Inspectors or men working on the Airplane finding defective or damaged parts must notify the Project Officer or Project Supervisor of this condition before accomplishing any work."

Doolittle's fliers landed one after the other at McClellan.

"Stick close to the field," Doolittle instructed his men. "I want every first pilot to make absolutely certain that his plane is in perfect shape."

He warned his crews that mechanics planned to remove the radios: "You won't need it where you're going."

Many now assumed that meant Japan.

The rubber gas tanks, cameras, and broomstick tail guns drew questions from the curious ground personnel, prompting a sharp retort: "Mind your own business."

Despite strict orders, problems persisted, as described by Lawson. "I had to stand by and watch one of the mechanics rev my engines so fast that the new blades picked up dirt which pockmarked their tips," he wrote. "I caught another one trying to sandpaper the imperfections away and yelled at him until he got out some oil and rubbed it on the places which he had sandpapered. I knew that salt air would make those prop tips pulpy where they have been scraped. The way they revved our engines made us wince. All of us were so afraid that they'd hurt the ships, the way they were handling them, yet we couldn't tell them why we wanted them to be so careful. I guess we must have acted like the biggest bunch of soreheads those mechanics ever saw."

Doolittle finally picked up the phone to Arnold.

"Things are going too slowly out here," he told the general. "I'd appreciate it very much if you would personally build a fire under these people."

Arnold obliged.

Another time Doolittle chatted with several pilots in base operations when he heard a bomber engine backfire. He looked over to see a B-25 cough black exhaust as a worker tried to start the engine. An expert had visited Eglin to tune all the carburetors, not to regulation but to help guarantee each plane could achieve the maximum range. Doolittle had specifically ordered that no worker touch any of the carburetor settings— and under no circumstances change them.

"What's going on here?" Doolittle demanded.

"We're just readjusting the carburetors," the mechanic countered. "They're all out of adjustment."

"I was madder than a son of a bitch," Doolittle later recalled. "I naturally blew my top."

He cooled down and picked up the phone again to Arnold.

The crews ran into a similar headache with the arsenal, forcing yet another call to Washington. Even Doc White battled the post's uncooperative medical supply officer. "In several instances he had the desired supplies on his shelves but apparently did not want to deplete his stores and by one excuse or another refused to fill most of my requisitions," White griped in his report. "The Surgeon refused to override his decisions in spite of my explaining the urgency of my needs."

As work progressed on the bombers, the men used the evenings to relax. Ken Reddy went bowling, danced at the Breakers, and even visited a honky-tonk with the daughter of a sheep rancher. Others hung out at the Senator Hotel, where some of the airmen stayed. One night a few of the fliers decided to drop dollar bills from the hotel window to see what kind of commotion might unfold on the street below, a plan that ran afoul after some of the bills landed on a ledge below. "We lowered Dean Hallmark head-first out of the window and held him by the ankles; he retrieved the bills and sent them down to the street," Holstrom recalled. "About this time some of the senior guys told everybody to knock it off before someone called the cops."

Greening, Jones, and York stumbled out of the hotel bar, only to find an elderly gentleman passed out in the lobby.

"Let's give him a hot foot," Jones suggested.

Jones stuck a lit match in the toe of the gentleman's shoe while the airmen retreated to the far side of the lobby to watch. The match burned down and went out as the gentleman slept soundly. Jones did it again, this time using two matches, but once again the trick failed to waken the man. The third time he decided to use the entire matchbook to line the sole of the gentleman's shoe.

"Shame on you boys!" a woman, who had watched the prank unfold, protested. "Why don't you leave the poor man alone?"

The gentleman suddenly woke up. Rather than target Jones, he turned on the woman. "Go away y'ol'bat!" he barked. "Let 'em have their fun."

He then promptly passed out again.

Other airmen used the downtime to write final letters home, including engineer Jacob Eierman. "This will be my last letter for sometime because we are on our way—I am not able to tell you where we are going, but you will read about us in the newspapers," he wrote. "If the information leaked out as to where we are going, none of us would ever come back." Engineer Melvin Gardner echoed him. "Please don't worry mother," he wrote. "Remember no news is good news."

A classified message arrived from Arnold, directing Doolittle to travel to nearby San Francisco for a meeting with Admiral Halsey, his chief of staff, Captain Miles Browning, and Duncan. After his briefing with Duncan at Pearl Harbor, Halsey wanted a face-to-face with Doolittle—the man for whom he was about to risk the remnants of the Pacific Fleet. Nimitz agreed, ordering him to fly to the West Coast. The officers met March 30 in the bar of the luxurious Fairmont Hotel atop Nob Hill, which afforded spectacular views of the bay. The men sat in the bar, but Halsey feared Doolittle had too many friends in the area who might recognize him, so the group moved up to Halsey's room. "It immediately occurred to me that a personal contact with Jimmy Doolittle, whom I did not know at that time, was desirable," Halsey later recalled. "First, so that we could size each other up, and secondly, to discuss way and means."

During the three-hour conference Halsey and Duncan walked Doolittle through the Navy's plan. The submarines *Trout* and *Thresher* would scout weather conditions and search out enemy naval forces the surface ships might encounter. The *Hornet*, two cruisers, four destroyers, and an oiler would depart Alameda on April 2 as Task Force 16.2 under the command of Marc Mitscher. After flying back to Pearl Harbor, Halsey would put to sea April 7 in command of Task Force 16.1, consisting of the carrier *Enterprise*, plus another two cruisers, four destroyers, and a second oiler. The two task forces would rendezvous at sea on Sunday, April 12, to create Task Force 16. These sixteen warships would then steam toward to Tokyo, refueling some eight hundred miles from Japan. At that point the oilers would remain behind while the carriers, cruisers, and destroyers steamed to within four hundred miles of the enemy's capital.

"We discussed the operation from every point of view," Doolittle recalled. "We tried to think of every contingency that might possibly arise and have an answer to that contingency." If the task force was within range of Japan, the bombers would immediately take off, execute the mission, and hopefully reach China or get picked up by submarines.

If the task force was within range of either Hawaii to Midway, the bombers would take off for those destinations. The worst-case scenario called for crews to push the B-25s overboard to clear the *Hornet*'s deck so the Navy could launch fighters. "This was understandable and I accepted this possibility," Doolittle wrote. "After all, if the two carriers, the cruisers, and the destroyers were lost, it would mean the end of American naval strength in the Pacific for a long time. The Navy was, therefore, taking an extraordinary risk in our attempt to bring the war to the Japanese homeland."

With the final modifications and tune-ups complete, aircrews prepared to fly to Alameda to board the *Hornet*. Only then did York learn that mechanics—in defiance of Doolittle's orders—had swapped out the carburetors on his bomber. "We just happened to find out, by looking the engine over and checking the serial numbers, that they were different," he recalled. "No mention was made, or notation made, to let us know that the carburetors had been changed. We accidentally found out about it."

York summoned one of the mechanics.

"We had to change the carburetors," he explained. "You had the wrong carburetors on this airplane."

York pulled Doolittle aside and shared the news.

"Oh, Christ," Doolittle said. "What do you want to do?"

Time was up—there was nothing he could do.

"I don't think it makes any difference," York answered. "A carburetor is a carburetor anyway you look at it."

That statement would later haunt him.

"Well, if you think so," Doolittle replied. "Come ahead."

Miller had continued to practice short-field takeoffs with the crews at an airfield near Willows, just north of Sacramento.

"How do you think everybody's doing?" Doolittle asked him.

"I think it's no strain at all," Miller replied. "Everybody's doing great."

Doolittle planned to take fifteen airplanes along with several extra aircrews aboard the *Hornet*. "Would you list the crews in order of take off expertise—1, 2, 3, 4, 5, 6, 7?"

Miller did so, turning the list over to Doolittle and Hilger to review. Hilger objected to Miller's exclusion of Bates.

"When you get on over enemy territory and you have some of those Japs chasing you, you've got to be really sharp and you've got to be thinking all the time," Miller said. "If you panic, you're lost. I wouldn't take Bates."

Bates would go aboard the carrier, but he would not fly the mission. Miller was reluctant to end his adventure, seizing an opportunity to make his case when Doolittle asked him again for his views on the readiness of the aircrews.

"You know, Colonel, if you want proof, I've had less time in the B-25 than anybody," he said. "You can take an extra one along—a sixteenth airplane—and when we get 100 miles out of San Francisco, I'll take it off, I'll deliver it back to Columbia, South Carolina, back to the Army, and go back to Pensacola."

Doolittle would think about it.

The veteran aviator prepared to depart when the operation's officer handed him a detailed report to fill out on the quality of the work performed.

"I haven't got time to read all this," Doolittle barked.

"But it's our standard procedure, Colonel," the operations officer countered. "You must report on how the work was done."

Doolittle snatched the form and scribbled one word diagonally across the page: "LOUSY."

"Just a minute, Colonel, you will have to give us a detailed report," the officer countered. "This will not do!"

Doolittle refused.

"If that's the case," the officer fired back, "I won't sign your clearance—regulations you know!"

Doolittle ignored him. He walked out to his plane, climbed inside, and taxied out to the runway.

Jack Hilger, who had witnessed the exchange, flashed a grin.

"Who is that guy?" the operations officer complained to Hilger. "I can tell you he is heading for a lot of trouble!"

"He sure is," Hilger agreed. "He sure is!"

Doolittle's final outburst prompted depot commander Colonel Clark to fire off a preemptive report to his superiors, hoping to counter any complaint. Though he noted that the war had drained the depot of talented men, Clark couldn't help blaming Doolittle and his men. "At less than 24 hours before scheduled completion the flight leader indicated sudden and complete disapproval and rumors became prevalent that pilots were doubtful of the condition of their respective airplanes. It has been this depot's repeated experience to note a tendency for pilots to begin to worry as the departure date approached on several major projects completed," Clark wrote. "In no instance have they been able to justify their fears by citing legitimate grounds."

CHAPTER 7

★

We believe the hand of God is on our side—the side of
justice, decency and humanity.

—COMMANDER RUSSELL IHRIG,
APRIL 3, 1942

THE *HORNET* TOWERED OVER Pier One at the U.S. Naval Air Station
in Alameda on the afternoon of April 1, 1942. The 19,800-ton carrier
had departed Norfolk on March 4, transiting the Panama Canal en route
to San Diego and then San Francisco, where it had arrived only the day
before. Secured with its starboard side to the pier—by no fewer than a
dozen manila lines and four wire hawsers—the $32 million *Hornet* made
an impressive sight. Shipfitters, welders, and electricians at Virginia's
Newport News Shipbuilding and Dry Dock Company had labored for
more than two years to hammer out the nation's eighth aircraft carrier.
Once completed, the *Hornet* stretched 809 feet, the length of more than
two football fields. Nine Babcock and Wilcox boilers generated superheated steam to power the carrier's four turbines at up to 120,000 horse-
power. Four manganese bronze propellers—each weighing more than
27,000 pounds—drove the *Hornet* through the seas at thirty-three knots
or about thirty-eight miles an hour.

The carrier functioned much like a small town for the complement of
some 170 officers and 2,000 enlisted men who called the *Hornet* home.

Sailors slept sixty or more in compartments with bunks stacked four high, while most of the officers bedded down in two- and four-person staterooms. A desalination plant made ocean water drinkable and provided fresh water for showers, galleys, and the boilers, while walk-in freezers, refrigerators, and pantries carried frozen steaks, chickens, and canned fruits and vegetables. Five doctors and a team of corpsmen stood ready to handle everything from a routine runny nose to an emergency appendectomy. The carrier featured laundry services, a barbershop, and even a small library. Sailors could pick up stamps and mail letters at the post office or buy cigarettes, razors, and toothpaste at the ship's store. The 565-foot enclosed hangar bay—complete with steel doors that rolled open to allow planes to warm up without creating deadly gas—doubled as a perfect movie theater.

Three times a day hungry sailors queued up at the mess deck to eat at long tables and benches bolted down to weather rough seas while officers enjoyed white linens and monogrammed silver in the wardroom that stretched the breadth of the carrier and showcased an emblematic hornet's nest that dangled from the overhead. Many marveled at the carrier's so-called mechanical cow, which churned dehydrated milk into ice cream, the perfect treat on long cruises in tropical waters. Despite the advances in naval shipbuilding, technology could not remedy everything. "The food on carriers is generally quite good for the first month after stocking up and putting to sea," remembered Frederick Mears, a pilot on board the *Hornet*. "Thereafter it begins to deteriorate. Fresh milk disappears almost immediately, and the next to go are fresh eggs, greens and fresh vegetables, and finally fresh meat. Officers and crew alike begin to live on powdered milk, powdered eggs, and canned fruit and vegetables and meat."

Life aboard the carrier centered on the wooden flight deck, which sailors joked made the warship resemble a bathtub with a barn door on top. General quarters sounded each morning at daybreak as the first patrol planes roared into the air, a ritual that followed again at sunset, the two vulnerable times of day when a carrier is silhouetted against the sky, easy prey for enemy submarines. The *Hornet*'s island rose some forty feet above the teak deck, containing the navigation bridge, chart house, bridge, and admiral's quarters. "There was always noise on the carrier deck—the ripping of the wind in the rigging on the island structure, the wash of water alongside, and the pounding of the great ship in the sea, if nothing else," Mears later wrote, "but these sounds tended to create peace rather than confusion." Captain Mitscher had ordered a special addition to the *Hornet*, a message painted in block letters on the ship's stack that was symbolic of the mission at hand: "Remember Pearl Harbor."

Doolittle arrived first at Alameda Naval Air Station and reported soon thereafter to the carrier's chain-smoking skipper in his long-billed hat. Marine Corporal Larry Bogart, who served as Mitscher's orderly, stood outside the skipper's door. He heard someone state, "Lieutenant Colonel Doolittle, Captain."

"I didn't think much about it," Bogart later admitted. "But after a while I heard our executive officer, Commander George Henderson, say, 'Hello, Jimmy.' Then it clicked. I knew who he was. Jimmy Doolittle! The guy who had all the flight records—speed, endurance, altitude, distance. He was going with us."

Bogart knew enough of Doolittle's reputation that he immediately upped his government insurance policy from a thousand to five thousand dollars.

Mitscher told Doolittle that he planned to turn his personal quarters over to him, a suite below the flight deck that included a large conference room, bedroom, and head, while he himself would relocate to a small room off the bridge.

"You'll be holding meetings with your people and it will be more convenient for you to have a place where you can do that. My quarters makes that possible," Mitscher said. "Besides, it's the only place on the ship large enough for private meetings."

Doolittle had originally planned to take eighteen bombers on board the *Hornet*, but only about fifteen B-25s would fit safely. With crews apprehensive about the carrier's short flight deck, he remembered Miller's suggestion to bring an extra bomber that the Navy lieutenant could use as demonstration. He ran the idea by Mitscher.

"All right with me, Jim," the skipper told him. "It's your show."

By the afternoon of April 1 all of the aircrews had departed McClellan Field for Alameda, where Doolittle greeted them upon arrival. He had instructed his pilots to spend at least an hour in the skies to give each bomber a final test to check for any mechanical problems. Any pilot who reported a problem—regardless of how insignificant—Doolittle instructed, would have to park the bomber. Otherwise he directed pilots to taxi to a ramp by the wharf. Doolittle planned to take all twenty-two aircrews on the *Hornet*, not only as a backup in case anyone dropped out, but because he didn't want to leave anyone behind who had gone through the extensive training. He couldn't risk any possible leak.

The crews arrived one after the other on a beautiful sunny day where the high temperature reached fifty-eight degrees. As Ski York and his copilot, Robert Emmens, approached Alameda, the aviators spied the Bay Bridge, which connected San Francisco to Oakland, a tempting opportunity for a little fun.

"What do you think?" York asked.

"We are off to see the Wizard of Oz somewhere out there in the Pacific," Emmens thought. "It will probably be the last chance we will ever have."

"Let's do it," he said.

York nosed the plane down and roared underneath the bridge, the bomber's belly just feet above the cool waters of San Francisco Bay. He landed soon afterward and introduced his new copilot to Doolittle, who stuck out his hand.

"How much time do you have in a B-25?" Doolittle asked Emmens.

"Sir, I have about 1,000 hours."

"Do you want to go on this thing?" Doolittle pressed. "It is strictly volunteer."

"Yes, sir," Emmens answered. "I do."

Doolittle turned back to York.

"All right," he said. "You are the new crew."

Emmens later reflected on his first impression of his new commander. "The moment York introduced me to Doolittle I knew why the mission was bound to be successful," he later wrote. "It was at once easy to understand why a personality such as his was a tremendous factor in bringing about the highest degree of morale, discipline, and confidence among all the participants in the raid—confidence in their leader, their airplane, and, most important of all, in themselves."

York and Emmens weren't the only ones who opted for some final fun with the Bay Bridge. Navigator Charles McClure carried a movie camera loaded with color film as the *Ruptured Duck* approached Alameda.

"What about flying under the bridge?" asked copilot Second Lieutenant Dean Davenport, who had the controls. "The Pan American boys do it all the time in the Clippers. It would make a good shot for Mac."

Pilot Ted Lawson didn't object, though he fought the urge to pull the plane up at the last moment, afraid there might be cables underneath. Just as the bomber soared beneath, McClure howled—his camera wouldn't work. He begged for a second pass, but Lawson objected, making his final approach to Alameda. "As I put the flaps down for the landing, we all let out a yell at the same time," he later wrote. "I guess the others got the same empty feeling in the stomach that I did. An American aircraft carrier was underneath us. Three of our B-25's were already on its deck."

"Damn!" one of the airmen said into the interphone, summarizing the views of all on board. "Ain't she small."

The *Ruptured Duck* landed, and Lawson taxied over to Doolittle and York, rolling back his window.

"Is everything okay?" Doolittle asked.

Lawson considered telling him that the bomber's interphone system didn't work well, but opted instead to ignore the problem.

"Taxi off the field and park at the edge of the *Hornet*'s wharf," Doolittle instructed. "They'll take care of you there."

Lawson did as ordered. Navy sailors drained all but a few gallons of the bomber's gasoline; then the aircrew watched as a "donkey" towed the *Ruptured Duck* down the pier, where a crane hoisted the B-25 up to the carrier's deck. The operation was so secretive that the *Hornet*'s deck log that day made no mention of loading the bombers.

"It was an eye-opener to me as I watched in wonderment and concern as my *land-based* bomber was being loaded aboard an *aircraft carrier*!" Jack Sims, a pilot, later wrote. "I suspect all the Raiders had similar feelings of apprehension as the lifting cables were connected to the aircraft hard-points followed by a Navy yard crane which lifted each aircraft aboard the carrier."

"I don't think any of us had ever been on board a carrier," recalled pilot Bill Bower, "let alone a naval vessel." The young lieutenant watched the cranes lift his bomber and felt the hackles rise on the back of his neck. Everything he had trained for had come down to this moment. "My heavens," he thought. "This is it!"

Others marveled at America's newest carrier. From the air the *Hor-*

net had, in the words of one pilot, resembled a "postage stamp," but pier side the flattop rose up like a skyscraper. "We knew we were going to fly off an aircraft carrier, but this was the first time I had been up close to one. And, boy, it was a pretty awesome looking thing," remembered pilot Travis Hoover. "I never saw anything so big in all my life."

"She was a great sight," recalled Lawson. "I can't describe the feeling I got, standing there, looking up at her sides. Maybe the thing I felt was just plain patriotism."

Lieutenant Henry Miller approached.

"Don't tell the Navy boys anything," he warned Lawson and his men. "They don't know where you're going."

Doolittle ran into the Navy lieutenant.

"You know, I talked to them about your idea of taking an extra plane along and they go along with it," Doolittle told him. "So we'll take sixteen and launch you 100 miles out."

"That's great."

The Army airmen filed aboard, each one saluting the American flag on the stern and the officer of the deck, just as Miller had taught them.

Curious *Hornet* aviators lined the decks, watching the Army fliers land at the nearby airfield. "My, don't those fellows come in slow, they don't come screaming in to the field, dive bombing in the average Army manner," one flier remarked. "Looks as if they had had a little naval indoctrination."

One of those watching was *Hornet* intelligence officer Lieutenant Stephen Jurika Jr., one of the few who knew the carrier's mission. "I think *our* initial reaction, most of the officers on the ship and certainly the captain's and mine, was that an all-volunteer crew like this had to be special in ability to fly and desire to do something as a group together," he recalled. "But in looks, in appearance, and in demeanor, I would say that they appeared undisciplined. Typical of this was the open collars and short-sleeved shirts—the weather was quite cool in Alameda— grommets either crushed or none at all in their caps, worn-out, scuffed-type shoes. They were not in flight clothing."

Jurika voiced his concerns to Miller. Were the Army aviators ready? Miller leveled with him. "I've done everything I can for them and there's nothing they don't know about short take-offs," Miller confided in his colleague. "It's just when that deck is moving and they're taking off, will they go through with it?"

The Army airmen watched as sailors spotted the B-25s, parking the bombers prop to tail before chocking the wheels and tying them down. The tight squeeze left the tail of the sixteenth bomber dangling off the carrier's fantail. While the *Hornet* may have inspired confidence, its short flight deck failed to impress, even though it had accommodated no fewer than four thousand people at the carrier's commissioning. "I never saw such a small, insignificant thing to be a called a runway in all my life," Hoover recalled. "And all my awe turned to goose pimples because it was a tiny thing."

The Army's enlisted men would dine and bunk with the *Hornet*'s chief petty officers, while many of the officers shared staterooms with Navy ensigns, often crashing on fold-up cots. "I was a First Lieutenant then and thus outranked the Ensigns, but that didn't seem to impress them very much," Lawson later wrote. "They crawled into their nice bunks and pointed to a cot for me."

Other airmen piled onto cots in the skipper's quarters, but pilots Richard Cole and Billy Farrow landed in the passageway outside. "You had to go down the hall to the head to brush your teeth and shower," recalled Cole, who served as Doolittle's copilot. "But outside of that, it was no problem."

San Francisco Bay resembled a Navy parking lot. In addition to the *Hornet*, the battleships *Maryland*, *Pennsylvania*, *Colorado*, *Tennessee*, *Idaho*, *New Mexico*, and *Mississippi* joined the oiler *Cimarron*, the cruisers *St. Louis*, *Nashville*, and *Vincennes*, and the destroyers *Cushing*, *Smith*, *Preston*, *Gwin*, *Meredith*, *Monssen*, and *Grayson*, among other ships. A high-pressure area just off the West Coast on April 1 promised a dense fog the following morning, perfect to help disguise the task force's departure.

With the bombers all lashed down on deck, the harbor pilot climbed aboard at 2:45 p.m. Thirty-one minutes later—and with the help of four tugboats—the *Hornet* departed the pier, anchoring that afternoon in Berth 9.

Doolittle assembled his men late that afternoon.

"All right, everyone is free. Boats will be running back and forth," he told them. "Everyone go and have a good time. Secrecy above all, but go ahead and visit anyone you want and do whatever you want."

Doolittle did the same, spending time with his wife, Joe, in a San Francisco hotel. He climbed into the elevator, where the operator spotted his uniform.

"Understand you're moving out tomorrow," the operator asked.

The comment shocked Doolittle, who wondered how much the operator actually knew. Doolittle didn't answer him, but rode up in silence. "His remark proved to me that it is extremely difficult to keep military movements secret," Doolittle wrote. "As anyone could plainly see, the *Hornet* was sitting in the middle of San Francisco Bay with 16 Army Air Forces B-25s aboard, obviously ready to go someplace."

Many of the men gravitated that night to the Top of the Mark, a rooftop bar located on the Mark Hopkins Hotel on Nob Hill. The cocktails flowed freely as the airmen relaxed after weeks of training. Many would party up until the departure of the last tender; a few would even come close to missing it. "We had enough time," remembered pilot Richard Knobloch, "to have a hell of a good time."

The mission would demand the most of the men—and not all would come back alive, a fact not lost on some. "It was a beautiful night and as I looked out across the city, the thought crossed my mind that maybe we would never see this again," remembered navigator Charles McClure. "So you had better stop and stare at it."

The moon rose, and the men could see the *Hornet* at anchor, the bombers silhouetted against the night sky. The Navy had put out the story that the planes were being transported to Hawaii; still, seeing them made many people uneasy.

"Just putting the aircraft on the carrier in itself was not that revealing," recalled Herb Macia. "But to trust a bunch of guys to be on the town getting drunk, talking to gals, that took a lot of courage."

"We had some concerns," admitted Hank Potter, Doolittle's navigator. "But they soon vanished in the blessings of whiskey and soda."

THE *HORNET* SWAYED at anchor in Berth 9 the brisk Thursday morning of April 2. The day had started early for the flattop's officers and crew. The Navy oil barge no. 4 pulled alongside the port quarter at 3:40

a.m., topping the *Hornet* off with 153,329 gallons of oil, a process that took just two hours and forty minutes and brought the total on hand to more than 1.4 million gallons. In preparation for the morning's departure sailors lit fires under boilers 2, 3, 6, 8, and 9 while the crew mustered at eight.

Doolittle had spent the night in San Francisco with Joe, rising early so that he could enjoy a farewell breakfast with her before packing his B-4 bag. He had not told his family a single word about the mission, though his weeks of shuttling between Washington, Florida, and Ohio had raised questions. "Hear sundry rumors as to your activities and am at present confused," his eldest son, Jim, an Army Air Forces pilot, wrote in a letter. "Would like to hear what's cooking."

Doolittle was equally mum with his wife of twenty-four years.

"I'll be out of the country for a while," was all he told Joe this morning. "I'll be in touch as soon as I can."

"We had had many separations before in our lives together, but I had the feeling she knew this departure was different," he later wrote. "I kissed her tenderly. She held back tears, but I'm sure she thought it was going to be a long time before she saw me again. I wondered if we would ever see each other again."

Doolittle returned to the carrier and met with Mitscher to discuss the *Hornet*'s departure plan, when an officer interrupted to deliver several messages, including one that alerted him that the arrangements for oil, gas, and airport markings were underway in China. He thumbed through the others to find farewell notes from Generals Arnold and Marshall. "You will be constantly in my mind," the Army chief of staff wrote. "May the good Lord watch over you." Even the acerbic Admiral King wished Doolittle good luck in a handwritten memo. "When I learned that you were to lead the Army air contingent of the *Hornet* expedition, I knew that the degree of success had been greatly increased," King wrote. "To you, your officers and men I extend heartfelt wishes for success in your job—and 'happy landings' and 'good hunting.'"

Doolittle readied himself to depart when he received word to report ashore for an urgent phone call. With a heavy heart he climbed into the captain's gig, suspecting that the call was from Arnold, a last-minute effort to yank him off the mission. Doolittle was surprised instead to find General Marshall on the phone.

"Doolittle?" the general asked.

"Yes, sir."

"I just called to personally wish you the best of luck," Marshall said. "Our thoughts and our prayers will be with you. Good-bye, good luck, and come home safely."

The call stunned Doolittle. The Army's top officer had personally phoned to wish him success, a gesture he felt communicated the importance of the mission to the nation's beleaguered war effort. Doolittle felt at a loss for words.

"Thank you, sir," he finally offered. "Thank you."

The warships pulled anchor one by one as a heavy fog hung low over the bay, slashing visibility to barely a thousand yards. The light cruiser *Nashville* got underway at 7:42 a.m. for a final calibration of the ship's radio direction finder, followed by Destroyer Division 22, consisting of the *Gwin*, *Grayson*, *Monssen*, and *Meredith*. The *Hornet*, with its guests of seventy Army officers and sixty-four enlisted men, departed at 10:18 a.m., followed a minute later by the cruiser *Vincennes* and then the oiler *Cimarron*. The ships steamed under the Bay Bridge at 10:33 a.m., sliding past Alcatraz Island less than half an hour later. In a single column separated by a thousand yards, the task force navigated through the gate of the antisubmarine net, then passed beneath the Golden Gate Bridge at 11:13 a.m., the majestic red symbol of San Francisco that divided the bay from the Pacific. The mission had finally begun, and for the *Hornet* the departure would prove particularly ominous—the carrier would never again return to the United States.

Sailors lined the flight deck as the *Hornet* headed to sea, a scene captured in the diaries of several of the Army airmen. "It was quite a thrill to look back at the Golden Gate," Bill Bower wrote. "The thoughts that ran through one's mind, at least mine, were mixed, many of anticipation for what was in store and others of the awe inspiring sight made by a naval convoy." "Our send off was the weary howling of light house warning horns," noted Ken Reddy. "Soon after we got out to sea a prevalent question in my mind was answered, as massive as this ship is, it still is capable of being rocked by the sea." Others couldn't help contemplating the danger. "As we passed under the great Golden Gate Bridge," George Larkin wrote, "we wondered if we would see it again."

Doolittle gathered with his men in the wardroom as the California coast vanished in the *Hornet*'s frothy wake. After weeks of training, many of the airmen suspected the nature of the mission, but the time had arrived to eliminate any doubts.

"For the benefit of those of you who don't already know, or who have been guessing, we are going straight to Japan," Doolittle told them. "We're going to bomb Tokyo, Yokohama, Osaka, Kobe and Nagoya. The Navy is going to take us in as close as is advisable, and, of course, we're going to take off from the deck."

Bombardier Horace Crouch no doubt summed up the feelings of many of his fellow fliers. "We all had a whoopee," he recalled, "and a hard swallow at the same time." For *Ruptured Duck* pilot Ted Lawson the news provided a concrete goal on which to focus. "I can't tell you how much of a relief it was to hear these words," he later wrote. "It took away the weeks of confused thinking and ended a period of hush that was gripping all of us. I could stand up and yell Japan at the top of my lungs now. I was no longer shooting in the dark. Here was a job, definite and tangible."

"All of the training we had received at Eglin added up to a new purpose," remembered Brick Holstrom, "to bomb Tokyo!" Bob Emmens was thrilled to realize that he had guessed wrong. "Douglas MacArthur was having a bad time in the Philippines at this time. We thought we were headed for Bataan to help him out someway," he recalled. "We didn't dream that it would be the capital of Japan itself."

Doolittle continued his briefing, informing his men of the plan to land at Chinese airfields, refuel, and then push on to Chungking. "Now, we're going to be on this carrier a long time, but there will be plenty of work for you to do before we take off."

He ended as always with the offer for anyone to back out.

None did.

The shrill boatswain's pipe reverberated throughout the *Hornet* late that afternoon before the executive officer's voice crackled over the loudspeaker: "Now hear this." Mitscher then took over. "This ship will carry the Army bombers to the coast of Japan," he announced to the officers and crew, "for the bombing of Tokyo."

"Cheers from every section of the ship greeted the announcement," Mitscher wrote in his action report. "Morale reached a new high."

"It was the biggest thrill of the war," remembered Lieutenant John

Lynch, a material officer on the *Hornet*. "We were going to bomb Tokyo!"

"I don't know who was more excited," recalled Army bombardier Robert Bourgeois, "we of the air force or the Navy personnel. It was a great thrill to know that at last we had a chance to strike back at the Japs."

Signalmen broadcast the news via semaphore to the other task force warships. *Life* magazine editor John Field sat in the wardroom of one when the loudspeaker broadcast Mitscher's announcement. "It froze everybody to his seat," Field later wrote. "We knew now what the purpose of this secret trip was."

"Carry me back to ol' Virginny," muttered one of the black stewards in the wardroom, while others soon sang a song set to the tune of *Snow White*. "Hi-ho, hi-ho, we're off to Tokyo; we'll bomb and blast and come back fast."

War planners had mapped a course for the 5,223-mile journey to avenge the attack on Pearl Harbor that closely paralleled the route Admiral Nagumo had taken only four months earlier. The task force would follow the fortieth parallel just south of a polar front that promised high winds, squalls, and rough seas. While the inhospitable weather would slash visibility and limit patrol flights, it also made it equally likely that Japanese naval and merchant ships would avoid this route as well, providing the American armada a back door to the empire's waters. "We went north to the 40th parallel and stuck on it just like a highway all the way across the Pacific," remembered John Sutherland, a *Hornet* fighter pilot. "It's a nice parallel to be on, because it was a very rough road and a very secure road, the weather was bad, the fog was heavy, it rained intermittently. That was the one time when the bad weather and the rocking of the ship did not make anybody unhappy at all. All of us wanted to go sight unseen."

Safety was paramount even as the warships cut through the swells just off the West Coast. Shore-based planes would guard the task force until nightfall. Then the ships would steam on alone in radio silence, zigzagging and darkened to avoid submarines. Its flight deck crowded with bombers, the *Hornet* was like a toothless tiger. Until the task force rendezvoused more than a week later with Halsey and the carrier *Enterprise*, Mitscher would have to depend on his escorts for protection. America's newest carrier, two cruisers, and a loaded fleet oiler would make an inviting target, a fact hammered home by the *Cimarron*'s skipper, Commander Russell Ihrig, in a war message to his men. "Our new assignment will probably place us under fire, not only from submarines, but from aircraft and surface ships," he warned. "Be fully prepared to go into action TO WIN. Knowledge of your job and careful performance of small duties become more important than ever. Remember, there is *no second place* in a sea-fight."

To prepare for such threats—an attack on an oiler loaded with more than six million gallons of fuel could prove particularly dangerous—Ihrig issued battle instructions. "Don't think of the Japs as faraway," he cautioned his men. "Think of them as HERE!" Sailors dressed in full winter underwear to guard against possible flash burns and passed out steel helmets and gas masks. Others tossed flammable rubber mats overboard and removed non-watertight doors and even shower curtains; only those necessary for blackout protection could remain. Ihrig ordered the glass ports on the bridge replaced with metal plates and officer staterooms readied as battle dressing stations. The skipper knew that he could take no chances. "I have served six years in the Orient in close association with the Japs, including two years during the current war in China. I have seen their brutality, bestiality—and bravery. If you expect to survive, you will have to do your best," Ihrig instructed his men. "This is a war to the death."

The reality of the mission sank in as the *Hornet* steamed toward Japan, each hour taking the carrier and crews closer to the enemy's homeland. Doolittle's meeting had hammered home the gravity of the mission. Lawson passed out pads of paper to his crew that afternoon, demanding each one write down any idea on how to improve the plane. Other nervous airmen paced the flight deck, counting off each precious foot. The boundaries were no longer marked by flags and white lines but by cold blue ocean waves. A missed takeoff meant a plunge into the Pacific. Even Doolittle—the legendary pilot—felt edgy. The first full day at sea he, too, stared down the deck.

"Well, Hank," he said to Miller. "How does it look to you?"

"This is a breeze."

"Let's get up in that airplane and look."

Doolittle climbed into the cockpit, and Miller joined him in the copilot's seat.

"This looks like a short distance," Doolittle observed.

"You see where that tool kit is way up the deck by that island structure?" Miller said. "That's where I used to take off in fighters on the *Saratoga* and the *Lexington*."

"Henry, what name do they use in the Navy for 'bullshit'?"

The men climbed down and Miller headed to lunch, while Doolittle rushed to find Mitscher. He told the skipper that he wanted to scrap Miller's proposed takeoff demonstration and instead take the sixteenth plane on the mission, a move that would increase the operation's firepower by four bombs.

Just as Miller shoveled down the last of his dessert, he heard his name broadcast over the loudspeaker, summoning him to the bridge. The young lieutenant arrived to find Mitscher. "Well, Miller," the skipper leveled with him. "I don't think I'll be able to give you 40 knots of wind over the deck."

"Captain, I don't need that anyway, because we have 495 feet," he replied. "I taught these guys how to take off from an aircraft carrier with 40 knots of wind and 250 feet. We have lots of room."

Miller concluded by sharing his story of his conversation with Doolittle right before lunch.

"Well, Miller," Mitscher replied. "Do you have an extra pair of pants with you?"

"Oh, yes, Sir," he answered. "I brought all my baggage with me because I'm going to fly nonstop to Columbia, South Carolina."

Mitscher leveled with him.

"We'll take that extra plane."

Miller, of course, was thrilled. He had wanted to go all along and now he would be trapped on board, able to watch all sixteen planes thunder down the deck and lift off, all airmen he had trained. Miller concluded with a dose of levity.

"Captain, will you drop me off at the next mail buoy, please," he said. "I'm a Lieutenant now but by the time I get back to Pensacola, I will have travelled half way around the world on a telephone call so I'll probably end up as an Ensign."

"The hell with them," Mitscher said. "I'll see that you make it OK."

★

ADMIRAL YAMAMOTO'S OBSESSION with preventing an attack on Tokyo had only grown as Japan's victories mounted and senior leaders debated the future direction of the war. The lightning successes in the conflict's opening weeks had caught many of the nation's strategists flat-footed. The great risks coupled with the preparations for the ambitious assault on Pearl Harbor and the seizure of the oil-rich southern territories had prompted senior leaders to postpone planning the next phase of the war, an oversight that became clear before the first month of the battle drew to a close. Combined Fleet chief of staff Matome Ugaki, who ordered his staff to prepare a blueprint of future operations by the end of February, captured that surprise in his diary. "We shall be able to finish first-stage operations by the middle of March, as far as the invasion operation is concerned. What are we going to do after that?" he wrote on January 5. "Advance to Australia, to India, attack Hawaii, or destroy the Soviet Union?"

War planners debated several options, including ending offensive actions and preparing a defense, an idea few supported. Another option was to invade Australia, robbing America of a launch pad to push back against Japan. Alternatively forces could push into the Indian Ocean, seize Ceylon, and finish off the British fleet, a move that would allow Japan to link up with Germany in the Middle East. The final option was to advance across the central Pacific and seize Hawaii, guaranteeing a showdown with America. Bogged down in China—and afraid of overextension—the Army resisted such moves. "We want to invade Ceylon; we are not allowed to!" complained Captain Yoshitake Miwa, the Combined Fleet's air officer. "We want to invade Australia; we cannot! We want to attack Hawaii; we cannot do that either! All because the army will not agree to release the necessary forces." Ugaki agreed. "It's annoying to be passive," he wrote in his diary. "Warfare is easier, with less trouble, indeed, when we hold the initiative."

Throughout this debate Yamamoto maintained a single-minded focus—annihilate America's Pacific Fleet. Despite the celebration that followed the attack on Pearl Harbor, Yamamoto saw the strike largely as a Pyrrhic victory. Japan had anticipated the loss of as many as three of its six carriers, but the attack in the end had cost just twenty-nine planes, five midget submarines, and fewer than a hundred men. Vice Admiral Chuichi Nagumo should have capitalized on his unexpected success that Sunday morning and ordered his pilots to rearm and attack again, spreading the assault over several days if necessary. Yamamoto knew that the shortsighted focus only on the battleships and planes—leaving the submarine base, repair facilities, and aboveground tanks with 4.5 million barrels of precious fuel—would only help accelerate America's rebound. Just two days after the attack—as the fires still smoldered at Pearl Harbor—Yamamoto ordered Ugaki to prepare a plan for the invasion of Hawaii. He had to clean up Nagumo's mess.

Yamamoto believed that the destruction of America's carriers—absent from Pearl Harbor that Sunday morning—coupled with the capture of Hawaii would give Japan the power to bargain a peace deal, one that would allow it to keep many of its conquests. Yamamoto's concerns on the surface appeared unwarranted, considering Japan's great successes, but the veteran admiral spied hints of trouble to come. That threat had first materialized in the form of an American carrier raid on the Marshall and the Gilbert Islands on February 1, just fifty-six days after the attack on Hawaii. The dawn strike had robbed Japan of a subchaser and the 6,500-ton transport *Bordeaux Maru*, as well as damaged eight other ships, including a light cruiser. The raiders had even managed to kill Marshall Islands commander Rear Admiral Yukicki Yashiro, a Naval Academy classmate of Ugaki's and Japan's first admiral killed in the war. "They have come after all," Ugaki wrote in his diary with disbelief. "They are some guys!"

Although derided in the Japanese press as "guerrilla warfare," the raid impressed senior leaders. "This attack was Heaven's admonition for our shortcoming," declared Miwa. "Our staff could only grit their teeth and jump up and down in frustration." Few believed that the audacious assault would prove to be the last. Such a bold strike reflected America's adventurous national personality, Ugaki noted, and would merely help make Japan's leaders look "ridiculous." "Pearl Harbor was a complete surprise, but we cannot say the same for this, which happened during the war," Ugaki confided in his diary. "It was fortunate for us that the enemy only scratched us on this occasion and gave us a good lesson instead of directly attacking Tokyo." Ugaki wasn't alone in his fears. Japan's lack of defenses would no doubt invite the Americans to attack again. "Whatever happens, we must absolutely prevent any air attack on Tokyo," Miwa said. "Against enemy aircraft carriers, the defensive is bad strategy, and worse tactics."

The United States followed up the raid on the Marshall and the Gilbert Islands with a February 20 strike against Rabaul, which the Japanese repelled but at a cost of nineteen planes. American carriers then hit Wake on February 24 and Marcus Island on March 4. Six days later carriers appeared off New Guinea, launching a strike of 104 fighters and bombers against Japanese forces at Lae and Salamaua. "The failure to destroy the U.S. carriers at Pearl Harbor haunted us like a ghost ever after," wrote Minoru Genda, one of the chief planners of the attack on Hawaii. "We always worried about them and had to reckon with their potential presence in every operation we planned." The raids convinced senior naval aviators that Japan wasted time with its own attacks against Australia and British forces in the Indian Ocean, particularly when America's carriers remained the only formidable force left in the Pacific. Mitsuo Fuchida, who led the air attack against Pearl Harbor, even warned Admiral Nagumo, "Don't swing such a long sword."

America's carrier raids did little damage, but the marauding flattops posed a much greater potential threat. As in a game of Russian roulette, it was only a matter of time before the barrel pointed at Tokyo, the seat of the emperor. Halsey's attack on Marcus Island had stirred up considerable concern, given that less than a thousand miles separated that island from the nation's capital. Senior naval officers sweated out America's attacks even as the oblivious Japanese public enjoyed victory celebrations. "If real enemy planes raided amidst the festivities, the mere thought of the result makes me shudder," Ugaki wrote in his diary on March 12. "A great air raid over the heads of the rejoicing multitude!" As American attacks grew more audacious, senior leaders began to contemplate what had long been considered unthinkable, a question Miwa raised in his diary. "How shall we defend our capital against an enemy air raid?" he wrote. "It is a big problem."

Yamamoto knew the only way to protect Tokyo was to destroy America's flattops. But that was no easy task. With its Pacific and Asiatic fleets wrecked, America treated its carriers like an endangered species, always retreating at the first sign of danger. Yamamoto's forces had no way to predict where, in an ocean that spread across sixty-five million square miles, to find them. The admiral needed a plan to lure them into combat, an objective so precious that Admiral Chester Nimitz would have no option but to send his carriers into battle. Since the Army would never sign off on the invasion of Hawaii, Yamamoto needed a plan the Navy could tackle largely alone. He set his sights on Midway, the two-and-a-half-square-mile atoll between Tokyo and Hawaii, some thirteen hundred miles northwest of Oahu. This former stopover for the transpacific flights of Pan American Airways Clipper seaplanes had evolved into a vital American naval air and submarine base, whose proximity to Pearl Harbor led Admiral Nagumo to dub it "the sentry for Hawaii."

Yamamoto saw in this wind-ravaged coral atoll not only the perfect launch pad for the eventual seizure of Hawaii but a priceless piece of Pacific real estate he knew America would never surrender. He greenlighted the plan to grab Midway, setting the stage for what he was sure would be a bitter fight with the Naval General Staff in Tokyo. Yamamoto sent Captain Kameto Kuroshima and Commander Yasuji Watanabe to Tokyo to press his case in a three-day session that began April 2, the same day the *Hornet* left California. Senior officers with the Naval General Staff believed America's eventual offensive drive would not come across the central Pacific but up from Australia, where the United States and its allies could amass bombers, warships, and troops on Japan's southern perimeter. Rather than risk resources on a quixotic hunt for a few flattops, officers favored seizing New Caledonia, Samoa, and the Fiji Islands, a move that would sever America's vital communication lines with its ally down under.

Captain Sadatoshi Tomioka and Commander Tatsukichi Miyo spearheaded the Naval General Staff's skillful attack on the Midway operation, an attack the men feared risked dangerous overextension in exchange for little strategic reward. Miyo argued tearfully at times that the United States had no doubt learned a valuable lesson on December 7. The Americans had likely reinforced Hawaii and now diligently tracked Japanese fleet movements, refusing to be caught off guard again. The atoll's proximity to Hawaii furthermore gave the United States the clear tactical advantage. While Japan would have to fight more than two thousand miles east of Tokyo and depend largely on its exhausted carrier forces, the United States could flood the waters with submarines and the skies with Hawaii-based bombers. Furthermore, there was no guarantee that America would even risk its precious carriers to protect Midway. Why not let Japan capture the austere atoll, then strangle it by blockade, making it impossible to reinforce?

Even if Japan managed to capture Midway, Miyo argued, what strategic value did the tiny atoll really offer? An advancing American armada could easily bypass the limited range of Midway air patrols. Furthermore, the atoll was so far from the West Coast that its capture would have a negligible effect on the morale of the American public. As the debate dragged on over several days, it became clear that Yamamoto's plan had less grounding in large-scale tactical goals and more in his fixation on destroying America's carriers. "One wonders whether C. in C. Yamamoto appreciated just how ineffective aerial reconnaissance using Midway as a base would be," Miyo wrote in an article published after the war. "Had he really taken into thorough account the enormous drain on resources and difficulty in maintaining supplies on such an isolated island, or the reduction in air strength necessary in other areas in order to keep it up, and the influence on the fleet's operational activities?"

With both sides reluctant to budge, Watanabe phoned Yamamoto for instruction on April 5. The admiral made it clear he planned to dictate, not negotiate. Japan would either seize Midway, or he would resign. "The success or failure of our entire strategy in the Pacific will be determined by whether or not we succeed in destroying the United States Fleet," he warned in a final statement. "We believe that by launching the proposed operations against Midway, we can succeed in drawing out the enemy's carrier strength and destroying it in decisive battle." Yamamoto had made a similar threat when faced with opposition over his plan to attack Pearl Harbor and the Naval General Staff had caved. Now this son of a former samurai warrior was more popular than ever. How could the Naval General Staff explain his sudden resignation? Rear Admiral Shigeru Fukudome, who headed the Naval General Staff's plans division, knew Yamamoto had again won. "If the C. in C.'s so set on it," he said, "shall we leave it to him?"

Miyo lowered his head and wept.

CHAPTER 8

═══════════
═══════════

★

We shall not begrudge our enemies the impressive victories
which exist in their imaginations and in the
ether waves of their radios.

—*JAPAN TIMES & ADVERTISER*,
FEBRUARY 8, 1942

LIEUTENANT STEPHEN JURIKA JR. met Doolittle and his men on
board the *Hornet* to brief them about what to expect in the skies over
Tokyo and Japan. Few in the Navy could compete with the thirty-one-
year-old's expertise. Jurika had grown up in the Philippines, where his
father had settled after the Spanish-American War, operating a plantation
on Sibuco Bay, on the southwestern tip of the island of Mindanao. His
adolescence was filled with exotic tales most children found only in adventure books. He had learned to swim and sail in azure seas infested with
sharks, hunted cobras that nested in abandoned coconut shells, and even
shot crocodiles in leech-infested swamps. The ethnic diversity of his childhood friends reflected the Philippines' historical role as the crossroads of
Asia—a mix of Filipino, Chinese, Spanish, and Japanese, all languages
Jurika picked up. As he grew older, his parents sought to further broaden
his experience, sending him to boarding school in the Japanese city of
Kobe and later in Shanghai, China.

When Jurika finished high school at fourteen, his father encouraged him to attend Stanford University, hoping he would return to the Philippines to run the family business, but Jurika balked. He had wanted to be a naval officer since he was a child, but even though he was an American citizen, he had no congressman or senator who could appoint him to Annapolis. Jurika had no choice but to enlist, serve two years, and then sit for the academy's entrance exam. He faked his age and joined the Navy at just fifteen. Jurika went on to graduate from the Naval Academy in 1933 and to serve on the cruisers *Louisville* and *Houston*, playing bridge on the latter against his commander in chief during Roosevelt's 1934 voyage to Latin America. Jurika later earned his wings, flying torpedo bombers for several years off the carrier *Saratoga*. The head of naval intelligence wrote Jurika in 1939, asking whether he was interested in serving as an assistant naval attaché in Tokyo. Jurika jumped at the opportunity.

The few attachés worked out of the embassy, collecting intelligence on the Japanese Navy. Much of the information came from open sources, ranging from newspaper articles to the Navy's annual ship construction budget, debated each year in parliament. Other times Jurika traveled south to Kobe to surreptitiously photograph the launches of new ships, reserving a fourth-floor room at the Oriental Hotel with a view of Mitsubishi's sprawling shipyard, which employed a wartime peak of almost 23,000 workers to hammer out freighters, submarines, and naval auxiliaries. Every three months the attaché hopped an American President Line ship south to the Philippines to log his required hours in a cockpit, persuading the skippers en route to steam near Japanese shipyards, which often used scaffolding and netting to block views from shore. Other days Jurika attended air shows—he once got to sit in the cockpit of a Mitsubishi Zero fighter—or played golf next to air stations so he could clock takeoffs and landings.

As the war in China raged—and tensions between Japan and America increased—authorities ramped up efforts to crack down on American spying. Military police interrogated Japanese guests who had visited the homes of the attachés, a move that discouraged locals from befriending the Americans. Meanwhile, police began to shadow the military diplomats. When Lieutenant Commander Henri Smith-Hutton rode the train past the naval base at Kure, the attendant entered the compartment, lowered the shade, and demanded that the embassy's senior naval attaché leave it shut. When the train stopped in Hiroshima—home to a large Japanese Army base—attendants again lowered the shade, this time barring Smith-Hutton from even leaving the compartment. "Tokyo is really a city of the living dead; so different from last year!" Jurika wrote in an October 1940 letter. "Most of the American and British women and some of the men have gone, and now everyone else is packing or about to pack."

Despite the added challenges, Jurika soldiered on, broadening his sleuthing into an area that would make him a vital asset to Doolittle's mission. "As an aviator I was interested in more than just ships," he recalled. "I became interested in targets." Oil depots, chemical plants, and blast furnaces—the beating heart of any steel mill. The industrial might that powered a nation and its war machine, Jurika knew, would prove the Achilles' heel in a life-and-death struggle—and in Japan's capital and sprawling suburbs, the studious attaché found such industry everywhere. "Each time I drove from Tokyo down toward Yokohama, going through the fantastic industrial district of Kawasaki, I would take a different route and go by the petro-chemical factories, the chemical factories, the iron and steel mills, and see for myself where these big things were located, factories that covered hundreds of acres," Jurika said. "It was really unending, just one succession of one big factory after another, all the way down."

Jurika and his colleagues realized in the summer of 1940 that they had no target maps of Japan or its principal industries. Some of that information, the officers discovered, was available through books and commercial brochures, published by steel mills, silk factories, and shipyards. The intelligence officers collected detailed land maps—printed by the Japanese government—that pinpointed homes, roads, and principal thoroughfares. Armed with the commercial data, the officers fleshed out the maps, labeling important industries and even specific buildings. "We started to fill in a host of what we considered primary targets, first, in the Tokyo area, and then on down through Kawasaki to Yokohama, where we identified the shipbuilding, the tank farms for fuel oil and gasoline, some major wharves, bridges that were strategic in the sense that the main Tokkaido line would cross, or tunnels where bombs could be dropped and possibly obstruct traffic for a considerable period."

But the American naval attachés, more accustomed to sizing up new ships and armament, struggled to complete the target maps, prompting Jurika to turn to an unlikely ally—the Russians. Though the Soviet attachés largely kept to themselves, despite Tokyo's vibrant diplomatic social scene, Jurika managed to befriend assistant Russian naval attaché Ivan Egoricheff one day on a local tennis court, scoring an invitation to lunch. When Jurika arrived at the Russian embassy, Egoricheff escorted him to his office, seating him next to a potted palm as he handed him a glass of straight vodka. Jurika took a few reluctant sips of his noontime cocktail, watching as his host downed his own drink. "When he went over to fill his," Jurika remembered, "I dumped mine into the flower pot." Egoricheff repeatedly refilled both drinks, and Jurika continued to feed his to the palm, never drinking more than a quarter of his vodka. "By the time I'd had one drink," Jurika recalled, "he'd had four."

Over lunch the officers complained about how difficult it was to pick up any real intelligence in Japan.

"We know that you get along much better with the Japanese than we do," Egoricheff observed.

Jurika insisted he must be joking. After all, America was on the verge of war with Japan. "Do you read the newspapers?" Jurika asked.

The Russian officer confessed that he didn't believe the papers. Despite the tensions between the two governments, Egoricheff repeated his view that American attachés enjoyed friendlier relationships with the Japanese and had better intelligence on the Imperial Navy. But maybe there was something America needed. What did Jurika want in exchange for details on Japanese ships?

Without compromising his hours of spying on launches and timing takeoffs, Jurika knew he could hand over information on the Japanese Navy he had culled from newspapers and magazines, all unclassified open-source intelligence that was available to anyone willing to dedicate the time to hunt for it.

"Well," Jurika said, "I've only recently begun to think in terms of some future day when we might want to know the location of a tank farm or shipbuilding or something like that."

"Ah," the Russian attaché replied. "We have all that information down. We've been collecting that type of information for years."

That was the news Jurika wanted to hear.

"I'll give you what you want to know," Egoricheff continued. "Where do you want to start?"

Jurika's answer was simple: Tokyo.

ANCHORED AT THE HEAD of Tokyo Bay and in the shadow of majestic Mount Fuji—an active volcano rising to more than twelve thousand feet—spread the sprawling capital of the empire of Japan. Tokyo served not only as the national seat of government and power but also as Japan's great commercial, industrial, transportation, and communications center, with the nation's top hospitals, universities, department stores, museums, and theaters. According to the 1940 census, the population had hit 6,778,804, making Tokyo home to one out of every ten Japanese and the third-largest city in the world, behind only London and New York. Divided into thirty-five wards, Tokyo stretched out across more than two hundred square miles; the density in some wards topping more than 100,000 people per square mile—a figure almost ten times that of Washington, D.C.

But Tokyo proved an urban planner's nightmare. Factories, homes, and stores were all crowded together. Areas classified industrial turned out to be densely populated, while homes often doubled as workshops. Visitors complained that the layout of city blocks failed to conform to any decipherable plan, complicated by the fact that streets often went unnamed, forcing residents to direct one another via nearby major intersections. A further challenge emerged from the city's practice of numbering properties not on the basis of a geographical sequence along a street but by the order constructed. A residence built on the site of a demolished property would retain the original address, a procedure that only exacerbated the confusion as Tokyo's density soared. One street had no fewer than a dozen homes—all with the exact same street number.

These quirks complicated navigation in a city that on the war's eve counted a staggering 1,057,921 homes, shops, schools, and government buildings. A network of buses, electric trains, and even a subway—albeit with only nine miles of lines—shuttled an army of commuters throughout the teeming capital. Workers at more than 45,000 factories and small workshops churned out products ranging from textiles and ceramics to machines and tools. There were two dozen banks in Tokyo, and the port welcomed an average of fifty ships each day. Wealthy patrons strolled along the Ginza—Japan's tony shopping avenue, dubbed the Broadway of Tokyo—where stores whisked customers between floors on escalators and in high-speed elevators. Others flocked to motion picture palaces that competed against traditional Kabuki and Noh theaters.

The Imperial Palace occupied the heart of this congested city. Protected by wide moats, ancient walls, and towering pines, the 531-acre compound and home of the forty-year-old emperor Hirohito was the largest open space in all of Tokyo, eloquently described by one American newspaper reporter as "a piece of heaven in which dwells a god in human form." A few blocks south sat the Imperial Diet, a Western-style political palace that housed Japan's bicameral legislature. Workers toiled for nineteen years to complete the $8.5 million parliament building—hailed as Japan's largest public structure—with 390 rooms spread across 597,000 square feet. The marble walls, carpeted corridors, and numbered elevators—as well as a central tower capped with a pyramid—prompted reporters to compare the Diet to Madison Avenue's Metropolitan Life Insurance Building and the Bankers Trust Company skyscraper on Wall Street.

But Japan's transformation from isolated island nation to modern power proved far from complete. New arrivals accustomed to the magnificent ports of San Francisco and New York found themselves underwhelmed—if not outright appalled—by the capital's rough and unpolished appearance. Tokyo represented a dichotomy, a city that straddled centuries with a wealthy Western veneer of shiny offices and wide boulevards loosely covering a primitive and agrarian past. How could a nation strong enough to seize control of one-tenth of the globe still have open sewers in some districts of its crowded capital? "It is a city old and new, backward and ultra-modern, Oriental and Occidental," observed one American newspaper reporter. "Stately Buddhist temples rise serenely against a background of smoke stacks. Shiba Park boasts the temples and tombs of the Shoguns as well as a modern swimming pool."

New York Times correspondent Otto Tolischus, who arrived aboard the SS *Coolidge* at daybreak on February 7, 1941, captured in his diary his impressions of the roughly twenty-mile drive from Yokohama to downtown Tokyo, a city permeated by the nauseating odor of rotting fish. "Both sides of the road were lined with dirty, dilapidated, ramshackle wooden shops and shacks, which had nothing in common with the pretty doll houses pictured in Japanese scenes at home. The people looked equally poverty-stricken. Most of them shuffled about in dirty kimonos or a bizarre array of Western dress, and most of them, though it was winter, walked about in bare feet shod in wooden clogs. Farmers, driving lumbering oxcarts, were completely in rags, sometimes covered with a raincoat made of straw. Ragged were also the innumerable children—tiny but chunky half-naked urchins," Tolischus observed. "Shantytown! That was the only word I could find for the scene. I looked at my companions, who smiled; they had seen that astonished look on the faces of other new arrivals."

More than four years of war with China had reduced the stream of imported luxuries to a trickle, replaced by a flood of tin boxes carrying the ashes of Japan's war dead. Scrap drives, food rationing, and fuel shortages abounded as the nation diverted all resources to the war. Tokyo was not spared. Guests hiked up the stairs at the landmark Imperial Hotel—designed by famed architect Frank Lloyd Wright—after the elevators stopped running in an effort to conserve electricity. The government discouraged travel and forbade dancing—an activity deemed out of touch with the nation's wartime mood—shuttering the city's eight large dance halls and more than one hundred nightclubs. Residents nursed rationed beers and guarded pet dogs and cats, often netted and killed for the promise of warm fur to insulate gloves. "I've seen housewives," wrote *Wall Street Journal* reporter Ray Cromley, "wait in line all morning to get two carrots, in another line all afternoon to get one sardine, and go away bragging at their luck."

American war planners knew that Tokyo made an especially inviting target for a surprise air attack for reasons far greater than the city's role as Japan's capital and hub of industry. Tokyo was cursed with an Achilles' heel, a fatal design flaw laid bare before the world at two minutes before noon on September 1, 1923. That warm Saturday morning, as residents headed to beach and mountain getaways, a 7.9-magnitude earthquake struck. The ground swayed and groaned before a sudden roar raced across the city, the chorus of collapsing offices, hotels, and restaurants. Police in neighboring Yokohama estimated that the quake toppled no fewer than ten thousand structures—one out of every ten in the city. But the earthquake and the forty-foot tsunami that slammed ashore proved to be only the start of Tokyo's nightmare. Ruptured gas lines and toppled stoves triggered an inferno—fueled by the strong winds of an approaching typhoon—that feasted on the region's dense mix of homes and shops built of little more than brittle wood and paper.

Terrified residents fled to the few parks as collapsing bridges and marching fires cut off exits. Some slathered their faces in mud to prevent their skin from burning, while sparks ignited the hair of other, less fortunate souls. Many dove into canals and ponds, only to drown among the tangled masses or boil as fires superheated the water. Of the 44,000 who had crowded onto the twenty-acre field of the Army Clothing Depot near Tokyo's sumo stadium, only 300 survived, many consumed by the unique phenomenon of a fire tornado. Henry Kinney, editor of the monthly magazine *Trans-Pacific*, later described the horror he witnessed from a hilltop above. "Yokohama, the city of almost half a million souls, had become a vast plain of fire, of red, devouring sheets of flame which played and flickered. Here and there a remnant of a building, a few shattered walls, stood up like rocks above the expanse of flame, unrecognizable," he wrote in the *Atlantic Monthly*. "It was as if the very earth were now burning."

The conflagration that burned for forty-six hours destroyed Yokohama and most of Tokyo, claiming an estimated 140,000 lives—more than Japan lost in the Russo-Japanese War. Though an earthquake had triggered the 1923 fire, incendiary bombs could just as easily spark the next blaze. To limit the spread of fire, engineers added six major avenues—each 120 feet wide—and cut more than one hundred other streets through the dense city. Workers constructed several large parks and fifty smaller ones to serve as firebreaks and refuges for victims, while Tokyo's newly rebuilt business district sported Western earthquake and fire-resistant technologies. But the lessons proved short-lived. The economic depression that dragged from 1927 to 1931 prompted officials to relax building regulations, a situation made even worse in 1938 when steel was banned for private construction. The Tokyo that Doolittle now set his sights on—much like the city destroyed nineteen years earlier—consisted of 98 percent wood and paper. "If you can start seven good fires," Jurika promised the men, "they'll never put them out."

★

DOOLITTLE DEBATED THE BEST plan of attack. One idea called for liftoff three hours before sunrise, which would put the raiders over Tokyo at dawn. That would assure an element of surprise and guarantee the planes maximum security. Bomb conditions would be ideal and crews would have plenty of time to reach China before nightfall. The Navy's refusal to light up the carrier at night—easy prey for any Japanese submarine—coupled with the uncertainty of taking off in the dark prompted Doolittle to abandon the plan. Another possible scenario called for a dawn liftoff, with the attack to take place early in the morning yet still allow enough time for crews to reach China before nightfall. Doolittle nixed this plan as well because it would force pilots to bomb during the day, exposing them to antiaircraft fire and fighters.

The plan Doolittle settled on called for a takeoff just before dark. He would lift off first and arrive over Tokyo at dusk, pummeling the most flammable sector of the city with incendiary bombs. The others would take off three hours later and use his fires to guide them into the city. This would allow the bombers to attack under the cover of darkness and arrive over China at dawn. Doolittle organized the fifteen planes into five waves of three bombers. Travis Hoover would lead the first flight and cover northern Tokyo. The second wave, under Davy Jones, would target the city's center. Ski York would lead the third flight over southern Tokyo and the north-central part of the bay area. The fourth wave, led by Ross Greening, would hit the southern suburbs of Kanagawa, Yokohama, and the Yokosuka navy yard. Jack Hilger would lead the final wave, tasked to bomb the industrial cities of Nagoya, Osaka, and Kobe.

Doolittle spread the flights over a fifty-mile front, a move that would give the attack maximum coverage and create the appearance of a greater aerial armada than just sixteen bombers. Such a wide front would furthermore help ensure surprise, preventing two bombers from passing over the exact same points. The approach likewise would help dilute any subsequent countermeasures. Doolittle allowed the pilots to pick the target city. Folders were then handed out with selected objectives, from oil refineries and tank farms to steel plants, ammunition dumps, and dockyards. Each crew was assigned a primary target as well as alternatives in case flak or fighters barred them from reaching the principal target. "I spent more time than most of the other crews evaluating the total target selection," Hilger recalled, "in order to assure a balance of targets that would do what we considered the greatest damage to the Japanese."

The fliers pored over the two-and-half-foot target maps, which showed highways, railroads, and even individual houses, while Jurika instructed them on major landmarks like the Tama River and the Diet. "Every outline of the coast which we were to approach was carefully studied and memorized," navigator Charles McClure later wrote. "So were the silhouettes of the particular plants, rail yards, and other military objectives we were to strike." Doolittle drilled his men hard. "We went over and over and over again the exact route that a ship should take," he recalled, "what they should see; the points that would identify the approach to the target; what the pilot, the navigator and bombardier would see as they approached the target; the point at which they were to pull up to the proper altitude; the appearance of the targets."

Much to Jurika's frustration not all the raiders paid close attention. "A briefing would be set up for 8:30 in the morning, after breakfast, they would saunter in and the briefing scheduled for 8:30 wouldn't start before 9:00 or 9:15, sometimes as late as 9:30," he recalled. "And their attention span was very short, half an hour at the most. They would be interested up to a point, and yet, from my point of view, their lives were at stake. The success of a raid was at stake." More than anyone else, Jurika understood the danger these men faced. "If they were captured dropping bombs on Japan, the chances of their survival would be awfully slim," he warned. "I figured they would be, first of all, paraded through the streets as Exhibit A, and then tried by some sort of a kangaroo court and probably publicly beheaded. This seemed to settle them down quite a bit."

Some of the raiders went so far as to cut a deck of cards to see who would bomb the Imperial Palace.

"We all wanted it," Chase Nielsen recalled. "There wasn't any of us had any love for the Japs. Besides that, we figured the Emperor was at the bottom of the whole thing and we wanted to get at the bottom of it all."

Doolittle heard the scuttlebutt and immediately put a stop to it. "You are to bomb military targets only," he ordered. "There is nothing that would unite the Japanese nation more than to bomb the emperor's home. It is not a military target! And you are to avoid hospitals, schools, and other nonmilitary targets."

Doolittle told them of his visit to Britain in 1940 when the Germans bombed Buckingham Palace, which he described as a useless attack that only rallied the British people. The same applied for the Imperial Palace. The mission was to sow disunity and spread doubts about the ability of the Japanese military to protect the people. That would be lost in the nationalistic uproar that would surely follow an attack on the emperor. "Even though I could have designated it a specific target, I unilaterally made the decision that we would not bomb it," Doolittle later wrote. "I consider this admonition one of the most serious I ever made to bombardment crews throughout the war."

The men learned about the ordnance that would be used in the mission. Each plane would carry four bombs for a total of 2,000 pounds. Most would carry a mix of 500-pound M-43 demolition bombs and M-43 incendiary clusters made up of 128 four-pound bomblets designed to scatter over an area 200 feet by 600 feet.

"You will drop the demolition bombs in the shortest space of time, preferably in a straight line, where they will do the most damage," Doolittle advised. "Avoid hitting stone, concrete, and steel targets because you can't do enough damage to them."

A pilot popped up and asked about targeting residential areas.

"Definitely not!" Doolittle warned. "You are to look for and aim at military targets only, such as war industries, shipbuilding facilities, power plants, and the like. There is absolutely nothing to be gained by attacking residential areas."

He reiterated his admonition not to bomb the emperor's palace. "It's not worth a plane factory, a shipyard, or an oil refinery, so leave it alone."

One of the pilots asked what Doolittle would do if his plane were hit.

"Each pilot must decide for himself what he will do and what he'll tell his crew to do if that happens," he answered. "I know what I'm going to do."

A silence hung over the men before the pilot asked the logical follow-up.

"I don't intend to be taken prisoner," Doolittle replied. "I'm 45 years old and have lived a full life. If my plane is crippled beyond any possibility of fighting or escape, I'm going to have my crew bail out and then I'm going to dive my B-25 into the best military target I can find. You fellows are all younger and have a long life ahead of you. I don't expect any of the rest of you to do what I intend to do."

The gravity of the raid sunk in for many. "We figured there was only a 50-50 chance we would get off the *Hornet*," Nielsen remembered. "If we got off, there was a 50-50 chance we'd get shot down over Japan. And, if we got that far, there was a 50-50 chance we'd make it to China. And, if we got to China, there was a 50-50 chance we'd be captured. We figured the odds were really stacked against us."

Each combat crew member received a pistol, a parachute knife, an extra clip of ammunition, one day's type C field ration, a flashlight, a full canteen of water, a Navy gas mask, and a hand ax. Not all of the gear passed muster. "I went through that box of 1911 pistols," remembered pilot Edgar McElroy of his .45. "They were in such bad condition that I took several of them apart, using the good parts from several useless guns until I built a serviceable weapon. Several other pilots did the same."

The airmen sat through myriad other classes and lectures. Jurika drilled into them the important Chinese phrase "*Lusau hoo metwa fugi,*" or "I'm American." He furthermore taught them that the easiest way to distinguish a Japanese soldier from a Chinese one was to look at the toes. "The Japanese wore *tabi*, which separates the big toe from the other four toes," he recalled. "The Chinese have all their toes together."

Greening continued to hammer the airmen on gunnery, firing on kites from the stern of the *Hornet*. One of the airmen who worked the hardest was Staff Sergeant Edwin Bain, tapped to join Jack Hilger's crew just before the *Hornet* left port after the original gunner was hospitalized.

"Know anything about a tail gun?" Doolittle asked him.

"Nossir," Bain replied. "I'm a radioman."

"That's what you *were!*" Doolittle told him. "You're a tail-gunner now."

Other times the fliers studied meteorology and practiced celestial navigation with the help of *Hornet* navigator Commander Frank Akers by shooting star shots with a sextant from the deck and from the bomber's navigator compartment. Mission adjutant Major Harry Johnson was impressed by the diligence of the aircrews, as evidenced by his report: "Pilots plotted and replotted courses with their navigators until I feel most of them could have almost discarded their maps."

Along those lines Doolittle cautioned crews on how best to dump the extra fuel tins. "I don't want you to throw them out as they're used," he instructed. "If you do, it will leave a perfect trail for the Japanese to follow back to the carrier. Use up the stuff in the cans first, of course, but save them and dump them all together. The Navy has been great to us. Let's show our appreciation in whatever way we can."

Mission doctor Thomas White administered the final vaccinations against the plague, weathering another round of teasing from the airmen. "One chap swore he'd bleed serum if he were ever wounded, since he was certain there was no room for blood in his veins. Another wanted to know when I was going to give him his latex shots," White wrote. "He wanted to be self-sealing like the gas tanks!" White reviewed sanitation dangers the crew would face in China, hammering into them the importance of avoiding cuts and of drinking only boiled water and eating cooked foods. "The way the Doc talked," Joseph Manske noted in his diary, "all disease must of started in China."

With the help of the *Hornet*'s medical department, White even rustled up a pint of whiskey for each member of the crew, ostensibly for snakebites.

"Are there snakes in China?" Knobloch asked.

"I don't know," the doctor replied. "But if there are, this'll sure help you."

CHAPTER 9

★

Four months today since Pearl Harbor—and the situation
has deteriorated every minute since.

—BRECKINRIDGE LONG,
APRIL 7, 1942, DIARY ENTRY

ROOSEVELT WATCHED THE NEWS in the Pacific worsen as winter
gave way to spring. Japan had seized the oil-rich Dutch East Indies, captured Rangoon, and severed the Burma Road, the vital lifeline of aid into
China. Japanese forces reached as far south as Australia, pummeling the
coastal city of Darwin in a raid that put every ship in the harbor on the
bottom. Powerless to stop Japan's advance, Roosevelt commiserated with
Prime Minister Winston Churchill, who sulked for weeks over the loss of
Singapore. "I do not like these days of personal stress and I have found it
difficult to keep my eye on the ball," Churchill confessed, later adding,
"The weight of the war is very heavy now and I must expect it to get
steadily worse for some time to come."

The pragmatic president urged Churchill to focus on the future. "No
matter how serious our setbacks have been, and I do not for a moment
underrate them, we must constantly look forward to the next moves that
need to be made to hit the enemy." Roosevelt pressed that theme again in
other correspondence. "There is no use giving a single further thought to
Singapore or the Dutch Indies," he advised. "They are gone." In a softer

exchange he encouraged Churchill to find a way to relax. "Once a month I go to Hyde Park for four days, crawl into a hole and pull the hole in after me," he wrote. "I am called on the telephone only if something of really great importance occurs. I wish you would try it, and I wish you would lay a few bricks or paint another picture."

Roosevelt struggled at times to take his own advice, letting the war's setbacks and continued attacks by isolationist rivals upset him. That was evident when he lashed out in a March 6 letter to prominent New York banker Fred Kent. "You wax positively gruesome when you declare solemnly that had it not been for the thirty million man-days lost by strikes since the defense program began, the Philippines, the Dutch Indies and Singapore would all have been saved. You sound like Alice in Wonderland," the president wrote. "Let me tell you something more fantastic than that. If, since the defense program started, we in the United States had not lost sixty million man-days through that scourge of Satan, called the common cold, we could undoubtedly have had enough planes and guns and tanks to overrun Europe, Africa and the whole of Asia."

The pressures on the president only increased as the struggle for the Philippines neared its tragic end. Under orders from Roosevelt, MacArthur had escaped in March, leaving Lieutenant General Jonathan Wainwright in command of 110,000 American and Filipino forces on the Bataan Peninsula and the fortified island of Corregidor. Cut off from reinforcements by a Japanese blockade, Wainwright's troops battled malaria and starvation, forced to slaughter and eat the cavalry's horses. "Our troops have been subsisted [sic] on one half to one third ration for so long a period," Wainwright radioed on April 8, "that they do not possess the physical strength to endure the strain placed upon the individual in an attack." MacArthur warned General Marshall to prepare for the worst. "In view of my intimate knowledge of the situation there, I regard the situation as extremely critical and feel you should anticipate the possibility of disaster."

The situation was hopeless. Roosevelt instructed Wainwright to do what he felt best. "I have nothing but admiration for your soldierly conduct and your performance of your most difficult mission," he messaged. "You should be assured of complete freedom of action and of my full confidence in the wisdom of whatever decision you may be forced to make." The Japanese overran Bataan on April 9—one week after the

Hornet left San Francisco—setting the stage for the infamous Death March that would kill thousands. Holed up on Corregidor with the last of the Philippines' fourteen thousand defenders, Wainwright listened that night as a "terrible silence" settled over Bataan. "If there is anything worse than a battlefield that shakes with explosions and the cries of men," he later wrote, "it is one that becomes mute and dead." He tried to sound optimistic in a message to the president. "Our flag still flies on this island fortress."

But it would not for long.

Wainwright knew it; so did the Japanese.

And so did Roosevelt.

The fall of Bataan exacerbated the pressure on Roosevelt. Americans had grown tired of retreat and defeat. "Bataan is a bugle call to tell us that only attack will win," argued the *San Francisco Chronicle*. "Attack is not only suited to our temperament," echoed the *New York Times*. "It is also the life-sparing road to a victorious peace." The Doolittle mission promised a potent tonic to the frustration brought on by Pearl Harbor, Wake, Guam, and now Bataan. But the recent disaster in the Philippines only magnified the enormous political risk of a mission grounded in the promise not of tactical gains but of positive headlines. How would the country react if Japan destroyed America's precious few carriers, cruisers, and destroyers? Was Roosevelt in his quest to boost the nation's morale pushing his Navy to commit suicide? That question would be answered soon enough.

THE ARMY AVIATORS SETTLED into life on board the *Hornet* as the task force cut through the swells west toward Japan. In addition to attending classes and lectures, the men worried about the bombers, which were exposed to everything from corrosive salt air and sea spray to gale-force winds and pounding rains. Crews paid careful attention to the auxiliary gas tanks, which were prone to leak. "Deck lashings had to be inspected and secured daily," wrote pilot Jack Sims. "Batteries ran down requiring regular recharging, spark plugs fouled, brakes failed, hydraulic component and system leaks occurred and generators sometimes broke down. It was a constant, never-ending battle against the elements."

On one of those inspections, Edward Saylor discovered a problem.

He drained the oil sump on the right engine and pulled out the magnetic plug, which is designed to pick up any metal shavings or particles that might have come loose. Attached to the plug he found two horseshoe-shaped keys that held the engine's five planetary reduction gears in place on the shaft. The loss of those two keys signaled the breakdown of the engine's gear system, a catastrophic failure. Saylor reported the news to Doolittle.

"Can you fix it?" Doolittle asked.

Saylor knew this was no easy job; it would require the removal and disassembly of the engine—on an aircraft carrier at sea.

"Probably," Saylor replied. "I've never done anything like this before."

Doolittle was blunt.

"You've either got to fix it or push it over the side."

Saylor set to work. The bomber with its tail dangling over the carrier's stern could not be transported below, forcing Saylor to remove the engine on the flight deck even as the winds at times reached thirty-five miles per hour. Navy sailors helped, constructing a tripod over the plane complete with a chain hoist to support the more than 2,000-pound Wright Cyclone engine. As he unfastened the bomber's engine, Saylor carefully packed each nut and bolt inside the aircraft so as not to lose them overboard.

The men transported the engine down to the *Hornet*'s hangar deck, where Saylor disassembled the back half of the engine, working amid a sea of parts. He directed the machine shop to make replacement keys and then carefully installed them. "There was nobody around that had ever done it before, none of the other mechanics," he recalled. "It was just a matter of using your head, taking it apart and putting it back together again, getting everything just right." Crews transported the rebuilt engine back up the elevators, and Saylor reinstalled it on the bomber. "Ran it up and it ran fine," Saylor said. "Normally we would have test flown the aircraft to see if everything was really working out okay on it after such a major rebuild, but of course we didn't have a chance to do that so we just had to make sure that everything was just right on it. "

The airmen took care of other issues, big and small.

Ted Lawson continued to order gunner Dave Thatcher to stop calling him "sir."

"All right, sir," Thatcher answered. "I won't."

Bobby Hite had come on board as the pilot of one of the backup crews. He hungered to go on the mission, complaining to his friend and fellow pilot Billy Farrow.

"I've been training my own crew and everything," Hite griped. "I want to go."

Farrow wasn't wild about his copilot and asked Hite whether he wanted to come along in his place, even though it meant a demotion in status from aircraft commander to copilot. Hite jumped at the opportunity. "I would have gone as bombardier, rear gunner, nose gunner," he recalled. "I would have gone in any position to be on that raid."

The airmen used the limited free time to take tours of the *Hornet*, visiting the hangar deck and the torpedo rooms. With a background in engineering, Hilger marveled at the boiler and engine rooms. As the mission's second-in-command, he enjoyed a stateroom to himself and caught up with an old high school friend, now an officer on the *Hornet*. Doolittle's navigator, Hank Potter, realized that, in his rush not to miss the last tender back to the carrier the morning the task force left San Francisco, he had left his dog tags in his hotel room. He persuaded technicians in the carrier's medical department to fashion him new ones. Richard Cole likewise spent a day in the optical repair shop, making a new screw for his sunglasses to replace one he had lost. Joseph Manske visited the ship's dentist and barber, while Herb Macia refereed an ongoing chess match between the two naval roommates, who seldom played face-to-face.

"Hey, has Bill been here?" one of the sailors would invariably ask Macia.

"No."

"I'm going to move that one back."

Chow time became a daily highlight for the airmen, as captured by Ken Reddy in his diary. "The meals in the Navy were not good, but excellent," he wrote. "The most elaborate meals to be consistent I have ever seen. Fresh fruit, vegetables and milk." Ted Lawson echoed him. "The Navy fattened us up like condemned men," he later wrote. "We even had chicken." As the *Hornet* steamed farther west—and fresh stores began to run low—the airmen got a taste of a Navy culinary tradition. "I had never eaten beans for breakfast," confessed bombardier Robert

Bourgeois. "Later in China those beans would have looked like ice cream."

When the novelty of the new surroundings faded, many of the airmen settled down to games of poker and craps, surprised to discover that the crew shared quarters with a billiard table. "What in the world would you ever do with a billiard table on the ship? Because even anchored, even at the dock, I don't know how you would use it," Davy Jones later said. "But at any rate, it was there and it made a helluva crap table. When we weren't studying, there was a crap game."

And what a game it was.

"I fear the dice games were the biggest and best ever held on the *Hornet*," recalled Charles McClure, Lawson's navigator. "All of the bomber officers had money and adopted the theory that it didn't make a damn bit of difference what became of it. We didn't have premonitions of disaster, but we realized that we were off on one of the most dangerous attempts to harm an enemy that had ever been conceived; money just didn't seem to mean much under the circumstances. There was solid logic behind this thought. Only by a miracle could all of us have escaped whole."

Even Ken Reddy, who swore off gambling after he lost $40 back at Pendleton, picked up the dice and cards again. "Since I've been aboard I have gone back on my better judgment," he confided in his diary. "I took a $5.00 bill earned in a crap game and ran it up to $104.00 playing poker for 4 days. One day I fell off $19.00 but out of the four I earned $104.00."

Not all of the raiders came out ahead.

Davy Jones shared a stateroom with Lieutenant William "Gus" Widhelm, the executive officer of Scouting Squadron Eight. Widhelm had not only one of the best record collections but a sizable appetite for cards as well—and an ego to match. "When you brag as much as I do," he often quipped, "you gotta live up to your words!"

That he did, wiping out the shipboard savings of many of the raiders, who would then gather in the passageways and mournfully sing "Deep in the Heart of Texas." "He forgot one thing, however," Ross Greening later noted. "There were still some Army crew who didn't go on the raid that were still aboard. By the time the task force reached Pearl Harbor revenge had been won—the Army cleaned Gus for 1100 dollars and cleaned every other Navy poker player of every cent they started to sea with!"

The Navy's senior officers ignored the illegal shipboard gambling, even though a deck court on board the task force's destroyer *Balch* found more than a dozen sailors guilty of the same offense, levying fines of as much as forty dollars.

Mitscher at one point even walked in on one of the *Hornet*'s games, looking over the shoulder of a young second lieutenant.

"How are you doing?" the skipper asked.

The Army airman with a cigar dangling from the corner of his mouth glanced up but failed to recognize Mitscher.

"OK, Joe," he answered, much to the embarrassment of Mitscher's marine orderly. "Want to take a hand?"

Though the skipper shrugged off such illegal games, other officers on board took offense at the airmen's lax behavior, including Jurika. "Most of them slept in. Few of them came down to breakfast," the lieutenant later griped. "Poker games were going, sometimes on a twenty-four-hour basis. I know there were games that went for two or three days. Somebody would go to the wardroom during a meal and bring back enough to keep them from starving. I know that there was also some booze on board." The airmen's winning irked the Navy in other ways. "Being so flush we bought enormously in their ship store," recalled McClure. "We bore down heavily on cigarets [*sic*] by the carton and candy bars by the dozens; we almost drained their supplies."

Not everyone gambled. "If you didn't play poker," recalled Cole, Doolittle's copilot, "you more or less had to generate your own amusement." The airmen spied whales one day near the ship. Another time a school of tuna jumped. Jacob DeShazer found himself drawn to the albatross that trailed the task force. One night on guard duty, he wrestled with loneliness and fear. He comforted himself by considering the statistics of World War I. Of all the soldiers who fought, only a fraction had died. Surely he, too, would be one of the lucky ones and survive. "I began to wonder how many more days I was to spend in this world. Maybe I wasn't so fortunate after all to get to go on this trip," DeShazer mused. "I shuddered to think where I would go if I was to die."

DeShazer wasn't alone. Others wrestled with the same fears, as evidenced by the crowded Easter service the Sunday morning of April 5. Those who couldn't find a seat inside the carrier's mess deck stood in the aisles. Others jammed the doorways. Lieutenant Commander Edward

Harp Jr., the *Hornet*'s chaplain, counted no fewer than thirty of Doolittle's men sitting shoulder to shoulder in the first two rows. "Looking down at those youngsters, I wondered what I could say to them. I knew that some of them would not get back," he later wrote. "However, men going into danger do not like to hear about it." Harp chose not to focus his sermon on the perilous mission ahead or even suggest that the men make peace with God. "I spoke, instead, of immortality. I told them that there were certain realms over which death had no control. The human personality was one of them," he wrote. "Death could not destroy them."

Harp led the men in singing hymns as he played the hand organ, performing songs the fliers had requested, mostly old Sunday-school psalms remembered from childhood; seven of the airmen would later ask him as well for copies of the New Testament to take on the mission over Tokyo. One of the fliers who listened that morning was Ken Reddy, homesick for his church back home in Texas. "The service was nice, but my mind was wandering over the benches in the Church at Bowie. Mr. Bellah on the front row; Mrs. Heard doing her best on the pianos; Bob Spain leading the singing, Dad standing respectfully while Mama did her bit to help the dragging music," he wrote in his diary. "Today, however, when the services were over, there was no argument as to where I would eat dinner. There was no after Church parley with Dorothy and Geo., Son, or Ed and Margaret. I just made my way to the wardroom and ate."

Fellow airman Joseph Manske captured a similar sentiment in his diary that day. "Easter Sunday on board ship was just another day," he wrote. "We had beans for breakfast and chicken for dinner. Nothing extra."

VICE ADMIRAL HALSEY HAD concluded his meeting in San Francisco with Doolittle and prepared to return to Pearl Harbor by April 2. The three-star admiral needed time to make final preparations for the mission. Strong westerly winds, however, stymied his plan, forcing the cancellation of all Hawaii-bound flights. The winds failed to die down the next day or the day after. By April 5, much to Halsey's frustration, he had no choice but to alert the *Hornet* to postpone the scheduled rendezvous by a day. Halsey's luck continued to deteriorate. The next day, as he prepared to return to Pearl Harbor, he was hit with a self-diagnosed case of the flu. "When I boarded the plane, I was so full of pills that I rattled, but I slept until a nosebleed woke me as we lost altitude for our landing," Halsey later wrote. "I stepped off at Honolulu with the flu licked."

Halsey spent April 7 meeting with Chester Nimitz and his planning staff, finalizing Operation Plan No. 20-42, which the laconic Pacific Fleet commander signed that afternoon. As part of his plan Halsey requested that two submarines patrol off Japan, tasked to monitor enemy forces that might jeopardize the mission. The Navy would divert all other subs south of the equator. That would allow Halsey to conclude that any ships sighted west of the rendezvous were hostile. The *Enterprise* sortied the next day at 12:32 p.m., accompanied by the cruisers *North Hampton* and *Salt Lake City*, the destroyers *Balch*, *Benham*, *Ellet*, and *Fanning*, and the oiler *Sabine*.

Journalist Robert Casey of the *Chicago Daily News*, who was on board the *Salt Lake City*, surveyed the scene as the ships departed. He had hopes of accompanying a massive task force of several carriers, battleships, and cruisers, but the eight ships that slipped out to sea appeared to be the "same old Punch and Judy show." "Maybe things are going to be different," Casey wrote in his diary that day. "But on the surface this looks like another assault on the outhouses of Wake."

Unlike the *Hornet*'s Mitscher, who shared the task force's destination with the crew soon after departure, Halsey sat on the news as hours turned into days, much to the frustration of many. The resourceful journalist Casey pressed everyone on board the *Salt Lake City* for details, including Commander John Ford, the Academy Award–winning director of *The Grapes of Wrath* and *How Green Was My Valley*, a naval reservist called to active duty. "All we know," Ford told him, "is that it's some sort of suicide."

Casey wasn't the only one to gripe about Halsey's secrecy, particularly as the warm Hawaiian days gave way to bitter nights as the carrier steamed north.

"Cold as all Alaska," one of the *Enterprise* aviators noted in his journal on April 12. "Only God and the admiral know what we are up here for. We're probably going to bomb Japan itself."

The frustrated journalist found he could do little more than take solace in the beauty of the vast and empty ocean. "The ships ahead of us in line on a glowing blue sea were misty gray like a procession of Gothic cathedrals," Casey wrote in his diary. "I stood for a time freezing and drinking in the terrific beauty of it all."

The *Hornet* had received news on April 9 of Halsey's delay and reversed course and slowed. The two task forces closed in on each other at 4:30 p.m. on April 12, when the *Hornet* detected radar transmissions 130 miles southwest. Lookouts on the *Hornet* spotted *Enterprise* search planes at 5:28 a.m. the next morning. Thirty-seven minutes later the masts of Halsey's force came into focus at a distance of 20 miles.

Enterprise pilot Tom Cheek towed a target for gunnery practice that morning. "As I flew over the *Hornet*, I looked down and saw those B-25s packed on the flight deck," he recalled. "Needless to say, I spent the next three and a half hours wondering about our destination. Tokyo wasn't even considered."

Cheek's surprise mirrored that of the sailors who crowded the deck of the *Enterprise*, peering through binoculars at the *Hornet*.

"They're B-25s!" announced one sailor.

"You're crazy, sailor," snorted one of the carrier's aviators. "A B-25 could never take off with a load—and if it did, it could never land aboard again."

"They won't have to carry a load, you dope, and they won't have to land. They're reinforcing some land base."

"Out here? Which land base?"

"I'll bet we're going through the Aleutians and deliver them to a secret Siberian base."

"Are they using army pilots on carriers? If so, our careers are over. Let's join the marines."

The two task forces merged. The *Hornet* took over as the guide and fleet center, with the oilers *Sabine* and *Cimarron* a thousand yards astern followed by the *Enterprise*. The cruisers *North Hampton* and *Vincennes* steamed in one column and the *Nashville* and *Salt Lake City* in another. The eight destroyers formed an inner and outer antisubmarine screen with a circular spacing of one mile as the force steamed due west. Weather permitting, pilots flew continuous daylight air patrols coupled with dawn and dusk search flights out to two hundred miles, sixty degrees off each bow.

On April 13 the *Enterprise*'s loudspeaker crackled as Halsey prepared to alert his men of the mission. "This force," he announced, "is bound for Tokyo."

"Never have I heard such a shout as burst from the *Enterprise*'s company!" the admiral later wrote. "Part of their eagerness came, I think, from the fact that Bataan had fallen four days earlier."

The admiral then messaged to the other ships in his task force details of the plan. "Intention fuel heavy ships about one thousand miles to westward," Halsey instructed. "Thence carriers cruisers to point five hundred miles east of Tokyo then launch army bombers on *Hornet* for attack. DDS and tankers remain vicinity fueling rejoin on retirement. Further operations as developments dictate."

Casey heard the news of the mission directly from the *Salt Lake City*'s skipper. This was no attack on Wake or Marcus Island, but an assault on the enemy's homeland. Casey surveyed the muscular task force of carriers, cruisers, and destroyers that cut through the swells. His earlier disappointment vanished. "This is a big force now," he wrote in his diary, "a force that the Japs would hardly dare take on without twice the number of ships and at least an even break of airplanes."

The skipper of the *Salt Lake City* came over the loudspeaker at 11 a.m. to warn his men to remain vigilant against enemy submarines.

"You are about to take part in a very historic event," he announced. "For the first time in the history of Japan, the home territory is about to be attacked. This attack will be in force and will undoubtedly have great effect."

The same day the task force crossed the 180th meridian, which serves as the international date line, skipping ahead one day to April 15. Casey noted the day's demise in his diary with a tombstone inscription:

Here lies
April 14, a Tuesday,
sacrificed to the west-bound crossing of the
international date line.

Each new day carried the task force another four hundred miles closer to Japan and at a cost to the *Hornet* of as much as fifty thousand gallons of fuel. Radiomen hunched over receivers twenty-four hours a day, monitoring Tokyo's commercial stations to decipher news and broadcast routines, while officers and crew manned battle stations at dawn and dusk. Mitscher ran his sailors through countless drills to prepare them for combat, from gunnery and damage control to abandon-ship exercises. The Navy's rigorous practice at times irked some of Doolittle's men. "It seemed to me," griped Robert Bourgeois, "that every time I started to sleep or eat that damn General Quarters would sound off."

The danger was reflected in *Cimarron* skipper Russell Ihrig's battle instructions, demanding that sailors toss all magazines overboard and use wet rags to wipe down bulkheads, light fixtures, furniture, overhead pipes, and wiring to eliminate flammable dust. He ordered officer state-rooms readied as battle dressing stations—complete with scissors or knives to cut off clothes—and instructed sailors to shave off beards and cut their hair to no longer than two inches. "Throw overboard *tonight all shoe polish*, hair oils and hair tonic. Wash your head and do not put on any hair-tonic or oils of any kind," he ordered. "Keep all unnecessary lights turned off throughout the ships at all times. Light takes electricity, electricity takes steam and steam takes oil. *We need that oil!*"

Bad weather continued to plague the mission, forcing the *Cimarron* to slow amid forty-two-knot winds to prevent structural damage. The *Vincennes* lost a man overboard on April 6—he was recovered from the fifty-one-degree seas by the destroyer *Meredith*—and the *Cimarron* lost another a few days later trying to refuel the *Hornet*, forcing a second rescue by the destroyer. Heavy seas one night cost the *Vincennes* a paravane along with a sixty-man lifeboat, including two oars and five gallons of water, while *Hornet* sailors had to rescue the raider Joseph Manske, trapped topside in a storm as he checked to make sure that his bomber was secure.

The hellacious seas, which caused the *Ruptured Duck*'s altimeter to vary by as much as two hundred feet, amazed even veteran sailors. "We ran into the God damnedest weather I've ever seen," recalled Lieutenant j.g. Robin Lindsey, a landing signal officer on the *Enterprise*. "For three days the waves were so high the deck was pitching so much that I had to have a person stand behind me to hold me on the landing signal plat-form so that I wouldn't fall down. Several times I did, and you can imag-ine the amazement on the pilot's face as he passed over with no signal officer there."

Tension mounted on board the ships as the task force closed in on Japan. "You could feel it in the wardroom, in the crew's mess, in the lookouts, and on the bridge," *Life* magazine editor John Field wrote. "How close to Tokyo could we get without being spotted? Nobody knew for certain."

Anxious for distractions, sailors listened over a shortwave radio to a San Francisco dance band. Others swapped jokes in the wardroom.

"Anybody seen the Staten Island ferry go by?" someone quipped.

The joke broke the tension, but all eyes soon drifted to the map that adorned the wardroom bulkhead, confirming what each sailor knew.

The task force was now on the enemy's home turf.

Even the *Hornet*'s chaplain, Edward Harp, harbored doubts.

"How are we going to make out on this deal?" he asked Mitscher.

"The mission has to be successful," the skipper replied. "The whole war does."

No one knew that more than Doolittle, whom Harp encountered one night after dinner up on deck near the bridge. "In the dusk I saw a lone figure there," the chaplain later wrote. "I stopped and watched a minute. It was Doolittle, walking up and down, his head bent characteristically. I could almost see him thinking, as he moved slowly from one rail to the other. In that moment I glimpsed the enormous responsibility resting on him. I left him there without speaking and retraced my steps."

Doolittle held a final inspection of each bomber several days before the mission's scheduled takeoff, passing out to every pilot a twenty-four-point checklist that included items ranging from guaranteeing that guns and bombs were properly loaded to stowing maps, charts, and first aid kits along with thermoses of fresh water and bagged lunches. Doolittle hoped the *Hornet* would deliver the raiders to within 450 miles of Japan. Even if crews had to launch from a distance of 550 miles, he predicted, the mission would in all likelihood prove successful. Doolittle set an outside limit of 650 miles. Beyond that, and he doubted his crews would have the fuel to reach China. Some of the raiders found the news unsettling. "It sure didn't sound very inviting," Joseph Manske wrote in his diary, "but it's too late now to start worrying about anything."

The Army airmen made personal preparations for the mission. Shorty Manch packed his portable phonograph, while Ken Reddy used his poker earnings to pay his mess bill, lending ten dollars apiece to William Birch, James Parker, and Harold Watson before packing up and mailing his watch home, careful to insure it for fifty dollars. Robert Emmens penned a final letter to his mother on *Hornet* stationery. "It may be quite some time before any of us can send anyone any word," he wrote, "so just don't worry, and feel that I'm doing something at last to help in this damnable mess."

The airmen received a shock a few days before takeoff when operators picked up an English propaganda broadcast from Radio Tokyo. "Reuters, British news agency, has announced that three American bombers have dropped bombs on Tokyo," the broadcast stated. "This is a most laughable story. They know it is absolutely impossible for enemy bombers to get within 500 miles of Tokyo. Instead of worrying about such foolish things, the Japanese people are enjoying the fine spring sunshine and the fragrance of cherry blossoms." The news alarmed Halsey and sickened the raiders, who had hoped to be the first to attack the enemy's capital. Doolittle in contrast doubted the report's veracity, which proved so fantastic that it made headlines in the United States. "The Japanese radio strangely denied today that three American planes had bombed Tokyo," the *New York Times* reported. "It was strange, because the Tokyo radio went to great lengths to deny something that apparently nobody reported."

The *Cimarron* came along the port side of the *Hornet* at 6:20 a.m. on April 17, topping the carrier off with 200,634 gallons. The oiler next refueled the *Northampton* and then the *Salt Lake City*, while the *Sabine* topped off the *Nashville*, *Enterprise*, and *Vincennes*. The seas crashed over the bows as gale-force winds blew out of the southeast at forty-one knots. A thousand miles east of Tokyo, visibility dropped to as little as one mile.

At 2:44 p.m. the *Hornet* and *Enterprise* accompanied by the four cruisers pulled ahead of the oilers and destroyers for the final run toward Tokyo. The *Hornet* guided the reduced force at twenty-five knots, trailed by the *Enterprise* at a distance of just fifteen hundred yards. The *Northampton* and *Vincennes* formed a column off the *Hornet*'s starboard bow, while the *Nashville* and *Salt Lake City* took up a similar position off the carrier's port bow. "I had left the destroyers behind so we wouldn't be hampered if we had to get out of there in a hurry as we approached Japan," Halsey recalled. "I was like the country soldier who wanted no part of the cavalry because he didn't want to be bothered with a horse in case of retreat. We didn't know what might happen."

Sailors brought the incendiary bombs up to the flight deck via the no. 3 elevator, while the demolition bombs rode up in the regular elevators. Others helped load the ammunition for the nose and turret guns, a mixture of armor-piercing, incendiary, and tracer rounds. Two freshly painted white lines on the flight deck served as guides—one for the nose-wheel, the other for the left wheel—promising pilots six feet of clearance with the carrier's island. Airplane handlers spotted the bombers for take-off half an hour before sunset. Even with the sixteenth bomber's tail dangling precariously over the carrier's stern, Doolittle in the lead plane would have just 467 feet to take off.

Mitscher summoned Doolittle to the bridge.

"Jim, we're in the enemy's backyard now," the skipper told him. "Anything could happen from here on in. I think it's time for that little ceremony we talked about."

The airmen assembled on the flight deck, joined by a Navy photographer. The U.S. Battle Fleet had in October 1908 visited Yokohama, where commemoration medals were presented by a representative of the emperor. Two Brooklyn Navy Yard employees, master rigger Henry Vormstein and shipwright John Laurey, who had received such medals as seamen on the battleship *Connecticut*, returned them to Navy Secretary Frank Knox after the attack on Pearl Harbor. "May we request," Vormstein wrote, "you to attach it to a bomb and return it to Japan in that manner."

Daniel Quigley, a former sailor on the battleship *Kearsarge* who now lived in Pennsylvania, wrote a similar letter to Knox, enclosing his medal. "Following the lead of my former Fleet mates," he wrote, "I herewith enclose the one issued to me and trust that it will eventually find its way back in company with a bomb that will rock the throne of the 'Son of Heaven' in the Kojimachi Ku district of Tokyo."

Jurika contributed his own medal, one he had received in the name of the emperor from his time as an attaché.

The reserved Mitscher gave a brief speech to the airmen and read aloud the messages from Admiral King, General Marshall, and General Arnold. Doolittle and his men then tied the medals to the bombs. Thatcher grinned as he attached one.

"I don't want to set the world on fire—just Tokyo," someone scrawled in chalk on one bomb. Other inscriptions read, "You'll get a BANG out of this!" and "Bombs Made in America and Laid in Japan." Marine Corporal Larry Bogart, the skipper's orderly, honored his girlfriend and his parents. "This one is from Peggy," he wrote on one, and on another, "This is from Mom and Pop Bogart." "We painted them all up with slogans and almost everybody autographed them," recalled Robert Noone, a signal officer on the *Hornet*. "We were proud to take part in the venture."

Men from the extra bomber crews pleaded to get on a flight, waving fistfuls of cash. "One of the most vivid memories I have of the Tokyo raid is of a group of men who were willing to pay $150 apiece to die," Thad Blanton later wrote. "These men tried every way they knew how to beg, borrow or steal a seat on the raid." None of the sixteen crews would give up a spot, a feeling well captured by Reddy in his diary. "It would take more than money could buy to secure my place on this trip."

Doolittle held a final meeting with his men in the wardroom. He kept his instructions brief, warning that takeoff could happen at any moment. Under no circumstances were the men to fly to Vladivostok. He reiterated his demand that no one target the emperor's palace or any other nonmilitary target. "If all goes well," Doolittle told his men, "I'll take off so as to arrive over Tokyo at dusk. The rest of you will take off two or three hours later and can use my fires as a homing beacon."

He gave his men, as always, a final chance to bow out.

None did.

Doolittle concluded with a promise.

"When we get to Chungking," he told them, "I'm going to give you all a party that you won't forget."

The men dispersed, and Lawson climbed into bed the night of the seventeenth. Across the task force others did the same; the risk of sudden danger prompted many to slip beneath the sheets still in uniform.

"Listen, you fellows, there's going to be no card playing in here tonight," one of Lawson's naval roommates ordered the others. "Lawson's got to get some sleep for a change. He might need it."

LIEUTENANT COLONEL EDWARD ALEXANDER and Major Edward Backus lifted off on April 13 from Chungking in a twin-engine DC-3 cargo plane to make final preparations for the Chinese airfields to receive

Doolittle and his men. The Army aviators planned to fly first to Chengtu and swap the lumbering American cargo plane for two Chinese fighters, before pressing on to Kweilin, Kian, Yushan, Chuchow, and Lishui. Special Aviation Project No. 1 remained a guarded secret. Rather than risk making arrangements via radio, the Army wanted Alexander to personally brief airfield commanders on the operation. Even the use of two Chinese fighters as opposed to a single cargo plane was designed to prevent any enemy spies from questioning why an American plane had visited such remote airfields. "My instructions were to maintain absolute secrecy," Alexander wrote in his report. "Therefore this flight was undertaken without advising the Chinese Air Force or any one in China of the intended destination."

Alexander's orders were to make sure local airfield commanders assembled everything necessary to help the Tokyo raiders. The airfield at Kweilin would need 10,000 gallons of 100-octane fuel and 100 gallons of 120-grade lubricating oil; each of the other stations would require just 5,000 gallons of fuel and 100 gallons of lube oil. Alexander also would have to instruct local personnel on how to rapidly refuel the bombers, allowing Doolittle and his men to remain on the ground as little as possible in a region that straddled the front lines with Japanese forces. Furthermore, local commanders would need English-speaking personnel, landing flares, and radio transmitters to broadcast homing signals to help guide the raiders. "Signal transmitted will consist of figure 57, key held down 1 minute, figure 57, key held down 1 minute, figure 57, then off for 1 minute," advised a cable from Chungking. "This signal will be repeated continuously for 2 hours before daylight on the date you specify."

That date was April 20.

The message traffic that filled folders in Washington and Chungking indicated that preparations in China progressed smoothly. Stilwell had requested a range of details, from the size of bomber fuel openings down to whether the fliers would need food and water. But those messages proved little more than a bureaucratic veneer over the ragtag efforts to make arrangements in China, driven in part by Arnold's refusal to brief Stilwell on the true nature of the operation. The forced secrecy, poor communication, and distrust of Chinese leaders and the remote and unsecure airfields at the mission's terminus combined to create a possible disaster for Doolittle and his men, a likelihood that only increased as the

Hornet steamed closer to Japan. As evidence of those challenges, Alexander's mission to inspect the airfields was not the first such attempt. Stilwell's air operations officer, Colonel Clayton Bissell, had ten days earlier dispatched a lieutenant in an aged C-39 cargo plane, instructing him to swallow his notes if captured. "Neither Lieut. Spurrier nor the C-39 are considered suitably equipped for the execution of the assigned mission," Bissell confessed in his report, "but there is no alternative."

Bissell's assessment proved sadly accurate. Spurrier's plane crashed before he could complete the mission, but Alexander drew an important lesson from Spurrier's failure—he elected to use two fighters this time, in part to double the mission's chances of success. Aside from logistical problems, other challenges arose that also threatened the operation. Japanese bombers accompanied by fighters twice blasted the two most eastern airfields on April 1, destroying 4,500 gallons of gasoline. Bombers returned the next day and targeted the three most eastern airfields, though this time inflicting negligible damage. The airfield at Lishui came under Japanese attack on April 3. Tokyo claimed in radio broadcasts to have launched the raids because America had lengthened the runways so as to be able to use them to bomb Japan. This struck Vinegar Joe as more than just a coincidence. "Three essential fields have all been bombed," Stilwell confided in his diary. "Leak? Or just precaution by the Japs? Suspect talk in Washington."

Alexander and Backus landed the DC-3 at Chengtu, departing again at 4 p.m. in two Curtis Hawk fighters. Weather reports predicted poor conditions around Kweilin. Alexander pressed on, only to find that the low-lying clouds over the mountains and valleys made it impossible to land. "The surface weather conditions at the place and time were approximately zero zero. The top of the overcast was at 12,000 feet," he wrote in his report. "The pursuit aircraft are not equipped for night flying or with radios." The pilots had no choice but to turn back toward Chungking. Arriving over the Chinese capital at 6:30 p.m., they found the area buried in clouds. Alexander dove through the clouds and managed to land his plane on a sandbar in the Chia-ling River, though his fighter struck river boulders and wrecked the landing gear. Backus refused to risk it and bailed out with his parachute. The men rushed by the fastest means possible to the nearest airfield, at Sui-ning, arriving there three days later.

Alexander and Backus set out again from Chengtu on April 17, this time in a DC-3 carrying four Chinese radio operators to be stationed at Kian, Yushan, Chuchow, and Lishui, each one conversant in English. Poor weather combined with radio failure, however, forced the plane to put down for the night at Kunming. The Army airmen refused to give up, taking off again the next morning. The urgency to complete the mission led Alexander to arrange through the Chinese air force for homing signals as well as radio assistance to help with the landing. Flying at times on instruments, the DC-3 finally reached Kweilin, circling for half an hour above cloud-covered peaks that reached up to fifteen thousand feet. Efforts to raise the ground by radio failed. Alexander had no choice yet again but to turn back. "It is to be particularly noted that concrete procedures and understandings had been arrived at with the Chinese as to radio assistance at Kweilin," he stressed in his report. "Yet, none was available."

Struggles continued to mount on the political front as well. Chiang Kai-shek had initially agreed to the use of the five airfields in late March, though he did not know the bombers would arrive after a raid on Tokyo. War conditions in China, however, continued to deteriorate, prompting Chiang to urge American leaders to postpone the operation until the end of May, a move he argued would give his ground forces time to protect Chuchow from possible Japanese occupation. The generalissimo further requested that the bombers be diverted to attack Japanese forces in Burma and in the Bay of Bengal. General Marshall fired off an urgent message on April 12 to Stilwell. Delay was not an option: a sixteen-ship task force and ten thousand sailors steamed toward Japan. "Execution of first special mission is so imminent that it is impossible to recall," Marshall cabled. "Their arrival at field agreed upon should be immediately anticipated and all arrangements perfected." Arnold followed up the next day. "First project cannot be stopped," he cabled. "We are depending on your assistance as regards flares for landing and guidance and supplies for refueling."

Stilwell met with Chiang on April 14, reporting that the generalissimo still pressed for a delay. The general followed up the next day with news that Chiang demanded that officials voice his concerns again to senior leaders in Washington. The generalissimo refused to allow the bombers to land at Chuchow, but reluctantly consented to the use of the other four airfields as well as one at Heng-yang. An astute politician as well as warrior, Marshall hastened to prevent any political fallout, directing Stilwell to explain America's position to the generalissimo. "We regret the apparent misunderstanding concerning the timing of the first special mission," Marshall instructed Stilwell to tell Chiang. "It appears that we must have failed to make our intentions sufficiently clear to the Generalissimo because we have understood for some weeks that the project was desired by him. The necessity for absolute secrecy did not permit reference to the matter except in the most guarded language."

Marshall framed the operation as though it were motivated by American altruism to help the generalissimo, noting that airmen and bombers would remain in China afterward to fly other missions. American leaders therefore assumed Chiang would want the operation to take place as soon as possible. Absent from Marshall's message was any mention of what the United States hoped to gain or of the horrific fallout everyone from Marshall down to Doolittle knew would soon befall the Chinese. "The project is now so far advanced that it is impossible to recall," Marshall concluded. "Please inform the Generalissimo that I deeply regret the lack of a complete understanding with him on this point and sincerely hope that no embarrassment will be occasioned to him by the incident." Marshall's final words were for Stilwell. "Please report to the War Department promptly," he ordered, "the first news you may have of the accomplishment of this special project with the strength of the detachment completing the task."

Chiang's repeated objections caused enough alarm that General Arnold ordered a one-page memo sent April 16 to Roosevelt. Marshall followed up the next day with a message to Chiang, directing Stilwell to present it personally. "I want personally to express to you my deep regret that this matter was not brought to your attention in detail, at its inception," Marshall wrote. "The president is fully appreciative of your difficult situation and is particularly anxious that all our operations in your region be under your complete control and in conformity with your desires. Since he has learned that you consider the execution of this mission undesirable at this time he would be very glad to cancel it if this were possible and he regrets that he cannot now do so because of the imminence of execution. He is therefore especially grateful to you for the very effective measures you have directed to be taken to make the venture a success."

Marshall messaged Stilwell on April 18. This time his concerns focused not on Chiang but on the actual operation. America wanted to keep the mission a secret. "Desire that there be no repeat no publicity of any kind connected with the special bombing mission," Marshall ordered. "It is our purpose to maintain an atmosphere of complete mystery including origin, nationality, destination, and results of this type of effort. So far as public information is concerned you are directed to deny all knowledge of the incident and of any connection therewith. You are directed also to make earnest request upon the Generalissimo to observe this policy and to cooperate with you in the effort. As quickly as you obtain any definite information of this affair, either through survivors or otherwise, you are directed to render a report by urgent message to the War Department."

CHAPTER 10

═══════

★

Measures now in hand by Pacific Fleet have not been
conveyed to you in detail because of secrecy requirements
but we hope you will find them effective when they
can be made known to you shortly.

—FRANKLIN ROOSEVELT TO WINSTON CHURCHILL,
APRIL 16, 1942

THE DARKENED TASK FORCE cut through the swells at twenty knots
in the predawn hours of April 18, 1942, more than eight hundred miles
from Tokyo. The *Hornet* led the armada on a course almost due west at
267 degrees trailed by the carrier *Enterprise*. The cruisers *Northampton*
and *Vincennes* steamed off the *Hornet*'s starboard bow while the *Nashville* and *Salt Lake City* covered the port. At 3:10 a.m. *Enterprise* radar
operators reported two surface craft off the port bow at a range of 21,000
yards, or twelve miles. Two minutes later a distant light appeared on
approximately the same bearing. General quarters immediately sounded,
and throughout the carrier sailors sprang from bunks and darted to battle stations, readying ammunition and yanking off gun covers. The news
broadcast to the crew was short: "Two enemy surface craft reported."

Though Halsey's four cruisers and two carriers far outgunned the
enemy vessels, the veteran admiral knew better than to engage and ruin
the element of surprise, if radar had not already alerted the enemy. The

overcast skies void of moon and stars shrouded his force in darkness at a time when he needed to push on as far as possible, even if that was only until dawn. Every hour—every mile—now mattered. Halsey ordered the task force via a high-frequency, short-range radio to come right ninety degrees. The contacts faded from the *Enterprise*'s radar at 3:41 a.m. at a range of fifteen miles. The ship relaxed from general quarters, resuming a westerly course at 4:15 a.m. At first light three scout bombers roared off the *Enterprise*'s flight deck to patrol two hundred miles west while three more bombers and eight fighters took off for combat and inner air patrols.

Dawn revealed how much the weather had continued to deteriorate as the task force closed in on the enemy's homeland. Low broken clouds swept across the empty horizon, peppered by frequent rainsqualls. Winds of as much as thirty knots whipped up white caps that broke across the bows of Halsey's force. Journalist Robert Casey on board the *Salt Lake City* captured the scene best in his diary. "Went on deck at 5 o'clock to face a howling wind. Sky gray. Sea pitching," the *Chicago Daily News* reporter wrote. "Water is rolling down the decks, sometimes a couple of feet deep. It's hard keeping upright." Doolittle raider Ken Reddy ventured up top of the *Hornet*, recording a similar scene that morning in his diary. "The sea was rough and the airplanes were pulling against their ropes like circus elephants against their chains."

Lieutenant j.g. Osborne Wiseman was patrolling the skies ahead of the task force at 5:58 a.m., when he spotted a small fishing boat bobbing atop the dark waters. The naval aviator, following orders, did not attack, but attempted to avoid detection. He circled back and buzzed the carrier, alerting Halsey via message drop of the boat forty-two miles ahead. Wiseman noted that he believed enemy lookouts had spotted him. Halsey again chose not to engage, but ordered the task force to swing southwest, a move that gave him only a brief reprieve as *Hornet* lookouts spotted another patrol at 7:38 a.m. at a range of more than eight miles. Radio operators on the ninety-ton *Nitto Maru No. 23*, part of Admiral Yamamoto's defensive net, fired off a message to Tokyo: "Three enemy carriers sighted. Position, 600 nautical miles east of Inubosaki."

The time to fight had arrived.

The *Nashville* sounded general quarters and via flag hoist requested permission to fire. Halsey gave the order at 7:52 a.m. The cruiser opened fire one minute later with its main battery at a range of nine thousand yards, or about five miles. The fifteen six-inch guns—mounted three to a turret—thundered across the open sea, each capable of hurling a 130-pound projectile almost fifteen miles. The guns barked again and again. Armor-piercing projectiles pounded into the waves around the target at 2,500-feet per second, throwing up so much spray that the *Nitto Maru* appeared to vanish.

The *Nashville* ceased fire at 7:55 a.m. to allow the spray to settle and then resumed the assault one minute later. Even firing at a rate of almost 150 rounds per minute, the hail of projectiles continued to miss. Heavy swells with a height from crest to trough of twenty feet obscured the trawler, leaving only the mast tops visible. Furthermore, many of the wave tops shielded the *Nitto Maru*, intercepting the cruiser's fire. The *Nashville* increased speed to twenty-five knots and closed to 4,500 yards, swinging to port in order to shoot straight down the wave troughs.

The cruiser's heavy gunfire sparked excitement throughout the task force as anxious sailors, airmen, and journalists all struggled for a glimpse of the battle. "Terrific barrage with 15 six-inch guns. Shells are tossed like machine-gun bullets—eight salvos in the air at once," Casey wrote in his diary. "Flashes run around ship like lights on an electric sign." The scene likewise amazed *Life* magazine editor John Field. "Her guns blazed big and red," he wrote, "and rolled like thunder."

Hornet fighter pilot John Sutherland found the experience surreal. "I remember thinking that it was a very curious way to watch my first active engagement," he recalled. "We stood out on the flight deck watching the fire between our ships and the meager return from the Japanese, much in the manner of tennis players that you see in the newsreels with their heads going back and forth watching the action."

"Well, if it's all like this," Sutherland thought to himself, "this will be fine."

Jurika climbed from the flight deck up to the bridge for a better view. "I could see the salvos from the *Nashville*," he remembered. "There were heavy swells and the picket boat was going up, it would be on top of a swell and then it would be seen, then it would be down, and you couldn't see a thing except perhaps the top of its mast. The splashes were all around it, but it was still there."

The gunfire startled many of Doolittle's men.

Brick Holstrom grabbed a Navy ensign in one of the *Hornet*'s passageways. "What's going on?" he demanded.

"I don't know," the officer replied. "I think they're firing at a submarine."

The *Nashville*'s thunderclap nearly took the hat off mission doctor Thomas White, while bombardier Jacob DeShazer stood in awe on the carrier's deck. "The whole side of that Navy ship looked like it was on fire," he recalled, "booming away."

Eight *Enterprise* fighters circled five thousand feet overhead as the *Nashville* blasted the *Nitto Maru*. The aviators dove to attack, only to spot a second patrol, the eighty-eight-ton *Nanshin Maru No. 21*. The pilots diverted to strafe the smaller boat, raking the tiny trawler from stem to stern with .50-caliber machine-gun fire. One of the pilots made eleven passes, burning through at least twelve hundred rounds. The obliterated boat began to settle, prompting the pilots to join the attack on the *Nitto Maru*.

Enterprise bomber pilot Ensign John Roberts hungered for action. He pushed his bomber over at 7,500 feet and dove on the *Nitto Maru*, but pulled out of the attack at 3,500 feet to avoid one of the fighters. Roberts returned with a glide-bomb attack, dropping one 500-pound bomb, which missed by about 100 feet. He joined the fighters to strafe the dogged *Nitto Maru* until most ran out of ammunition. Lieutenant Roger Mehle summed up the attack in his report: "Liquidation of enemy personnel. Vessel placed out of operation. When left it was wallowing in a trough of the waves." Another pilot was more succinct, describing his fellow fliers as "a bloodthirsty bunch of bastards."

The *Nitto Maru* erupted in flames at 8:21 a.m. and finally slipped beneath the waves two minutes later, exactly half an hour after the assault began. Two survivors bobbed in the water, neither of whom could be recovered; the skipper watched one of the injured sailors drown. The *Nashville* had hoped to silence the *Nitto Maru*, but radiomen picked up continual transmissions for twenty-seven minutes after the cruiser fired the first shot. There was no doubt Japan now knew of the approaching armada.

The ninety-ton fishing boat had robbed the Nashville of 928 rounds of six-inch ammunition, including 13 rounds needed to clear the guns after the battle ended. The skipper was mortified, blaming the poor shooting on his inexperienced gun crews and the churning seas that helped shield the *Nitto Maru*. "Expenditure of 915 rounds to sink a sampan appears ridiculous, and obviously was excessive," he wrote in his report, "but in this instance was not wholly inexcusable."

DOOLITTLE HAD WATCHED the battle alongside Mitscher on the *Hornet*'s bridge.

"It looks like you're going to have to be on your way soon," the skipper told him. "They know we're here."

Halsey flashed a message about that time to the *Hornet*. "Launch planes," the admiral ordered. "To Col. Doolittle and gallant command, good luck and God bless you."

Doolittle shook hands with Mitscher and then darted below to his cabin to grab his bag, yelling at his men he encountered to load up. Many of the raiders had just sat down to breakfast in the wardroom when the carrier's loudspeaker crackled to life. "Now hear this! Now hear this! Army pilots, man your planes!"

Others proved equally ill prepared. Ross Greening had just finished a letter to his wife, while Edgar McElroy relaxed with a copy of the *Hornet*'s Plan of the Day. News of the aircrew's imminent departure caught Jack Sims in the most precarious position. "I happened to be in the 'head' when I heard the order," the pilot recalled. "Believe me; that was the best catharsis one could ever ask for!"

Doolittle ran into Miller.

"Would you help get the pilots in the airplanes?"

Miller agreed.

Sailors darted across the wet decks to help the Army airmen yank off engine and gun turret covers. Others topped off fuel tanks, rocking the bombers back and forth to get air bubbles out. Crews handed five-gallon gasoline cans up through the rear hatches to the gunners, as others untied ropes and removed wheel chocks so Navy handlers could position the bombers for takeoff. Airmen armed the ordnance already loaded in the bomb bays, as crews brought up the last of the incendiaries from below deck. "We had spent months preparing for this first bombing of Japan," navigator Chase Nielsen recalled, "and we were keyed up like a football team going into the big game."

Problems soon arose.

Davy Jones had suffered a leak in his bomb bay tank only the day before, forcing technicians to patch the bladder and then leave it empty overnight to dry. As crews now rushed to fill the 225-gallon rubber sac and top off the wing tanks, they discovered that the Navy had shut off gas lines, a common procedure in the event of a surprise attack. Ross Greening ordered his crew chief to haul his extra tins over to Jones, optimistic that the Navy would turn the lines back on in time to allow him to finish fueling.

Harold Watson had green-lighted the replacement of his bomber's fouled spark plugs that morning before general quarters. "When the alarm sounded, I found all the cowling off the left engine and all the plugs out!" he recalled. "The last piece of cowling was snapped in place as the ship ahead started its engines."

Shorty Manch appeared alongside Ted Lawson's *Ruptured Duck* with a fruitcake tin in hand. "Hey," he shouted up to bombardier Bob Clever. "Will you-all do a fellow a big favor and carry my phonograph records under your seat? I'll take my record-player along in my plane and we'll meet in Chungking and have us some razz-ma-tazz."

Miller stopped by as well, extending his hand for a farewell shake. "I wish to hell I could go with you."

Airmen checked in with the *Hornet*'s navigation room for the latest weather reports, wind information, and the ship's location. Crews knew that the magnetic compasses, after more than two weeks aboard the steel carrier, were far out of calibration. Furthermore, the squalls would prevent navigators from using a sextant to shoot sun or star shots. Pilots would have to fly dead reckoning to Japan. Compounding the challenge was a twenty-four-knot headwind they would have to battle. The biggest concern, however, came down to distance. The *Hornet* remained 824 statute miles east of Tokyo, almost twice as far as Doolittle had originally planned.

Ross Greening was inspecting each plane, making sure the bombs were all armed, when navigator Frank Kappeler approached.

"Captain Greening, we are over 800 miles from Tokyo," Kappeler exclaimed. "I didn't know we were going to be this far away."

Greening chased down and informed Doolittle, who merely nodded and did not utter a word.

He already knew.

News of the *Hornet*'s distance from Japan soon spread throughout the crews. "I wasn't concerned about it," recalled Hank Potter, Doolittle's navigator. "We had full confidence in our pilot. We had full confidence in our airplane; we had full confidence in ourselves, and we had this to do."

Others didn't share Potter's confidence.

The likelihood of running out of fuel loomed large. "The way things are now, we have about enough to get us within 200 miles of the China coast, and that's all," Jack Hilger leveled with his crew. "If anyone wants to withdraw, he can do it now. We can replace him from the men who are going to be left aboard. Nothing will ever be said about it, and it won't be held against you. It's your right. It's up to you."

Hilger's men absorbed the news.

Bombardier Herb Macia remembered his parents and his wife, Mary Alice, pregnant with the couple's son. He thought of everything he wished he had told them before he left, drawing comfort in the idea that his death would at least be honorable. "This couldn't have happened to me, but it's happening to me, so I'm going to go in and really do it right," he concluded. "That's all I care about!"

Others in the crew shared Macia's determination.

"Not a man withdrew," Jacob Eierman, Hilger's engineer, later wrote. "Although I don't suppose any of them felt any better than I did."

Brick Holstrom warmed up the engines; then his navigator climbed in and delivered the bad news. "What the hell do we do now?" he thought.

Pilot Billy Farrow asked bombardier Jacob DeShazer whether he knew how to row a boat, while a sergeant shouted to DeShazer as he climbed in the back, "We just got one chance in a thousand of making it."

It wasn't just the airmen who were worried.

"We knew that the pilots really didn't have a Chinaman's chance of getting to China with those airplanes," Miller recalled. "It was just too far."

Despite the poor prospects posed by the added distance, aircrews still hurried to prepare for takeoff, stowing gear, warming up engines, and going over checklists. Carl Wildner did so even as his stomach churned. "I was scared," the navigator on the second bomber later wrote.

"We knew the odds were against us and it seemed to me we were doing things without thinking—like automatons. I guess we were and maybe that's the way it was supposed to be."

The *Hornet* swung into the wind at 8:03 a.m. and increased speed to twenty-two knots. The seas crashed against the flattop's bow, alarming even the most veteran sailors. "It's the only time in my life," Halsey recalled, "I ever saw green water come over the bow and right onto the flight deck of a carrier."

Navy handlers positioned the bombers as far back on the flight deck as possible, two abreast and crisscrossed. The near-gale-force winds coupled with the revving engines made it difficult for the flight deck crew to maneuver, each of whom wore a safety line to keep from getting blown into the whirling props. "It sure was windy!" recalled George Bernstein, a flight deck crewman. "We had to literally drop to the deck and hang on with our fingers in the tie-down fittings when the B-25s revved up."

Over this roar Miller shouted instructions to the pilots: keep the trim tabs in neutral and the flaps down. Any changes he would display on a blackboard. "Look at me," Miller demanded, "before you let your brakes off!"

Doolittle climbed into the lead bomber alongside his copilot, Second Lieutenant Dick Cole. Throughout the plane sat the navigator, Second Lieutenant Hank Potter, the bombardier, Staff Sergeant Fred Braemer, and the gunner and crew chief, Staff Sergeant Paul Leonard. Rain beat down on the cockpit windshield as Doolittle stared down the 467-foot flight deck. The days of practice and the nights of worry had come down to this moment—not just for Doolittle but for all sixteen aircrews. "We all stood around, watching and sweating it out," recalled Eierman. "We had done plenty of practicing—on land—but this was going to be the first real take-off from a carrier with one of our big bombers."

The loudspeakers crackled on board the other ships in the task force: "*Hornet* preparing to launch bombers for attack on Tokyo."

Troops ranging from cooks and quartermasters to engineers and gunners crowded rain-soaked decks for a chance to witness the historic event—a few even saw an opportunity to profit. "Sailors, like stockbrokers, work everything out by betting, and there was soon heavy money down on both sides: would they make it, would they not?" recalled Alvin Kernan, an *Enterprise* plane handler. "The odds were that the B-25s wouldn't have been on the *Hornet* if there had not been successful tests somewhere, but with all the skepticism of an old salt about anything the services did, I put down ten dollars at even money that less than half of them would get into the air."

Doolittle revved up the bomber's twin engines and checked the magnetos. The carrier's speed and the furious storm combined to create as much as fifty miles per hour of wind across the *Hornet*'s deck, perfect conditions for takeoff. He flashed the thumbs up sign to Lieutenant Edgar Osborne, the signal officer who clutched a checkered flag. Sailors pulled the wheel chocks out as Osborne waved his flag in circles, signaling Doolittle to push the throttle all the way forward.

"Everything all right, Paul?" Doolittle asked his crew chief.

"Everything okay, Colonel."

Osborne watched the *Hornet*'s bow so as to release Doolittle just as the carrier began to dive down the face of a wave. The time required for a B-25 to traverse the flight deck meant that the bomber would reach the bow on the upswing, catapulting the plane into the air. Osborne dropped the flag and Doolittle released the brakes. The bomber roared down the flight deck at 8:20 a.m. "The scream of those two engines, the excitement and urgency, made an incredible sight. I was lying face down on the wet deck, clutching tiedown plates to keep from being blown back by the terrific wind. When Doolittle's B-25 began to move, it seemed unreal," Greening later wrote. "I had chills running up and down my spine from excitement."

Doolittle's left wheels hugged the white line that ran down the deck. He passed fifty feet, then one hundred.

Then two hundred.

"He'll never make it," someone shouted.

The bomber charged toward the end of the flight deck and then appeared to vanish.

"Doolittle's gone," McClure thought to himself. "We'll have to make it without him."

The plane then roared up and into the gray skies over the bow.

"Yes!" Knobloch shouted. "Yes!"

Sailors crowded along the flight deck and carrier's island erupted in cheers. "The shout that went up should have been heard in Tokyo," Thomas White, the mission's doctor, remembered. "We were all yelling and pounding each other on the back. I don't think there was a sound pair of vocal cords in the flotilla."

On board the cruiser *Salt Lake City* journalist Robert Casey captured the moment in his diary. "First bomber off the *Hornet*. Miraculous," he wrote. "The carrier is diving, deluging deck with white water. The big plane is just about catapulted as the ship lifts out of the sea."

In the skies overhead Doolittle instructed Cole to raise the wheels as he circled over the *Hornet*, where the carrier's course was displayed in large figures from the gun turret abaft the island. Doolittle paralleled the flight deck, allowing Potter to calculate any error with his magnetic compass before he pressed on toward Tokyo.

On deck below First Lieutenant Travis Hoover throttled up his bomber. The aircraft shook and shuddered. Hoover's mouth was dry as he stared down the flight deck at the bow, now buried in a wave. Osborne dropped the flag and Hoover released the brakes, charging down the runway just five minutes after Doolittle. "I was running out of deck," he recalled. "I came back on the yoke and she stood up like a bucking bronco."

The bow wash pushed the bomber's nose even higher. Sailors and airmen alike looked on with horror, convinced the aircraft would stall and crash. Hoover and copilot Bill Fitzhugh stiff-armed the controls to wrestle the bomber's nose back down as the plane appeared to dive toward the waves.

"Up! Up!" airmen on deck shouted. "Pull it up!"

Hoover did and soon regained control; a sense of relief washed over him. "I felt wonderful, almost euphoric," he recalled. "We're airborne."

The graceless takeoff failed to impress some of the naval aviators, one of whom compared his vacillating takeoff to that of a "kangaroo."

The third pilot in the queue, Bob Gray, stunned his fellow fliers when he roared down the flight deck at 8:30 a.m., trading brown lace-ups for cowboy boots. "They are the most comfortable shoes in the world," he professed. "Just the thing for walking."

Miller watched Gray climb into the skies, then scrawled a note on his blackboard, reminding pilots to keep the stabilizer in neutral. The fourth, fifth, and six bombers took off successfully over the next ten minutes.

Ted Lawson had tested the *Ruptured Duck*'s flaps during the engine run-up, but in the excitement failed to lower them again before he released the brakes at 8:43 a.m. "We watched his plane disappear before the bow of the ship," Greening recalled, "then come waddling back up like some big bullfrog, right on the water ahead of the carrier."

In his report Miller reflected on Lawson's near disaster with a bit of humor, noting the most important fact: "He got away with it."

York shot down the flight deck next, at 8:46 a.m.

"Nice take-off, Ski," Emmens said. "How did it seem compared to the practice take-offs you've been making on the ground back at Eglin?"

"How the hell should I know?" York answered. "I never made one."

The pilots now settled into a rhythm, as bombers nine through thirteen followed one another at just three-minute intervals. Each plane that took off safely not only added a few extra feet of deck space for the next pilot but also helped boost the confidence of all the others. That was certainly the case for pilot Bill Bower. "It seemed like he was as unconcerned about this raid as he could possibly be," recalled his navigator, Bill Pound. "My impression was that it was just another cross-country trip to him. Only difference was that the take-off strip was a little shorter than usual."

Greening didn't quite share the sureness of his colleague. "I could see many faces peering down from the bridge and navigation rail on the carrier's island. All of the crewmen whose aircraft hadn't been brought aboard were there," he later wrote. "I wondered how many still were willing to change places with us now."

By 9:15 a.m. all but one of the bombers had safely lifted off; the earlier thrill now waned. The tail of the *Bat out of Hell*, the final plane, dangled over the carrier's stern just as a strong wind swept across the deck at 9:19 a.m., lifting the B-25's nose and threatening to topple the bomber into the ocean. "Sailors, slipping on the wet decks and fighting the wind, swarmed around our plane," recalled copilot Bobby Hite, "every available man grabbing a handhold on the nose and front wheel."

Seaman First Class Robert Wall, amid the struggle, tumbled into the *Bat out of Hell*'s left prop, gouging his back and cutting his left arm at the shoulder.

DeShazer was on the deck to pull the wheel chocks when the accident occurred. He surveyed the bloody scene with horror.

"Give them hell for me," Wall muttered, a message DeShazer couldn't hear over the roar of the engines, but could read on the seaman's lips.

"Help me get him to one side," DeShazer barked at one of the other sailors. The two men pulled the injured the seaman to safety.

The tragedy shocked the crew.

"The seaman's arm was practically cut off," navigator George Barr recalled. "This accident unnerved me and it was all I could think about as we lined up for our takeoff. I hoped it wasn't going to be a taste of worse to come."

DeShazer climbed up into the bomber, only to discover more problems. The tail of the previous plane had punctured a hole in the Plexiglas nose.

"Should I tell the pilot," he wondered.

Doolittle had warned that crews would push any defective plane over the *Hornet*'s side. DeShazer had worked too hard to let a busted nose stop him. He would tell Farrow about the hole—after the bomber was airborne. Farrow released the brakes seconds later and the *Bat out of Hell* shot down the flight deck.

Across the task force sailors watched Farrow's bomber climb into the gray morning skies. "When the last plane had left there was a physical let down all over the ship," remembered Ensign Robert Noone, a signal officer. "Everyone was exhausted from the nervous tension of watching them take off. We mentally pushed every plane off the deck." Exhaustion soon turned to euphoria. "We all cheered loudly and choked down a few patriotic tears," added Kernan, the *Enterprise* plane handler who had bet on the loss of at least half the planes. "I thought my ten dollars well lost in a good cause, as if I had actually contributed the money to success in the war."

One sailor clasped his hands above his head; another blessed himself. "For a few minutes the sky was full of them," *Life* magazine's John Field wrote. "With the deep-throated roar of their twin motors, their beautiful lines, and their American insignia painted boldly on their wings and fuselages, they made us all feel proud." Fellow journalist Robert Casey recorded the scene in his diary. "Quiet on the horizon," he wrote. "There hasn't been a hitch. All have shot straight up in the teeth of the hurricane."

Mitscher had watched the takeoffs with a mix of disbelief and shock. The veteran aviator had tensed up each time one of the bombers roared down the deck, his arms instinctively moving as though he sat before the controls. "With only one exception, take-offs were dangerous and improperly executed," he complained in his report. "Apparently, full back stabilizer was used by the first few pilots. As each plane neared the bow, with more than required speed, the pilot would pull up and climb in a dangerous near-stall, struggle wildly to nose down, then fight the controls for several miles trying to gain real flying speed and more than a hundred feet of altitude."

Other senior naval officers were more forgiving. "The job that was done in launching those planes was to me a miracle," recalled Captain Frederick Riefkohl, the skipper of the *Vincennes*, who watched the take-offs from astern of the *Enterprise*. "I expected at any time that those big planes would crash into the sea, but the timing was perfect." No one was more pleased than Lieutenant Hank Miller, who had trained all eighty of the airmen. "Without a doubt every officer and man aboard the *Hornet* would have pinned every medal in the world on those people who went off that deck in those airplanes," he later said. "They really had what it took."

DOOLITTLE SETTLED IN FOR the long flight to Tokyo, pleased to have successfully answered the question of whether a loaded B-25 could lift off from a carrier. "Take-off was easy," he later boasted in his report. "Night take-off would have been possible and practicable."

The wind blew out of the northwest as Doolittle guided the bomber down to wave-top level, skimming just two hundred feet above the dark waters. He reviewed plans for the arrival that night in China, hoping that Lieutenant General Stilwell had made the necessary arrangements at the airfields.

In the seat next to him copilot Dick Cole also wondered what China would be like, confident that despite the added distance his crew would make it: "It never once occurred to me that there was a possibility that we would never get there." Cole instead hummed the folk tune "Wabash Cannonball," failing to notice that he had attracted the attention of others: "One time I was singing and stomping my foot with such gusto that the boss looked at me in a very questioning manner like he thought I was going batty."

Half an hour into the flight First Lieutenant Travis Hoover's bomber closed in on Doolittle, who soon banked to give wide berth to what appeared to be a camouflaged naval vessel. Hoover spotted patches of white smoke around the ship, indicating possible gunfire. Carl Wildner felt the tightness return to his stomach. "Why am I here," he thought, "when it would have been so easy to be somewhere else?"

All sixteen bombers had successfully lifted off from the *Hornet* with an average interval of less than four minutes, forming a loose string some 150 miles long. Most flew due west, aiming to cross the Japanese coast at Inubo Saki, a rocky cape topped with a lighthouse east of Tokyo. "There was no rendezvous planned, except at the end of the mission," Lawson recalled. "Those who took off early could not hover over the ship until a formation was formed because that would have burned too much gas in the first planes. This was to be a single file, hit-and-run raid—each plane for itself."

Airmen emptied the five-gallon gas cans, hacked holes in them, and tossed them into the seas as the pilots hedgehopped across the blue waves, some buzzing so low that salt water occasionally sprayed the windshield—*Bat out of Hell*'s props even nicked a wave once and sent a shudder through the bomber.

Soon after takeoff pilot Davy Jones asked engineer Joseph Manske for an update on the bomber's total fuel, which the young airman provided.

"Well, boys," Jones announced over the interphone. "We don't have enough gas to make our destination, but we'll go as far as we can."

A hush fell over the bomber.

"What in the world have I gotten myself into?" Manske thought, realizing there was only one thing to do. "Being brought up in a good Christian home," he later wrote, "I got down on my knees and prayed."

The harried takeoff had left Corporal Bert Jordan frazzled. Once in the air he organized his space and tested the .50-caliber machine guns, only to discover that the turret didn't work; the electrical lead was not connected, a fact he would not learn, however, until after the mission. The frozen turret rendered the guns worthless. Jordan, meanwhile, noticed that the left wing tank leaked. He tried to alert pilot Brick Holstrom, but couldn't communicate with him over the roar of the engines. When the crawlway tank was finally empty, Jordan climbed forward to the cockpit to deliver the bad news.

Other planes suffered similar problems. Davy Jones realized his bomber was short thirty gallons in its left rear tank, and the *Whirling Dervish*'s turret tank started to leak at the corner seams about fourteen inches from the top. Technical Sergeant Eldred Scott alerted pilot Harold Watson over the interphone and hurried to transfer the fuel as fast as he could. Scott likewise found that the left gun hydraulic charger failed, forcing him to charge the .50-caliber machine guns by hand.

With the bomber en route, DeShazer got on the phone to Farrow, informing him of the busted nose. "We've got a hole in this thing about a foot in diameter."

"What did you say?" Farrow replied, struggling to hear over the roar of the engines.

DeShazer repeated the news.

Copilot Bobby Hite climbed down to examine the damage. "Take your coat off," he instructed DeShazer." We'll see if we can stuff our coats in that hole."

At 160 miles per hour, the coats blew out.

A few Japanese civilian and naval vessels plowed the seas below; their numbers would only multiply as the bombers closed in on Japan.

"We're entering the danger zone, now," pilot Donald Smith warned his crew over interphone. "Keep on the alert. Surface vessel on our right-hand side."

"I see it, sir," Edward Saylor replied, manning the gun turret.

A few of the bomber pilots, including Doolittle, spotted enemy patrol planes in the skies as well. "A twin-engined land plane came out of a cloud ahead of us and passed us on the right," Jones recorded in his report. "I maintained course while it turned to avoid us. The Japanese markings were plainly visibly on it."

Joyce also encountered a twin-engine patrol just an hour and a half into the flight. "It immediately dove out of the clouds and pursued me," he noted in his report. "I increased power and was able to out distance the patrol plane which did not fire on me but I think recognized that I was the enemy."

These brushes foreshadowed the danger ahead, prompting many of the crews to fire a few test rounds, including *Ruptured Duck* gunner Dave Thatcher.

"Damn, boy," copilot Dean Davenport announced over the interphone when the .50 calibers started to rattle. "This is serious."

The *Ruptured Duck* buzzed a merchant ship.

"Let's drop one on it," Davenport joked.

Others on board agreed.

Lawson let them joke.

"Okay," navigator McClure finally said, giving up the idea, "but I bet that guy is radioing plenty to Tokyo about us."

Pilot Donald Smith in the *TNT* killed time tuning radio stations, picking up a Japanese broadcast several hundred miles out. "A normal program seemed to be in progress," he logged in his report. "I listened to it at intervals for over an hour."

Smith wasn't the only one who tuned into Tokyo radio station JOAK, the same station Lieutenant Jurika had monitored over the past week for any news of the task force's detection as the Hornet closed in on Japan. "That's what you've got to follow," Chase Nielsen, the navigator of the Green Hornet, instructed pilot Dean Hallmark. "Just keep that needle centered and you'll split Tokyo right in the middle."

The early flow of adrenaline that had propelled the airmen off the *Hornet*'s flight deck waned as the bombers droned on toward Tokyo, the cold blue swells of the Pacific tumbling below as the minutes turned to hours. "We kept going in and, after two or three hours, it got tiring," Lawson recalled. "I was keyed up enough, but at our low level and sluggish speed it was a job to fly the ship."

The crew of the *Green Hornet* rode in silence. "We were too busy thinking, and our nerves were kind of taut," Nielsen wrote. "I got to thinking about my wife, Thora. She and I were married December 8, 1941, the day after war was declared. We had 40 happy days together before I volunteered for the Doolittle flight."

"Conversations were short and to the point," recalled Emmens. "Every man was going over again in his mind each item for which he knew he was responsible. Of course, little black thoughts like an engine going out over that expanse of salt water, and the possibility of a reception committee of Jap Zeros, crept forward often enough to keep our minds well occupied with imaginary forced landings and combat tactics."

Emmens distracted himself with a mental inventory of all his purchases from the *Hornet*'s store. "I thought about the stack of razor blades, candy, and cartons of cigarettes," he recalled. "I then laughed at myself for buying such things as if I would be gone a year, when actually here we were on our final mission, and it would be over that same day. And we would be starting back home, probably, in a few days."

The sun burned away the morning clouds as the planes pressed on toward the enemy's homeland. Pilots kept close watch on the fuel consumption. Lawson smarted over the fact that the morning's warm-up on board the *Hornet* had forced him to burn through the equivalent of eight of his five-gallon tins. "Forty precious gallons," he later wrote, "gone before we were on our way!"

Jones had an almost fatalistic acceptance of the challenge he would face, estimating that he needed an extra 150 gallons of gas to make up for the added distance. "Navy got jittery and booted us off 10 hours too early," he griped in his diary. "810 miles to Tokio—guys all knew they couldn't make it. Oh well."

Ski York busied himself with calculations of the bomber's fuel consumption.

"Hey, Bob, take a look at this," he said around 11 a.m., more than two hours into the flight. "Am I screwy or are we burning this much gas?"

Emmens reviewed the numbers. Was the gas gauge inaccurate, he wondered, or had the plane developed a leak.

"Hell, Ski," he replied, "if that's right we're not going to get *near* the Chinese coast."

Navigator Nolan Herndon dropped his charts and inspected the bomb bay fuel tank. The lieutenant reported the bad news: the gas gauge was correct.

"Great," David Pohl, the gunner, said it himself. "Mrs. Pohl's young hero is headed for a ditching somewhere in the China Sea—provided we get through the flak and fighter screen over Tokyo. Here I am, a Boston boy of 20, the youngest of the 80 Doolittle raiders, a sergeant whose future just passed."

The crew had few options, none of them good. The airmen could land in Japan, but after an attack a landing there would likely lead to the crew's torture and possible execution. The fliers could attempt to reach China, ditch in the sea, and pray for a long-shot rescue by an American submarine before sharks ate them. The final option was to fly to Russia, a much shorter distance. Even then the crew faced the possibility the Russians would mistake them for an enemy and shoot them down.

"Have you got a course from Tokyo to Russia plotted, Herndon?" York asked.

"I've plotted all possibilities."

"Russia's neutral, isn't she?" engineer Staff Sergeant Theodore Laban asked.

"Doolittle didn't exactly issue a direct order not to go to Russia, but he made it plenty obvious that it wasn't a good idea," York added. "They'd probably give us gas and we'd be on our way across occupied Korea and China tomorrow morning."

"We hope!" Emmens answered.

The debate was soon interrupted.

"There's the coast," someone shouted. "This is it!"

THE *NITTO MARU'S* REPORT reached Admiral Yamamoto on board the *Yamato*, his flagship, just after breakfast at seven thirty on April 18. Efforts to follow up with the ill-fated picket boat had so far failed, but few doubted the report's veracity. Increased American message traffic in recent days—coupled with radio intelligence developed on April 10— had led many to conclude that Yamamoto's long-feared raid on the nation's capital was imminent. Japan had mistakenly concluded that America had lost a carrier in a submarine attack near Hawaii in January, leaving the United States with only three flattops. According to *Nitto Maru's* errant contact report, the entire Pacific Fleet carrier force now steamed straight toward Tokyo. Yamamoto's worst nightmare had come true. He ordered Tactical Method No. 3, Japan's plan for the defense of the homeland. "Enemy task force containing three aircraft carriers as main strength sighted 0630 this morning 730 miles east of Tokyo," he flashed. "Operate against American fleet."

Most inside the Naval General Staff believed Japan had at least a day to prepare. The short range of carrier fighters and bombers meant raiders would not strike in all likelihood until the morning of April 19, given that the flattops would have to steam within two hundred miles of Tokyo in order to launch and recover planes. That was the tactic the United States had taken on previous raids against the Marshall and the Marcus Islands, not to mention the one Japan had used for the attack on Pearl Harbor. Senior leaders in the meantime hurriedly cobbled together all available air and naval forces to repel the invaders. Many of Japan's frontline forces were still at sea; others had just returned in need of rest. Resourceful leaders went so far as to pilfer fighters and bombers from the carrier

Kaga, a Pearl Harbor veteran now in Sasebo for repairs after striking a reef. Within a few hours Japan amassed no fewer than ninety carrier fighters, eighty medium bombers, thirty-six carrier bombers, and two flying boats.

Rear Admiral Seigo Yamagata, commander of the Twenty-Sixth Air Flotilla, which was tasked to perform defensive air patrols east of the home islands, alerted his attack and reconnaissance units of the impending strike. Four twin-engine medium bombers crewed by up to six airmen had lifted off from Kisarazu Air Base near Tokyo at 6:30 a.m. for a routine morning patrol flight that extended out 700 nautical miles. Three hours and fifteen minutes into the flight, pilots spotted two twin-engine enemy bombers at a range of 580 and 600 nautical miles and at a distance from the Japanese planes of just two miles, though surprisingly this unusual report failed to dissuade Japan's leaders that the American attack would not come at least until the next morning. Anxious to go on the offensive, Japan launched three medium bombers at 11:30 a.m. Twenty-nine more, armed with aerial torpedoes, roared into the skies at 12:45 p.m. accompanied by two dozen carrier fighters equipped with extra fuel tanks.

Japanese warships likewise readied for battle. Vice Admiral Nobutake Kondo, the Second Fleet commander, who had just returned to Yokosuka from southern operations the day before, prepared to return to sea at once in charge of all available surface forces. That included the fleet's Fourth Cruiser Division, made up of the *Atago*, *Takao*, and *Maya*, as well as the Fifth Cruiser Division's *Myoko* and *Haguro*. Vice Admiral Shiro Takasu, commander of the First Fleet with its four battlewagons, would depart Hiroshima Bay to support him. Forces at sea likewise raced to intercept the Americans, including a submarine squadron of six boats some five hundred miles off Honshu. Another squadron of five submarines abandoned its mission to Truk to search north of the Bonin Islands. In the Bashi Strait, off the southern coast of Formosa, Vice Admiral Chuichi Nagumo ordered his powerful carriers *Akagi*, *Soryu*, and *Hiryu* east. Fighter pilot Mitsuo Fuchida, who led the Pearl Harbor attack, raced to the *Akagi*'s operations room.

"Well," Commander Minoru Genda, the First Air Fleet's operations officer, announced upon Fuchida's arrival, "they've come at last!"

The Japanese public had long braced for the possibility of air raids, given the nation's proximity to the Soviet Union and China. Throughout the 1930s Japan held annual air-raid drills for the six major cities of Tokyo, Yokohama, Osaka, Nagoya, Kyoto, and Kobe, emphasizing first aid, blackouts, and poisonous gas defense. Department stores and public buildings often displayed exhibits of World War I–era German bombs as well as mock-ups of miniature cities, complete with planes, bombs, and underground shelters. No less than 70 percent of Tokyo adults had invested in inexpensive gas masks. The war with China had only increased the importance of such precautions, prompting Japanese leaders to enlist Tokyo's 140,955 neighborhood groups, a communal system made up of ten to twenty families whose roots stretched back to the feudal era. Armed with hand pumps, buckets, and shovels, these groups served on the front line of civilian defense in the event of an air raid.

Though these precautions contrasted with the government's boastful declarations that an enemy raid was impossible, Tokyo residents had learned to accept the drills as a normal inconvenience of wartime life, similar to rationing and the loss of imported foreign goods. Outside of these frustrations little else had changed for many residents. Just two weeks earlier several thousand people had turned out for the cherry blossom festival. Music lovers still chatted about the Wednesday and Thursday night performances of famed piano soloist Kazuko Kusama at the Hibiya Public Hall, while gadflies buzzed about the upcoming House elections in which a hundred candidates vied for just thirty-two Tokyo-area seats. No fewer than 230 campaign rallies had taken place the day before in the nation's capital. The Tokyo university baseball spring league—made up of the teams of six rival schools—planned to kick off the new season at 1 p.m. with two games, Wasdea versus Tokyo Imperial and Keio versus Hosei.

News of the war filtered out to the public through the government-controlled media, which painted a jingoistic picture of Japanese forces as great liberators throughout Asia and the Pacific, casting off the imperial chains of Europe and America. Articles in the press just that week claimed that Japanese textbooks already were bestsellers in recently captured Hong Kong. Other accounts stated that residents on Sumatra celebrated the two-month anniversary of the day Japanese forces parachuted onto the tropical island and that schoolchildren in Singapore were thrilled to learn to sing the "Kimigayo," Japan's national anthem. Closer to home the first of more than 30,000 families of the nation's war dead had begun to pour into the capital for the Yasukuni Shrine Festival set to begin April 24, a four-day celebration that would include the enshrinement of 15,017 service members killed in the war with China. "I am overwhelmed with awe," one widow told reporters, "that the spirit of my husband is going to be deified."

Editorials meanwhile gloated over the capture of Bataan. "With the imminent fall of Corregidor the entire waters of the Southwestern Pacific will become an exclusive lake for the Japanese Navy," bragged an editorial that morning in the *Japan Times & Advertiser*. "Warships of the United States and Brittan have been made into inglorious, baseless vagabonds on high seas. But fortunately, the matter was much simplified inasmuch as most of them already have been sent down to the bottom by Japanese warships which have swept Anglo-American ships clean of these waters." The editorial went on to ridicule rumors of a possible Allied offensive in the weeks ahead. "Without any base for their fleet to start out from, how can they carry out their plans?" the paper asked. "All their ballyhoo about a summer offensive is the wishful thinking of the desperate Allied leaders who hope to keep their people from dwelling upon the numerous disasters their army and navy have suffered at the hands of the Japanese."

The war would make a brief intrusion this morning into the otherwise busy weekend lives of many Tokyo-area residents. Newspapers two days earlier had alerted residents of a practice air-raid drill scheduled for the morning of April 18, a fact local police communicated just the night before to the detained diplomats at the American and British embassies. About the same time the last B-25 roared off the deck of the *Hornet*, Tokyo responded to what officials referred to as the "first alarm." No sirens sounded, nor did the government mandate that residents seek shelter. Only the city's firefighting companies and air-raid wardens participated. Two firefighting squadrons appeared that morning outside the British embassy, while the detained American diplomats simply tugged shut the blackout curtains in the embassy and the chancery. The drill, however, soon ended. By 9:30 a.m. the air-raid wardens at the British embassy had stood down, and by 11 a.m. the one from the American embassy had teed off for a round of golf.

Air maneuvers over the capital were frequent, and this Saturday morning was no different. Tokyo residents enjoyed celebrations in advance of Emperor Hirohito's forty-first birthday at the end of the month as well as the Yasukuni Shrine Festival, which would feature a flyover of five hundred Army airplanes. The press had announced the maneuvers several days earlier, and authorities had alerted diplomats at the American embassy that morning. Firefighters lingered on the streets to watch the maneuvers while detained diplomats with little else to do gazed skyward as Japanese fighters battled one another in mock dog-fights. Troops along the city's waterfront floated barrage balloons, large inflatables anchored with metal cables that proved hazardous to any low-flying enemy planes. These activities wound down around noon. One detained American official, who had received special permission to visit a doctor, caught a streetcar at 12:15 p.m. Others traded small talk. Across the sprawling city of Tokyo, life returned to normal, residents no doubt comforted that for 2,600 years no invader had ever touched Japan.

CHAPTER 11

===

★

Once off the carrier, everything was peaceful
until we hit the coast.

—CHARLES MCCLURE,
NAVIGATOR ON PLANE NO. 7

DOOLITTLE CLOSED IN ON Japan, the bomber skimming just two
hundred feet above the blue Pacific swells. The weather had cleared seventy miles out, and numerous civilian and naval vessels crowded the seas.
Second Lieutenant Hank Potter, the twenty-three-year-old navigator
from South Dakota, had struggled to obtain an accurate fix ever since
takeoff. The airmen sighted the shore ahead.

"We're either fifty miles north of Tokyo or fifty miles south of it,
that's the way I figure it," Doolittle told Potter.

"I think we're about thirty miles north," Potter replied.

Doolittle's bomber charged ashore about fifty miles north of Inubo
Saki. "Was somewhat north of desired course but decided to take advantage of error and approach from a northerly direction," he wrote in his
report, "thus avoiding anticipated strong opposition to the west." The
sighting by the patrol boats coupled with other reports made Doolittle
suspect that fighters and antiaircraft batteries would anticipate the
bomber's arrival from the west. Approaching from the north would
throw them off.

"We've got company, Colonel," copilot Richard Cole interjected, motioning out the cockpit at a B-25 that dipped its wings.

First Lieutenant Travis Hoover, lead pilot of the first flight of three bombers, cruised off of Doolittle's port side.

The two bombers roared in over airfields north of Tokyo. The fields and the skies above were full of planes, mostly small biplanes that appeared to be primary or basic trainers. Gunner Staff Sergeant Paul Leonard in the turret counted as many as forty. "Japan looked green, peaceful and picturesque," Cole later wrote. "The people on the ground waved to us and it seemed everyone was playing baseball." Braemer echoed him. "We looked down and saw the street cars running and people walking in the streets," he recalled, "so we knew our little party was going to be a complete surprise."

Doolittle flew as low as the terrain would allow, heading due south over the capital's outskirts. The bomber roared over Tega Numa, a large lake northeast of Tokyo, with the plane almost "on the water." The awful weather that had plagued the mission for days had cleared, and the ceiling over Japan this Saturday was unlimited, though a haze reduced visibility to about twenty-five miles. The pilots and gunners scanned the skies for fighters, while Potter sought to orient the plane, a much greater challenge than he expected. The maps showed that mountains as high as five thousand feet ringed northwest Tokyo, but Potter looked down and saw only miles of flat lands. Furthermore, although highways did not stand out, he found that rivers, canals, and railroads did, including the gigantic Tobata railway yard. He picked up the Ara River, which sliced through the landscape north of Tokyo—and was crossed by large bridges—as well as the easily identifiable Tachikawa railroad, which started by the palace and ran due west out of Tokyo.

About ten miles out, Doolittle spotted nine fighters in three flights of three. The planes charged through the skies as much as eight thousand feet above. Doolittle kept the bomber low, hoping to avoid being detected. As the fighters roared past, the airmen spotted five barrage balloons over east central Tokyo and more in the distance.

Twenty minutes after crossing the coastline, the bombers reached the Sumida River, which wound through northern Tokyo. Hoover banked west in search of his target, while Doolittle pressed on into Tokyo. His primary target was the armory just a few miles north of the

Imperial Palace. In the bomb bay sat four incendiary bombs, which he hoped would serve as the match for a much larger explosion. The airmen could now clearly see the high-rises that crowded Tokyo's business district as well as the palace and even the muddy moat that encircled Emperor Hirohito's home.

Doolittle was now poised like a dagger to stab at the heart of the empire of Japan. He pulled up to twelve hundred feet and banked southwest to prepare to bomb.

"Approaching target," he told Staff Sergeant Fred Braemer, the twenty-four-year-old bombardier from Washington.

Braemer mashed the button, and the bomb bay doors yawned open, the roar of the engines now loud inside the plane.

"All ready, Colonel," Braemer announced over the interphone.

Antiaircraft fire thundered into the sky as Doolittle leveled off for the run, buzzing his target by less than a quarter mile. Braemer sighted the arsenal. A red light on the cockpit instrument panel blinked as the first bomb plummeted to the ground below. Braemer noted the time was 1:15 p.m., though the time on the ground was one hour behind. The red light on Doolittle's instrument panel flashed again.

Then again.

And again.

Four incendiary bombs—each packed with 128 four-pound bomblets—tumbled down to Tokyo.

On the ground below, several teachers at the Tsurumaki national school looked up as Doolittle's bomber roared overhead, low enough that the American insignia was clearly visible. "Bomb-like objects fell from the plane," one recalled. "On their way down they opened up like umbrellas and came down like leaflets."

About thirty of the bomblets landed on the school, including fifteen in the yard near where some 150 students gathered on the playground after lunch before kendo class. Others came down on the street, killing a pedestrian and setting fire to several stores and homes. Startled resident Seikichi Honjo charged outside in such a rush that he didn't put on his pants. Still other bomblets set fire to the nearby Okazaki Hospital, where orderlies rushed to carry out the sick.

About two hundred yards beyond the hospital sat Waseda Middle School, where faculty discussed attending the funeral of a colleague as students played outside in the yard. One of the bomblets hit fourth-grader Shigeru Kojima in the shoulder; he collapsed and started convulsing. Seconds later he fell still and died.

All told, Doolittle's attack killed two people and injured nineteen others, four seriously. Japanese investigators would later recover 425 incendiary bomblets, including 31 unexploded ones. As many as 250 others set fire to homes; fire brigades extinguished another 150, which caused minor damage. Another 100 came down on area roads and fields. Firefighters hurried to extinguish the blazes, but not before thirty-six buildings containing forty-four homes burned to the ground. The attack partially destroyed six other buildings, which included a total of twenty homes.

Antiaircraft fire thundered. With the bombing complete, Braemer slipped the .30-caliber nose gun in place and loaded it, only to suffer a jam at this most inopportune time. He discovered a round jammed in the T slot. He pulled back on the bolt handle and fished the round out with his finger and then reloaded the gun.

Antiaircraft shells exploded in the skies around the bomber. The elevation of the fire was good, but most shells burst a hundred yards to the right or left of the bomber.

"Everything okay back there, Paul?" Doolittle asked his gunner.

"Everything's fine," he answered.

"They're missing us a mile," Doolittle added.

A shell burst shook the bomber.

"Colonel," Leonard replied, "that was no mile."

Doolittle dove the bomber down to the rooftop level and flew over the western outskirts into a low haze and smoke. Smoke from the fires tickled the sky. He then turned south and headed back out to sea, passing over a small aircraft factory with a dozen newly completed planes on the line.

"Colonel, can't we burn up some of those Jap planes?" Braemer asked.

"It would only alert them down there," Doolittle replied. "This would give them a chance to raise hell with any of the boys coming after us."

The anxious Braemer spotted what appeared to be either a tank or an armored car on a highway below, once again asking permission to fire.

"Relax, Fred," Doolittle said. "They probably think we are a friendly aircraft. Let them keep on thinking that. And knocking off one tank isn't going to win this war."

★

FIRST LIEUTENANT TRAVIS HOOVER reached his target at almost the exact same time as Doolittle. The lead pilot in the first wave of three bombers, Hoover had scanned the skies all morning for First Lieutenants Robert Gray and Everett Holstrom, but had never spotted them. The only other bomber he had seen was Doolittle's.

First Lieutenant Carl Wildner, the navigator, had set a course upon takeoff of 272 degrees, virtually due west. Following that heading meant Hoover should have come ashore over a rocky promontory topped by the Inubo Saki lighthouse, but instead he looked down on white sandy beaches that stretched for miles. Wildner knew this was bad.

Real Bad.

So did Hoover.

"What'll I do?" the pilot asked.

All Wildner could suggest was to follow Doolittle.

Wildner scanned his maps and peered out the window, desperate for any clue of his location. He had ended up as a navigator only after he had washed out of pilot training. The experience had left him with a major inferiority complex. With each passing minute—and as the plane plunged blindly deeper into Japan—his fears mounted. "In all my life I have never felt so helpless," he wrote. "We passed over rice paddies, streams and a few temples but I couldn't identify a single landmark on my maps. I knew the maps had been made up from very poor information but it seemed to me that the maps I was holding were of another part of the world. Nothing matched."

Unsure of his position, Hoover opted to trail his commander, zigzagging west across the rural landscape at an altitude of barely a hundred feet. The airmen remained surprised at the lack of concern. Despite the battle with the *Nitto Maru*, coupled with sightings of various other ships and planes, Japan seemed oblivious to the inbound aerial armada. Even the military bases the bomber buzzed appeared not to be on alert.

"There were no pursuit planes or anti-aircraft," Wildner wrote in his report. "The populace had shown no alarm at our coming."

"The people that I observed on the ground," added Richard Miller, the bombardier, "casually looked up and watched us go by."

His plane armed with three 500-pound demolition bombs and one incendiary, Hoover had orders to target a powder factory and magazines near a bend in the Sumida River. "Nothing of military importance was observed until we reached the outskirts of northern Tokyo," he noted in his report. "I recognized the Sumida River and immediately turned west along it toward our target. We started the climb."

Hoover scanned the congested riverbanks below but failed to spot the powder factory where the map indicated it. He hustled to pick an alternative target, spotting two factory buildings and storehouses near the river. The entire area was congested with small buildings, which would no doubt burn.

Perfect.

"There's our target," Hoover shouted.

Hoover didn't have time to pull up to fifteen hundred feet, so he leveled off at nine hundred. Second Lieutenant Richard Miller raced to set up the shot, unaware Hoover had swapped out the targets. "I spotted a large factory with several small warehouses around it which fit the description of our target," he wrote in his report. "I immediately opened the bomb-bay doors and took a very quick aim at the center of the large factory and released all four of my bombs at half-second intervals by means of the manual release switch."

"Bombs away," Miller yelled as he closed the doors. "Let's get out of here."

Hoover banked the plane just as the bombs detonated. At less than nine hundred feet, the explosions jolted the crew, hurling debris as much as one hundred feet above the low-flying plane. "The concussion of the three demolition bombs," Wildner later noted in his report, "lifted us before I realized that they had been dropped."

Even Richard Cole, Doolittle's copilot in the skies several miles away, saw debris cloud the air, while gunner Paul Leonard in the turret thought the blast would bring down Hoover's plane.

But Hoover survived, roaring through the smoke and debris. The massive explosions near an Asahi Electrical Manufacturing Corporation factory would level or set ablaze thirty-eight buildings, all but eight completely destroyed. Fifty-two homes were lost and fourteen others damaged. The blast blew one woman out of her second-floor; miraculously she landed unhurt in the street atop a tatami mat.

Ten others would not be so lucky, including several who burned to death in collapsing houses. The attack injured another forty-eight people, thirty-four seriously. Ruptured water lines hindered efforts to fight the fires, as did the low tide of the Sumida River, which made it difficult for firefighters to pump water. Investigators would later measure two bomb craters thirty feet wide and fifteen feet deep.

"I looked back and saw about half of our target covered with black smoke," Staff Sergeant Douglas Radney, who manned the .50-caliber machine-gun turret, wrote in his report. "Near the base of the target there were flames and smoke."

The anxious airmen in the front of the bomber asked Radney whether he had seen the explosions.

"Yes, sir," the gunner informed Hoover. "All four hit close together and there's smoke all over the area. We got it all right!"

"OK, gang, hold your hats," Hoover announced over the interphone. "We're going down."

The pilot pushed the bomber into such a steep dive that loose items floated upward, along with Wildner's stomach. "I glanced at the airspeed indicator and saw that it was close to the redline," the navigator later wrote. "Outside all I could see were rooftops—millions of them."

The bomber skimmed barely thirty feet above the city's rooftops until Hoover spied a power line dead ahead.

"Over or under it?" he asked

"You better not go under," Wildner shot back, before instructing Hoover to ease back on the gas. China was still a long way to go.

"I want to get out of here fast."

FIRST LIEUTENANT GRAY TORE ACROSS the Japanese coastline fifteen miles south of the Inubo Saki lighthouse and due east of Yokohama at 1:35 p.m.—some twenty minutes after Doolittle and Hoover had attacked.

The bombers had lifted off from the *Hornet* at average intervals of only 3.9 minutes, but mechanical troubles and navigational errors had slowed the aerial armada's advance across the Pacific. This respite of as much as half an hour had given the Japanese vital time to recover from the shock. Air-raid sirens sounded throughout Tokyo at approximately

12:35 p.m. local time, while pilots scrambled into fighters and troops manned antiaircraft batteries. The element of surprise had vanished.

Gray roared across the Boso Peninsula, the arm of land that curled south and protected Tokyo Bay from the Pacific. The aircrew spied men in blue uniforms in the hills before the bomber reached the bay, approaching the capital from the southeast. Gray's route into the city would lead him across the flank of the antiaircraft batteries that covered the Tokyo's waterfront, a dangerous course he would then have to retrace on his escape. Gray's journey was made all the more perilous in that Doolittle had flown over his targets, no doubt alerting ground forces.

The flak thundered as Gray charged across the bay, the puffs of smoke creating a trail through the skies toward his targets: a steel mill, chemical factory, and gas company in the densely populated industrial district northwest of the palace.

"They're shooting at us," exclaimed copilot Shorty Manch, making what his fellow fliers would later joke was a brilliant observation.

Gray pressed on through the flak and climbed to 1,450 feet; ten miles east an oil tank appeared to burn.

"Dropped our bombs in four individual runs," wrote Sergeant Aden Jones, the bombardier. "Then hit the deck and got the hell out of there."

Gray didn't see the first bomb hit, but he felt the concussion. He believed he scored direct hits with his second and third attacks against the gas company and chemical works, the latter appearing to set the entire factory ablaze. He scattered his lone incendiary bomb over a densely populated small-factories district. Second Lieutenant Charles Ozuk Jr., *Whiskey Pete*'s navigator, peered out the window, later describing the scene in his report. "Observed heavy smoke from the target area."

Gray had scored a direct hit on the Japan Diesel Manufacturing Corporation, the bomb tearing through the timber roof of warehouse no. 3 and punching an eighteen-centimeter dent in the concrete floor before detonating. Employees had scattered for lunch, and no one had sounded the air-raid alarm. The massive explosion killed twelve workers and injured another eighty-eight, including forty-seven seriously. The attack leveled the warehouse and damaged eight other buildings, sparking a fire in warehouse no. 2 that crews eventually extinguished. Another one of his bombs partly destroyed two additional buildings and injured nine people. Gray's incendiary bomblets spread out over a largely civilian area, destroying four buildings containing twenty-seven homes. One of those was the Sanrakuso apartment building and another a clothing factory dormitory.

Gray immediately began evasive maneuvers to throw off the heavy antiaircraft fire as he banked sharply right and began his retreat.

Jones manned the .30-caliber nose gun, opening fire on the buildings and streets a thousand feet below; the distinct rattle of the machine gun filled the cockpit. Ozuk saw some of the tracers tear into wooden buildings below, appearing to set some on fire. Jones then set his sights on what appeared to be a factory complete with an air defense surveillance tower perched atop the roof. "I saw fifteen to twenty bodies which had fallen as if they were hit by our bombardier's fire," Ozuk wrote in his report. "The rest of the men just scattered and ran in all directions."

Sadly, those weren't men.

Teachers at Mizumoto Primary School had earlier dismissed the students for the day, though many of the children remained behind to help clean classrooms. About 150 of the students had started to walk home moments before Gray's plane thundered in the skies overhead and Jones squeezed the trigger of his machine gun, blasting the first and second floors of the school.

Terrified students ran back toward the school, where teacher Yukiteru Furusawa directed them into the classrooms for shelter. High school freshman Minosuke Ishide suddenly collapsed. Furusawa thought the boy had stumbled and helped others into a classroom, returning minutes later to find Ishide still on the floor. He examined the boy and realized he had been shot, a hole visible through one of the glass window planes. "This student was immediately taken to another room and it was found that his pulse was very weak," Furusawa recalled. "The student died on the way to the hospital which was about one hour and fifteen minutes after being hit by the bullet."

FIRST LIEUTENANT EVERETT HOLSTROM, at the controls of the fourth bomber to take off from the *Hornet*, felt apprehensive as he approached Japan. One of his wing tanks leaked, the .50-caliber machine guns didn't work, and he was the last bomber in the first wave of attacks aimed at northern Tokyo, meaning that local air defenses would no doubt be on high alert. He decided his only hope was to outsmart the Japanese.

He instructed his navigator to make landfall just south of the capital, a move he believed would allow him to slip past any fighters that might anticipate more attacks from the east. Holstrom had flown due west all morning without realizing the bomber's compass was off as much as fifteen degrees. He made landfall at just seventy-five feet on a small group of islands south of Tokyo.

Far south.

A check of the map revealed the bomber's position 75 miles south of the capital, a finding that would add 150 miles to his trip. Holstrom soldiered on, however, banking north toward Tokyo. If the Japanese jumped the bomber, he told his men, he planned to dump the bombs and run. Holstrom's orders called for him to bomb a powder magazine and clothing depot in northern Tokyo. He would never reach those targets coming up from the south, so he decided to drop his three demolition bombs and one incendiary on alternate targets—an oil storage tank farm and troop barracks.

Holstrom's hope to outsmart the Japanese backfired. The outbound bombers raced out to sea, followed by Japanese fighters. Holstrom flew straight toward them—in a plane low on gas and without workable .50-caliber machine guns.

Copilot Lucian Youngblood was climbing back to transfer the last of the fuel from the bomb bay to the wing tank, when Holstrom spotted the first two fighters over Sagami Bay, the scenic body of water southwest of Tokyo. He shouted for Youngblood to return to his seat as he immediately banked under them. "The red dots on their wings looked as big as barns," Youngblood wrote in his diary. "We were really in a spot."

One of the fighters opened fire.

Holstrom watched as tracer bullets zinged over the cockpit.

"When I saw 7.7-millimeter bullets bouncing off our wing," he recalled, "I figured the hell with this!"

Youngblood spotted two more fighters zoom past the bow at fifteen hundred feet.

"I made up my mind that we should try to escape," Holstrom wrote. "I thought that if we continued, it was a certainty that we would be shot down."

Holstrom ordered the bombardier to dump the ordnance. Sergeant Robert Stephans opened the bomb bay doors, placed the arming hammer in the safe position, and salvoed the weapons at an altitude of just seventy-five feet. Holstrom's four eggs vanished into the water below. He turned south to outrun the fighters.

The crew felt depressed.

"It's kind of a sickening feeling," navigator Harry McCool recalled. "There's all this effort for nothing."

CAPTAIN DAVY JONES CHARGED ashore north of the Inubo Saki lighthouse at just fifty feet above the waves, with Dean Hallmark and Ted Lawson close behind. These three pilots made up the second wave of bombers tasked to pummel central Tokyo. Jones throttled up to 200 miles per hour as he punched inland, but when the expected enemy fighters failed to materialize, he slowed to 180 miles per hour.

His relief over his lack of opposition soon gave way to a more pressing concern. Fields, streets, and villages raced beneath the bomber's belly as Jones and his crew searched for landmarks that might help orient them. Five minutes turned into ten before Jones had to make a painful confession: "We didn't know where in the hell we were."

"Well," he finally decided. "We'll turn south."

Ten minutes more passed.

Then fifteen.

Every gallon of fuel burned hunting for Tokyo, Jones knew, was one gallon less he could count on to reach China.

The flustered flier decided to bomb the first target he found just as his B-25 crested a ridge and passed over the mouth of Tokyo Bay. He instantly recognized his location. Rather than approach Tokyo from the north, Jones had turned south too soon, flying down the Boso Peninsula and bypassing the Japanese capital. He entered the bay due east of Yokosuka, banked north, and pressed on toward Tokyo.

His orders were to bomb several targets east of the Imperial Palace, including an armory. With his gas running low, however, Jones opted for an alternative. The cockpit windshield revealed myriad possible targets packed along the bay shores. He informed bombardier Denver Truelove of his new plan.

Jones pulled up to twelve hundred feet as Truelove coached him in over the targets by voice, sighting an oil tank two blocks from the waterfront. Truelove next targeted what appeared to be a brick power plant several stories tall. Jones banked left in search of more targets, a move that allowed him to witness the second explosion. "The building assumed the shape of a barrel," he recalled. "The sides rounded out and the top became circular. Then the 'barrel' burst. Smoke and dust and bricks were everywhere."

The raiders scored another hit with an incendiary bomb on a two-story building with a saw-toothed roof. The massive structure, which stretched more than two city blocks, reminded Jones of North American Aviation's California factory. "It was easy to hit," he wrote in his report. "Every one of the bombs in the cluster hit on the roof of this plant."

The antiaircraft fire had prompted Jones to increase his speed to as much as 270 miles per hour, causing Truelove to overshoot his final target. The demolition bomb appeared to blow off only the corner of a two-story building with windows and ventilators on the roof and a canal running along the west side.

A postwar analysis would reveal that one of the bombs ripped through the top of a roofing factory and exploded on a support beam ten feet above the ground, killing twelve workers and injuring eleven others on lunch break. Only the structure's steel frame prevented the total loss of the building. Another bomb tore through the roof of a Yokoyama Industries warehouse, which doubled as an office. The bomb hit a pile of firewood and exploded, killing fifteen workers and injuring another eleven within a sixty-five-foot radius of the blast, including some in a factory next door. All told, the attack killed twenty-seven people—the most by any single bomber.

Jones now dove down to rooftop level to make his escape, as the Japanese antiaircraft fire and even machine-gun bullets buzzed the bomber, terrifying Joseph Manske in the turret. "When I saw the tracer bullets," the gunner recalled, "I got out of that turret in a hurry and never fired a round."

SECOND LIEUTENANT HALLMARK AND THE crew of the *Green Hornet* marveled at the ease of entry into the enemy's homeland. No antiaircraft fire. No fighters. Just a warm Saturday afternoon. "It was so pleasant and serene then you'd think we were a commercial airliner coming in for a visit," navigator Chase Nielsen recalled. "The fine weather made us feel good. We figured it was a sign that our mission would be successful."

That serenity ended when the bomber closed in on Tokyo.

Zooming in at more than 220 miles per hour, Hallmark pulled up to fifteen hundred feet. The bomb bay doors swung open as the antiaircraft fire thundered, some of it from warships moored in the bay. One round struck Plexiglas near copilot Second Lieutenant Robert Meder. Dark smoke curled above the horizon from the previous attacks, as six Japanese planes roared overhead at ten thousand feet.

Hallmark's orders were to target the steel mills and foundries in the northeastern corner of the capital that crowded the banks of the bay, a massive target Nielsen estimated to be no less than six hundred feet by two thousand feet. The Texas pilot now poised to fulfill a prophecy he had made just days after the attack on Pearl Harbor. "The Japs sure did make a big mistake," he wrote then in a letter to his parents. "I imagine they will be awfully sorry they ever heard of the U.S. in a few months."

Sergeant William Dieter, the bombardier, stared down his Mark Twain sight at the congested Japanese capital below. Nielsen pressed him on where he planned to drop the bomber's lone incendiary.

"I'll figure that out," Dieter answered.

Hallmark interrupted the debate.

"I've already figured out what he's going to do with the incendiary," the pilot instructed. "I'm going to circle and come back and we're gonna go over the target area and spread it all over."

"Are you sure you're not going to circle and go over the Imperial Palace?" Nielsen joked.

Hallmark leveled off and made his run. He then circled back; his total time over the target was just three minutes.

"We couldn't miss from 1,500 feet," Nielsen later wrote. "We saw the bombs explode, watched the smoke and fire and then circled."

Hallmark's first bomb detonated on the concrete road in front of Japan Steel Fuji Steelworks, blasting a crater some thirty feet wide. The explosion destroyed seven nearby homes and damaged eleven others, seriously injuring one person. The *Green Hornet*'s second bomb hit steelmaker Nippon Yakin Kogyo, tearing through the roof and denting the concrete floor. The massive explosion blew apart the wooden building and took the roof and windows off the neighboring factory building. Alerted workers had begun to evacuate, though flying shrapnel cut some of them. Hallmark's incendiary bomblets spread across a residential area 1,000 feet long and 150 feet wide. Sixty-nine of the explosives landed on homes, injuring three people. The others burned up on roads and in nearby fields, and Japanese investigators would count eleven duds.

Nielsen would later dispute Japanese charges that the *Green Hornet* strafed civilians on the ground, arguing that no one on board the bomber had ever even fired the machine guns. Nevertheless, postwar Japanese records would show that preschooler Yoshiro Nakamura was hit in the back and killed in the area where the bomber's incendiary bomblets fell, possibly from bomb shrapnel or even antiaircraft fire.

Hallmark and his crew strained for a final glimpse of the damage as dark puffs of antiaircraft fire flooded the sky, turning white as the shells exploded.

"I didn't feel any sort of emotion until we began to circle after we dropped our bombs," Nielsen recalled. "But when we saw that we'd scored with our bombs we let go."

"That's a bulls-eye!" Hallmark yelled.

The others joined him to congratulate Dieter.

Hallmark dove down to just fifty feet and tore across the bay, joining his navigator in a duet of "We Don't Want to Set the World on Fire."

The crew relaxed, the mission accomplished. "We felt good," Nielsen wrote. "We figured the worst was over now."

He was wrong.

FIRST LIEUTENANT TED LAWSON ROARED ashore in the seventh bomber, the last one charged with bombing central Tokyo. He was surprised at how basic it looked. "I had an ingrained, picture-postcard concept of Japan. I expected to spot some snow-topped mountain or volcano first," he wrote. "But here was land that barely rose above the surface of the water and, at our twenty feet of height, was hardly distinguishable."

The beaches gave way to green fields and farms, carved into the landscape with an almost mathematical precision. Lawson realized that after nearly three weeks at sea—surrounded by grays and blues—the vibrant colors were a welcome change. "The fresh spring grass was brilliantly green. There were fruit trees in bloom, and farmers working in their fields waved to us as we pounded just over their heads," he wrote. "A red lacquered temple loomed before us, its coloring exceedingly sharp."

Even Corporal David Thatcher, who manned the .50-caliber machine guns to ward off enemy fighters, couldn't help stealing glances at the exotic landscape that raced beneath the bomber. "I saw quite a few good highways in Japan but no cars, only bicycles," he wrote in his report. "As we passed over the rooftops the people in the fields and on the roads would stop whatever they were doing and look up at us. From the way they acted it seemed as though no Japanese planes ever flew that low."

The *Ruptured Duck* buzzed a school. Children flooded out into the yard, many waving to the airmen. The calm scene was strangely disarming, until Lawson caught sight of the school's flagpole. Fluttering in the warm April wind was the Japanese flag, the bright red sun plastered against the white background. "It was like getting hit in the chest very hard," the pilot recalled. "This was for keeps."

"Keep your eyes open, Thatcher," he ordered.

"I'm looking."

Lawson followed several valleys toward Tokyo, the surrounding hills hiding the twin-engine bomber. The minutes ticked past. Lawson, copilot Second Lieutenant Dean Davenport, and bombardier Robert Clever spotted six enemy fighters at the same time, racing toward them in two formations at fifteen hundred feet. The first buzzed overhead, followed by a second, though one fighter peeled off and started to dive.

"I saw him," Thatcher assured his pilot.

Lawson asked whether he wanted to power up the turret.

"No," he replied, "wait awhile."

With each second, Lawson grew more fearful.

"I don't know what the dickens happened to him," Thatcher finally announced. "I think he must have gone back in the formation."

The *Ruptured Duck* crested a hill, then swooped down on Tokyo Bay, skimming the surface at just fifteen feet.

"Nowhere was there any evidence of a warning," recalled McClure, the navigator. "Shipping lay in the harbor. We passed close to an aircraft carrier which looked almost deserted—not a plane on deck. We could have bombed it with ease. But we didn't. Our orders were to hit specific targets and we passed up everything else."

Lawson closed in on the Japanese capital, charging over wharves and docks that crowded the shore. Through the cockpit he saw the city stretched out before him. "In days and nights of dreaming about Tokyo and thinking of the eight millions who live there, I got the impression that it would be crammed together, concentrated, like San Francisco. Instead it spreads all over creation, like Los Angeles," Lawson wrote. "There is an aggressively modern sameness to much of it."

The aircrew spied several large fires from previous attacks and a smoky haze settled over northeastern Tokyo. The antiaircraft fire thundered as Lawson pulled up to fourteen hundred feet, executing a run west from the waterfront toward the Imperial Palace. Though tasked to bomb Nippon Machine Works, Clever instead sighted a factory almost half the size of a city block with several 100-foot chimneys.

The red light on Lawson's instrument panel flashed as the first demolition bomb plummeted toward Tokyo, landing in a canal next to a Japan Steel Piping factory and causing only minor damage. Clever sighted two more factories. The red light flashed again and again. The second bomb exploded atop a pile of coke, an important fuel used in steel mills, while the third landed nearby with little damage.

Clever took a final look down the Mark Twain sight, releasing his incendiary bomb over Japan Steel Piping's shipbuilding factory. The explosives scattered across an area that measured some nine hundred feet by two hundred. Others came down on roofs and sparked fires, which sand bucket brigades raced to extinguish. All told, the attack injured four people, two seriously, with most suffering burns to the arms and legs.

The *Ruptured Duck* blew past the emperor's home, the towering walls and greensward visible to the airmen in the cockpit. McClure flipped on his movie camera to capture the damage done by Doolittle and his men. "I became disgusted when I noticed little specks of dirt on the camera lens. What a time, I thought, for a lens to show up dirty," he wrote. "I took the camera from my eye and saw what the trouble was. Those weren't dust specks but the bursts of antiaircraft shells."

The batteries on the ground below zeroed in on the *Ruptured Duck*. Thatcher saw one burst just off the right wing about the same time Lawson dove to escape.

"That's flak—flak," the airmen shouted in unison. "Let's get out of here."

A BRITISH PROFESSOR AT the University of Tokyo—and one of the few English subjects the Japanese had not interned—John Morris was wandering that Saturday afternoon down the Ginza, Tokyo's main shopping boulevard, when an air-raid alarm suddenly screamed. Morris assumed it was a routine noontime drill, until he looked up and saw an American bomber tear through the skies overhead, the plane's insignia clearly visible. He saw no Japanese fighters, though minutes later he heard the distant roar of antiaircraft fire over the city's suburbs. The puzzled Englishman looked around at other shoppers. "There was not the slightest sign of panic," Morris later wrote. "The police halted the traffic, but nobody made any attempt to take shelter; the general sentiment was one of bewildered interest, everybody wondering what was going to happen next."

Morris's experience proved far from unique. The raid had managed to catch most Tokyo residents completely unaware. The attack by sixteen bombers on a city spread across more than two hundred square miles meant few of the capital's nearly seven million residents would witness firsthand the raid's destruction, though many would see the enemy marauders either en route to targets or afterwards. The low-flying bombers that hedgehopped over homes, restaurants, and businesses prompted people to press against windows, while others ran out into the streets for a better look. "Most of the people did not believe it, thinking it was just another drill," remembered Bruno Bitter, a Catholic priest at Tokyo Sophia University. "But when they learned it was a real raid, nobody could hold them back to go outside, to climb the roofs or the chimneys to get a better view. In other words, it was a thrill rather than a frightening event."

That was the case for French journalist Robert Guillain, who was at home near the city's center when the attack started. He heard a series of powerful explosions. "Bombs?" he wondered before he heard what sounded like antiaircraft fire. "Still," he thought, "if it were a raid, we'd have heard the sirens." Less than four minutes later, an alarm pierced the Saturday air. "A raid at high noon!" Guillain exclaimed. "Our first raid! So *they've* come!" The reporter charged down the street toward Toranomon, a major intersection near the city's principal ministries. He followed the skyward point of many fingers just in time to spot a bomber zoom past. "Everyone was out of doors; they had watched the raid from the middle of the street to get a better view," he later wrote. "The people were not visibly worried, but at least they showed a lively excitement."

The raid likely made the Stanford University–educated Kazuo Kawai, chief editorial writer for the *Japan Times & Advertiser*, question the wisdom of his morning pronouncement that the Pacific was now an exclusive lake for the Japanese. "The sirens did not even go off until the planes were over the city and the sky was full of antiaircraft fire," he recalled. "I was out and saw the firing, but thought it was just practice, although it seemed strange to be practicing with what appeared to be live shells. Then I saw the planes and realized it was a raid. Then finally the sirens were sounded." The attack made others question the nation's preparedness, including a primary school principal in a village just outside Tokyo who watched the planes buzz over his school. How had the enemy penetrated Japan's defensive net? "As for military weapons, we had bamboo spears. We were instructed to use bamboo spears in case parachute troops landed," he would later tell American investigators after the war. "It was truly comical."

Captain Sadatoshi Tomioka was enjoying lunch at the Army and Navy Club with Colonel Takushiro Hattori. The two officers discussed the proposed seizure of Midway, which both opposed, when the distant rumble of bombs interrupted them. Tomioka surmised the planes came from carriers, calculating that Yamamoto could abandon the Midway plan and destroy the American fleet right off the shores of Japan.

"Wonderful!" he exclaimed.

American ambassador Joseph Grew had just finished a morning meeting with the Swiss minister before departing his embassy office to wander up the hill toward the residence for his Saturday lunch. The mustached statesman spotted several fires in the distance, which he dismissed as the ordinary blazes that periodically erupted throughout the wooden capital. Grew reached the residence and wandered out into the garden with several other interned Americans. Additional fires soon broke out in the distance, forming a 180-degree arc that stretched from northern Tokyo south to Yokohama, the dark columns of smoke curling skyward. Antiaircraft fire suddenly thundered. Just then the ambassador spotted a twin-engine bomber charge through the skies less than a mile from the embassy. The plane suddenly dove, buzzing the rooftops to the west.

"My goodness—I hope that is not an American bomber," Grew blurted out. "I think it is crashing."

Grew realized that the low-flying bomber was actually executing evasive maneuvers about the time he spotted a second plane to the east, this one trailed by a line of black puffs of smoke that he recognized as the bursts of antiaircraft shells. "All this was very exciting," he wrote in his diary, "but at the time it was hard to believe that it was more than a realistic practice by Japanese planes."

Naval attaché Lieutenant Commander Henri Smith-Hutton was relaxing in his office with his wife when he heard the first explosions. The couple hurried outside. The Army's language officer, who had climbed up to the roof, called down, telling him this was the most realistic drill he had ever seen. The officer reported smoke from several fires, while another blaze appeared to have just started. Smith-Hutton ran into the departing Swiss minister, asking whether it could be a real raid. The European diplomat doubted it. Smith-Hutton headed on to lunch in the compound, where the dining room doors opened to the garden. The attaché spotted a policeman on a nearby rooftop about the time an explosion rattled the embassy. His wife ran out into the garden just as a bomber roared overhead, vanishing before anyone identified the insignia. "Half of our group thought it was a genuine air raid, but no one could be sure of the nationality of the planes," Smith-Hutton recalled. "The other half of our group still thought it was a drill."

The diplomats decided to settle the dispute with a $100 wager that the bombers were part of the earlier planned drill. "We saw three bombers altogether and six big fires," Grew recalled. "Even then, however, we didn't know whether it was a real raid or whether it was a well-managed show put on by the Japanese in accordance with their air-raid precautions. There was a great difference of opinion among my own staff— quite a lot of money changed hands on that issue, I may say."

"Well," someone finally said to the policeman at the gate, "that was a very successful show you put on today."

"That was no show," the guard responded. "That was the real thing."

A similar response played out at the British embassy, where the drone of American bombers coupled with dark smoke on the horizon finally convinced the eighty-seven interned diplomats that the attack was real, including Frank Moysey, a cipher officer. "Our fondest wish," he later said, "had come true." Embassy staffers manned air-raid posts. He guarded the entrance to the compound's cellar, where he was supposed to aid stretcher bearers, watching the smoke rise from behind a hill until he could no longer stand idle. "I ran into a building and climbed to the roof; it was a beautiful sight," recalled Moysey, whose colleagues would spend the rest of the afternoon toasting the American fliers. "There, surging up from Tokyo's heavy industrial district, were six enormous columns of smoke, dense and black. No smoke bombs could have caused them. While we watched the smoke increase and spread with the wind, a big twin-engined bomber suddenly roared across the sky a half-mile away."

"It is so unfair that you should bomb us," complained one of the embassy's local staffers. "Our houses are only made of wood, while yours are of stone."

The Danish minister to Japan, Lars Tillitse, watched the attack from his home window. Only the night before, he had attended a dinner the Japanese foreign minister hosted for diplomats of neutral countries. Tillitse had overheard the foreign minister's wife insist to another woman that there was no need to build an air-raid shelter or even to ship her furs, jewels, and wines out of Tokyo. America could never bomb Tokyo. He thought of the conversation again as he saw one of the bombers streak overhead.

Argentinian commercial attaché Ramón Muñiz Lavalle likewise watched the attack unfold, albeit from the roof of the embassy. He saw four bombers zoom barely a hundred feet over the city's rooftops, sparking one of the few noted scenes of chaos. "I looked down the streets. All Tokyo seemed to be in panic. Japs were running everywhere, pushing, shouting, screaming," Lavalle recalled. "I could see fires starting near the port. Our two Japanese interpreters in the embassy were frightened out of their skins."

"If these raids go on," one maid complained, "we'll all go mad."

American reporters who worked in Japan at the war's outbreak had endured far worse treatment than the diplomats. "It is true," one Office of Strategic Services report later noted, "that there seemed to be a special animus against newspaper correspondents." No one knew that better than *New York Times* reporter Otto Tolischus, who had spent months locked up, praying for "an American air armada come to smash the whole town into smithereens, and the whole blasted prison with it." The shriek of a siren followed by the rush of guards down the passageway alerted Tolischus that his prayer had finally been answered. "My friendly floor guard opened my door long enough to indicate to me that this was no drill, but the real thing. He made a long face and shook his head," Tolischus wrote in his diary. "An air raid—a real honest-to-goodness air raid—was apparently something the Japanese had not counted upon. I felt like cheering."

Associated Press correspondent Joseph Dynan sat out the war in an internment camp halfway between Tokyo and Yokohama, along with a dozen other Americans. The police had grabbed the reporter as soon as he came home from church the day the war started. Dynan's long wait for the Japanese to ship him home was interrupted by what he later described as "the thrill of a lifetime." "We were having coffee and toast when the police rushed into our camp excitedly and told us to extinguish the fires in the stoves and close the windows because there was an air raid. We thought it was only a drill—even when we heard two tremendous explosions in the direction of the Kawasaki industrial area," Dynan wrote in an article after his release in July. "One of the United States planes flew directly over our camp and the music of its motors was sweeter than Beethoven's Fifth symphony, which our phonograph was playing at the time."

CHAPTER 12

★

Tokyo is our capital and center of our divine country, so in
this sense any enemy air raid on there cannot be allowed to
take place under any circumstances.

—CAPTAIN YOSHITAKE MIWA,
FEBRUARY 8, 1942, DIARY ENTRY

WITH THE GAS DWINDLING, Ski York roared into Tokyo, piloting the
eighth bomber off the *Hornet* and the first flight of three planes aimed at
the capital's south side. His objective: an aircraft engine manufacturing
plant known simply as target no. 331.

Calculations showed that the bomber burned through an average of
ninety-eight gallons an hour, far more than the seventy-two to seventy-
five gallons it should have. York had used up his auxiliary tanks, which
were supposed to last through the raid, forty-five minutes before even
reaching the coast. Ted Laban's latest check of the tanks revealed the
bomber would not come within three hundred miles of China.

"Kee-rist," York exclaimed, "that sure looks like a carrier up ahead
there!"

York banked left to avoid the flattop, which with guns and a deck
full of fighters could prove problematic for the unescorted bomber.

"Where in the hell is Mount Fujiyama?" Emmens asked, scanning
the approaching coastline. "I'd seen lots of Jap laundry calendars and I

thought old Fujiyama, snow-covered and pink, would be looming up to meet us long before now," he wrote. "But only a rugged mountainous sky line began appearing inland."

The cockpit windshield framed a view of the breakers leading into the beaches.

"Course from Tokyo to Vladivostok, three hundred degrees," Herndon called out.

"Damn it, Bob," York griped again, "I can't get over that gas consumption. Can you figure it out?"

"Not unless we've got a gas leak—and hell, there's no evidence of that."

The men agreed Russia offered the only hope.

"I sure wish we could let them know we're coming," Emmens added, "so they'll know who we are when and if we get there."

The bomber roared ashore. The crew looked down on a fenced-off encampment filled with a couple hundred people. A guard tower with a white roof stood in one corner. Many of the people below waved frantically. Others jumped up and down. The crew noted that most had Western features, leading the crew to surmise that the compound was likely an internment camp. "Maybe a ray of hope pierced their black existences for that brief moment," Emmens wrote. "I hope so."

The bomber zoomed over villages and rice paddies and buzzed the heads of schoolchildren. David Pohl in the gun turret spotted nine fighters some ten thousand feet overhead, but the enemy fliers never saw the ground-hugging B-25. "After flying for about 30 minutes after our landfall was made, we still hadn't spotted Tokyo itself, so I started looking for any suitable target; something that was worthwhile bombing," York said. "We came across a factory, with the main building about four stories high. There was a power plant, and about three or four tall stacks, and railroad yards."

York pulled back on the yoke, climbing to fifteen hundred feet.

"Open your bomb bay doors, Herndon," York said, then turned to Emmens. "That would be a fine thing at a time like this—to forget to open your bomb bay doors!"

Herndon did as ordered, repeating the Twenty-Third Psalm: "Though I walk through the valley of the shadow of death, I fear no evil."

Four eggs plummeted down.

"Bombs away!" Herndon called out.

The explosions jolted the bomber, hurling debris above the plane. Smoke and steam climbed into the sky. The first bomb narrowly missed the Nishi Nasuno train station and railway buildings, blasting a crater more than six feet deep and thirty feet wide. The explosion blew out the windows and doors of a nearby home, whose family was away at the time. The second bomb hit a largely unpopulated area, while the third exploded in a rice field and shattered the glass windows of nearby buildings. The incendiary likewise caused little destruction. All told, York's attack managed to damage only a single building and neither killed nor injured anyone. Japanese investigators would later recover a casing labeled "Chicago ACME Steel Company."

York dove back down to rooftop level. Rather than turn back to sea, like the other crews, the bomber continued northwest.

"Keep your eyes peeled back there, Pohl."

"Yes, sir," the gunner answered. "All clear."

The foothills west of Tokyo soon grew into 8,000-foot peaks, the wide mountain range that served as the spine of Honshu. York eased back on the yoke, and the bomber climbed, soaring over the snow-covered peaks below. In the distance the aircrew spied the Sea of Japan, a streak of silver on the distant horizon.

"Okay," Pohl announced as the plane began its descent on the western slope of mountains. "All clear."

"I'll bet we're the first B-25 crew of five to bomb Tokyo and cross Japan at noon on a Saturday," Emmens joked.

"And took off from an aircraft carrier called the *Hornet*," York replied with a smile.

FIRST LIEUTENANT HAROLD WATSON piloted the *Whirling Dervish*—the ninth bomber off the *Hornet*—ashore thirty-five miles north of Tokyo. He had come straight across the ocean, catching up with planes that had taken off ahead of his.

Watson buzzed the beach and over a coastal airport with eighteen twin-engine bombers dispersed on the ground and fighters warming up on the ramp. The pilot banked southwest and climbed above the haze to 4,500 feet, passing over four more airfields en route to his target, the

Kawasaki Truck and Tank plant. The aircrew saw fires near the Electric Light plant, the radio station JOAK, and the Japanese Special Steel Company. Others burned north of the palace near where Doolittle had attacked.

Watson flew across the northwest corner of Tokyo Bay, diving as he approached his target, which sat along the waterfront. Barrage balloons floated over the water at altitudes of as much as three thousand feet—some anchored on barges in the bay. Antiaircraft fire thundered from the time Watson reached the capital's outskirts all the way to the target, prompting the *Whirling Dervish*'s gunner, Technical Sergeant Eldred Scott, to describe the afternoon as "a nice, sunshiny day with overcast anti-aircraft fire."

"I expected to see holes opening up any minute," Scott would later tell reporters, "but never saw one."

Watson pressed on through the flak toward his target, holding the bomber steady in what one witness on the ground would later describe as "majestic deliberation." The bomber zoomed between the Imperial Palace and the bay waterfront, buzzing over the Japanese Diet and the *Nichi Nichi* newspaper plant. A photo of the *Whirling Dervish* would even appear in the paper the following morning.

Watson leveled off at 2,500 feet and a speed of 230 miles per hour, lining up for a ten-second run. Wayne Bissell sized up the target, which sat on a sand spit along the edge of the bay and consisted of eight or nine buildings about 50 feet by 200 set in rows with about 100 feet between them. "I dropped two demolition on our target area," the bombardier wrote. "There was a 4½ second delay for our incendiary bundle and I released the remaining demolition and the incendiary bundle at the end of that time."

The first bomb tore through the roof of a hazardous-materials warehouse filled with gasoline, heavy oil, and methyl chloride. The 500-pound weapon bounced off gas cylinders and landed in the wooden building next door before it exploded. The second bomb detonated sixty feet away, leaving a crater six feet deep and thirty feet wide. Alerted to the raid by antiaircraft fire, workers had begun to evacuate, but shrapnel from the second bomb killed one and injured forty-one others, three seriously; one victim with a shrapnel wound to the head later died. The attack damaged five of the factory's buildings. The incendiary came down in a residential area, partially burning one home. The final demolition bomb proved a dud, but it still ripped a nearly two-foot hole through the tiled roof of a home, passed through the wooden floor and buried in the wet red clay, forcing the military to form a 650-foot perimeter to later dig it out.

When gunner Eldred Scott looked back to see the damage, he found the crew in trouble. The Japanese jumped the bomber. "Tracers were looping up at us from behind and below from a single fighter that was only a hundred yards away from us and pointing straight at me!" he wrote. "I opened fire only to find that my sight fogged up. All I could do was keep my finger on the trigger and aim with my tracers. As my bullets came closer and closer, the enemy fighter fell off on the left wing and I never saw it again. I think I got him but I'll never be able to swear to it."

FIRST LIEUTENANT RICHARD JOYCE PILOTED the final plane tasked to bomb the capital's southern end, specifically the Japan Special Steel Company's plants and warehouses in the Shiba Ward about a mile and a half north of the Tama River.

As the pilot of the tenth bomber, Joyce expected opposition, prompting him to pull up to three thousand feet and hide in the clouds as he charged across the Pacific. He hit the coast at Inubo Saki and banked south, flying another ten miles before he turned west and headed across the Boso Peninsula and into Tokyo Bay.

Navigator and bombardier Horace Crouch mentally prepared himself as Joyce closed in for the attack. "When we were a short way out from the target I read briefly from the Testament that I carried," he recalled. "I also said a short prayer, then I figured it was time to get back to the job at hand."

Joyce dropped down to 2,400 feet and slowed to 210 miles per hour as he lined up on his target, the bomb bay doors now open. An aircraft carrier steaming out of the bay toward the Yokosuka naval base opened fire, but the flak proved woefully inaccurate.

Crouch lined up his shot and released the bombs. "The targets were so thick and we were so low," he recalled, "we couldn't miss."

Joyce's first bomb blasted a wharf; the second hit a building that served as a study room and dormitory for workers, many of whom had evacuated to volunteer standby spots once the air-raid alarms sounded. Not everyone, however, had left. New workers who were still waiting for volunteer assignments loitered in the dormitory. The bomb exploded and killed five instantly, plus two female office employees, who had remained behind to collect important records. Seven other workers died hours later from injuries. Joyce's third bomb exploded in a home just north of the Ministry of Railways Supply Bureau clothing factory in Shinagawa, leveling several wooden houses in a forty-foot radius and killing six residents, two of them children. Shrapnel riddled the clothing factory a hundred feet away, where five workers died, including several female office employees. Seven others were seriously injured, as were many others at the railway ministry. Joyce's attack killed a total of twenty-five men, women, and children—second only to Jones's in the number of fatalities—and seriously wounded twenty-three. Another hundred and fifty people suffered minor injuries. All told, he leveled nine buildings with sixteen units and damaged eight others, which contained another twenty units.

The antiaircraft fire thundered around the bomber. Joyce's long and straight target run had allowed the enemy gunners to zero in on him. Americans imprisoned in a school in the Denenchofu district watched Joyce's frantic escape, afraid the Japanese would shoot down the bomber. One shell exploded so close that shrapnel tore a hole eight inches in diameter in the fuselage forward of the horizontal stabilizer.

Joyce's luck went from bad to worse. Nine enemy fighters appeared overhead at about five thousand feet. Two immediately peeled off to attack, closing to within six hundred yards. Joyce pushed the controls forward. The bomber's speed jumped to 330 miles per hour as Joyce dove under the fighters. The steep dive caused the ammunition to fly out of the can and tangle up, putting the bomber's turret out of commission. Larkin frantically worked to remedy it, as enemy machine-gun rounds tore into the left wingtip. One fighter passed so close that Crouch felt as if he could reach out and touch it. The bombardier jumped back against the bulkhead: "I remember looking down to see how many holes he had shot in me because I was sure that he had fired on us from there."

Joyce charged west along the Tama River toward the mountains, buzzing treetops along the way. Two more fighter formations attacked. Joyce outran three fighters, but another three pursued, held off only by Larkin's gunfire. One fighter closed the distance, pulling alongside and above the bomber. "I turned south at the mountains to go out to sea and we fired at him with everything we had," Joyce wrote. "I believe that we hit him but none of us are sure whether or not we knocked him down."

As Joyce passed over Sagami Bay, antiaircraft fire again erupted. Two more fighters jumped the bomber. Joyce increased power and pulled back on the yoke, climbing at two thousand feet per minute. "It seemed that when the Japs saw the tracers coming after them, they were afraid to come close." Larkin wrote in his diary. "We were finally able to climb to the clouds and lose them."

CAPTAIN ROSS GREENING, in the eleventh bomber off the *Hornet*, led the attack's fourth wave, designed to target Kanagawa, Yokohama, and Yokosuka. First Lieutenants Edgar McElroy and Bill Bower in the twelfth and thirteenth bombers flew close behind, until the trio reached the coast and split off in separate directions.

"Let's be nonchalant about this," suggested Ken Reddy, Greening's copilot. "What do you say we have a sandwich? We can say when we go home, 'We were eating a sandwich when we were bombing Tokyo.'"

Greening took a bite of his, but he was so wound up that he could neither chew nor swallow. The *Hari Kari-er* made landfall northeast of Tokyo, and Greening aimed south at 170 miles per hour toward Yokohama, the industrial suburb south of Tokyo. "I don't think I'd ever flown so low in my life, dodging down creek beds and ducking between trees rather than going over them," Greening wrote. "I'm not sure it was necessary, but it gave a sense of security. Those minutes seemed like hours."

The bomber was roaring across Kasumigaura Lake when four Japanese fighters attacked. Machine-gun rounds pinged off the bomber's right wing. Gunner Melvin Gardner let loose with the .50-caliber machine guns. "Two of these were shot down, one on fire," Greening would later report. "Neither were seen to hit the ground."

The other two fighters appeared to back off until Gardner's gun jammed and then the turret motor burned out, filling the rear of the bomber with smoke. The fighters dove to attack. Greening had no choice but to dive and outrun them. "We hugged the ground as tightly as we could and even flew under some power lines in the hope that some of the ships might crash into them. They didn't," the pilot recalled. "I flew so low over an agricultural plot that I can't understand how I missed hitting a farmer plowing with his ox. I wonder what he thought when our B-25 suddenly went thrashing past his head, with two Japanese fighters shooting at us in furious pursuit."

Greening looked out the cockpit window and saw one of the fighters score a line of as many as fifteen hits, from the trailing edge of the *Hari Kari-er*'s right wingtip to the prop. He had to unload his bombs—fast. He ordered Bill Birch to get ready; the bomb bay doors shuddered open. Greening carried four incendiaries to blast Yokohama's oil refineries, docks, and warehouses, but with the fighters hugging his tail he needed an alternative. "I could see a concentration of buildings ahead and figured we'd better use it as a target while we still could bomb anything," he wrote. "We noticed refinery pipelines and tanks camouflaged by thatched roofs, appearing to look like a cluster of houses. We rationalized, if we were going to bomb a refinery this one would do just fine. "

Greening lined up for his run and pulled back on the yoke, climbing to just six hundred feet, far less than the desired fifteen hundred.

"Oh, if my wife could see me now," he thought to himself.

The red light on the cockpit instrument panel flashed again and again. Four incendiaries tumbled out in train, followed immediately by a large explosion and several successive ones, each rocking the bomber. "There were great sheets of flame and a terrific explosion that threw the co-pilot and me right up out of our seats, even though we were belted, and banged our heads against the top of the cockpit," Greening would later tell reporters. "Once we had unloaded our bombs our speed increased and we ran right away from the two pursuit ships that were following."

Greening had hit not an oil refinery but the half-built Katori naval air station, which was covered at the time by scaffolding. The attack destroyed six buildings, including a dormitory for workers, but it neither killed nor injured anyone. Greening looked over to see blood running down Reddy's face from where he had hit his head, a small price to pay for the mission's success. As the bomber roared out to sea, Greening finally swallowed his bite of the sandwich. "When we turned and looked back," Reddy wrote in his diary, "we could see huge billows of smoke towering at least ½ a mile high."

★

FIRST LIEUTENANT BILL BOWER IN the twelfth bomber came ashore north of Choshi, a city due east of Tokyo. Bower and his crew struggled to orient themselves, so he flew an irregular course south, paralleling the coast of Japan anywhere from five to twenty miles inland toward a point east of Yokosuka.

Bower then hedgehopped, keeping the *Fickle Finger of Fate* just a few feet off the ground. "I became a busy boy trying to harvest the rice crop for the natives," he wrote in his diary. "Pretty rough job flying at zero altitude."

Despite the tough flying, Bower couldn't help admiring the lush countryside. "Why on earth," he wondered, "do they want war with us?"

Bower buzzed an airfield, interrupting a traffic pattern of as many as ten medium bombers preparing to land. East of the capital and near Sakura, the aircrew spotted a huge fire, Greening's handiwork. Several fighters tailed the bomber, but never closed to within a thousand yards. When Bower neared Yokosuka, he banked west, flying south of the Kisarazu naval air station. "Ahead was the bay," he wrote in his diary. "Down to the surface we went, mouths like glue, eyes wide open, and the target in sight."

Bower's orders were to blast the Yokohama dockyards. Barrage balloons encircled the target, making an attack impossible. He ordered Waldo Bither to pick another target. The bombardier settled on what he thought was an Ogura oil refinery—it was actually Japan Oil—as Bower leveled off at roughly eleven hundred feet. "About that time," the pilot later wrote in his diary, "all hell broke lose."

Antiaircraft shells exploded in the skies. Bower ignored the black clouds of smoke and pressed on toward his target. The red flight flashed.

"Bombs away," Bither called out.

Bower banked the plane, and the red light flashed several more times. The total time to unload the bombs was just four seconds, which, with a speed of two hundred miles per hour, spread the destruction over a quarter-mile area. Bither watched the first tear through the roof of a warehouse near the docks, while another hit a railroad track that ran down between the two piers. He had aimed another at three oil storage tanks and thought he either hit them or came close as a massive black cloud suddenly enveloped the area. "I was watching through the driftmeter and saw them hit," navigator Bill Pound later wrote.

"There was no doubt but that a lot of work was stopped on the docks that day." Copilot Thad Blanton echoed Pound: "Our bombs were right on the nose."

A postwar analysis would reveal that one of the bombs missed a massive Japan Oil tank by just thirty feet and an army oil tank by ninety, instead destroying six underground gas pipes and a steel-reinforced concrete wall. Workers dove inside a recently built, though not yet activated, furnace to escape. Two other bombs hit a Showa Electric factory, blasting roads inside the compound and leaving a crater eight feet deep and almost forty feet wide. The explosion hurled a sixteen-foot piece of rail line nearly two hundred feet, where it crashed into a roof of a nearby factory, while shrapnel tore into a hydrogen tank, triggering a fire. Several dozen incendiary bomblets fell across the Showa Electric factory and the neighboring Japan Steel Piping, destroying a two-story building. Some seventy other bomblets fell harmlessly in the canal that ran between the two factories; investigators would later collect thirteen unexploded ones. All told, Bower's attack destroyed two buildings and damaged a third. No one was hurt or killed.

Bower dove back down, hedgehopping over rooftops toward the sea, dodging the dark bursts of antiaircraft fire. Only when the bomber buzzed the breakers did the fliers finally relax. "Because we were not allowed to smoke, I was chewing gum," Pound wrote. "My mouth had become so dry that the gum got stuck all over the inside of my mouth and I felt I really had a mouth full of cotton."

FIRST LIEUTENANT EDGAR McELROY, the last one tasked to bomb the Tokyo suburbs, spotted the coastline in the distance at 1:30 p.m., and there he ordered bombardier Robert Bourgeois to ready the nose gun.

"Mac, I think we're going to be about sixty miles too far north," navigator First Lieutenant Clayton Campbell announced. "I'm not positive, but pretty sure."

Campbell was close. The *Avenger* charged ashore about fifty miles north, prompting McElroy to turn back to sea and parallel the coastline south. The bomber buzzed many small fishing boats and at least four freighters before McElroy turned inland again at 2:20 p.m. The *Avenger* passed an airfield on the southeastern shore of Tokyo Bay. Antiaircraft guns thundered as Campbell pinpointed the bomber's precise location. McElroy banked northwest and bore down on the target: the Yokosuka naval station. "It was a thrilling sensation to see the sprawling metropolis below," Bourgeois later wrote. "This was it, our answer for Pearl Harbor."

Copilot Richard Knobloch spotted several cruisers anchored in the harbor, but the real prize, the airmen soon realized, was in the dry docks, where Japanese workers were converting the former submarine tender *Taigei* into a new 16,700-ton carrier, *Ryuho*. Bourgeois couldn't believe how accurate his preparation was. "I had looked at the pictures on board the carrier so much that I knew where every shop was located at this naval base," he later wrote. "It was as if it were my own backyard."

McElroy pulled back on the controls and climbed to thirteen hundred feet, his speed two hundred miles per hour. "There were furious black bursts of antiaircraft fire all around us," the pilot later wrote, "but I flew straight on through them, spotting our target, the torpedo works and the dry docks."

"Get ready!" McElroy shouted.

Bourgeois opened the bomb bay doors as McElroy lined up for his east-to-west run over the base's shops and building slips. Bourgeois stared down the rudimentary sight, knowing that the low altitude combined with the large target guaranteed success. "A blind man," he later joked, "could have hit my target."

The red light flashed again and again as Bourgeois dropped his three demolition bombs, followed by his single incendiary.

"Bombs away!" he shouted.

Knobloch had picked up a candid camera at the Sacramento Air Depot's base exchange. He and Campbell now snapped pictures out of the cockpit and navigator's side window, the only ones that would survive the raid.

"We got an aircraft carrier!" shouted engineer and gunner Adam Williams, who manned the turret. "The whole dock is burning!"

The bomb had ripped a massive hole twenty-six feet tall and fifty feet wide, through the port side of the *Taigei*, damage that would set back its conversion to an aircraft carrier by four months. Another thirty incendiary bomblets came down inside dock no. 4, igniting a fire that burned five crew members, carnage McElroy would capture in his report of the attack. "The large crane was seen to be blown up and a ship in the building slips was seen to burst into flames," he wrote.

"When some 30 miles to sea, we could see huge billows of black smoke rising from target."

The view looked much worse to Kazuei Koiwa, a nineteen-year-old civilian who worked out of the Yokosuka naval arsenal. He was on the phone with the staff of the Sasebo naval arsenal when the air raid alert sounded and explosions shook the building. "I looked out the window and saw a ferocious cloud of black smoke rising rapidly," he recalled, charging out onto the roof for a better view. "Large numbers of wounded were being carried on stretchers to the infirmary next to the docks."

Vice Admiral Ishichi Tsuzuki, chief of the arsenal, appeared behind him, a mournful smile on his face. "The enemy," the admiral said, "is quite something."

MAJOR JACK HILGER MADE LANDFALL on the cliffs just north of the Katsura lighthouse, a point almost due east of Yokosuka. Doolittle's second-in-command led the fifth and final wave of attacks, aimed at the industrial cities of Nagoya, Kobe, and Osaka. For Hilger the mission was personal: the Navy had just announced that his younger brother was lost when the Japanese sank the destroyer *Pillsbury* off Java.

Hilger banked southwest and paralleled the coast toward Nagoya Bay, buzzing over dozens of fishermen, many of whom waved. Donald Smith, in the fifteenth bomber, flew on Hilger's wing, finally separating to make his run on Kobe. Hilger never saw Billy Farrow, in the sixteenth bomber, who should have been on his other wing.

South of Nagoya, Hilger turned inland and at a hundred feet zoomed north up Chita Wan, a narrow inlet crowded with industrial installations that paralleled the much larger Nagoya Bay.

Hilger planned to skirt the east side of Nagoya, a move that would allow him to circle back and make a north-to-south run over the city. Herb Macia scanned the empty skies for any sign of enemy opposition. "Where are those fighters?" the navigator wondered with relief. "Thank God, we're not going to be shot down."

The aircrew marveled at the landscape. "It was a beautiful spring day with not a cloud in the sky," Hilger wrote in his diary. "The Japanese country is beautiful and their towns look like children's play gardens. It is a shame to bomb them but they asked for it." Macia agreed. "We climbed over some low-lying, beautifully cultivated country; very green, spotless," he recalled. "Every inch of land seemed to be fully utilized."

"Look, they've got a ball game on over there," Hilger announced to his crew. "I wonder what the score is."

No one suspected an air raid.

Macia noted that some people even stood up and waved.

The city of Nagoya defied the aircrew's expectations. Most thought the industrial powerhouse—Japan's third-largest city, with about 1.3 million residents—would be much larger than it actually was. Viewed from an altitude of fifteen hundred feet, the city's canals proved tough to spot and the waterfront area poorly defined. "While over Japan our entire crew was impressed with the drabness of the cities and the difficulty of picking out targets," Hilger later noted in his report. "All buildings were grey and very much the same in appearance. The cities did not look at all the way we expected them to look from the information in our objective folders and on our maps."

Hilger thundered in over the city. His orders were to target the barracks of the Third Division Military Headquarters adjacent to the Nagoya castle, Matsuhigecho oil storage northwest of the business district, the Atsuta factory of the Nagoya arsenal in the city's center, and the Mitsubishi aircraft works along the waterfront. Two minutes before Hilger lined up for his run, the antiaircraft batteries opened fire, filling the empty skies above and behind the bomber with puffs of black smoke.

"Major Hilger, sir," Bain called over the interphone, his voice filled with indignation. "Those guys are shooting at us!"

Engineer Jacob Eierman spotted one antiaircraft battery of four guns on a parade ground of the army barracks, which was the target. He saw a second battery on the side of the Mitsubishi aircraft factory. "Some of the stuff was so far off it didn't seem that they were really trying," Eierman later wrote. "I saw only one mark on the plane—a little hole near the running light on the left wing tip."

Hilger leveled off for his run at a speed of 220 miles per hour. Copilot Jack Sims asked him whether he was hot.

"No," Hilger replied.

"Then what the hell are you sweating so for?"

Hilger carried four incendiary bombs, hoping to do as much damage as possible. Macia sited the army barracks on the ground below. The red light flashed as the first incendiary dropped, the individual bomblets spreading out over several rows. Bain watched the destruction from the rear gun turret: "I saw some ten to fifteen fires in this area and another twenty or more columns of greenish smoke."

Macia prepared next to bomb the oil and gasoline storage warehouses. He selected the largest building in the cluster, which resembled a massive college gymnasium, complete with a curved roof.

Hilger bore down on his third target, the arsenal. "A tremendous building," he noted in his diary. "Macia could have hit it with his eyes shut." The bombardier agreed. "All I had to do was just drop the bomb," he recalled. "I couldn't have missed."

Antiaircraft batteries continued to roar, throwing up flak and filling the skies with dark puffs of smoke. "Our fourth and last target was one that I had been waiting to take a crack at ever since this war started," Hilger later wrote. "It was the Mitsubishi Aircraft Works. It turns out a bimotored medium bomber very similar to a B-25. The main building was about 250 yd. square and Macia hit it dead center."

Others agreed. "That was a beautiful hit," Eierman wrote. "I could see the bombs strike and flames burst up all over it." He spied something else. "As we passed over, a cleaning woman rushed out of one door and shook a mop at us!"

Hilger dove the bomber, buzzing past two oil storage tanks. "I fired a burst of some thirty to fifty rounds but did not set fire to the tanks," Bain noted in his report. "From the tracers I am certain the tanks were hit."

Hilger's attack destroyed twenty-three buildings and damaged six others. He had missed the army barracks and instead hit the Nagoya army hospital, destroying eighteen buildings; among the burned structures were six wards, but orderlies were able to evacuate the patients. Unable to put out the blaze, Army firefighters called in civilian assistance. Even then the inferno burned until the next day. The raid likewise burned up a food storage warehouse and Army arsenal, and destroyed five buildings at the Nagoya engine depot and damaged five others. No one was killed or injured.

Eierman looked at Bain and couldn't contain his laughter. "His left fist was clenched tight and his fingers were oozing peanut butter and jelly from that sandwich he had started to eat as we swept in over Japan," the engineer later wrote. "The whole raid had taken us about eight minutes, and he had never let go."

The bomber buzzed just a few feet above the bay and headed back out to sea. A mushroom-shaped column of heavy black smoke rose as much as six thousand feet above the city, visible to the airmen at a distance of thirty miles. Sources picked up in China would later confirm that fires raged for the next forty-eight hours.

"Boy," Bain called out. "You ought to see that place burn."

FIRST LIEUTENANT DONALD SMITH piloted the fifteenth bomber off the *Hornet*, staying off Hilger's wing as he listened to radio station JOAK. An alarm interrupted the regular broadcast at about 1:25 p.m., consisting of a forty-five second bell followed by what sounded like someone shouting three words. "This took place about 10 times," Smith logged in his report. "That was the last we heard of the station."

There was little doubt the raid had begun.

"Oh-oh!" copilot Griffith Williams called out. "There's the land."

"We ought to be seeing some action pretty soon," added Doc White.

Smith banked south for the hour-and-fifteen-minute run down the coast, flying barely a hundred feet over the heads of the fishermen.

"Here's a good chance to sink some of these ships, Smitty," Howard Sessler called out from the bomber's nose. "Fly over them and I'll give a few bursts."

"Better not," Smith replied. "They may think we're friendly aircraft if we don't fire. This is supposed to be a surprise."

"Guess I'll unbutton my collar," engineer Edward Saylor announced, the tension rising. "Getting a little tight."

Smith turned into Nagoya Bay, zooming past lighthouses and coastal defense batteries without drawing any fire. "The only person we bothered," White wrote in his diary, "was one fisherman who jumped into the water!"

Hilger waggled his wings at about 2:30 p.m. and headed for Nagoya. Smith pressed on toward Kobe, piloting the *TNT* just a few feet over the waters crowded with small and colorful boats. "We had our first opposition as we zoomed over the beach heading inland," White later wrote.

"Four small boys who were playing along the shore threw rocks at us as we skimmed by a few feet over their heads."

Smith pulled back on the yoke and started to climb up to several thousand feet to cross the mountains. "Say, Saylor, start pushing," copilot Griffith Williams joked. "Seems like we're stopped up here."

The airmen scanned the skies and the ground below. "Very pretty and interesting countryside, rice paddies terraced clear to the tops of the hills," White wrote in his diary. "Only airplane seen was a commercial airliner which flew by overhead. No pursuit seen though we flew by several airfields."

The bomber passed just north of Osaka, Japan's second-largest city, with almost two million residents. The airmen saw no evidence that the nation's largest commercial center had been bombed, but instead marveled at the congestion. No line appeared to mark where Osaka ended and Kobe began, while the city's factories belched a heavy smoke that left a thick haze in the air, slashing visibility and prompting White in his diary to label the city the "Pittsburgh of Japan."

Smith followed the Shinyodo River as White snapped photos of the industry that crowded the banks. "Trains, streetcars and buses were still running on the streets, people were out walking about," he later wrote. "We even passed a commercial airliner heading in the other direction," the Greater Japan Airlines daily round-trip flight from Fukuoka to Tokyo, carrying twenty-one passengers that afternoon and bound to arrive in the capital at 4:40 p.m. The sea breeze blew back some of the haze as the bomber neared Kobe, the nation's sixth-largest city, with a population of about a million. The airmen spotted Koshien stadium, the largest ballpark in Asia, able to seat some fifty thousand fans and even boasting flush toilets. On the same field where Nankai battled Taiyo this afternoon, Babe Ruth and Lou Gehrig played during a 1934 visit, later commemorated on a plaque at the stadium's entrance. "Everything looked very much as the objective folder had shown, and we had no trouble in finding our targets," Smith wrote in his report. "No anti-aircraft fire was encountered, and nothing hindered us from completing the mission."

Japan's confidence that America would never raid its cities was on display in Kobe, where the airmen observed no effort to camouflage important factories and plants. The skies likewise proved empty of any fighter opposition, barrage balloons, or even antiaircraft fire as the *TNT* droned toward its targets, carrying four incendiary bombs to use against the city's warehouses, shipping docks, and aircraft factories.

"There's the steel foundries straight ahead, Smitty," Sessler said. "That's where we'll start our bombing run from."

"I see it," Smith replied. "Give 'em hell!"

Smith lined up for his run at two thousand feet and 240 miles per hour.

"Bomb bay doors open," Sessler announced.

"Okay."

Sessler stared down the Mark Twain sight, dropping the first bomb immediately west of the Uyenoshita Steelworks and aiming the second at the Kawasaki Dockyard Company. The third fell west of the Electric Machinery Works, an area populated by small factories, machine shops, and residences. Sessler aimed the fourth at the Kawasaki aircraft factory and the Kawasaki Dockyard Company aircraft works. Only then did antiaircraft batteries open fire, from positions near the mouth of Shinminato River.

"Hey, when you going to start dropping those things," Smith blurted out, unaware that the red light on his cockpit instrument panel had burned out. "It's getting kind of hot up here and I'm starting to sweat."

"I've already dropped them," Sessler called back.

"Bet they got a bang out of that!" Saylor quipped.

"Hope they don't lose their heads over it," added Smith.

A postwar analysis showed that the *TNT* largely missed its intended targets. One of the bombs destroyed eighteen homes in the Nishide neighborhood and damaged eleven others, killing one person, who was hit by an incendiary bomblet. Another bomb burned up three homes and damaged two others in the neighborhood of Minami Sakasegawa, while most of the final incendiary bomblets came down harmlessly in a canal alongside the Kawasaki aircraft factory. All told, Smith's attack killed one person and injured five others, while destroying twenty-one homes and damaging fourteen others.

White took photographs throughout the attack, spotting the aircraft carrier *Hiyo* under construction at the Kawasaki dockyard. When he shot all thirty-two frames, the doctor removed the film, slipped it in a canister, and taped the edges.

Smith swooped down over the bay and headed back out to sea as the airmen marveled at how easy the mission was. "Nobody realized we were enemies until the bombs dropped," Saylor later said. "The Japs simply didn't think it could be done." Smith agreed. "It was like the old sleeper play in football," the pilot recalled. "We caught them napping and got away with it."

SECOND LIEUTENANT BILLY FARROW roared in last, in the *Bat out of Hell*, the encore of America's first attack against Japan. Farrow's orders allowed him to target either Osaka or Nagoya; he chose the latter. "We came in over the Japanese mainland at hedgehopping height," recalled navigator George Barr. "The sun was shining and the people in the streets below were all waving. They'd been so indoctrinated that Japan would never be bombed that they couldn't imagine it could really happen."

When enemy fighters appeared in the skies, Farrow increased speed and pulled back on the controls, climbing up to seven thousand feet and vanishing in the clouds. The airmen flew dead reckoning toward Nagoya, diving through a hole in the clouds over the city.

"Get set to drop bombs at five hundred feet," Farrow ordered bombardier Jacob DeShazer. "There is the first target."

The *Bat out of Hell* carried four incendiary bombs to target an oil refinery and an aircraft factory. Farrow lined up his run as DeShazer looked down the sight.

"See that gasoline tank?"

DeShazer did.

The red light flashed on the cockpit instrument panel as the first three bombs dropped. Farrow banked the plane. DeShazer smelled smoke and wanted to see the refinery burn. "To the left of us I saw where the first bombs had dropped. There was fire all over the tank, but it had not blown up yet," he recalled. "What I was smelling, however, was powder of the shells that were being shot at us instead of the bombs I had dropped. I had noticed a little black smoke cloud right in front of us, and evidently the hole in the nose of our airplane allowed the smoke to come inside."

Farrow pressed on toward the next target, a long flat building that the pilot suspected was an aircraft factory.

"Let your bombs go," he ordered DeShazer.

The red light flashed a final time.

The *Bat out of Hell* hit the Toho Gas Company's no. 3 tank, sparking a massive fire. Japanese workers rushed to prevent an explosion by releasing gas throughout the city. Farrow's final attack hit Mitsubishi Heavy Industries' Nagoya Aeronautical Manufacturing, a plant that produced the famed Zero fighter. Damage was light, but the attack killed five people and injured eleven others, two seriously.

"We didn't miss," Deshazer and copilot Bobby Hite wrote. "We bombed from 500 feet with ack-ack bursting all around us, but we never got hit. We circled fast, took a look at the fires and then headed west and a little south for the China coast."

CHAPTER 13

═══════

★

*Saturday's experience has shown that despite the series of
crushing defeats which he has suffered so far, the enemy still
has the spirit left to make air raids on this country.*

—*NICHI NICHI* NEWSPAPER,
APRIL 19, 1942

HALSEY DID NOT WAIT to see the bombers vanish over the horizon.
Three minutes after Farrow's B-25 roared off the *Hornet*'s deck, the admiral ordered his task force to turn back to Pearl Harbor. The *Enterprise* took over as guide, the force charging through the swells due east at twenty-five knots. Sailors hustled to ready the *Hornet*'s idle planes for action, bolting wings onto torpedo, bomber, and scout planes before sending them up the carrier's three elevators to the flight deck. The *Nitto Maru*'s contact report would no doubt trigger a Japanese response, but the force remained far outside the range of enemy fighters and would soon slip beyond the reach of multiengine bombers. The only real threat came from enemy surface ships or submarines.

Sailors hurried to help Seaman First Class Robert Wall, chewed up by Farrow's propeller, down to the carrier's sprawling sick bay. Doctors and corpsmen stopped the bleeding, then x-rayed his mangled left arm. The prognosis was bad.

Real bad.

Lieutenant Commander Edwin Osterloh, an assistant medical officer, summoned Chaplain Harp. "It will have to come off," he said. "See if you can console him."

Harp approached the bunk, noting that Wall appeared pale and in shock. He wondered what to say, when the ship's loudspeaker interrupted his thoughts: "The U.S.S. *Hornet* has reversed its course and is heading for Honolulu."

Harp seized on the announcement as his segue. "That's good news, isn't it?"

Wall was silent for a moment before he answered, skipping the banter. "Please don't let them cut it off," he pleaded.

Harp pulled a chair alongside the bed. "There is only one thing I can tell you," he said, noting that the injured seaman studied his face as he spoke. "Please listen."

Wall turned away. Harp knew his tone had only confirmed the sailor's fears. The chaplain pressed on with his impromptu speech, telling him that there wasn't a man on board from the skipper on down who would not sacrifice an arm to help make the mission a success. "You gave yours in freeing one of his planes, possibly saving the life of its crew," Harp said. "If that plane had crashed, it could never have flown over Tokyo, and the mission would have been weakened by just that much."

Wall listened.

"The crew of that plane has a mighty slim chance of getting through alive. Compare yourself to them. There is a serious danger that they will be shot down or crash. They knew that; nevertheless, they went ahead. You have already made your sacrifice toward the success of that mission. May theirs be no more serious than yours."

Harp watched as the sailor regained his composure then nodded. The doctor appeared moments later alongside the bed.

"All right, Sir," Wall said. "Let's get on with it."

Officers would later take up a collection on behalf of the injured sailor, raising $2,700. Wall broke down in tears when presented the money.

The task force continued to battle rough seas, winds of up to thirty miles an hour, and low broken clouds. Halsey took no chances with the force's security. The *Enterprise* turned into the wind and launched four scout bombers at 11:15 a.m. to search south, where radar had earlier indicated the presence of enemy vessels. Twelve minutes later a dozen more lifted off, tasked to search up to two hundred miles astern. Eight fighters roared into the skies for an inner air patrol joined by eight *Hornet* fighters.

The bombers soon went to work. At 11:50 a.m. Ensign Robert Campbell spotted a dark gray patrol boat that he estimated to be about 125 feet long. He charged in and dropped a 500-pound bomb at 1,200 feet, but missed by about 100 feet. Campbell circled back and dropped two 100-pound bombs, this time at an altitude of just 800 feet. Again he missed. The dogged naval aviator then circled back and strafed the picket boat with his .30- and .50-caliber machine guns, firing more than three hundred armor-piercing, tracer, and incendiary rounds. "The enemy maneuvered radically but did not return the fire," he noted in his report. "Minor damage topside due to strafing was observed."

Lieutenant Ralph Arndt led three planes in an attack on a seventy-five-foot motor patrol boat equipped with a radio mast at 12:26 p.m. In repeated bombing and strafing attacks, the aviators unleashed three 500-pound bombs and five 100-pounders, scoring only one near miss, which managed to knock out the patrol's lone gun. Ensign John Butler picked up a third patrol at 12:45 p.m., this one towing a small white boat. He dropped two 100-pound bombs, both duds. He then released his 500-pound bomb, which appeared to strike the target's port side. The patrol cut the smaller boat adrift and charged in circles, firing on Butler as he strafed the vessel. His plane took three minor hits, including a .25-caliber machine-gun bullet later recovered from the aircraft.

Radar at one point picked up an enemy patrol plane, passing north of the task force at a range of more than thirty-five miles, oblivious to the escaping armada. More patrol boats crowded the seas, giving the naval aviators a workout. Lookouts on the *Enterprise* sighted two such vessels at 2:01 p.m. Two minutes later carrier planes pounced, firing some 6,000 incendiary, tracer, and armor-piercing rounds. One of the patrols sank, and aviators damaged the other. The *Nashville* charged in for the kill, opening fire on the wooden patrol boat at a range of six thousand yards. The guns roared again and again, firing 102 six-inch rounds and another 63 five-inch rounds, reducing the patrol to little more than timbers. "Her whole starboard side," the cruiser's gunnery officer wrote in his report, "was riddled before she finally sank."

Sailors threw lines in the water and lowered a makeshift sea ladder, fashioned from a cargo net. Five enemy prisoners, suffering from shock and immersion, climbed aboard, one with a bullet wound in the cheek. Through sign language *Nashville* sailors learned that six other Japanese crewmen had died. "One was wounded and another virtually exhausted," the cruiser's action report noted, "yet all were recovered without great difficulty although the ship was rolling heavily."

Despite his wounded cheek the injured prisoner later recounted the attack. He had tried unsuccessfully to rouse his sleeping skipper when he first spied American planes at dawn. The sailor returned a few hours later when he spotted the task force.

"Two of our beautiful carriers ahead, sir!"

News of the carriers finally rallied the Japanese skipper, who climbed out of bed and marched up to the deck. He studied the American task force through binoculars. "They're beautiful," he admitted, "but they're not ours."

The Japanese skipper retreated below deck; this time he put a pistol to his head and squeezed the trigger.

The *Nashville*'s work was not over. One of the *Enterprise*'s bombers, hit in the engine by machine-gun fire while strafing the patrols, ditched at 3:03 p.m., some nine thousand yards astern of the carrier. The cruiser plucked the two airmen from the water, but the plane vanished beneath the swells.

The task force resumed its twenty-five-knot run east. Halsey's forces in a matter of hours had ripped a gaping hole in Japan's defensive net, destroying the *Nitto Maru* and *Nagato Maru* and so heavily damaging the *No. 1 Iwate Maru* and *No. 26 Nanshin Maru* that Japanese forces would later sink them. The Navy likewise damaged the merchant cruiser *Awata Maru*, along with the guardboats *Chokyu Maru*, *No. 2 Asami Maru*, *Kaijin Maru*, *No. 3 Chinyo Maru*, *Eikichi Maru*, and *Kowa Maru*. Enemy casualties totaled no fewer than thirty-three dead and another twenty-three wounded.

The *Nashville*'s guns drew much of the praise.

"She had a grand day," recalled Robin Lindsey of the *Enterprise*. "She loved it, nothing to do but not get fired at but to sink sampans. She chased all over the ocean after them as fast as our pilots would report them."

Throughout the task force officers and crewmen alike crowded around radio receivers, anxiously awaiting news of the raid. The entire mission—the work of sixteen ships and ten thousand men—came down to this moment. Had Doolittle succeeded?

At Mitscher's request Jurika settled in the *Hornet*'s flag plot, where he monitored Tokyo's AM broadcast stations via headphones. Others scanned the airways with personal radios or crowded inside the carrier's air plot, which was so jammed men could barely move. "All the ship's radios that morning were tuned in on Japan, picking up the programs from Tokyo, Kobe and Yokohama," recalled Chaplain Harp. "Our public-address system in turn relayed the programs along to the ship's personnel, so that from one end of the *Hornet* to the other there was the weird sound of Japanese broadcasters intoning their various versions of the day's news in the Axis world."

One broadcaster cited the Reuters report of an alleged American raid, assuring listeners such an attack was impossible. Jurika translated this morsel for the crew.

"Boy, oh boy, are they going to be surprised!" exclaimed one of the pharmacist's mates in the sick bay. "Whoopee!"

Jurika calculated the expected time the bombers should appear in the skies over Tokyo. That time came and went. Fifteen more minutes passed. Then twenty. The Tokyo announcers rattled on unfazed. "There was nothing to indicate from the broadcasts that there was any unusual event taking place," he recalled. "Nothing."

Jurika wasn't alone in his fears.

"We began to worry," Harp wrote, "suspecting that the fliers had either become lost in the dreadful weather or that they had been intercepted somewhere along the way."

Many of the sailors had taken to calling a female English announcer with JOAK "Lady Haw Haw," the same name the British used to describe a female Atlanta native who made similar propaganda broadcasts from Germany. The announcer suddenly interrupted her afternoon broadcast with a shrill scream just as the radio went dead.

Sailors waited in anticipation.

"A moment before, the continued broadcasting had worried us," Harp later wrote, "but now the silence was almost unbearable."

The *Hornet*'s quartermaster recorded the first official news of the attack in the ship's log at 2:45 p.m., when the broadcast resumed. "Enemy bombers appeared over Tokyo today shortly after noon for the first time in the current East Asia War," the announcer stated in English. "Heavy and telling damage was inflicted on schools and hospitals, and the populace shows much indignation."

The announcement was followed by another in Japanese, designed for domestic audiences. "A large fleet of enemy bombers appeared over Tokyo this noon and caused much damage to non military objectives and some damage to factories. The known death toll is between three and four thousand so far. No planes were reported shot down over Tokyo. Osaka was also bombed. Tokyo reports several large fires burning."

Cheers erupted throughout the *Hornet*.

On board the *Enterprise* Halsey listened as the airwaves filled with sudden excitement, then fell silent.

"They made it," the admiral said.

Others agreed.

"It doesn't take much imagination to follow through as to what had happened," observed Lieutenant Elias Mott, an assistant gunnery officer on the *Enterprise*.

Chicago Daily News reporter Robert Casey listened on board the *Salt Lake City* as afternoon turned into evening. One bulletin claimed Chinese, American, and Russian planes executed the attack, an identification the Japanese later abandoned, as military leaders struggled to determine who was actually responsible. The official Nazi news agency later reported that Yokohama had been bombed, while the British United Press announced carriers in Japanese waters had launched the raid.

The sailors bounced back and forth between the announcements intended for an international audience and the local broadcast bands designed for Japanese ears. Over one of the nation's domestic frequencies the sailors listened as a female announcer shrieked hour after hour about the need for blood donors.

"Even if she had been talking of nothing more unusual than new ways to cook rice, you would know that terror had arrived in Tokio," Casey noted in his diary. "It is her voice, rather than the subject, that gives you the notion."

The *Salt Lake City* skipper, Captain Ellis Zacharias, who was in Japan when the 1923 earthquake struck, joined his men to listen.

"The woman's had a shock," he said, "*a bad shock*. Japanese women don't get that way over nothing. Maybe this bombing amounts to something after all."

The announcer continued.

"Give your blood as the men at the front are giving theirs," she cried. "Give your blood. Your lives are in danger. Tomorrow—tonight—your children may be blown to bits. Give your blood. Save them—save Japan."

"An interesting moment, gentleman," Zacharias added.

Sailors listened as Japanese broadcasters depicted the American raiders as barbarians who targeted civilians.

"There has been no damage at all to military objectives, but several schools, hospitals and shrines have been destroyed," a male broadcaster announced in English. "Thirty primary school children on their way home from morning classes were machine-gunned in the street."

"You notice that nobody on the Jap radio yet knows whose planes they were. They give themselves away guessing," one of the cruiser's senior aviators noted. "On the face of the evidence it looks as if this bombing has been a great success."

The broadcaster announced that nine unidentified planes had been shot down, drawing a laugh from the same flier. "More evidence the bombing was a success," he added. "We shot down nine planes but we don't know whose."

On board the *Hornet* Chaplain Harp worked most nights from 7:30 until 11 p.m., typing up the news reports that came over the radio and mimeographing them into a makeshift daily paper for the officers and crew, the *News Digest*. Stenciled across the top of the edition that he prepared for April 19 was the same slogan that Mitscher had ordered painted on the carrier's stack: "REMEMBER PEARL HARBOR!!" Just beneath that Harp ran a cartoon of Uncle Sam spitting a stream of bombs on an island emblazoned with the caption "Japan or where it used to be."

A seaman contributed another cartoon, which Harp, though he felt it was "rowdy," still chose to publish. The sketch showed several bombers targeting an outhouse, revealing a Japanese man squatting with his trousers around his knees. The caption read, "How does it feel to be caught with your pants down?"

Commander Stanhope Ring, the carrier's air group commander, penned a four-stanza poem, the first of which read,

Twas the eighteenth of April in forty-two
When we waited to hear what Jimmy would do,
Little did Hiro think that that night
The skies above Tokio would be alight
With the fires Jimmy started in Tokio's dives
To guide to their targets the B-25s.

Such humor wasn't restricted to just the *Hornet.* An anonymous sailor on board the *Enterprise* wrote a mock business letter to Japanese prime minister Hideki Tojo. "It gives me great pleasure to inform you, in case it has not been brought to your attention, that, in accordance with the terms of your contract, accepted by us on 7 December 1941, the first consignment of scrap metal has been delivered to your city. You understand, of course, that shipping conditions being what they are it is necessary for us to effect delivery via air," the creative sailor wrote. "I wish to remind you that we are in a position to continue deliveries for years to come."

That night the tired officers crowded into the *Hornet*'s wardroom, peppering Jurika with questions as the carrier steamed farther away from the enemy's homeland, the mission now a clear success. America had struck its first blow in the war against Japan. "No one could get enough of talking and asking that night. We tried to eat, but couldn't taste our food," Harp later wrote. "We talked for hours. When I finally went to my quarters and got to bed, I was too tense to sleep. I took sleeping powders, but they were useless. I lay awake until morning, thinking about the Doolittle fliers. I could almost hear 'Deep in the Heart of Texas' booming along my passageway."

CHAPTER 14

═══════

★

There have been thousands and thousands of sorties in all
these wars and what's different about ours is only that we
knew when we took off that we weren't going to make it.

—DAVY JONES,
PILOT OF PLANE NO. 5

DOOLITTLE SETTLED IN FOR the long flight to China, trailed by fourteen other bombers—all but that of York, who had diverted to Russia.
The pilots had executed the attacks and returned to sea, vanishing over
the same horizon where the B-25s had first appeared, a move designed to
confuse the Japanese as to the mission's true terminus. Once at sea the
pilots turned south and paralleled the Japanese coast, buzzing the corner
of Kyushu before banking west along the twenty-ninth parallel to cross
the East China Sea.

Despite the *Nitto Maru*'s advance warning, the raid had so far
proven a success. The Japanese failed to shoot down a single raider. Richard Joyce's bomber was the only one of sixteen hit by antiaircraft fire,
and his dogged aircrew managed to fend off more fighters than did the
rest of the mission combined. All except one of the crews had bombed
targets. That so many of the planes got lost en route to the targets helped
spread the assault across an even wider front than Doolittle had initially

planned, making it harder for Japanese forces to anticipate where to intercept the attackers.

That alone did not excuse Japan's weak defense. Antiaircraft guns had roared and fighters had peppered the skies, but the flak proved wildly inaccurate and the pilots either blind or timid. Doolittle and his men had flown right underneath many of them, while those pilots who spotted the bombers often refused to engage or did not press home the attacks. "The sky was just purple with anti-aircraft but their aim was awful," one flier later told the *New York Times*. "Had our plane been brought down, it would have been because we flew into the fire, not that they hit us."

Others agreed.

"The most opposition we had was from a group of Japanese kids playing on a beach," another later quipped. "We passed over them at about twenty feet and they threw stones at us." Even the veteran aviator Doolittle, in his more sober analysis, confessed his shock at the weak defense entrusted with guarding such an important target as Tokyo. "I was amazed at the small number of enemy fighters," he later said. "We were opposed by only about one-tenth of the fighter opposition we had anticipated."

The raid not only exposed Tojo's poor decision not to employ a more rigorous domestic defense but also the complacency that had developed in the wake of months of lightning successes. "The over-all picture is one of inadequate defense," noted one American report. "The warning system did not appear to function; interception by fighters was definitely cautious; and anti-aircraft fire, responding slowly, did not reach the intensity one would expect for so important a city as Tokyo."

On board the bombers that flew on toward China, euphoria over having survived such a perilous mission seized some of the men. "As we paralleled the south coast of Japan, we had lunch and relaxed. It had all seemed a little unreal to me and I don't think any of us really realized that we had just made our first real bombing run," Carl Wildner recalled. "It had almost been like a training mission. It was a beautiful day in Japan and I felt like a tourist wanting to land and see the sights on the ground." A similar scene played out on board Billy Farrow's bomber. "We sang songs and kidded each other a lot about what daring young men we were," Robert Hite and Jacob DeShazer later wrote, "because, actually, the bombing wasn't anything at all."

Tensions remained high for others.

"Wow!" Dean Davenport exclaimed as the *Ruptured Duck* rounded the southern coast of Kyushu for the push to China. "What a headache I've got."

Others experienced a similar release, including mission doctor Thomas White. "About this time I sat down and had a good case of the shakes," he remembered, "a reaction to all the excitement and suspense."

But the excitement was far from over.

The *Hari Kari-er* buzzed a Japanese picket boat as the bomber headed out over the East China Sea. Gunner William Birch opened fire with the machine guns, spraying the patrol. "Just as Birch cut loose," Reddy wrote in his diary, "our right engine began to cough & sputter, throwing flames clear out the front of the nacelle." Greening and Reddy both hit the mixture control at the same time, which regulated the ratio of fuel and air. "It soon stopped but none too soon to suit any of us," Reddy wrote. "I'm sure that they would have had no mercy on us if we had gone down there."

The crew of the *Whirling Dervish* looked down three hours out of Tokyo and spotted two Japanese cruisers and a battleship. One of the cruisers opened fire, first with antiaircraft guns, then with the main battery. "One of the shells landed so near it sprayed water all over our plane," gunner Eldred Scott recalled. "There I was, firing back with a .50 caliber machine gun. Might as well have had a cap pistol."

With the added gas cans and fuel tanks empty, the airmen could smoke cigarettes, which helped ease the tension. Saylor uncapped his bottle of snakebite whiskey and took a long pull, the only time in his career he ever drank on duty. He had earned it—and he wasn't alone. Lawson, McClure, and Thatcher toasted the mission in the cockpit of the *Ruptured Duck*.

As the minutes ticked past and the adrenaline wore off, attention turned to the question of fuel: would the bombers have enough to reach China? "Up until now, we had been flying for Uncle Sam, but now we were flying for ourselves," pilot Edgar McElroy wrote. "We had not had time to think much about our gasoline supply, but the math did not look good. We just didn't have enough fuel to make it!"

That reality now hit home for many. "My feelings of exhilaration soon evaporated and I once again felt the same stomach knot as when we left the *Hornet*," added Jack Sims, Hilger's copilot. "The odds of reaching the Chinese coast were considerably against us and we didn't think we were going to survive with hundreds of miles to go over hostile territory, land *and* sea."

Airmen furiously computed the distance and fuel consumption, then ran the numbers again, hoping against all odds. "By stretching our calculations to the utmost, we knew our gasoline would run out some 250 miles short of the Chinese mainland," bombardier Robert Bourgeois wrote. "It seemed certain that we were headed for the end. All we could do was just fly on and hope for a miracle."

Even Doolittle, the amazing airman who time and again had pushed himself and his aircraft to the limit, faced the same fate as his men when navigator Hank Potter informed him that he expected the bomber to run out of gas 135 miles short of China. "I saw sharks basking in the water below and didn't think ditching among them would be very appealing," Doolittle recalled. "Fortunately, the Lord was with us."

"We've got a tail wind," Potter suddenly announced.

The headwind the bombers had long battled now turned into a twenty-five-mile-per-hour tailwind that pushed the planes toward China, lifting the spirits of the exhausted aircrews. "For the first time since morning we knew that we had a chance of seeing the night out," Jack Hilger confided in his diary. "We were all pleased and proud of the success of our bombing but now we were like a bunch of kids for we knew we had a chance to live long enough to tell about it."

As the bombers closed in on China late in the afternoon, the weather began to deteriorate. The beautiful skies turned overcast as fog settled in and raindrops pelted the cockpit windshields. Visibility declined further as night approached. The low fuel light glowed on most instrument panels, rekindling earlier worries. "Chances of reaching land were almost nil," Sims recalled. "It felt like walking the last mile."

Doolittle feared he might not make it. "See that the raft is ready," he ordered bombardier Fred Braemer. "We're going to keep going until we're dry."

Copilot Dick Cole studied the water below. The change in color from blue to brown indicated the presence of mud and sediment, the discharge of a river. The cockpit windshield now framed a sliver of land in the distance.

"There it is," Paul Leonard yelled. "Damned if I don't feel like Columbus."

The charts showed mountains as high as five thousand feet, but Doolittle didn't trust the maps. Crossing the Chinese coast, he pulled back on the yoke, climbing up to eight thousand feet. He went on instruments and looked down at the occasional twinkle of dim lights far below, unaware that the same tailwind that had rescued him and his men from a watery grave had stymied the desperate efforts to ready the airfields. Doolittle tried to raise Chuchow on 4495 kilocycles, but got no answer. The airfield was nestled precariously in a valley twelve miles long and just two wide. "Without a ground radio station to home in on, there was no way we could find it," Doolittle wrote. "All we could do was fly a dead-reckoning course in the direction of Chuchow, abandon ship in midair, and hope that we came down in Chinese-held territory."

"We'll have to bail out," Doolittle announced to his crew, ordering Leonard to go first, followed by Braemer, Potter, and then Cole. Doolittle would jump last. "Got it?"

"Got it, Colonel," Leonard replied.

Doolittle addressed his navigator. "When we get as close as you think we are going to get to the airfield, we will leave the airplane."

Potter folded up the navigator's seat and table and yanked open the hatch as Doolittle switched on the bomber's autopilot.

The time to jump arrived.

"Get going," Doolittle ordered.

Leonard and Braemer left the plane within seconds of each other at 9:10 p.m., followed two minutes later by Potter.

"Be seeing you in a few minutes, Dick," Doolittle said to Cole, helping to free his copilot's parachute from the seat and then patting him on the shoulder.

Cole hovered over the hatch, staring down at the dark void. "I was one scared turkey," he recalled. "Being in an airplane that was about to run out of fuel and looking down at the black hole that would exit you into a foreign land, in the dark of night, in the middle of bad weather was not exactly what one envisioned when enlisting."

Cole vanished out the hatch, leaving Doolittle alone in the bomber. He had flown for thirteen hours and traveled 2,250 miles. The legendary pilot had accomplished the impossible: he had bombed the Japanese capital for the first time in that nation's history. Doolittle thought he had enough fuel for maybe another half hour, but he couldn't be certain. The decision was made; it was time to go.

He shut off the gas valves and dropped through the forward hatch.

The night swallowed him.

Doolittle's jump marked the third time he had been forced to bail out of an airplane to save his life. He drifted down through the darkness worried about his ankles, which he had broken fifteen years earlier in Chile. He feared he might snap them again if he landed too hard. Doolittle hit the ground and bent his knees to cushion the blow, only to find that he had landed in a rice paddy filled with night soil, fertilizer made from human waste. He climbed out of the paddy and unhooked his parachute.

Doolittle spotted a light emanating from what appeared to be a small farmhouse. He hiked over and banged on the door, repeating the phrase that Jurika had taught him. "I heard movement inside, then the sound of a bolt sliding into place," he later wrote. "The light went out and there was dead silence."

Cold, wet, and filthy, Doolittle wandered on, finding a small warehouse. He went inside and discovered an elongated box perched atop two sawhorses. Peeking inside the box, he discovered a dead Chinese man. He set off again and soon came upon a water mill that offered him shelter from the rain. He spent most of the night performing light calisthenics to keep warm.

Other members of his crew endured similar experiences. Cole yanked his parachute's rip cord so hard that he hit himself in the face and gave himself a black eye. "First you hear the roar of the airplane and then it's just like that; it's quiet," he recalled. "I tried using my flashlight, but it was like being in fog, and it just reflected back. You couldn't see anything. I thought I would be able to see the ground, but I couldn't do it." Cole drifted down, his chute snagging atop a pine tree. He managed to untangle it and fashioned a hammock to spend the night, grateful he had made it down safely. "I was in all one 'scared piece,'" Cole wrote, "and I do mean scared."

Leonard landed on the side of a hill near the top. He rolled up in his parachute and slept until morning. Potter likewise landed on a mountainside and sprained his ankle. He slipped off his parachute and spotted a path in the dark. He started down the mountain until he realized it was futile to walk out at night. The navigator stretched out under a tree, pulling his goggles over his eyes to block the rain. Braemer did the same. "Couldn't see," the bombardier wrote in his report. "Crawled about 20 ft. down hill, got no place, went uphill 20 ft. past chute, got no place. Came back to chute, cut some from shroud lines. Rolled up in it, put arm around bamboo tree and went to sleep."

DEAN HALLMARK ROARED JUST fifty feet above the waves, afraid to fly any higher and risk battling a fierce headwind. The weather had started to deteriorate about a hundred miles from the Chinese coast. He pressed on even as a heavy fog soon slashed visibility to zero. The pilot of the *Green Hornet* planned to make landfall around Hangchow Bay, a move that would allow him to follow the river south toward Chuchow. He had long since disabled the nagging low-fuel light, hoping that he had a least a few more miles worth of gas. He asked navigator Chase Nielsen how much longer to the coast.

"Three minutes," Nielsen answered.

Hallmark spotted the coastline through the dark and pulled back on the controls, intending to fly as far inland as possible before the crew bailed out. Bill Dieter remained in the nose, resisting Hallmark's suggestion to climb out. "No," the bombardier insisted. "I'd better stay down here because then if I see a building or a tree sticking up or something maybe I can warn you soon enough so you don't run into it."

The bomber bore down on the coast just as the left engine cut out. Seconds later the right coughed—then quit.

The *Green Hornet* fell silent.

"Prepare for crashing landing," Hallmark yelled.

Nielsen didn't even have time to buckle his safety belt. "Well," he thought as the plane plunged. "I won't have to use this parachute."

The left wing struck the water first, snapping off. The fuselage then hit and the bomber's belly split wide open, like a gutted fish. Nielsen heard Dieter scream and saw water rush up over the nose. "All went black momentarily," the navigator recalled. "When I came to, I was standing in water up to my waist and was bleeding from gashes on my head and arms. My nose hurt and I knew it was broken. The two pilots were gone and so was Dieter from the nose section. Not only was Dean Hallmark gone but so was his seat, which had catapulted right through the windshield."

Nielsen grabbed the crash ax and smashed out the top window of the navigator's compartment. He climbed atop the fuselage along with copilot Bob Meder. Hallmark struggled to free himself from his cockpit chair and then joined them. "The gunner was crawling out of the back, and he was bleeding all down his face. He had a big hole in his forehead," Nielsen recalled of Donald Fitzmaurice. "The bombardier finally came up under the wing, and he was in an awful mess, I don't think he was using either arm."

Meder yanked the release to inflate the life raft, but the cable broke off the air cartridge. The aviators scrambled to tie themselves together as waves battered the filleted fuselage, tossing them into the water. Hallmark ordered the men to stay together and swim to shore. The rain poured down and the waves churned. The fliers yelled out in the darkness, hoping to locate one another, but the voices soon fell silent and the men drifted. "I thought about my family," Nielsen recalled. "I began to worry about whether my navigation had been accurate. Were we only a few miles off the coast of China or a couple hundred? I prayed that I was right but was overcome by doubt."

Nielsen wasn't sure where to swim. He fired his .45 automatic to alert the others, but the ammunition was water logged. He unbuckled his gun belt and let it drop. He had studied the tidal timetables on board the *Hornet* and assumed the seas would eventually deposit him on shore. "I figured there was no use in trying to swim because you don't know which way you're swimming. You can't see the coast. You can't see anything. And if you swim you might just be swimming toward the open ocean," he said. "So I floated for awhile, and floated, and finally I ran into some fishing nets that had been hung on some bamboo poles about eight inches in diameter."

Exhaustion threatened to overwhelm him, but Nielsen knew the nets signaled he was close to shore. He thought about waiting for the fishermen to come and retrieve him, but realized the owner of the nets might be Japanese. Nielsen swam on until he heard the sound of breakers. He put his feet down and touched the bottom. Making his way to shore, he discovered his legs wouldn't work, so he crawled, but the waves would break over him and pull him back toward the water. He refused to give up. "I crawled until I figured I was past the tide line and then I collapsed completely," he wrote. "I was fagged out. Everything, my mind and body, was numb. All I wanted was sleep."

THE *RUPTURED DUCK* CLOSED in on the Chinese coast, skimming just fifty feet above the wave tops. The heavy fog and rain clouded the windshield and forced pilot Ted Lawson to roll back his side window to see out.

"I think we ought to go a little farther south," navigator Charles McClure said as the bomber cruised past one of the many islands that guarded the coastline. "It must be all occupied along here. I can't tell much about anything, with this visibility."

The plane pressed on south as McClure's frustration mounted. "I don't think we'll ever find anything this way."

Lawson felt he had no choice but to pull up and go on instruments, a move that would allow the crew to bail out. He eased back on the controls and the *Ruptured Duck* began to climb even as Lawson continued to wrestle with his decision to abandon the bomber. This was not how he had hoped to conclude what had so far been a flawless mission. A break appeared in the clouds, offering the aircrew a glimpse of long white sandy beach below. Lawson estimated that the *Ruptured Duck* still had about a hundred gallons of fuel. If he could land the bomber on the beach, the crew could wait out bad weather, lift off at dawn, and find the airfield.

Lawson nosed the plane down and twice buzzed the concave beach. He saw no logs that might chew up the bomber, and the rain appeared to have pounded the sand down hard enough to support the *Ruptured Duck*'s delicate nosewheel. "It was by all means," he wrote, "the best thing I had seen for twelve hours or more."

The crew rushed to trade parachutes for life jackets as Lawson lowered the flaps and wheels and aimed up for the beach, whose crescent shape meant the bomber had to come in over the water and then bank to land. He was approaching at 110 miles per hour when both engines coughed, then died, just a quarter mile from shore. Lawson hit the throttles and pulled back on the stick, desperate to keep the nose up.

Just as McClure reached up to grab the aircrew's pistols, the wheels struck the wave tops, and he heard the horrible sound of metal ripping. "We're crashing," the navigator thought with disbelief.

The *Ruptured Duck* dove, then flipped upside down. The impact threw the bombardier Bob Clever headfirst through the nose of the plane and catapulted Lawson and copilot Dean Davenport out of the cockpit, still strapped in their seats. McClure crashed with his shoulder into the armor plate before he, too, landed in the water.

Lawson came to moments later, still strapped in his seat about fifteen feet underwater, the roar of the engines replaced with total silence. He thought of his wife, Ellen, wishing he had left her money. He remembered his mother as well. "I'm dead," he thought. "No, I'm just hurt. Hurt bad."

Lawson unbuckled his safety belt. The crash had broken the dioxide capsule that triggered the pneumatic life belt, so he shot to the surface, the quiet replaced by darkness and driving rain. Lawson felt numb and disoriented, but he knew enough to unfasten his parachute and wade toward shore, the waves lifting him up. He banged into a solid object. He looked down only to realize it was one of the *Ruptured Duck*'s wings. The crash had torn the engine off. Lawson stared at the tangled wires and cables and felt nauseous as the gravity of the crash hit him. A wave pushed him forward, and he turned to spot the tail rudders rising out of the waves, an image that reminded him of tombstones.

He tried to crawl up on the beach, but the waves kept pulling him back out to sea. Finally a wave pushed him up on shore. Lawson rose and walked in a circle, his legs numb. He cursed himself over the crash only to realize that his voice sounded strange and muffled. Lawson reached up to feel his mouth. "The bottom lip had been cut through and torn down to the cleft of my chin, so that the skin flapped over and down," he later said. "My upper teeth were bent in. I reached into my mouth with both of my thumbs and put my thumbs behind the teeth and tried to push them out straight again. They bent out straight, then broke off in my hands. I did the same with the bottom teeth and they broke off too, bringing with them pieces of my lower gum."

Lawson stared down at his handful of teeth and gums before dropping them and trudged up the beach. Davenport appeared in front of him. He grabbed Lawson's head and examined it.

"Good God!" Davenport exclaimed. "You're really bashed open. Your whole face is pushed in."

Lawson asked his copilot whether he, too, was hurt badly.

"I think so," Davenport said. "I don't know."

McClure came to underwater, estimating he was at least ten feet down. "I must go up," he thought. "But where the hell is up?"

The navigator felt his feet touch the sand, and he kicked toward the surface and immediately popped through the waves in the chest-deep water. He started toward shore. "I reached out with one hand to help the wading with a paddle strike. To my astonishment I couldn't get the hand above the water. I looked at the hand and arm. Then I decided to reach the other hand over toward the upper arm on the opposite side. That was a no go either," he recalled. "Gradually I realized that both were broken."

McClure found Clever in the shallow surf. The bombardier was woozy. "Help me in," he pleaded with McClure.

"Can't," McClure answered. "I think both my arms are broken."

"You wouldn't kid me, would you?"

McClure said he wouldn't.

"Come on, you son of a bitch," Clever shot back. "Come help me!"

The two airmen shouted at one another in the surf. "He called me fighting names and I gave some back," McClure wrote. "Then we looked at each other disgustedly and dragged ourselves out of the water to collapse on the beach."

Dave Thatcher came to his senses in back of the *Ruptured Duck*. He had hit his head on impact, leaving a small gash on top of his head, one he felt would have been far worse had he not remembered to slip on his flight helmet right before the crash. Water rushed in through the gun turret, which in his disoriented state Thatcher thought was the rear escape hatch. He pulled the string on his life vest then tried to climb through the turret. Only then did he realize the bomber was upside down. He pushed out the escape hatch and climbed up on the belly of the bomber, making his way toward the smashed nose. Thatcher heard McClure call to him from the beach. The gunner stepped off the fuselage and into the waist-deep water, wading toward shore.

After he joined the others, two men appeared atop a nearby embankment. The gunner unholstered his pistol and aimed. "Should I shoot 'em?"

"Hell, no," McClure answered. "They're Chinese fishermen."

"How do you know?"

"Well," he said. "I've read the *National Geographic* magazine."

The fishermen climbed down the embankment and approached, dressed in conical hats and straw raincoats. A half dozen others appeared and followed them down. "Chinga," one of the locals said, pointing to his chest.

The aircrew repeated the phrase Jurika had taught them, and the fishermen nodded. One of the villagers then made a show of counting the airmen. He then pointed to the plane, questioning whether there were any more.

The fishermen helped carry the battered airmen to a nearby hut, a feat that amazed McClure. "Under other circumstances, the man appointed to carry me off the beach would have been the basis for a joke," the navigator later wrote. "He was a little bit of a squirt, hardly more than four feet tall and weighing not more than 100 pounds, wringing wet. But he backed up manfully and tried to take my arms over his shoulders—my weight was about 205. My pained expression stopped him, and I tried with such sign language as I had to tell him what was wrong. Then he backed up again with his back bent and I mounted piggyback with my hands resting on his shoulders. Somehow he made it to a house that must have been 200 yards away."

Inside the two-room hut made of mud bricks and with a thatched roof, the fishermen helped Lawson, Davenport, and McClure to bed. Clever passed out on the floor. Thatcher set to work tending his wounded crew by the faint light of a single lamp. The prognosis was bad. Davenport had cut his right leg so bad between the knee and ankle that within a day he would not be able to walk. McClure's injured shoulders had already begun to swell down to his elbows, making it difficult for him to use his hands. Within days his right arm would turn black. Clever sprained his hips and back so that he was unable to stand up and walk, forcing him to crawl on his hands and knees. Cuts above one eye and below the other caused his eyes to swell shut while his headfirst exit through the bomber's nose had nearly scalped him. "The top of his head," Thatcher wrote in his report, "was so badly skinned that half his hair was gone."

Lawson was the most seriously injured. He had suffered a long deep gash just above his left knee, causing a serious loss of blood. The wound

looked so bad that the airmen were convinced his kneecap had been severed. Lawson suffered another short but deep cut between the left knee
and ankle through which Thatcher could see the bone. His foot below
the ankle was so bruised it would turn black within days, and he suffered
another deep gash on his left arm. His face looked as if someone had
slashed it with a razor, and by Thatcher's count he had lost up to nine
teeth. "If he'd only had one of these injuries it wouldn't have been so bad,
but with the four serious ones he lost so much blood it made him very
weak," Thatcher wrote. "I was afraid he would die or that gangrene
would start in his leg before we reached a hospital."

Thatcher used the bandage in the first aid packet on his gun belt for
the large wound on Lawson's knee. He then improvised, applying his
handkerchief to the cut on Lawson's arm. He had no choice but resort to
dirty rags the fishermen gave him for Lawson's other wounds as well as
those of Davenport and Clever. Thatcher knew he needed more supplies.
Later that night with the injured men settled, he took a lantern and
returned to the plane, hoping to find the first aid kit stored in the *Ruptured Duck*'s tail. He reached the beach, only to discover that the tide
had come in and submerged the bomber. There was no hope of finding
the kit that evening. Thatcher would have to care for the others as best he
could in what would prove to be a long night.

The shock of the crash wore off as the hours marched past. "My
shoulder pains got worse. I couldn't lie down and I couldn't stand. There
was no position that I could bear very long," McClure said. "Thatcher, at
my request, would lift my head carefully and leave it up a little while;
then he would lower my head and let me rest my hands on my knees.
Every movement was excruciating pain."

The navigator thought he would feel better without his clothes. He
ordered Thatcher to cut away his coat and shirt, but Thatcher was afraid
to ruin them. McClure lashed out at the young gunner, who finally
agreed to split the sleeve and cut across the lapels, allowing him to peel
his coat off. Shock soon seized McClure. "I felt that my body was going
to leap without my will from the bed. It is no exaggeration to say that I
expected to go crazy," he wrote. "After a little of this I passed out."

McClure woke at one point in the night to hear Davenport pleading
with one of the locals. "Hospital—soon," he begged. "Get coolies—carry."

Lawson likewise wrestled with his injuries. With the help of the fishermen, he removed his ripped-up pants, anxious to inspect his wounds. "I had no idea that there would be anything wrong with my left leg except a bruise," Lawson wrote. "It was cut from my upper thigh to my knee, and cut so deeply that it lay open widely enough so that I looked into it and saw the gristle and muscle and bone. It wasn't bleeding badly—just oozing. My circulation probably had slowed down because of the shock and the cold. I just stared at it, hypnotized and detached. I had never seen anything like it."

The door suddenly sprang open and another fisherman appeared. The airmen watched the excited whispers among the Chinese. Through sign language the fishermen made clear to Thatcher that Japanese patrols now searched the island for a downed plane. His only hope was to abandon the four injured aviators and escape. Thatcher looked at the others: Lawson, Davenport, McClure, and Clever, immobile and in pain.

"No," Thatcher made clear with a headshake.

Lawson looked up at one point to see a Chinese man dressed in heavy shoes, Western-style pants, and a shirt open at the collar enter the hut. The new arrival inspected each of the injured airmen, paying careful attention to uniform buttons and insignia. Lawson wondered whether he planned to sell them to the Japanese.

"Me—Charlie," the stranger finally announced.

Lawson and the others felt stunned to encounter an English-speaking local, pelting him with questions.

"Me—Charlie," the man repeated.

Davenport repeated the phrase Jurika had taught them.

"Melican," Charlie said with a nod.

Through a mixture of pidgin English and sign language the airmen learned that the nearest hospital was several days away; Chungking, even farther. "Many day," Charlie informed them. "Many."

The men struggled to communicate as the night waned and dawn approached. Charlie finally left, promising to return soon to help. Lawson ordered Thatcher to return again to the plane to attempt to recover the first aid kit and morphine.

"Yes, sir," the gunner said.

Thatcher arrived at the beach to find that the tide had washed much of the bomber's wreckage up on the shore, though the engines remained in the water. The gunner picked through the debris, finding only a few scattered packs of waterlogged cigarettes. He saw no sign of the first aid kit. "The nose was just a mangled mass clear back to the bomb bay," he later wrote in his report. "It was only by the hand of God that any of us got out of there alive, let alone all of us."

CHAPTER 15

★

We must always give our best, and when we die we want
to feel that our life has been lived as fully as
we could have lived it.

—BILLY FARROW,
UNDATED LETTER TO HIS MOTHER

SKI YORK'S BOMBER CLOSED in on Russia after an uneventful flight across the Sea of Japan in which the airmen saw only a single freighter; otherwise the two pilots and navigator feasted on a candy bar split three ways.

"What do you think we ought to tell these people when we land?" York asked. "Think we ought to tell them who we are and what we've done?"

"Let's wait till we see if they already know," Emmens suggested.

Shortly before 5 p.m. the cockpit windshield framed the distant coastline, where dark mountains climbed up out of the sea, putting an end to the day's fears of running out of gas over the water. "Lord," Emmens wrote, "what a welcome sight!"

Armed with poor maps, the airmen feared making landfall over Japanese-occupied Korea, just fifteen miles south of Vladivostok. Navigator Nolan Herndon studied the coastline and confirmed the bomber had reached Russia. The plane buzzed the rocky coastline, where the airmen felt relieved to spot no antiaircraft guns.

The bomber passed an airdrome with as many as forty navy planes parked on the tarmac, prompting the pilots to realize that the sooner the bomber was on the ground, the better. "You can't fly around over the seaboard area of a country at war," Emmens wrote, "without someone in that country eventually doing something about it."

The bomber buzzed a second, smaller field, and the airmen spotted several buildings. A few men stood outside dressed in long black coats. A fighter dove out of the sky overhead just off the bomber's right side.

"For Christ's sake," Emmens said, "let's get our wheels down to let him know we're going to land and he won't have to *shoot* us down."

The fighter hugged the bomber's tail until touchdown. Relief washed over the crew, who had flown for more than fourteen hundred miles across hostile territory and open water. "Now, at last, dry, good ground," Emmens wrote. "It was a wonderful feeling."

York taxied over toward a parked plane, hidden under camouflage netting.

"Leave fifteen degrees of flaps down and let's take a look at these jokers to see if they've got slant eyes," York said. "If they have, we'll take off straight ahead!"

The fliers studied the faces of the men on the ground, which confirmed that the bomber was in Russia and not in Japanese-controlled territory. York and Emmens pulled the flaps up, locked the brakes, and killed the switches, listening as the aircraft fell silent. A dozen Russians, all dressed in long black coats with black leather belts, gathered off the bomber's wingtips. The fliers relaxed upon seeing the Russians all grinning.

"You guys stay in the ship and keep me covered—just in case!" York said as he climbed out.

"We've got you covered," Emmens answered, pulling his pistol out and opening the side window. "By the way, do you know any Russian?"

"Hell, no."

York approached the Russians. Emmens heard laughing and watched as the grins morphed into wide smiles. York looked back and shot his copilot a smile, which the fliers interpreted as a positive sign and climbed out to join him. York kept repeating the need for gasoline, which none of the Russians understood. Three older and obviously higher-ranking Russians approached from a nearby office, prompting the others to scatter.

York asked the leader whether he spoke French, but got only a shrug. Emmens then asked whether he spoke German, only to receive a blank stare in return.

"Americansky," the Russian asked.

The raiders confirmed and everyone laughed.

The Russians ushered the fliers to an unheated office in a rundown building, inviting them to sit in chairs while the leader barked into a phone. The men waited, deciding not to say anything about bombing Japan until the American consul arrived and could advise them. Half an hour later the Russians escorted them across the field to another equally decrepit building. The sun had set and the temperature dropped.

The Russians led the men into a large office with a desk at one end and a large conference table in the center. Another Russian arrived moments later with a world map that measured roughly four by five feet, tacking it to a wall. The leader pointed to the map. Reluctant to admit having bombed Japan, York pointed to the Aleutians, tracing a route across the Sea of Okhotsk to Vladivostok. "Good-will flight," he said.

To the airmen's relief the Russians appeared to buy it and for the next hour attempted to engage the fliers in small talk, even bringing in a portable gramophone at one point to play music, along with a chess set and decanter of water.

The door finally swung open, revealing a young officer dressed in a fur-lined cap and jacket. The raiders immediately recognized him as a pilot, who in all likelihood had just landed. He motioned for York to repeat the story of his flight.

"This guy's no dummy," he said as he rose from his chair.

York repeated the story of his flight from the Aleutians. The Russian officer listened intently and then shook his head and put his finger on Tokyo. York again traced the fictitious route, this time prompting the Russian to laugh. "Not sneeringly," Emmens later wrote, "more as if he were enjoying a good joke."

"I guess that guy wasn't fooled," York said when he finally sat down.

About 9 p.m. a colonel arrived, accompanied by a civilian translator. The Russian officer shook hands with each of the raiders and welcomed them to Russia. York stuck to his story of flying from the Aleutians, prompting the colonel to congratulate the men on the successful completion of such a long and difficult flight.

"Colonel, we would like to make our rendezvous with other ships in Chunking," York said. "Do you have hundred-octane gasoline here?"

"Yes, such a question will be decided soon," he answered through the interpreter. "But now you must be hungry and tired."

The interpreter told the men that a room had been prepared in the building for them to spend the night. After each raider printed his full name and rank on a piece of paper, the interpreter escorted the fliers upstairs to a large room with five cots. The bathroom was down the hall, equipped with a bar of soap and a single towel. "It was like the Three Bears," Emmens recalled. "There were five of us. They had five cots, five little tables between the cots, five chairs at the end of the bed, and that's all."

The interpreter returned for the airmen at 9:45 p.m., informing them that dinner was ready. He led the fliers downstairs to a large room set up with two tables, covered with wine and liquor glasses as well as platters of pickled fish, caviar, black bread, and various meats and cheeses. Servers poured clear liquid into each raider's glass.

"A Russian always begins and ends his meal with vodka," the colonel said through the interpreter. "I toast two great countries, the U.S. and the USSR, fighting side by side for a great common cause."

The fliers downed the vodka, which Emmens noted by the third sip felt as though "someone had drawn a hot barbed wire across my tonsils." The dinner was foreign to the airmen, but delicious after the long day.

Each time the fliers asked about fuel, the Russians brushed them off. York leaned over to Emmens toward the end of the meal. "I think we should tell this guy the true story," he said. "I'll get him and the interpreter and we'll go upstairs."

Emmens watched soon thereafter as York asked the interpreter whether he might speak alone with the colonel. The three left, returning fifteen minutes later.

"In behalf of my government, I congratulate you for the great service you have rendered your country," the colonel announced. "You are heroes in the eyes of your people." The colonel raised a glass of vodka to toast the raiders. "To your magnificent flight today and to the victorious ending of the war for both our great nations!"

The men returned to their room after dinner, bellies full and heads swimming with vodka. "When we went to bed that night," York would later tell investigators, "we were fully confident we were going to leave the next morning."

One of the men began snoring in two minutes. "I thought about home and my wife and wondered how I could let her know we were all right," Emmens recalled. "I wondered how the other fifteen planes had fared. Had they all met as little opposition as we? Had they all proceeded to their destination, and were they all together somewhere in China, celebrating, that night? All but us? Had we actually bombed Japan that day and were we really in Russia? Or was all this a dream?"

PILOT DONALD SMITH HIT the Chinese coast twenty-five minutes earlier than he expected and barely ten miles north of his planned landfall. Fog and rain slashed visibility to zero with a ceiling of barely three hundred feet. The approach of nightfall only made his challenge worse. Smith spotted the outline of a mountain climbing up out of the sea dead ahead and banked right, increasing his throttles so that he could climb and head back out to sea. Smith estimated that he had two hundred gallons of fuel—enough to fly for another two hours—but he found that his engine gave him little power. The left started to cough. He knew the *TNT* would not remain in the air much longer.

"Brace yourselves," Smith announced over the bomber's interphone. "I'm going to set her down in the water!"

The airmen hustled to trade out parachutes for Mae West life vests, as Smith buzzed the coast of an island about four hundred yards from shore. He rolled back his side window, noting that the water appeared calm with no whitecaps. Engineer Ed Saylor in the rear of the plane slipped his winter coat on over his life vest, sat with his back against the turret tank, and wrapped his arms around the footrest. Bombardier Howard Sessler climbed atop the navigator's table, bracing his feet against the steps leading into the cockpit while holding on with his arms to the bars overhead.

Smith planned to make a wheels-up landing. He cut back on the throttles and ordered the flaps down at 110 miles per hour, slowing to 85. As the plane skimmed the wave tops, copilot Griffith Williams killed the switches.

The bomber glided down tail first in the water, giving the crew only a slight jolt. A second later the nose came down with barely any more impact than the tail. The plane sliced through the swells like a ship, making a gradual swing to the right before it finally came to a stop. The landing smashed the fragile Plexiglas nose, and cold seawater now poured inside, flooding the cockpit up to the seat level, but the wings rested atop the waves, giving the crew precious minutes to escape.

Smith, Williams, and Sessler climbed out the top hatch. Smith went back to retrieve the life raft, then kicked out the glass in the navigator's compartment, fishing out the crew's gun belts and rations. Saylor tried to squeeze out the rear escape hatch, but realized he couldn't fit with his thick jacket. He had no choice but to shed the cumbersome coat and then dive through the muddy water, swimming out from under the plane. Doctor Thomas White remained inside the sinking bomber despite calls from the others to escape. White tuned out such demands and instead hurriedly salvaged his gun and emergency medical kit, passing them out one of the side windows.

The plane settled rapidly in the water until the wings were awash and the tail began to climb skyward as the bomber prepared for its final dive. The inflated raft sloshed about the left wing inboard of the engine nacelle, as the airmen raced to load the rubber boat with guns, rations, parachutes, and extra clothing. A wave crashed against the plane and forced the raft against the sharp metal edge of the flap, tearing a small hole through which air now slowly leaked out. The flooded nose began to pull the bomber down, forcing the airmen at last to climb aboard the punctured raft and shove off. The men had barely cleared the port rudder when the bomber, its landing lights still ablaze, slipped beneath the dark waves, just eight minutes after touchdown.

The fliers paddled toward shore, bucking the wind and current, aiming for a break in the cliffs that White suspected might offer a beach. Two men rode atop the raft armed with oars, while the others clung to the sides, swimming and pushing. Sessler realized that the damaged raft couldn't support all of them, so he struck out for shore on his own, hoping to lighten the load for the others. The men watched as he soon disappeared beyond voice range. "The sea was so rough you couldn't swim very much," recalled Saylor. "We were just being splashed under by the waves, and then brought back up on top by our life vests, spit out the salt water and look around and see where everybody else was and point toward the island again."

As the air seeped out, the raft increasingly listed. The men hunted for the leak but could not find it in the darkness. A wave capsized the boat, tossing all the gear the men had worked to salvage into the dark waters, with the exception of a single bag of rations that Smith rescued. The men climbed aboard only to capsize again—and again. "Turned over three times," White would later write in his diary. "The last time I was too tired to climb back on, so popped my life vest and swam, towing the raft." The exhausted aviators finally stopped fighting the sea and drifted. "Current nearly swept us past the point but finally we made it," White wrote in his diary. "Tried to save the raft but too tired—cold and dark and the raft was waterlogged, so I tied it to a rock."

Sessler had beaten the others to shore, climbing up a rocky embankment about twenty feet above the surf. The *TNT*'s exhausted navigator lay down and passed out. The others emerged after a two-hour battle in the surf only to face an eighty-foot ascent up a steep rock wall, collapsing at the top. "There was a cold rain falling and a keen wind blowing which cut through our wet clothing like a knife," White wrote. "We tried huddling together in a small depression to get a little rest and mutual warmth, but soon found that it wasn't enough of a windbreak." The men needed to find real shelter, but did not know who controlled the island. A quick tally of the gear proved disheartening. "We had one waterlogged flashlight which gave a weak glow," White wrote, "and our total armament consisted of a sheath-knife Sgt. Saylor had on and my pocketknife!"

The airmen spotted a dim light across a valley and set off, reaching a fisherman's hut with mud walls and a thatched roof. The fliers banged on the door, shouting the Chinese phrase Jurika had taught them. No one answered. "We decided to curl up in the goatpen which was dirty, but dry and protected," White later wrote. "It looked like the Ritz to us!" The airmen had just bedded down when the fisherman came out of his house, armed with a lantern. He ushered the aviators inside, building a fire with straw on the floor. White noted there was no chimney and that the smoke filtered through the thatched roof. The fisherman roused his wife and mother, who fired up a small stove and prepared tea and dinner. "We warmed our chilled bodies," White wrote. "Soon we had some hot tea and rice and some dried shrimp to eat. Then I became the object of envy of the whole crew since I could eat with chop-sticks while they had to use their fingers."

The tea and food revived the exhausted aviators, who tried to communicate as a stream of villagers crowded inside the room. "For most of these people it was the first time they had ever seen a white man and their curiosity knew no bounds," White recalled. "We weren't too sure of the political affiliations of our friends, but their hospitality could not be doubted." The airmen drew pictures of flags in the dirt, but made little progress communicating their nationality. White switched gears, holding up four fingers then pointing to the other airmen. The doctor then held up a fifth finger, indicating a lone man. The villagers understood and locals soon departed to search for Sessler. One of the villagers then produced an almanac that had four English words across the top of each page along with the Chinese and Japanese equivalent. Leafing through the book White communicated that the airmen were Americans. "We told them that we had just come from bombing Tokyo, at which news their joy knew no bounds," he later wrote. "They literally gave us the clothes off their backs to wear while ours dried."

The villagers explained that the airmen had landed on Tan Do San, the only island in the area not in Japanese control. There were two nearby lighthouses, one still in Chinese control. White explained that the aviators needed to reach Free China and then head to Chungking. The villagers said a motor launch could be arranged the following evening. The warmth of the hut coupled with the long day soon took its toll. The host ushered the other villagers from the hut and pointed the Americans to the family bed that consisted of a primitive raised platform covered with a single quilt. "No springs, no mattress, no pillow. We lay down two each way and in spite of the hardness of the bed were soon asleep," White later wrote. "The last thing I remember that night was 'Grif' saying sleepily that he was going to come back after the war and make his fortune selling the Chinese innerspring mattresses!"

THE WEATHER WAS SO BAD as the sixteenth bomber roared over the Chinese coastline that copilot Bobby Hite spotted waterspouts, reminding him of the dust whirlwinds he knew back home in Texas.

Navigator George Barr worked frantically, trying to pinpoint the *Bat out of Hell*'s precise location, while the pilots scanned the airwaves, hoping for the promised homing beacon, which never came. "The weather was bad and foggy," Barr recalled. "Visibility was zero. It was raining hard, we couldn't see the ground."

The bomber reached the area around Chuchow and circled. Barr suggested the men fly west for fifteen minutes then turn south, a course he felt certain would deliver them safely to Chinese territory, but pilot Billy Farrow objected. The South Carolina native wanted to save the plane and chose instead to fly farther west, hoping for a break in the weather that would allow him to make a forced landing, even though such a course would take them closer to Nanchang, an area occupied by the Japanese.

The bomber flew west as the gasoline ran low. The men spotted a break in the clouds—and lights on the ground below—just as the low-fuel light glowed.

"We're out of gas," Farrow announced. "We'll have to jump."

"Are we in Free China or in occupied China?" bombardier Jacob DeShazer asked.

"I don't know," Farrow replied.

But Barr did. The constellation of lights that twinkled far below only confirmed Barr's navigation—and his worst fears. "That's Nanchang."

It was too late for the men to divert; the *Bat out of Hell* was out of gas. The airmen would have to jump and hope to avoid capture.

Gunner Harold Spatz would bail out of the rear, while the bombardier, navigator, and two pilots would go out the forward escape hatch.

"Jake, you're first," Hite announced.

DeShazer, who had reluctantly volunteered for the mission, now found himself first in line to bail out over Japanese-held territory. "Boy," DeShazer thought, "I'd like to see somebody else go."

The bombardier followed orders, sitting down and dangling his feet out the hatch. The wind hit his legs and blew them back against the fuselage. DeShazer pushed himself out the hatch and then counted to ten, yanking his rip cord. The chute unfurled and he drifted down, crashing into a dirt mound with enough force that he fractured several ribs. He surveyed the scene and realized that he had landed on a grave in a cemetery. Despite his injuries DeShazer felt so relieved to have survived the jump that he hugged the grave. He fired his pistol in the air several times, hoping to signal the others, but heard no response. DeShazer then whipped out his knife and sliced up his silk parachute, fashioning a cover for his head to protect against the rain.

"I'll go towards the west," the bombardier thought. "If I ever can figure out which way is west."

DeShazer trudged through the muddy rice paddies until he stumbled across a small brick enclosure that housed a shrine, complete with irons used for burning incense. Cold, wet, and exhausted, DeShazer pushed aside the irons and crawled inside, sheltered from the wind and rain. He closed his eyes and soon passed out.

George Barr stuffed cigarettes and candy bars in his coveralls and then pulled on his flight hat and jumped. "As soon as I went through the hatch the hat blew away," he recalled. "It's funny but my first thoughts were about losing that hat."

The *Bat out of Hell*'s navigator landed in a rice paddy, sinking up to his waist in water. He jolted his back and scraped his ankle, but otherwise was fine. Barr saw the flames in the distance from the bomber's crash; the last plane off the *Hornet* was down. He shed his chute and climbed out of the rice paddy, wandering around through a maze of connected fields. He hiked on until he came across a small bamboo bridge that had been dug out for fortification. He had no option but to wander through it. Just as he passed through, a sentry shoved a rifle in his back. "My heart stood still," he recalled. "Was he Japanese or Chinese? Was he going to shoot me in the back or what?"

The guard prodded Barr to proceed to a nearby dugout in the embankment, where he roused several other soldiers. The guards searched Barr, then bound him, his hands in front of him, elbows behind his back. The men marched him down the road toward Nanchang, about a mile or two away. "I was still hoping they were Chinese just doing their duty but when we got to the town I was brought into a room where there were about 10 or 15 Japanese officers in full military dress, sitting around a table overloaded with a variety of wines, whiskies, cigarettes and delicacies," Barr recalled. "They were delighted with their captive. I was a rare prize."

Bobby Hite's gun belt had two .45s, one with a loaded clip and the other without. The *Bat out of Hell*'s copilot could not fit the belt on under his parachute, so he hung on to it with his left hand and jumped, tugging the rip cord seconds later. The jerk yanked the gun belt out of his left hand. Hite instinctively shot his right hand out and managed to grab the .45 by the grip, his finger even sliding through the trigger area. The only problem—he saved the gun without a clip.

Hite drifted down into a rice paddy, sinking, like others, waist deep in the water, mud, and slime. The Texan pulled himself out, shed his parachute, and climbed atop a dike. He could hear the tinkling of running water. "I was standing there and I was thinking of a little song that I had heard as a boy, 10,000 miles away from home and sitting in the rain," he recalled. "It was kind of a lonely, eerie feeling." Hite pressed on, wandering along the dikes until he found a cemetery. Unsure of where to go in the dark, he lay down on the leeward side of the graves, hoping to keep out of the rain.

DeShazer awoke around daybreak and set off west, passing several villagers, none of whom paid him much attention. He felt his spirits rise; maybe he was not in Japanese-occupied territory. His feeling of good fortune was soon replaced by the shock at the poverty he saw in the villages he passed. "I could see inside their mud houses," DeShazer recalled. "Chickens, pigs, and children were wading around together in filthy mud inside the house. The people had heads about the size of a four-year-old child in America. The skin on their faces was wrinkled and old looking."

DeShazer tried several times to question the villagers he passed but without any luck. He continued down the road until he spotted a camp with soldiers outside, rinsing uniforms in a ditch. Unable to tell whether the troops were Chinese or Japanese, he backtracked until he came across a house riddled with bullet holes. He spotted a couple of young men in uniform, who DeShazer estimated couldn't be older than fifteen, playing with children in a yard. He decided to approach.

"China?" the bombardier asked. "Japan?"

"China," one of the young men replied.

"America," DeShazer answered.

One of the young soldiers disappeared, which spooked DeShazer. He started to leave, but the other motioned for him to stay. "China," he repeated. "China."

DeShazer offered him a cigarette, hoping to gain some information, but he soon realized it was futile. Just then ten more soldiers arrived, armed with rifles and bayonets. DeShazer raised his pistol and cocked the hammer. "China?" he asked. "Japan?"

"China," several of the soldiers assured him.

The soldiers made a show of shaking hands and patting DeShazer on the back before motioning for him to follow them. The men set off down the road toward the camp DeShazer had seen earlier. The bombardier felt nervous.

"We think you better let us have your gun," one of the soldiers said.

DeShazer stopped and turned around. The soldiers fanned out around him with rifles drawn. His spirits sank. "Their guns were all pointed right at me," he recalled. "There wasn't anything I could do. I let him take my gun."

The soldiers ushered him down the road to the camp, offering him *yokan*, mashed beans with sugar. DeShazer hadn't eaten in twenty-four hours.

"How did you get here?" one of the soldiers pressed.

DeShazer refused to answer, repeating his earlier questions to his captors. "Are you Chinese or Japanese?"

"Chinese," the soldiers insisted.

The bombardier spotted photos of high-ranking officers on the walls, asking the interpreter who the men were, hoping it might confirm whether the forces were Japanese. The solider rattled off the names, which meant nothing to DeShazer.

"You're in the hands of the Imperial Japanese Army," the interpreter announced.

DeShazer felt terrible.

"Aren't you afraid?" the interpreter asked.

"What should I be afraid of?"

Roosters rallied Bobby Hite in the cemetery shortly before daybreak. The copilot of the *Bat out of Hell* had suffered a miserable night, trying to duck the rain while occasionally running in place to keep warm. He set off to find a friendly local. Barking dogs drove him away from the first few houses he encountered. Hite pressed on until he found a home without a dog. The family invited him inside. "I had a pocketful of Lucky Strike cigarettes and Mounds candy bars and about $5 in silver," Hite recalled. "I was prepared to offer anything that I had for help."

As the family feasted on his candy and the wife chain-smoked his cigarettes, Hite repeated the phrase that Jurika had taught them. The husband then slipped on a shawl, a large hat, and wooden shoes before motioning for Hite to follow him. The aviator followed his host for twenty minutes through the rice paddies until he found a Chinese soldier. To Hite's relief, the soldier spoke English. Hite paid the farmer his silver and watched as he set off to return home. He told the Chinese solider that he was an American and had come to help Chiang Kai-shek.

"Well," the solider told him, "let's get something to eat."

The men started toward a cluster of homes just as fifteen Japanese soldiers charged out and surrounded him with bayoneted rifles. The soldiers searched Hite and confiscated his .45 and then with bayonets motioned him into the back of 1938 Ford truck, which galled him, and drove him half a mile to Nanchang.

Private First Class Tatsuo Kumano, who served in Japan's Eighteenth Army in China, worked in the military's press bureau in Nanchang. Kumano had turned in the night of April 18, only to have a fellow soldier later shake him awake, instructing him to report to the Nanchang Military Police Headquarters. The graduate of Saint Francis Xavier College in Shanghai, who spoke English, arrived to find Harold Spatz seated in a room barely eight feet by six feet with an intelligence officer. Kumano was instructed to sit and serve as the interpreter. The intelligence officer asked Spatz his name and rank and then pressed him for details of the mission, but the gunner rattled off a bogus story of flying off a mysterious island in the Pacific. Spatz chatted with the interpreter alone, telling him of his growing up in Kansas. Kumano told him of studying English.

Kumano's work had only begun. Over the course of that night and the following morning, Japanese soldiers had rounded up all five of the airmen from the *Bat out of Hell*, each one now marched through the interrogation room.

After Spatz, officers brought in navigator George Barr, who refused to cooperate. "I am not saying anything."

Then came Hite, but he, too, declined to talk.

So did DeShazer.

Billy Farrow came last, giving only his name and rank. "I am under oath," he said, "not to reveal any military secrets."

CHAPTER 16

★

When we hit the ground we could just as well have been
some place in Arizona for all we knew of the whereabouts.

—FRED BRAEMER,
BOMBARDIER ON PLANE NO. 1

DOOLITTLE HAD SUFFERED a long night in the mill, performing calisthenics to fight off the cold while wrestling with the uncertainty of the mission's outcome and the fates of his seventy-nine men. The fifteen bombers that had flown to China had all reached the mainland or the islands off shore. There amid the blinding fog and rain—and faced with the glow of the low-fuel light—aircrews had wrestled with the same dilemma as their commander. Outside of Ted Lawson and Donald Smith, only pilot Travis Hoover had attempted to land, putting his bomber down on a mud flat that had fileted the fuselage, but miraculously left not a single scratch on any of the fliers. The crew then torched the plane, watching it burn from a trench atop a nearby mountain.

The rest of the aircrews had done just as Doolittle, climbing high above the mountains in preparation to abandon ship. Men had slipped on parachutes and stuffed their pockets with emergency rations, Baby Ruth candy bars, and cigarettes. Others had filled canteens with water, and a few of the navigators sketched out rudimentary maps to pass around. Shorty Manch seized a 40-40 Winchester rifle, two .45 automatics, a .22

automatic, and a German Luger along with an ax and a bowie knife. Last, but not least, he grabbed his phonograph. The men then yanked out the hatches. "It was the blackest hole I've ever looked at in my life," recalled Davy Jones, who urinated on the cockpit controls before he bailed out. "I hated to do that more than anything else."

Eight of the bombers had gone down in the general vicinity of the eastern airfields, while five others had crashed along the coast near Hang-chow. Two had flown deep into the Chinese interior. Not a single plane—with the exception of York's—had survived the mission. The forced bailout sadly claimed the life of gunner Leland Faktor, whose remains local villagers would find the next morning alongside the wreckage of the bomber. The jump and subsequent hard landings injured several others, including pilot Harold Watson, who broke his right arm after tangling it in his parachute shroud line. Navigator Charles Ozuk smashed into a cliff face, gouging his left shin, while gunner Edwin Bain hit so hard he broke a tooth and cracked another. Shorty Manch realized when he landed that all he had left of his phonograph was the handle.

Other airmen had come down in precarious positions, including gunner Eldred Scott, who landed in a tree. The darkness prompted most of them to forgo the risk of hiking out of the mountains and to curl up instead under parachutes and wait until dawn. Snakebite whiskey and cigarettes helped fend off the weather and fear; the latter may even have saved bombardier Waldo Bither's life. "I lit a cigarette and remained very quiet," he wrote in his report, "listening for a signal from some of the crew." Not hearing any, Bither finished his cigarette and flicked it away, watching the glowing butt plummet into space. "I immediately decided not to try to move until daylight. I wrapped up in my parachute and in spite of rain and cold I was able to sleep very well."

The aircrews that would awake on mountainsides, in valleys, or along the sandy beaches were spread across more than four hundred miles and several provinces, an area peppered with Japanese forces that within hours would be on alert for downed American aviators, some of whom had already been captured. The scattered crews now faced the challenge of reaching Chuchow and ultimately Chungking as dawn revealed just how primitive the region was, an impression best captured by Jack Hilger in his diary: "I had landed in the China of a thousand years ago." The subways, buses, and cars that the men were accustomed to back home were here replaced by little more than footpaths, burrows, and sedan chairs. Though the airmen had been warned on board the *Hornet*, few really grasped just what to expect. "I had the idea that I would reach this road and then walk to a gas station where I could use a phone to call for help," navigator Hank Potter recalled. "None of us had ever been out of the U.S. or even away from home, for that matter. As far as I was concerned, the rest of the world was like the United States."

Far from it.

Doolittle set off at daybreak on April 19, hiking down a worn path toward a village. The rain had stopped, but gray clouds crowded the skies. Before long, Doolittle encountered a local farmer who he quickly discovered spoke no English. The veteran aviator improvised, using his notepad to sketch a picture of a train. The farmer nodded and set off with Doolittle in tow, delivering the marooned airman to a nearby military garrison. Doolittle was relieved to meet a major who spoke a little English, though his relief proved short-lived when the Chinese officer demanded he hand over his pistol. Doolittle refused. He explained that he was an American who had parachuted into a rice paddy the night before. The major appeared doubtful, no doubt sizing up the filthy airman still caked in dried night soil. Doolittle worried he might be shot.

"I'll lead you to where my parachute is," he finally offered.

The major agreed.

Accompanied by a dozen armed soldiers, Doolittle retraced his steps. He reached the rice paddy, only to discover his parachute was gone. Doolittle felt the tensions rise as the major glared at him. He explained that the farmer he visited the night before could corroborate that he had appeared at his door, but to Doolittle's shock, the farmer, his wife and even his two children denied ever having seen him.

"They say they heard no noise during the night," the major told him. "They say they heard no plane. They say they saw no parachute. They say you lie."

The Chinese officer had had enough. The soldiers approached Doolittle to seize his gun, just as two others emerged from a search of the farmer's house, holding up his parachute. "The major smiled and extended his hand in friendship," Doolittle recalled, "and I was thus admitted officially to China."

Copilot Dick Cole rolled up his parachute at daybreak and with his pocket compass set out west. After a few hours he picked up a trail and followed it until he ran into a Nationalist soldier, who led him to a small compound where Cole noted the Chinese flag fluttered. "He showed me a picture that somebody had drawn with a two-tailed airplane with five parachutes coming out," he recalled. "I pointed to the next to the last one and that was me." Chinese soldiers escorted Cole to the military garrison at Tien Mu Shen, where he was reunited with the artist of the sketch—Doolittle.

Hank Potter wandered down a mountain path at dawn until he reached a small village, where the locals welcomed him. One of the village elders sketched out Chinese characters on a sheet of paper that Potter couldn't read, but the villagers were able to help the navigator pinpoint his location on a map. He looked up a few minutes later to spot bombardier Fred Braemer trotting down the same path. "When I saw him, I must say that my spirits rose," Potter recalled, "because at least I had a friendly face."

Potter's novelty immediately vanished. The presence of two foreign airmen rattled the locals. One grabbed Braemer from behind and yanked his pistol from his shoulder holster as well as his knife. Others disarmed Potter.

"Let's get out of here," Braemer announced.

The airmen hurried out of town with five of the locals following them, armed with handguns, knives, and a rifle.

"Well," Potter thought, "we are in trouble here."

Half a mile outside the village the locals robbed them again, stripping the airmen of cash and watches. Potter lost both his navigational watch and a Hamilton wristwatch his parents had given him as a Christmas gift in 1940.

The disheartened airmen set off west again, running into a young boy who had been schooled by local missionaries. "Me China boy," the youth announced, motioning for Potter and Braemer to follow him.

The aviators followed the youth to a house, where local adults soon crowded inside, offering the men tea and eggs. Both felt reluctant to eat, remembering the many warnings on board the *Hornet*.

"Well," Braemer finally said, "hot tea can't hurt you."

A local guerrilla chief arrived, and the airmen told him that some of the locals had robbed them. The guns, knives, and even Potter's navigation watch soon reappeared, but the airman decided to press his luck.

"Hey," he said, "how about my other watch?"

The navigator realized the impoverished locals probably questioned why he needed two watches, but Potter insisted, after all it was a treasured gift.

"We go," one of the guerrillas finally said.

Paul Leonard had meanwhile set off at daybreak, hiking up a valley in search of his fellow fliers. The crew chief walked an estimated six miles before he turned back, running into four armed men. "One motioned to me to raise my hands while the other three proceeded to cock rifles," he recalled. "One took aim."

Leonard pulled out his .45 just as the other man fired. The airman fired two shots then turned and charged up a hill. He could see the men and others gathering below. Leonard decided to remain hidden and escape after dark.

About an hour and a half later, he saw a crowd march down through the valley. To Leonard's surprise Potter and Braemer led the pack. He reloaded his clip and charged down the hill, only to discover the others were in the hands of friendly guerrillas.

"I didn't know whether you were amongst the friends or enemies," he said. "But I wasn't going to stay up there alone again. I was going to join you."

The airmen continued the trek, up a hillside, when a villager suddenly appeared next to Potter and handed him his Hamilton watch. The exhausted fliers arrived at the military headquarters that afternoon to find Cole and Doolittle.

The locals had meanwhile found Doolittle's crashed bomber, which had gone down about seventy miles north of Chuchow. He and Leonard set off that afternoon to investigate the wreckage, hoping to salvage any gear or supplies. "There is no worse sight to an aviator than to see his plane smashed to bits," Doolittle later wrote. "Ours was spread out over several acres of mountaintop."

Doolittle combed through the debris, but locals had already picked the bomber's carcass clean, even plucking the brass buttons off one of his shirts. He dropped down next to one of the wings and surveyed the scene. The B-25 that had carried him and his crew in the skies over Japan had been reduced to little more than tangled metal, twisted cables, and shattered glass. He felt certain the other fifteen bombers had suffered similar fates, all low on gas and battling rain and fog. Doolittle would be lucky if the others had even survived. "This was my first combat mission. I had planned it from the beginning and led it. I was sure it was my last. As far as I was concerned, it was a failure," Doolittle later wrote. "I had never felt lower in my life."

Leonard recognized the depth of Doolittle's despair, writing in his diary that the veteran aviator was "disconsolate."

"What do you think will happen when you go home, Colonel?" the crew chief dared to ask.

"Well," Doolittle answered, "I guess they'll court martial me and send me to prison at Fort Leavenworth."

"No, sir," Leonard fired back. "I'll tell you what will happen. They're going to make you a general."

Doolittle offered a weak smile, recognizing Leonard's efforts to buoy his spirits.

"And," the crew chief continued, "they're going to give you the Congressional Medal of Honor."

Doolittle did not respond.

"Colonel, I know they're going to give you another airplane and when they do, I'd like to fly with you as your crew chief."

Doolittle felt tears in his eyes. "It was the supreme compliment that a mechanic could give a pilot," he wrote. "It meant he was so sure of the skills of the pilot that he would fly anywhere with him under any circumstances."

The men started to return, but darkness enveloped them. The Chinese major found a farmhouse where the men could sleep on the floor. The accommodation looked perfect to the exhausted aviators, who within minutes were asleep. Doolittle awoke later to hear strange guttural sounds. He reached out to feel bristles; he had managed to bed down in the spot of the family pig. He shoved the pig away and fell asleep again.

Doolittle arrived back at the governor's house the morning of April 20 to learn that four other aircrews had been located. He requested that General Ho Yang Ling, director of western Chekiang Province, post lookouts along the coast, from Hang Chow Bay south to Wen Chow Bay. He also wanted all sampans and junks ordered to search for any bombers that went down at sea or along the shore.

Word reached Doolittle that at least some of his airmen had been captured along the coast and others near Lake Poyang, the latter Billy Farrow's crew. Doolittle had obtained $2,000 in Chinese money prior to leaving the United States and questioned whether that cash could be used to buy the captured airmen along the coast from the local puppet government. He also asked about seizing Farrow's crew by force, a move the Chinese discouraged, given the high concentration of Japanese forces around Nanchang. Doolittle then drafted a wire to be sent to General Arnold through the embassy in Chungking. "Tokyo successfully bombed," he wrote. "Due bad weather on China Coast believe all airplanes wrecked. Five crews found safe in China so far."

The general hosted a banquet for Doolittle and his men, one that featured a large bowl of soup with a dead duck floating in it.

"Now you guys, don't make any remarks. Eat what you have and don't cause any problems," Doolittle warned his men. "You are guests here now."

The airmen needed to travel from Tien Mu Shen south to Chuchow as soon as possible, where they could hop a flight to Chungking. They climbed aboard the general's boat, hiding in the cabin as the vessel set off on a winding journey along several rivers that ultimately would deliver them beyond the reach of the Japanese. The aviators peered out as the searchlights of enemy patrol boats pierced the darkness.

Missionary John Birch had fled his church in Hangchow after the attack on Pearl Harbor, when the Japanese rounded up all the Americans in the area and put them into internment camps. The twenty-three-year-old Baptist, born to missionary parents in India and later raised in rural Georgia, had settled in Kiangsi Province, starting a new mission in Shangjao. Birch had heard the news of the Tokyo raid over the radio just as he planned to set off on a preaching trip through the Ch'ien T'ang River valley. He stopped a few days later in the village of Yien Tung Kuan for lunch at a restaurant overlooking the river. A Chinese officer came inside and spotted the missionary, striking up a conversation in the hope of practicing his English. The officer commented that there were several Americans on the general's boat tied up below. Birch protested that he must be mistaken, prompting the officer to point out the policeman in a black uniform standing guard on deck. Birch decided he had to check it out for himself.

"Have you any Americans on this boat?" the missionary demanded of the guard.

"No," the policeman answered in Chinese.

"Are there any Americans in there?" Birch repeated, this time shouting.

Doolittle and his men crouched inside the cabin, listening to the exchange. "Well, Jesus Christ," Paul Leonard blurted out.

"That's an awfully good name," Birch answered. "But I am not he."

The door sprang open, and Birch spotted several bearded faces inside. "Come in here!" came the chorus.

Birch climbed inside the cabin and came face-to-face with Doolittle and his men. The aviators were thrilled to meet Birch, whose language skills and knowledge of the area would be assets. Doolittle briefed the young missionary on the operation and asked whether he would travel with them and help interpret. "Of course, I was glad to," Birch later said. "The first time I'd associated with celebrities."

Birch traveled with Doolittle to Lanchi, relating stories of the Japanese atrocities. The missionary confessed to Doolittle that he wanted to help American forces. Doolittle bade farewell to Birch, assuring him that he would recommend him up the ladder and asking him to remain ready to help other raiders. Doolittle and his crew then pressed on toward Chuchow, a journey that would involve rail, bus, and rickshaws.

The trip across rural China at times proved so exhausting that Doolittle at one point protested to his guide that he couldn't go any farther.

"I will see if I can find a donkey for you to ride," the Chinese officer volunteered. "You just wait here."

The officer returned half an hour later from a nearby village. "Here," he told Doolittle. "You can ride this donkey."

Doolittle felt relieved, circling the donkey to inspect the animal. As he passed the animal's backside, the donkey kicked him in the chest. The veteran aviator tumbled back down the trail, clutching his chest and gasping for air.

The Chinese officer volunteered a few added words of caution.

"He bites too!"

CHASE NIELSEN AWOKE ABOUT 8 a.m. on April 19 on the beach where he had collapsed after the *Green Hornet* had crashed into the sea the night before. On looking up, he spotted two vultures perched on a rock overhead.

"Good lord," he thought. "The Jap high command is here already."

The sun was high, and only a few clouds drifted across an otherwise clear sky, a drastic change from the fog and rain that the aircrew had recently battled. The crew would have had no trouble finding Chuchow in this weather. "Why," Nielsen wondered, "couldn't it have been this way yesterday?"

The navigator surveyed his surroundings. He had collapsed the night before on the beach of a small bay. In the distance he spotted docks with a couple of patrol boats tied up. He could see the Rising Sun flags flying off the stern.

"Boy, this is a fine pickle," he thought. "Here you are 6,500 miles from home, your aircraft carrier is gone, your airplane is sunk, you don't know where your crew is, you're in enemy territory and you don't speak Japanese or Chinese."

The news worsened.

Down the beach Nielsen spotted two washed-up bodies, both in orange Mae West life vests. He knew the remains had to be men from his crew. He pulled himself up and started toward them, crawling through the bushes that lined the beach. Nielsen parted some bushes and found himself staring at a pair of split-toed canvas-and-rubber shoes. His eyes drifted up to see laced leggings. "The next thing I saw was a rifle pointing right at my head that looked like the bore of a cannon," he recalled. "It was that big around."

"Stand up or me shoot!" the man ordered.

Nielsen considered his options. "I might be able to overcome him," he reasoned, "but all he would have to do would be to squeeze the trigger." Nielsen decided not to risk it and instead got to his feet.

"You Japanese or you American?" the man continued.

"You Chinese or you Japanese?" Nielsen countered.

"Me China."

"Me American."

On his feet Nielsen had a better view of the bodies. He recognized them, bombardier Bill Dieter and gunner Don Fitzmaurice.

The Chinese man noticed Nielsen's gaze.

"They dead," he said. "Bury them in hour. You go with me."

The roar of boat motor interrupted the men, who looked up in time to spot a patrol boat charging around the bend.

"Japanese come," the guerrilla said. "You run this way. If Japanese catch us they kill us."

The men set off on a trail through the brush, ducking into a bamboo thicket with a view of the Japanese base, where the boats soon docked. Nielsen asked him where he had learned English, and the guerrilla said he had picked it up as a cabbie in Shanghai.

Nielsen reached the garrison, where he found more than two dozen guerrillas, a ragtag operation. "It was a welcome sight but as a military garrison a far cry from anything I had even seen before," he recalled. "Facilities were meager but the stench from human waste and rotten fish was outstanding."

Nielsen was pleased to find Dean Hallmark there. The pilot's leg was severely banged up from his exit through the *Green Hornet*'s cockpit windshield. He struggled to walk. Copilot Bob Meder arrived soon afterward.

The men returned to the beach that afternoon to bury Dieter and Fitzmaurice atop a small knoll near where the men washed ashore. The Chinese had fashioned simple wooden caskets, and the aviators laid the two men inside them dressed in their uniforms and packed in wood shavings. The waves crashed in the distance.

"Hallmark, Meder and myself each said a prayer over our beloved friends' caskets and that was all the services consisted of," Nielsen would later write to Dieter's mother. "As then, I have many times since, with tears running down my face, regretted the fact that we could not linger longer and see a better service given, but the Japs were scattered all through that area and delay meant our capture."

Two of the five airmen were dead.

"Hurry, hurry, hurry," the interpreter urged. "Japs come pretty soon. You hurry. Get away."

The airmen covered the graves and returned to the garrison.

Nielsen and the others felt anxious to escape, but each time the aviators addressed the garrison commander, he stalled them. "Soon," he promised. "Soon."

"We felt we had to rely on the Chinese, but the longer we stayed the more certain we became that the Japs would catch up with us," Nielsen later wrote. "We agreed we'd probably be executed if they caught us, but deep in our hearts we did not believe it. I never gave up hope and I don't think the others did, either."

One day passed.

Then another.

By late in the morning of April 21—three days after the crash—Nielsen knew the men had waited too long. A commotion erupted at the front gate.

"Japanese come," a winded Chinese man announced to Nielsen and the other aviators. "Japanese come."

The airmen slipped up toward the front gate, spotting what Nielsen estimated to be several hundred Japanese soldiers armed with rifles, bayonets, and hand grenades. "We talked briefly about making a run for it, but we decided we'd be shot down at once," he recalled. "It was better to take a chance of the Chinese hiding us."

The men ran back to their quarters, but the effort proved futile. "The Chinese led the Jap captain to us," Nielsen later wrote. "I can't blame those Chinese too much. They were out-numbered and out-gunned."

The captain, who Nielsen noted had a moon-shaped face and a tiny mustache, spoke through an interpreter. "You now Japanese prisoner," the enemy officer announced. "You no worry. We treat you fine."

The men would soon learn otherwise.

DAVID THATCHER RETURNED TO the hut around daybreak, soaking wet and clutching nothing but a carton of waterlogged cigarettes and a life belt. "I got to the plane," the *Ruptured Duck*'s gunner announced. "But this is all I could find."

The injured aviators now stirred. It had been a long night, and without morphine the pain throbbed; copilot Dean Davenport could no longer even walk. Charlie returned soon thereafter with an entourage of local Chinese men, who loitered outside the hut in the rain. Lawson noticed that some of the men carried ten-foot bamboo poles, while others hauled ropes and latticework squares. The men set to work, fashioning litters that consisted of a rope seat that dangled from a pole carried on the shoulders of the local laborers. Thatcher paid the fisherman ten dollars for four blankets, and the group set off just as the weather started to clear. McClure sized up his new transportation. "It was no comfortable sedan chair; it was a primeval makeshift," he later wrote. "We had gone in a few hours from man's most speedy transportation to his slowest."

The travel proved arduous as the barefoot Chinese labored under the weight of the injured airmen, particularly the 205-pound McClure. "They slipped in the mud frequently and every slip jolted my torn shoulders," the navigator later wrote. "We were all disgusted. We kept hollering at each other. Why didn't we have autos or a plane, or a carriage? Why hadn't we been fed, and why hadn't a doctor come? For one, I was too sore to reason about the facts as they were." The overgrown path soon gave way to rice paddies and then verdant hills. The guerrillas slogged on, one step at a time as the minutes soon turned into hours. "As we rose to still higher ground, the men climbed mossy rocks as if they were steps," Lawson recalled. "Their toes gripped the rocks like fingers. I hung on as I swung between them like a butchered hog."

They stopped at a large house in a meadow with grazing cattle. A motley band of guerrillas loitered outside, armed with a mix of guns from all over the world, each decorated with bright colored tassels. Lawson wondered how these impoverished fighters could resist the temptation to sell the injured Americans to the Japanese. "One of the toughest-looking men in the bunch now got up and advanced on me as I lay there, too exhausted from the trip over the hill to care what he would do to me," he recalled. "He reached down quickly toward my mouth and when he pulled his hand away I felt a lighted cigarette between that part of my lips which still met. I tried to smile back at him, but I felt more like crying. Maybe from relief. Maybe shock. I don't know. Anyway, I closed my eyes now and I thought that wherever I was I was among good men—men who were fighting for about the same thing I was fighting for."

The injured men were sipping boiled water when one of the guerrillas charged up the path, warning that the Japanese were advancing. The guerrillas picked up the airmen and set off, this time at a trot escorted by half a dozen armed guards. The group passed through a village and then boarded a flat-bottomed boat, which McClure estimated was twelve feet long and five feet wide. A single man propelled the boat with a pole down a canal. "It was hard not to moan incessantly now, even though the warm sun felt good," Lawson recalled. "We passed slowly down the canal for a couple of hours, the only sound being the thump of the pole against the back of the boat and the occasional jumble of conversation from the guerrillas. Sometimes the canal became so narrow that we could have reached out and touched the sides. Sometimes the limbs of overgrowing trees made the silent boatman bend low. I just lay there, hurting, and wondering what lay at the end of this ride and how I'd ever be able to walk when the ride did end."

The group disembarked later that afternoon, and the guerrillas carried the injured aviators through rice paddies. McClure spotted others perched on higher ground, serving as scouts. The men reached a ridge, overlooking a bay where a Chinese junk sailed toward the beach. Only then did Lawson realize the men had crashed on an island. As the guerrillas carried the men toward the junk, a Japanese gunboat charged around the promontory, prompting them to drop the injured aviators in a ditch. The men peered over the embankment at the gunboat. "With sick, mingled fears I watched it come up briskly to the side of the junk. I could hear the Japanese questioning the men on the junk," Lawson recalled. "It was torture to lie there in the ditch, waiting. Physical and mental torture. The Japanese must have spotted us, I reasoned. They must be wild to catch us, for certainly they had been informed of the raid and our route to China. They surely had found the plane by now. They would make one of the men on the junk tell."

Moments later, to Lawson's surprise, the gunboat backed up and charged off. The guerrillas waited until the boat vanished, then darted across the beach, sloshing through the shallow surf to the waiting junk. Lawson and the others tumbled over the side, coming to rest in a mix of sawdust and bilge water. The guerrillas climbed in after them. Chinese sailors rolled down the lattice blinds over the side as the boat set off around 6 p.m. The pain and the spring heat—coupled with weak winds—made the voyage unbearable. "We moved along like a snail," Lawson recalled. "We groaned and began begging for water. Any water. When it seemed as if there wasn't another breath of air to gulp in that darkening hole, it began to rain. The guerrillas understood about the water, then. They picked up bowls they found on the junk and set them out in the rain. They'd reach them in to us and we'd gulp the cool rain water and hand them back for more."

As he had done the night before, Thatcher moved among the injured fliers, helping make each as comfortable as possible. The dried blood that caked Bob Clever's scalped head blinded the bombardier, but Thatcher felt reluctant to wash his wounds and risk exposing him to infection. Clever's headfirst exit through the bomber's nose had so jarred his back that he could not sit up. "Only after getting tired of laying in one position for awhile would he ask me to help him move into a different position," Thatcher later wrote. "For instance if he was laying on his back he would want me to help him move over on one side. His being able to sleep and get some rest helped a lot." McClure, whose right arm had begun to turn black, suffered the opposite. "With this injury of his shoulders he was unable to lay down; had to be sitting up all the time," Thatcher wrote. "He could not get any sleep either."

Lawson likewise continued to battle his injuries. His left thigh and ankle oozed blood and grew increasingly numb. "He tried to sleep but it was almost impossible," Thatcher observed. "He was in such intense pain all the time."

Exhaustion finally overtook him.

"Don't let them cut my leg off," Lawson mumbled.

Davenport shook him awake. "You were having a nightmare."

Lawson made Davenport promise that if he passed out he would not let any doctor cut his leg off.

The junk reached a guerrilla hideout about midnight, scraping against a dock as the boat came to rest. A couple of the guerrillas hopped off the boat, pointing at their mouths to communicate the intent to collect food. Thatcher followed them up to a house, retrieving a bowl of noodles topped with egg slices. "I was pretty darned hungry," he wrote, "but couldn't eat very much of the stuff." The guerrillas gave him a bowl for each of the others, as well as spoons, sparing the injured aviators the use of chopsticks. To wash it down the men provided a jug of rice wine. McClure refused to eat, but Lawson managed to gum down a few egg slices. Much as he wanted the wine to numb his pain, the battered aviator couldn't drink it. "It was like raw, uncut alcohol," he recalled. "It burned my busted mouth and torn gums like lye."

The junk set out again after only about twenty minutes, sailing on into what McClure would later describe as "the blackest night" he had ever known. Thatcher once again resumed his nursing duty. The twenty-year-old gunner had been awake now for fully thirty-six hours; bandaging wounds and helping to feed and comfort his injured mates. The exhausted corporal once again set out his cup and a few saucers to try to collect rainwater; the demand for his services remained constant. "Lawson was wanting water all the time because his throat was dry from the blood in his mouth where his teeth had been knocked out. I didn't think that terrible night would ever end," he later wrote. "The most disheartening part of the trip was that we understood the guerrillas to say it would only take two hours but it took two days."

The boat tacked west through the night. Clever was the only one of the four who was able to sleep. The others hovered in various states of semiconsciousness, never far from their pain. Lawson lifted the lattice blinds around daybreak and saw that the junk had reached the Chinese mainland and now headed up a wide river. The boat sailed on as morning turned into afternoon, finally docking late in the day at a settlement. Thatcher set off to find a telegraph office, eventually wiring word of the crew's fate to Chungking. New porters helped offload the injured aviators—this time on more standard stretchers—and hauled them to the magistrate's headquarters, arriving close to dark. "I was carried on a flat board," McClure recalled. "The pain of the shoulders was at its height and with lack of food I certainly was not a genial person to be near."

The guerrillas set the injured men down on a patio, where Lawson noted that China Relief posters plastered the walls. From inside he heard someone speaking accented English. A bespectacled Chinese man walked out and extended his hand. "Anything we got is yours," he said to Lawson. "We know what you have done."

Lawson told him that the men needed a doctor, anesthetic, and sedatives—demands that elicited an unfortunate sigh from his host. "They had nothing at this station, except bandage and a little food and water," Lawson recalled. "Not even a sleeping pill, not even an aspirin tablet or any kind of antiseptic. No doctor, of course."

The locals fed the men boiled rice and water and helped bathe the aviators. All modesty had long since vanished. "Sitting in one of the anterooms," McClure recalled, "a Chinese girl, whom I suspected was a nurse, helped me out of my clothes and I stood in the wooden bucket while she gave me a complete bath."

Nurses washed the caked blood from Clever's face, allowing him to see for the first time since the crash. Others cleansed McClure's infected right ankle, which he found now under attack by a "man-eating bug." Nurses removed the belt and necktie tourniquets from Lawson's left leg and then carefully cleaned the pilot, discarding the filthy quilt he had clung to since they were in the fisherman's hut. Attendants gave the men heavy blankets, but sleep remained elusive, despite the exhaustion of battling pain without the aid of morphine for two days. "I didn't get much rest," McClure recalled. "I still had to sit most of the time with my hands on my knees and I seemed to be forever developing new pains." Lawson suffered the same. "I tried to go to sleep," the pilot later wrote. "But I just lay there full of pain, everything on me wanting care."

Dr. Chen Shenyan arrived at the magistrate's headquarters at about 3:30 a.m., after a grueling twelve-hour journey on foot. The graduate of Ting-nan Medical College, a private institution in Shanghai, had received a phone message at 3 p.m. the preceding day, requesting he come right away to help care for five injured American aviators. Chen and his father owned the En-Tse Hospital, about forty miles up the road in Linghai, a former missionary clinic the family had purchased from the Episcopalian church a decade earlier. Chen had heard the air-raid alarm on the afternoon of April 18, but had not thought much more about it until he received the message the afternoon of April 20. The doctor quickly packed a small surgical kit, grabbed a colleague, and departed just thirty minutes later for the half-day trip.

Chen surveyed the airmen's injuries. He found McClure sitting up, unable to lie down because the severity of his pain made it difficult for him to breathe. Both of the navigator's arms were severely swollen and numb, and he could barely move them. Davenport had cut up his right leg and left hand and lost considerable blood. So had Clever. Lawson clearly had suffered the worst. He had shattered his left knee joint and lacerated wounds covered his face and lower jaw. "There was a compound fracture of the mandible with the loss of 8 teeth," Chen noted, "all on the right side." The crash was so violent that Lawson had not only lost his canines and incisors but also his upper and lower molars. "He also had multiple wounds of the left leg and foot," Chen observed, "and was unconscious for a considerable length of time."

Chen needed to move the men to his hospital. He dressed the wounds as best he could and then phoned four missionary friends in Linghai. He was going to require help.

A lot of help.

The group set off at 8 a.m. on April 21 to cover the forty-mile return trip, with Lawson on a stretcher and the others in sedan chairs. "We were given a royal send-off," Thatcher wrote, "with a band and everything." A company of Chinese troops, standing at attention, lined the path out of the village, saluting as each airman passed. "It brought a lump to a fellow's throat," Lawson recalled. "Those of us who could, returned the salute. I wondered if there was ever a more grisly parade."

The journey once again proved arduous as the porters climbed the steep and rugged terrain. "At the top of a ridge we halted for tea and were offered—of all things!—cookies," McClure later wrote. "This homelike touch was another morale builder as well as a hunger killer." The morning gave way to afternoon as the injured airmen continued to suffer. "There were times when I thought I could not stand one more jolting bounce," Lawson recalled. "When I felt I'd have to cry out and ask them to leave me behind, I'd suck on the bitter oranges and try to concentrate on the way the juice burned my mouth, the number of seeds the oranges had, and other things, so I wouldn't think about the leg and arm and hands. I couldn't pass out."

Night soon fell. The porters trekked onward, navigating through rice paddies before arriving late that evening at Chen's hospital.

"You're safe here," George Parker, an English missionary, told the men.

Lawson asked about medical supplies.

"You'll get more care than anything," Parker answered. "We have an antiseptic fluid, a little chloroform and bandage. Nothing else."

To the injured airmen that was relief. "It was a hospital now—a real hospital and real medical care at last!" McClure wrote. "It had iron beds with real springs. Best of all it was sanitary. What a pleasure it was to dare to drink cold water."

Thatcher was exhausted. For days he had cared for the *Ruptured Duck*'s injured crew, helping the men escape to safety. He shunned any credit, pointing instead at what his injured mates had endured. "It was forty miles and took us twelve hours," he wrote in his final report. "I can't see how Lawson was ever able to stand it."

CHAPTER 17

★

I had many things to thank God for at the end of that day.

—KEN REDDY,
APRIL 18, 1942, DIARY ENTRY

THE RUSSIANS WOKE YORK and his crew on April 19 at around 9:30 a.m., informing them that breakfast would be served in half an hour. The fliers sat down soon afterward with the colonel and his staff in the same downstairs room they had been in the night before, asking right away about obtaining gasoline to fly on to China.

"Business must never be discussed over meat and wine," the colonel said. "All decisions will be made in due time. First you must eat and drink heartily."

Caviar, cheeses, pickled fish, and black bread crowded the table along with other delicacies. The first course consisted of a cream soup followed by roast goose and fried potatoes. The fliers next feasted on a roast pig, which was served whole to allow the men to slice off individual portions. A hot chocolate drink rounded out the five-hour meal. "During this time, we had toasted the Red Army; they had toasted the US Army. We had toasted the Red Navy; they had toasted the US Navy. We had toasted the Russian Air Force; they had toasted the US Army Air Corps," Emmens recalled. "We toasted victory to the free people of the world about three times."

"Tell you what," York finally said to the colonel. "How'd you like to see the inside of our ship?"

The Russian eagerly accepted the offer. York even offered, despite the vodka, to give the colonel a flight, which he smartly refused. The Russians explored the bomber, enjoying a laugh over the broomstick tail guns.

"Are you sure you wouldn't like a little ride?" York asked the colonel as he fired up the B-25's twin engines. The terrified colonel almost knocked Emmens over as he rushed to climb out of the bomber.

The fliers returned to their rooms about 3:45 p.m., no closer to the goal of securing gasoline and flying to China. The inebriated airmen stretched out, only to be awakened by the interpreter forty-five minutes later.

"You must hurry and get up," he demanded. "You are leaving at once. The airplane is waiting!"

"My God, I have never flown in this condition, but so be it," Emmens thought. "If they have gassed our airplane, let's get the hell out of here and get on it."

Emmens could at least get out of bed. "I finally had to pull York up to a sitting position," he recalled. "We were in bad shape, easy to handle."

The Russians ushered the fliers onto an aged bus and drove them out to a waiting DC-3, which the locals dubbed the "Roosky Dooglas."

"Where are we going," one the fliers asked, "and what about our bags?"

"You will learn everything in due time."

The DC-3 roared into the afternoon sky and the airmen soon fell back asleep, a journey interrupted only by the occasional trip to the rear of the plane that left Emmens paler each time. The airmen deduced that the plane flew in a northerly direction, but could discern little else over the two-and-a-half-hour trip.

"Khabarovsk," the colonel announced as the plane circled an airport at nightfall in preparation for landing.

A large industrial city in eastern Siberia, Khabarovsk sat along the Amur River just north of Manchuria. The raiders disembarked and climbed into several waiting cars, which drove them to a nearby building. The Russians led them inside and to an office occupied by a Russian officer, who stood behind a large desk.

"May I introduce to you General Stern commanding general of the

Far Eastern Red Army, who wishes to ask you a few questions," the interpreter said.

Stern's physical stature wowed Emmens, who counted at least four stars on his shirt's collar. "General Stern was the nearest to a human ape I think I have ever seen," Emmens recalled. "His shoulders must have been three feet across, narrow hips, and his arms hung almost to his knees, practically no neck. I remember just being amazed at his totally bald head. There wasn't a hair on it anywhere."

The general interrogated the fliers about the raid, about targets, the route across Japan, and whether any enemy planes had followed them, a question he repeated several times. The airmen answered candidly but refused to reveal the role of the *Hornet*. The general concluded the half-hour interview with a lengthy statement, which the interpreter translated. "The General has asked me to tell you that according to a decision reached between our two governments and by direction of orders from Moscow, you will be interned in the Soviet Union until such a time as further decisions are made in your case," the interpreter said. "You will commence your internment immediately in quarters which have been prepared for you outside the city of Khabarovsk. You will be given proper protection and attempts will be made to make you comfortable."

The Russians loaded the raiders back into the cars and drove them along narrow and unpaved streets. The car's single headlight illuminated men and women dressed in rags. Factories stood behind tall fences, often overseen by guards atop watchtowers.

After about an hour the cars rolled up outside a one-acre fenced property that the fliers would later learn the Russians called a dacha, a country house often used for Red Army officers on rest. The primitive property had enough bedrooms for the raiders and guards as well as a kitchen, dining room, and odiferous toilet.

"Well, here we are," York said.

The disheartened fliers had awakened that morning expecting to obtain gasoline and fly on to China. Now they faced an uncertain future. Would the internment last a week or a year—or worse, the war? No one knew, though the airmen definitely doubted the general's claim that this was a joint arrangement, decided by both the American and the Russian governments. "There wasn't anything to do but sit down," Emmens later wrote. "We had no baggage with us, no unpacking to do."

A Russian officer appeared at the door, introducing himself as Mihaiel Constantinovich Schmaring, a name the raiders would soon shorten simply to Mike. "I speak a little English," he said. "I will be staying with you."

Mike invited the raiders to enjoy a late dinner of black bread, salmon caviar, and cheese followed by soup, meat, and potatoes and, of course, vodka. Around midnight the news came over the radio, which Mike translated for the information-starved internees. The broadcast's final report claimed that Japan had shot down eleven bombers in the recent raid on Tokyo. The airmen had no way to know whether the report was true or just enemy propaganda, but the possibility floored the raiders. "My God, there had been only sixteen airplanes on the whole raid, and if eleven had been shot down over Japan we were one of five surviving aircraft!" Emmens later wrote. "I can tell you we felt pretty sad that night as we turned in—our first night as internees in the Soviet Union."

The men spent the next day exploring the dacha, which included an unkempt yard that sloped down toward the Amur River, whose dark waters were all that separated the airmen from Japanese-controlled Manchuria. News reports revised down the number of bombers lost over Tokyo, from eleven to seven, prompting the raiders to conclude all such reports were likely propaganda. The airmen's bags arrived several days later, though the raiders discovered the Russians had searched them and pilfered all candy and American cigarettes. "Anything that resembled airplane equipment was kept by them," York would later tell American investigators, "including our pistols."

Despite a trip to a primitive bathhouse, as well as lessons on the various types and potencies of vodka, the raiders soon grew restless. "Every day had been almost exactly the same," Emmens wrote. "We got up at about nine-thirty, had breakfast at ten, lunch at one, supper at seven, and rounded up each day with the news and tea at midnight. The drinks of vodka were beginning to be looked forward to as a relief from boredom, but the gaps of time in between were pretty hard to fill up. We slept quite a bit, whittled wood, and attempted now and then to get a start on the language."

A car pulled up one night at the dacha after the raiders had spent some ten days in Khabarovsk. Two Russian officers who had left earlier that day returned, summoning Mike from the dinner table. He came back moments later, sat down, and finished his dinner before he announced that the raiders were leaving.

"Leaving!" the raiders replied. "When?"

"You must be ready tonight."

"Where are we going?" the raiders pressed.

"You will find out," Mike replied. "Everything in due time."

AN INFLUX OF VISITORS at dawn aroused Don Smith and the crew of the *TNT*. The locals appeared to show particular deference to one man, who was better dressed than the others, though much of his nose was eaten away by what Doc White suspected was leprosy. He looked over the battered fliers and then left. The host told the aviators via sign language that he departed in a boat, which the fliers feared meant he planned to betray them to the Japanese. The men scarfed down a breakfast of rice, dried shrimp, and garlic greens, pulled on their wet clothes, and left. The first person the fliers met was a fisherman with bombardier Howard Sessler in tow. "He was still intact, though chilly, having spent the night in a sheltered cleft in the rocks, about two miles from where we landed," White wrote in his diary. "A native explained that because of a Jap gunboat in local waters we should have to wait till dark to go. Nothing for it but to go back and keep under cover."

The raiders returned to the hut to find that the leader had come back with the news that the Japanese were near. The aviators had no choice but to remain in the hut that day, napping and drying their clothes. Five men arrived at dusk and escorted the fliers down to a small junk in a cove. The airmen crawled into the boat, where the Chinese had them lie on the bottom and covered them with mats before sculling out to sea. No wind and a cold drizzle made the passage slow. "Several times other boats passed nearby and we always kept very quiet until they were out of earshot. Once we heard motors and saw a searchlight in the distance," White wrote. "We got awfully cramped and uncomfortable lying still in the bilge of the little junk so the fishermen gave us some rude raincoats made of tree bark to cover our clothes in case we should be seen. We could then sit up and look around, though there wasn't much to see in the dark and drizzle."

The boat reached the island of Nandien—where Lawson's *Ruptured*

Duck had crashed—around midnight, and the crew tied up at a small stone pier. The fliers remained in the boat except for White, who set off down the pier with two of the Chinese men and a couple of lanterns. The trio hiked for over an hour along narrow footpaths that snaked between rice paddies, over steep hills, and through crevices. There was no wind, but a heavy mist hung in the air; the sole relief from the darkness came from the two lantern candles. "The only sound was the croaking of innumerable frogs and the scrape of our feet," White later wrote. "The utter alien-ness of the surroundings made it seem as though I were taking a stroll on another planet."

After an hour the group reached a farmhouse, where White met guerrilla leader Jai Foo Chang, whom Lawson had referred to simply as Charlie. He informed White that another B-25 crew had crashed on the island and that he had helped the men escape. Charlie produced a few mementos from the crew, including a card with Davenport's name. White knew immediately that the crew was Lawson's. Charlie informed him that most of the crew was injured, mimicking broken teeth, arms, and legs and injured eyes. White wanted to know how quickly the airmen could follow, but Charlie told him the men would have to wait. White sent a note back to the boat with one of Charlie's men, telling the others to come to the farmhouse. White then sat up for a couple of hours, drinking tea and chatting. Charlie was disappointed to learn that the men had been unable to salvage any guns from the plane. He likewise was pained to hear about the fall of Singapore.

"Damn and fuck," he said.

The others arrived, and the fliers set off to a nearby farmhouse, where the locals provided them mats to stretch out on atop the dirt floor. Charlie appeared soon after daybreak with several chickens. The presence of a Japanese garrison on the island forced the men to spend the day hiding out. White passed out coins and pictures of his kids. Sanitation he noted was nonexistent, though it didn't stop the airmen from feasting on the chickens. The plan was to travel that night, and Charlie detailed five men to guard the fliers. Word arrived late that afternoon that the Japanese were coming, so the aircrew split up into small groups and set off, hiking through the lush hills.

The various groups reassembled on the banks of a canal, bidding Charlie farewell before climbing into a flat-bottomed skiff. Villagers would run out and shout information, part of what the airmen dubbed the grapevine telegraph. At other times locals would offer up hard-boiled eggs. The journey down the canal fascinated White, who described the primitive scene in his diary. "I noticed the extreme age of everything we saw," he wrote. "Carving on the ridgepoles of tiled roofs; others thatched; sluice gates of carved stone; extensive canals and terraces. Everything was just as it had been for thousands of years except for us and the guns of our companions."

The boat reached the end of the canal around dusk. The aviators disembarked and walked about a mile to a local barracks, where they ate eggs, rice, and shrimp and drank tea and wine before pushing on another couple miles in the dark, arriving at an abandoned house. The group waited until the moon set, then climbed aboard another small boat for a short trip before continuing on foot to an old temple. A local priest greeted them. "The old priest had fine features, wild hair and beard, and wore a black gown," White wrote. "Our leader and the priest offered up prayers for us and then tested the omens via the jumping sticks three times. Once for them, once for us, and once for Chiang Kai-shek!"

The men had a late dinner of eggs and tea and then shivered as they tried to sleep on mats on the floor without any blankets. The next day the fliers remained hidden in the temple. White shared chocolate and crackers with the priest; in exchange he offered hard black Chinese candy. Around 3 p.m. one of the scouts arrived with the news that sixty-five Japanese soldiers were en route to the temple.

The fliers gathered up their few belongings, and the Chinese hustled them down the trail to a nearby farmhouse. After much debate the owner escorted them inside and through a secret panel hidden behind a bed that led into a cave dug out of the hillside. The airmen sat on a platform built against the far wall, which the Chinese covered with mats. A single candle placed in a wall niche provided the only light. The men heard scuffling outside before half a dozen Chinese entered, sitting between the fliers and the door, guns cocked and ready to fire. "We felt trapped like rats," White wrote in his diary. "I had some of the worst moments of my life while we waited for the Japs to find us."

The Chinese men waited and smoked, fogging the cave and threatening to choke the airmen. The fliers heard the Japanese soldiers arrive outside, splitting up to search for the airmen. "Several times we heard the questing footsteps cross the roof of our hiding-place and then we heard them enter the house which hid the entrance to the cave," White wrote. "From there presently arose sounds of struggle and screams and shouts. One of our escorts turned to us and made whipping motions across another's back. The Japs were beating the owner of the house trying to make him tell where we were."

Edward Saylor studied one of the guerrillas closest to him, who he noted had a dated and rusty rifle and cloth ammunition belt, filled with various rounds of all shapes and sizes, ammo Saylor surmised he had scrounged. "I don't know whether he could have helped us or not," Saylor recalled. "He was there to try." The cigarette smoke became unbearable as the men waited. "The air in the cave, none too fresh to start with, became suffocating," White wrote. "It was all we could do to keep from coughing and thus betraying our position." The men heard a sudden confrontation. "Clattering noises outside, then many men talking, sounds of blows, screams," one report noted. "The Japanese had come—they beat the old man, they beat the villagers, but nobody squealed."

Finally after two hours the Japanese left. "Everyone relaxed and crawled out," White wrote in his diary. "I was never so glad to see the light of day." The priest met the men and through sign language told of the ordeal he had suffered. "They had evidently entered his temple, defaced his idols and had even beaten him, but he showed us how he had cried, torn his hair and wrung his hands and had sworn that he had never seen us," White wrote. "Any of these poor people could have made a very nice bit of change by betraying us to the Japanese, but the thought apparently never entered their minds. Their sense of responsibility for us and their hatred of the Jap were enough."

The fliers trudged on that afternoon and into the night, winding along narrow trails and around rice paddies. At a house near the water the men ate chicken, rice, shrimp, and eggs before climbing aboard a junk bound for the mainland. The clear night and breeze offered a chance for the men to relax and watch how the Chinese handled the boat. It turned out the Japanese occupied the intended destination, forcing the men to divert around 4 a.m. to a sleepy village. They stopped off at a home above a dry goods store for breakfast and an opportunity to wash with soap before continuing on foot throughout the day. "Fascinating countryside," White noted in his diary. "Our feet were sore and blistered, the soles of our shoes cracked from drying them out over a fire."

The men finally boarded two small junks for ferryboats and headed several miles upriver before disembarking and walking another five miles. The magistrate gave the crew a royal welcome, and the men learned that Lawson's crew had passed through two days earlier. The fliers afterward visited the local army headquarters, where the Chinese gave them soap for bathing and clean civilian shirts and shorts. "Glad to get off my lousy underwear!" White wrote in his diary. "Had a very nice dinner and entertainment. Small girls brought us flowers, danced, and sang about the wonders of flight." The Chinese asked whether the fliers needed the service of women. "We replied that we appreciated the offer," White wrote, "but were just too tired!"

The airmen awoke the next morning refreshed for the first time in days. "Had a gorgeous night's sleep and then breakfast," White wrote in his diary. "Washed our teeth for the first time since leaving the ship." The Chinese offered to let the airmen send telegrams. White sent one to his wife, Edith, that read simply, "Safe and well," but she would never receive it. The Chinese then hosted a reception that morning in honor of the fliers attended by town officials, schoolchildren, and soldiers. The fliers looked past the out-of-tune bugle and enjoyed the cheers and singing. The magistrate and others made speeches followed by short remarks from each of the airmen. Officials presented the airmen with a silk banner. A photographer who had traveled some thirty-five miles on foot documented the event with a 12 x 12 camera, one with no shutter or diaphragm. White reciprocated and gave the magistrate's son his helmet.

The fliers set out that morning to find Lawson and his crew, walking through town in what White described in his diary as "a triumphal procession—soldiers, firecrackers, confetti, cheers and songs." Outside town the aviators climbed into wicker sedan chairs for the long trip to the hospital in Linghai, escorted by ten soldiers. "We went up a long valley," White wrote in his diary. "The broad stone-paved road degenerated to a single muddy track at times. Rice paddies everywhere, right up the hillsides. Pumps and bailers; scattered farming settlements; hay drying in trees. The age of everything and lack of repair noticeable."

The procession passed through a small village where schoolchildren and teachers greeted the fliers, holding up banners, cheering, and singing songs about airplanes. The fliers passed down the village's main street, lined with shops, mostly selling food. The aviators ate eggs, pork, and sausages for lunch, then continued on up into the mountains, a trail of children following behind. "Everywhere we went people crowded around to see us," White wrote in his diary. "One baby crawled under my chair. Its mother yanked it out and slapped it, and it started to cry. I gave it a penny and it stopped instantly."

The men stopped that night at an army outpost, then pressed on the next morning to Linghai, arriving around 10 a.m. on April 24. White went to the hospital and found the crew of the *Ruptured Duck*. Lawson's condition had worsened. The Chinese doctor, Chen, had extracted some of the pilot's loose teeth and enlarged the wound on his left knee to remove loose fragments of his patella. Lawson floated in and out of consciousness, responding only by opening and closing his eyes. He could not eat and was administered glucose intravenously. White wired Chungking for an airdrop of supplies, specifically an officer's medical field kit, a complete blood transfusion kit, morphine, surgical dressing and either sulfadiazine, sulfathiazole, or sulfanilamide.

In his first report White noted that Lawson had a compound fracture of the left patella with a deep laceration six inches long, extending into the knee joint and nearly severing the tendons. He had other lacerations on his left shin, chin, and lip, and a deep gash on his cheek, plus two more on his scalp. By White's count Lawson had lost his upper three incisors and canine teeth. "All of the wounds were hideously infected with a very virulent organism, apparently one of the fecal-contamination type of symbiotic, anaerobic bacteria," he later wrote. "The whole leg was swollen, crepitant and fluctuant with a foul watery discharge issuing from every opening. There was an area of dry gangrene over the inner aspect of his ankle. Motion of the knee-joint was of course extremely painful and Ted was delirious most of the time from weakness and toxic absorption."

The worst injury was the one to Lawson's left leg. White was determined to save it if possible and tore apart the hospital in search of precious medicines, finally finding some Japanese brand sulfanilamide, though he doubted its potency. He immediately started Lawson on it and then drained his infected wounds. "The area of gangrene over his left ankle was insensitive and I was able to excise with scissors with a minimum of discomfort," he wrote. "My labors were rewarded when over a cupful of stinking material gushed forth." White couldn't help marveling at how Lawson and the other injured fliers from the *Ruptured Duck* had gone four days without any medical help, a point he would later highlight in his report. "The fact that Ted and Dean were still alive," he wrote, "is just one of the many miracles which occurred on that memorable April 18th!"

THE JAPANESE LOADED THE CREW of the *Bat out of Hell* onto a transport plane to Nanking the afternoon of April 20, touching down around five. Guards ushered the raiders into the back seats of separate 1938 four-door Fords with guards on either side. Hite could look out from under his blindfold at the chaotic city where dogs, donkeys, and children scattered about the streets. Guards tossed the fliers into individual cells with wooden bars that measured just four by eight feet. A can served as the toilet; the only other furnishing consisted of a damp blanket to cover up with atop the hard wooden floor. Watchful guards paced the prison passageways.

The Japanese pulled DeShazer out of his cell that evening and dragged him into an interrogation room occupied by several officers, one of whom spoke English with a lot of slang. The exhausted airman had been blindfolded now for twelve hours and had gone even longer since his last meal, but he still refused to cooperate. The officers taunted the blindfolded bombardier, threatening to execute him if he didn't talk, at other times getting into his face and laughing. This proved to be only the warm-up until guards dragged him into yet another room and yanked off his blindfold. DeShazer looked up to find a squat Japanese man with a large paunch who smoked a cigar.

"I'm the kindest judge in all China," the Japanese man said through an interpreter. "You're very fortunate to be questioned by me."

Everyone sat down.

"Doolittle was your commanding officer, was that true?" the judge asked.

"I won't talk," DeShazer answered.

"You're our property and we want you to talk," the judge admonished him. "We'll treat you very good."

The interrogation continued.

"How do you pronounce H-O-R-N-E-T?"

"Hornet," DeShazer answered.

"That's the aircraft carrier you flew off of to bomb Japan," the judge stated.

"I won't talk," DeShazer repeated.

"Sixteen B-25s took off the *Hornet* and bombed Japan," the judge continued. "Is that true?"

"I won't talk."

The judge continued to pepper DeShazer with questions, and each time the flier refused to answer, prompting the judge to finally slam his fist down on the table. "When you speak," he demanded, "look me straight in the eye!"

DeShazer did as ordered, but the judge only grew more enraged, finally yanking his sword from his side. DeShazer's eyes focused on the bright steel blade.

"Tomorrow morning when the sun comes up, I'm going to cut your head off," the judge barked. "What do you think of that?"

DeShazer had no idea how to respond, but knew he needed to say something—then it hit him. "Well," the bombardier answered, "I think that would be a great honor to have the kindest judge in all China cut my head off."

The courtroom erupted in laughter.

The Japanese likewise pulled Bobby Hite from his cell, dragging him into an interrogation room with a major and an interpreter. Four guards stood watch.

"You will please to sit down," the interpreter said. "Do you care to smoke?"

Hite spied a package of White Owl cigars and cigarettes on the table. He reached out for the latter, but the interpreter pulled them back.

"You may have them afterward," he said.

"After what?"

"After you tell us what we want to know."

"I'm a prisoner of war," the Texan replied. "I am not required to give any more than my name, rank and serial number which I have done."

"You will give us more!" the interpreter screamed at him. "If you don't, we will have you shot where you sit!"

The Japanese proceeded to drill Hite about the *Hornet* and Doolittle, but the pilot decided to dodge, claiming that he had flown instead from the Aleutians.

"You couldn't fly that far," the Japanese countered.

"We could and we did."

George Barr suffered a brutal night after he, too, refused to answer questions put to him by a board of officers. Guards led him downstairs and past a room where he spotted DeShazer surrounded by Japanese shoving pencils between his fingers.

Barr landed in his own interrogation room along with several Japanese enlisted men. Handcuffed and blindfolded, the navigator never saw the punches; he could only feel the pain as the Japanese pummeled his face and body. An officer entered the room and ordered the men to stop. The Japanese pulled Barr's blindfold off but left him handcuffed, questioning him with the aid of a civilian interpreter.

Barr refused to talk. The Japanese laid him on the floor, shoved rags in his mouth, and poured water over his face. He felt the water run down his nostrils, but he couldn't cough it out. He felt he would drown.

The Japanese stopped, and the officer asked Barr whether he was ready to talk. The navigator refused and the torture started again. "The water was going down into my lungs," Barr later testified. "It just stopped your breathing."

The officer looked on as Barr struggled. The torture continued for twenty minutes before Barr felt he could no longer tolerate it. He would talk. Barr confessed that the fliers had taken off from an aircraft carrier. The guards led him back to his cell.

The raiders suffered a long night in the vermin-infested jail. Someone even stole DeShazer's watch. "My hands were tied and my legs were tied," he recalled. "I laid there with my clothes on, the lice just crawling all over me."

The guards hauled the Americans outside the next morning, photographed them, and then loaded them aboard an airplane, handcuffed, blindfolded, and tied with ropes. DeShazer stole peeks outside the window and saw only empty water as the plane droned on for hours. He eventually spotted an iconic landmark—Mount Fuji—that told him exactly where he was going. His destination, he knew at that moment, was Tokyo.

★

THE JAPANESE LOADED Dean Hallmark, Bob Meder, and Chase Nielsen into chairs and carried them several miles over a mountain trail to the garrison, arriving around 5:30 p.m. "Nobody said anything to us on the trip, but the soldiers kept looking at us, grinning and nodding. I couldn't think much," Nielsen later wrote. "I tried to work out a plan, but nothing seemed feasible. I made up my mind I'd do the best I could and if I had to I'd kill some Japs before they killed me."

At the garrison the Japanese fed the men boiled eggs and vegetable sandwiches before marching them down to a dock and aboard a diesel-powered boat. The airmen changed boats at Ning-po, but otherwise spent the four-day trip handcuffed in a tiny cabin, the only furnishing a grass mat. At night the Japanese even cuffed the airmen's legs together. Meals consisted of eggs, vegetable soup, and pastries. At about 2:30 p.m. on April 24, the boat reached Shanghai, a fact Nielsen surmised when he spotted signs along the waterfront for the Shanghai Power Company and Shanghai Docks.

The Japanese blindfolded the airmen upon arrival and tethered each one to a guard with a rope around the waist. Guards then placed the fliers in separate cars and drove them to an airport about twenty minutes away, locking them into narrow individual cells. Nielsen hardly had time to settle in before guards pulled him out and led him to an interrogation room. The cramped room was hot and had a single window, the bottom half of which was frosted and blocked his view outside. Six officers sat around a table along with one enlisted man and a civilian interpreter. The Japanese offered Nielsen a cup of tea, which he awkwardly drank with handcuffs.

One of the officers started the interrogation. Where did Nielsen come from and what was he doing in China?

The navigator gave only his name, rank, and serial number.

The interrogators slapped him about the face and head—by his own estimate as many as thirty times—making his ears ring. Others kicked him in the shins hard enough to draw blood. With his hands cuffed behind the chair and his ankles tied to the legs, he was powerless to defend himself.

"We have methods of making you talk," the interpreter told him. "You understand, nobody in your country know you alive. If we happen to torture you to death your people think you missing in action. You want to talk now?"

Nielsen again refused. "That crack about my folks never knowing what became of me sort of got me, but I was so tired that my feelings didn't register," he recalled. "He was watching me closely and he seemed disappointed at my reaction."

The officer snapped his finger and issued a guttural order, triggering the door to burst open. Nielsen watched as four husky enlisted men marched inside. "There was absolutely no expression on their faces," he later wrote. "They seized me, hauled me to my feet and though I tried to resist at first they tossed me on the floor without any trouble. One held my handcuffed arms. Two others held my legs. The fourth put a towel over my face, arranging it in a cup-like fashion over my mouth and nose."

The guard then poured water over his face. To his horror Nielsen felt the tepid liquid run into his mouth and nostrils. "A man has to breathe," he recalled. "Every breath I took I sucked water into my lungs."

Nielsen struggled to fight back. He turned his head and managed to suck in a mouthful of air before the guard forced his head back. He likewise fought without success to move his arms and legs. He started to lose consciousness. "I felt more or less like I was drowning," he recalled, "just gasping between life and death."

Seconds before he blacked out, guards jerked him upright. He coughed and sputtered as the interpreter pressed him to talk.

Nielsen again refused.

A snap of the fingers once again started the horror. "With the water trickling steadily into my mouth and nose I began to go out—quicker this time," he later wrote. "I was too weak to struggle. Just as a black cloud seemed to be settling over me I was jerked to my feet, slugged in the jaw and shoved into the chair."

"Talk," the interpreter barked.

Exhausted and half drowned, Nielsen shook his head no. He couldn't help noticing the smile that crept across the faces of the guards, one of whom retrieved a large bamboo pole about three inches in diameter. Nielsen thought the men might beat him with it, but instead the Japanese slid it behind the back of his knees and then twisted his handcuffed arms backward until he kneeled. Pain pierced his legs. The officers grinned at Nielsen, now in such pain he felt himself begin to panic.

"I can't stand this too long," he thought.

Noises echoed down the hall and Nielsen suspected Hallmark and Meder suffered the same. "The sweat was pouring down my face and into my eyes," he wrote. "I felt dizzy and weak. I could see the sun shining through the upper part of the window and I thought if I could just get outside I might have a chance to make a break for it."

One of the officers slipped off his shoes. He then brought the heel of his foot down on Nielsen's knees. "With each blow it felt as though my kneecap was actually coming loose, but the pain wasn't so great now because my legs had grown numb," Nielsen later recalled. "It was something like the sensation you feel when a dentist pulls a tooth he has first deadened with novocaine."

The torture dragged on for ten minutes before the guards jerked Nielsen to his feet. He collapsed as soon as the Japanese released him, his legs unable to support him. The officers laughed at him as he struggled to pull himself up.

Guards reached down and picked Nielsen up, dumping him back in his chair. Though exhausted and battered, Nielsen now fumed. The officers stared at him and he glared back. The interpreter asked if he wanted to talk.

"I've given you all the information I have," he replied.

The Japanese then slid a pencil-sized rod between his forefinger and middle finger, then squeezed his fingers together while another guard slid the rod back and forth. "I could feel the edges of the pencil slowing cutting the membrane and the sides of my fingers," he later wrote. "I could feel when the blood started. It was a nasty pain, quite different from the bamboo rod torture. It got to your nerves more."

Nielsen refused to surrender.

"Well," the interpreter told him, "this is the start of your treatment and you might be interested to know that we have a lot more splendid devices like this. We'll get the information we want if we have to torture you to death."

"We'll see about that," Nielsen thought.

Some of the officers left the interrogation room, but one returned moments later, bragging that Nielsen's friends had confessed. Why

Flames engulf American planes at the naval air station during the Japanese attack on Pearl Harbor on the morning of December 7, 1941. (NATIONAL ARCHIVES)

American troops scan the skies for enemy attackers as the battleship *California* burns during the attack on Pearl Harbor. (NATIONAL ARCHIVES)

Admiral Isoroku Yamamoto, the architect of the attack on Pearl Harbor, had studied at Harvard and understood American resilience. His number one fear was an American strike against Tokyo, the home of the emperor. (NATIONAL ARCHIVES)

In response to President Franklin Roosevelt's demand that America strike back against Japan, Admiral Ernest King, U.S. Fleet commander, encouraged his subordinates to deve a plan for a carrier raid against Tok (NATIONAL ARCHIVES)

Lieutenant General Henry "Hap" Arnold, chief of the U.S. Army Air Forces who had learned to fly from the Wright brothers, tapped his staff troubleshooter Jimmy Doolittle to plan the raid, which would involve flying Army bombers off a Navy carrier. (NATIONAL ARCHIVES)

Lieutenant Colonel Jimmy Doolittle, a famed racing and stunt pilot, was a pioneer in American aviation. (NATIONAL MUSEUM OF THE U.S. AIR FORCE)

Vice Admiral William "Bull" Halsey Jr. commanded the Navy's task force of sixteen warships and ten thousand men. (NATIONAL ARCHIVES)

Captain Marc Mitscher served as the skipper of the *Hornet*, the 19,800-ton flattop that carried Jimmy Doolittle and his raiders to Japan. (NATIONAL ARCHIVES)

Sailors look on as sixteen Army B-25 bombers, tied down
and with wheels chocked, crowd the deck of the carrier *Hornet*
en route to bomb Japan. (NATIONAL ARCHIVES)

A smiling Jimmy Doolittle, surrounded by his raiders, fastens a Japanese medal to the fin of a 500-pound bomb in a ceremony on the *Hornet*'s deck on the eve of the raid. (NATIONAL ARCHIVES)

Army airmen on the deck of the *Hornet* hustle to load ammunition in advance of the raid. Each plane carried four bombs to drop on Japan, as well as .30- and .50-caliber machine guns for defense against Japanese fighters. (NATIONAL ARCHIVES)

The task force encountered a string of Japanese picket boats early in the morning of April 18, 1942, including this one, which was destroyed by a combination of gunfire and attacks from American planes. (NATIONAL ARCHIVES)

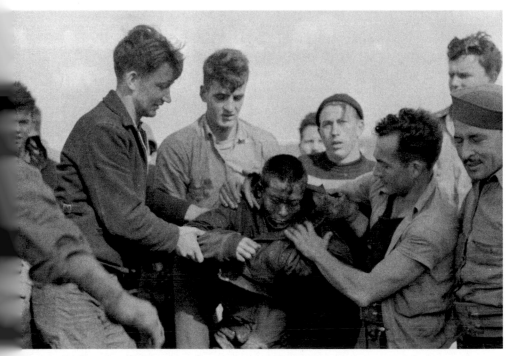

Nashville sailors hold up an exhausted Japanese prisoner of war, rescued from one of the destroyed picket boats. (NATIONAL ARCHIVES)

One of the sixteen B-25s races its engines in preparation for takeoff for the raid against Tokyo. Heavy winds and fierce seas sent waves over the bow of the towering carrier. (NATIONAL ARCHIVES)

Sailors throughout the task force cheered as each bomber lifted off from the *Hornet*'s flight deck. (NATIONAL ARCHIVES)

This photograph of the Yokosuka naval base, shot from one of the bombers, is one of the few images of the raid to have survived. (NATIONAL ARCHIVES)

A Japanese official stands in a crater more than six feet deep and almost forty-three feet wide, surrounded by the debris of a destroyed wooden factory building in the Tokyo area. The attack by pilot Dean Hallmark not only leveled the structure but also blew out the windows of the adjacent building. (NATIONAL INSTITUTE FOR DEFENSE STUDIES)

This bomb crater near an Asahi Electrical Manufacturing Corporation factory in the Tokyo area measured more than fifteen feet wide and almost ten feet deep. (NATIONAL INSTITUTE FOR DEFENSE STUDIES)

The attack led by pilot Travis Hoover, in the second bomber to leave the *Hornet*, destroyed this Tokyo-area home, killing one person. (NATIONAL INSTITUTE FOR DEFENSE STUDIES)

Lieutenant General Joseph Stilwell, pictured here with Generalissimo Chiang Kai-shek, struggled with his disdain for the Chinese leader.
(NATIONAL ARCHIVES)

Local Chinese survey the wreckage of Doolittle's B-25 after the raid on Japan.
(NATIONAL MUSEUM OF THE U.S. AIR FORCE)

Locals carry some of the raiders in sedan chairs, one of the many forms of native transportation the airmen depended on in China, including rickshaws and miniature ponies. (NATIONAL ARCHIVES)

Chinese soldiers escorting the crew of the fifteenth bomber, including, *from left*, Herb Macia, Jack Sims, Jacob Eierman, and Jack Hilger. (NATIONAL ARCHIVES)

Pilot Ted Lawson was badly injured in the crash of the *Ruptured Duck* in the surf along the Chinese coast, leading to the amputation of his left leg by mission doctor Thomas White. (AIR FORCE HISTORICAL RESEARCH AGENCY)

Jimmy Doolittle and his second-in-command, Major Jack Hilger, listen to Madame Chiang Kai-shek after she presented them with medals in Chungking following the raid on Japan. (NATIONAL ARCHIVES)

President Franklin Roosevelt presents Jimmy Doolittle with the Medal of Honor at the White House on May 19, 1942, as Lieutenant General Henry Arnold, Joe Doolittle, and General George Marshall watch. (NATIONAL ARCHIVES)

Blindfolded by his captors, pilot Bobby Hite is led from a Japanese transport plane. He would spend forty months in captivity. (U.S. AIR FORCE MUSEUM)

Missionary priests and Sisters of Charity ford a stream in their flight from the Japanese following the Doolittle raid. (DEPAUL UNIVERSITY)

The Japanese reduced the town of Ying-tan to little more than rubble in the wake of the Doolittle raid. (DEPAUL UNIVERSITY)

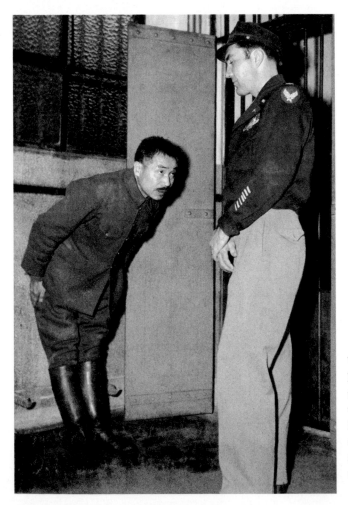

Warden of Kiangwan Milita
Prison, Sotojiro Tatsuda, be
to Chase Nielsen during the
war crimes trials in Shangh
in 1946 for those accused o
executing some of the Dool
raiders. (NATIONAL MUSEUM O
U.S. AIR FORCE)

should Nielsen continue to suffer since the Japanese now knew all the details of the raid?

"Tell it to me and I'll see if you got it right," Nielsen said.

"Oh, no," the officer said, chuckling. "You tell it to us."

Nielsen again refused.

Guards twisted the navigator's arms until he dropped to his knees. Others slapped his face and kicked him in the shins.

"How do you like that?" the interpreter would occasionally interject. "Do you want to say anything now?"

The abuse dragged on until the guards appeared to tire. "If you insist on not telling us anything we might as well finish the job right away," the interpreter told him. "You will face the firing squad for execution immediately."

Guards slipped a blindfold over Nielsen's eyes and led him outside. He felt the sun on his face and gravel under his feet. The guards pushed him along, holding tight to his arms. He always knew that, if he was captured, the Japanese might execute him, but he never truly believed it—until now. "My mind was in a whirl and I couldn't think straight," he recalled. "It's awfully hard to understand that you are about to die, especially when you are not conscious of having done anything wrong. I didn't feel fear then; just a numbness in my body and an empty feeling in my stomach."

Nielsen heard men marching behind him and thought it must be the firing squad. His throat went dry and his heart stopped. Guards had marched him about a thousand feet down the path when he heard a guttural command. The soldiers stopped, and he heard rifle butts hit the gravel. Guards pushed Nielsen a few feet farther down the path and then turned him. "The sweat was pouring down my face and neck now," he recalled. "I wanted desperately to wipe my face, but my hands were cuffed."

He heard another command and the sound of what he suspected were rifles being raised and aimed. No one held on to him now. He thought he might run for it, but he knew it would be futile with his blindfold and handcuffs. "My whole life flashed in front of my mind's eye," he later wrote. "I remembered how my dad and I used to go hunting and fishing back in Utah when I was a boy. I thought of my wife, Thora. I realized suddenly that my folks might never know what had become of me and that thought was agonizing. Somehow a man feels a little better if he is certain that those he loves know what happened to him. I began to feel weak. I thought my heart was actually going to stop. It would pound and jump and there seemed to be long pauses between the beats."

"Well, well, well," the interpreter said. "We are all Knights of the Bushido of the Rising Sun and we don't execute men at sundown. It is now sundown, so your execution will take place in the morning. We will shoot you then unless you decide to talk in the meantime."

Nielsen felt his heartbeat finally slow as his rage increased. "If you boys don't shoot me now," he thought, "you won't shoot me in the morning."

Guards dragged him back to his cell. He heard Hallmark's voice down the hall as the Japanese likewise locked up the *Green Hornet*'s pilot after an afternoon of similar treatment. Several guards arrived at Nielsen's cell around 6 p.m., hanging him by his handcuffs on a wooden peg high up on the wall. His toes barely touched the floor. He realized he was helpless; any movement only hurt his wrists more. "Panic seized me then. I didn't think I could stand that punishment very long," he later wrote. "In a few minutes the pain in my wrists was so intense that I was almost sick to my stomach. Then stabs of pain began to shoot through my chest and shoulders."

He shouted for help, but no one came. The minutes ticked past. An hour turned to two and then three. He finally passed out. "There were periods of consciousness," he recalled, "but the entire night is like a horrible dream in my memory."

Nielsen woke the next morning at daybreak as the guards pulled him down off the wall. "When I let my arms down I thought they were both going to drop off," he said. "My arms were numb, my shoulders were numb, I was numb clear to the waist."

Guards blindfolded him and led him out of his cell. When the Japanese removed his blindfold, he spotted Hallmark and Meder. The men looked haggard, but exchanged the thumbs-up sign. Guards blindfolded the fliers, drove them to the airport, and loaded them aboard a transport plane, tying each of the handcuffed aviators to his seat. The plane roared down the runway. "I could see a little bit out of my blindfold and we seemed to be flying toward the sun," Nielsen recalled. "I figured Tokyo was the goal."

CHAPTER 18

★

Far from winning the war, we have just begun to fight.
But we have begun.

—*PITTSBURGH PRESS*,
APRIL 20, 1942

JAPAN'S LEADERS FUMED OVER the attack on Tokyo. Almost more humiliating than the assault was the fact that it literally followed an air-raid drill. Shouldn't Japanese forces have been on alert? The raid not only made a mockery of the earlier exercise but also exposed the flawed assumptions of Japan's senior leaders, a sentiment captured best in the diary of Captain Yoshitake Miwa. "As the enemy position was 700 miles east of Tokyo, it was thought that an enemy air raid would be made early tomorrow morning. Therefore, when a telephone call came in from Tokyo saying that Tokyo and Yokohama area was bombed, it seemed entirely unbelievable," Miwa wrote. "We cursed ourselves for this, but there is no other way to do. We only thanked God for our not being inflicted much damage, especially no damage sustained to the Imperial Palace."

The lack of widespread damage did little to comfort Yamamoto, who was physically sickened by the news of the attack. The veteran admiral who once had two fingers blown off in the Russo-Japanese War retreated to his stateroom aboard the battleship *Yamato*, refusing to come out. His chief steward, Heijiro Omi, had never seen the admiral so depressed. Yamamoto battled the shame of having failed not only the emperor and the people of Tokyo but even his own mistress, Chiyoko Kawai, who was in bed with pleurisy at the time of the raid, a scene she captured in her diary. "Helped in my hard-labored breathing and got up in spite of myself. Abandoned by doctors, there is no other way but to leave myself in the hand of destiny," she wrote. "Sad indeed."

Yamamoto's incapacitation left Rear Admiral Matome Ugaki to handle the attack's fallout. Early reports showed that the raiders had used twin-engine bombers—Ugaki incorrectly speculated about possible B-26s—and had targeted at least nine spots in Tokyo, plus others in Yokohama, Yokosuka, Nagoya, Wakayama, and Kobe. Ugaki learned that one of the bombers had hit the bow of the submarine tender *Taigei*—undergoing conversion to an aircraft carrier—while reports claimed another targeted Niitsu's oil wells in Niigata Prefecture. Early casualty figures revealed that the attacks had killed twelve and wounded more than a hundred. The raiders had burned fifty houses and left another fifty partly or completely destroyed. Ugaki could not figure out how the bombers had escaped. Did the planes return to carriers or fly on to Russia or China?

The Japanese bombers and fighters that had sortied shortly before 1 p.m. had flown as far out as seven hundred miles without locating the enemy task force. By 5 p.m.—and with no sign of the attackers—Ugaki could do little more than vent. "We have missed him again and again. This is more than regrettable, because this shattered my firm determination never to let the enemy attack Tokyo or the mainland," he wrote in his diary. "If the enemy carried out attacks from such a long distance, which is about the same as an expected one-way attack, we shall have to revise our countermeasures fundamentally, studying their type planes. In any case, this is one up to the enemy today. As we have no information whether he'll attack again tomorrow, going north toward Hokkaido or south heading for Marcus and Wake, we shall have to let it up to him."

Erroneous reports of new attacks kept Japanese leaders on edge. At 2:02 a.m. on April 19 observation posts at Sawara, Kagoshima, and Togane all reported hearing large explosions and issued an aircraft alert. Two flying boats took off at 2:45 a.m. to search the waters east of Tokyo, but found nothing. The Japanese lifted the alarm half an hour later, but as a precaution kept fighters in the air and dozens more on a fifteen-minute standby alert. A 12:15 p.m. telephone call from the central military district claimed enemy planes had been sighted over Osaka and the suburb of Sakae. More than two dozen fighter and scout planes again roared into the skies, only to learn that several Japanese bombers had triggered the false alarm. These measures coincided with a search of the waters out to seven hundred miles by eighteen land-based bombers.

Reports indicated the enemy task force might head north, creating fear of a raid on Hokkaido. No one had heard from the doomed *Nitto Maru* or the *Nagato Maru*, though Ugaki learned that the Americans had damaged at least three other picket boats. Twenty-four hours after the raid the casualty count climbed to as many as 363 killed and injured. "The reason," Ugaki wrote in his diary, "for the comparatively large number of casualties versus the number of bombs might be splinters from our own antiaircraft fire." News that at least one American bomber had crashed in China initially added to the confusion. "What relation there was between the powerful enemy task force sighted in the east sea of Japan yesterday and the movement of this Army air force is still beyond our judgment," Miwa wrote in his diary. "Did they take off from carriers? Did they operate separately, or, did they intend a simultaneous attack?"

Ugaki did soon catch a break. The Japanese captured five raiders, though the initial interrogation reports out of China proved a muddled mess, thanks to the wild and conflicting stories made by members of the *Bat out of Hell*'s crew. Harold Spatz had told interrogators that the aviators took off from a fictitious island west of Midway, while Bobby Hite claimed the men flew from the Aleutians. One check of the charts revealed to veteran sailor Ugaki that it was all bogus. "They never told the truth," he griped in his diary. "It couldn't be helped, as the interrogators must have been some army officers of lower rank with little knowledge of foreign languages and the sea. We must investigate further promptly so that we can take proper measures for the future."

Even through the blatant falsehoods the Japanese gleaned some valuable details, deducing that at least thirteen North American B-25s—each with a five-man crew—all headed for China. Based on that, Ugaki pieced together the plan. "What the enemy intended in this attack, I suppose, was to launch long-distance planes from converted carriers after closing in our homeland supported by carriers, heavy cruisers, and destroyers. After flying over our homeland, the bombers were to go to the mainland of China, where they would use bases for carrying out raids on our country. In view of this recent success, undoubtedly the enemy will repeat this kind of operation while attempting raids from China. Therefore, we must take steps to watch far to the east and, at the same time, always keep a sharp lookout on the threat from the west."

By the following evening—and after the Americans failed to attack Hokkaido—Japan suspended Tactical Method No. 3 against the U.S. Fleet, the nation's plan for the defense of the homeland. Even forty-eight hours after the raid, Ugaki clearly was still irritated. "The enemy, already withdrawn far to the east, through radio must have observed our confusion with contempt," he wrote. "Thus, our homeland has been air raided and we missed the enemy without firing a shot at him. This is exceedingly regrettable." Yamamoto had since recovered and shared the outrage. "One has the embarrassing feeling of having been caught napping just when one was feeling confident and in charge of things. Even though there wasn't much damage, it's a disgrace that the skies over the imperial capital should have been defiled without a single enemy plane being shot down. It provides a regrettably graphic illustration of the saying that a bungling attack is better than the most skillful defense."

The Japanese had transferred the crew of the *Bat out of Hell* to Nanking, where after waterboarding and other tortures the airmen had talked. Ugaki knew by April 21 that the *Hornet*, loaded with sixteen bombers, had left San Francisco around the first of the month accompanied by two cruisers, four destroyers, and a tanker, joining up at sea with another carrier plus more cruisers and destroyers. He knew that detection by the Japanese had prompted the early takeoff and that the bombers had flown due west across the Boso Peninsula to targets. Ugaki not only knew that all the fliers were volunteers, but he knew the approximate wind speed across the carrier's deck at takeoff. Ugaki's frustration over the raid appeared tempered only by his professional curiosity and even admiration for the plan's ingenuity. "How the sixteen planes were accommodated remained unsolved," he wrote. "Work harder to solve the riddle!"

A final tally revealed that the attack obliterated no fewer than 112 buildings—containing 180 units—and damaged another 53 buildings, with 106 units. In Tokyo, raiders had torched more than 50 buildings around the Asahi Electrical Manufacturing Corporation's Oku factory, another 13 around the National Hemp Dressing Corporation along with the Communication Ministry's transformer station. In nearby Kanagawa Prefecture, they targeted the foundries, factories, and warehouses of the Japanese Steel Corporation and Showa Electric. They had blasted the Yokosuka naval station and experimental laboratory and wrecked the Japan Diesel Corporation manufacturing in Saitama Prefecture. The attacks on Nagoya had completely burned one of Toho Gas Company's massive storage tanks as well as damaged the Mitsubishi Heavy Industries aircraft factory. Six wards of the army hospital had gone up in flames, along with a food storage warehouse and army arsenal.

Civilians were not immune. The attack burned homes in places ranging from Tokyo to Kobe. A postwar analysis would count 87 men, women, and children killed in the raid and another 151 seriously injured, including a woman shellfishing near Nagoya who was shot through the left cheek and thigh. More than 311 others suffered minor injuries. Most of the deaths had occurred in just a few of the attacks— namely, those led by the pilots Hoover, Gray, Jones, and Joyce, which accounted for 75 of the mission's total fatalities. The deaths of children in the attacks by Doolittle, Hallmark, Joyce, and Gray would become a flashpoint as newspapers in the weeks ahead begged parents of those killed to share their views on how Japan should treat the captured raiders. "One father wrote to a leading daily telling of the killing of his child in the bombing of the primary school," stated the interrogation report of one Japanese prisoner of war. "He deplored the dastardly act and avowed his intention of avenging the child's death by joining the army and dying a glorious death."

While Ugaki and others in the Navy struggled to decipher the details of the raid, the Army and government likewise wrestled with the question of how to handle publicly the news of the attack, given the long-standing claim that such a raid was an impossibility. Japanese leaders juggled several goals, including informing the public and minimizing blame as well as covering up the abysmal fact that the defense forces failed to intercept or shoot down any of the bombers. On a larger level Japanese leaders wanted to paint themselves as victims in the inevitable propaganda war with the Americans. The official communiqués issued throughout the afternoon reflected those goals and differed greatly from the frantic broadcasts intercepted by radiomen on the *Hornet*. That was evident by the first bulletin issued by Eastern District Army headquarters at 2 p.m.:

"Today, April 18, at about 12:30 p.m., enemy planes from several directions raided the Tokyo-Yokohama district. Countered by the air and land defense corps of the Imperial forces, the enemy raiders are being repulsed.

"Thus far nine enemy planes are known to have been shot down, while damage inflicted by the enemy appears to be slight.

"The Imperial Household is in no way affected, it has been learned."

That was followed by a similar bulletin at 3 p.m. from the Central District Army headquarters, stating that two bombers had raided Nagoya, but caused only slight damage, while another had targeted Kobe with incendiary bombs, again without causing any real destruction. "The time has come," the bulletin declared, "for the people to rise to the occasion by defending the sky courageously and with absolute confidence in victory." Authorities with the Central Nippon Army headquarters put out more details an hour later, again deemphasizing the raid's damage. "Incendiary bombs were dropped by the enemy at six different places in the vicinity of Nagoya, but they are practically extinguished by now," the bulletin stated. "In Kobe one incendiary bomb each was dropped at three different places. They were, however, extinguished."

Bulletins proved quick to congratulate the air defense forces, which not only were slow to sound the alarm but failed to shoot down any of the invaders. "The corps guarding the air was very prompt to locate the enemy planes, with the result that the air raid alarm could be sounded in time," stated a 4:30 p.m. bulletin from the Eastern District Army headquarters. "Thanks to the efforts of the air and land defense units and the presence of mind and quick action of the people, the damage inflicted by the invading planes could be limited to the minimum." The deceptive alerts stunned senior naval officers. "The Army announced that nine enemy planes were shot down, which was entirely untrue. In fact, even one enemy plane was not shot down," Miwa wrote in his diary. "What for, I wonder, did the army make such a false announcement?"

At the same time the government sought to reassure the public, leaders looked to spin the raid for the rest of the world, as evidenced by a message from Foreign Minister Shigenori Togo to Berlin that America intercepted: "In connection with the recent air attack by enemy planes, in order to circumvent enemy propaganda we had Domei and the radio broadcast the facts immediately to the outside world." Japan's version of the attack, playing up the civilian loss of life, went out over the airwaves in eight different languages. "This afternoon a few spots in Tokyo had some bombs dropped by enemy planes," Japanese broadcasts declared. "The cowardly raiders purposely avoided the industrial centers and important military establishments, and blindly dumped their incendiaries in a few suburban districts, especially on schools and hospitals. The shameless raiders, however, were almost all downed by our surface guns and bombing planes, to the open view of the Tokyo residents who shouted Banzai at the sight."

Newspaper headlines in the days after the attack parroted those themes, championing Japan's alleged success in destroying nine American bombers, while others sought to assure the public that the nation's air defense network was impenetrable. One of the more comical write-ups appeared in an April 22 editorial in the *Japan Times & Advertiser*, which boasted that of the hundreds of planes American flattops carry, only ten could penetrate Japan's protected airspace. "The few enemy planes that did manage to slip through the defense cordon failed to get near any of the establishments of military importance which were too well guarded," the paper boasted. "Hence the planes were forced to fly around aimlessly over the suburbs of Tokyo, dropping incendiary bombs on schools and hospitals, machine-gunning innocent civilians and hitting at least one elementary school pupil, before being brought down or driven away."

The schizophrenic press, when not decrying the slaughter of civilians, portrayed the raid as so inconsequential that it had no effect on daily life. Even Emperor Hirohito could not be bothered to seek shelter, opting instead to listen to a 2 p.m. report on other matters from Home Minister Michio Yuzawa. Others noted that motion picture and stage theaters refused to cancel shows; the only exceptions were the Kabukiza and the Imperial Theater, which chose simply to postpone afternoon performances. Financial markets likewise took no hit; the press even bragged that the stock market opened stronger on Monday on news of the nation's great defense. Public officials spoke out often in the media, describing the raid if anything as a "valuable experience." "Air raids are nothing to be feared," stated Mamoru Shigemitsu, the ambassador to China, who was in England during the German blitz. "Compared with German raids on London, today's air attacks cannot be called an air raid in any sense of the word."

"The truth is that the American raiders were easily repulsed by the iron-wall air defense of our country," asserted Tomokazu Hori, a spokesman for the board of information.

"Air raids alone, no matter how intensive, have not ruined any nation," declared Lieutenant General Asasaburo Kobayashi, chief of staff of the Defense General Headquarters.

To bolster the reports of so many planes shot down—and no doubt to help obscure the fact that Japan in the short term could produce no wreckage—the press published colorful accounts of two pilots who claimed to have blasted enemy bombers, though neither could confirm seeing the enemy planes actually crash.

"I pursued this plane, showering machinegun shots. The enemy plane strove to flee south," reported Lieutenant Ryosaburi Umekawa, who in fact had pursued Ross Greening's bomber. "I caused her to burst into flames."

"We saw her right engine in flames," added the other pilot. "There can be no doubt that the enemy plane crashed into the sea."

Editorial pages meanwhile helped peddle the government's spin, applauding the valiant Japanese forces and ridiculing America.

"The enemy's daring enterprise failed to achieve any results worth mentioning," argued the *Nichi Nichi* newspaper.

"The manner in which the invading planes were driven back conclusively showed that air defenses in Japan Proper are perfect," added the *Miyako*.

"Their weak attacking strength was a sort of comic play," declared the *Mochi* newspaper.

Others sought to remind the public how the government expected them to behave in the event of a future attack. "The most important thing is that the people at large should remain calm and collected under all circumstances," advised the *Chugai Shogyo*. "The sense of alarm and consternation which the public may betray would be most deplorable, as it will then be only playing into the hands of the enemy."

Not all editorials were so laughable. Some precisely outlined America's true motivation behind the surprise attack. "It was a mere gesture made for its psychological effect on the American public," argued the *Japan Times & Advertiser*. "The harassed and embarrassed leaders at Washington had to do something to quiet the mounting tide of criticism from their own people. Something dramatic, even if desperate, had to be done. The air attack on Japan was the answer."

Despite the bravado and efforts to belittle the raid, Japan could not suppress all the news. Some practical information had to be released. Reports revealed that the Industrial Bank of Japan and the Hypothec Bank of Japan would take over claims of financial institutions that were creditors to air-raid victims and that life insurance companies would pay unconditionally the entire insured amount to anyone killed in the attack. Other reports noted that prefectural governors would dole out aid to victims under the Wartime Sufferers Protection Law. "The law provides that family members of those killed and injured as a result of wartime disaster such as air-raids will be given temporary or continuous protection for a fixed period of time from the viewpoint of stabilizing the people's living," the news stated. "Besides being housed, the afflicted will be supplied with food, clothes, bedding, and other daily necessities."

Americans and other captive Allies pored over the papers, looking for clues that might provide a sense of the attack's success. Under house arrest inside the American embassy, Ambassador Joseph Grew had long since grown accustomed to the government's propaganda. "It is sometimes so poor that it is surprising that they can even fool themselves," he later quipped. "After the fall of Bataan they published in all the vernacular newspapers a photograph of an arch with a lot of Japanese soldiers around it waving helmets and shouting. On the arch was painted, 'United States Naval Vase' with a base spelled with a v. Our Navy is able to spell at least. The next day the same picture was published in the *Japan Advertiser*, an English language paper owned by the Japanese government. The v was scratched out and a b was substituted."

The veteran diplomat scanned the papers for telltale signs of bomber wreckage. If Japan had indeed shot down nine bombers, he knew the government would display the burned wreckage as a trophy of its airmen's great success. Not until April 26—eight days after the attack—did the *Japan Times & Advertiser* finally run such a photo, accompanied by the colorful headline "Miserable Remains of Wrecked Enemy Raider." To maintain the charade Japanese authorities had gone so far as to hunt down bomber wreckage—the Chinese army would later report that it was Farrow's plane—and import it to Tokyo, putting it on display for the crowds to see at the Yasukuni Shrine. To verify the wreckage's authenticity, the press highlighted a stamp on a gasoline tank that read, "North American Aviation Company." Authorities included a parachute, again noting the tag "Made by Switlik Company, Inglewood, California."

Grew wasn't the only diplomat on the lookout for wreckage. "We expected photographs of the planes to appear in the papers. We waited and waited and waited," recalled Frank Moysey, the cipher officer at the British embassy. "Finally, a week later, the papers published an explanation for the lack of photographs—all the planes had been shot into the sea. We finally concluded that all the planes shot down were Japanese fighters." Moysey added that the raid led servants who had long been friendly with the diplomats to suddenly cool toward them. "For two weeks after the raid the Japs were jumpy as cats," he recalled. "Trips to do necessary shopping and to hospitals for treatment were immediately abolished. We were not permitted out of the compound, so it was impossible to determine the amount of damage."

Other Westerners likewise noted a psychological change, including Ramón Muñiz Lavalle, the commercial attaché at the Argentine embassy. "The raid by Doolittle was one of the greatest psychological tricks ever used. It caught the Japs by surprise. Their unbounded confidence began to crack," the diplomat would tell reporters after his arrival in the United States in April 1943. "The results of Doolittle's raid are still evident in Japan. They are stamped into the daily living habits of the Japanese people. Where before they imagined themselves safe from aerial aggression, they now search the skies each morning and each night. Japanese newspapers carry pictures of American planes and say these planes are practicing in Texas on how to bomb Tokyo. Fire brigades have been organized. Fire drills are practiced. Fearlessness has turned to fear."

French journalist Robert Guillain concluded that the flat-footed response of both the military and the civilian population served as an important lesson for the Japanese, who redoubled efforts to prepare for the possibility of future attacks. "The raid did the Japanese more good than harm," Guillain later wrote. "Air defenses were reinforced; in

Tokyo, rooftops in the business and ministerial districts sprouted spot-
ters and heavy machine guns. Parks were dug up for antiaircraft batteries. Barrage balloons soon encircled the capital and new bases were built
for fighter squadrons. Air-raid drills were frequent and for a full day,
sometimes two, every month, normal activity was suspended in an entire
quarter, occasionally in the whole city, by firefighting drills in which hundreds of thousands of men and women took part."

Interviews with repatriated Americans aboard the Swedish vessel
Gripsholm in the summer of 1942 echoed those themes. "The Doolittle
raid produced noticeable results in the attitude of the Japanese," stated a
report by the Office of Strategic Services. "One man from Kobe saw a
plane above his house, heard the explosion of bombs, and observed four
fires, one of which was in a lumber yard and burned for more than a day.
The air raid is reported to have shaken the Japanese because many of the
common people were firmly convinced that, after all, Japan could not be
successfully attacked. The raid is, therefore, to be regarded from the
point of view of its psychological effect as well as from the point of view
of its material consequences. We found no one who could make any estimate of the extent of the damage. At the same time we found no one who
thought it unimportant in its effect upon the attitude of the people."

Senior Japanese leaders privately agreed. "It could hardly be called a
real raid," Yamamoto complained in an April 29 letter, "but I feel it was
just enough of a taste of the real thing to warn the people of Tokyo
against their present outlook." Shigenori Togo, Japan's foreign minister,
was more blunt. "The bombing of Tokyo," the diplomat later wrote,
"produced a serious shock in Japan, as it proved the falsity of the military
assurances of the inviolability of the Imperial capital." Mitsuo Fuchida,
the pilot who led the attack on Pearl Harbor, agreed. "In point of physical damage inflicted, it was true enough that the raid did not accomplish
a great deal," he later wrote. "But the same could not be said of its impact
on the minds of Japan's naval leaders and its consequent influence on the
course of the war at sea. From this standpoint, neither 'do-nothing' nor
'do-little' were accurate descriptions. On the contrary, it must be regarded
as a 'do-much' raid."

The effects of the raid rippled through the military's and public's
mindset, both in Japan and beyond, as was noted by Saburo Sakai, one of
Japan's top fighter pilots down in New Guinea. "The attack unnerved

almost every pilot at Lae," he wrote. "The knowledge that the enemy was strong enough to smash at our homeland, even in what might be a punitive raid, was cause for serious apprehension of future and heavier attacks." His cousin Hatsuyo had witnessed the attack. "The bombing of Tokyo and several other cities has brought about a tremendous change in the attitude of our people toward the war," she wrote. "Now things are different; the bombs have dropped here on our homes. It does not seem any more that there is such a great difference between the battlefront and the home front. I know that I, as well as the other girls, will work all the harder to do our share at home to support you and the other pilots who are so far away from Japan."

The biggest effect of the raid was on the proposed plan to capture Midway. Even though Yamamoto had strong-armed approval of the operation within his service, the Navy had since encountered complications with the Army. Just six days before Doolittle's bombers appeared in the skies over Tokyo, Captain Sadatoshi Tomioka had presented the plan to Lieutenant General Shinichi Tanaka, chief of the operations section of the Army general staff. The general saw the Midway operation as a stepping-stone for the Navy's desired capture of Hawaii, a move Tanaka warned risked a dangerous overextension of Japan's defensive perimeter and could ultimately undermine the nation's entire war effort. The Army refused to cooperate. Tomioka soldiered on, preparing a report on the proposed operation that Navy chief of staff Admiral Osami Nagano presented to Emperor Hirohito on April 16.

No final decision had been made when American bombers thundered over the capital, ending all debate. "It was just as if a shiver had passed over Japan," recalled Kameto Kuroshima, one of Yamamoto's senior staff officers. "The Doolittle raid had a pronounced effect on the Midway operation," added Yasuji Watanabe, another senior aide. "With the Doolittle raid the Japanese Army changed its strategy and not only agreed to the Midway plan of the Navy but agreed to furnish the troops to occupy the islands." Mitsuo Fuchida concurred. "Even the most vociferous opponents of the Midway plan were now hard put to deny that the threat from the east, if not greater than the potential threat from Australia, was at least more pressing and immediate," Fuchida wrote. "The Midway operation was now definitely decided. Combined Fleet had gained its way, thanks to the unwitting assistance of Colonel Doolittle and his fliers."

★

BACK IN WASHINGTON, General Hap Arnold anxiously awaited word from Doolittle regarding the outcome of the raid. There was little doubt that at least some of the bombers had hit Tokyo. American newspapers had all but screamed the news in bold headlines that ran across the top of papers nationwide—all of it picked up from Japanese radio broadcasts. But Arnold was unable to balance out the Japanese propaganda with the actual results. Did the raiders really blast schools and hospitals? Had the Japanese in fact shot down nine of Doolittle's bombers? Arnold had no way of knowing.

Absent any real information, American leaders remained quiet, much to the frustration of the press. "Why, everybody wants to know, does Washington keep silent as to the bombing attacks on Japan?" asked the *Boston Globe*. "For the best news of the war—the sensational American air attack on Japan—the United States yesterday had to depend entirely on enemy radio broadcasts," noted the *Washington Post*. "Our own Army and Navy were silent. No communiqués on the raid were issued, and none were promised: indeed, there was no confirmation of any kind here in Washington."

Washington's silence baffled even the Japanese, who had expected the U.S. government to celebrate the attack. "I wonder why the publicity-minded Americans did not make a fuss out of this air raid," Captain Yoshitake Miwa wrote in his diary on April 22. "Is it that all of the attacking bombers made a forced landing, thus making it difficult for them to assess the result of the air raid? Is it because most of them failed to return to the designated base with too much damage sustained to announce it? Or, is it that they are thinking of more contemplated plans?"

As the days marched past—and the silence continued—Japan's curiosity gave way to desperation, prompting Tokyo radio to fish for news. "The American papers are talking big, but not a whisper from the Army or Navy," announced one broadcast picked up by United Press in San Francisco. "We will be very interested in knowing their claims of damages, which, according to them, no doubt will be great."

Members of Congress proved happy to sound off, many boasting that the raid was a prelude to continued assaults, which America was in no position to execute. "This will prove TNT in boosting morale," declared Representative John Snyder of Pennsylvania, while Senator Joseph Hill of Alabama described it as "hardly a token compared with what we're going to give them." "This is the only way we are going to win the war," said Senator D. Worth Clark of Idaho. "Start right in bombing them at home."

No one was more pleased than President Roosevelt, who had left two days before the raid for an unannounced visit to his home at Hyde Park. Only when the task force bore down on the Japanese homeland did Admiral King finally share the full details of the impending assault with the president, who, of course, had known the principal concept of the mission, just not the final logistics. "Until twenty-four hours before the raid only seven people—King, Low, Duncan, Arnold, Doolittle, Nimitz, and Halsey—knew of the *complete* plan," King later wrote. "President Roosevelt and even Secretary Knox were not told until the planes had taken off from the *Hornet*."

Armed with that news, the president had stewed. He phoned his distant cousin and confidante Daisy Suckley around 10:15 a.m. on April 17.

"Hell's a-poppin'," he told her.

The president drove over to pick up Daisy, accompanied by speechwriter Sam Rosenman, aide Marvin McIntyre, and secretary Grace Tully. Daisy climbed into the front seat, and the car set off through the New York countryside. The president confided in Daisy that he was in a "bad humor—needed fresh air & a change." The hourlong ride along narrow wooded roads and past fresh-cut lumber appeared the perfect tonic for the commander in chief. "So many things were coming to life," Eleanor Roosevelt noted in her "My Day" column, "lilies of the valley, bulbs of various kinds and lilac bushes."

That evening the president and Eleanor dined with Treasury Secretary Henry Morgenthau and his wife, who celebrated their twenty-sixth wedding anniversary. Roosevelt had settled into work Saturday with Rosenman and Tully on his seven-point anti-inflation message for Congress and the fireside chat that would follow, when word of the raid arrived from Washington. "The President was, of course, overjoyed by the news," Rosenman later wrote. "He knew the heartening effect it would have on American morale and the morale of our Allies, and the blow to the prestige of the Japanese, to have American bombers over Tokyo even for a short, fleeting time."

Roosevelt spent much of Saturday on the phone. While Arnold fretted over the logistical outcome of the mission, Roosevelt had only to worry about the morale of the American people. Any effort to strike back against the Japanese, he knew, would be seen as a victory. The president realized he would soon need to answer the question of where the bombers had originated, a sensitive issue he brainstormed with Rosenman.

"Mr. President, do you remember the novel of James Hilton, *Lost Horizon*, telling of that wonderful, timeless place known as Shangri-La," Rosenman asked. "It was located in the trackless wastes of Tibet. Why not tell them that that's where the planes came from? If you use a fictional place like that, it's a polite way of saying that you do not intend to tell the enemy or anybody else where the planes really came from."

Roosevelt immediately liked the idea. He phoned Steve Early and briefed him on the plan. The president then tried out the line the next morning on Assistant Secretary Bill Hassett when he entered Roosevelt's bedroom.

"What's the news?" the president asked.

Hassett relayed to him the latest headlines and recounted how all the papers were filled with speculation over the mysterious raid on Japan.

"You know," Roosevelt said, "we have an airplane base in the Himalayas."

A former journalist with the Associated Press and the *Washington Post*, Hassett thought about the president's answer for a moment. "That seemed to me, geographically, a prodigious distance from Tokyo," he wrote in his diary.

The president then brought the joke to its climax. "The base," he continued, "is at Shangri-La."

The befuddled Hassett stared at the commander in chief. "I was unfamiliar with James Hilton's book *Lost Horizon*," he later admitted, "and so was dumb enough until I sensed that he was kidding."

Roosevelt ordered the train readied that night to leave at eleven and return to Washington. The reference from Hilton's book stayed in his mind. He liked it so much that he confided in his cousin Daisy over breakfast the next morning, on the train as it approached the nation's capital, that he planned to use that phrase with reporters.

When a journalist brought up the raid during the 4:10 p.m. press conference in the Executive Office on April 21, Roosevelt immediately segued to the question over where the bombers originated. "I think the time has now come to tell you," the president announced. "They came from our new secret base at Shangri-La!"

The press erupted in laughter, though as Daisy recorded in her diary, only about half of them understood the joke. Reporters pressed Roosevelt for details of the raid, which only served to highlight how little the White House still knew.

"Would you care to go so far as to confirm the truth of the Japanese reports that Tokyo was bombed?" one reporter asked.

"No. I couldn't even do that," Roosevelt said with a laugh. "I am depending on Japanese reports very largely."

Like Roosevelt, the press soon took to the joke about America's mythical base in the Himalayas, using it days later in an April 24 press conference.

"Is there any news today from Shangri-La?" one reporter asked.

Roosevelt would have particular fun with the theme during a May 26 press conference. "A southern newspaper editor," he told reporters, "was asked in a letter to the editor where Shangri-La was, and he said that he had examined carefully the maps of every parish in the State of Louisiana and been unable to find Shangri, L-A."

The press howled with laughter.

"When is the ambassador of Shangri-La going to present his credentials?" one reporter asked to even more chuckles.

"I understood that was an American possession," another countered.

"Have you any Shangri-La stamps for cancellation?"

"Yes," Roosevelt answered. "I have a special album sent me by the 'Lama.'"

Roosevelt would later go so far as to dub the new presidential retreat in Maryland's Catoctin Mountain Shangri-La, a name future president Dwight Eisenhower changed in 1953 in honor of his grandson to Camp David. The Navy followed Roosevelt's lead in 1944, inviting Joe Doolittle to christen the 27,100-ton aircraft carrier *Shangri-La*. Even her husband would embrace the president's humor, recording the famous mission in his flight log simply as "Shangri-La to Shangri-La."

The president's jocular humor in the days after the raid helped mask the administration's lack of information. At other times Roosevelt simply deflected questions, arguing that he knew only what had been reported in the press.

"Mr. President, there are complaints in Tokyo that our Army and Navy are keeping too quiet," one reporter asked on April 24, addressing the official silence that had surrounded the mission. "Could you do anything about that?"

"I read that too," Roosevelt cryptically answered, ending the discussion.

Privately the president couldn't help gloating, firing off a message to Winston Churchill. "As you will have seen in the press we have had a good crack at Japan by air and I am hoping that we can make it very difficult for them to keep too many of their big ships in the Indian Ocean," Roosevelt wrote. "I am frank to say that I feel better about the war than at any time in the past two years."

The military hustled to keep the president informed of any news. The same day Roosevelt first joked about Shangri-La, Arnold sent him a one-page memo, noting that sixteen bombers had left the carrier and successfully attacked targets in the Tokyo-Osaka area, but had encountered bad weather over China. "The number of airplanes forced down or shot down over Japan are not definitely known," the general wrote. "We have received reports of nineteen crew members landing safe and uninjured in the area south of Hangchow." Arnold's opinion of the mission's success was mixed. "From the viewpoint of damage to enemy installations and property, and the tremendous effect it had upon our Allies, as well as the demoralizing effect upon our enemies, the raid was undoubtedly highly successful," he wrote. "However, from the viewpoint of an Air Force operation the raid was not a success, for no raid is a success in which losses exceed ten per cent, and it now appears that probably all of the airplanes were lost."

Arnold's view improved drastically the next day. The general had finally received Doolittle's cable, which had been sent to the Chinese embassy, translated, and forwarded to Arnold. The general quoted it in full to the president. He likewise cited reports from Chungking, noting that he could now account for eleven bombers, meaning the Japanese could have shot down at most only five. He further noted that despite early discovery, the dogged Doolittle had charged ahead with the mission, a fact that clearly impressed Arnold. "Everything points to Doolittle having accomplished a most remarkable flight. He knowingly and willingly took off twelve hours ahead of time, which put him over Japan at the worst possible time of day. He also knew that this would put him over China at night where, if the weather broke against him the chances of getting in safely were very very poor," he wrote. "Thus, he had the breaks against him on the take off, at the time he did his bombing, and also at the time of landing in China."

William Standley, the American ambassador, messaged Washington on April 22 that York's crew had landed in Vladivostok, news Russia didn't want public: "The Soviet military authorities would like to have this information kept secret and especially do not wish that the press should know that a United States Army plane had landed in the Soviet Union," Marshall informed the president the next day. "The crew," he wrote, "was apparently uninjured and is being well cared for." Major General Dwight Eisenhower drafted a message to the embassy on Marshall's behalf with a plan to get the crew out. "It would appear desirable, if consistent with the views of the Soviet Government, to remove the crew and plane from eastern Siberia as quickly as possible," he wrote. "This would minimize the danger of the enemy discovering their presence and demanding explanation. If this can be accomplished, it is further suggested that these individuals might be attached for the time being to the United States Embassy. If Mr. Stalin desires to take possession of the plane you are authorized to offer it to him for use in Russia."

The raid did create real fears of possible Japanese retaliation in some observers, including Admiral William Leahy, who that summer would become Roosevelt's chief of staff. "This might have been of some assistance to our war effort by requiring defensive Japanese air forces to remain in Japan," the admiral later wrote, "but I feared it would bring reprisal bombing attacks on American Pacific Coast cities." So, too, did Henry Stimson, though the public's enthusiasm over the raid coupled with the Japanese government's hysteria initially tamped down the war secretary's concerns. "I have always been a little bit doubtful about this project, which has been a pet project of the President's," Stimson confided in his diary the day of the attack. "But I will say that it has had a very good psychological effect on the country both here and abroad and it has had also a very wholesome effect on Japan's public sentiment."

After news of the attack settled, Stimson's earlier concerns returned. He summoned Generals Marshall and Arnold on April 21 for a "few earnest words," expressing his fear that Japan would have no choice but to counter with a carrier raid against the West Coast. The war secretary made similar predictions during a press conference in an effort to prepare the public for just such a possibility. "The United States government," Stimson told reporters, "administered a stinging, humiliating, surprise blow when it bombed Tokyo. This was shown by the fact that at the time of the raid the Japanese were boasting about their invulnerability. To any one who knows Oriental psychology, as I do, this meant to the Japanese a serious loss of face, which can only be wiped out by a return blow, possibly a little bigger than the one suffered. We have a paramount necessity to set our house in order for what seems inevitable."

Such concerns prompted major cities across the nation to review air-raid precautions. "Don't forget the payoff," warned New York City's police commissioner, Lewis Valentine. "If we can do it, they can do it, too." Brooklyn held a massive blackout just a few days after the raid that affected 968,000 residents spread across seventeen square miles. Tensions remained so high that two men got into a fistfight at the intersection of Russell Street and Norman Avenue after one refused to snuff out his cigarette. Similar fears triggered a three-hour shutdown of San Francisco—the longest so far of the war, leaving motorists stranded on the Golden Gate and Bay Bridges—after authorities reported the discovery offshore of an "unidentified target."

Despite those anxieties—coupled with the lack of concrete details—Americans applauded the raid, both those at home in the United States and those serving overseas. "We drank a bottle of champagne to celebrate the event," Major General Lewis Brereton wrote in his diary when news reached him in New Delhi. "Good for Jimmy!"

Editorials across the nation lit up with the news. "Tokyo bombed! Yokohama bombed! Kobe bombed!" trumpeted the *Washington Post*. "After four months of defeats in the Pacific War these words have abruptly electrified the pulse of America."

"If we can do it once, we can do it again—and again," added the *Pittsburgh Press*. "We have sweat and bled. Now it is her turn."

The *New York Times* called it a "blow at the heart of the Japanese Empire." "For 2,600 years Japan's warriors have suffered no invaders on the sacred soil of the homeland. Now they have suddenly swarmed out of the sky," the paper wrote. "A reverse so striking and portentous is bound to reverberate throughout the Orient."

Many news outlets characterized the raid as a reprisal for Japan's horrific attack in December. The Associated Press went so far as to describe it as a "balm for the wounds of Pearl Harbor and Bataan," while the *Los Angeles Times* suggested that Japan "consider this another installment on our debt to her."

Amid the celebration and demands for more attacks, other editorial voices cautioned Americans to temper expectations, pointing to the long fight still ahead. "Encouraging as the news is, it will be a mistake for our people to give it too much weight," wrote the *Chicago Daily Tribune*. "Japan is a powerful nation." The *Boston Globe* agreed. "Satisfaction felt in this country because of this daring exploit should not lead us to forget that air attacks of greater power and persistence will be needed before there is any real diminution of Japan's strength," argued the paper. "The trail blazers have marked out the way, but the task ahead remains formidable."

CHAPTER 19

★

Don't forget, America—make sure that every flier that
comes here has a special pass to hell, and
rest assured it's strictly a one-way ticket.

—TOKYO RADIO,
APRIL 21, 1943

THE AIRCREWS TRICKLED IN day after day to Chuchow. Davy Jones and his men arrived first on April 19, followed by the crews of Bill Bower, Ross Greening, and Jack Hilger. Sometimes an entire crew arrived; occasionally, just a single aviator. By the time Doolittle appeared on April 26, fifty-six airmen had been found. After days alone in the Chinese wilderness the reunions among friends were heartfelt, a sentiment best captured by Hilger in his diary. "It was like a homecoming and we were all as happy as kids," he wrote. "There's nothing like a familiar face in a foreign country."

Arrival in Chuchow capped an exotic adventure for most of the raiders, who had hiked down out of the mountains, often aided by Chinese guerrillas, villagers, and even a few foreign missionaries. "Everywhere we went we were the center of attraction and everyone seemed to know all about us," navigator Carl Wildner recalled. "We were oddities as well as celebrities." In many cases the Americans found themselves welcomed in villages and towns by local politicians and military leaders; a few even held parades. That was the case for Jones and his copilot, Hoss Wilder, who stepped off a train in Yushan to find a beaming gentleman dressed in Western clothes at the forefront of a crowd of hundreds. "I am Danny Wang, mayor of Yushan," he announced in English. "This reception is in your honor as American heroes!"

The raiders had marveled at the ancient walled cities of Iwu and Kuangfeng, the latter's cobblestone alleys rubbed smooth by more than a millennium of passing footsteps. "It was the kind of Chinese city I had read about," Hilger wrote in his diary, "but never really believed in." Others, such as navigator Eugene McGurl, were shocked by the poverty and sickness he witnessed: "Signs of every known disease could be seen even on smallest children," he wrote in his journal. "Shops were dens of filth & disease." Though gunner Adam Williams went so far as to shoot and roast a pheasant, many of the others choked down the local cuisine, from rice and greens to delicacies like fried snake and boiled pigeon eggs. Navigator Clayton Campbell even got a special taste of what he referred to as chow dog: "The Chinese pluck the hair from a dog like feathers are plucked from a chicken and the animal is cooked with the skin on."

At Chuchow the Chinese housed the aviators at barracks about ten miles from the airfield, complete with a bomb shelter dug out of rock. Local officers translated newspapers with datelines from London, Berlin, and Tokyo that recounted the raid's success, and they spoiled the American aviators with long-saved luxuries of condensed milk and tinned beef and even the last of the two-year-old canned butter. The after-action reports and personal diaries of the raiders universally praised the warmth and aid of the Chinese, to many of whom the raiders gave trinkets as small tokens of appreciation, from cigarettes to pocket change. One of the pilots gave his white silk parachute to an engaged missionary couple so that she could use it to fashion a wedding dress. "These people are the most sincere, grateful, and just plain wonderful people I have ever seen," Jones raved in his diary, "and they have been fighting for 5 years."

The celebrations were tempered by the confirmed death of Leland Faktor. The Chinese had stripped the gunner naked—no doubt to salvage his clothes—and carried him out of the wilds lashed to a long pole, much like a slaughtered animal. Rumors circulated that two other bodies had been spotted along the coast and three more discovered in the wreckage of a plane. Reports indicated the Japanese had captured at least a few of the aviators, while others had suffered serious injuries, including Lawson. Many of the fliers saw such injuries firsthand when Charles Ozuk limped into Chuchow, a scene captured by Joseph Manske in his diary: "He had the worst cut in his leg I'd ever seen in my life." Some of the fliers blamed the losses on the Navy for forcing them to take off early, rechristening the *Hornet* with the diminutive nickname the Housefly.

The airmen passed the days playing poker. Davy Jones, whose mustache had grown so long that he earned the nickname Fu Man Jones, lost seven dollars in a single night. Other times the aviators swapped stories of their adventures in China, trying to outdo one another. "When we met up," Hank Potter recalled, "each had a story of a horrible ordeal and wanted to tell it. But none of us wanted to listen because we all had one of our own." One such tale that would even find its way into an official report concerned a sergeant, found after two days in the wild by a Chinese couple. The family invited the airman home, fed him, and then put him to bed. Much to the exhausted aviator's surprise, the couple climbed in with him. "He was so tired that he didn't even mind when the man took care of his husbandly duties," the report stated. "If they didn't mind his presence, he sure as hell didn't care, just so they didn't keep him awake."

Japanese bombers pummeled Chuchow daily in retaliation for the raid, forcing the aviators to spend long hours crowded inside the shelter. The Chinese had no forces to counter the attacks, and the American fliers felt frustrated to sit idly by as the enemy returned again and again. "We called our home the Chu Chow bombing range," Ken Reddy wrote in his diary, "for that is all it amounted to—practice for the Japanese." Bill Bower agreed. "It's a crime," he griped in his diary. "No sign of opposition. Just one airplane would be all we need. Too bad one of us couldn't have landed." The men emerged each day to see the horrific results of the Japanese assaults, particularly the strafing attacks against civilians. "Frequently, bodies were stacked like cordwood along the roadside until they could be taken away for burial," Greening later wrote. "It was a depressing sight to us. We hadn't encountered anything like this before."

Under Greening's command the first group of twenty raiders—each presented with a new white silk shirt—climbed aboard a train the evening of April 25 to begin the first leg of a four-day journey west to Chungking. The aviators crowded inside wooden berthing compartments and were soon asleep in the hard narrow bunks. "The rails don't click, they jolt," Bower complained in his diary, "but it's much better transportation than that of last week." Chinese trains ran largely at night to avoid Japanese attacks, so at dawn the raiders disembarked at Ying-tan, enjoying a delicious breakfast at the Catholic mission with a Dutch priest and Father Bill Glynn of Chicago; these were some of the same missionaries who had helped Harold Watson and Edgar McElroy. "Ham and eggs," Bower wrote, "but best of all cornfritters with brown sugar and molasses."

The aviators crowded aboard a rickety bus after breakfast and set off on an eleven-hour trip over dirt roads that would cover barely 150 miles, stopping for the night in a nice hotel in the ancient city of Ning Lee. "The courtyard outside is without a doubt the most beautiful sight I've seen in China," Jack Hilger wrote in his diary when he visited a few days later. "There is a small lake with a pavilion and bridge and the entire courtyard is shaded by an immense camphor tree which must have a spread of 200 feet. The full moon shining through completes the effect and makes all of us lonesome." The raiders enjoyed the newfound luxury even if the hotel still depended on oil lights. "I got my first Chinese shave here," Reddy wrote in his diary. "If you don't stop them they shave your ears, nose, forehead, and between your eyes."

The raiders set out again early the next morning for another long and tiresome bus ride, passing through miles of uncultivated lands void of even cattle or sheep. The bus stopped in Toho, where the fliers dined with a local commissioner and met the governor, before pressing on to Kian, spending the night of April 27 in a new hostel operated by the American Volunteer Group under Claire Chennault. The journey began again early the next morning in a new bus, which crossed several rivers on ferries before reaching a hotel in Heng-yang near midnight. Chungking planned to dispatch a cargo plane to collect the raiders, giving the airmen time to relax that morning. Bower sunbathed, while Reddy enjoyed the spoils of war, a scene he described in his diary: "I rode a Japanese horse, bareback, as the saddle had not been captured, just to say I had been on one."

A C-47 buzzed the hotel the afternoon of April 29, promising an end to the long journey. "When it flew over with our insignia on the side we all shouted with joy," Reddy wrote. "It was the most beautiful sight we had witnessed in China." Colonel Clayton Bissell, General Stilwell's air operations officer, greeted the airmen as they climbed aboard. The plane never shut down its engines, but roared back into the skies, arriving less than three hours later in China's wartime capital. Perched atop a promontory between the Yangtze and the Chia-ling Rivers, Chungking was a damp and weathered city whose hot and humid climate left the walls coated with a green slime. Mosquitos clouded the air, while armies of rats and cockroaches marched through narrow streets and alleys that reeked of rotting food, urine, and feces. "There was no escape from the stink that attacked our nostrils at every turn," one American nurse would later write. "A thin fog hovered around the city; the moisture undoubtedly made the smells more pungent."

The improvised capital had long been battered by the twin ills of poverty and war. The *Time* and *Life* magazine publisher Henry Luce visited in 1941, writing that it was impossible to "distinguish between the great masses of bomb-rubble on the one hand and, on the other, shacks, temporary structures and ordinary homes of the poor." The Japanese had launched routine raids against Chungking—the world's first capital to suffer systematic bombings—almost as soon as the Nationalist government arrived, pummeling the city from 1939 to 1941 no fewer than 268 times. The single most savage attack had occurred the afternoon of May 4, 1939, when the Japanese killed 4,400 people and injured another 3,100, an assault witnessed by missionary and author Robert Ekvall. "The city of Chungking boiled in a sudden upheaval of flying wreckage and black dust," he wrote. "By nightfall the entire horizon was red with fires that threatened to burn the rock of Chungking clean of human life and habitation."

The war-torn city—named the most bombed spot on Earth by *Life* magazine in March 1942—showed those scars, prompting one reporter to colorfully compare the clobbered capital to Pompeii. Bombs and fires had leveled and blackened many of the city's buildings—some rebuilt up to half a dozen times—while the acrid stench of wet ashes hung heavy in the air. Air-raid sirens screamed daily, forcing the city's half million residents to crowd inside twelve hundred shelters dug deep into the sandstone cliffs, the largest a mile-and-a-half-long tunnel that could accommodate up to twenty thousand people. "Downtown Chungking was all bedlam. The narrow streets crawled with people cawing like flocks of hungry crows," observed Frank Dorn, one of General Stilwell's top aides. "The people in the streets, for all their weary smiles and courage, looked whipped and beaten down by the years of struggle that had driven them to this ant hill of a city as a last refuge. Despair was etched deeply in their eyes, profiles, and sagging shoulders."

The raid against Tokyo eleven days earlier had given Chungking a brief moment of celebration. Residents had crowded around radios, listening to Japanese broadcasts, while Chinese newspapers quickly sold out of extra editions, the ink barely dry. Movie theaters flashed details up on screens, drawing cheers from the audiences. Firecrackers exploded in the skies, while residents stopped Americans on the street to congratulate them. Government officials even declared the day of the attack a holiday. "The nightmare of the Japanese militarists can be shattered only by bombs," announced Ho Ying-chin, Chungking's war minister. "These raids on Japan proper are only the beginning." Just as Americans had hungered to avenge Pearl Harbor, so, too, did the Chinese desire payback for years of bombing. "We have been waiting almost five years for this day," one resident told the Associated Press. "We are glad that the Japanese people know at last the din of bombs and the smell of explosives."

Doolittle's men disembarked from the C-47 that afternoon and were escorted to the American military mission, a small outpost located on a terraced hilltop. The aviators dined that night with Brigadier General John Magruder, the outgoing chief of the American military mission to China, who told them to expect some good news in the morning. Around 9 a.m. on April 30 Bissell, Magruder, and his staff gathered with the twenty raiders. Bissell congratulated the airmen for the successful mission and shared the appreciation of the president, General Marshall, and General Arnold. He then announced that each man had earned the Distinguished Flying Cross, a medal first awarded to Charles Lindbergh in honor of his solo flight across the Atlantic.

"We were all astounded," Ken Reddy wrote in his diary. "For a minute it was as if someone had belted me one in the stomach," Bill Bower noted in his. "I couldn't breathe very well," recalled Ross Greening. "It was the biggest thrill of my life."

The Chungking-based officers invited the raiders to celebrate that night at a house by the river. Engineer George Larkin cut up his parachute and made scarves, giving them out to the party's hosts. Wartime inflation had driven the price of a bottle of booze up as high as eighty dollars, forcing the officers to cater the party with bathtub gin made by a local ice company, a fact that didn't dissuade navigator Eugene McGurl, who wrote in his diary, "Started drinking wine (Chinese variety & potent) about 4:00 p.m. & capped off the evening with Chungking Gin— arguably a highly explosive mixture."

Chiang Kai-shek invited the raiders to lunch the next day, a scene described by Reddy in his diary: "His home was very lovely inside, having indirect lighting of a Chinese design, soft modernistic chairs, and heavy padded cushions without backs to sit on, individual silver ashtrays, herring bone hardwood floors, and a soft glowing fireplace." The home's elegant furnishings contrasted with the battered and bruised raiders. "I'll bet it was the motliest bunch of men who ever dined with the ruler of any country," Bower wrote in his diary. "Coveralls, leather jackets, several ties, and everything containing a varied assortment of spots and mud."

Madame Chiang Kai-shek welcomed the airmen, stealing all the attention. Born in Shanghai to a wealthy family, May-ling Soong started boarding school at age ten at Wesleyan Female College in Macon, Georgia, the world's first chartered women's college. She went on to study at Wellesley College near Boston, majoring in English literature and wowing faculty with what the press later called her "Scarlett O'Hara accent." The forty-four-year-old had returned to China after graduating in 1917, able to speak English better than her native tongue. Beautiful, slender, and often dressed in tight long gowns, Madame Chiang married the generalissimo in 1927, forming a powerful political partnership. General Joseph Stilwell found her far more impressive than her husband, describing her in his diary as "a clever, brainy woman." "Direct, forceful, energetic, loves power, eats up publicity and flattery, pretty weak on her history," he wrote. "Can turn on charm at will. And knows it."

The raiders loved her. "The Madame is the most impressive character I have ever had the privilege to meet," Reddy wrote. "She speaks excellent English, and better still she has control of the American slang; she's brilliant, witty and *beautiful*."

The airmen feasted on a multicourse lunch that began with a delicious onion soup, followed by potatoes and cold ham and beef. After that came a dish of chicken, green peas, and noodles. For dessert the aviators enjoyed lemon pie and ice cream, the only time the men savored the sweet frozen treat in China. They washed it down with cups of American coffee. "It was," Reddy wrote, "our best meal in China."

The generalissimo arrived midway through lunch. Speaking through an interpreter, he toasted first the airmen and then Roosevelt and victory. Compared with his wife's, Chiang's appearance was unremarkable. "He entered the room, apparently harassed and hurried, and made a very short speech," Greening recalled. "Then he came over, shook hands with me as the ranking representative of our group, and left."

After lunch the raiders adjourned to the living room with Madame Chiang. Reddy asked her to sign the map in the front of his diary and his Short Snorter Dollar, but Colonel Bissell intervened to halt the autographs seekers. Bissell presented a pair of American wings to Madame Chiang, who confessed that she would also like to have a flight cap, prompting several of the raiders to hand them over. The airmen soon realized that it would probably be best for Doolittle to send a new one once he returned home. "In order to get the size she tried Capt. Greening's on, and then mine," Reddy wrote in his diary. "The latter fit OK." Greening presented her with a set of Air Forces and Seventeenth Bombardment Group insignia. "I had a bit of an embarrassing time," he later wrote, "fumbling around trying to find somewhere to pin them on her."

The airmen returned to their quarters at the mission that afternoon, only to be summoned again around 9:30 p.m. to the drawing room. They received instructions on how to behave moments before Madame Chiang arrived with an entourage of local officials. Reddy noticed she wore the wings the men had presented her earlier in the day "in a conspicuous place over her heart." Camera flash bulbs popped and motion picture cameras rolled as she presented the raiders with distinguished service medals. She then posed for pictures with the airmen, standing in front of Reddy.

"This should make my girl at home jealous," the pilot mumbled to the aviator next to him.

"Blonde or brunette?" Madame Chiang asked.

She also presented each airman with a personal letter, thanking him for the raid. "The entire Chinese people are grateful to you," she wrote. "May you continue to vindicate freedom and justice so that by your efforts a happier and more unselfish world society will evolve when victory is ours."

The raiders were thrilled by her graciousness. "Praise be it. Red Letter day," Bower wrote in his diary. "We all never expected anything like this and surely know of others who have sacrificed much more often in this war for no recognition."

The airmen used the downtime in Chungking to unwind from the adventures of the previous few weeks. Bower explored the chaotic city but got lost, which he noted in his diary was "almost as bad as being lost in the Chinese mountains." He managed to buy a bottle of vodka and three orange squeezes, which set him back eighty-five dollars. Joseph Manske spent much of his time on his back, recovering from malaria, while Reddy visited a doctor to x-ray his banged-up knee and stitch up the cut on his head.

The first group of twenty aviators shipped out for India on May 3, piling into the same C-47 cargo plane that had just delivered Doolittle, Jack Hilger, and nineteen more raiders to Chungking. The second group of airmen had followed the same course as the previous ones, traveling by train, bus, and plane to the wartime capital. Doolittle had left Davy Jones and Brick Holstrom in Chuchow to await any stragglers and bring them along later. He also sent for John Birch, requesting that the missionary oversee the burial of Leland Faktor.

Birch held a memorial for Faktor near Chuchow—the same afternoon Doolittle touched down in Chungking—attended by thirteen of the raiders. Birch tried to use the $2,000 in Chinese currency Doolittle left him to buy a burial plot, but the Chinese informed him that international law prohibited the sale, offering instead to lease a plot for free for a hundred years. "Shall accept," Birch cabled Chungking, "if not otherwise instructed." The country magistrate at Sheui Chang donated the coffin, though air raids slowed preparation of the grave and stone for two weeks. At 5 p.m. on May 19 near the military headquarters at Wan Tsuen—and with two hundred of the base personnel in attendance—Faktor was buried with military honors provided by the Chinese air force.

Doolittle meanwhile arrived in Chungking to learn that his earlier fears were unfounded. Arnold had cabled a congratulatory message on April 22. "On your truly wonderful and magnificent flight I wish to congratulate you and all members of your organization in behalf of myself personally and for the entire Army Air Forces," the general wrote. "Fully realized are the conditions unforeseen which arose to make your task an almost impossible one. Your achievement is made all the more glorious by the fact that you surmounted these unforeseen conditions."

A message from General Marshall also awaited him. "The President sends his thanks and congratulations to you and your command for the highly courageous and determined manner in which you carried out your hazardous mission and for the great service you have rendered to the nation and to the Allied cause," Marshall cabled. "Your nomination as a brigadier general goes to the Senate this morning. To me your leadership has been a great inspiration and fills me with confidence for the future."

Doolittle had learned on April 28 that Arnold had promoted him to brigadier general. He would for the second time in his career skip a rank, a promotion he knew would only reinforce the idea of some of his contemporaries that he was Arnold's fair-haired boy. Doolittle did not have any stars to wear, so Clayton Bissell, who also had just been promoted to general, gave him a set. "He offered me a swig from his high-priced Scotch whiskey in celebration and I took a large gulp, which he didn't appreciate," Doolittle recalled. "He estimated my gulp was worth about $80." Doolittle's men were thrilled at the news of his promotion, as Hilger recorded in his diary: "We're all as happy as if each one of us had been made a general too."

The rest of the raiders received the Distinguished Flying Cross, and, like the earlier group, met with Chiang. Doolittle later had the cap he wore over Tokyo cleaned and then gold braid sewn into it before he sent it to Madame Chiang. "My second in command, Jack Hilger, received the highest Chinese decoration," he recalled. "Then when I walked in, Chiang and his wife looked at each other and realized that something had gone wrong with the presentation ceremony—they didn't have a decoration to give me. Chiang looked toward one of his highly decorated generals, approached him, and removed a beautiful decoration from around his neck. He then hung it on me. It is said that the Chinese are emotionless, but that general sure showed emotion when stripped of his medal by the Generalissimo!"

Doolittle's copilot, Dick Cole, used his downtime in the Chinese capital to fire off a letter to his parents back home in Ohio. "I realize you are probably both worried and wondering as to my whereabouts and safety. The long silence on my part was imperative and someday you will know why," he wrote. "It is pretty hard to write a letter without writing about your activities, but I guess it's O.K. to tell you that I have had my first taste of combat and find it not too bad. 'Lady Luck' is still riding on my shoulder and I hope she stays there in the future." Cole closed with an observation of how the raid had affected him and his views. "The last four weeks have vindicated my life-long opinion—that there is no place as good as the United States—No place."

Each of the raiders who passed through Chungking sat down and completed a detailed report of the raid and its aftermath under the supervision of Colonel Merian Cooper, one of the Army Air Forces's more colorful officers. A forty-eight-year-old former bomber pilot, Cooper was wounded in aerial combat behind enemy lines during World War I, suffering severe burns and sitting out the rest of the war in a German hospital. He recovered and flew volunteer missions against the Russians in the 1919–21 Polish-Soviet war, where in July 1920 he was shot down again and captured. Cooper managed to escape after ten months in prison, a feat that required him to slit the throat of a Russian soldier. Cooper's thirst for exploration and adventure proved a natural fit in Hollywood—*The New Yorker* dubbed him the "T. E. Lawrence of the movies"—where he went on to create the 1933 film classic *King Kong*. Like Doolittle, Cooper had remained in the Army Reserves, requesting foreign duty as soon as the war broke out.

As the debriefing officer for the raid, Cooper would ultimately sit down with fifty-nine of the raiders, including Doolittle. "I can remember you well—open neck, unshaved, dirty clothes, but still full of fire," Cooper wrote in a 1971 personal letter to Doolittle. "You gave me the map I still have, marking where you thought your lost crews were, in your handwriting." Hilger described the debriefing experience in his diary. "It seems that I have done nothing but write all day long," he griped on May 5. "It has taken us longer to write the reports on this mission than to fly it."

Doolittle departed May 5 for the United States flush with the one hundred dollars Cooper had lent him to cover any expenses, a debt the general repaid to Cooper's wife in Alexandria, Virginia. "Had it not been for his kindness—and affluence, I would have had the Devil's own time getting home," Doolittle wrote her. "As it was, I arrived just about destitute." Just before Doolittle left, Cooper made him a promise. "I told you I would do the best I could for all your men," he later wrote to him. "I did."

Armed with Doolittle's map of where the missing crews likely were captured—and information provided by the generalissimo's chief of intelligence and secret police—Cooper proposed a rescue operation and requested $10,000 in gold coins for bribery. "I had used gold coins in my explorations in the 1920's in Persia, Arabia, Siam, Abyssinia, etc., and found they worked magic when paper money meant nothing," he wrote. "I felt gold coins would do the same in China and among the Japanese."

Cooper outlined his plan to Bissell, who then gave him the go-ahead. "I told him that I would either bring back the prisoners alive, or I would not come back. I meant I would be dead. I did not intend to be captured and tortured by the Japanese and then executed," Cooper later wrote to Doolittle. "If it was evident that I was going to be captured by the Japanese, I intended to kill myself; but I didn't think this would happen. I felt quite confident I could bring out the Doolittle crew prisoners alive."

The next morning, when Cooper went to retrieve the gold, Bissell told him the operation had been killed. Cooper never learned why, though it would haunt him for decades. "I was pretty broken up by the cancellation of my proposed rescue mission. I thought I was eminently qualified to carry it through successfully. After all, I had escaped from a Russian prison near Moscow—after ten months there—and walked over 200 miles, living in the open, in dangerous Communist country, stealing and begging food from the peasants, sleeping in the melting snow, and swimming over one hundred ice-cold streams and rivers," he wrote years later to Doolittle. "I have never written the story of my escape, as it looks too fantastic and incredible. But I considered it more difficult than rescuing your men—but they didn't let me."

TED LAWSON'S CONDITION continued to deteriorate. He suffered a terrible night on April 25, forcing Doc White to give him a blood transfusion. The doctor recruited Griffith Williams to serve as the donor, since he and Lawson shared type A blood. "I had no means of doing a proper crossmatching so had to take the chance of sub-groups and a reaction," White later wrote in his unpublished memoir. "We had the expected trouble with clogging needles and syringes, but managed to get in 150 cc the first try and later after cleaning and boiling the outfit, 200 cc on the second try. Ted seemed stronger afterward."

Missionary Frank England held a prayer service at the hospital the next morning for the aviators, and then White accompanied England to his home, where he built a modified Rodger Anderson splint to help Lawson's leg. "Installing the splint was a painful process," White wrote, "but immobilizing the knee joint and elevating the leg made him more comfortable and I hoped would improve drainage."

The magistrate brought the aviators a large basket of oranges, while other municipal and military officials arrived with gifts of raisins, grapefruit, wine, and canned butter. A group of children came from a town forty miles away to deliver 450 eggs.

On April 27 Smith, Williams, Sessler, Saylor, and Thatcher departed via sedan chair for Chuchow, leaving behind White and the injured airmen. "We all sent letters out with them," White wrote. "We felt pretty lonesome after they had gone."

Lawson continued to struggle, prompting White the next day to give him chloroform and operate on his leg to enlarge his wounds and improve drainage. The procedure almost proved too much for Lawson. "Ted stopped breathing," White wrote. "I had some anxious moments before we could get him going properly again."

The surgery appeared to help. The next day White dressed his wounds, which he noted in his diary looked much better. Afterward he went into town, where he bought a thermos for $120 and twenty tablets of sulfanilamide for $40. Lawson's reprieve proved short-lived. By May 1 his leg again looked bad, leading White to grind up his entire supply of sulfanilamide tablets into power, which he applied to his wounds.

A local doctor from the Plague Prevention Unit and Public Health Hospital at Kinwah arrived with morphine, more sulfanilamide, and a blood transfusion kit. White went to work immediately. Both Clever and McClure were still weak, so rather than take a full pint from either, he took just enough from both to give Lawson 500 cubic centimeters. "Lawson no better," White wrote in diary on May 3. "I'm afraid he'll lose that leg."

White wired Chunking the next day after the Sunday service to see whether it might be possible to dispatch a seaplane that could land on the river, but he received no response. "By Monday Lawson was in such poor shape that it was evident that both his leg and his neck could not be saved," White later wrote. "So we decided to amputate."

The doctor appeared next to Lawson's bed on May 4. The pilot sensed White's sudden unease and asked whether he planned to take his leg.

"Yeah," the doctor said. "I think so."

White was stoic; the situation, nonnegotiable. "Doc didn't ask me how I felt about it," Lawson later recalled. "So, after a bit, I said I wished he'd get started. All I could think of now was getting rid of that damned thing."

"That's all I wanted to know," White answered.

The Parkers entered and tried to comfort Lawson with talk of his wife and soon-to-be-delivered baby, while Chen explained that the men planned to use spinal anesthesia, an ampoule of novocaine smuggled out of Shanghai at White's request.

Lawson tried to joke that the surgery would make him walk with a shoe with high instep, but White failed to answer. He knew then the doctor planned to amputate more than just his foot and ankle. He pressed White on where he planned to cut.

"Above the knee," he said. "I'll leave you as much as I can."

Lawson asked why he couldn't cut lower.

"If I did that, I might not get enough off. Then there would have to be another one," White said, "and your system couldn't take it."

The men rolled Lawson on his side, and White injected the novocaine into his lower spine. Attendants moved him onto a stretcher and carried him to the second-floor operating room in a nearby building.

Mrs. Smith sterilized the packs and instruments, many of which, White noted, were of 1890s vintage. She and Chen then scrubbed in along with White. Lawson would be awake during the surgery, but numb from the waist down.

The surgical team used drapes to block off the infected part of Lawson's left leg and cinched a tourniquet as high on the thigh as possible. "We had to make our skin incision about the middle of the thigh in order to get a decent margin of healthy tissue above the infected area," White later wrote in his memoir. "I made fairly large skin flaps and undercut each layer of muscle as I came to it. The large vessels were clamped and tied as we came to them, though because of the tourniquet they naturally didn't bleed. The large nerves were dissected up a short ways and cut."

Lawson remained awake as the doctor worked. "I couldn't see any blood, or feel anything. But I knew he was cutting," he later wrote. "I could see his arm moving and see him lift my leg up so he could cut underneath."

Sensation started to return to the toes on Lawson's right foot. He told White that he could feel his ankle. The anesthetic was wearing off—and there wasn't any more. Two Chinese nurses came alongside Lawson and held his wrists down.

Lawson watched as White prepared to saw off his leg. "Doc stepped away and walked back quickly with a silver saw," he wrote. "It made a strange, faraway, soggy sound as he sawed through the bone. Except for the tugging fear that I was coming back too soon, the actual amputation was almost as impersonal to me as watching a log being sawed. I could hear the different sounds of the saw as Doc's elbow bent and straightened, bent and straightened and the teeth went through thicker and thinner sections. Then there was an almost musical twink, and deep, deep silence inside me as Doc laid aside the saw. The Chinese nurses let go of my wrists. The nurse on the right walked around to the left side of the table. She picked up the leg by the ankle. The other nurse picked up the other, thicker end. I watched the two nurses carry it out the door."

White beveled the edges of Lawson's bone and then began to close the wound layer by layer, using raw silk suture ties. More sensation returned to Lawson's right leg, making the pilot nervous.

"Just a few more now," White assured him.

Lawson watched the doctor's arm rise and fall with each suture.

"Just one more," he said and then finished.

White gave Lawson another blood transfusion. He had tapped out his type A donors, so he used his own. It was fortunate in that his blood was type O, commonly known as the universal blood type because it can safely be given to anyone. "The next day," White wrote, "Ted was better. He was comfortable for the first time since the accident and was lucid for the first time in weeks."

The news of the May 6 surrender of American forces on Corregidor arrived as Lawson convalesced, a sad final chapter to the five-month struggle to hold the Philippines.

The following day White noted with alarm that Lawson was running a low-grade fever, leading the doctor to give him a second pint of his own blood, but Lawson continued to deteriorate. The next day his stump was infected, he stopped eating, and he grew delirious. White could do little more than change his dressing—the wound continued to discharge pus—and give him an intravenous injection and morphine.

Lawson fell into a semiconscious state plagued by the same bad dream. "It was screwy," he said. "I thought I was in a small rowboat, off the coast of China. I was rowing and making good time, but someone would always make me change into another boat. The new boat would have no oars. I'd tried to get back in my old boat, but I could never find it. I'd find a lot of rowboats but they'd have no oars."

The other aviators watched in alarm as one of the Chinese hospital attendants entered Lawson's room with a Bible. "He is very sick," the attendant told the men. "Maybe he won't be here long."

The news rattled Lawson's fellow fliers. "We were all solemn and silent," McClure recalled, "hoping he would come thru."

Chen got a lead on some sulfathiazole, which White encouraged him to pursue. That Sunday, May 10, $410 worth of the drug arrived, the answer to White's prayers. He started Lawson on the drug immediately, then removed the stiches from his leg. The stump had healed, but still showed some signs of infection. "Lawson's temperature normal for the first time!" White wrote in his diary the next day. "Seems on the mend."

White helped him out of bed twice and let the pilot rest in a chair. Lawson continued to improve, so much so that a week after his surgery he could drink milk, which the Chinese had boiled, poured into a bottle, and lowered into a well to cool. He followed that with strained soup and mush. A local carpenter made him crutches.

White busied himself filling teeth and doing eye exams. "Had three more dentistry patients and three eye patients!" he exclaimed in his diary. "Opthalmoscopy and retinoscopy by candlelight!" He even had time to whittle a dagger and buy stamps for his collection, while the locals presented each raider with a cane inscribed, "A keepsake to the officers of our friends and allies of the American Air Force." "Whatever people can say about the unsanitary conditions, etc., of the Chinese, no one can ever complain about their hospitality," White wrote in his diary. "They are great people."

The other airmen found ways to keep busy as Lawson healed. Through Davy Jones the men learned that most of the raiders had survived, and other news came over the hospital's radio, which could pick up station KGEI in San Francisco. McClure cheered the success of his beloved St. Louis Cardinals, who would go on to beat the New York Yankees that summer in the World Series, while all the men rejoiced at the news of the American Navy's victory over the Japanese in the Battle of the Coral Sea. "We whooped and yelled like Indians when we got the score on that one," McClure later wrote. "Any time we could hear of bad fortune for the Japs the day was a success."

Japanese bombers droned overhead daily, en route to attack other towns, a constant reminder of the enemy's advance. White knew time was running short and began to make preparations to press on to Chuchow. The locals threw a farewell feast for the raiders, complete with nine courses and five extras that began with roast watermelon seeds, followed by buffalo, pork, and even shark fins. "It looked like white rubber," McClure recalled of the delicacy, "and tasted the same."

The Japanese onslaught continued; the airmen were out of time. "News not so good. The army and the banks have already left town!" White wrote in his diary on May 17. "Have to leave tomorrow, rain or shine."

The men woke early on the morning of the eighteenth to find it cold and rainy. Exactly one month had passed since the raid on Tokyo. White dressed Lawson's stump, while others helped him into a pair of trousers, the left pant leg pinned up. The aviators then climbed into sedan chairs, pulling oilcloths over them to keep dry

"I want to show you something," Chen said to Lawson.

The porters carried the airman around the hospital and set his chair down alongside a wooden coffin. "It was a new one, made by the same Chinese carpenter who had made my crutches," Lawson wrote. "It was to have been mine."

The airmen set off in the rain, accompanied by the Smith family, Chen, porters, and armed escorts. "We crossed the pontoon bridge over the river and headed up the valley," White wrote. "We followed the river, crossing and recrossing its stream many times, sometimes on bridges, more often by ferries—small boats poled by coolies or towed across by ropes. The countryside was lovely and green and as the day progressed it slowly cleared and we dried out."

The men broke for lunch at 2 p.m. and then set out again. "Many of the hills along the way had beautiful old pagodas on them," White recalled. "New patches of rice seedlings looked like rich lawns. Occasionally we would pass through a small grove of young pine trees. It was very interesting and beautiful country."

The aviators stopped that night at the Smiths' house. White redressed

Lawson's leg and sent a cable to Chungking. "En route Chushien with four injured officers," he wired. "ETA 22 May. Request plane meet us."

The Smiths remained behind as the aviators set out again the next morning, despite protests from the fliers to evacuate. "The spirit and pluck of these people," White wrote, "never ceased to amaze me."

"See you in Chungking," Mrs. Smith said.

The Japanese advance forced the aviators to hurry; traveling the next several days in rickshaws and sedan chairs, winding past rivers and through the mountains. "It seemed to me," Lawson said, "that I could feel the very breath of the Japanese on my neck."

The hospitality at each stop was grand, including Boy Scouts who awaited them at one village with banners that read, "Welcome to American Air Heroes."

White's winded rickshaw driver often fell behind the others, prompting his fellow fliers to shout, "Shift him into high-blower!"

"It's no use," the doctor replied. "He's conked out. I've got to hit the silk!"

Transportation improved as the men reached more populated areas, allowing them to trade in the rickshaws and sedan chairs for a 1941 Ford station wagon, complete with bullet holes from a Japanese strafing. "One had evidently went through the windshield and gone through the back of the driver's seat," White wrote. "It had been neatly patched but it gave us something to think about!"

Most of the raiders piled into the station wagon, but White loaded Lawson into the back of a charcoal-burning truck, believing the injured pilot would be more comfortable stretched atop three blankets. The vehicles traveled only at night, so as to avoid air attacks by Japanese planes. "Every time we'd hit a bump, and we must have hit a million, I'd leave the floor. The next bump would get me coming down," Lawson later wrote. "I used both my hands to keep what was left of my leg from banging. That didn't help much. It just thumped and bled and throbbed."

The station wagon in contrast proved a smooth ride. "It was a real luxury," White recalled, "to lean back on the leather cushions and whiz down the road at ten to twenty times the speed at which we had traveled for the previous five days!"

The aviators could hear explosions in the distance behind them. Lawson asked Chen, who rode with him in the truck, what they were.

"Japanese too close," he replied. "So Chinese blow up road behind us, just after we pass."

The men arrived in Lishui the night of May 21 at one of the airfields the raiders had tried to reach the night of the raid. The Chinese had been forced to blow up the field to keep the Japanese from seizing it. No plane would come for them now. The fliers turned in, but awoke at 3 a.m. to the news that Japanese forces were bringing mechanized gear over the same roads the Chinese had just destroyed.

White dressed Lawson's stump, and the raiders set out a little after 4 a.m. in a small camphor-burning bus with a driver whose love of the horn soon earned him the nickname Johnny Beep-beep. "The bus's brakes were only third in importance in his mind. The horn was first and the steering wheel second," Lawson recalled. "He was the damndest driver I ever saw. Nothing bothered him, including our yells."

They stopped that night, May 22, at a local mission. Lawson was too exhausted to participate much in the feast and soon went to bed, wondering aloud why he found the same overpowering smell everywhere he slept.

"It must be some sort of national disinfectant the Chinese use," he told himself.

White administered a dose of morphine to ease his pain and only then could Lawson bring himself to admit the truth about the stench. "It was my leg, not disinfectant," he later wrote. "I had been trying to kid myself."

The men reached Nancheng about 2 a.m. on May 24, only to learn the airfield there had also been destroyed. "We had talked of little else for two days except getting the plane there," Lawson wrote. "Now it would have to be Kian." They took small consolation in the fact that the Nancheng headquarters at least could offer them iodine, a precious commodity that none of the fliers had seen in the five weeks since the crash. "All of us were welted and sore with bedbugs and lice," Lawson recalled. "I still had the bed sores on my back. Doc dabbed all of us from head to foot."

They slept late the next morning and enjoyed a much-needed day of rest. White wrote a few letters, and Clever's battered face had healed enough that the bombardier attempted to shave. "It was his first crack at a straight edge but he made out all right," White observed. "At least he didn't cut his throat."

At about six the following morning the fliers set out in another Ford station wagon, arriving twelve hours later at an American Volunteer Group hostel. The Flying Tigers had moved on from Kian, leaving behind a radioman and a few Chinese employees. The news was the same as before. "There was no plane. The field was gone," Lawson recalled. "We were numb with disappointment."

They had no choice but to press on to Heng-yang, picking up an overnight train bound for Kweilin, where the fliers settled into an American Volunteer Group hostel. Lawson continued to suffer. "It was a battle to keep from giving him morphine," White recalled. "There are times when a doctor must be cruel in order to be kind. So I had to let him suffer quite a bit of pain to keep from making an addict out of him."

The days ticked past as the fliers awaited a plane to fly them out. Lawson had suffered a brutal six weeks. He had survived a violent crash in the surf, endured a battle with gangrene, and the primitive amputation of his left leg. His personal agony was incalculable, but now, after forty-six days, rescue was finally at hand. On June 3 a DC-3 with U.S. Army Air Forces markings appeared in the skies overhead. The raiders erupted in cheers. The airfield was a few miles away, and the hostel's jeep was already down there. Half an hour later the airmen heard the drone of the vehicle's engine and looked up to see their fellow raiders Edgar McElroy and Davy Jones, the latter armed with a medical kit. "I knew I'd start crying as soon as I heard Davy's voice," Lawson wrote, "and damned if I didn't."

CHAPTER 20

★

I was beaten, kicked and pummeled pretty regularly by the
Japanese and systematically starved every day.

—GEORGE BARR,
MAY 12, 1946

THE CREWMEN OF THE *Green Hornet* were not so lucky. The plane
carrying Chase Nielsen, Dean Hallmark, and Bob Meder touched down
in Tokyo at 7 p.m. on April 25. Guards ushered the men into cars, and
after an hourlong ride the fliers arrived at the headquarters of the gendarmerie, whose brutal reputation was best described in a 1942 intelligence
report. "The gendarmerie is the worst element in the Japanese Armed
Forces," the report stated. "They have no respect for man, woman or
child. Gambling, narcotics, kidnappings, deliberate murder, prostitution,
graft of all kinds and terrible torture are all in the day's work. They will
even deliberately kill their own nationals to create an incident if this is
the only excuse they can find to obtain the end they desire."

Once inside, guards removed Nielsen's blindfold, exposing to him a
bare room that contained only a table and three chairs. He was joined by
an unarmed Japanese civilian. Nielsen was still handcuffed, but a guard
stood by the doors. The civilian told him his name was Ohara and that
he was a graduate of Columbia University.

"But Ohara is an Irish name," Nielsen said.

"I realize that," he answered. "But it is still my name."

Nielsen guessed the short-statured Ohara was in his late twenties and appeared confident to the point of cockiness. He started to rattle on about baseball, talking about how much the Japanese worshipped Babe Ruth. The interrogator then changed topics. "I suppose you know Tokyo was bombed last week?"

"It was?" Nielsen replied, feigning surprise. "Who did it?"

Ohara chatted again about sports, but this time Nielsen interrupted him. "What do you think about President Roosevelt?"

"I'd like to hit him in the face with a rotten tomato," Ohara barked.

"You can say that now that you're back in Tokyo," Nielsen said with a smile.

Ohara assured Nielsen he would not be mistreated. "You can play baseball and golf and enjoy the hot baths of Japan."

Nielsen would soon learn how far from the truth that assurance was.

The door opened, and a Japanese officer with short hair entered. Ohara left, replaced by a short baldheaded interpreter who Nielsen estimated was in his midsixties. He told Nielsen and the other airmen he had graduated from Stanford University and spent thirty-five years in Sacramento, working as a lawyer for Japanese farmers along the West Coast. Nielsen would spend a lot of time with the interpreter, who began every sentence with a stock answer. "Well, well," he would always say, "we'll have to see about that." Nielsen and the others soon nicknamed him Well-Well.

"I made a fortune," Well-Well said, "and came back to Japan to retire, but they cleaned me out and here I am."

The questioning began again. Where did Nielsen come from? Had he bombed Tokyo? Was he stationed in China or the Philippines?

The interrogation by three guards, two reporters, and the interpreter dragged on until about 4 a.m. as the Japanese alternatively slapped and kicked the American aviator, whose legs were tied and hands bound behind the chair. The abuse reopened the wounds on his shins, causing blood to run down his legs.

Guards finally hauled the exhausted airman back to his cell, a cubby barely four feet wide and eight feet deep with a latrine in the corner. Nielsen collapsed atop the grass mat with several blankets and slept until 7 a.m., when guards brought him a breakfast of watery rice and a cup of miso soup.

The interrogation began again right after breakfast, but Nielsen refused to offer more than his name, rank, and serial number. "We didn't get the brutal treatment we'd received right after we were captured," the navigator later wrote. "A more subtle form of torture began at Tokyo— the endless days and nights of solitary confinement in stinking, filthy cells with just enough food to keep us alive."

The other airmen suffered the same. "The first two weeks, it seemed like they interrogated us about twenty-four hours a day," Bobby Hite recalled. "They would run us in and out of the cell and we didn't know if it was night or day, really. The main thing they seemed to want to know was, where in the world did we come from?"

The interrogator's intent was to wear down the aviators—and as one boasted to navigator George Barr, "Japanese method scientce-fic."

The scientific method, the red-haired New Yorker discovered, was a sucker punch; one such hit would cost him most of his hearing in his right ear.

The Japanese likewise walloped Nielsen on the back with a black rubber hose, prompting him to ask one day about the unusual choice of weapon.

"Hose don't make marks," the interrogator responded.

"Well," the bombardier thought, "what difference does it make if you're going to kill us whether we've got marks on us or what?"

The airmen were often shocked by how much the Japanese knew, prompting Barr to wonder, "Is it chance or is their espionage better than we had suspected?"

Jacob DeShazer recalled one such experience that floored him.

"You were the bombardier," one of the interrogators pressed him. "You know all about the Norden bombsight. We want you to draw us a picture of that Norden bombsight. Put the knobs on and show us how it's built."

"You know," DeShazer replied. "I'm one of the worst persons. I can't draw anything, even a house."

"You can surely draw a picture of an airplane."

DeShazer sketched an intentionally terrible picture. "That's an airplane," he said. "That's about the best I can do."

The interrogators weren't dissuaded. "You should be able to make some kind of picture of that bombsight."

Then to DeShazer's surprise one of the interrogators picked up a pencil and drew the bombsight. "It was just perfect," the bombardier recalled. "I could tell there wasn't a thing out of order."

"Is that a Norden bombsight?" the interrogator asked.

DeShazer felt there was no use denying; the Japanese clearly had nailed it. "It sure is," he confessed.

The long days of interrogation and abuse coupled with endless hours of solitary confinement wore down the aviators. The Japanese forced them to wear leg irons with just a few inches of chain that hobbled the airmen at all times, even in their cells. "Sanitation facilities were worse than primitive," Nielsen said. "There was no water in the cell. The toilet was a hole in one corner. I tried to get permission to wash my hands and face and teeth and 'Well-Well' said he'd see about it, but nothing happened."

The only reprieve came from a few curious guards who attempted to chat with the airmen in broken English, mostly asking about American actors such as Gary Cooper, Dorothy Lamour, and Jean Arthur. The airmen welcomed even that scant interaction. "Nothing is the hardest thing in the world to do," Nielsen later wrote. "I just sat in my cell—no exercise, nothing to read, no radio, no nothing."

Others agreed. "We had just come out of a full American life with all kinds of goodies," Hite recalled, "good food, good life, and suddenly we were in a solitary cell and were being harassed, slapped, and kicked. Our rations were meager, and we just wondered if the world was going to hold together."

Well-Well pestered the captives. "You can't smoke or drink now," he told Nielsen. "So you will lose all of your bad American habits."

Nielsen fired back: who said those were bad habits?

Well-Well just grinned.

The Japanese had managed to locate at least one of the downed bombers, salvaging maps and charts that interrogators laid out before the captured fliers. Nielsen spotted stationery with the aircraft carrier's crest and name. His heart sank.

"What's a *Hornet*?" the interrogator asked.

Nielsen attempted to explain that it was a bee that stung, but the Japanese officer didn't buy it. Instead the interrogator produced a crew list of each plane and pointed to Doolittle's name at the top. "Do you know him?"

"Yes."

"Well, we captured him several days ago," he said. "We killed him."

"Oh."

The interrogator ran his finger down the list until he hit crew six. He stopped beside Nielsen's name. "I know you know this guy," he said.

"Yes," Nielsen admitted.

"Your friend, George Barr, the red-haired guy," the interrogator continued. "He told us all about it."

"Oh, he did?" Nielsen said, though he didn't believe it. "Why don't you tell me, and then I'll tell you whether he is right or not?"

"Oh, no, you tell us."

Nielsen felt it was futile. The airman had resisted for weeks, but he believed there was no point in holding out any longer; to do so invited only more beatings, abuse, and agony, particularly now that the Japanese had found some of the mission's most vital records. "We confessed to bombing Tokyo, told them the areas we had bombed and confessed of leaving an aircraft carrier," Nielsen said. "Other than that, a small sketch of our life's history—where we went to school, where we had our army training, that was all it consisted of."

The Japanese prepared statements allegedly based on the confessions and then read them back to the aviators, who never saw actual English translations. Nielsen recalled that his statement as read to him noted only that he had bombed steel mills; there was no mention of targeting civilians or schools and churches. The others recalled similar statements. The Japanese demanded the men sign them, each one dated May 22. Nielsen refused, but after the Japanese threatened him, decided it wasn't worth a fight.

The airmen's confessions proved far different from the ones the Japanese claimed the men made. Excerpts of the alleged statements that the gendarmerie forwarded to General Hajime Sugiyama proved so outlandish and contradictory as to be almost unbelievable. On the one hand, they painted the raiders as incompetent cowards, so terrified of Japan's powerful fighters that they dropped bombs on any target and fled. This was intended, no doubt, to cover up the incredible defense failures that had allowed sixteen bombers to penetrate the homeland, pummel the capital, and escape unmolested. On the other hand, the alleged confessions portrayed the airmen as bloodthirsty marauders who wanted to kill women and children, statements Japan could use against them in future criminal proceedings as well as in the court of world opinion.

"What were your feelings when bombing Nagoya?" an interrogator asked Hite, according to excerpts of his alleged statement.

"I thought it natural to drop bombs without locating the targets, destroying civilian houses and wounding civilians. I thought that this was one of the objectives of guerrilla warfare," the Texan supposedly answered, characterizing America's tactics with the same language the Japanese government had used in the press to describe previous carrier raids. "While bombing I was filled with feelings of fear and thought it would be much more prudent to drop the bombs anywhere as quickly as possible and flee. At that time I thought it was too much for me to bomb accurately."

"Did you fire your guns while fleeing from Nagoya?" the interrogator continued.

"I did not mention this point before today but, honestly speaking, five or six minutes after we left the city, we saw a place that looked like a primary school and saw many children playing," he allegedly said. "The pilot lowered the altitude of the plane rapidly and ordered the gunner to get prepared. When the plane was in the oblique position, the pilot ordered us to fire; therefore, we fired at once."

Billy Farrow's supposed confession echoed Hite's.

"Although you say that you aimed at military installations, in reality you injured innocent civilians?" the interrogator asked.

"I'm sorry about that," Farrow supposedly answered. "We are only temporary personnel and did not receive full training, so we cannot be sure of hitting the target. Moreover, at the time the Japanese Army was firing anti-aircraft guns at us so all I cared for was to drop the bombs as quickly as possible and go. This is why homes were destroyed and civilians were killed."

"You fired at the children in the primary school on your way out to the sea after leaving the city of Nagoya, didn't you?"

"Really, I'm sorry about that," the South Carolinian repeated. "There was a place which looked like a school, with many people there. As a parting shot, with a feeling of 'damn these Japs,' I made a power dive and carried out some strafing. There was absolutely no defensive fire from below."

The Japanese likewise cast Harold Spatz as a gunner bent on revenge. "I aimed at the children in the school yard and strafed," he supposedly said. "My personal feeling at that time was to feed these 'Japs' their own medicine."

The raid had in fact killed civilians and some children, which the Japanese used as a political weapon. Just as Roosevelt had capitalized on the mission's success to help bolster American morale, the Japanese used the attack to outrage and unite the rattled public. The bogus confessions served as the perfect tool to ignite that fury—and set the stage for a trial that could land the captured airmen in front of a firing squad.

Although many of the bogus confessions incriminated the aviators, the Japanese used others to tar senior American leaders, particularly Doolittle—the nation's new hero. That was the case with Jacob DeShazer's confession. "We thought that it would be permissible to drop the bombs as rapidly as possible, killing, injuring, and confusing as many as possible," the bombardier said. "Col. Doolittle and other senior officers, and of course, the pilot, too, did not give us any special precautions. Of course, the original target was the oil tanks; though the civilian homes around the tanks were also sought."

Bob Meder's confession went even further, not only blaming Doolittle but also pointing out that this savage new form of warfare was how America fought. How else could the United States weaken Japanese resolve?

"You bombed many homes of civilians and killed many of them, besides hitting the factories; what do you think about that?"

"We didn't mind their casualties too much because Col. Doolittle, in his order, did not specially caution us to avoid bombing them."

"Don't you even feel sorry about injuring innocent women and children?"

"As an individual, I personally feel sorry, but I think that it is inevitable in modern warfare. We cannot help but ignore such conditions because demoralization of the people achieves one of our objectives."

ONE OF THE OBJECTIVES of William Standley, America's ambassador to Russia, was to sort out the diplomatic mess caused by Ski York and his crew. Standley had been shocked by the news that one of Doolittle's crews had landed in Vladivostok—information the Russian government failed to disclose for three days. The first report the ambassador had received was that the Russians planned to intern the raiders near Khabarovsk, a decision made without consultation with the American authorities—just as the crew had suspected.

A four-star admiral who had served as chief of naval operations from 1933 to 1937, Standley had arrived in Russia to begin his ambassadorship barely two weeks earlier. He sat down for his first meeting at the Kremlin with Soviet leader Joseph Stalin two days later, on April 23, a meeting that touched on the fate of the raiders.

"Of course, Mr. Ambassador, they should not have landed on Soviet territory," Stalin said. "We'll have to intern them in accordance with International Law."

To Standley's relief, Stalin displayed "no annoyance" over the matter and "regretted" the need to intern the crew. The Soviet leader said the airmen were safe and would be well cared for in Russia, adding that the pilot claimed to have run out of fuel and been forced to divert. Standley told him that the other bombers had flown to China as ordered and that this one must have been unable reach Chinese territory.

The United States still hoped to smuggle the aviators out—a plan that involved assigning them to the embassy as assistant military attachés—since so far only the Russian and American governments knew of the bomber's diversion. That hope was dashed the following day in a press conference in Kuibyshev, Russia's wartime capital, located on the banks of the Volga River some five hundred miles east of Moscow.

"What would happen if an American plane was forced to land on Soviet territory after bombing Japan?" an American reporter had asked.

The question floored Solomon Lozovsky, head of the Soviet Information Bureau, who knew Japanese correspondents were present. "There's no use talking about something which may never happen," he stammered.

The Russians feared the ruse was up. Afraid of possible Japanese retaliation, Russia opted to release the news, blaming America afterward for the leak. Standley was embarrassed. "Look, fellows," he told reporters. "I've really nothing for you. The Soviet Government acted in the only way they could, once the news was out."

Standley sat down on the evening of April 25 with Foreign Minister Vyacheslav Molotov, who complained that the bomber's diversion to

Russia had only complicated relations with Japan. Standley told him that General Marshall expressed appreciation for the courtesy Russia had extended to the crew and assured them that the landing was "wholly unintentional." "After thanking me for this message Molotov asked me to request my Government to take adequate steps to prevent such landings in the future," the ambassador wrote in his report of the meeting. "I stated that I felt sure that my Government had already issued such instructions."

Standley followed up with a personal note to Molotov, requesting permission for an American representative to visit the interned airmen. The Russian foreign minister responded on April 27, "stating in effect that since the crew was being transferred to a region nearer the center of the USSR the visit could not be made at the present time; that upon the arrival of the crew at the new place of residence I would be advised when and where my representative might visit the crew."

The possibility of a visit with the crew excited officials at the War Department, where analysts were busy sifting through Japanese propaganda broadcasts to decipher important details of the raid. Secretary of State Hull fired off a telegram to Standley with eight questions the War Department wanted answered. Those included the route flown as well as details on the enemy opposition encountered, from fighters and barrage balloons to antiaircraft fire. The department further requested specifics on the targets attacked and the results as well as on the measures Japan took to camouflage its factories and industries. "Of course, information regarding the welfare and living conditions of the crew and their treatment is desired," the message concluded. "It might also be possible to take from them messages for relatives and friends in the United States."

American officials weren't the only ones interested in the crew. Of the eighty airmen who had participated in the raid, Japan had managed to capture just eight. York's crew represented a chance to increase that number. The ambassador to Russia, Naotake Sato, a career diplomat and former Japanese foreign minister, threatened his Soviet counterparts, according to American intelligence intercepts. "If the Soviet merely intern American aircraft which lands in Maritime provinces after raiding Japan, they will, in effect, be providing Americans with a base, inconsistent with the neutrality treaty and dangerous to Soviet-Japanese relationship," Sato argued. "If the incident were repeated on a large scale Japan could not accept responsibility for consequences." Further instructions from Tokyo days later told Sato to make clear that it was not all right for Russia to "merely intern the planes and crews."

Russia refused to be bullied, arguing that internment was in line with international law and therefore did not violate the Soviet-Japanese Neutrality Pact. Though Russia would "endeavor to avoid" any misunderstandings, officials emphasized that Japan needed to back off. "Whatever steps are taken the Soviet government is to decide," Russia countered on April 30. "Any criticisms of the steps we take must be made on the principle of friendly nations. Any act contravening this principle is to be condemned. No complaints should be made unless made in a friendly spirit."

Tokyo ordered Sato to again press the issue. "If the United States sees that the Soviet winks at this sort of mischief, the United States will keep doing it on a larger scale. Therefore, it is essential to stop it before it starts," Tokyo instructed Sato to argue. "The United States cannot bomb Japan unless she does so from someone else's territory." Then there was the matter of York's bomber. "Since the other planes which escaped headed for Central China, it is evident that this lone plane fled intentionally in the direction it took," Tokyo warned. "One more occurrence will necessitate measures on our part and have a tremendous influence on our mutual relations."

Despite Japan's threats, its pressure was limited. While Russia was bogged down in the west against Germany—and reluctant to open a second front in the east—Japan likewise could not risk another fight so close to home. If war broke out between Japan and Russia, America would no doubt flood the latter with bombers that would then day after day pound Tokyo, Osaka, and Nagoya, forcing Japan to recall its forces to defend the homeland. Sato understood this reality and on May 7 cautioned his superiors to back down: was the fate of this one bomber crew worth another war? "I advise that we discard all small feelings against the Soviet Union and work towards a softening of feelings," Sato wrote. "Basically, the main idea is for us to take a friendly attitude toward the Soviet Union and make them become less watchful of us and eventually to draw them toward us."

Against the backdrop of these contentious negotiations, Russia relocated York and his crew in late April. Guards at the dacha in Khabarovsk ushered the airmen into several cars around 10 p.m. and drove for half an hour, stopping alongside a single railcar parked at a siding outside of the city. The raiders climbed aboard to find an aisle on one side with compartments along the other. The dim glow of candles—shielded from the outside by blackout curtains—illuminated primitive compartments that featured little more than wooden benches without cushions and no floor carpeting. Overhead racks held rolled-up straw mattresses, and the smell of dirt hung in the air. "It didn't take us long," Emmens recalled, "to figure that we were going to be sitting on those hard benches in the daytime and at night we would be sprawled on those straw mattresses."

Crews outside loaded the car with loaves of black bread, three-foot bolognas, tins of caviar, and cases of vodka—all of which the airmen realized pointed to a long trip. A train engine soon arrived and attached to the railcar, pulling it to a nearby station to link it up with a longer train. About midnight the train set out west for what turned out to be a twenty-one-day journey along the Trans-Siberian Railroad. The scenery at times was beautiful as the train rolled through forests and alongside rivers. Some days the conductor pulled onto sidings to allow other trains to pass, including many loaded down with troops headed to fight the Germans. Unlike the raiders, who traveled in compartments, Russian forces crammed into boxcars without bunks and only straw to cover the floor. Horses and men occasionally even crowded together.

The poverty amazed the fliers; everyone seemed to be dressed in rags. Beggars crowded around the windows in train stations, pleading for bread crusts. "The children were the most impressive," Emmens wrote. "Bands of them dressed in absolute tatters, no shoes, and covered with filth—completely black, some of them—roved the railroad station area and begged for food." A scene in Omsk particularly troubled the pilot. "One of the children had nothing on but a piece of dirty cloth with a hole cut in it for his head," Emmens wrote. "It had no bottom and no sleeves. The lower half of him was as naked as the day he was born. His stomach, like those of 80 per cent of the children we saw, protruded from lack not only of proper food, but of any kind of food."

After seventeen days the train neared Kuibyshev, Russia's wartime capital and home to all the foreign embassies.

"I think your people will be expecting you," Mike, the translator-guard, announced.

The news thrilled the airmen, who after a month in Russia, had yet to see anyone from the American embassy or consulate. The night before the train arrived, they hustled to get ready. "We shined our brass. We made a list of things we were running out of. We needed toothpaste, toothbrushes, soap, shaving cream, and lotion. And we would ask for some cigarettes," Emmens later wrote. "And, of course, we would give them messages to send home to our families saying that we were okay."

The train pulled into the station at 5:30 a.m. Mike locked the airmen in the compartments and departed with a final request from them to contact the embassy and make sure American officials knew they were there. The airmen waited anxiously. An hour passed, then two; morning turned into afternoon. The fliers grew glum. Mike and the other guards arrived back at dusk, smelling of soap and vodka, having spent the day bathing and drinking, as opposed to tracking down diplomats. "Not one word did we hear from the American Embassy," Emmens recalled, "nothing."

The train pulled out of the station that evening, once again chugging west. A few days later, on May 19, it reached Okhuna, a small village about ten miles from Penza. A half dozen Soviet officers welcomed the fliers, ushering them into waiting cars for a twenty-minute ride through an area with no paved streets or sidewalks. "The same sad and bitter-looking people were trudging slowly along the paths," Emmens recalled. "Again, only rags constituted their clothing."

The cars rolled up to the compound, which was surrounded by a tall wooden fence and guarded by a gate. Inside the men found three buildings, including a guesthouse where York settled alone in one bedroom, while the others paired off into shared quarters. The rooms offered clothes racks along with iron cots and kapok-filled mattresses. Despite the coarse sheets and blankets, the men considered the quarters comfortable.

"Well, here we are!" Emmens announced to his roommate, Nolan Herndon.

"Yeah," Herndon replied, "where?"

CHAPTER 21

★

DOOLITTLE ARRIVED BACK IN the United States on May 18, after a two-week journey that took him through India, North Africa, and even South America. A staff car awaited him at the airport in Washington, whisking him directly to the War Department, where he met with General Arnold. Doolittle debriefed the general about the mission, pointing out his concerns for the captured aircrews and the loss of the bombers. Arnold assured him the loss of the bombers was not a problem. The two men then met with General Marshall, whom Doolittle found in surprisingly good humor.

Afterward Arnold instructed the new brigadier general to go to the uniform store and buy some new clothes and then head home to his apartment at 2500 Q Street, in northwest Washington, and remain out of sight until Arnold called him. Joe Doolittle meanwhile was in Los Angeles, tending to her sick mother. Arnold had secretly phoned her in advance of her husband's arrival, inviting her to Washington. Joe Doolittle flew all night on a commercial plane to Pittsburgh, landing the morning of May 19; there an Army officer ushered her onto a military transport to Washington.

Arnold rang Doolittle late that morning and told him he would swing by the apartment and retrieve him in a few moments. The general just two weeks earlier had sent a final memo to the president, giving him an ultimate tally of the mission's outcome and taking a swipe at the Japanese. "With the 15 planes reported located in East China, 1 interned in Siberia, and 1 which the Japanese claim is on exhibition, there is a total of 17 accounted for—which is 1 more than we sent over."

The car pulled up outside Doolittle's apartment, and to his surprise both Arnold and General Marshall sat in the back seat. Doolittle saluted and climbed in the front with the driver. The car pulled away from the curb. Doolittle waited for someone to tell him where the men were headed, but neither Arnold nor Marshall spoke. Doolittle finally could not contain his curiosity any longer and asked.

"Jim," Arnold answered, "we're going to the White House."

"Well, I'm not a very smart fellow and I don't want to embarrass anyone," Doolittle said. "What are we going to do there?"

"The President is going to give you the Medal of Honor," Marshall interjected.

The raid had thrilled Marshall, who later wrote that it "was successful far beyond our most optimistic hopes." He had a week earlier sent a secret memo to Arnold, outlining the details of Doolittle's honor and his ideas for an elaborate media rollout. He had directed Arnold to prepare a press release and even a proposed statement for Doolittle. "It will be necessary to keep this citation secret for a long time," Marshall advised. "However, the fact of the award of the Medal of Honor should be made public the day it becomes known that Doolittle is in town. I wish to arrange the affair so that he is kept under cover until received by the President and decorated."

Doolittle was floored by the honor—and immediately protested. "General, that award should be reserved for those who risk their lives trying to save someone else," Doolittle argued. "Every man on our mission took the same risk I did. I don't think I'm entitled to the Medal of Honor."

Doolittle watched as Arnold's cheeks turned red with anger and Marshall suddenly scowled. He knew he had just offended them both.

"I happen to think you do," Marshall shot back.

The car fell silent. "This was the only time Hap ever got mad at me and General Marshall ever spoke sternly to me," he later wrote. "The highest-ranking man in Army uniform had made his decision. It was neither the time nor the place for me to argue."

The officers arrived at the White House, where Doolittle was pleasantly surprised to find Joe. He had last seen her forty-seven days earlier in San Francisco. The two had little time to catch up before aides ushered them into the Oval Office at 1 p.m., followed by a gaggle of reporters and photographers.

President Roosevelt, who had pushed his military leaders to develop the raid, perched behind his desk. He greeted Doolittle and shook his hand, telling him that the raid had accomplished everything he had hoped.

The president pinned the Medal of Honor on Doolittle just above the left pocket of his uniform shirt as Marshall read aloud the citation. "Brigadier General James H. Doolittle, United States Army, for conspicuous leadership above and beyond the call of duty, involving personal valor and intrepidity at an extreme hazard to life," Marshall read. "With the apparent certainty of being forced to land in enemy territory or to perish at sea, General Doolittle personally led a squadron of Army bombers, manned by volunteer crews, in a highly destructive raid on the Japanese mainland."

Generals Arnold and Marshall both saluted Doolittle, while Joe rewarded her husband with a kiss.

News photographers shot stills and motion pictures of the historic event. The War Department handed out a three-page press release and a two-page statement attributed to Doolittle, giving the country the first real details of the mission, from hedgehopping across Tokyo to the types of targets bombed. The statement even mentioned the baseball game Jack Hilger's crew witnessed.

Doolittle then took to the airwaves in a radio talk broadcast the following evening, where he graciously credited the mission's success to the seventy-nine young pilots, navigators, bombardiers, and gunners who volunteered. "No group of men could have thrown themselves into a task more whole-heartedly," Doolittle told listeners. "They did not seek the path of glory. They merely volunteered for a hazardous mission, knowing full well what such a phrase implied concerning their chances for personal safety. They followed the finest traditions of American fighting men."

Reporters lapped it up, peppering Doolittle with questions in a press conference after the Medal of Honor ceremony.

"We flew low enough so that we could see the expressions on the faces of the people," Doolittle remarked.

"And what was that expression?" someone asked.

"It was one, I should say, of intense surprise," Doolittle replied with, as one reporter noted, a twinkle in his eye.

He went on to tell reporters that nine Japanese fighters attacked his bomber over Tokyo. "I was able to run away from all of them," he said, before turning to face the journalists. "Better make that 'evade all of them.'"

"Are you going back again?" a reporter asked.

"That is in the laps of the gods and the hands of the War Department."

Doolittle couldn't resist a little fun—albeit off the record—when asked whether he could have bombed the palace. "Why," he said. "I could have blown that chrysanthemum-painted bedpot right out from underneath the imperial throne."

Reporters wanted to know what losses America suffered.

"No planes were left in Japan," Doolittle said. "Some were damaged, but none was shot down. No plane was damaged to an extent that precluded it from proceeding to its destination."

He likewise refuted claims that the enemy had the wreckage of one the mission's bombers on show in Tokyo. "The Japanese do not have one of our planes on display," he said. "They may have painted up one of their own to look like ours, or they may have gotten an American plane from somewhere else, but not from us."

Reporters followed up by asking a stunned Joe Doolittle her thoughts. "I'm too thrilled to speak," she replied.

Absent from all the details released, of course, was any mention of the *Hornet* or the fact that the bombers had taken off from a carrier. More important—and what would later pose a problem for the War Department and the administration—was Doolittle's dodge over the fate of the bombers. The press and as a result the American public were left with the deliberately false impression that all of the bombers as well as airmen had made it through the mission safely, even though by then Doolittle and his superiors knew that fifteen of the sixteen bombers had in fact crashed and that two of the crews had been captured. "Doolittle emphasized," noted a story the next day in the *Chicago Daily Tribune*, "that all planes and men came thru safely and hooted at Japanese claims that they have one or more of the American planes on display."

The world had waited in anticipation to learn who had master-minded and executed the stunning assault on the Japanese capital. One month and a day later it had its answer in what would prove a public relations masterpiece, just as Marshall had envisioned. America's aviation darling Jimmy Doolittle, the newly promoted general and recipient of the nation's highest award for heroism, was a hero many already knew. The MIT-educated racing and stunt pilot, who had captivated Americans for decades with his aerial feats, was the perfect face to put on America's war effort.

The photo of the president pinning on the five-pointed star plastered the front pages of newspapers across the nation, accompanied by stories filled with the harrowing details of the raid that Doolittle now shared in his statement and interviews. Long profiles of the famed aviator followed in papers and magazines, reminding readers of his past heroics. Typical was the 1,797-word article in the *Washington Post* that carried the head-line "His Life Story Reads like a Thriller, but with Perfect Timing."

Articles and editorials alike glowed with praise for America's new hero. More than a few made a play on Doolittle's ironic surname.

"Jimmy Doolittle is a man whose exploits utterly belie his name," declared the Baltimore *Sun*.

"He should be named Doomuch," recommended the New York *Daily News*.

"Jimmy did it," heralded *Time* magazine.

Other newspapers argued that only someone of Doolittle's caliber could have been trusted to organize and lead such a dangerous mission. "This was a test of skill and courage," wrote the *New York Times*. "It took a splendid flier like Doolittle, resolute, intrepid and resourceful, to carry it through."

The *Chicago Daily Tribune* echoed that sentiment. "The bombing of Tokio may seem compounded of magic and the spirits of evil to a Japa-nese, but the American people will know that to Jimmy Doolittle it was a job," the paper argued. "It was a job of planning, of organization, of nav-igation, of flying, of finding the target and releasing the bomb loads— and all of this has been Jimmy Doolittle's life."

Doolittle's family beamed.

"I'm pretty cocky about my old man!" James Doolittle Jr., a second lieutenant in training in Dayton, told a reporter.

Doolittle's youngest son, John, who was about to begin his studies at West Point, was even more succinct: "Yippee!"

Even Roosevelt scored political points off the mission's success. "I think you should have gone a little farther by giving him the privilege of having his name changed to Doobig," Mrs. T. J. Dykema of Pittsburgh cabled the president. "I hope my two boys in the Army have a similar opportunity."

"Give us more Doolittles," added James Jordan of Portland, "we will take our chances in the west."

Personal congratulations poured in to both Jimmy and Joe Doolittle from friends, colleagues, and even strangers from around the country.

"We only know that if ever any one could do it—it would be you," Marty Moore wrote from Florida. "God-bless you."

"It is glorious news for the whole nation," cabled Herb Maxson from New York. "He will always be tops in any league."

"*So* your Jimmie performed the miraculous feat!!" wrote Maude Howell from Los Angeles. "It is too marvelous to believe."

Hank Potter's mother wrote from South Dakota. "Among the scores of congratulatory messages that you are receiving there will be none any more sincere than ours; especially so since our son Henry was navigator for your husband on his flight to Japan," she wrote. "I rejoice that all came back safely; and feel very proud—and humble—that the boys not only had the *courage* to volunteer but that they had the *ability* to do their job—and to your husband is due credit & praise."

One of the letters Doolittle would treasure most came from none other than Admiral Halsey, written April 24 as the task force neared Pearl Harbor. "I hated to dump you off at that distance, but because of discovery there was nothing else to do," Halsey wrote. "I stated to my Staff, that on landing you should have had two stars pinned on each shoulder, and the Medal of Honor put around your neck." Halsey added that he knew of no other deed in history more heroic than the raid Doolittle led. "You have struck the hardest blow of the war directly at the enemy's heart. You have made history," he concluded. "Keep on knocking over those yellow bastards."

Even old aviation rivals couldn't help congratulating Doolittle, including famed racer Roscoe Turner. After the attack on Pearl Harbor, Turner had suggested to Doolittle that the veteran aviators recruit some younger fliers and bomb Tokyo. Doolittle had brushed him off, arguing the former racers were too old to serve as combat pilots. "Congratulations, you dog!" Turner now cabled. "Guess you have shown the world we old boys can still be of service as combat pilots."

Turner went so far as to fire off a letter to Joe. "The day the bombs fell on Tokyo I told all of my friends that that could be no one but Jimmy Doolittle's work," he wrote. "He is the greatest guy that ever climbed in an airplane."

DOOLITTLE SAT DOWN WITHIN days of his return to write letters to the families of all seventy-nine raiders, an exercise that made him take stock of the mission's outcome, of what happened to each young man who had raised his hand and volunteered. The raid had claimed the lives of twenty-year-old gunner Leland Faktor, twenty-three year-old engineer Donald Fitzmaurice, and twenty-nine-year-old bombardier Bill Dieter, though Faktor's death was the only one so far confirmed. The Japanese had captured eight other airmen from Dean Hallmark's and Billy Farrow's crews, and the Russians had interned Ski York and his men. Several others had been injured, a few seriously.

Many of the letters were easy, and a form letter would suffice, echoing the May 20 note Doolittle sent to copilot Dick Cole's mother in Dayton:

"I am pleased to report that Dick is well and happy although a bit homesick. I left him in Chungking, China, a couple of weeks ago. He had recently completed a very hazardous, extremely important and most interesting flight—the air raid on Japan. He comported himself with conspicuous bravery and distinction. He was awarded the Distinguished Flying Cross for gallantry in action, and also was decorated by the Chinese Government.

"Transportation and communication facilities are extremely bad in the Far East and so it may be sometime before you hear again from Dick directly. I assure you, however, that everything is going smoothly with him and although plans for the future are uncertain he will probably be returning home sometime in the not too distant future.

"I am proud to have served with Dick, who was my co-pilot on the flight, and hope that I may have an opportunity to serve with him again."

Doolittle sent similar letters to the families of navigator Hank Potter, bombardier Fred Braemer, and his loyal crew chief, Paul Leonard, as well as the wives and parents of the members of the eleven other crews who had safely escaped. He mentioned Charles Ozuk's leg wound and Harold Watson's injured arm. To the wife of his second-in-command, Doolittle wrote that he was requesting orders that day for Jack Hilger to return to the United States. "Under separate cover, I am sending one of several scrolls that were presented to the outfit in China," he added. "Jack particularly liked this one and I am sure the Smithsonian Institute, where we planned to send it, will not miss the one."

The remainder of the letters Doolittle wrote over a two-day period proved far more painful, none more so than the one to Faktor's uncle in Iowa. The gunner had been killed bailing out over China. Had his chute failed or had he failed to pull the rip cord in time? No one would ever know. The only fact was that he had died. "It is with the deepest regret that I am obliged to inform you that your nephew, Corporal Leland D. Faktor, was killed in action in the raid on Japan. He was buried with military honors in a field specially set aside at Chuchow in China," Doolittle wrote. "He was a fine boy and is mourned by the entire group. I am proud to have served with him."

Information on the two captured crews was spotty—and incorrect. Reports indicated that two of Farrow's crew were missing, when in fact the Japanese had captured all five. "The latest news we are able to get is that the plane piloted by your son landed near Japanese occupied territory and that two of the crew members are missing and three have been taken prisoner by the Japanese," Doolittle wrote to Farrow's mother. "We are unable to definitely authenticate this report, and are also unable to determine which of the crew members are missing and which captured. An attempt is being made today, through the American Red Cross, to obtain more definite information. As fast as we obtain any additional information you may depend on my passing it on to you. I am sincerely sorry that I am obliged to give you such an unfortunate report."

That misinformation likewise led Doolittle to pen far more upbeat reports to Hallmark's father in Dallas and to relatives of the other crew members of the *Green Hornet*, including the families of Dieter and Fitzmaurice, who had died in the surf and been buried on a sandy knoll along the Chinese coast. "I am extremely sorry to have to bring you bad news. However, it is not as bad as it might be," Doolittle began. "Your son, according to the most reliable information that we are able to obtain, landed in Japanese occupied territory in China and has been taken prisoner. Every effort was and still is being made to extricate him from Japanese hands but to date we have not been successful. You may depend on everything possible being done in this direction."

Doolittle advised the families of Ski York's crew that American diplomats were now working to secure the airmen's release, though he was vague about the extent of injuries suffered by Ted Lawson and others on board the *Ruptured Duck*, no doubt hoping to spare them worry. He was far more candid about the gravity of the crash in his letter to Dave Thatcher's parents, praising the twenty-year-old gunner for having rescued Lawson and the others. "All of the plane's crew were saved from either capture or death as the result of his initiative and courage in assuming responsibility and in tending the wounded himself day and night," Doolittle wrote, noting that Thatcher had already received the Distinguished Flying Cross. "I have today recommended that he also be awarded the coveted Distinguished Service Cross for outstanding heroism."

Doolittle's personal letters cheered the families and elevated the already high opinion most held of the general, a sentiment captured in a letter from Harold Watson's father. "I doubt if the rules and regulations of the Army require a Commanding General, after completion of a mission, to write a personal letter to the parents of each participating member," he wrote. "However, because in addition to being an able officer, General Doolittle is a father and a gentleman, he chose to do just that."

Many of the mothers, fathers, and wives responded with glowing telegrams and letters, congratulating Doolittle on the raid. "I can't express in words how thrilled and proud I am to be the wife of one of the men who participated in the bombing of Tokyo," wrote Thelma Bourgeois, wife of bombardier Robert Bourgeois. "Congratulations to you and your volunteers for achieving a completely victorious mission."

Others wrote to ask favors. Fred Braemer's wife inquired whether Doolittle could expedite the return of her husband, who had been deployed to India. So did Melvin Gardner's fiancée. "I am hoping to get married as soon as he comes back and wanted some idea so I would know whether to go ahead with some wedding plans."

Gardner would sadly never walk down the aisle; three days after his fiancée wrote her May 30 letter, he died in a plane crash after a raid over Burma.

Pilot Richard Joyce's father questioned whether publishing the names of the raiders, particularly those still fighting in Burma, only put them at greater risk if later captured. Douglas Radney's father wanted to know whether Doolittle might help him find his son's 1940 Chevrolet, which he had left parked back in Pendleton, Oregon.

Pilot Robert Gray's parents, like many others, shared their son's admiration of Doolittle. "Robert is mighty proud to serve under you, you are his ideal as a soldier, a flyer and a man," the couple wrote. "We too are mighty proud that our son is with you and that you feel he is worthy of the place. May God bless you and keep you and our son and all his brave companions for the glory and honor of our great, free America." Thomas White's mother echoed that in a telegram. "Your leadership inspired all of your men," she cabled. "Our Bob's part is a glory to us all. He would follow you anywhere."

The letters Doolittle received from the parents of the captured airmen proved much more difficult to reconcile. Families were desperate for information, and many would continue to write to Doolittle as spring turned into summer. Chase Nielsen's mother went so far as to write President Roosevelt, asking what treatment her son would likely suffer at the hands of the Japanese. "My heart grieves, and my burden seems almost unbearable without mentioning what he must be enduring," she wrote. "I would be so very grateful for any information I might receive about my boy."

Bobby Hite's mother wrote that her husband's death in July 1941 coupled now with the capture of her son proved more than she could handle. "I just pray God," she wrote, "that he still lives." Bill Dieter's mother, despite her own worries, still found the strength to applaud the mission's success, a grace that amazed Doolittle. "Your kindness in congratulating us on the raid touched me deeply," the general responded. "Congratulations should go to you, the mother of a gallant boy who served his country heroically and effectively in time of great national peril."

Billy Farrow's mother wrote that she depended on her faith in God.

"If it is His purpose to have my son give his life, I am very proud to say that he was ready and glad to give his life in the noble defense of his own land," she wrote. "He felt it a *very* high privilege to serve with you, and to be chosen as one who was capable of doing the job." She shared her son's final letter, encouraging her despite her woes in Washington to remain strong, signing the note simply: "Chin up!" "He knew then he was going on a hazardous mission, probably never to return," she wrote Doolittle. "Such courage as that makes me able to carry on just now. I would be a very unworthy mother who could not manifest some of that same spirit and keep her chin up and hopes high."

THE ARMY BRASS, which had promised the raiders the Distinguished Flying Cross in Chungking, prepared to deliver. Doolittle fired off a cryptic letter on June 15, addressed "To All Officers and Men with me at Shangri-La." He instructed them to come to Washington and report to Major Sherman Altick in room 4414 in the Munitions Building. "You will grant no interviews with the press nor pose for photos and in your communications to your homes will advise them simply that you are back in the United States. Use the utmost caution until such time as you have been given a directive by Major Altick on what you can say and do," he wrote. "In others words, be most cautious with everyone except authorized Intelligence officers of the United States Army."

The returning raiders promised another public relations victory for the military, just as the announcement the month before of Doolittle's Medal of Honor. Army Air Forces officials initially had hoped for a reception with the president at the White House—followed by a noontime parade in New York City from the Battery to the Waldorf Astoria Hotel—but in the end had to settle for a scaled-back ceremony at Washington's Bolling Field on June 27. More than two dozen raiders had returned to the United States, but just twenty officers and three enlisted men could be on hand for the ceremony, including Jack Hilger, Ross Greening, David Jones, and Thomas White, the mission doctor. In place of the president stood Hap Arnold, displaying his trademark grin.

"These officers and enlisted men are cited for extraordinary achievement while participating in a highly destructive raid on the Japanese mainland on April 18, 1942," announced Colonel Leslie Holcomb, reading the citation. "They volunteered for this mission, knowing full well that the chances of survival were extremely remote, and executed their parts in it with great skill and daring. Their achievement reflects high credit on them and on the military service."

Arnold walked down the line and pinned the medals, which had come packed in three green wooden boxes, above the left shirt pocket of each of the raiders, as Doolittle beamed. A half dozen of the airmen's wives watched the fifteen-minute ceremony, but navigator Bill Pound's spouse arrived too late, having gotten got lost en route and then stopped in an air-raid traffic test. Tears streamed down her cheeks.

"Don't cry, honey," Pound urged his wife.

"When I heard they used B-25's I had an idea my husband was there," she told reporters once she recovered. "Then when I heard of Doolittle's promotion I was certain of it."

The press, of course, soaked it up, begging the raiders to describe the historic flight. "Something like a picnic," joked bombardier Denver True-love. "They waved at us until we dropped the bombs."

Though the military designed the ceremony to shine a light on the young heroes—allowing the airmen to tell personal stories of the raid—officials once again adhered to strict limits on what details could be released to the public. The military was keen on preserving the secret of Shangri-La—and the loss of all the planes. "No information should be made public which indicates the starting point of this raid or the ultimate destination after the raid was accomplished, or the ultimate disposition of the aircraft used in the raid," a briefing memo warned. "Information such as the distances flown or the time in the air or the amount of fuel consumed and all other related matters should not be made public as they furnish a key to the prohibitions mentioned above." Part of the secrecy stemmed from the reality that America had not ruled out future attacks on Japan; in fact, Arnold had challenged his staff to devise just such a scenario. "You fellows use your imagination and see what ideas on this subject you can present me."

Doolittle meanwhile worked behind the scenes to secure additional awards for some of the raiders. He recommended that Hilger, Greening, Jones, and Hoover—the senior officers who had overseen aspects of the mission such as gunnery and intelligence—each receive the Distinguished Service Cross or the Distinguished Service Medal. The Army ultimately denied Doolittle's requests, but did award Silver Stars to Thomas White and the *Ruptured Duck*'s Dean Davenport and David Thatcher; the latter's story particularly wowed debriefing officer Merian Cooper in Chungking, as evidenced by a report he sent to Doolittle. "Beyond the limits of human exertion, beyond the call of friendship, beyond the call of duty, he—a corporal—brought his four wounded officers to safety," Cooper wrote. "Medal of Honor? Pin it on him. He earned it."

Doolittle likewise recommended all officers and enlisted men for promotion with one exception—Ski York's crew. After his many warnings not to fly to Russia, York had done just that, and a clearly irritated Doolittle wanted answers. He also held back on recommending York for the Distinguished Service Cross or the Distinguished Service Medal. "The crew of the airplane that went to Siberia has not been recommended for promotion," the general wrote in a memo, "and will not be until such time as it is possible to ascertain why they were in apparent direct violation of orders."

The plane carrying Ted Lawson meanwhile touched down in Washington on the afternoon of June 16. Walter Reed Army Hospital sent an ambulance to collect the injured pilot along with *Ruptured Duck* navigator Charles McClure.

The men landed in ward five in a room with raider Harold Watson, who had just undergone surgery to repair his broken arm. The fliers traded stories that evening until Doolittle arrived. "I tried to stand up when he came in," Lawson recalled, "but he put his hands on my shoulders and wouldn't let me."

Doolittle apologized that he was not at Bolling Field to greet them, but no one had told him of the airmen's arrival. "How about the family situation?" he asked.

Lawson stalled. He said he wanted a good night's sleep before he figured out how to proceed.

"Do you know about your mother?" Doolittle pressed. "She's had a stroke. She's pretty bad off. I'm sorry."

Lawson fell silent.

"What do you want to do about your wife?"

Lawson wasn't ready for his wife to see him. Not yet. He asked Doolittle to tell her he was still out of the country.

"I've already written your wife and told her you were injured and on the way back, but that I didn't know the extent of your injuries," Doolittle advised. "You'd better do something about it."

The general decided to intervene, phoning Lawson's wife in Los Angeles, where she had gone to be closer to her family. Though Doolittle did not go into details about Lawson's injuries, he told her he was going to send her an airmail letter.

"Well, what do you think I look like," Ellen Lawson told Doolittle on the phone. "I'm eight months pregnant!"

Doolittle wrote that he had spoken at length with Lawson. "He is in good health but quite depressed. The depression results from the fact that a deep cut in his left leg became infected and it was necessary that the leg be amputated. He also lost some teeth and received a cut on his face," Doolittle wrote. "He is receiving the best medical attention that is possible to obtain, here at Walter Reed Hospital, but I feel that his recovery is being retarded by a fear of how his misfortune is going to affect you and his mother. Ted will probably be hospitalized here for some time and it is my personal belief that his recovery would be expedited through your presence."

Ellen Lawson sat down and fired off an airmail letter of her own, assuring her husband of her love. "I'm glad to know the truth. My imagination has been running away with me," she wrote. "Darling, it could be so much worse. I've had so many nightmarish dreams that you didn't come back at all, and others in which you completely lost your memory and refused to believe I was your wife. Those were horrible. There is no reason in the world why we can't lead a perfectly normal life and do the things we've planned. When I do see you I'll do my best to control my tears. But, should there be any, please don't misinterpret them. Because they'll be tears of happiness and joy. "

Lawson was overjoyed to receive the letter and even more so when she appeared in his hospital doorway days later after Doolittle arranged a flight. "I jumped up to go to the door, forgetting everything. Forgetting the crutches," Lawson later wrote. "And when I took a step toward her I fell on my face in front of her."

Lawson would have to endure a second amputation on his left leg followed by oral surgery to reshape his mouth as well as remove the broken nubs of his teeth, including one that had gone up through his gums into his sinus.

"He's still got some of that beach sand in there!" Lawson heard one of the doctors comment during the surgery.

McClure likewise faced two surgeries to repair his battered shoulders, though his stay in the hospital proved personally beneficial. He fell in love with the occupational therapist Jean Buchanan and would marry her the following January.

The chief of the Army air staff, Major General Millard Harmon, and Treasury Secretary Henry Morgenthau visited on July 6 to present the three raiders along with Howard Sessler and James Parker with the Distinguished Flying Cross. Press accounts either made no mention of how the fliers were injured or noted that the airmen "were injured in an airplane crash some time after the raid on Japan."

Since the injured raiders had bypassed Chungking, Major General Chu Shih-ming, the military attaché for the Chinese embassy, stopped by on July 25 to present them with the Military Order of China. Doolittle was, as always, on hand for the ceremony. "You have exploded the myth of Japanese invincibility," the Chinese general told them, "and set up a fine example for other military men of the United Nations to emulate."

DOOLITTLE WRAPPED UP THE mission's postmortem, finalizing his thirty-one-page report and shipping a box of cigars to the Sacramento worker who packed the parachute that had saved his life. He requested that the raiders suggest for possible awards any Chinese individuals who had helped them. Recommendations soon flooded his in-box. Harold Watson suggested Father Wendelin Dunker, who had aided the crew of the *Whirling Dervish*, while Dave Thatcher recommended guerrilla leader Jai Foo Chang, better known to most of the crew simply as Charlie. Thomas White nominated Chen and his father. The two physicians had graciously opened up their hospital to the crew of the *Ruptured Duck*, whose badly injured men drained the hospital of much of its precious medicines. "Neither man would take a penny for their services or their supplies saying that they felt it was their part in the fight against Japan," White wrote. "I feel that Lawson and possibly Davenport owe their lives to Dr. Chen's prompt and skillful treatment, and we all owe him a lot for his help and our comfort while at Linhai."

The military planned to cash in on the success of the raid, asking the stateside airmen to volunteer to travel the country to sell war bonds and deliver morale speeches to factory workers eager for stories from the front. Most of the raiders jumped at the chance—a far safer volunteer assignment than their previous one. Pilot Bill Bower chatted up workers at the B. F. Goodrich Company in Ohio, while navigator Tom Griffin mingled with employees at the Dumore Company in Wisconsin. Pilots Griffith Williams and Ken Reddy spoke at a Birmingham luncheon attended by more than four hundred people, and the Army bragged that engineer Jacob Eierman on his tour of New England factories was seen by as many as twenty-five thousand. "Even though Ross was embarrassed to tears," a Pierce County War Bond staff official wrote of Greening's visit to Tacoma, "he helped us sell thousands and thousands of dollars worth of bonds and stamps."

Doolittle himself jumped into the action, posing alongside enlistment posters that read, "Fly to Tokyo: All Expenses Paid." He sent a congratulatory telegram to workers at the Wright Aeronautical Corporation in Paterson, New Jersey, the maker of the B-25's twin engines. "Jap planes couldn't do a thing to stop us," he cabled. "They will never stop us if you keep up your great work." He fired off another telegram to employees at the Western Electric Company in the nearby town of Kearny, who helped build the radios that aided the raiders. "Through those radios we issued commands between ships that sent our bombers on their marks," Doolittle wired. "Through those radios we cheered each other on as our bombs crashed into vital Japanese naval and military installations. And, perhaps best of all, through those radios, we heard the hysterical Japanese broadcasters, too excited to lie, screaming about the damage we had done."

Doolittle stopped by the California factory of North American Aviation—the manufacturer of all sixteen B-25s used in the raid—congratulating workers in a noontime speech on June 1. "Don't tell a soul, but Shangri-La is right here in this North American plant. This is where our B-25 bombers came from," he told the twelve thousand attendees at the Inglewood plant. "Our bombers—your bombers—functioned magnificently." Company president James Kindelberger was so impressed with the speech that he sent a personal letter to Doolittle's wife. "He not only made a fine talk, but his going around the plant chatting with people caused more goodwill than anything that has ever happened here," he wrote. "I have taken many people of fame and prominence through the plant, but this is the first time that anyone has actually stopped the show."

Doolittle was no stranger to celebrity, but the raid catapulted his fame to a new level. He was now a hero not just to the aviation community but to a grateful nation, the leader of a mission so dramatic that both Universal Pictures and Warner Brothers begged for the rights to tell it. In the eyes of the public, Doolittle personified bravery—the hero, as the *Chicago Daily Tribune* noted, with "the plain, honest American face." Accolades, tributes, and even gifts soon flowed. The Rotary Club of Saint Louis elected Doolittle an honorary life member, as did the San Diego Consistory of the Ancient and Accepted Scottish Rite of Freemasonry. The Dayton district commissioner wrote that teens aged fifteen to eighteen wanted to form an air scout squadron named in Doolittle's honor. Fan mail arrived by the bundle as people asked for autographs, photos, and even old envelopes the general had used, anything he had touched. An Oklahoma woman sent him a flag she crocheted with 3,620 stitches. Total strangers wrote songs—a few went so far as to set such tunes to music and publish them—and poems about Doolittle, including Patsy Browning of New Jersey:

> There is a man in this world
> As proud as he can be,
> For he fights for just one thing,
> And that is "Victory."
> This man's power and strength
> Is not just a riddle,
> For this is the great—
> Jimmy Doolittle.

Tony Mele of Brooklyn sent this poem:

> Doolittle did plenty when he let the Japs know
> That American pilots could bomb Tokyo
> His calling card said, "I'll be back some day
> And when I do there'll be hell to pay."

Long forgotten friends from Doolittle's past surfaced, including Everett Hastings, a schoolmate from his youth in Alaska. Hastings confessed in a letter that his mother had referred to Nome's scrappy young brawler by the diminutive nickname Dooless. Much had changed since those days. "My son gets in a fight every now and then. When he happens to tell some kid that his Dad went to school with you, they give him a laugh and tell him he is a liar," Hastings wrote. "You and your 'Gang' are the idol of all the sprouting fliers to come."

Doolittle's fame grew so much that an autographed war bond poster for the Cleveland Athletic Club would fetch a staggering four million dollars. A newly incorporated Missouri town of 220 residents in the Ozarks even decided to name itself in the general's honor. "We may not be big," Mayor Alfred Cook boasted, "but we have a good name and enthusiasm." Not until after the war did Doolittle's schedule permit a visit, but when it did city leaders unveiled a bronze plaque of his likeness. As always he attributed his success to others. "I deeply appreciate the honor you have done me," he said. "However, I should like always to believe that the tribute you have paid me you also intended for the men of vision who made aviation as we know it today possible—and also for the gallant people with whom it was my pleasure and privilege to serve."

CHAPTER 22

★

One cannot imagine the barbarism of the Japs till one
witnesses it with his own eyes.

—FATHER LOUIS BERESWILL,
JANUARY 29, 1943, LETTER

JAPANESE LEADERS FUMED OVER the Tokyo raid, which had revealed
China's coastal provinces as a dangerous blind spot in the defense of the
homeland. American aircraft carriers not only could launch surprise
attacks at sea and land in China but could possibly even fly bombers
directly from Chinese airfields to attack Japan. Military leaders needed
to eliminate that threat by wiping out the airfields in the provinces of
Chekiang and Kiangsi. The Imperial General Headquarters ordered an
immediate campaign against those bases, issuing an operational plan in
late April: "The primary mission will be to defeat the enemy in the Chekiang area and to destroy the air bases from which the enemy might conduct aerial raids on the Japanese Homeland."

Japanese forces occupied the area along the lower reaches of the
Yangtse River. The Imperial General Headquarters ordered the main
force of the Thirteenth Army, along with elements of the Eleventh Army
and the North China Area Army, to execute the operation. That force
ultimately swelled to fifty-three infantry battalions, along with as many
as sixteen artillery battalions. The plan called for the capture of the

larger airfields at Chuchow, Lishui, and Yushan—all fields Doolittle had hoped to use—as well as the destruction of many other, smaller bases in the region. Orders left little doubt about the horror to come. "The captured areas will be occupied for a period estimated at approximately one month," they demanded. "Airfields, military installations and important lines of communication will be totally destroyed."

The United States had neither boots on the ground nor faith that the Chinese military could repel a Japanese invasion. Details of the destruction that would soon follow—just as officials in Washington and Chungking, and even Doolittle, had long predicted—would come from the records of American missionaries, some of whom had helped the raiders. The missionaries knew of the potential wrath of the Japanese, having lived under a tenuous peace in this border region just south of occupied China. Stories of the atrocities at Nanking, where the river had turned red from blood, had circulated widely. "When the Japs come into a town the first thing that you see is a group of cavalrymen," Herbert Vandenberg, an American priest, would recall. "The horses have on shiny black boots. The men wear boots and a helmet. They are carrying sub-machine guns."

Vandenberg had heard the news broadcasts of the Tokyo raid in the mission compound in the town of Linchwan, home to about fifty thousand people, as well as to the largest Catholic church in southern China, with a capacity to serve as many as a thousand. Days after the raid letters reached Vandenberg from nearby missions in Poyang and Ihwang, informing him that local priests cared for some of the fliers—Watson's and Knobloch's crews. "They came to us on foot," Vandenberg said. "They were tired and hungry. Their clothing was tattered and torn from climbing down the mountains after bailing out. We gave them fried chicken. We dressed their wounds and washed their clothes. The nuns baked cakes for the fliers. We gave them our beds."

The arrival of the raiders worried Vandenberg and the other priests; Japanese forces were entrenched just fifty miles north in Nanchang. By late May reports circulated that those forces were on the move. Father Steve Dunker suggested Vandenberg set off June 1 for Hangpu—about twenty miles away—and take forty-five of the Chinese orphans over the age of ten. Fathers Dunker and Clarence Murphy would remain behind with about fifty Chinese girls who were too small to make the difficult journey. Each day the news worsened as Japanese forces closed in on Linchwan. On June 4 Dunker and Murphy decided it was time to get out. The priests packed a wheelbarrow of supplies and planned to set off to follow Vandenberg the next morning.

But at 1:30 a.m. on June 5, Japanese soldiers arrived armed with machine guns. A heavy rain fell as troops pounded on the gate of the mission residence. The gatekeeper peered out the window and stalled, claiming he could not find the key, as he alerted the Americans inside. Dunker and Murphy darted from bed, slipped outside, and hid in the mission's air-raid trenches in the garden. The soldiers forced the local priest Father Joseph Kwei to escort them through the entire compound, demanding that he open all the doors to facilitate the search. The soldiers looted the valuables and then trashed the church.

"Where are the Americans?" the Japanese demanded.

Dunker and Murphy stayed in the air-raid trench until about 4 a.m. and then shortly before sunrise grabbed a ladder, leaned it against the fourteen-foot wall, and started up. A sentry spotted them and opened fire just as the clergy hopped over the wall. The two priests escaped and trudged through the flooded rice paddies to join Vandenberg at Hangpu, arriving later that night exhausted and with blistered feet. On Sunday, June 7, while the three priests gathered with the orphans for services in the mission, machine guns rattled on the outskirts of Hangpu. The Japanese had caught up to them.

"Come on!" Vandenberg shouted. "Run for your lives."

The orphans and priests fled again. "It was a mad screaming flight across swollen creeks up into the hills," Vandenberg recalled. "At night we slept in the straw in a Chinese temple. We had no food." The priests headed for the village of Ihwang, figuring that the Japanese would never go that far. "Ihwang was in the mountains; on the road to nowhere; unimportant militarily; hard to get to, etc.," recalled Father Wendelin Dunker—Steve's cousin—who had helped care for Harold Watson's crew. "I just could not seem to believe that they would come there in any manner, shape or form."

News reached Dunker that the priests and orphans were en route, so he saddled his horse and rode out to meet them on the afternoon of June 8. Days on the run had left them exhausted. Though Dunker believed the Japanese would never come, he began to pack supplies and sent a man to hire a boat. If necessary, the priests could go to Ou-tu, about seventeen miles away, where the mission had a small church and school. The exhausted priests stretched out at 1 p.m. An hour later machine-gun fire rattled outside the north gate, followed soon by bullets zipping over the residence. Steve Dunker darted downstairs. "The Japs are here," he shouted. "The Japs are here."

The priests and orphans charged out of the mission. Wendelin Dunker waited only long enough to grab a briefcase of cash before he followed the others. "Was out the back gate in about two minutes but at that I was the last one," he later wrote in a letter to his parents. "Boy, oh boy, was this place emptied in a hurry!"

The priests and orphans joined the local masses, who fled across the bridge out of town. "We thought we were fast but we were slow compared to a lot of the people in the town," Dunker wrote. "There were hundreds and hundreds ahead of us and thousands behind." He described the scene again in a letter to Bishop John O'Shea. "Believe me," he wrote, "a record was made in getting out of town and across the river."

The Japanese pursued the escapees, opening fire on them. "Bullets whistled over our heads," Vandenberg recalled. "As we ran we looked up on the mountainside where lay the gleaming wreckage of one of the Doolittle bombers. It was a fearful sight for we knew that we were paying a price for the work of that plane."

The priests hiked throughout the afternoon, resting that evening in the home of a local Catholic. "When we stopped to make an inventory," Dunker wrote, "we were six priests with the clothes on our backs, some money, but not a thing else." The priests not only had no supplies, but Dunker realized that in his escape he had failed to consume the Blessed Sacrament. "The more I thought of it," he wrote, "the more convinced I became that it would be a relatively simple matter, and probably not too dangerous either, to return to Ihwang and get some things out of the residence, consume the Blessed Sacrament in the church, and do so without being caught by the Japs."

Dunker recruited three of the mission's workmen and set out that night for the five-mile hike back to town. "The Lord was with us," he wrote in a letter, "for we found one bridge unguarded." The men slipped across and headed for the mission. "When I entered the back gate of the residence I could see no light of any kind in any of the buildings, nor could I hear any sound," he later wrote. "I felt sure if the Japs were sleeping in any of the buildings there, they would have had guards, and likewise some sort of light somewhere. Nevertheless I approached the priest's house very cautiously, and listened for any sort of sound. But not a sound was to be heard."

Dunker slipped inside the church, where he opened the tabernacle and consumed the Blessed Sacrament. He next went to the stable, stunned to find that the Japanese had left the mission's two horses, though one soon ran off. Dunker and the workmen rounded up baskets of clothes, flour, and Mass wines that would be needed to survive in the hills, each tasked to carry as much as eighty pounds. Rather than use a saddle, Dunker draped five blankets over the horse, making his return comfortable "in body if not in mind." "I had to ride pretty carefully tho," he wrote, "for with all those things wrapped around the horse it was like riding an elephant in width if not in height."

Dunker and the workmen made it back to the others at daybreak. After breakfast the group set out again, reaching Ou-tu that night. Dunker's money allowed the priests to buy rice and vegetables. Reports of the Japanese advance continued, prompting the group to press on to Kenkwo-gee, a village of less than a dozen families where the missionaries owned a building that doubled as a chapel and priest's room. "It was half way up a mountain, in a small valley, and the only way of getting to it was by a small path that wound through the mountains," Dunker wrote. "We used doors, boards and what not for beds, and for the first time in about a week felt relatively safe."

Dunker's group wasn't alone. Throughout the region foreign priests and villagers alike sought refuge from the Japanese fury in the mountains, including the California native Bishop Charles Quinn, the vicar apostolic of Yukiang. Quinn had met Doolittle when he passed through en route to Chungking. "We found a package of American cigarettes and were able to give each boy one cigarette," he recalled. "I believe they appreciated them more than they did the breakfast." Accompanied by eight priests and five Sisters of Charity, Quinn led some two hundred orphans into the hills about fifty miles from Yukiang. An Italian priest, Father Humbert Verdini, had begged to remain behind along with thirty-eight orphans, many of them children or elderly. Quinn relented, assuming that, since Japan had allied with Italy, Verdini would be safe.

The journey proved difficult with small children and elderly nuns. "With haste we moved children, food, clothes from our residence," recalled Father Bill Stein, "first by boat then by short stage to fit the traveling of the young people, moving farther than farther, trying to distance ourselves from town, and bringing us to the mountain vastness where we would hide." The group settled first in an abandoned temple, but the locals feared Japanese reprisals and encouraged them to move farther, telling them of an abandoned bandit hideout in the woods. Quinn went so far as to buy guns and to station guards at the foot of the mountains, a move Stein opposed.

"Bill, what are we to do?" the bishop replied. "We have these children and Sisters to protect should the Japs find us. We must give them a chance to escape. Our duty is to protect them."

The group set out to make a camp, constructing huts and digging toilets, a job made all the more difficult by a lack of nails. "Under the tutorage of the local farmers," Stein recalled, "using crude instruments, we felled the trees, dug holes in the granite soil, bound trees with vines, thatched our seven framed huts with straw, constructed beds of bamboo frames—all this done under the damp heat of summer." Smith had bought a lot of salt before evacuation, which the missionaries used to trade with local farmers for vegetables and the occasional chicken or duck. "All of us lost much weight," Stein recalled, "but God helping, we survived."

WENDELIN DUNKER WAITED ABOUT ten days before news reached him in the hills that the Japanese had moved through Ihwang. The anxious priest recruited Father Clarence Murphy to return with him to survey the damage and protect mission property from looters. "What a scene of destruction and smells met us as we entered the city!" he later wrote. "There were packs of dogs, whose masters either had fled or had been killed, and who had no one to feed them. Consequently even though many of the cadavers had been covered after a fashion by people who had returned to the town, the dogs usually dug them out to get something to eat. The big maggot-producing flies were almost as thick as snowflakes in a snow storm," Dunker continued. "They swarmed about you, and you had to keep your mouth closed lest they fly into your mouth."

The Japanese came through again days later, forcing Dunker to evacuate once more. This time the Japanese burned most of the town. "They shot any man, woman, child, cow, hog, or just about anything that moved. They raped any woman from the ages of 10–65, and before burning the town they thoroughly looted it. When they wanted something to eat they would shoot any hog that they saw, then cut off a few pounds of meat that they wanted at the moment, and then leave the rest of the animal on the ground to rot. There weren't many cows, but those they saw they did the same to them," Dunker wrote. "None of the humans shot were buried either, but were left to lay on the ground to rot, along with the hogs and cows. This part of the Japanese army were absolute barbarians. The men of the Roman Legions could not have been more barbaric."

Dunker found the mission wrecked, though fortunately not torched like so much else in Ihwang. "Things were dumped out, turned over, broken, burned," he wrote in a report to Bishop O'Shea. "All things of value were carried off." The Japanese had gone so far as to smash Dunker's typewriter and steal his razor, though he managed to salvage two bottles of beer in the basement that the soldiers had somehow missed, which the priest savored. "If you are unfortunate enough to have the Japs come your way, it would be a good thing to give them a wide path. Every town they enter is another Nanking on a small scale," he warned O'Shea. "Absolutely no one would be able to stop them from dragging off young— and also not so young—women, and maybe when a dozen or more are through with her, to run a knife through her body."

The destruction of Ihwang proved typical, even mild compared with the horror the Japanese visited upon some of the villages and towns in the provinces where Doolittle and his men had bailed out. Quinn returned to Yukiang after almost three months in the mountains. "The sight that met our eyes was appalling," the bishop said. "Part of the town had been burned. As many of the townspeople as the Japs had been able to capture had been killed." Father Vincent Smith echoed Quinn. "Death came in horrible forms," he said. "We learned that with our own eyes." Local villagers related for the priests some of those horrors. "Jap soldiers would stand on bridges being used by refugees streaming into the interior," Quinn wrote. "As the aged Chinese would pass by, Jap soldiers would push them off the bridge and into the water. Those who could not swim, of course, drowned; those who could swim afforded tragic targets for Jap riflemen."

Quinn returned to the mission to find that the three-story residence of thirty-three rooms had been reduced to charred timbers and ashes. Soldiers had looted or smashed all the windows, doors, and furnishings of the mission's church and three schools, even tearing down the altars. The biggest tragedy involved Father Verdini, who had remained behind with several dozen orphans and elderly unable to travel. "In a pond, in the garden, we found Father Verdini's body," Smith recalled. "Nearby were the bones of the orphans and the aged men and women. Few met the merciful death of a bullet." The Japanese had bayoneted many. Two of the dead had been burned to death, used as "human candles." The scattered remains of as many as forty others who had sought refuge at the mission littered the garden. "The total number," a church report stated, "cannot be ascertained for certain, because no one escaped."

The walled city of Nancheng would prove one of the worst hit after the Japanese marched in at dawn on the morning of June 11, beginning a reign of terror so horrendous that missionaries would later dub it "the Rape of Nancheng." Soldiers rounded up eight hundred women and herded them into a storehouse outside the east gate, assaulting them day after day. "For one month the Japanese remained in Nancheng, roaming the rubble-filled streets in loin clothes much of the time, drunk a good part of the time and always on the lookout for women," wrote the Reverend Frederick McGuire. "The women and children who did not escape from Nancheng will long remember the Japanese—the women and girls because they were raped time after time by Japan's imperial troops and are now ravaged by venereal disease, the children because they mourn their fathers who were slain in cold blood for the sake of the 'new order' in East Asia."

At the end of the occupation, Japanese forces systematically destroyed the city of fifty thousand residents, bringing in technical experts in fields ranging from communications to medicine. Teams stripped Nancheng of all radios, while others looted the hospitals of drugs and surgical instruments. Engineers not only wrecked the electrical plant but pulled up the railroad lines, shipping the iron out through the port at Wenchow. The Japanese lastly sent in a special incendiary squad, which started its operation on July 7 in the city's southern section.

"Broken doors and partition boards were placed in the center of every house according to plan and kerosene was poured over," wrote the *Takung Pao* newspaper. "A long torch was then applied from the outside. When there was a high brick wall between two houses, torch was applied on the next one. There was a group of soldiers assigned to this task for every street and lane and larger buildings. This planned burning was carried on for three days and the city of Nancheng became charred earth."

The Japanese spared little in this summertime march of ruin, driving what Claire Chennault later described as a "bloody spear two hundred miles through the heart of East China." Enemy forces looted towns and villages of precious rice, salt, and sugar, even stealing honey and then scattering hives. Soldiers devoured, drove away, or simply slaughtered thousands of oxen, pigs, and other farm animals; some wrecked vital irrigation systems and set crops on fire. At other times troops burned wooden water wheels, plows, and threshers and stole all the iron tools. Along the way the Japanese destroyed bridges, roads, and airfields, reducing some twenty thousand square miles to smoldering ruins. "The thoroughness of the Jap work of destruction is amazing!" wrote one unnamed clergyman. "Beyond Words!" Dunker would later echo that sentiment: "Like a swarm of locusts, they left behind nothing but destruction and chaos."

Outside of this punitive destruction came stories of sadistic torture and murder, including the abduction of a thousand boys between the ages of twelve and sixteen whom the Japanese enslaved as orderlies and later shipped to Nancheng to be trained as spies. In Yintang troops smashed headstones and dug up graves, plucking the jade rings off the fingers of the dead; in Linchwan soldiers tossed entire families down wells so that the bloated bodies of the dead would contaminate the village's drinking water. One woman crawled out and later described how nine members of her family had drowned. Soldiers did the same in Ihwang, murdering several generations of a schoolteacher's family. "They killed my three sons; they killed my wife, Angsing; they set fire to my school; they burned my books; they drowned my grandchildren in the well," he recalled. "I crawled out of the well at night, when they were drunk, and killed them with my own hands—one for every member of my family they had slaughtered."

In the town of Kweiyee soldiers raped the mayor's niece twelve times, tied her naked to a post, and burned her body with cigarettes. Troops in Nancheng tore the hair off the head of an albino child, while others in Samen sliced off the noses and ears of villagers. "I cannot tell you the full story of the brutalities inflicted on these helpless people, on men, women and children, even upon babies," Smith recalled. "No civilized mind can conceive the tortures which were inflicted on all. Whole towns of from 15,000 to 20,000 people were wiped out, the populace killed and the homes and places of business leveled by fire." Father George Yaeger recounted similar atrocities. "The whole countryside reeked of death in every form," he later told reporters. "From some of the villagers who had managed to escape death we heard stories far too brutal and savage to be related. Just one charge was not heard—cannibalism. But outside of that take your choice and you can't miss the savage nature of the Japanese army."

The Japanese refused to spare religious institutions or the clergy. Troops beat and starved French priest Michael Poizat so badly that he died within a month. "You want to go to heaven, don't you?" soldiers asked Father Joseph Kwei before cutting his head off with a sword. The Japanese looted or wrecked two-thirds of the Vincentian's twenty-nine missions or parishes, many burned or totally destroyed. On the wall of one torched church the Japanese chalked, "Christ is defeated." Vandenberg would describe the destruction he found on his return to Linchwan. "It was a fearful sight," he said. "Our priests house, schools, and orphanage had been burned. Our stone church was still standing but its interior was a shambles. The Japs had chopped up the altars, torn down the pulpit and wrecked the sacristy. The feet and the hands of statues of Christ, Mother Mary, and the saints had been slashed off and the eyes gouged out."

The Japanese reserved the harshest torture for those discovered to have helped the Doolittle raiders. In Nancheng soldiers forced a group of men who had fed the airmen to eat feces before lining up a group of ten for a "bullet contest," testing to see how many people a single bullet would pass through before it finally stopped. In Ihwang the Japanese found Ma Eng-lin, who had welcomed injured pilot Harold Watson into his home. Soldiers wrapped him in a blanket, tied him to a chair, and soaked him in kerosene. The Japanese then forced his wife to torch him. Troops likewise burned down the hospital of a German doctor who had helped set Watson's arm. "Little did the Doolittle men realize," the Reverend Charles Meeus later wrote, "that those same little gifts which they gave their rescuers in grateful acknowledgement of their hospitality—parachutes, gloves, nickels, dimes, cigarette packages—would, a few weeks later, become the tell-tale evidence of their presence and lead to the torture and death of their friends!"

A missionary with the United Church of Canada, the Reverend Bill Mitchell traveled in the region, organizing aid on behalf of the Church Committee on China Relief. Mitchell gathered statistics from local governments to provide a snapshot of the destruction. The Japanese flew 1,131 raids against Chuchow—Doolittle's intended destination—killing 10,246 people and leaving another 27,456 destitute. Enemy forces likewise destroyed 62,146 homes, stole 7,620 head of cattle, and burned 30 percent of the crops. "Out of twenty-eight market towns in that region," the committee's report noted, "only three escaped devastation." The city of Yushan, with a population of 70,000—many of whom had participated in a parade led by the mayor in honor of raiders Davy Jones and Hoss Wilder—saw 2,000 killed and 80 percent of the homes destroyed. "Yushan was once a large town filled with better-than-average houses. Now you can walk thru street after street seeing nothing but ruins," Stein wrote in a letter. "In some places you can go several miles without seeing a house that was not burnt. Poor people."

But Japan had saved the worst for last, summoning the secretive Unit 731. A clandestine outfit, Unit 731 was led by Major General Shiro Ishii, a fifty-year-old doctor and army surgeon who specialized in bacteriology and serology. Flamboyant and outgoing, Ishii once developed a field water filtration system, demonstrating its effectiveness by urinating in it and then guzzling the output. He was one of Japan's early proponents of bacteriological warfare. The operation that had begun almost a decade earlier in an old soy sauce distillery in Manchuria had since grown into his personal bacteriological empire, occupying a three-square-mile campus near the town of Pingfan. Shielded from prying eyes behind towering walls and electric fences, some three thousand scientists, doctors, and technicians toiled in the secret compound that boasted its own powerhouse, rail access, and even airfield. To disguise the true nature of the unit, the Japanese publicly labeled it the Epidemic Prevention and Water Supply Unit of the Kwantung Army.

Researchers with Unit 731 focused on such diseases as anthrax, plague, glanders, dysentery, typhoid, and cholera, determining which ones would be best suited for bacteriological warfare. At full capacity Ishii's so-called death factory could crank out more than 650 pounds of plague bacteria a month, 1,500 pounds of anthrax germs, 2,000 pounds of typhoid, and more than 2,200 pounds of cholera. To test these awful germs, Ishii's scientists experimented on humans, from bandits and communist sympathizers to spies and the occasional Russian soldier. The Japanese often kept kidnapped subjects in a special holding cell under the consulate in Harbin, transferring them to the unit headquarters at night in vans. At Pingfan, Ishii's older brother Takeo ran the secret two-story prison, through which six hundred men and women passed each year. As a macabre souvenir the Japanese even kept one Russian subject pickled in a six-foot jar. "No one," recalled one of the unit's senior leaders, "ever left this death factory alive."

Experiments ran the gamut from pressure chambers and frostbite to injecting humans with horse blood, but most focused on bacteriological warfare. Researchers fed prisoners cantaloupes injected with typhoid, chocolate laced with anthrax, and plague-filled cookies. At other times the Japanese staked prisoners down and set off nearby bacteria bombs. In one of the more horrific practices, pathologists autopsied living prisoners without anesthetic, which doctors feared might affect the organs and blood vessels. A former medical assistant later recounted the autopsy of a Chinese prisoner infected with plague. "The fellow knew that it was over for him, and so he didn't struggle when they led him into the room and tied him down," he said. "But when I picked up the scalpel, that's when he began screaming. I cut him open from the chest to the stomach, and he screamed terribly, and his face was all twisted in agony. He made this unimaginable sound, he was screaming so horribly. But then he finally stopped."

Researchers struggled to devise the best delivery mechanism for a bacteriological attack. Strong air pressure and high temperatures generated by bombs killed many germs, making it difficult to use common ordnance. During his travels before the war in Europe, Ishii had developed a fascination with the plague, which had spread via fleas, a natural yet effective delivery system. Since the plague still occurred throughout Asia, Ishii realized that by employing it he could disguise a biological attack from the enemy. Researchers at Unit 731 set out to breed fleas in some 4,500 nurseries or incubators that allowed the parasites to feast on rodents, churning out as many as 145 million fleas every three to four months. Ishii tested those theories in the summer of 1940 around the Chekiang Province port of Ning-po, dropping some 15 million plague-infested fleas from a low-flying airplane. Of the ninety-nine people ultimately infected, all but one died. A thrilled Ishii released a documentary film of the operation.

The Doolittle Raid provided Ishii with another chance to target Chekiang and surrounding provinces. After returning from Tokyo in May, Ishii summoned his senior chiefs, informing them that the general staff had ordered the unit to prepare for a large expedition in China. The plan was to target the areas around Yushan, Kinhwa, and Futsin to coincide with the withdrawal of Japanese forces. In what was known as land bacterial sabotage, troops would contaminate wells, rivers, and fields, hoping to sicken local villagers as well as the Chinese forces, which would no doubt move back in and reoccupy the border region as soon as the Japanese departed. Over the course of several conferences, Ishii and his divisional chiefs debated the best bacteria to use, settling on plague, anthrax, cholera, typhoid, and paratyphoid, all of which would be spread via spray, fleas, and direct contamination of water sources. For the operation Ishii ordered almost three hundred pounds of paratyphoid and anthrax germs.

In late June and early July 1942 about 120 officers and civilian employees left Pingfan for Nanking by rail and air. The mission was initially slated for the end of July, but the slow progress of the Japanese operation in the region pushed it back into August. Technicians filled peptone bottles with bacteria, packaged them in boxes labeled "Water Supply," and flew them to Nanking. Once in Nanking, workers transferred the bacteria to metal flasks—like those used for drinking water—and flew them into the target areas. Troops then tossed the flasks into wells, marshes, and homes. The Japanese also prepared three thousand rolls, contaminating them with typhoid and paratyphoid. Guards handed out the rolls to hungry Chinese prisoners of war, who were then released to go home and spread disease. Soldiers likewise left another four hundred biscuits infected with typhoid near fences, under trees, and around bivouac areas to make it appear as though retreating forces had left them behind, knowing that hungry locals would devour them.

The region's devastation made it difficult to tally who got sick and why, particularly since the Japanese had looted and burned hospitals and clinics, cutting off means for many to seek treatment. The thousands of rotting hogs, cows, and humans that clogged wells and littered the rubble only contaminated the drinking water and increased the risk of diseases. Furthermore, the impoverished region, where villagers often defecated in holes outdoors, had been prone to such outbreaks and epidemics before the invasion. Anecdotal evidence gathered from missionaries and journalists shows that many Chinese fell sick from malaria, dysentery, and cholera even before the Japanese reportedly began the operation. Chinese journalist Yang Kang, who traveled the region for the *Takung Pao* newspaper, visited the village of Peipo in late July. "Those who returned to the village after the enemy had evacuated fell sick with no one spared," she wrote. "This was the situation which took place not only in Peipo but everywhere."

Kang recounted how a pallid and clearly ill woman answered the knock on the door of her home. "Everybody is sick," the woman told Kang. "All are sick people." "She was perfectly right," Kang wrote. "She herself was sick. Her daughter was having malaria. Her elder grandson was having dysentery and the younger one's face was pallid and swollen." In Tsungjen, Kang asked a child on the street what ailed him. "Belly ache," the boy responded. "Belly seems burning." "His eyes and nose were so swollen that they seemed to have disappeared altogether," she wrote. "He was about eleven and there are bigger and smaller ones as sick as he all along the road." Australian journalist Wilfred Burchett accompanied Kang on her travels, finding that outbreaks of disease had left entire cities off limits. "We avoided staying in towns overnight, because cholera had broken out and was spreading rapidly," Burchett wrote. "The magistrate assured us that every inhabited house in the city was stricken with some disease."

In December 1942 Tokyo radio reported massive outbreaks of cholera, and Chinese reports the following spring revealed that a plague epidemic forced the government to quarantine the Chekiang town of Luangshuan. "As a note of some interest," an American intelligence report stated, "previous to the Sino-Japanese war, bubonic plague had never been known to appear south of the Yangtze River." Chinese authorities knew better. "The losses suffered by our people," one later wrote, "were inestimable." Some of Unit 731's victims included Japanese soldiers. A lance corporal captured in 1944 told American interrogators that upward of ten thousand troops were infected during the Chekiang campaign. "Diseases were particularly cholera, but also dysentery and pest," the report stated. "Victims were usually rushed to hospitals in rear, particularly the Hangchow Army Hospital, but cholera victims, usually being treated too late, mostly died." The prisoner saw a report that listed seventeen hundred dead, most of cholera. Actual deaths likely were much higher, he said, "it being common practice to pare down unpleasant figures."

The three-month campaign of terror across Chekiang and Kiangsi Provinces infuriated many in the Chinese military, who understood that local farmers and villagers were raped, murdered, and poisoned as a consequence of America's raid, one designed to lift the spirits of people thousands of miles away in the United States. None of Japan's reprisals were unexpected by officials in either Chungking or Washington, who had purposely withheld details of the raid from Chiang Kai-shek, knowing the Japanese would surely retaliate, a vengeance that claimed an estimated 250,000 lives.

Chiang Kai-shek cabled the horrors to Washington. "After they had been caught unawares by the falling of American bombs on Tokyo, Japanese troops attacked the coastal areas of China, where many of the American fliers had landed. These Japanese troops slaughtered every man, woman and child in those areas," he wrote. "Let me repeat—these Japanese troops slaughtered every man, woman and child in those areas."

Lieutenant General Stilwell received his first report of the destruction in October after one of his aides visited the region. He blamed Chiang Kai-shek and what he viewed as cowardly Chinese forces. "It was even worse than we thought," he wrote in his diary. "A bitched-up action at Ch'u Hsien, buggered completely by the Generalissimo, and then orders to retreat, which were thoroughly carried out. The 'reconquest' was merely reoccupation after the Japs had gone, allowing plenty of time to make sure." Chennault noted that the Japanese had so thoroughly wrecked the airfields at Chuchow, Yushan, and Lishui that it would be easier to build new ones than to repair them. "Entire villages through which the raiders had passed were slaughtered to the last child and burned to the ground. One sizeable city was razed for no other reason than the sentiment displayed by its citizens in filling up

Jap bomb craters on the nearby airfield," he wrote. "The Chinese paid a terrible price for the Doolittle raid, but they never complained."

The slaughter drew some notice in the American media when news trickled out in the spring of 1943 as missionaries who witnessed the atrocities returned home. A few major papers even published editorials, including the *New York Times*. "The Japanese have chosen how they want to represent themselves to the world," the paper wrote. "We shall take them at their own valuation, on their own showing. We shall not forget, and we shall see that a penalty is paid." The *Los Angeles Times* proved far more forceful, calling for vengeance and arguing that the destruction of the Japanese Empire would only partly atone for such atrocities. "To say that these slayings were motivated by cowardice as well as savagery is to say the obvious," the paper argued. "The Nippon war lords have thus proved themselves to be made of the basest metal, and offer considerable evidence that the Japanese race is subhuman. It would be unfair to the lower animals to call it bestial. It might even be libelous to hell to call it demoniac."

CHAPTER 23

═══════════
═══════════

★

I went through ninety-two days of hell and no words
can adequately describe the mental and
physical torture I had to endure.

—W. N. DICKSON, BRIDGE HOUSE PRISONER,
AUGUST 31, 1945, STATEMENT

SKI YORK AND HIS CREW settled in at the new dacha near Penza, anxious to forget the three-week train ride across Siberia. The raiders enjoyed
decent quarters and food, complete with plentiful Russian cigarettes and
vodka. "Most important of all, we were near the capital," Emmens wrote.
"They would probably keep us here a few days and then slip us into Moscow and turn us over to the embassy, or maybe back to Kuibyshev. On the
other hand, this present setup certainly did have an air of permanency
about it. But why the secrecy, and why deny us the right to contact our
own people?"

The raiders adjusted to a daily routine that began at 9:30 a.m. with
breakfast followed by lunch around 1:30 p.m., a late-day snack of tea
and sweet rolls at 6 p.m. and dinner at 9 p.m. Afterward the fliers listened to the radio until midnight. Outside of meals the men played chess
or chatted with the guards and the female housekeepers, attempting to
learn some of the language. Every other day the raiders bathed in a log
hut with a copper tub and two showerheads. "We later learned,"

Emmens recalled, "that the frequency with which we demanded baths astonished them."

In an attempt to keep the airmen busy, the Russians brought movies and a projector, including the local films *Suborov* and a four-hour slog, *Peter the First*, as well as the American movie *One Hundred Men and a Girl*, the 1937 musical comedy staring Deanna Durbin. The Russians likewise provided a small gramophone and phonograph records, allowing the airmen to dance with the housekeepers, who taught them a few folk steps. "Always the thought was in the back of our minds: When?" Emmens recalled. "When will we see someone from our embassy? When will we be leaving?"

The long-awaited answer to that question came on May 24, 1942, with the arrival of Colonel Joseph Michela, the American military attaché, and Edward Page Jr., the second secretary of the embassy. The Russians had alerted the crew of the visit only the night before, prompting the airmen once again to shine boots and clean uniforms. "Now we would find out a lot of things. Had they received any of our messages in the embassy? Had they known we were in Kuibyshev that day we waited all day locked on the train? Would they have news of the rest of the Tokyo raiders?" Emmens later wrote. "And one very important thing—was I a father yet?"

Three cars pulled up around 12:30 p.m., one with the two American diplomats and the others filled with Russian officers. After a brief tour of the dacha Michela suggested the airmen meet privately in York's room.

"How long have you been here?" the attaché began.

The raiders walked him through the six-week ordeal, including the grueling train trip and daylong layover in Kuibyshev in which the airmen had hoped for a visit from embassy personnel. York asked whether the officials even knew the raiders were there.

"We knew you were being moved from the east, but we were told that you had been in Kuibyshev only after you had left there."

The airmen answered the formal questions about the raid that the War Department had requested, and they asked how America planned to get them out of Russia. Michela dodged the question, assuring them that life was far better in Penza than in Moscow, with more available food and freedoms.

"Getting out is not so easy," added Page, jumping into the conversation, no doubt sensing the airmen's frustration. "These people are worried about a war in the east right now. And they are afraid that the Japs might be offended if you are released."

The news sapped the airmen's spirits. In an effort to be more upbeat, Page said the embassy was developing a plan and hoped to have them out in two to three weeks. In the meantime he promised to keep in touch weekly.

The airmen pressed for any information from home, prompting the diplomats to ask Emmens whether he had received the news from his family that the embassy forwarded. Emmens confirmed he had not.

"Congratulations! You have a son!"

Page translated the telegram from Russian: "You have a small, redheaded son. Everyone well including grandmothers. Wish you were here. Love, Justine."

"I wish I had some cigars to pass," a thrilled Emmens told the others.

York asked about the Tokyo raid and the fate of the others, but Michela could offer no concrete details, other than to confirm that Japanese news reports were greatly exaggerated—just as the airmen had suspected.

The diplomats gave them a few boxes of supplies that included a couple of cartons of cigarettes, shirts, socks, soap, and a few magazines collected around the embassy, such as issues of *Collier's*, *Saturday Evening Post*, and *Life*. The raiders passed along letters to family members for the diplomats to mail and asked whether the embassy could send some more toothbrushes and toothpaste.

"In the meantime," the diplomats requested, "keep your eyes open for any bits of intelligence that you can give us."

The report Ambassador Standley forwarded to Secretary of State Hull commended the Russians for how well they had cared for the interned airmen. "Athletic facilities, books, billiards and other distractions are provided; in fact, the Soviet authorities have been most considerate in looking after the crew," Standley wrote on May 25. "The food is better than that obtainable by the Diplomatic Corps in Kuibyshev and the men are accorded about the same freedom of movement as chiefs of mission. They appeared to be in excellent physical and mental condition and stated that they had no complaints as to treatment save that they are urged to eat and drink too much."

May soon gave way to June and then July as the interned crew stewed in the dacha. "We were completely shut up in that house," York would later complain to American authorities. "We were never allowed outside of it." The supplies began to run low. Cigarettes soon vanished—forcing the raiders to roll their own using Russian tobacco and the newspaper *Pravda*—followed by meat. Meat suddenly returned, but then vegetables vanished—all, of course, except cabbage. Even vodka grew scarce as news of the war on the German front only worsened. "Food and cigarette shortages were quite common now. We would go for days without meat or vegetables, or sometimes both," Emmens later wrote. "Some days we had only rice and cabbage."

A Russian newspaper in early August carried a story about twenty-three members of the raid receiving decorations in Washington. The news shocked the crew. "Were there only twenty-three survivors? Or were the rest still overseas?" Emmens later wrote. "The plan had been that all of us would return to the United States immediately following the raid. Twenty-three was a peculiar number to mention. Maybe the article was wrong. We didn't ask the questions because there could be no answer."

The men grew increasingly bored and restless. The plan to have them out in three weeks never materialized, nor did the weekly updates from the embassy, leading the raiders to consider other alternatives.

"What do you think our chances would be of escaping?" York asked Emmens one day as the airmen sat on the dacha's steps.

"I don't know," he replied. "It sure would be a help if we could speak the language."

"I think there is no intention on the part of these people of letting us out of here and therefore no possibility of our own people getting us out," York continued.

"I think you are right."

A German reconnaissance plane appeared one day in the skies high overhead, followed by the thunder of antiaircraft fire from Penza that sent a piece of shrapnel through the dacha's tin roof. Russian antiaircraft guns began to fire regularly as the war moved closer. *Pravda* ran a map in August that showed that Saratov had been bombed, a city not far from Penza. This occurred around the time that an official package arrived with long underwear, a sign that the airmen weren't going home anytime soon.

Mike disappeared for most of the day on August 15, returning that night just as the raiders finished dinner.

"We are leaving," he announced. "We must pack everything right after we have finished eating."

"Where are we going?" York asked.

"You'll find out!"

THE JAPANESE PULLED THE eight captured raiders from the *Green Hornet* and the *Bat out of Hell* from their Tokyo cells on June 16. The wounds on Chase Nielsen's battered shins had long since grown infected, as had the myriad bedbug and lice bites that covered his body after fifty-two days in a filthy cell. For once the navigator wasn't blindfolded, and he stood blinking in the bright sunlight. When his eyes adjusted, he spotted his fellow fliers. The aviators couldn't talk but flashed each other grins and the thumbs-up sign. The Japanese loaded the trussed-up Americans aboard an overnight train south to Nagoya. "The coal soot," DeShazer recalled, "made us look as though we had been living in a pig sty." Guards in Nagoya prodded them up the gangway of a small ship bound for the Chinese port of Shanghai. On their June 19 arrival guards once again blindfolded the aviators and carted them off to the infamous Bridge House jail, better known to most as the "dreaded 'Hell Hole' of Shanghai."

Located off Szechwan Road in the heart of Shanghai, the cream-colored Bridge House served as the headquarters of the Special Service Section of the gendarmerie. The Japanese took over the seven-story stone apartment building in 1937, converting the basement and ground floor into primitive cells made of wood and concrete where "the walls," one captive recalled, "oozed a cold, clammy moisture." Up to forty prisoners crowded into each cell, the only contents a corner bucket that served as a latrine. A single overhead light burned day and night. Guards forbade any talking and forced prisoners to either kneel or sit cross-legged all day. Only at night could the captives lie down, but even then conditions were miserable. "We all slept, most of the men with large pus-filled sores covering their thin-clad bodies, packed like sardines against each other on the hard wooden and damp concrete floor," recalled American Alfred Pattison. "So small was the sleep space that when one man moved all men had to move with him."

Prisoners broiled in the summer heat and froze throughout the winter. A starvation diet of watery rice and a few ounces of bread caused fillings to fall out of teeth, and some inmates suffered vision loss. One Chinese prisoner starved to death after going twenty-five days without food. Filth was another constant. There were no baths, no haircuts, no shaves. Prisoners filed down their fingernails by rubbing them against the concrete walls. The Japanese refused to provide females with sanitary napkins, leaving them with bloodstained legs and dresses that served as a source of endless amusement for the guards. Fleas, lice, and centipedes swarmed the cells, and rats often tugged at the hair of sleeping captives. Disease was rampant, from dysentery and tuberculosis to leprosy. The communal latrine forced others to witness the horrific and untreated venereal diseases some prisoners suffered. "I had no idea when entering Bridge House," recalled one captive, "that I was going to one of the worst prisons in the world." An American intelligence report was more blunt: "it is truly a hell on earth."

"The guards," one captive later testified, "seemed to be have been selected for their callowness and brutality." The Japanese punched one prisoner so hard it drove his dentures into the roof of his mouth, while guards bashed others with rifle butts, hung them up by their thumbs, and bent fingers backward until the digits snapped. Captors used cigarettes to burn the bottoms of hands and feet—some as many as five hundred times—and even shoved them up nostrils. "It isn't so bad," one American would later tell reporters, "because the membranes inside the nose put out the cigarette and you don't feel pain very long."

Some guards jammed metal and chemical spikes under fingernails, set up mock firing squads, and waterboarded prisoners, adding pepper, salt water, and even kerosene to the mix. A few of the tortures were perverse. One of the guards played with a captive's genitals, squeezing his testicles, while others burned the skin off a prisoner's penis and testicles with a cigar. Another prisoner endured iodine poured down his urethra. "The torture chambers were immediately overhead," recalled William Bungey, a British civilian. "We could hear the cries of the victims day and night." "The screams," added another, "were so terrifying that I had to put my fingers into my ears to try not to hear."

"Are you a Christian?" one of the torturers asked an American prisoner, who answered in the affirmative. "Then let's see if your God can help you now."

The Japanese burned a cross on the prisoner's chest with a cigarette.

A British employee of Shanghai Telephone Company, Henry Pringle, endured 114 days at the Bridge House in 1942, during which time he suffered one of the prison's more notorious forms of torture. "I was seized and strapped down on two benches," Pringle would later tell war crimes investigators. "Three pairs of handcuffs were used to secure my feet to the benches and thin cords were used to tie down my body and arms. My shirt was then opened and water was sprayed over my stomach, face and chest, after which the man named Suzuki applied an electrical shocking electrode to my body, one electrode being placed on my navel and the other alternately on the nipples, lips, throat, ears, nose and head. The pain was excruciating. My torturers seemed to be highly amused at my cries and contortions as they roared with laughter."

American journalist John Powell, the editor of *China Weekly Review*, spent five months there after the outbreak of the war. His weight plummeted from 145 pounds to just 70, while his bare feet froze and turned gangrenous, forcing doctors to later amputate both up to the heels. "I wouldn't say it was terrible," Powell said upon his release. "We got off with our lives." Not everyone would be so lucky, including British officer William Hutton, imprisoned in a nearby interrogation substation at 94 Jessfield Road. The Japanese beat him, stripped him naked, and hogtied him so tight the cords bit into his flesh. Hutton went mad in just two weeks. "He was in a pitiable condition, stark and staring, filthy and stank," recalled fellow prisoner John Watson. "Hutton was dripping saliva at the mouth, trying to imitate various animals."

He died two days later.

To the eight captured Tokyo raiders, Bridge House was now home. The Japanese forced the new arrivals into cell no. 6, already packed with fifteen other prisoners of various races and nationalities. Guards would move the others out after several days—no doubt to isolate the raiders as well as limit knowledge of their presence. Until then, the exhausted airmen searched out spots to sit on the floor of the filthy cell, which measured barely twelve feet by fifteen feet. The poor health of the other prisoners shocked the airmen. "A Jap and a Chinese were on the floor, nearly dead from dysentery," Nielsen later wrote. "It was impossible to sleep. We simple leaned against each other and tried to rest."

Allied prisoners in neighboring cells were anxious to learn more about new arrivals, all but one of whom appeared to stand well over six feet tall. The men were clearly aviators, dressed in khaki trousers and windbreakers. All sported heavy beards; some of the prisoners would recall George Barr's bright red hair.

Frederick Opper, an associate editor with the *Shanghai Evening Post* who had languished in the Bridge House since March, listened as the newcomers attempted to make conversation with others in the neighboring cell.

"What's Shanghai like?" he heard one of the men ask. "I always wanted to see it but not this way."

The next morning guards led the new prisoners to a spigot outside. Prisoners in nearby cells struggled for a glimpse. As the raiders walked past Opper's cell, one used his hand to imitate a bomber, swooping down just as he said "Tokyo."

"We grinned cheerfully and gave them a thumbs up signal," Opper later wrote. "They grinned back, about the sole means of communication we had."

Since the raiders had already confessed, the Japanese spared them the torture other prisoners endured but little else of Bridge House's misery and discomfort. "The building was infested with rats, centipedes, lice, bed bugs, fleas, every other kind of bug that walked, crawled or jumped," Nielsen recalled, noting that the rats soon proved to be the worst. "We maintained a guard at night to keep them from biting us. They'd crawl into our cell, big fellows and awfully bold. We didn't try to kill them because we were afraid they'd crawl away and die, and that would make the stench worse. One big female rat had a lot of little ones and we used to watch them crawling around."

Guards liked to wake up the raiders at night and force them to stand. Other times the airmen witnessed them beat fellow prisoners. One even hit Bobby Hite once with a sheathed sword. "It was the first time that I had ever been in such a wicked environment," DeShazer recalled. "There is bad in America, but the bad in America does not begin to compare with that which we observed." The distress was exacerbated each night when the raiders heard American music waft across the bustling city, the same popular tunes the fliers would have heard that last night in San Francisco at the Top of the Mark. Tears welled up in Hite when he heard the song "Smoke Gets in Your Eyes." "It was hard to take," he recalled, "and think that here we were, we could hear music like that, and then to realize where we were and what had happened to us."

Days turned into weeks and then months as the fliers wallowed in filth. Hite reminded Farrow that he had invited him to join his crew. "Bill, I don't know," Hite told him one day. "Maybe I shouldn't have come with you." The fliers were at least thankful to be together. "We would have gone stark mad if it were not for the opportunity to talk," Nielsen later wrote, though the airmen had to be careful not to be overheard. "We talked plenty. We used to talk about football and baseball and things we'd done in our lives, and we talked about food. Brother, how we talked about food. We'd plan meals we'd order if we ever got out—thick, juicy steaks and plenty of pie and ice cream." The uncertain future prompted deeper discussions. "We talked a lot about religion," Nielsen recalled. "A fellow thinks a lot about God at a time like that."

Diarrhea coupled with a diet of wormy soup and stale bread continued to weaken the airmen, many of whom soon developed beriberi, a painful thiamine deficiency caused by malnutrition. Hite found that he could press on his leg and leave a dimple in the muscle; another one of the airmen went seventeen days without a bowel movement. Dysentery hit Dean Hallmark hard in the middle of August. "He had no control over his bowels whatsoever and he could hold nothing in his stomach," Nielsen said. "We had to continuously help him. He was just at a state where he didn't know he was there or what was going on."

The men had lost so much weight and body fat that sitting for hours on the hard wooden floors proved painful, causing boils to erupt on their hips. To help comfort Hallmark, who was ravaged by aches and fever, the men took turns holding his head in their laps. "He wanted me to sing songs to him," Hite recalled. "He wanted to remember all of the tunes and things that he had heard through the years."

Faced with their precarious fate, the raiders scratched a message on the wall of cell no. 6, one that a British prisoner would later commit to memory and relate to investigators upon his release in August 1945:

"Notify Chief of Army Air Corps, Washington, D.C."

American B-25
Detachment

D. Hallmark
W. Farrow
R. Meder
R. Hite
G. Barr
C. Nielsen
J. DeShazer
H. Spatz

We crashed!"

The Japanese finally came for them on August 28, after the airmen had endured seventy days in Bridge House. Hallmark was by then too weak even to walk, so Billy Farrow and Bobby Hite carried him out on a stretcher, loading the Texan into the back of a truck. The Japanese transported the handcuffed raiders to Kiangwan Military Prison on the outskirts of Shanghai.

Guards marched the fliers into a courtroom that measured approximately thirty feet by sixty at about 2:30 p.m. Lieutenant Colonel Toyoma Nakajo, who served as chief judge of the Thirteenth Army military tribunal, perched behind a desk on a dais. On either side sat associate judges First Lieutenant Yusei Wako and Second Lieutenant Ryuhei Okada. Prosecutor Major Itsuro Hata and a court reporter flanked the judges, while armed guards stood watch in the rear and at the doors along both sides of the courtroom.

Hallmark remained on his stretcher, his condition so poor that Nielsen suspected he didn't know what was happening. "The flies buzzed around and covered his face," the navigator recalled. "He was too weak to brush them away."

George Barr likewise was so exhausted that he collapsed, prompting the Japanese to provide the red-haired navigator a chair. The other six airmen stood, but after seventy days in a cell, they all struggled with balance.

The airmen were not provided with any defense counsel or allowed to call any witnesses. No one even informed them of the charges against them or offered them the opportunity to enter a plea. "As a matter of fact," Nielsen would later tell war crimes investigators, "we didn't even know it was a court martial."

The judges ordered each man to describe his education and military training. The airmen mumbled through. Fellow prisoner Caesar Luis Dos Remedios, whose father was Portuguese and mother Japanese, served as the translator.

Barely half an hour into the proceedings Hata made his brief closing argument. "It is evident that they are guilty in a view of military law," the prosecutor said. "Therefore I request that the penalty be death."

All three judges agreed.

"What is it?" Nielsen asked the interpreter of the punishment.

"The judge has ordered that you not be told of your sentence."

Guards ushered the seven healthier prisoners into cells no. 2 through no. 8 at Kiangwan Military Prison, while Hallmark returned alone to cell no. 6 at Bridge House, now occupied mostly by Chinese and a few Russian prisoners. His health continued to deteriorate. Dysentery had reduced Hallmark's five-foot-eleven-inch frame to a skeleton; his eyes were sunken and his cheekbones protruded above his filthy beard. He spent his days lying on the floor, dependent upon fellow prisoners to lift him onto the latrine. "His bowels," recalled his cellmate Alexander Hindrava, "would just move themselves." When pressed by war crime investigators to describe Hallmark's weight, Hindrava would later note that he weighed "only as much as his bones."

The seven other raiders settled into individual cells at Kiangwan that measured five feet wide and nine deep, with floors made of wood, walls of concrete, and a single window eight feet off the ground. A hole in the corner served as the latrine. Prisoners had a grass mat and several blankets to sleep on—albeit infested with lice and fleas—while rations consisted of white rice and soup three times a day. Each man was allowed a bath once a week and a haircut every thirty to forty-five days, though the fliers still wore the same tattered uniforms from the mission. Guards allowed the raiders to be outside for half an hour a day, but the weakened men had little energy for exercise. "We had nothing to read, no one to talk to, nothing to write with," recalled Hite and DeShazer. "Torture isn't limited to physical punishment. Solitary confinement in a filthy little cell can be more horrible than even the most fiendish physical torments."

As the raiders languished in prison, Japanese military leaders wrestled with the question of their punishment. Ten days after the attack Hideki Tojo sat down with his senior military leaders to determine what to do with the airmen. Tensions ran high. Admiral Osami Nagano, the

Navy chief of staff, had watched the attack unfold in Tokyo. "This shouldn't happen," he declared at the time. "This simply should not happen." Despite the government's best efforts to play down the raid, many in the general public remained outraged, firing off angry letters to the Navy that only added to the combustible situation and made Captain Yoshitake Miwa take to his diary to question the patriotism of such individuals: "Should they deserve to be Japanese?" In the April 30 election one anonymous voter went so far as to cast his ballot for Doolittle over Tojo, jotting down on his ballot, "North American Aircraft, Banzai!"

General Hajime Sugiyama, the Army chief of staff, humiliated that Japanese forces had failed to shoot down a single bomber, had fumed over the attack, going so far as to threaten to court-martial every single air-defense commander. For Sugiyama the question of what to do with the captured airmen had an easy answer: execute them all. He made that demand directly to Emperor Hirohito, who reprimanded him. Sugiyama likewise pressed his case to Tojo, who also found the raid reprehensible. "It was not against troops but against non-combatants, primary school students, and so forth," Tojo later said. "We knew this, and since this was not permitted by international law, it was homicide." Despite that view, the war minister was reluctant to execute the raiders, even as he understood the intense public pressure that the attack had provoked. "This was the first time Japan had been bombed," Tojo testified after the war. "It was a great shock. Public feeling ran very high."

Others shared Tojo's reluctance, including Sugiyama's subordinate Lieutenant General Moritake Tanabe, though the vice chief of the general staff would later change his mind, no doubt under pressure. Lieutenant General Heitaro Kimura, the vice minister of war, likewise agreed with Tojo, fearing that such executions would only jeopardize the welfare of Japanese residents in the United States. Top commanders on the ground in China—Lieutenant General Shigeru Sawada of the Thirteenth Army and General Shunroku Hata of the China Expeditionary Army— also voiced opposition, maintaining the airmen should be afforded the rights of prisoners of war. Not everyone was even convinced that the civilian deaths were intentional. Major General Ryukichi Tanaka singled out the case of the shooting of a primary school student. "I believe it was due to a mistake," he later said. "That is, the plane took that child for a soldier or something."

Tojo's meeting on Tuesday, April 28, adjourned without a decision. Sugiyama pressed forward with his plan to try the raiders in China before a military commission. General Hata not only opposed such a plan but went so far as to tell his aides that he would be as lenient as possible on the raiders. He directed his chief of staff to spell out his concerns in a letter to the vice chief of the general staff. Rather than simply write back, Sugiyama dispatched an emissary, Colonel Arisue. The colonel made it clear that Sugiyama not only demanded a trial but expected the death sentence. "Arisue was sent," Tanaka recalled, "to notify Hata that he was to do as he was ordered and that no theory or logic on his part with reference to this case would be accepted by Tokyo." Staff officer Colonel Masatoshi Miyano echoed Tanaka. "At no time were we permitted or were we in any position to either alter or change any of those decisions or to offer our own recommendations," he said. "Tokyo assumed control of the entire matter."

Japan had failed to ratify the 1929 Geneva Convention, which would have provided the airmen the traditional rights of prisoners of war. At the same time it had no legal mechanism to carry out Sugiyama's demands. In an effort to punish Doolittle's men and discourage any future raids, legal experts that summer drafted the Military Law Concerning the Punishment of Enemy Airmen, or what would more commonly be known as the Enemy Airmen's Act. In a July 28 message to Hata's chief of staff, Sugiyama's staff asked for a delay in the airmen's trial—and the scheduling of the subsequent execution—to make sure the law could be put in place. The ex post facto law, which went into effect on August 13, stipulated that any enemy airman who killed civilians or even destroyed private property in an air raid over Japan or its territories could be shot. As soon as the judges handed down the death sentence, Sugiyama went back to Tojo and demanded that the airmen's executions be carried out immediately.

Tojo remained reluctant to execute all eight of the airmen. He decided to go over Sugiyama's head. On October 3 the war minister went to see the emperor, pleading his case to Hirohito's senior adviser Koichi Kido, who recorded the conversation in his diary. "At 11:30 Premier Tojo came to see me in my room and requested me to inform the Emperor regarding the details of the treatment of American prisoners who participated in the raid last April 18th," Kido wrote. "From 1:05 to 1:15 I reported to the Emperor as Premier Tojo requested." Tojo's message, as he later related in an affidavit for the war crime trials, was to compromise: "Being fully aware of His Majesty's gracious concern on such matters, I, as the War Minister, after an informal report to the Throne," he wrote, "took measures to have the death penalty of five of the prisoners commuted."

The Japanese worked out a precise plan over the next week, spelled out in a message dated October 10 from Sugiyama to Hata. Hallmark, Farrow, and Spatz would be shot, whereas the death sentences of Hite, Nielsen, Barr, Meder, and DeShazer would be reduced. "The five whose death sentences are commuted are hereby sentenced to life imprisonment. They are adjudged war criminals and as such should receive no consideration as prisoners of war," the orders stated. "In no case will they be repatriated as prisoners of war in the event of an exchange of prisoners."

The job of carrying out the execution fell to Sotojiro Tatsuta, Kiangwan's warden and chief guard. Tatsuta had grown up in a poor family in Ishikawa Prefecture, on the western coast of Honshu, concluding his education after only primary school. He joined the Army in 1923 as a court reporter and worked his way up by 1938 to the post of warden. Over the course of the war the father of four—two sons and two daughters—would participate in as many as fifty executions. He now set out to prepare the logistics for one of those. On October 14 Tatsuta ordered workers in the carpentry shop of the Thirteenth Army's regimental headquarters to build three crosses and then three coffins.

By that point, Hallmark was over the worst of his dysentery, though he still needed help just to stand and use the latrine; he was so swollen, in fact, that it was impossible to distinguish the last three toes on his feet. He repeatedly told fellow captives that if only he could leave Bridge House and go to a proper prisoner-of-war camp his health would improve. The same day workers started on the crosses, guards appeared at Hallmark's cell door to transport him to Kiangwan. Fellow prisoners helped him out; he felt his prayers had finally been answered. That evening with the help of Remedios the warden directed Hallmark, Farrow, and Spatz to sign several sheets of blank paper that would serve as receipts for the airmen's belongings. Tatsuta then gave them additional paper on which to write final letters to loved ones back home, letters that would never be mailed. Though handwritten originals would vanish, investigators after the war would find translated copies of the airmen's final farewells.

Hallmark wrote to his parents and sister in Dallas. He had left Bridge House that day, believing his horrible ordeal was about to improve. Now he learned that within hours he would be shot. His shock over the sudden course of events showed. "I hardly know what to say," the twenty-eight-year-old wrote. "They have just told me that I am liable to execution. I can hardly believe it. I am at a complete loss for words." Hallmark asked his parents to please share the news of his fate with his friends. Even in his final hours he worried about his parents, particularly his mother, to whom he had once confided in a telegram, "All that I am or hope to be I owe to you." "Mother you try to stand up under this and pray. And Dad you do the same and sister," he now wrote. "I don't know how to end this letter but will end by sending you all my love."

Spatz wrote to his father in Kansas. His was the shortest of all the letters; just six sentences that barely totaled more than a hundred words. The twenty-one-year-old gunner told his father that he was entitled to all his personal property, which amounted to only his clothes. "I want you to know that I died fighting for my country like a soldier," Spatz wrote. "I love you and may God bless you."

Farrow's letters were the most upbeat. The South Carolina native, whose father had once warned him that he lived in "a cold, hard cruel world," had long struggled with life's challenges, a fact that made him particularly protective of his family. "We've both been cheated of a decent home through our beloved drunken rot of a father," he once wrote to his sister. "I'd fight a duel or walk through fire for you." Farrow's self less instincts returned as he encouraged his mother and family to remain strong. "Here's wishing you, Marge, all the family, and Lib a most happy future—please carry on for me—don't let this get you down. Just remember that God will make everything right, and that I will see you all again hereafter," the twenty-four-year-old wrote. "Life has treated us well as a whole, and we have much to be thankful for. You are, all of you, splendid Christians, and knowing and loving you has meant much in my life. So for me, and for America, be brave, and live a full, rich life, pray to God, and do your best."

Farrow dedicated the final paragraphs of his three-page letter to his mother. "I know, Mom, that this is going to hit you hard, because I was the biggest thing in your life—I say I am sorry not to have treated you with more love and devotion, for not giving you all that I could, and will you please forgive me? It is usually too late that we realize these things," he wrote. "You are, I realize now, the best Mother in the world, that your every action was bent toward making me happy, that you are, and always will be, a real angel. So let me implore you to keep your chin up, like you wrote in your last letter that I always did—be brave and strong, for my sake. I love you, Mom, from the depths of a full heart." He ended with the practical news that she could find his insurance policy in his bag. "My faith in God is complete," he concluded, "so I am unafraid."

Farrow also penned a letter to his beloved aunt, Margaret Stem, whom he knew simply as Marge. "Well, here we've come to the parting of our ways for the present. But you have helped give me faith to go forward with steadfast heart—I've built my house upon a rock. That we will meet again, I am sure," he wrote. "All will be right in the end." In another letter Farrow asked his best friend, Ivan Ferguson, to cherish the good times the young men shared. "Do you remember Spokane and Glacier Park, and what we said about a place full of so much that is good and beautiful—what it's worth to us? And Crater Lake, Oregon Caves, the giant Sequoias, the Golden Gate—how splendid they were? And the thrill of flying—that we experienced together too—it was the most wonderful part of my career. So—keep 'em flying, Fergie, and remember me to all the guys in the squadron." He closed by asking his friend to do him a final favor and reach out and help comfort his mother. "She will need your sympathy."

Farrow addressed his final letter to his red-haired, green-eyed girl-friend of two years, Elizabeth "Lib" Sims, whom he had once described in a note to his sister as so "full of pep." "You are to me the only girl that would have meant the condition of my life. I have realized the kind of life being married to you would have meant to me and to both of us, and I know we would have found complete happiness. It is a pity we were born in this day and age. At least we had part of that happiness," he wrote. "I go over each time we were with each other, the lovely nights at your home before the fireplace; the never-to-be-forgotten weekend spent at Caroline's; your balalaika played so many times; the flights we took at Columbia and at Augusta where you no doubt learned to love flying; the meals we had together; the walks in the woods, enjoying the fresh air and the smell of growing things; all these times were the greatest pleasure to me." Farrow closed with what was no doubt a painful yet unselfish final wish that she move on with her life. "Find yourself the good man you deserve, Lib, because you have so much to give the right one," Farrow wrote. "Goodbye and may God be with you."

Farrow entrusted Remedios with the few personal belongings he had managed to hold on to since he jumped from the *Bat out of Hell*, including his Social Security and American Red Cross cards and eleven signed Bank of America travelers checks, in ten-dollar denominations. Lastly, he slipped him the photograph of a girl.

AROUND 10 A.M. ON October 15 Tatsuta visited Public Cemetery no. 1 accompanied by several guards to prepare the grounds for the afternoon's execution. Shigeji Mayama cut the grass while Yoneya Tomoichi planted the three crosses made from fresh lumber in front of the ruins of a Chinese temple. Tatsuta instructed the workers to erect a stand to hold incense burners and flowers.

Guards came for Hallmark, Farrow, and Spatz that afternoon, ordering them to leave their personal belongings behind. The Japanese ushered the exhausted and emaciated fliers from the prison to several waiting trucks, transporting them the few miles to the cemetery, which overlooked a fairway golf course and stood opposite the race track. Four staff cars sat parked outside the gate.

The record of the execution included four official witnesses: chief prosecutor Colonel Akinobu Ito, clerk Chosei Fujita, medical officer Lieutenant Maruo Masutani, and interpreter Yasutoshio Miura. In addition, Ito invited more than half a dozen spectators, including a few officers with the Shanghai Military Police and several medical officers and corpsmen. Associate Judge Yusei Wako, who had sentenced the raiders, also showed up to watch. Several guards patrolled the cemetery grounds as security.

The medical officer pronounced the three raiders fit for execution, including Hallmark, who was still so weak he needed help to go to the bathroom. Major Itsuro Hata, the prosecutor, informed the fliers through an interpreter he was there to carry out the order of execution and told them to die like brave soldiers. He then bowed.

"I do not know what relation I had with you in the previous life but we have been living together under the same roof," Tatsuta told them. "On this day you are going to be executed, but I feel sorry for you. My sympathies are with you. Men must die sooner or later. Your lives were very short but your names will remain everlasting."

"Please tell the folks at home that we died very bravely," Tatsuta recalled Farrow requesting.

The warden informed the airmen that in a moment guards would bind them to the three crosses in preparation for execution. "Christ was born and died on the cross and you on your part must die on the cross," Tatsuta added, "but when you are executed—when you die on the cross you will be honored as Gods."

Tatsuta concluded by asking the raiders to pray as he made the sign of the cross. He asked whether the men had any final words.

None did.

Guards escorted the raiders to the crosses and forced them to turn around and kneel. The Japanese tied each flier's forearm and upper arm with new white cloths to keep them from falling over once shot. Tatsuta helped secure Spatz to the cross on the left while others tied Hallmark to the center cross and Farrow to the one on the right. The Japanese then placed a white cloth around the airmen's heads, each with a black dot drawn to mark the center of the forehead just above the nose.

First Lieutenant Goyo Tashima commanded the firing squad, which consisted of one noncommissioned officer and nine enlisted men. Six of the soldiers were designated as riflemen with two assigned to each raider—one a primary shooter, the other secondary. The other three enlisted men served as security guards.

"Attention," Tashima demanded. "Face to the target."

The rifleman turned toward the fliers just twenty meters away.

"Prepare."

Tashima watched as the firing squad members kneeled and took aim. He raised his arm and then dropped it as he shouted his final order.

"Fire!"

All three guns roared.

Hallmark, Farrow, and Spatz slumped forward.

"The men who fired were all expert marksmen," Tatsuta testified, "and only fired one shot each."

Tashima ordered the firing squad to cease fire and about face. He directed them to march forward, stop, and remove the spent cartridges.

The medical examiner checked each raider to make sure he was dead, later telling Tatsuta that he detected a slight pulse, though only briefly before each expired. The doctor certified the deaths and bandaged the wounds before guards laid the bodies in the caskets side by side in front of the dais. The Japanese saluted them.

Tatsuta ordered the bodies of the dead airmen taken to the Japanese Residents Association Crematorium. He planned to hang on to Hallmark's leather flying jacket, ordering Remedios to have his name removed from the coat and to find a tailor in Shanghai who could cut it down to fit him.

FOUR DAYS AFTER THE execution of Hallmark, Farrow, and Spatz, Radio Tokyo announced the "capture, trial, and severe punishment" of an unspecified number of raiders, claiming the airmen had intentionally attacked nonmilitary targets and civilians. The Japanese listed the names of only four of the captured airmen—Hallmark, Farrow, Spatz, and DeShazer—though it reported that all had confessed to bombing hospitals and shooting children. "I saw school kids playing around a building which looked like a grammar school," the broadcast quoted Farrow as having said. "I felt I might as well give the Jap kids a taste of bullets while I was at it. So I dived down toward them and machine-gunned them. I felt sorry for them, but hell, ain't they enemy kids?"

News that any of the raiders had been captured—much less punished—shocked the American press and the nation. Though Doolittle had informed the families of the captured airmen, he had requested in each of his May letters that the news remain a secret. Rumors that at least a few of the raiders had been captured had circulated among reporters, but the nation at large had assumed that all the airmen had safely escaped. The Japanese looked to exploit America's secrecy, using the fate of the raiders as a wedge to drive between the government and the people. "The American public has a right to know the extent to which they are being treated in the official announcement," Tokyo broadcast. "Two facts are laid before the public. One is that the United States War Department on October 20 flatly denied that any of their airmen had been made prisoners in Japan. The other is that the United States War Department, in a cablegram dated August 19, inquired of the International Red Cross headquarters in Yokohama requesting that they send the name of the eight missing men. Let the public judge."

Japan in another particularly cruel broadcast urged any doubters to seek out the families of two of the captured raiders. "For those who are skeptical, these observers suggested that they enquire as to the present whereabouts of 21-year-old Robert Hite and Lieutenant William G. Farrow," the English-language broadcast announced. "Next of kin of these men, who are but part of the captured crew, should make all efforts to obtain a satisfactory reply from the United States War Department."

The press initially questioned whether such broadcasts were bogus, but American leaders knew the ruse was up. At an October 22 press conference War Secretary Henry Stimson confirmed that the four names Tokyo broadcast were raiders, but made no mention of any other captive airmen, an omission Japan exploited days later when it dribbled out the names of the others in what the United Press described as a "sly propaganda campaign." The government's decision to withhold the fact that Japan had captured some of the raiders drew a sharp rebuke from some in the media, including syndicated columnist Raymond Clapper. "The news is released just now, after Tokyo breaks it," he wrote. "There was no news in that to be withheld from the enemy. It was withheld only from the American people, who have been as much interested in the Tokio raid as in any one thing we have done in this war. Some of our officials call this a people's war. It would help if we also considered this an American people's war."

Reporters hungered for information about the captured fliers, a void Washington columnist David Lawrence soon filled by offering up a personal testimony from Billy Farrow. One of the pilot's close friends had held on to a memo Farrow wrote to himself in 1940 when he decided to go into aviation, titled simply "My Future." The South Carolinian, who had once meticulously logged instructions on the front flap of his algebra notebook, had likewise taken stock of his life. "The time has come to decide what rules I am going to set myself for daily conduct," Farrow wrote. "First I must enumerate my weaknesses and seek to eliminate them. Then I must seek to develop the qualities I need for this type of work. It's going to be hard, but it's the only way. Work with a purpose is the only practical means of achieving an end."

Farrow unflinchingly charted his flaws, ranging from a lack of curiosity and sober thought to lapses in self-confidence. He then outlined strengths he hoped to build upon, from his health to his faith. "Stay close to God—do His will and commandments. He is my friend and protector," he wrote. "Fear nothing—be it insanity, sickness, failure—always be upright—look the world in the eye." Lawrence's column listing each of Farrow's twenty-one bullet points ran in newspapers nationwide just seven days after the Japanese forced him to kneel, tied him to a cross, and shot him in the forehead. The young flier from the tiny town of Darlington represented any one of the millions of soldiers, sailors, airmen, and marines who over the course of the war would fight in every corner of the globe, from the deserts of North Africa to the jungles of Guadalcanal. "He was neither poet nor scholar," Lawrence wrote, "but just a lieutenant in the U.S. Air Corps."

Letters of support arrived at Farrow's mother's home from as far away as New York, Georgia, and Ohio. Churches across the country seized on the young airman's inspirational message, publishing it in Sunday bulletins, while businesses such as Minnesota's Northwestern National Life Insurance Company churned out patriotic pamphlets with headlines like "An American's Creed for Victory." Students at Henry Snyder High School in Jersey City gazed up at posters plastered on classroom walls that carried Farrow's message, and the University of South Carolina's president, J. Rion McKissick, turned the creed into a speech for the 1943 graduating class at the raider's alma mater. "No matter what has happened to my boy, I know he has served a wonderful purpose in the war," Jessie Farrow told reporters. "My son is an average American willing to face life fearlessly and die for ideals of right and freedom."

The United States meanwhile scrambled to determine what punishments the Japanese had meted out, only to learn the unfortunate news in a note passed through the Swiss on February 23, 1943, accusing the airmen of purposely bombing schools, hospitals, and crowds of civilians. "What may be more stigmatized," the note stated, "is the fact that they wounded and killed little innocent school children who played in the grounds of their school by machine gunning, deliberately mowing them down although recognizing them as such." Because the airmen had allegedly confessed to intentionally targeting civilians, the Japanese refused them the protections traditionally afforded to prisoners of war. "The American Government will understand that such persons are unpardonable as enemies of humanity," the Japanese wrote. "The guilt of such persons having been established by court inquiry, the death penalty was pronounced according to martial law. However, following commutation [of] punishment granted as special measure to larger part condemned, sentence of death was applied only to certain of accused."

Roosevelt refused to inform the public even as the State Department struggled to decide how best to handle the crisis, a job that initially fell to Assistant Secretary of State Breckinridge Long, who drafted a detailed memo of America's options: "The full texts of the Japanese note concerning the execution of some of the Doolittle fliers now having been received and studied leaves no room for the doubt I hoped would exist that it was not a definite and positive statement that they had been executed." The first option on Long's list: "proceed immediately to retaliate by executing a comparable number of Japanese officer prisoners of war in our custody." He went on to rule out the scenario, doubting it would have any effect on the Japanese government other than to spur it to retaliate, a dangerous proposition since the fall of the Philippines had led to the capture of many Americans. "I am not unmindful of the fact that the Japanese hold 18,000 of our prisoners and we a few handfuls of theirs," he wrote, though the number of American military and civilian prisoners was actually much higher. "It is true we hold many of their civilians but I am differentiating between civilians and prisoners of war."

Long proposed that the government could publish the note and inform the American people, though he questioned whether that would only inflame the anxiety of the captured airmen's families as well as spark a backlash against people of Japanese descent. More importantly, America had only weeks earlier made a request to exchange forty-five hundred prisoners. "Any deterioration in that situation," he wrote, "would be deplorable if there is a chance for the exchange to be effectuated." The plan Long advocated was for the United States to make a strong protest and demand that the Swiss determine the names and locations of those alive and the details related to the execution of the others. He added that America could include a "statement to the effect that this is such a barbaric departure from the rules of civilized warfare and such a violation of the definite agreements which Japan undertook in connection with prisoners of war that we reserve the right, though delaying its use until further information is received, to retaliate by the execution of an equal number of officer prisoners of war in our hands."

Long ordered a draft protest readied by noon of March 22, recommending in the meantime that the United States withhold all information. "Until we know the exact number of prisoners involved in the execution, we are not in a position to announce the names or give publicity to the execution or to retaliate in kind—if retaliation should be decided upon." Officials inside the State Department prepared a seven-page letter accusing Japan of violating the Geneva Convention and extorting confessions from the airmen through "bestial methods." "If, as would appear from its communication under reference, the Japanese Government has descended to such acts of barbarity and manifestations of depravity as to murder in cold blood uniformed members of the American armed forces made prisoners as an incident of warfare," the State Department wrote, "the American government will hold personally and officially responsible for those deliberate crimes all of those officers of the Japanese Government who have participated in their commitment and will in due course bring those officers to justice."

Secretary of State Cordell Hull presented the protest to Roosevelt for approval on April 7. "Questions of retaliation had been considered and discarded with the consent of the War and Navy Departments," Hull wrote. "The supporting memorandum and the green telegram raise questions of the highest policy in the conduct of war and I must submit it you for your consideration and approval." The president read the protest, writing at the end of the last page, "OK, FDR." Roosevelt sent an accompanying memo back to Hull the next day. "I am deeply stirred and horrified by the execution of American aviators," he wrote. "In view of the severe tone of this note and especially of the warning in the last paragraph that we propose to retaliate on Japanese prisoners in our hands, I can see no reason for delaying a public announcement on my part. The note to the Japanese Government is so strong that it will not further hurt the persons of Americans now in their custody—civilians and members of the armed forces if I give out the full facts, together with a copy or paraphrase of the note."

Roosevelt misinterpreted the final paragraph of the protest, which stated only that the United States would "visit upon the officers of the Japanese Government responsible for such uncivilized and inhumane acts the punishment they deserve." An unsigned April 9 memo on White House stationery pointed out his error: "Our note to Japan did not threaten retaliation—but punishment of Jap officers guilty of executing U.S. prisoners of war." The president suggested going public with the news of the execution of the raiders the following Tuesday, though he found the State Department's proposed public announcement insufficiently strong or comprehensive. "Please let me have a redraft of it which will be less official and more human."

The Japanese once again looked to scoop the American government as the raid's anniversary neared. Elmer Davis, the Office of War Information director, announced at an April 14 press conference plans to release the full story of the raid within days.

"Will we be told where Shangri La really is?" a reporter pressed.

Davis confirmed with a smile.

Two days later he had to reverse himself. "After consultation with the War Department this office finds that clearance of the Tokyo raid story has not been completed," the director of war information announced. "It is impossible to predict at present a date when this story will be released."

Many in the media howled over the government's continued secrecy, including the *New York Times*. "The Japanese captured some of the American fliers," the paper wrote. "It is altogether probable that the Japanese Government now knows much more about the details of the Tokyo bombing than the American public has been permitted to know. In justice to the magnificent exploit of the men who participated, as well as in justice to our own public, which is always entitled to know at least as much as the enemy knows, the full story of that daring raid ought now to be told."

The Japanese seized on the opening, releasing a detailed and largely accurate report of the raid's planning, execution, and conclusion, down to the precise number of airmen and bombers involved. "I take pleasure," Major General Nakao Yahagi, chief of the Japanese Imperial Headquarters Army press section, told reporters, "in telling the people of the United States the full story." The Japanese not only revealed the *Hornet* as Shangri-La, but even singled out Stephen Jurika's intelligence briefings en route to Tokyo. The Japanese did mix some fact with fiction, claiming to have shot down many of the planes and accusing Doolittle of being so scared that he fled to China without ever dropping his bombs. "We have the pleasure of conferring upon him the title 'Did Little,'" Yahagi's report stated. "We may expect the next commander which Roosevelt is likely to appoint as his successor will be Colonel 'Do Nothing.'"

America had no choice but to counter with its own version, an eleven-page press release that many newspapers printed verbatim and that the Japanese ridiculed as a hurried and "patched-up production" designed to camouflage a "flop raid." The way both countries fought to control the narrative reflected the major effect the raid had for leaders in Japan and in America, a surprise given how truly insignificant the attack was compared with the raids that would dominate the war's final months. Japan's humiliated leaders still smarted over the audacity of the attack and hoped to deflate American enthusiasm for what had proven an early victory in the war, particularly now that Japan had suffered a reversal of fortunes in losses in the Coral Sea, Midway, and the Solomon Islands. American leaders, by contrast, had built up a mythology about the raid, exaggerating its success, which Japan's continued challenges only undermined.

The release of the information placed American leaders once again in a tough spot. The military had told the public when Doolittle received the Medal of Honor that all of the planes had escaped safely, but later had to admit that at least eight of the pilots had landed in Japanese captivity. Now American leaders confessed that, with the exception of the one aircrew that diverted to Russia, the United States had lost all fifteen of the other bombers. Few disputed the need for secrecy in war, but the government's carefully crafted releases designed to deceive infuriated many. "The American people will never forget that Tokyo was raided, but at the same time they will never forget that they were fooled," argued the *News*, the daily paper in Lynchburg, Virginia. "Not uninformed of what happened, but intentionally and with purpose fooled." Even some members of Congress protested. "I believe that any government is playing with dynamite when it tricks its own people," argued Representative Walter Judd of Minnesota. "We do not want soothing syrup; we want to be treated as grown-up free men and women."

The battered White House struggled to regain the public relations advantage over Japan—and rally the nation. Hours after the release of the raid's details, Roosevelt issued a statement while on a tour of military posts in Texas. He admitted that the United States had learned weeks earlier that Japan had executed several of the captured raiders and ordered the State Department to release its April protest. "It is with a feeling of deepest horror, which I know will be shared with all civilized peoples, that I have to announce the barbarous execution by the Japanese Government of some of the members of this country's armed forces who fell into Japanese hands as an incident of warfare," the president said. "This recourse by our enemies to frightfulness is barbarous. The effort of the Japanese warlords to intimidate us will utterly fail. It will make the American people more determined than ever to blot out the shameless militarism of Japan."

The strong response from the normally relaxed and jovial commander in chief shocked some in the media. "President Roosevelt has issued the most powerfully worded statement of his whole career," proclaimed Robert St. John of NBC. "The statement is full of strong, red blooded words. Call them hate words, if you will."

The reaction from members of Congress proved equally fierce. A few lawmakers went so far as to demand like reprisals, while others insisted America dedicate more resources to the war in the Pacific.

"We are fighting a bunch of beasts," argued Representative John Rankin of Mississippi, "not a nation of human beings."

"So gruesome it defies comment," asserted Speaker of the House Sam Rayburn of Texas.

Senator Tom Stewart of Tennessee seized on the execution to build support for his bill to intern all Japanese and even Americans of Japanese descent, arguing in a speech that he hoped his fellow lawmakers would strip citizenship from the "yellow devils." "Where there is a drop of Jap blood, there is treachery," Stewart howled. "They cannot and never will be honest. The execution of the American airmen confirms that statement. They are unworthy of the rights of citizens."

Even William Douglas, an associate justice of the Supreme Court, sounded off. "Those boys were not killed," Douglas said. "They were murdered. They have laid on us obligations from which we cannot escape."

Letters of outrage poured into the White House, many exposing the nation's long-simmering social tensions. Rollie Toles of Pasadena argued that acts just as barbaric had been committed against the nation's blacks. Other letters targeted people of Japanese descent, just as Breckinridge Long had feared. "In the face of your report of the horrible manner our flyers were treated by Japan do you still feel any Jap of any standing whatever should be permitted the freedom of this West Coast area," asked Ira Seltzer of Los Angeles. "We out here definitely do not."

W. A. McMahon of Reno was far more hostile in his letter to the president. "With horror, we hear of the execution of some of Gen. Doolittle's men, by these goddam Japs," he wrote. "I despise them, as they are nothing but heathens, cannibals and rats. They should be treated as such, and KILLED and eliminated."

In response to the executions, North American Aviation announced that its workers named eight new bombers after the captured raiders, while the Wright Aeronautical Corporation's chief field engineer told reporters that he used a Japanese-made slide rule—complete with the Rising Sun markings—to perfect the power control calculations used by the Tokyo raiders. Bond sales soared, and newspapers that had been critical of the military's evolving story of the raid now rallied in horror at the execution of the American airmen, targeting the enemy in outraged editorials with headlines such as "Japanese Beasts," "The Savages of Tokyo," and "Those Jap Murderers."

Many broadcast journalists likewise vilified the enemy. "Never before has Japan committed an act so arrogant, so vicious and so impelling to immediate retaliation, as the execution, in cold blood, of American prisoners of war," declared Joseph Harsch of CBS. "They were not killed when they had a chance to defend themselves. They were taken prisoner, tortured, finally executed on a charge which was trumped up."

More than a few newspapers and magazines resorted to racist stereotypes, including an editorial cartoon in *Time* magazine that depicted a cocked pistol labeled "Civilization" pointed at the head of an ape on whose chest was written, "Murderers of American Fliers."

"The Japs are even lower than the apes," echoed the *Independent Tribune* of Anderson, South Carolina. "The sneak Pearl Harbor attack should have been ample warning of what the Monkey Men would do to war prisoners."

Amid such calls for retaliation a few voices in Congress and the press urged restraint, a sentiment captured by an editorial in the *Washington Post*. "Horror breeds a demand for reprisals and we must avoid reprisals on the Japanese pattern like the plague," the paper argued. "Any such reprisals would indicate that, far from delivering Japan of its virus, we were letting the Japanese inoculate us with it. Then we should have lost the war. We must crush Japan, but without doing violence to our values."

The executions, the loss of the bombers, and the retaliation suffered by the Chinese made some observers question whether the raid was even worth it, including syndicated columnist David Lawrence, who had previously published Billy Farrow's creed. "The raid on Tokyo can be classed, therefore, as a stunt—a token affair designed for its psychological effect rather than its military value," he wrote. "Stunts play a part, but they are not usually worth the risks unless they are integrated in a well-sustained military plan."

The execution of the raiders hit hard in the military. "We must not rest—we must redouble our efforts until the inhuman war lords who committed this crime have been utterly destroyed," Hap Arnold declared in a message sent to the entire air force. "Remember those comrades when you get a Zero in your sight—have their sacrifice before you when you line up your bomb-sight on a Japanese base."

Admiral Halsey, who commanded the Tokyo task force, was less politic. "We'll make the bastards pay!" he snarled through gritted teeth as the birthmark on his neck turned bright purple. "We'll make 'em pay!"

Doolittle's fury was evident as he addressed reporters at the Allied headquarters in North Africa, vowing that America would bomb Japan until the empire crumbled and its leaders begged for mercy. "We will drop each bomb in memory of our murdered comrades," vowed Doolittle, who was joined by his fellow raiders Rodney Wilder and Howard Sessler. "Such a hideous act violates all our principles of right and justice—all the things we are now fighting for. After my first feeling of regret that such wanton barbarity could still exist in a civilized world, I could only feel a deep loathing and resentment toward the war leaders who were responsible for the act."

"The day will come when these atrocities will be avenged," Sessler added. "I hope I am among the avengers."

Raiders elsewhere promised payback.

"We won't forget!" Joseph Manske wrote in the *New York Herald Journal*. "We've been over Tokio once—and we'll be over it again."

The families of the captured raiders struggled with the news that the Japanese had executed some of the airmen. The rushed release of information meant that most had learned the news from the radio or newspapers. Sid Gross, the head copyboy at the *Cleveland Press*—and close friend of Bob Meder's family—called and broke the news to Meder's mother, an experience he described in an angry letter to Steve Early, the White House press secretary. "She was very upset. In addition she was shocked that the news had to be given to her over the phone and not by official notification from the government. It is cruel and thoughtless for the families," he wrote, "to learn of the unhappy news without being previously warned."

Reporters sought out the families for interviews, some of whom were in denial. "The Japanese just can't be so heartless and inhuman as all that," Meder's mother told the press. "They just couldn't resort to such vile and insane acts with our boys."

"I don't see how any one who professes to be of the human race can be so cruel and inhumane," said Chase Nielsen's mother.

The mother of Donald Fitzmaurice, who had drowned in the surf after the crash of the *Green Hornet*, told reporters she was convinced her son was now fighting alongside the Chinese guerrillas, whereas Billy Farrow's mother was more pragmatic. "What the Japs are dealing out to those left," she said, "may be worse than death."

CHAPTER 24

───────────
───────────

★

For victory, the black heart of Japan must be
bombed again and again.
—*PHILADELPHIA INQUIRER*,
APRIL 22, 1943

SKI YORK AND HIS CREW traveled almost a week by train, followed by
several more days in a flat-bottomed ferry boat on the Kama River, before
finally disembarking at the village of Okhansk, located at the foot of the
Ural Mountains. Poverty was rampant in this communal farm village.
"There was no pavement in the town at all," Emmens recalled. "Everything was just dirt and these almost hovels."

The raiders settled into a primitive home—albeit one with a fresh
coat of paint—that boasted a kitchen, a dining room, a bedroom for
York and Emmens to share, and another for Ted Laban and David Pohl.
Nolan Herndon would have to sleep on a bed in the small hall. The single
bathroom consisted of a hole in the floor that emptied out under the
home. "The odor," Emmens later wrote, "can be imagined."

The Russians measured the airmen for winter clothes. After the first
week, a bundle of forty letters arrived. York counted thirteen and
Emmens ten, while the others split up the rest. "I will never forget the
thrill of receiving news from home," Emmens recalled. "Both Ski and I
received pictures from home of our new offspring."

"I wonder how old our kids will be when we get out of this place?" Emmens asked.

"Jesus," York answered, "I wonder."

Hope seemed to arrive when Major General Follett Bradley, who was in Russia on a mission from Roosevelt to speed up the delivery of lend-lease supplies, visited the crew. Joined by Ambassador Joseph Standley and recently promoted Brigadier General Michela, the three departed Kuibyshev the afternoon of September 11, flying in a twin-engine Douglas transport to Molotov. There the Americans boarded the provincial governor's yacht, a side-wheel riverboat. "The countryside was even more beautiful from the steamer than it had been from the air, the foothills of the Ural mountains rising gently from the river, forested with deciduous trees flaming with the gorgeous colors of Autumn," Standley wrote. "Turbulent mountain streams tumbled down the hills, so crystal clear and beautiful that I longed for a chance to wet a fly in one of them."

The American officials disembarked the next day at Okhansk. The raiders watched from the top of the riverbank, marveling at the governor's yacht.

"Boy," York said, "that's not exactly consistent with the communism this country preaches, is it?"

The ambassador caught sight of the anxious airmen. "I saw a little group of men in American khaki uniforms at the top of the bluff," Standley later wrote. "They waved excitedly and we waved back."

The raiders saluted the senior officers on arrival, and the group made introductions of everyone and shook hands.

"Wonderful country," Standley said, trying to make conversation.

"Yes, sir," York replied, "except when you are stuck in it."

Everyone laughed.

The group returned to the house. The primitive conditions surprised Standley, who described the home as resembling a "log cabin." The Americans sat down at the dining room table. "Not exactly like home," the ambassador said, "is it?"

York asked about the war, and Bradley gave the men a brief update. "What news do you have of the rest of our gang from the Tokyo raid?" Emmens asked.

"The raid made quite an impression back home," Bradley said.

York mentioned that Japanese reports broadcast in Russia claimed the loss of as many as seven bombers.

"None of the ships was lost over Japan itself," Bradley said. "Some of them did have trouble when they got to China. In fact, I think the Japs got one or two of the crews, but I don't think any of them was shot down."

One of the Russians brought in a box of supplies for the raiders, including more magazines, toothpaste, and a Russian grammar book that the fliers had requested. "It's not much," Michela said, "just a couple of shirts and some toothpaste sample tubes."

The airmen appreciated the supplies and asked for the possibility of getting some new clothes and shoes. Michela instructed them to write down their sizes.

"Have they been feeding you well?" Standley asked.

"No, sir," York replied. "They have not! We have been living on rice and cabbage and black bread and tea until the word came of your visit. All that food that you see was brought in last night for your benefit."

The American diplomats were appalled, but powerless to do much to help—and the raiders knew it. "I felt a tremendous letdown creeping over me, and I think the other boys felt it too. Here were our own countrymen, the only people in Russia who could do anything for us, but their hands were tied," Emmens wrote. "They had no more chance of getting the Russians to do something for us than we did."

Standley had to balance bigger concerns and carefully chose his battles. These were just five fliers out of what one day might be thousands who would land on Soviet soil. The ambassador couldn't push the Russians too far. "I felt terribly sorry for the boys, but, after all, like the rest of us, they were caught up in the maw of a vast war which might go on for years," he later wrote. "I wanted to help them and to establish a procedure for all the others who would land in Russian territory as the home islands of the Japanese came within the bomber line of our advancing forces."

York leaned across the table toward Michela.

"General, we are having a rather bad time. This enforced idleness is not good," he said. "If nothing has happened by the time the spring thaws come, I'm afraid we are going to have to try getting out on our own, even from up here. In that event, is there anything you can do for us? We would need maps and a compass."

Michela said he suspected the raiders might be planning an escape, but cautioned that the embassy could not help. "I don't blame you for feeling that way, but you can imagine what would happen if the embassy were caught aiding you."

"You would all be taking pretty much of a chance trying anything like that," Standley added.

Bradley intervened, informing the raiders that he was trying to arrange a route to ship lend-lease bombers to Russia via Alaska. "If I am successful, it just might be worked out that you could all be absorbed into the crew setup of Americans who will be flying airplanes into Russia," the general said, warning the men not to get too excited. "On the other hand, if these people want to keep you here in the Soviet Union, there is nothing I can do, you can do, or anybody else can do about it to change their minds."

York said the news was encouraging. "You must all try not to lose your powers of reason. You must remember that, after all, there is a war being fought, a big war, and it will last a long time," Bradley added. "You are five Americans up here in Siberia. Your getting out or staying here will not change the course of that war."

The general then produced a carton of smokes from his briefcase. "Oh, boy, American cigarettes!" York exclaimed. "We'll have to really ration these."

The raiders passed along lists of desired supplies and letters for the embassy to mail and then accompanied the ambassador and generals down to the dock. "I felt as if we were saying good-by to our only hopes of leaving, our only connection with the outside world," Emmens wrote. "Actually, we were!"

Standley would note in his report to Secretary of State Hull that he found the raiders in "good health, comfortably housed, adequately fed and in general well taken care of," but the ambassador empathized with the airmen's frustration. "I knew how the men felt," he later wrote. "I tried to cheer the boys up as best I could without arousing false hope. They were still standing on the ferry barge looking after us and waving, as the little yacht rounded the first bend in the Kama River."

SEPTEMBER GAVE WAY TO October and then November. The weather grew cold and wet as the village's dirt roads first turned to mud and then froze. By October a foot of snow blanketed the area, and large pieces of ice floated down the Kama, a brief prelude before the entire river froze, making river passage impossible until spring. Unaccustomed to such brutal cold, the raiders remained mostly indoors. "Our morale was becoming lower day by day," Emmens wrote. "It was becoming necessary to be extremely careful of the things we said and the manner in which we said them to one another. Any serious rift among ourselves would be bad, in our close quarters."

As the group's leader, York enforced discipline, insisting that his men use formalities such as "yes, sir" and "no, sir." Though he was best friends with Emmens, he likewise required the junior officer do the same in front of the others, though in private the two used each other's nicknames. "I knew we had to maintain discipline," York later said. "Instead of coming out like a bunch of bums, we would come out like a bunch of troops." The raiders split firewood outdoors and studied Russian, chuckling over the grammar book's propagandist sentences, such as "In America, the workers are poorly fed, poorly clothed, and are generally mistreated by the ruling class." "I spent about ten hours a day studying Russian," York recalled. "I figured this would probably be the only chance in the world where I would want to learn the language, but as long as I had to be there, I was going to come out with something."

The raiders played hearts each night after dinner until the evening news came on at midnight, devising a system to reward the winner as well as solve petty grievances. "The heaviest loser had to put his head down in the seat on the divan with his bottom toward the center of the room," Emmens later wrote. "Each of the other players was allowed to render him one swat on the stern with an open hand. The swat could be helped by a running start from the opposite wall. The second loser received similar treatment from the remaining three, the third loser from the remaining two, the fourth loser from the winner only, and the winner suffered only a sore hand. This offered some vent to ill feeling which any of us might build up during the week."

In late November, assistant military attaché Major Robert McCabe and naval physician Commander Frederick Lang visited the crew, arriving by horse-drawn sleigh with magazines, books, and several bottles of American whiskey.

"Well, what are we waiting for?" Lang announced.

"By God," Emmens said, "it is the cocktail hour, isn't it?"

The raiders retrieved glasses from the kitchen and ice from an outside fence post and settled in for an afternoon and evening of heavy drinking that lasted until 2 a.m. Lang gave each raider a physical the next day, calling them all together afterward. "I see some indications of pellagra and scurvy in all of you," he told the men. "It is caused by improper diet. The serum and the pills should reach here in about ten days. Stop worrying, all of you. Get some exercise and get outdoors as much as you can."

The embassy cabled McCabe's report on the raiders to Secretary of State Hull on November 30. "Based on Soviet standards the food, housing and heating conditions are excellent. Winter clothing issued by the Soviets was not adequate but the military commander at Okhansk has promised the immediate issue of better clothing from Molotov. Except for moderate vitamin deficiencies the health of the crew is satisfactory," McCabe wrote. "Morale is still excellent due to the outstanding leadership displayed by Major York, although continued inactivity, especially during the winter, is causing a decline. The Soviet attitude toward the crew is very friendly."

McCabe unofficially warned that the continued idleness would prompt the raiders to try to escape, which would create an embarrassing situation. "It would be desirable if some way could be found for the internees to be assigned some useful work. He also states that they have expressed the desire for a transfer to a more southerly climate since all of them are from the southern part of the United States," the report noted. "It might be possible during some of the conversations which are taking place between American and Soviet military authorities for the American representatives to propose that the internees be released on parole for work with the Soviet Air Force in the Caucasus."

Heavy black coats arrived a week later, made from reversed goatskin and cheap black dye that would soon leave the raiders ink stained.

"Looks like we're here for the winter," Emmens said.

"Was there any doubt in your mind before he brought us this stuff?" York quipped.

One local froze to death on the road near the house as the temperatures dipped below zero. Food grew scarce. The raiders lived off little more than cabbage and black bread, causing York's weight to drop from

180 pounds to just 135. Nothing was ever wasted, a scene best captured after the locals secured several chickens. "We turned down the heads and the feet, but the women in the kitchen ate the feet and the heads, cracked them open and ate the brains," Emmens recalled. "They ate so many of the insides of the chicken that I didn't realize existed—lungs, of course, the gizzard and the liver, little round things that are kidneys, I guess, about as round as the end of your little finger. They made the most of chicken that I have ever seen made."

The airmen battled lethargy as time seemed to stand still, the days and even weeks blurring together. The fliers would sleep all afternoon yet lie awake at night, struggling to summon enough energy at times even to study or read. In a desperate effort to fight off boredom, the men held a contest to see who could catch the most rats, tormenting the captured rodents for amusement. "We would stake a live one outside in the snow—the things you think of—and tie a piece of thread around its legs so it couldn't get away and the stake on the ground; give it about 1½ or two feet," Emmens recalled. "It would scramble around on top of the snow, and a bird or a hawk or something would come down and grab it and take off with it. What else did we do?"

Even these diversions failed to help. "Our spirits had reached an unbelievable depth. It was difficult to realize that we had been in the country as long as we had," Emmens wrote. "My son would be seven months old on the eighteenth of December. I wondered what he looked like." Thanksgiving passed with little notice, but the approach of Christmas felt different as homesickness exacerbated the airmen's daily miseries. "On one of the trips to the forest for wood, we brought back a Christmas tree," Emmens recalled. "It was a small one, but we decorated it with bits of cotton and put it on the table. Somehow, it helped our morale just a bit."

Mike, the interpreter, brought a filthy Gypsy woman home, and at night the raiders would listen to him having sex with her in his room, which further eroded morale. "Our gums were bleeding whenever we brushed our teeth. We found that we could even spit blood by just sucking on our gums," Emmens later wrote. "Our skin was dry and flaky. We were all losing weight. And our morale was pretty well shot."

Hungry, exhausted, and desperate to escape the frozen wasteland, York proposed writing a letter directly to Stalin.

"Are you serious?" Emmens replied. "What makes you think a letter would even reach him?"

"Maybe it wouldn't," York replied. "But it's like everything else—we won't know until we try."

Emmens asked what he planned to tell him.

"Exactly what we think! We'll tell him we want to get out," he said. "If he can't arrange that, we ask him to move us to a warmer climate and to put us to work."

York soon sat down and started a lengthy letter. "You don't know about us, of course," he wrote. "We are a trained combat crew, and we are not doing anybody any good. We could be fighting against our common enemy." York suggested several possible courses of action, including simply releasing the airmen. After such a long time the release could be done with certain secrecy. If that was not an option, York suggested that the fliers be allowed to fight alongside Russian forces or at a minimum to work in some other capacity that might take advantage of their skills, preferably somewhere warmer. Mike helped the raiders translate the letter.

"I will mail it at once," he said.

"I think he will too," York told Emmens, "because I think he would be afraid not to—a letter addressed to Stalin."

January proved a long and bitter month. "We never stopped hoping to hear from the embassy, that someone was coming, that we might be leaving, that the medicine we had asked for might arrive, that the clothing might arrive—anything," Emmens wrote. "But nothing came." By February the days began to warm up to zero degrees. The icy river, long frozen solid, started to break up. The raiders talked openly of escaping that spring, planning which boat to steal and how best to travel south, aiming to leave sometime between the middle of April and the middle of May.

"God, won't it be a day, the day we leave this goddamned place," York said one afternoon, as he and Emmens watched the ice float downriver.

"We don't know when we are leaving this place, but we do know that someday we will," Emmens said. "Think of all these people around us. They'll never get out."

The raiders were continuing to prepare for the spring escape when a well-dressed Russian captain and major arrived from Moscow late in the morning of March 25. The major removed a document from his briefcase.

"This letter was received in Moscow a short time ago," the Russian officer announced. "Did you write it?"

York confirmed.

"We are here to tell you that the first of your requests cannot be granted. That is the request to be released from the Soviet Union," the major said, a smile stretched across his face. "But our government has decided to grant you the second two requests. You will be moved to a warmer climate and you will be allowed to work."

York translated the news for the others.

"Ee-ow-ee!" Herndon shouted.

"You have been here for many months," the major continued. "When can you be ready to leave?"

"Ready?" York asked, still floored by the news. "I couldn't believe my ears," he later recalled. "I could be ready in five minutes."

The raiders gathered up their few belongings and then sat down with the Russian officers for a final meal of black bread, tea, and cabbage.

"Where are we going?" York asked.

"In due time you will know everything."

THE AIRMEN SET OFF around four that afternoon with the Russians in a motorcade of four cars, thrilled after seven months to finally see the dismal village of Okhansk disappear in the rearview mirror. Snow fell as the Russians drove through the afternoon and evening to the city of Molotov, a journey that took twelve hours and several spare tires to cover barely a hundred miles. In Molotov the officers checked the raiders into a hotel. "We had to walk up. The elevators didn't run, but the walls were still red plush; the old gaslight fixtures were still there but didn't burn any more," Emmens recalled, "evidence of a more luxurious time way back when the czars lived."

The major took the airmen's chest, waist, and shoe measurements and outfitted them in Russian uniforms, complete with felt boots, fur caps with the red star insignia on the front, and shirts with buttons emblazoned with the hammer and sickle. The major informed the raiders that he had tickets for them that evening to see the Leningrad Ballet perform *Swan Lake*. The return to civilization proved startling. "At the end of the ballet we stood up with the rest of the audience and applauded," Emmens later wrote. "The ballerina took her curtain calls gracefully, and each time she came out, after first bowing to the audience, she came over and made her special bow to our box."

After several days the Russian officers escorted the raiders to an airport for the flight south to the city of Chkalov, located northeast of the Caspian Sea. The airmen looked down as the plane approached, amazed to see camels on the ground below, a sense of wonderment bested only by the discovery of the first and only flush toilet the fliers would see in Russia. "Chkolov presented the same dismal picture that every other place had," Emmens recalled. "The same ragged people trudged along in silence. There were no stores, no signs of business, as we know the meaning of the word. Doorways and windows of what had apparently once been stores were boarded up."

After spending a few days in Chkalov, which included a night at the opera, the raiders climbed aboard a train. Unlike the passenger car on the Trans-Siberian Railroad, this one had red carpet on the floor and red plush seats. "Well worn," Emmens noted, "but not worn out yet." The train chugged south for eight days through Tajikistan and Uzbekistan, as the temperatures rose and vendors held up various fruits at each stop. York shared a compartment with a stocky young Russian named Kolya, who welcomed the opportunity to practice his English. Kolya oversaw lend-lease supplies imported through Iran, and beneath his seat he carried suitcases loaded with Spam, Maxwell House coffee, and, of course, vodka, which he gladly shared with the raiders.

"Where are you going?" Kolya asked at one point.

"We haven't the faintest idea," York answered.

"That's typical of my country, especially with strangers."

York never missed an opportunity to press his new friend for help with escape, though Kolya always demurred, arguing that he was sympathetic to the interned raiders, but reluctant to go against the wishes of his government.

"You must be patient," Kolya advised. "You will fight again."

The train pulled into the station in Ashkhabad, the capital of Turkmenistan, separated from neighboring Iran by rugged mountains with peaks that reached as high as ten thousand feet. The raiders bid farewell to Kolya, who also disembarked, and climbed into several cars, driving to a small adobe house surrounded by a high mud fence. The airmen's primitive new home consisted of a couple of rooms, one with two beds, the other with three, all-iron cots, each with a single blanket but otherwise void of mattresses, sheets, and pillows. The property's only water came from a spigot in the backyard; a hole in the ground shielded by a three-sided wooden fence served as the toilet.

"I had nothing to do with choosing this place," the embarrassed major confessed to the raiders.

"Home sweet home!" Emmens said. "We sure went from bad to worse."

York was less politic.

"These bastards!" he exclaimed. "These dirty, goddamned bastards!"

The major soon departed. A local officer would check on the airmen each night, and an elderly and toothless groundskeeper would prepare meals for them. The raiders climbed aboard a bus each morning starting on April 10 and headed to work in a local factory that specialized in overhauling two-wing trainer planes. The factory's foreman put York and Emmens to work dismantling a plane fuselage, while Herndon and Pohl cleaned instruments and Laban worked on small engines. The workday ran from 8 a.m. until 5:30 p.m., interrupted by a morning and afternoon break as well as an hour-and-a-half lunch that consisted of bread and noodles, measured out by the gram.

The only information of the outside world came from a newspaper, posted on the factory's bulletin board, which the airmen perused daily. In that paper York and his crew read about President Roosevelt's release of details of the Tokyo raid as well as the fact that the Japanese had executed some of the airmen. "This news was a shock to us," Emmens later wrote. "It made us feel ashamed of complaining about our lot. But it did not lessen our determination to get out of the Soviet Union."

Kolya knocked on the door one night soon after the raiders settled into Ashkhabad, beginning a series of clandestine meetings with the Americans, often at his house over dinner. Each time the raiders pressed upon him their desire to escape, wearing Kolya down over several weeks. "Very well," he finally told them. "I can help you and I will. You must place yourselves completely in my hands." Kolya warned the raiders to be patient and under no circumstances try to escape alone. "The border is manned by Russian troops, dogs, mines, and barbed wire," he said. "You cannot do it alone. Do not try!"

Kolya's offer to help thrilled the airmen, as best noted by Emmens: "Our spirits rose to the heavens." That spike in morale soon waned as several days passed and then a week. Koyla told the men his initial plan had collapsed, cautioning the raiders to remain patient and not to try to escape on their own. The airmen's frustration came to a head at dinner one night at Kolya's house when Laban drank too much.

"Sergeant, why don't you eat something?" York said. "You'll feel better."

The inebriated airman instead stood up at the dinner table and exploded at Kolya. "You and that goddamn boss of yours named Stalin can go piss up a rope," Laban shouted. "You are nothing but a bunch of goddamn SOBs."

"Laban," York said, jumping to his feet with clenched fists. "Shut up."

"And you," the sergeant countered, turning to address his commanding officer, "you SOB, can go to hell."

York shot a glance at Emmens. "You and Herndon and Pohl get Laban out of here," he demanded. "Take him home."

Herndon and Pohl each grabbed Laban under one arm and dragged him out the door. Emmens told York to try to salvage the situation and then followed the others. Laban yelled and swore as the airmen dragged him up the street.

"Laban, for Christ's sake," Emmens said when he caught up to them. "Straighten up, will you?"

Laban whirled around and punched Emmens. The pilot felt blood spurt from his left eyebrow and grew enraged. He punched Laban so hard on the side of his nose that his upper plate of false teeth flew out, hit the ground, and broke.

York arrived home half an hour later, telling Emmens that despite Laban's outburst Kolya agreed to still help. The lamplight illuminated his friend's black eye.

"What in the hell happened to you?"

Emmens related the story of the fistfight.

"Let's court-martial him when we get out," York said.

Kolya soon came up with a new plan, referring the raiders to a local smuggler who might be able to help them get across the Iranian border.

"I can't be seen with him. I can't introduce you, but I know the man by sight," Kolya told them. "He walks around the town square very often. On Sunday I will sit with York in the town square on a bench. When I spot the man, I will point him out, and then I will leave. The rest is up to you."

The plan unfolded just as outlined. Kolya pointed out the pacing smuggler, and York fell in behind him.

"You're Abdul Arram, aren't you?" York asked.

The man turned and looked at the airman, shook his head, and continued walking. York chased after him. "You're Abdul Arram," he repeated. "I know you are!"

"And if I am Abdul Arram?" the man said, turning to face York.

"I want you to do some work for me."

"What kind of work?"

York told him he needed five Americans smuggled out of Russia into neighboring Iran. The man refused.

"I can pay," York said. "Five hundred rubles."

"Impossible," the smuggler countered. "Do not speak to me any more!"

"—or in dollars!"

The mention of American currency stopped the smuggler. He demanded $800 to transport the Americans to Mashhad, the first major city across the border and home to the British consulate. York had won about $250 playing poker on board the *Hornet*. Emmens had another $60, and the three other airmen combined had about $40.

"One hundred dollars," York offered.

The smuggler countered at seven hundred, but York continued to beat him down. "Four hundred," Arram stammered, "or no go!"

"Two hundred fifty is all that we have," York said.

"Agreed!"

The plan sounded exceedingly simple. A truck would arrive in front of the airmen's adobe house just before midnight on May 10. When the driver killed the engine, the men would climb into the back and lie flat. By sunrise the raiders would be in Iran. "It seemed like a dream," Emmens recalled. "There it was—we were leaving!"

The next few days crawled by as the raiders worked at the factory and anxiously awaited the night of escape. The airmen counted out the smuggler's $250 fee and gave the rest to Kolya, who prepared a special departure bag of vodka and caviar for the raiders and sketched them a map of Mashhad, pinpointing the British consulate. The airmen stood by anxiously that Monday as the clock approached midnight. "There was only silence in the night outside," Emmens recalled. "None of us talked. We were all straining to hear the sound of an automobile engine."

Midnight came—and went. "Suddenly we all heard it at once," Emmens wrote. "There was the unmistakable racing of the motor of a truck as the driver shifted from high into second gear. It was turning the corner onto our street."

The raiders slipped outside and opened the gate, watching as the truck came to a stop out front. This was it—the moment the airmen had long awaited. The fliers climbed into the back of the truck. A match illuminated Abdul Arram, who wanted his money. York gave him a down payment of $100, but the smuggler demanded all $250.

"More—Mashhad," York countered. "In Mashhad—more money!"

The smuggler reluctantly agreed and hissed at the airmen to lie down before he climbed into the truck's cab with the driver. The raiders heard the driver turn the ignition key, but the truck refused to start. "It ground over and over just trying to get started," Emmens later recalled. "It wouldn't catch."

Arram climbed out of the cab and peered over the side of the truck, telling them that the driver had to run into town to get a part. He suggested that two of the raiders wait in the truck and the other three go back inside the adobe house. The minutes dragged until the driver returned as promised with the part. A few minutes later the truck grumbled to life. The raiders climbed into the back, covering up in the tarp. "The bottom of that truck was certainly hard, but it felt like a bed of roses to us," Emmens wrote. "It was carrying us out of that godforsaken and godless country—we hoped!"

The truck started and set off down the road, turning onto a paved highway and rattling as it picked up speed and headed toward the mountains. "We could tell we were going south," Emmens recalled. "We took the tarpaulin down. It was night, and nobody could see us. There was no traffic on the road or anything."

The raiders felt the driver shift into a lower gear as the truck began to climb into the mountains. Another hour passed. The truck slowed down and pulled off the road. The airmen heard a screwdriver on metal as the driver swapped out the license plates. The truck then started off, only to pull over again soon thereafter.

"Out," someone demanded.

The raiders climbed out just as a man emerged from the bushes, his face obscured in the dark.

"Pssst," the stranger beckoned. "Come on."

The airmen set out on foot in a single file, following the mysterious guide up the mountain. After the men had traveled barely a few hundred feet, the truck shifted into gear and pulled back onto the highway. The hike proved tough, because the mountainside consisted mostly of shale and was void of any vegetation. "You would take one step up, and you would slide back two," Emmens recalled. "We were having a hard time frankly in our physical condition keeping up with the guy."

The hike soon exhausted York, who vomited in darkness. "I don't think I can go up this thing any farther," he said. "Why don't you guys go ahead?"

The others refused, insisting the guide slow down. The airmen heard a rifle shot in the distance that echoed off the canyon walls followed by a barking dog. The raiders began finally to descend the mountain, which made for a far easier trek. At one point the guide demanded the men drop down and worm forward on their bellies, which the fliers later surmised was likely the actual border crossing. Shortly before daybreak the exhausted raiders, their clothes now ragged and torn from the hike, collapsed in an irrigation ditch alongside a highway. The same truck that had first carried the men into the mountains soon appeared, pulling off the highway. The fliers scrambled into the back. "The guy who had been our guide disappeared," Emmens recalled. "We never did see him. He was just sort of a mythical character who led us over there."

The driver slipped the truck into gear and pulled back onto the highway. Even though the airmen were now in Iran, Russian forces still occupied certain areas close to the border. The raiders felt the truck again slow. Emmens peeked out from under the tarp and saw a checkpoint. A wooden arch crossed the highway with a red star in the center and a picture of Stalin. The truck stopped, and Emmens could hear an animated conversation between the driver and the Russian troops. He then heard boots on gravel approaching the rear of the truck. Suddenly someone yanked the tarp down. "I was staring directly into a face a bare twelve inches above mine. There was a growth of stubble on the face, and a fur cap with a red star on it above the face."

"Oh, my God," the airman thought. "We have been caught."

Emmens closed his eyes and froze. The conversation outside the truck continued, and when Emmens opened his eyes the Russian face was gone. He suddenly felt the truck begin to move. "Slowly the guardrail, the arch, Stalin, and the red star passed over our heads and behind us," he recalled. "I began to breathe again."

The truck continued down the highway. The sun was now coming up as the airmen surveyed the scene. "It was desolate country; no trees in sight, just shale rock, stretching way ahead," Emmens recalled. "Way down in the valley ahead of us, there was a glint of a gold dome as the sun was just breaking over that horizon."

The truck motored on throughout the morning, pulling off onto the shoulder of the highway around noon. Abdul climbed out of the cab and came back.

"Out," he ordered. "Money."

"Mashhad," the raiders protested.

The smuggler pointed to the town a few miles down the road. "Impossible," he told the raiders. "Guards—Russians."

The men climbed out and handed over the remaining $150. The truck turned around and headed back down the highway. The fliers scrambled off the highway and into a nearby bomb crater about a hundred feet away. Tired and hungry, the men tore into the sack of supplies Kolya had given them.

"Well, here we are!" York announced. "A couple of miles out of Mashhad, Persia, sitting in a bomb crater eating black caviar, black bread, and drinking vodka. I wonder how many other Americans have done this."

"We're not in Mashhad yet," Herndon cautioned.

The men decided York and Emmens would sneak into town, find the British consulate, and return with help, while the others remained hidden in the crater. To mark the spot the raiders lined up the vodka bottles on the crater's rim.

The two pilots set off down the highway. Closer to town other locals appeared on the highway, coming and going. No one seemed to notice the airmen. A bridge led into Mashhad, guarded by a Russian sentry. Each time a cart passed over the bridge, the Russian would stop and search it, a process that took a few minutes but distracted the guard from the foot traffic that continued to flow into the town.

The airmen waited for the perfect time, committing Kolya's diagram of the city to memory about the time a truck rolled up toward the bridge.

"Now's our chance!" York announced.

The guard stopped the truck and started to search it, while the raiders blended in with the other foot traffic over the bridge. "It wasn't more than fifty feet across the thing. The temptation to break into a run was almost irresistible," Emmens recalled. "We didn't look back after we had passed, but we did increase the speed of our steps."

The fliers entered the town, surprised to see stores that sold cigarettes and other commodities unavailable in Russia. Up ahead the raiders spotted a Russian patrol. The airmen hustled across the street and pressed against a storefront, pretending to window-shop while watching in the reflection as the patrol marched past. The fliers hurried the final few blocks to the consulate, turning on the street to see the whitewashed walls and the arched entrance. Several soldiers stood guard. "We took a deep breath," Emmens recalled. "We sauntered very casually on that side of the street until we got exactly opposite the arch door. We just turned and rushed inside the gates."

Iranian soldiers poured out of the guardhouse and pinned the raiders against the wall with bayonets.

"American! American!" the raiders shouted. "British consul!"

A turbaned officer approached, looking the airmen over. "British consul not here," he finally said. "Vice consul here."

"Fine," the airmen said. "Vice consul."

Guards led the airmen inside, who marveled at the consulate's immaculate lawns, flowers, and swimming pool. A tethered gazelle played at the end of a long leash staked in the yard. The paradisiacal scene reminded Emmens of the Garden of Eden.

"Did you ever see anything as beautiful as this?" York asked.

"Never!"

The airmen jotted their names and ranks on a sheet of paper, identifying themselves as members of the U.S. Army Air Forces. The guard vanished, and less than a minute later the door burst open and the vice consul appeared.

"My God," he announced. "Where in the hell did you guys come from?"

The airmen instructed the British on how to find the other three raiders, and forty-five minutes later the crew was reunited. The exhausted raiders would within days begin the long voyage home through India, North Africa, and South America before finally touching down in Washington, but in the meantime the British showered them with hospitality, beginning that afternoon with the vice consul.

"Would you like a scotch and soda?"

CHAPTER 25

★

In war as it is fought today only a few rules are left—only a
few shreds of law and custom which, it was thought,
governed the relations of belligerents to each other.

—ERNEST LINDLEY, COLUMNIST,
APRIL 23, 1943

THE SAME DAY THE Japanese executed Hallmark, Farrow, and Spatz, guards came for the other five raiders in Kiangwan. Dressed in crisp uniforms and armed with rifles and sabers, the Japanese pulled the aviators out one by one that gray and foggy morning. "Though we were in separate cells and had no chance to talk to each other, we had all come to the same conclusion—if the verdict was execution we were going to try to make a break," Bobby Hite and Jacob DeShazer would later write. "It was a strange thing, but most of us armed ourselves with toothbrushes. We figured we might jab a guard in the face with a toothbrush to start the break."

The guards marched the airmen back into the courtroom. The raiders realized with alarm that there were only five of them: Hite, DeShazer, Chase Nielsen, George Barr, and Bob Meder. Hallmark's one-night stay at Kiangwan was in a different cellblock, so as far as the others knew, the pilot was still at Bridge House, recovering from his battle with dysentery. The Japanese had taken Farrow and Spatz out of their cells the night before, but the airmen never returned. Where were the others? They didn't have to wonder long. "We lined up before the bench," Hite and DeShazer recalled, "and looked our judges straight in the eye."

The Japanese read a short statement and then turned to the interpreter, whose hands trembled, sweat dripping from his face.

"For bombing and strafing school areas you have been sentenced to death," the interpreter began.

The airmen crouched, ready to make a break for it if the verdict was death. Guards sensed the tensions and clutched their sword hilts.

"But through the gracious majesty of the emperor," the interpreter continued, "you have been spared to life imprisonment with special treatment."

With that the sentencing was over. The entire proceeding lasted less than three minutes. The guards marched the raiders back to their cells and solitary confinement. "I could not help feeling a strange sense of joy, even though solitary confinement and a long war awaited any possible chance of freedom," DeShazer later said. "At the same time it seemed almost hopeless to think of ever being free again, since the most probable thing would be that we would be executed when America did win the war."

On the floor of cell no. 3, Meder scratched the date, followed by his name, rank, and serial number. He noted that he was in the Army Air Forces and a member of a B-25 detachment. He concluded with a plea for anyone who might one day read his missive: "Notify U.S. Army—Life Imprisonment."

Other raiders likewise used old fish bones and bits of seashells to carve messages on the floors. To pass the time, Barr scratched a calendar. He marked out the days from the first of October through the twenty-third, before he gave up. He never even wrote out the dates for the rest of October or filled in the squares for the November calendar he started. Four boards in from his cell door, the navigator etched a personal testament that war crimes investigators would later find:

Lt. G. Barr, USAAC—34th Bomb Sqdn.—Columbia, SC., USA—Took off from AC Hornet 4/17/42—Bombed Nagoya Japan—Flew 17 hours to China—No gas. Jumped—Captured 4/18/1942.

The heat and humidity of summer gave way to a long and bitter winter as temperatures dipped below freezing. The airmen struggled in unheated cells with little more than a few blankets to keep themselves warm. In December the Japanese moved the raiders into one large cell. "We were so thrilled and so hungry to be together," Hite recalled, "that we just visited, visited, and visited for days and days and days."

The meager diet of rice and turnip or onion soup continued to wear down their health, though the airmen tried to perform calisthenics. DeShazer shimmied up the narrow cells walls by pressing his feet against one wall and his hands against the other. Up high he had a view out the window of the countryside that stretched for miles. Hite set a goal of twenty pushups, only to discover in his weakened state that he could hardly do ten. He pushed himself one time and blacked out and hit his head.

Dysentery soon added to Hite's troubles. The Japanese moved the other raiders out of the cell, but left Meder to help care for his sick friend. Hite had managed to hang on to a few dollars when captured, which he used to convince some of the guards to buy him extra food to help him recover. He had failed, though, to consider sharing it with his fellow raiders, a fact he later regretted. "These are things that happened to you as a prisoner," he recalled. "Sometimes things that you discover about yourself are not too pretty."

The Japanese moved the men out of Kiangwan on April 17, 1943, almost a year to the day since the men had lifted off from the deck of the *Hornet*. Guards ushered the handcuffed prisoners aboard a plane, tethering them to their seats, but removing their blindfolds. The airmen welcomed the chance to see the landscape far below. "It was flat country dotted with rice paddies," DeShazer and Hite recalled. "We thought now how fortunate we were not to make a break for liberty. There was no place to hide. We would have been captured easily and probably shot at once."

The men arrived at the Japanese military prison in Nanking—a new facility constructed of brick and concrete and surrounded by a high wall—which boasted barely a dozen cells; fortunately most proved vermin free. The raiders once again landed in solitary confinement in nine-by-twelve cells, though Nielsen's and Barr's were several feet larger. A single window seven feet off the ground let in only limited light. Guards could look in on the prisoners through a screen slot in the wooden door and pass food through a six-inch panel near the bottom. "The furnishings consisted of a grass mat and three very thin cotton blankets," Hite and DeShazer said. "When we sat we sat on the concrete floor."

The raiders settled into life in the new prison, where the lone highlight of each day consisted of a half hour of exercise in the prison yard at 10:30 a.m., but only if the weather permitted. "The rest of the time," the men recalled, "we just sat or trudged around our narrow cells, like caged animals." Days turned into weeks and then months as the men battled the loneliness and fatigue of hours spent solo in a concrete cell. "Day in and day out it was the same thing—sitting in our cells with nothing to occupy our time," Hite and DeShazer wrote. "After we got to know our guards better we sometimes kidded them about Japan losing the war. Generally, this infuriated them and often they'd draw their swords and threaten us. Then we'd laugh and beckon them to come into the cells and carry out the threat, but they never did."

The Japanese found other ways to retaliate, as Barr later testified: "Some guards would torment us by calling us to the little window and then spitting in our faces or have a fellow guard douse our already shivery body with cold water." Though the airmen were largely spared the beatings given fellow Chinese prisoners, whose screams at times reverberated through the cellblock, their punishment was more subtle but no less severe: the withholding of food. The guards had the power to control who lived—and who died. It wasn't wise, the raiders realized, to push them too hard.

One day Nielsen turned over his aluminum drinking cup to discover a message scratched on the bottom: "Connie G. Battles, United States Marines." The Japanese had captured Battles on Wake in December 1941. This was the first time the airmen surmised there might be other captured Americans in the Nanking prison. Nielsen rubbed out Battles's name and scratched his own. The cup went from cell to cell until it eventually returned to Battles, who had managed during his time in a Shanghai prison camp to pick up various reports on the war's progress that he now shared. The men dubbed this primitive communications system the "tincup news service."

"Russians on German border," one message read.

The raiders in exchange could offer little more than each of their names, scratched on the bottom with either a nail or an old fish bone. Whoever found a message would rub it off so that Battles knew the information was received. The men would then whisper the news among themselves at exercise time. "That way we learned that the Yanks were making plenty of progress, both in Europe and Asia," Hite and DeShazer later wrote. "It was awfully sketchy information, of course, but at least it was good news and it did more to keep us sane and full of hope than any other thing."

The guards over time figured out the system, forcing the men to adapt. Meder devised a rudimentary way to communicate via Morse code: a rap on the wall equaled a dot and a scratch meant a dash. The creative pilot likewise came up with most of the nicknames the airmen used for the guards, names such as Big Ugly and Little Ugly, the Goon, the Mule, and Frankenstein. "He could see something funny in even the grimmest of our experiences with the Japs," Hite and DeShazer recalled. "He was certain that he would get out alive and he used to tap out his post-war plans through the cell wall. He wanted to start a men's furnishing store back in Lakewood, Ohio."

Dysentery struck Meder in early September about the time the hot and humid summer gave way to cooler fall weather. The meager rations had already so whittled his five-foot-eleven-inch frame that fellow fliers described him as a "toothpick." Beriberi soon added to his troubles. The pilot grew so weak that by November he stopped leaving his cell each morning for exercise. He could do little more than wallow on his mat. "We begged to go in to nurse him," Barr recalled. "Kindness was all the medication we had, but it would have helped. We were refused."

The other raiders persuaded Meder on December 1 to come outside for exercise. His feet were so swollen that all he could do was sit on the steps in the sun. One of the guards harassed him, and Meder rose to the challenge.

"Listen," he said in a mix of English and Japanese. "Sick as I am I can lick the whole damn bunch of you."

He took a swing only to miss and fall down. "It was sort of sad, but it was sort of good to see that even in as bad a shape that he was in, that the spirit was still willing," Hite recalled. "Bob knew that he was in real bad shape. He was just sort of a skeleton."

Hite asked him whether there was anything he could do for him.

"Just pray," Meder answered.

The others helped Meder back to his cell afterward. Hite was in the cell next to him. He heard his fellow pilot tell the guard known as Cyclops the address of his parents and ask him, if he died, would he please write them and send them his clothes.

Barr helped distribute dinner that evening for the guards. He slid Meder's mess kit through the slot but didn't hear anyone move. The navigator summoned a guard, who unlocked the cell door and found Meder dead.

The Japanese medical report of his death, discovered after the war, painted a heroic, albeit bogus, picture of efforts made to save Meder, from giving him special glucose and vitamin B injections when he first fell sick to the desperate final effort to resuscitate him when he died. "Immediately artificial respiration was tried and 3.0 cc of camphor was injected under the skin and 1.0 cc of adrenaline was injected into the heart," the report stated, "but the patient failed to recover."

The sounds of saws and hammers filled the prison the next day. Unaware that his friend had died, DeShazer peered out the window, startled to see guards building a coffin. On December 3 guards marched each of the prisoners into Meder's cell. The Japanese had stuffed cotton in his mouth. "The body was in a rough box and there were a few chrysanthemums on Bob's breast," Hite and DeShazer recalled. "Each of us said a silent prayer, but there were no religious services."

Meder's death pained the others; the Japanese seized on it as a means to torment them. "For several days after that, the guards would shout out Bob's number (it was three) when they passed his cell," Hite and DeShazer later wrote. "They'd wait for an answer, which couldn't come, of course, and then they'd laugh."

Meder had often said he would rather be dead and his family know it than be alive with no one knowing it. He had left a letter for his parents and sister, sealing it with the message: "To be opened only in the event of my death."

"I am writing this letter on December 7, 1941—that fateful day when the Japanese started the spark of this conflagration. As it has been the will of God I have answered my country's call and I pray that whatever efforts I may have exerted have been to some avail," Meder began his final farewell. "The main purpose of this letter to you is to try at this very last minute to comfort you. During this time of strife for all, those of you that have had to sacrifice loved ones are the real heroes of any struggle.

The word hero is truly inadequate. Just remember that the soul of a person is greater than his own physical body; therefore, you have not lost me, my spirit shall ever be with you, watching, and aiding if possible from wherever the 'Great Beyond' may be. Be brave, not bitter, be determined, not overcome. That is the job for those of you that I love most dearly. Democracy shall continue. It is our sacrifice for that cause."

Meder begged of his family one final request. "Please promise to never let anything separate you," he wrote. "Mend any petty disagreements—continue as a loving family on its way to do its part in this world. Mother and Dad, never let anything become so mistakenly important to cause such a thing as a separation or a divorce. And Doris-Mae, never let your love for Mother and Dad taper off. I ask these things of you in my memory. I know you will not fail me!" Meder reiterated his hope that his parents and sister would not allow his death to overwhelm them. "I bless and love you all very dearly; some day I feel very certain that we shall all be united in a happier life in the life ahead," he concluded. "God bless and protect you. Keep up your courage!"

After the war Doolittle would deliver a speech in Cleveland on October 18, 1945. Meder's parents were in attendance. "His mission was accomplished—gloriously," Doolittle told them and the audience. "He was not only one of the outstanding heroes of the war, but a martyr to the cause of your freedom and mine. Bob was a victim of the barbarism of the Japs who sacrificed him on the altar of hate."

Meder's sacrifice meant the others got two extra buns with each meal, but it also taught them a lesson. "Any of us can die at any time," Hite thought. "We could all die and they could do away with us and nobody would ever know the difference."

As the months marched past, the raiders grew increasingly withdrawn. The solitude tortured them. "We had to fight ourselves," Hite and DeShazer said, "to keep from going mad." The men lived inside their imaginations. Nielsen envisioned the house he would one day build for himself, while Hite planned out a farm back home in Texas. "I would think about the wonderful meals I'd have when I got out. Or I'd plan escapes in minute detail, going over every step in my mind," Barr remembered. "And then in my mind I'd raise sheep, rabbits, hogs or wheat. I'd go through every step, planting, fertilizing, weeding. I raised chickens in imaginary batteries. Maybe I'd 'work' on one occupation for a couple of days, go on to another, and then go back to the first one. It's amazing what your mind can do under such circumstances."

The men on occasion still battled with the guards. That happened after exercise one day when the guards tried to make Barr wash his feet in the snow. The navigator refused and started back toward his cell. The guard struck him on the legs with his sword. "I saw red," Barr later wrote. "I whirled and punched him in the nose. He went down and the other guards ran to help him. I was weak, but the Japs don't know how to use their fists and I did all right until I was overpowered by sheer numbers."

Guards dragged Barr back outside into the exercise yard. A couple held him while others slipped on a straitjacket, lacing it up so tight that it squeezed his chest and he gasped for air. "Panic comes quick when you cannot get your breath or move your arms to help yourself. There was no pain at first, only the horrible choking for air. I rolled over on my side because it seemed I could gulp a little more air in that position," he recalled. "Then the pain began. At the start there is only numbness, but when the blood forces its way through the constricted channels the pain becomes frightful. I could hear myself making animal-like noises as I fought for breath. There was enormous pressure at my eyeballs and in my nostrils. I was almost hysterical with panic and pain."

The other prisoners, forced back into their cells, listened as Barr suffered. "We could hear him making a sobbing noise," Hite and DeShazer recalled, "but there was nothing we could do to help."

A half hour later the guards pulled the laces even tighter. The prison commandant calmly stared at Barr, ticking off the minutes with a stopwatch. "My lungs, heart, liver were all crushed together with the ribs sticking in," Barr wrote. "The perspiration poured down my face and into my eyes, although it was a cold day."

Finally after an hour the guards released him. Barr's brutal punishment angered Misake, one of the few guards who showed compassion to the navigator. "Misake was among the guards standing by watching me groan and sweat in the snowdrift into which I had been thrown, but he did not laugh," Barr recalled. "When the order came for my release, he was the first to jump to my rescue." Misake escorted the exhausted airman back to his cell and in a surprise gesture offered him a cigarette. "He took a frightful chance doing that," Barr remembered, "and I'll never forget it or him."

The men battled the nagging physical pains of starvation, surviving on watery rice and unsweetened tea. "After awhile you get so you do not want to eat, and yet you are ravenously hungry," Barr recalled. "You eat because instinct tells you that you must eat to live, but I had to force the food down my throat." The fliers lost so much weight that the concrete floors pained them. Beriberi only compounded the misery. "At times the swelling from beriberi was so intense that we were required to push it back from around our eyes to be able to even open them," Nielsen later wrote. "Also our feet, hands, arms, and legs would puff up until our hands and feet looked like they were clubbed. Our joints ached continually and at times it was difficult to walk."

The dark days of hunger and hopelessness forced the men to wrestle with difficult questions. "We began to think a lot about death," admitted Hite and DeShazer. "During our exercise periods we talked about it and wondered why Meder had to be taken. Our only consolation was that it had to be the will of God."

"We thought a lot about religion," added Barr. "When you're in tough straits God is the only one you can rely on." Nielsen agreed. "Faith kept me alive," he said. "Faith in my nation. My religion. My creator."

Hite wrote to the prison commandant, requesting a Bible. To his surprise, one soon arrived; the King James version, still stamped with a $1.97 price tag. "It was sort of like a man being in the desert and finding a cool pool," he recalled. "We hadn't had anything to read. We didn't have newspapers. We didn't have radio. We didn't have books. We didn't have anything. So this Bible was really a tremendous thing that happened to us."

The men took turns reading the Bible, passing it from cell to cell as each man pored over it in the dim light. "I lived on hate for the first year and a half. Hatred is a very strong emotion," Hite recalled. "I think we were able to kind of keep ourselves together living on hate, instead of laying down and giving up." DeShazer echoed Hite, later writing that his hatred of the Japanese nearly drove him crazy. "The way the Japanese treated me, I had to turn to Christ," he remembered. "No matter what they did to me, I prayed. I prayed for the strength to live. And I prayed for the strength, somehow, to find forgiveness for what they were doing to me."

That hostility and anger soon vanished. "We decided that we had no hatred for our guards, vicious as they were. They were ignorant and mean, but perhaps—we thought—there was some good in them. The only way to develop that goodness would be by understanding and education—not by brutally mistreating them as they were doing to us," Hite and DeShazer later wrote. "The officers were different. They were educated men. They gave the orders for punishment. They must be punished in return. But the retribution should be just. They would not be beaten as we were. They should be tried in a court of justice and disciplined as we do our own criminals."

DeShazer was the most affected. "One day in my cell I felt the call as clearly as though a voice were speaking to me," he said, looking back. "I don't mean I heard a voice. It was more like a flash of truth. I even tried to think about something else, but I couldn't." He decided there in that awful cell in Nanking that if he survived the war he would return to Japan as a missionary. He felt his burden lift. "Hunger, starvation, and a freezing cold prison cell no longer had horrors for me. They would be only a passing moment. Even death could hold no threat when I knew that God had saved me," he recalled. "There will be no pain, no suffering, no sorrow, no loneliness in heaven."

The bombardier put his newfound faith to the test. He ignored the hostility of the guards and instead tried to befriend one of them.

"How are you?" he asked each day with a smile.

To his surprise after six days of this the guard presented DeShazer with a sweet potato. "Boy," he thought. "This really works."

Hite fell ill around the summer of 1944, right after the Japanese administered a round of vaccinations. The six-foot flier's weight fell to around eighty-eight pounds, and his body burned for five days with a 105-degree fever. The Japanese moved him to a cell with a screen door, but even then he was too weak to talk. "I was so sick I couldn't even raise my head," he said. "I just lay there."

The pilot heard Nielsen and DeShazer outside his door one day. "Hite won't be here tomorrow," Nielsen said. "I don't think he can make it."

The news rattled Hite. "I thought I was going to die. I prayed to the Lord, told him I was willing to die if that's what he wanted, that mother was a widow and she might need me, but that I wasn't afraid to die and I was trusting in him," he later said. "It was the most amazing thing. I started getting well right there."

The weeks slid past as summer turned into fall and 1944 rolled into

1945. Guards came for the raiders finally at 6:30 a.m. on June 12, 1945, armed with hoods and handcuffs. The airmen boarded a train later that morning for the forty-hour journey to Peiping, as Peking was officially named since 1928. Guards removed the hoods, but tied the fliers to the seats. The train transported Japanese officers, so the airmen enjoyed the same meals, which included beef. "It was the best food we'd had in three years. But our guards declined to give us any water. The result was that we had nothing to drink for 48 hours," Hite and DeShazer wrote. "When we got to Peiping we were literally sick with thirst."

The raiders reached Peiping around noon on June 14. Guards slipped hoods over the airmen's heads, then drove them to what was known as the North China Prison 1407, on North Hataman road about four miles outside of the city, a place a fellow prisoner of war would describe in an affidavit after the war as "hell." There raiders landed in cells that measured ten feet by ten feet. Two small windows provided the only light, one on the heavy wooden door that faced an inside passageway. Guards allowed the prisoners to bathe once a week. "We were placed in solitary confinement again, and in Peiping we didn't even have the half hour exercise period that was part of our Nanking regime," Hite and DeShazer wrote. "Our cells were just as primitive."

The mood of the guards served as a barometer of the war's progress. America's maritime offensive had reached a climax in the summer of 1944 with the capture of the Marianas, the ultimate prize of the Pacific. The volcanic archipelago of Guam, Saipan, and Tinian—just fifteen hundred miles south of Tokyo—provided bases for American B-29 bombers to reach Japan, to reduce its industrial cities to rubble, to continue the fight started by Jimmy Doolittle and his seventy-nine raiders. Japan's loss of the Marianas led not only to the ouster of Hideki Tojo and his cabinet but to four of the most telling words of the war, uttered by Fleet Admiral Osami Nagano, Hirohito's supreme naval adviser: "Hell is on us."

And hell it was.

Day after day, week after week, B-29 Superfortresses darkened the skies over Japan by the hundreds. Engineers had spared nothing in the creation of Boeing's aeronautical monster, a plane so powerful that even Doolittle said it "staggers the imagination." The four-engine bomber could not only fly twice the distance of the Tokyo raid but also haul five times as much ordnance as each of Doolittle's planes. America demonstrated the B-29's terrifying power in an incendiary raid against Tokyo on March 9–10, 1945, triggering an inferno so intense that pilots en route used the flames to navigate from two hundred miles out while the soot blackened the bombers' bellies. The attack would prove the war's single most destructive assault on an urban area, killing 83,793 people, injuring another 40,918, and leaving a million homeless. "I have never seen such a display of destruction," wrote *Boston Globe* journalist Martin Sheridan, who flew in one of the B-29s. "I not only saw Tokyo burning furiously in many sections, but I smelled it."

Bombers pounded Japan's major cities night after night in raids Doolittle could only have dreamed of years earlier when he throttled up his B-25 that rainy morning on the deck of the *Hornet*. As workers punched out more bombers, the airborne armadas only grew larger; on some nights more than five hundred Superfortresses thundered in the skies overhead. In the war's final months B-29s would fly more than 28,500 sorties against Japan, dropping almost 160,000 tons of bombs across sixty-six cities. The results were staggering. America would level some 158 square miles of Japanese cities, including more than 50 square miles of Tokyo, 15 of Osaka, and 11 of Nagoya. According to postwar Japanese records, the raids killed 330,000 people, injured another 475,000, and left 8.5 million homeless. "Japan eventually will be a nation without cities," Doolittle declared in July when he arrived in the Pacific after Germany's surrender. "A nomadic people."

These attacks built up to the muggy morning of August 6 when Colonel Paul Tibbets Jr.'s B-29 roared down the coral runway on the tiny Pacific island of Tinian at two forty-five. His payload consisted of the single atomic bomb "Little Boy," an ironic nickname considering experts predicted it would take two thousand loaded B-29s to rival the force of this one weapon. Tibbets appeared over Hiroshima and droppd his bomb at 8:15 a.m. Forty-three seconds later, the weapon detonated. Temperatures surpassed 3,200 degrees Fahrenheit, bubbling clay roof tiles and vaporizing human victims. American investigators after the war estimated that the attack, which leveled more than 4 square miles, killed approximately 80,000 men, women, and children and injured another 100,000. Three days later a second B-29 roared down Tinian's darkened runway, carrying the atomic bomb dubbed "Fat Man." The attack on

Nagasaki flattened another 1.8 square miles and killed approximately 45,000 people and injured as many as 60,000.

DeShazer awoke that morning in his prison cell in China to hear an inner voice urging him to pray. The health of the Doolittle raiders had reached a new low. Beriberi had stricken both Hite and Barr; the latter was at times delirious.

"What shall I pray about?" DeShazer asked.

The voice told him to pray for peace. DeShazer did, unaware of what had happened on the Japanese homeland. He prayed that Japanese leaders would welcome peace and that the public would not be demoralized or taken advantage of in postwar Japan. He prayed from 7 a.m. until 2 p.m., when he heard the voice again. "You don't need to pray anymore," the voice told him. "Victory is won."

CHAPTER 26

★

The recent uninvited visit of U.S. bombers to our country
seems to be President Roosevelt's method of flattering the
ignoramus within the United States.

—OSAKA MAINICIII,
APRIL 29, 1942

RAY NICHOLS LOOKED DOWN from the B-24 at the Peiping airdrome at 5:15 p.m. on the afternoon of August 17, just two days after Emperor Hirohito had taken to the airwaves to announce Japan's surrender. A major with the Office of Strategic Services, Nichols commanded a seven-man team code-named Magpie. On board the B-24 with Nichols sat Captain Edmund Carpenter; First Lieutenant Mahlon Perkins; First Lieutenant Fontaine Jarman Jr., the mission doctor; Staff Sergeant Dick Hamada, the Japanese translator; Corporal Melvin Richter, the Chinese interpreter; and Private First Class Nestor Jacot, the radioman. The team's mission as outlined in the four-page orders was to immediately contact all Allied prisoner-of-war camps in the area, notify headquarters of the number and health of the prisoners, and begin emergency medical assistance.

Magpie was just one of many teams the OSS had assembled to parachute into China, Manchuria, Korea, and Indochina the moment the war ended to search out the estimated 22,000 American prisoners. News of Japan's surrender, which would not formally take place until September 2, in a ceremony aboard the battleship *Missouri*, had been slow to trickle out, making such missions all the more perilous. But Nichols and others knew time was imperative when dealing with sick and injured captives, many of whom battled starvation. The B-24 had lifted off from Hsi-an that afternoon and was loaded down with everything from blankets and rations to blood plasma. "The weather was perfect—hot, sunny, and beautiful," Jarman later wrote. "We arrived over Peking fully expecting to be met by swarms of Kamikaze fighters foresworn to knock us down and make the supreme sacrifice doing so. There were no other planes in the air."

To prepare officials on the ground, the B-24 dropped hundreds of leaflets, many of which blew right back into the plane. Others missed the airdrome and drifted down atop the Pa Dao Wan Convent, where the mission report later noted that "the nuns found them quite interesting reading." In addition, team members each carried a letter from General Albert Wedemeyer, who had replaced Vinegar Joe Stilwell in 1944, explaining the purpose of the mission. If Wedemeyer's letter didn't suffice, there was always cash. Each flier packed $10,000, with the exception of Nichols, who carried $50,000. As the last of the leaflets fluttered out of the bomber, the men looked down and saw hundreds of Japanese soldiers take up positions around the airfield. "We were low enough so that I could see they were all armed with rifles and pistols," Jarman recalled. "I was praying that they had all gotten the word to quit but I had no way of knowing."

The team members crowded around the opening of the belly gun turret, which had been removed to allow the men to bail out.

"Happy hunting!" the jumpmaster announced.

One after the other they bailed out, pulled the rip cord, and drifted down to the airfield below. "The plane circled once more, dropped our equipment and supplies, and then departed," Jarman later wrote. "An almost overwhelming feeling of desolation swept over me as the B-24 faded away."

Nichols, Perkins, and Hamada started toward the hangar, leaving the others to guard the team's equipment. "A long shot rang out, evidently fired by some over eager solider, and a couple of our group hit the ground," the team's report stated. "The Japanese, on the whole, seemed rather disconcerted by our arrival."

A flatbed truck loaded with Japanese troops rolled up. A lieutenant climbed down, along with several soldiers armed with rifles and bayonets, who surrounded the Americans. "What is going on here?" the Japanese officer asked.

"The war is over," Nichols said and Hamada translated. "We're here to retrieve our prisoners."

"No," the lieutenant barked. "The war is *not* over yet!"

The Japanese drove the soldiers to the airfield's headquarters, where the officer of the day told Nichols he would have to wait for Lieutenant General Takahashi, commander of forces in central China. The general finally arrived at 6:30 p.m., in a Buick sedan "with much flourish, clicking of heels and presenting of arms." Nichols again pressed his case, demanding the release of all Allied prisoners of war. "The General," the mission's report noted, "was courteous, but he flatly refused permission to see the POW's until word arrived from Nanking. He pointed out that the war is actually not yet over, and though he would like to oblige, it was impossible." Nichols expounded in a personal note in the report: "Relations were courteous, although I carefully refused 'regretfully' to dine with him or to accept any social invitation from his officers."

The Japanese escorted the Americans to the Grand Hotel des Wagons-Lits in the city, where the frustrated rescuers spent August 18 awaiting permission to visit the area's prisoner-of-war camps. "During all this day, it should be noted that we were virtually prisoners in the Grand Hotel," the mission's report stated. "The Japanese had warned us against wandering around promiscuously, for they asserted that their soldiers were still inclined to be trigger happy. Thus we had no news from the outside."

Not until 5 p.m. the next day did a Japanese lieutenant colonel and captain finally arrive at the hotel. Nichols showed them Wedemeyer's letter, and the officers explained that Japan planned to move the prisoners into town.

"We are anxious to get started on our job as soon as possible," the major stated, according to a transcript of the meeting. "How many POW's and internees are there?"

"Twelve POW's and 317 internees," the lieutenant colonel replied.

"We understood there were more POW's."

"Just twelve."

"May we see the POW's tomorrow?" the major pressed.

"Well, no," the lieutenant colonel said, running through a list of excuses. "Perhaps the day after."

Finally, on the afternoon of August 19, the Japanese took the soldiers to visit all the major internment centers, which housed mostly Allied civilians such as missionaries captured by the Japanese. Nichols messaged headquarters that the team located 317 internees, including 117 Americans, spread across ten locations. "It was much like calling on friends on New Year's," the team's report stated. "Enthusiastic welcomes everywhere, and everywhere something to drink. We were obliged to insult our stomachs with a perfectly impossible combination of red wine, white wine, champagneted wine, pop, coffee and tea, but it was well worth it to see how happy we made everyone. We were even able to enjoy ten separate renditions of 'God Bless America,' sung by Dutch, Belgians, French, British, Germans, Chinese—not to mention Americans, and always with the kind of fervor that tends to bring an unexpected tear to the eye."

At noon the next day the Japanese finally allowed the Americans to visit the prisoners of war, whom guards had relocated into town, lodging them at two hotels. The prisoners rejoiced at seeing uniformed Americans.

"Give it to 'em, lads," many said.

Nichols sat down that afternoon with the commander of Fengtai, a large prisoner-of-war camp located about eight miles southwest of the city. The colonel with a walrus mustache assured Nichols that Japan had released all the prisoners. "While all this discussion was going on, the POW's and internees were peering in the doorways and indicating disapproval of all that was said," the team's report stated. "A few of the internees sidled up to the officers who were not engaged in the conferring with the Japanese and pointed out that there were four prisoners whom the Japanese colonel had not mentioned at all and that they were even now dying in a prison in Peking. These men, they said, were the last of the Doolittle Raiders and were under sentence of death."

ON AUGUST 16 THE RAIDERS noticed that the Japanese did not hold the usual morning drill, an aberration followed the next day by soldiers' torching maps and charts outside in the courtyard. Throughout the day more trucks arrived loaded down with papers, which soldiers continued to feed to the fire. "We watched them from our windows and called to each other from our cells," Hite and DeShazer wrote. "It was a rainy, nasty day, but our hearts were happy. We knew something was going to happen."

The guards were all dressed in crisp new uniforms and began escorting certain captives out of the prison, including Winfield Scott Cunningham, the famed commander of American forces at Wake. None of the airmen had known he was even in the prison. On the night of August 19 a guard entered each of the airmen's cells.

"Ima amata watachi tomoduce," he said. "We are now friends."

The raiders received extra food the next day, before guards pulled them from their cells around 6 p.m. and clipped their thick and matted beards. A barber then shaved them with a straight razor. "We had to stand up during the shave and he lathered our faces with cold water," Hite and DeShazer wrote. "Our faces were pretty sore."

Guards then offered the aviators a real prize—the chance to take a bath, albeit only in a bucket of hot water. "You can go to your country now," one of the Japanese officers announced as the raiders cleaned themselves.

The airmen stared at him in disbelief.

"You can go to your country now," the officer repeated. "The war is over."

The airmen had grown alarmed at the absence of George Barr, who the raiders knew had struggled in recent days with dysentery. A guard finally brought the navigator in while the other three bathed. "We were so happy and excited that we slapped each other on the backs and cheered, but poor George was too sick to comprehend," Hite and DeShazer wrote. "He kept asking us where we were going."

American soldiers arrived at the prison that evening around seven thirty. One of them paused in front of the door to Chase Nielsen's primitive cell. "He looks like an American," the soldier said. "Are you an American?"

Nielsen couldn't speak. After three years, three months and thirty days, the moment of liberation had arrived—yet his voice failed him.

"He looks like an American," the soldier repeated. "Open his door and let him out."

Nielsen's weight had fallen to just 103 pounds, leaving him a gaunt ghost of a man.

"Are you an American?" the soldier pressed again.

"Yes," the former navigator muttered, finding his voice. "I'm an American."

"Where were you taken prisoner?"

"Back in April of 1942 I flew off a carrier, the U.S.S. *Hornet*, in a B-25 with a guy named Jimmy Doolittle," he said. "We bombed Tokyo."

The soldier stared at him in disbelief. "Hell, those guys were all executed years ago," he said, turning to the others. "You want to watch him, he's out of his head."

"No, I'm not," Nielsen protested, his voice stronger. "There's three more of them right down the hall here, too, that are with me. We've been kicked around from Japan, through Shanghai, through Nanking, and now we're up here. Who are you guys?"

"The war's over," the soldier said. "Let's go home."

The soldiers loaded the raiders into a truck and evacuated them to the Grand Peking Hotel, offering them their first real meal in years. "A smiling little Chinese caterer brought us four lovely, heaping plates of Irish stew and nothing ever tasted so good," Hite and DeShazer wrote. "We sang, talked and ate all night."

To the emaciated raiders, who had survived on little more than rice and water, even the soldier's military rations proved a delicacy. "Lord, that was so good!" Hite said of the K rations. "The chocolate was the best thing."

"To us," added Nielsen, "Spam was like eating steak."

One of the rescuers spotted DeShazer slipping food inside his clothes. "From now on, you don't have to worry," he told him. "You'll get enough to eat."

"What did you say?" the bombardier asked, realizing he had been in solitary confinement so long he had trouble comprehending.

"From now on," the soldier repeated, only slower, "you'll get enough to eat."

The Magpie team radioed the spectacular news of the rescue of the raiders. "Have secured release of 4 Doolittle fliers who were charged with murder under Japanese law for Tokio Raid," the message read. "They are now quartered Grand Peking Hotel and receiving best care possible."

The news quickly reverberated up the chain of command. "Theater desires any info which 4 recovered Doolittle fliers may have concerning fate of other 4 captured Doolittle fliers similarly charged with murder," an August 23 message stated. "Kindly relay this and advise soonest."

In a report filed two days later Nielsen, Hite, and DeShazer confirmed the deaths of Bill Dieter and Donald Fitzmaurice in the crash off the China coast as well as Bob Meder's death in prison. The rescued raiders reported that the Japanese waterboarded them and then put them on trial for targeting children. "Hallmark, Farrow and Spatz sentenced separately and taken away," the report stated. "This was last subjects saw them. Subjects believed these three executed."

Hap Arnold would ultimately confirm those deaths in letters to the families, noting that he had prayed for the safe return of all the raiders. "There is nothing that one can say that will be of comfort to you I know, but one thing I hope you will always remember—the fire kindled in the heart of every American by your son and his fellow flyers led to the inevitable and conclusive defeat of Japan," he wrote to Hallmark's family. "The courage displayed by Lieutenant Hallmark throughout life was still evident when he faced his cowardly assassins. He died with honor and valor for his country."

Though both Hite and Barr struggled with beriberi, Barr proved in far worse shape. The navigator's weight had gone from 187 pounds to just 97, and his mind had begun to unravel. "He arrived in a state of stupor with weak pulse," the medical report stated. "Physical exam showed oedema of both feet and wide spread loss of tactile sensations." Doctors immediately gave him fifty milligrams of vitamin B_1 and continued him on injections twice daily, supplemented by vitamin tablets. He was also administered a ferrous sulfate solution three times a day before meals, along with calcium lactate tablets afterward; in addition doctors gave him two transfusions of blood plasma. "Present condition," the report concluded, "pulse improving but still weak, tactile sensations returning, knee jerks weakly present with reinforcement."

Nielsen, Hite, and DeShazer flew to Chungking on August 24, but Barr remained too sick to be evacuated. Former prisoner of war Karel Mulder sat vigil at the navigator's bedside, watching as Barr drifted in and out of consciousness. Barr's hand would occasionally creep up Mulder's shirt and grasp his long white beard. "I would then gently disengage his hand and put it down on his bed," Mulder recalled, "but a little later his hand would creep up and get hold of my beard again."

Jack Van Norman, the copilot of the C-47 transport that flew the others out of Peiping, wrote about the experience in his diary. "Brought back a load of Jap prisoners that were at Mukden. Three of them were Doolittle's men. They have been prisoners since April 1942. Left them at Chungking & took the rest to Kunming. Really had a reception waiting for them at Chungking," he wrote. "Most of them were in pretty bad shape, the Doolittle boys had been in solitary confinement most of the time. Went up to the club when we got back, a big time was had by all."

News of the rescue of the Doolittle raiders ran on the front pages of newspapers across the nation, including the *New York Times*. Reporters now anxiously awaited the chance to interview the fliers, who sat for a press conference in Chungking soon after arriving in a small room at the headquarters that overlooked the sluggish Chia-ling River. "The three men were so weak from malnutrition that they staggered when they walked down the gangplank of the C-47 transport that brought them here," wrote a reporter for United Press. "They were assisted to the ground."

"They looked at first glance," noted an Associated Press reporter, "as if they had never smiled nor ever would smile again—but they did."

The raiders recalled details of the attacks on Tokyo and Nagoya, which now seemed like old news in a war that was finally over. Hite nervously fingered his throat, his voice so low reporters struggled to hear him.

"It's good to get some GI food into your belly after that hollow feeling," DeShazer told reporters.

"I feel that I'm an American again," added Nielsen, who found a message waiting for him in Chungking from his wife, Thora. "He was a different man," one reporter noted, "after he read it."

General Wedemeyer fired off a telegram to Doolittle with the news of the rescue. "Three members of your Tokyo raid have been recovered. They are Lt. Nielsen, Lt. Hite and Sgt. DeShazer. Are now in Chungking leaving tomorrow for Kunming and then home," Wedemeyer wrote. "They wish to be remembered to you."

Hite, Nielsen, and DeShazer returned to the United States at 12:45

a.m. on September 4 and checked into Walter Reed General Hospital for an exam. The emaciated airmen had gained on average one pound a day since their rescue. There were other issues as well. After forty months without a toothbrush, Nielsen had to endure nineteen fillings. The raiders drew years of back pay, which totaled $8,832.91 for Nielsen, $7,547.80 for Hite, and $5,571.16 for DeShazer. The War Department put out a press release two days later, condensing three years of horror into just three pages. The raiders then sat for another press conference. "Their gaunt and prematurely aged faces," wrote a *New York Times* reporter, "bore silent witness to the suffering and privation they endured."

As the three men improved, Barr continued to unravel, believing his rescue was really just a ruse. "I was convinced that the whole thing was a Jap trick," he later wrote. "That this was some new form of torture." When he recovered physically, the Army flew him to Kunming on September 12, but Barr's suspicions followed. "I was a bed patient in the hospital; I saw no one I knew," he wrote. "A voice kept telling me this was a trick and to be careful. Even the hospital seemed like a prison."

Barr suffered a breakdown a few days after his arrival, described in a nurse's report. "Awoke suddenly at 2 a.m. Jumped out of bed screaming," the report stated. "Restrained by three men. Gritted teeth and uttered animal-like sounds with occasional threats to his 'torturers.'" The outburst landed Barr in the hospital's psychiatric ward. "All my past suspicions and doubts were now confirmed," he later said. "The barren room, the bars on the window, the occasional face at a slot in the locked door, and the solitary confinement spelled prison as far as I was concerned. I lay there a long time thinking things over and decided that I would pretend to go along with anything my captors were trying to make me do— but I would try to escape when the opportunity arose."

Barr saw his chance when a medical corpsman escorted him across the tarmac to a waiting C-47 for the flight out in October. He could see the distant mountains unobscured by towering fences and walls that for more than three years had defined his life and caged him like an animal. Barr felt his adrenaline soar; his freedom finally at hand. He broke free of the corpsman and ran, his feet carrying him toward the horizon.

An unseen blow knocked him unconscious. Barr awoke in a straitjacket in the back of a transport plane. His suspicions only deepened when he reached the Calcutta hospital. "I was regaining some strength," he later wrote, "but I still had those horrible nightmares and with them the persistent notion that the Japs had concocted some fiendish trick which would be made clear eventually."

Barr had spent his captivity with Hite, Nielsen, and DeShazer, all of whom were now gone. He scanned the faces of the doctors, nurses, and other patients, looking for anyone familiar. "Why don't I see someone I know," he asked himself.

"This is a trick, another Jap trick," an inner voice warned him. "Pretty soon you'll see you are still a prisoner."

Barr arrived at San Francisco's Letterman General Hospital on October 12. He carried no medical records or even identification and struggled to answer the admittance clerk's basic questions. The frustrated clerk finally summoned an orderly.

"Show the lieutenant to a room and get him some pajamas."

The orderly escorted Barr to a room with two beds, a nightstand, and a chair. "Take your clothes off," the orderly told him. "Put these pajamas on."

Barr did as told, and the orderly left him alone. The navigator's earlier fears now returned. This was no hospital, he believed, but another prison. Mentally and physically exhausted, Barr could no longer take it. He spied a pocketknife on the nightstand and picked it up, flicking open the blade. Barr plunged the knife into his chest. To his shock he felt no pain nor did he bleed much. He looked out his second-floor window, contemplating jumping, but realized he was not high enough. Barr found a heating lamp and ripped off the cord, fashioning a noose. He slid a chair under the overhead light fixture and climbed up. Barr tied the noose to the light and slipped it around his neck, careful to tighten it up. He kicked the chair out from under him.

Barr felt his head snap, and then he crashed to the floor as glass, metal, and sparks rained down on him. A report five days later noted that the Air Transport Service had failed to classify Barr as a disturbed mental patient. "The administrative failure," the report stated, "almost meant this individual's life." Doctors ordered Barr transferred to Schick General Hospital in Clinton, Iowa, a three-day train ride he made in a straitjacket. "He will require maximum care en route," his doctor's report noted. "Unless this is observed he can be counted upon to injure himself."

Orphaned at a young age, Barr had been cared for in part by a social worker, Eleanor Towns, who had spent the weeks since the war's end working the phones trying to find him. She finally located Barr in Iowa and alerted his sister, Grace Maas, who visited him along with her husband, Bill, and close friend Betty Alexander. The familiar faces of his friends and family proved the healing tonic he so desperately needed. "I knew then it was true," Barr wrote. "I knew I was free. I knew that the horror was over."

Eleanor Towns had likewise reached out to Doolittle during her frantic search. Once she located Barr, she relayed the information to the general, who promptly visited. On a walk across the hospital grounds, Barr recounted the horrors of his forty months in prison to the man who had led him over Japan. "He tried to tell me everything he could. He was hesitant at first, but then the tears flowed and the words began to pour out," Doolittle recalled. "Catharsis was obviously what was needed."

Barr's problems persisted. He told Doolittle he had not seen a doctor since his arrival. He likewise had no uniforms or money, even though he was entitled to years of back pay. Doolittle was shocked—then outraged. "The last of my Tokyo Raiders to come home needed help," he later wrote, "and I was going to see that he got it."

Doolittle marched to the hospital commander's office. "I unloaded Doolittle's worst verbal fury on his head. I won't repeat what I said because it would burn a hole in this page," he later wrote. "I will say that George was quickly outfitted in a new uniform, complete with the ribbons he didn't know he had earned, and was given a check for over $7,000 in back pay, and orders promoting him to first lieutenant. Best of all, he was seen immediately by a psychiatrist and began the slow road back to recovery."

Doolittle's fury reverberated at the highest levels of the Army Air Forces, which soon transferred Barr to Pawling Air Force Convalescent Center, on Long Island. Brigadier General Malcolm Grow, the air surgeon, promised to personally update Doolittle. "I have instructed our facility at Pawling to inform me as soon as Captain Barr arrives so that I can in turn inform you," Grow wrote in a letter to Doolittle. "I plan to keep myself informed of Captain Barr's condition and progress so that we can be sure that everything possible is being done to promote his recovery."

Before he left Schick General Hospital that afternoon Doolittle asked Barr whether he remembered his promise aboard the *Hornet* to throw a party for all the raiders.

"Yes, sir," Barr answered, "I do."

"Well, George, we never had that party because you and the rest of the fellows couldn't make it. But I'm going to keep that promise. The whole gang is invited to be my guests in Miami on my birthday," Doolittle told Barr. "I want you to come. I'll send an airplane for you."

CHAPTER 27

───────────
───────────

★

I don't want revenge. I want peace.

—GEORGE BARR,
MAY 13, 1946

RECOVERY WOULD PROVE DIFFICULT for the four former prisoners of war, who struggled after years of solitary confinement to readjust to life in civilization. The men often found themselves agitated and plagued by nightmares. "Lord, I was nervous and I kind of wanted to be alone. I think I was just sort of frightened of people," Hite recalled. "We had been in that solitary confinement so long that I don't know whether we wanted to see anybody or not. It had almost grown on us. Our people, at the time, didn't know what to do with us, really. I think they tried to push us and treat us like everybody else, which was probably a good thing in a lot of ways. But they didn't know the state of our minds or our psyche." In an article published a few months after their release, Hite and DeShazer described their struggle to readjust. "We have memories we can express only to each other," the men wrote. "They will be with us always."

The raiders not only wrestled with their own adjustment to freedom after forty months in horrific prisons but also battled the guilt of having survived when their friends had not. Despite his own struggles Hite felt he owed the families of his fellow raiders the courtesy of telling them what he could. In an October letter to Dean Hallmark's family in Dallas, Hite described the sham trial that had condemned his friends to death. "We never saw our buddies again," he wrote of the sentencing in October 1942. "The Japs took us to the room in which our clothes were stored; there we found Dean's clothing also the clothing of Spatz and Farrow. We were confused and struck by the indication, but nevertheless held to the theory that they had only been separated to another prison. Ourselves doomed to life in prisonment in solitary confinement it was hard to keep up our morale as we were entirely alone."

Hite confessed that his grief, upon his release from prison and receiving the confirmation of the execution of his friends, had delayed his writing. He tried to remain upbeat in his five-page letter written on U.S. Army Air Forces stationery, noting that Hallmark and the others were heroes to a grateful nation. "Dean was a splendid example of American youth and courage, hoping until the very end and then his hopes justified in his faith in the God of us all. It is a matter of deep concern to me that your son, loved by millions, is gone. He was noble, courageous and an uplift to all of us in our moments of despair, knowing not what the Japs were going to do with us." Hite concluded with a promise to come visit. "Neither Dean nor Meder or Farrow and Spatz are really gone," he wrote. "I know they are justified in the sight of our God. I can see them now and they are there indelibly inscribed on the hearts of all our American people."

Hite followed through with his plans to visit, sitting down with Hallmark's parents in their home at 808 Wayne Avenue in Dallas, an address he would never forget. The conversation proved difficult.

"Why are you here and not my son?" Ollie Hallmark asked. Hite struggled to respond. "Those were answers," he said, "that were sort of hard to come by."

Hite likewise wrote a letter to Harold Spatz's family in Lebo, Kansas. "I want to extend to you my deep felt sympathy and love for Harold," he began. "I know that the uncertainty has been hard on you as it has been on my mother, as she did think that I was executed. I cannot understand why three members of our flight were executed except that it was the treacherous act of the bloody Japanese. We were all kept blind as to what the Japs intended to do with us. Sometimes the Japs would say we were all going to be executed and again that we would be kept alive but not allowed to return to our country; the pressure has been trying and the disappearance of Harold, Hallmark and Farrow a grief to us all." Hite concluded by telling Spatz's mother that her son had remained strong until the end. "I know they are now happy and at rest," he wrote, "though it grieves us to know they are physically gone, they still live with us in spirit."

Chase Nielsen likewise wrote to Bill Dieter's mother in California, relaying the details of the *Green Hornet*'s violent crash in the Chinese surf, the injuries Dieter and Donald Fitzmaurice sustained, and the burial of the airmen the next day on the sandy knoll overlooking the beach. "Bill and Fitz were two simply grand fellows, and although we had not been acquainted very long we were all like brothers," Nielsen wrote. "I have spent many hours in sorrow thinking of my dear departed friends. I know that you too Mrs. Dieter have been carrying a heavy burden. But I know the Gracious God who comforts all will help you to bear up under your load. I also pray that he bless you in every way and that he grant Bill the privilege of preparing a beautiful place of meeting and rest for all his loved ones in the Kingdom where we all will meet again."

Nielsen gave the location of Dieter's and Fitzmaurice's graves to American forces in China in 1945. The Graves Registration bureau contacted him the next year, asking whether he would help find the remains. That spring Nielsen traveled back to that spot along the Chinese coast. Armed with shovels the men dug through the sand and found the wooden boxes the fliers had used to bury their friends four years earlier. "In each coffin with the remains," Nielsen wrote Dieter's mother, "was enough of their flying jackets left so as to identity each by the name plates." May Dieter had grown close with Donald Fitzmaurice's mother over the years as the women awaited word of what happened to their boys. The two mothers decided on a final request, which May Dieter outlined in a letter to Doolittle. The airmen had died together in the surf that night after the raid, and for the last four years they had lain side by side in graves in China. It would be a shame now to separate them. "Do you think," she added, "it would be too much to ask to have them in Arlington?"

American investigators after the war set out on what might have first appeared a quixotic hunt to track down the remains of the executed fliers. Despite Tatsuta's promise to the airmen that their ashes would be returned to the United States, the cremated remains of Hallmark, Farrow, and Spatz languished in a Shanghai funeral parlor, where the Japanese had placed them on November 14, 1942. When the war ended, uniformed Japanese troops visited the funeral home, changing Hallmark's name to J. Smith, Spatz's name to E. L. Brister, and Farrow's to H. E. Gande, a move designed to cover up the crime. A fellow prisoner and translator, Caesar Luis Dos Remedios, who worked with war crime investigators, located the remains. Though the Japanese had changed the names, Remedios discovered, no one had changed the birth dates, allowing investigators to link the ashes back to the raiders. Each box, nine inches long, nine wide, and twelve deep—covered by a flag—would serve as prosecution Exhibit C in the case of the United States of America versus Shigeru Sawada, Yusei Wako, Ryuhei Okada, and Sotojiro Tatsuta.

All that was left was to find the remains of Meder, who had died in Nanking on December 1, 1943. Captain Jason Bailey, a former agent with the Federal Bureau of Investigation from San Francisco, visited Kiangwan in late September, accompanied by journalist Irene Kuhn. Guards had just invited the American investigators to enjoy a cup of green tea when Captain Maszumi Shimada appeared, clutching a small wooden box wrapped in a fine white silk. The silk was open at the top, and a label stenciled in black read, "USA Commissioned Officer's Ashes."

"These are Captain Meder's ashes," Shimada announced. "They have just arrived from Nanking. You will take them back to Shanghai with you, perhaps?"

Bailey was shocked. "None of us," Kuhn later wrote, "was prepared for this."

"Give the box to me," Bailey ordered.

Shimada handed him the box, which he placed on his knees and stared down at silently. "I put out my hands," Kuhn wrote. "Perhaps because I was a woman responding to some inner urging that, miraculously, this young man understood, he handed me the box without a word. I cradled it in my arms on my lap and bent my head to hide my face from the inquisitive Japanese around us. Not for worlds would I have let them see the tears that were in my eyes and that I was fighting desperately to hold back."

The Japanese produced a second box, this one wrapped in unbleached muslin, which Bailey demanded opened. Shimada's aide untied the muslin knot, opened the top, and handed the box to Bailey. Inside he found Meder's personal effects.

"A book of traveller's checks, $10 denomination each, Bank of America, San Francisco," Bailey read, pulling the items out one by one.

"A personal check book, National Bank of Fort Sam Houston. Last check, according to the stub, made out to the U.S.S. *Hornet* Mess—for $17," he said. "The stub just ahead of that shows he drew a check to the Midland Mutual Life Insurance Co. for $21.25—premium on his life insurance policy. That was on February 2, 1942."

Bailey produced a membership card to the Round Up Room of the Temple Hotel in Pendleton, Oregon, the home of the Seventeenth Bombardment Group, as well as a Phi Kappa Tau fraternity card from Meder's days at Miami University in Oxford, Ohio. He also found a compass, comb, and Social Security card. "There was a picture of a very pretty girl," Kuhn wrote, "smiling out at us from the discolored paper in the mildewed leather case the young Lieutenant had carried with him until the last."

The raiders' remains were eventually brought back home. Harold Spatz was laid to rest at the National Memorial Cemetery of the Pacific in Honolulu. Hallmark, Farrow, and Meder's ashes were buried in Arlington. Herb Macia captured the scene in a letter to Hallmark's mother after he laid roses from his own garden on his friend's grave. "Dean is buried between Bob Meder and Bill Farrow," he wrote. "Their graves lie under a beautiful tree which shades and protects them."

With the war finally over and the guns now silent, America and its allies convened the International Military Tribunal of the Far East, the Pacific counterpart to the Nuremburg Trials, which prosecuted German political and military leaders for atrocities. This years-long legal process ultimately led to the investigation and prosecution of more than five thousand Japanese defendants, including some of those involved in the trial and execution of the Doolittle raiders. Authorities arrested Hideki Tojo and Shunroku Hata, the former commander the China Expeditionary Army, both of whom would stand trial for other war crimes. Hajime Sugiyama, the former Army chief of staff and vocal proponent of the airmen's execution, shot himself days after the war ended. Prosecutor Itsuro Hata had also died; so had Chief Judge Toyoma Nakajo.

Authorities arrested Shigeru Sawada. Hata had ordered the former commander of the Thirteenth Expeditionary Army in China to appoint the military tribunal that prosecuted the airmen. Investigators likewise arrested tribunal judges Ryuhei Okada and Yusei Wako as well Sotojiro Tatsuta, the warden and executioner. The four defendants stood trial together at the Ward Road Jail in Shanghai in what prosecutor Lieutenant Colonel John Hendren Jr. told reporters would be an "open and shut case." Opening statements began the morning of March 18, 1946. Unlike the case against the raiders, which had lasted barely half an hour, this one stretched on for nearly a month. Defendants were provided counsel, access to exhibits, and the opportunity to cross-examine witnesses. Defense lawyers even flew to Tokyo to search out witnesses and collect evidence. The record of the proceedings along with exhibits would ultimately run to some 750 pages and include a wide range of testimony, from Hallmark's cellmates at the Bridge House to a doctor who described Meder's death of malnutrition and Japanese teachers who witnessed the raid. Court members even visited the cemetery where the raiders were shot.

Nielsen served as the prosecution's star witness, noting in a letter to Doolittle how the defendants cringed when he entered the courtroom to testify. A photo of Tatsuta bowing to him would later run in newspapers nationwide. "I sit here with tears in my eyes," Nielsen wrote, "when I think what has happened to the ones who were in the Jap prison camps, and feel that I want to do what little I can to help those who came back and to help prosecute those who were responsible for the executing of the others." Nielsen testified for several days, recounting in detail the plans and training for the mission, Doolittle's strict orders to avoid all nonmilitary targets as well as his personal recollections of the raid. The *Green Hornet*'s navigator then recounted in painful detail the torture and punishment he and the others suffered after their capture in China, from the beatings and waterboarding to their forced confessions.

George Barr contributed testimony from Schick General Hospital in Iowa, a forty-three-page transcript ultimately included in the record. Hite and DeShazer in Washington likewise provided a joint four-page affidavit. Doolittle sat for questions at the Pentagon, resulting in a three-page transcript for the record in which he denied that any of his men had intentionally targeted schools or hospitals, as the Japanese had claimed. "Crews were repeatedly briefed to avoid any action that could possibly give the Japanese any ground to say that we had bombed or strafed indiscriminately," Doolittle testified. "Specifically, they were told to stay away from hospitals, schools, museums and anything else that was not a military target." He did concede that Japan's dense cities made it difficult to guarantee no civilian casualties. "It is quite impossible to bomb a military objective that has civilian residences near it without danger of harming the civilian residences as well," Doolittle said. "That is a hazard of war."

Prosecutor Robert Dwyer in his closing statement addressed the fallacy of the trial that had condemned some of the raiders to death and others to life in prison. "In all my life I have never seen, and I doubt whether I have even read, of any trial which was quite the mockery of justice that this one was," he said. "The evil began when these men were placed before a tribunal, a tribunal of any kind, and secondly, once they were placed before it they had no more chance or opportunity of a fair and honest trial than I have with my right hand to stem the fall of Niagara's waters, and these men having paid the supreme penalty, I say they stand here in spirit." The prosecution asked the commission for the maximum punishment. "We have charged these men with the violations of the laws of custom and war," he concluded. "We have proven it by a wealth of evidence and we close by asking for the death penalty against all four accused."

The defense lawyers, in contrast, blamed the trial and execution of the raiders on officers higher up the chain of command as well as on Japan's passage of the so-called Enemy Airmen's Act. The defendants had simply followed orders. "Every detail was decided in Tokyo and the defendants in this case in their respective official capacity acted only mechanically," Shinji Somiya argued. "They were nothing but the men of straw manipulated at the tip. They had entirely no freedom of will to do or not to do." In his closing statement the lawyer begged the justices to show mercy, asking them to remember the words from the Bible's book of Matthew: "I say unto you, love your enemies, bless them that curse you, do good to them that hate you, and pray for them which despitefully use you and persecute you."

After deliberating for two days, the five-member commission decided to spare the lives of the defendants, agreeing that the men had only followed orders. "The offenses of each of the accused resulted largely from obedience to the laws and instructions of their Government and their Military Superiors," the commission concluded. "They exercised no initiative to any marked degree. The preponderance of evidence shows beyond reasonable doubt that other officers, including high governmental and military officials, were responsible for the enactment of the Ex poste Facto 'Enemy Airmen's Law' and the issuance of special instructions as to how these American Prisoners were to be treated, tried, sentenced and punished. The circumstances set forth above do not entirely absolve the accused from guilt. However, they do compel unusually strong mitigating considerations, applicable to each accused in various degrees."

The commission sentenced Sawada, Okada, and Tatsuta each to five years of hard labor. Wako received nine years, the tribunal reasoning that since he had prior legal training he was in a better position to recognize the airmen's bogus confessions, yet he had accepted them without question. War criminals who could have swung at the end of a rope would instead walk free in just a few years. Although unable to increase the punishments, the reviewing authority blasted the weak sentences in August 1946. "The Commission by awarding such extremely lenient and inadequate penalties committed a serious error of judgment," the review found. "It is clear that when they found the accused guilty of the capital offenses of mistreatment and murder under the laws of war, the penalties should have been commensurate with such findings."

Reporters who covered the trial noted that the defendants appeared impassive as the commission read the lenient sentences, even as the Japanese defense counsel wept with surprise. A member of the defense team, Moritada Kumashiro, wiped away tears before addressing the court. "On behalf of the Japanese Counsel, I would like to express my hearty thanks to this Commission to the fair and sympathetic verdict in the case," Kumashiro said with a choked voice. "We deeply appreciate everything that has been done." The punishment outraged Americans across the nation. "Have you any comments on leniency court martial showed Japanese murderers of your son. Please wire collect," the managing editor of the *Philadelphia Daily News* cabled Hallmark's parents in Texas. "We will be glad to print any criticism you wish to make." A handwritten note in the Hallmark family files captured the anguish of the airman's mother. "In my estimation the representatives of our country have fallen down in avenging the murder of our son. I am amazed at the light sentence given the murders. We have heard from people all over the nation and they feel the same," she wrote. "This won't ever be forgotten."

Few were as outraged as Chase Nielsen, who had returned to China on a mission to seek justice for his friends. He promised Hallmark's mother that he planned to protest the sentences with Doolittle, his senator, and even President Truman. "I thought if I went back to Shanghai to testify it would help but it looks as though I've been made a fool of," he wrote. "I'll do all I can Mrs. Hallmark as the death of my three buddies by execution and the loss of three more through the raid, means much to me and a 5 to 9 year sentence is not a just one." Nielsen appeared to have calmed down almost two weeks later when he wrote to Dieter's mother. "I am sorry justice could not see fit to even its sides for the Mothers and families of the three executed," Nielsen wrote. "I feel I have done all in my power, and feel I have lost, but justice will be meted out some day yet."

The four convicted Japanese landed in Tokyo's Sugamo Prison to serve their sentences, where the former general Sawada lobbied American officials to release Okada and Tatsuta, who he argued were only following his orders. The duo's incarceration, he wrote, tormented his "heart day and night." "Since this was the tribunal of the Japanese Army which I had ordered and summoned in accordance with the order from my superior," Sawada wrote in 1949, "I should be responsible for all the consequences arising therefrom, and it has been a tremendous pain for me that my subordinates were punished for that matter in line with myself." Sawada, Okada, and Tatsuta would walk free on January 9, 1950, having served a total of just 1,365 days.

Yusei Wako was found guilty again in December 1948, this time for overseeing the beheading of eight B-29 airmen in June 1945—he personally decapitated two—and for his assistance with the execution of eight others that August. The commission this time sentenced Wako to death, a punishment Douglas MacArthur commuted in July 1950 to life in prison at hard labor. Even then he would not serve his full term, but was paroled in 1956, serving just six months for each man he was convicted of helping kill. Wako's prison record shows he spent most of that time crafting musical instruments and farming. On an application for clemency the prisoner who had helped kill twenty American airmen outlined a future career path that in all likelihood startled the review board. "I intend," Wako wrote, "to become a lawyer, public prosecutor or a judge."

★

WAR CRIME INVESTIGATORS likewise doggedly pursued former general Sadamu Shimomura, who had replaced Sawada as the commander of the Thirteenth Army on the eve of the raiders' execution, reportedly personally signing the airmen's death order. In December 1945, investigators orally requested that American authorities in Tokyo arrest him. General Douglas MacArthur's staff refused. Not unlike other suspected war criminals whom American officials would prove reluctant to prosecute, Shimomura had become a valuable asset in postwar Japan. He served as the nation's minister of war, working closely with American authorities to demobilize the army. He had given an important speech in October, publicly falling on the sword as he argued that Japanese military leaders must apologize for all of the military's transgressions. "It is common knowledge now that extermination of militarism and the military clique is being voiced both at home and abroad," he said. "Looking back on the past, this is only a natural consequence."

To American investigators in China, none of this mattered. If Shimomura played a role in the execution of the raiders, he should be prosecuted. In a January 3 memo Lieutenant Colonel John Hendren Jr., an assistant staff judge advocate, argued that evidence showed Shimomura had replaced Sawada at the time of the execution and had even issued the instructions to Tatsuta for how the deaths should occur. It would be unfair to try only Sawada if both generals were culpable in the trial and execution. "It is believed that if permission is not given to try Shimomura that Sawada should not be tried," Hendren argued. "If these two top Generals are left out of this case it will appear to the Military Commission and the public that we are attempting to hold junior officers for offenses which they were ordered to commit on command of higher authority."

War crimes investigators filed a formal request for Shimomura's arrest on January 11, 1946. MacArthur's staff again refused, this time claiming the case would be considered from an "international standpoint." Investigators filed a second arrest request on January 23 and followed up with a visit to Japan, arousing the international press. Now MacArthur's staff had no choice but to allow the arrest of Shimomura, who was interned at Sugamo Prison on February 9, 1946. Rather than hand him over to stand trial in March alongside the other four defendants, MacArthur's staff put up a fierce defense of the former general, tracking down hotel receipts and witnesses who might exonerate him. In the end, Brigadier General Charles Willoughby, MacArthur's chief of intelligence, fell back on the defense that Shimomura was simply following orders. "As the final decision for the execution of the fliers had been made by Imperial General Headquarters, Tokyo, on 10 October," Willoughby wrote in a memo, "the signature of the Commanding General 13th Army on the execution order was simply a matter of formality."

Willoughby's argument, of course, was the same made by the other four defendants, yet the court still tried and convicted them. His long delay did in the end accomplish its goal. "The War Crimes mission in China is about to close," Major Ralph Hinner wrote in September. "Further action by this Headquarters with respect to trial of General Shimomura is no longer possible. Accordingly, this Headquarters is not disposed to take any action in the case." Willoughby personally oversaw the details of Shimomura's secret release, which involved bypassing the required written instructions from the Japanese government as well as the stealth elimination of his name from the prison's daily reports. A private sedan would pick him up at the prison and drive him to his home in Ichikawa at noon on March 14, 1947, before officials sent him away "to a quiet place for a few months." The man who had allegedly inked his name to the execution order of Doolittle's raiders in the end would never serve another day in jail. "It is directed," orders stated, "that this release be given no publicity."

EPILOGUE

Immortality will always be theirs.

—HOWARD PYLE, ADMINISTRATIVE ASSISTANT TO
DWIGHT EISENHOWER, 1955

ON THE EVE OF the Tokyo raid, as his seventy-nine men crowded around him on board the *Hornet*, Doolittle had made a promise. "When we get to Chungking," he told them, "I'm going to give you all a party that you won't forget."

But the airmen had trickled into Chungking in waves, and the party never materialized. Doolittle held a reunion in 1943 in North Africa for about two dozen of the fliers, but that was not the party he wanted to have, not the party he had promised.

So with the war over—and the last of his airmen home—Doolittle sent a letter to his raiders. "Now seems to be the right time to have our get-together and I, for one, would appreciate nothing more than a chance to swap handshakes, yarns and toasts with the old, original gang," he wrote in November 1945. "I plan to throw a dinner with all the food you can eat and whatever liquid you choose to float the food on."

The first reunion in Miami the weekend of December 15, 1945, started a tradition that would carry on for nearly seven decades. The responses were overwhelming as telegrams and letters clogged Doolittle's in-box.

"I will be there with bells on," Davy Jones wrote. "In fact, I'm going in training this week so that I will be in good drinking shape by the time the 15th rolls around."

"General, I want to see those men and be at that party so badly that I can taste it," replied Shorty Manch.

"You may count on me," wrote Ross Greening, "unless the Empire State Building falls on me."

The prospective party gave pause to Chase Nielsen, still adjusting to his new life as a free man. "When I realize that I am the only one left of the crew on my ship," he wrote, "I feel almost alone, but exceedingly lucky."

Of the eighty men who roared off the *Hornet*'s deck, sixty-one had survived the war. The raid had claimed the lives of Leland Faktor, Bill Dieter, and Don Fitzmaurice. The Japanese had executed Billy Farrow, Dean Hallmark, and Harold Spatz, and Bob Meder had starved to death in prison. Twelve others had died in the war: Bob Clever, Bob Gray, Denver Truelove, Donald Smith, Richard Miller, Ken Reddy, Edwin Bain, George Larkin, Eugene McGurl, Omer Duquette, Melvin Gardner, and Paul Leonard. The last was Doolittle's trusted crew chief, who the day after the Tokyo raid had stood amid the B-25's wreckage on the Chinese mountainside and assured his commander he would not only make general but receive the Medal of Honor.

Doolittle was with Leonard when he was killed in 1943 in Algeria, hit by a bomb in a German attack on the airfield. "The softening point of this tragedy is that he never knew that it was coming and never knew that it hit him," Doolittle explained to Leonard's widow in Denver in what he later described as "the saddest letter I ever wrote." "If he had to go it was the way he would have preferred, quick, clean and painless." Doolittle spared her the awful reality of what the bomb did to her husband, though the horrible scene would haunt the general for decades. "I found what was left of Paul. It was his left hand off at the wrist, with a wristwatch still in place. This was all that remained of the wonderful boy who had tried to cheer me up in China in my saddest moment," he wrote. "Paul's loss was my greatest personal tragedy of the war."

That April 1942 Doolittle and his raiders had accomplished the impossible, taking off at such a great distance that most knew the chance of survival was slim at best, yet the airmen still managed to bomb Japan and escape. That more were not captured or killed is miraculous, saved only by a tailwind that pilot Harold Watson later described as the "hand of heaven." The Tokyo raid had not only buoyed the morale of a wounded nation, but postwar records and interviews with senior Japanese leaders would reveal the raid's effect on the plans to capture Midway, an unintended consequence that would yield the mission's greatest success. The June 1942 battle, which cost Japan four aircraft carriers, shifted the balance of power in the Pacific, setting the stage for America's offensive drive across the Pacific. "The carrier action at Midway," concluded the U.S. Strategic Bombing Survey, "was perhaps the decisive battle of the war."

But the raid came at great expense. Claire Chennault, leader of the Flying Tigers, later complained that the intense secrecy cost the mission all the bombers. Had he been informed of the operation, Chennault wrote, radiomen could have talked Doolittle's men down to friendly airfields. "My bitterness over that bit of bungling," he wrote, "has not eased with the passing years." That in part led to the government's deception, keeping secret the loss of the bombers and the capture of two of the crews. But the greatest toll, of course, came in the human and property losses suffered by the Chinese, a consequence of the raid that American leaders knew was a possibility yet decided was worth the risk. The estimated 250,000 Chinese killed was a by-product of the raid that drew far too little notice by the American public at the time and in the years since. "The invaders made of a rich, flourishing country a human hell," wrote one Chinese journalist, "a gruesome graveyard, where the only living thing we saw for miles was a skeleton-like dog, who fled in terror before our approach."

At that first reunion in Miami, the raiders swam, drank, and enjoyed the camaraderie of old friends. They returned to Miami in 1947 for a second reunion. Nielsen asked Doolittle whether he might invite the prosecutors from the war crimes trials, which had recently wrapped up in China. The party proved a raucous good time, as evidenced by the memo the following morning from the hotel's night attendant:

> The Doolittle boys added some gray hairs to my head. This has been the worst night since I worked here. They were completely out of my control.

I let them make a lot of noise in 211 but when about 15 of them with girls went in the pool at 1:00 A.M. (including Doolittle) I told them (no swimming allowed at night) Doolittle told me that he did not want to make trouble and that they were going to make one more dive and would leave. But they were in the pool until 2:30 A.M.

I went up twice more without results. They were running around in the halls in their bathing suits and were noisy up until 5:00 A.M.

Yes, it was a rough night.

More than two dozen raiders would autograph that complaint, which is now preserved in the archives of the Air Force Historical Research Agency at Maxwell Air Force Base, in Montgomery, Alabama. They had such a great time that they would continue to gather yearly until 2013, skipping only 1951 and 1966 because of the Korean and Vietnam wars. At each reunion they would reach out to the families of the men killed, reminding them that their sons were not forgotten. "Bill is here with us in spirit just as he is with you today," they wrote to Farrow's mother during the first reunion in Miami. "He will ever be with us through the years to come."

Ski York and Bob Emmens maintained a decades-long debate over whether the Russians had moved them south in order to allow them to escape. York later said he always believed the Russians had; Emmens disagreed. Neither airman would live long enough to learn the truth. A formerly top-secret cable from October 1944 contains an important clue that indicates York's hunch was likely true. The American ambassador to Russia, working with that nation's foreign minster, had arranged for twenty-eight internees to be sent from Siberia to Tashkent, on the Iranian border, to join sixty-two others, most of them Navy airmen. "When this is done," the cable stated, "an escape will be arranged for these prisoners similar to the one that took place last February."

The war receded into the background as the raiders moved on with their lives, found jobs, married, and raised children. Jacob DeShazer followed through with his vow to return to Japan as a missionary; there he was stunned to discover that the Japanese had created a park in Doolittle's honor. Over more than three decades, he would go on to start twenty-three churches, including one in Nagoya, the city he had first seen through a bombardier's sight. In an unlikely twist of fate, DeShazer's powerful tale of forgiveness helped persuade Mitsuo Fuchida to convert to Christianity, the famed pilot who had led the attack on Pearl Harbor. Fuchida was baptized in DeShazer's church. "I was very lost," he later said, "but his story inspired me to get the Bible."

DeShazer's fellow prisoners of war would wrestle for years with the pains of that traumatic experience. George Barr, with the help of Doolittle, finally began to heal. "He appears to have complete faith in his full recovery," Eleanor Towns wrote the general in February 1946. "For the first time since his capture I feel he now has a sense of security." Barr recounted his own battles in an article published two months later by International News. "The nightmares are less frequent now," he wrote. "I'm back to 170 pounds. I feel good. I want to forgot those three years as fast as I can."

A heart attack would claim Barr in 1967, at the age of fifty. Doolittle rallied to help his fallen raider's family after the Veterans Administration denied benefits to Barr's widow and four children, arguing that his death was not related to his time in the service. Doolittle disagreed, offering to go to court as a witness. Under pressure, the agency backed down. "I do not believe that anyone could have been in such bad physical shape as George was at the end of the war without having some permanent deleterious organic effect," Doolittle wrote, "in this case on his heart."

The other former prisoners likewise suffered long-term problems. Bobby Hite's wife in 1971—more than a quarter century after his release from prison—outlined her husband's daily struggles in a statement to the Veterans Administration, ranging from chronic stomach pains to a half dozen bowel movements per day. Nightmares had long haunted him. "He would awake screaming, still talking in his sleep, gritting his teeth and flinging his arms as if to ward off the enemy," she wrote. "I really don't believe that he has had one sound night's sleep in the nearly 25 years we have been married."

The men put aside these battles to celebrate with one another each year. At the center of it all was Doolittle. Over the course of the war the general had commanded many airmen, but he never denied he had favorites. "It's not that I love any of them the less," he said at a reunion in 1955, "but only that I love these boys the more."

The feeling was mutual.

"Young guys like us would go to hell and back for him," remembered navigator Nolan Herndon. "And we did."

The raiders were family. "It wasn't only teamwork," recalled pilot Harold Watson. "It was brotherhood."

"I flew 40 missions during World War II, but there was nothing to pass that mission," added bombardier Robert Bourgeois. "That Tokyo raid, that was the daddy of them all."

But the raiders long dismissed the idea that they were heroes, a sentiment captured best by engineer Douglas Radney: "I think we're all average American citizens who were afraid when we took off but more afraid not to."

At the raiders' seventeenth reunion, in Tucson in 1959, civic leaders presented the airmen with eighty silver goblets, beginning a storied tradition. Each goblet was engraved twice with the name of an airman. Doolittle's copilot Dick Cole built a velvet-lined mahogany traveling case to allow the airmen to transport the goblets to reunions.

At each gathering the raiders would hold a private ceremony and toast their fellow fliers who had passed away, turning the deceased airmen's goblets upside down. The second engraving allowed the name to be read. Doolittle presented his men with a bottle of Hennessy cognac from 1896, the year he was born. Tradition demanded the last two surviving raiders would open this special bottle and toast the others.

Over the years the raiders slowly passed away. Jimmy Doolittle, the legendary racing and stunt pilot, seemed to defy the odds of a man with his adventurous nature and lived to the age of ninety-six. In 2013 with just four of the raiders remaining—and all in their nineties—the men decided to amend tradition and hold the final toast on November 9 at the National Museum of the Air Force, in Dayton, Ohio.

The airmen opened this final toast to family members, friends, and dignitaries, who sat on folding chairs in one of the museum's sprawling hangars. Dick Cole was joined on stage by Edward Saylor and Dave Thatcher, the latter the then twenty-year-old corporal who had managed to save the lives of Ted Lawson and the badly injured crew of the *Ruptured Duck*. Former prisoner of war Bobby Hite, unable to attend because of his health, held his own celebration at his home in Tennessee.

Official raid historian Carroll Glines read aloud the names of the eighty volunteers, who on that stormy morning seventy-one years earlier had without question climbed into sixteen bombers crowded on the deck of the *Hornet*. The ninety-eight-year-old Cole, who sat right next to Doolittle at the controls on that legendary flight over Tokyo, then rose. "Gentleman, I propose a toast to those we lost on the mission and those who have passed away since," Cole said. "May they rest in peace."

The three raiders raised their glasses and drank.

And then taps began to play.

ACKNOWLEDGMENTS

Writing a book is a collaborative effort, and I am indebted to many people who helped me along the way. It was a privilege and an honor to meet four of the surviving raiders, Richard Cole, Dave Thatcher, Edward Saylor, and the late Tom Griffin, several of whom were kind enough to sit for lengthy interviews. I want to offer special thanks as well to Dave Thatcher, who graciously read an advance copy of the book.

I owe a debt to the family members of several raiders, including Jeff Thatcher, who was a tremendous help to me in my research and even proofread the book prior to publication. Furthermore, he made sure that I had a seat at the Final Toast in November 2013 in Dayton, Ohio. I also want to thank Becky Thatcher-Keller and Sandra Miller, who made me feel like part of the family that weekend. I likewise am grateful to Cindy Chal, daughter of raider Dick Cole. Cindy has spent years poring over raider records and photos and generously provided me with dozens of them. She not only spent several days going through files with me at the University of Texas at Dallas but was also kind enough to read the manuscript in advance of publication. I also owe a debt to Adam Hallmark, a cousin of pilot and executed raider Dean Hallmark, who shared with me scores of powerful records from his family's collection, as well as raider business managers Tom and Catherine Casey, who gave of their time to read an advance copy of the book.

Nonfiction books are like historical scavenger hunts, and I therefore owe much to the army of archivists and researchers who helped me hunt down the various pieces of the narrative puzzle. At the National Archives, I want to thank Nate Patch and Eric Van Slander as well as independent researchers Katie Rasdorf and Susan Strange. Archie DiFante and Sylvester Jackson were of great assistance during my time at the Air Force Historical Research Agency. I also want to thank my good friend George Cully in Montgomery, who has tirelessly helped me over the years and may very well have the most impressive home library I have ever seen. At DePaul University I owe a special thanks to Morgen Hodgetts and Carly Faison, who helped me unlock the records of the Japanese atrocities in China. Likewise, researcher Ken Moody was a terrific help at the Franklin D. Roosevelt Presidential Library, as was archivist Bob Clark. I am appreciative also of Ann Trevor for her assistance at the Hoover Institution Archives.

Others I owe thanks to include Bob Fish with the USS *Hornet* Museum; Tom Allen at the University of Texas at Dallas; the Navy Department Library's Davis Elliot; Evelyn Cherpak at the Naval War College Library; Air Force Academy librarian Mary Elizabeth Ruwell; the University of Maryland's Anne Turkos; Brett Stole with the National Museum of the U.S. Air Force; André Sobocinski with the Navy's Bureau of Medicine and Surgery; the National Museum of the Pacific War's Reagan Grau; Mike Lott and Buddy Sturgis at the South Carolina Military Museum; Kay Williamson with the Darlington County Historical Society; and James D'Arc at Brigham Young University. I am indebted to Doolittle Raid researcher Ted Brisco, who shared records from his personal collection. Françoise Faulkner likewise provided me with a copy of her unpublished biography of the Reverend Charles Meeus. In Tokyo, I am especially grateful to translator Terrance Young, without whose help I would have been lost.

Closer to home, I owe a special thanks to the kind staff at the Charleston County Public Library. Over the years Linda Stewart has been a great help with my research, along with my friend Stephen Schwengel. I have always found an open door and courteous staff at the Citadel, where I would like to thank Pamela Bennett Orme and David Goble. The College of Charleston's Claire Fund likewise has always gone the extra distance to assist me in my research. Several other writers provided me with records and leads, including my good friend Steve Moore, who has written more books than I can list. Thanks as well go to Nigel Hamilton, author of the terrific book *Mantle of Command*, and Greg Leck, who wrote the excellent *Captives of Empire*. Official Doolittle

Raid historian and author Carroll Glines graciously read my manuscript in advance of publication, while my good friends and fellow writers Craig Welch in Seattle and Jason Ryan here in Charleston helped keep me sane.

I am indebted to my wonderful editor at Norton, John Glusman, who also happens to be the author of one of the best World War II books in years, *Conduct under Fire*. John spent hours going line by line through this manuscript, helping me at each step improve the narrative. I also want to thank his superb and ever-patient assistant, Jonathan Baker. Special Projects Editor Don Rifkin and copyeditor Otto Sonntag did a tremendous job and helped make sure I didn't embarrass myself, while Norton's marketing and publicity departments have proven invaluable. I have been blessed over the years with a remarkable agent, Wendy Strothman, whose strong business sense and grace have guided me through three books. Last but not least, I owe an incalculable debt to my amazing wife and best friend, Carmen Scott, who has for years, often at her own sacrifice, allowed me to indulge my passion for history and storytelling. Without her unfailing support, coupled with that of our two wonderful children, Isa and Grigs, this book never would have happened.

NOTE ON SOURCES

To tell the story of the Doolittle Raid I consulted more than three dozen archives and libraries scattered across four continents. Mission commander Jimmy Doolittle's voluminous personal papers are divided among several institutions, including the Library of Congress, which holds copies of his original mission reports as well as his extensive correspondence with many of the raiders and the families of the airmen captured and executed by the Japanese. Other important Doolittle personal records are on file at the University of Texas at Dallas, including his extensive correspondence with his family, speeches he made after the war, and his logbooks. The National Personnel Records Center in Saint Louis holds the legendary flier's military file, totaling more than one thousand pages and including his medical records, efficiency reports, and commendations.

Another important collection is the Doolittle Tokyo Raiders Association Papers, also at the University of Texas, which includes a file for each airman, complete with letters, diaries, oral histories, and newspaper clippings collected over more than seven decades. The Air Force Historical Research Agency, at Maxwell Air Force Base, in Montgomery, Alabama, holds copies of many of the original mission records as well as excellent oral histories, photos, and important raider correspondence. The National Archives and Records Administration (NARA) in College Park, Maryland, contains the deck logs, war diaries, and action reports of the raid's naval task force, as well as the voluminous war crimes files. NARA also holds the debriefing report compiled by Merian Cooper, one of the most valuable records of the raid and one that more recent writers have failed to locate. The prize of Cooper's report is the individual narratives of the raid and aftermath—drafted in May 1942—by fifty-nine of the eighty raiders who passed through Chungking.

One of the most important, and until now untapped, collections are the missionary files located at DePaul University. The scores of previously unpublished letters, affidavits, and personal narratives provide an important window into the horrific Japanese retaliations against the Chinese in the wake of the raid that for too long have been glossed over. The Franklin D. Roosevelt Library and Museum in Hyde Park, New York, contains the records related to the attack on Pearl Harbor as well as policy papers dealing with the capture and execution of some of the raiders. Other important collections include those of Henry Arnold, Ernest King, and Marc Mitscher, all on file at the Library of Congress, as well as a second collection of King's and Mitscher's papers at the Naval History and Heritage Command. Many other smaller institutions, from the Darlington County Historical Commission to Ohio University, contain the individual papers of specific raiders.

A number of important records chronicle the Japanese side of the raid, including the diary of Combined Fleet chief of staff Matome Ugaki. The *Osaka Mainichi* newspaper and the *Japan Times & Advertiser* published the detailed bulletins and alerts issued during the attack. Historian Gordon Prange's papers at the University of Maryland house important interviews with many senior Japanese leaders, who provide valuable insight into how the Doolittle raid shaped military policy and led to the disaster at Midway. Other important and previously untapped Japanese sources include *Senshi Sōsho*, a 102-volume history that tells the story of Japan's war. Volumes 29 and 85 devote significant space to the Doolittle Raid. Also, Japanese historians Takehiko Shibata and Katsuhiro Hara published an important study of the raid in 2003 that includes excellent breakdowns on the precise damage done by each bomber, though the work fails to explore the horrific aftermath of the raid in China. There unfortunately exists no English-language translation of any of these titles. I am indebted to Terrance Young in Tokyo, who translated these records for me.

As with any topic that has been covered before, I am indebted to the authors of several previous books. Most notable are the works by Doolittle Tokyo Raiders Association historian Carroll Glines, including *Doolittle's*

Tokyo Raiders, *The Doolittle Raid*, and *Four Came Home*. I likewise consulted James Merrill's 1964 *Target Tokyo* and Duane Schultz's 1988 *The Doolittle Raid*. Most of my book, however, is based on primary source materials—reports, diaries, letters, and oral histories, for which I have provided extensive endnotes. I have chosen to include only a select bibliography of the books I consulted. All quotations and dialogue come from official reports, memos, press conference and trial transcripts, cables, letters and diaries, the *Congressional Record*, ships' logs, news stories, memoirs, both published and unpublished, and, in a few cases, from the recollections of those involved.

Place-names are rendered throughout the book as they were current in 1942. Likewise, ranks are often tricky, particularly in a fast-moving war, where promotions are frequent. As such, all raider ranks are given as they were on the date of the attack on Japan. To guarantee accuracy, I cross-referenced all ranks with Doolittle's official report, each individual raider's report, and documents related to post-raid promotions, which are on file with Doolittle's papers in the Library of Congress.

ARCHIVES AND LIBRARIES

Air Force Historical Research Agency, Montgomery, Ala.
American Airpower Heritage Museum, Midland, Tex.
American Catholic History Research Center and University Archives,
    Catholic University of America, Washington, D.C.
Australian War Memorial, Canberra, Australia
Charleston County Public Library, Charleston, S.C.
Daniel Library, The Citadel, Charleston, S.C.
Darlington County Historical Commission, Darlington, S.C.
Eugene McDermott Library, University of Texas at Dallas, Richardson, Tex.
Filson Historical Society, Louisville, Ky.
Franklin D. Roosevelt Presidential Library and Museum, Hyde Park, N.Y.
Harold B. Lee Library, Brigham Young University, Provo, Utah
Hornbake Library, University of Maryland, College Park, Md.
Hoover Institution Archives, Stanford University, Palo Alto, Calif.
Imperial War Museum, London, England
J. Willard Marriott Library, University of Utah, Salt Lake City, Utah
John T. Richardson Library, DePaul University, Chicago, Ill.
Library of Congress, Washington, D.C.
Marlene and Nathan Addlestone Library, College of Charleston,
    Charleston, S.C.
National Archives and Records Administration, College Park, Md.
National Museum of the Pacific War, Fredericksburg, Tex.
National Personnel Records Center, St. Louis, Mo.
Naval History and Heritage Command, Washington, D.C.
Naval War College Library, Newport, R.I.
Navy Bureau of Medicine and Surgery, Falls Church, Va.
Navy Department Library, Washington, D.C.
Nicholas Murray Butler Library, Columbia University, New York, N.Y.
Robert F. McDermott Library, U.S. Air Force Academy, Colorado Springs, Colo.
South Carolina Military Museum, Columbia, S.C.
South Caroliniana Library, Columbia, S.C.

Thomas Cooper Library, University of South Carolina, Columbia, S.C.
United Church of Canada Archives, Toronto, Canada
University of Texas at El Paso Library, El Paso, Tex.
U.S. Army Center of Military History, Washington, D.C.
U.S. Naval Institute, Annapolis, Md.
Vernon R. Alden Library, Ohio University, Athens, Ohio
Willis Library, University of North Texas, Denton, Tex.

NOTES

ABBREVIATIONS

AFHRA	Air Force Historical Research Agency, Montgomery, Ala.
DOMPF	Doolittle Official Military Personnel File, National Personnel Records Center, St. Louis, Mo.
DPLOC	James H. Doolittle Papers, Library of Congress, Washington, D.C.
DPUT	James H. Doolittle Papers, University of Texas at Dallas, Richardson, Tex.
DRMA	DeAndreis-Rosati Memorial Archives, Special Collections and Archives Department, DePaul University Library, Chicago, Ill.
DTRAP	Doolittle Tokyo Raiders Association Papers
FDRL	Franklin D. Roosevelt Presidential Library and Museum, Hyde Park, N.Y.
GPO	U.S. Government Printing Office
GWPP	Gordon W. Prange Papers, University of Maryland, College Park, Md.
HHAP	Henry H. Arnold Papers, Library of Congress, Washington, D.C.
LOC	Library of Congress, Washington, D.C.
NARA	National Archives and Records Administration, College Park, Md.
NDL	Navy Department Library, Washington, D.C.
NHHC	Naval History and Heritage Command, Washington, D.C.
OF	Official File
RG	Record Group
USSBS	United States Strategic Bombing Survey

PROLOGUE

1 "Hawaii is just": Matome Ugaki diary, Dec. 6, 1941, in Matome Ugaki, *Fading Victory: The Diary of Admiral Matome Ugaki, 1941–1945*, ed. Donald M. Goldstein and Katherine V. Dillon, trans. Masataka Chihaya (Pittsburgh, Pa.: University of Pittsburgh Press, 1991), p. 38.

1 The fifty-four-year-old: Background on Nagumo comes from Gordon W. Prange with Donald M. Goldstein and Katherine V. Dillon, *At Dawn We Slept: The Untold Story of Pearl Harbor* (New York: McGraw-Hill, 1981), pp. 107–8; Hiroyuki Agawa, *The Reluctant Admiral: Yamamoto and the Imperial Navy*, trans. John Bester (New York: Kodansha International, 1979), pp. 130, 253–54.

1 "I hope he": Matome Ugaki diary, Oct. 29, 1941, in Ugaki, *Fading Victory*, p. 17.

1 Nagumo's anxiety: Ryunosuke Kusaka interview, March 7, 1949, Box 58, Series 5.2, Gordon W. Prange Papers (GWPP), University of Maryland, College Park, Md.; Mitsuo Fuchida interview, Feb. 25, 1948, Box 15, Series 5.2, GWPP.

1 He seemed to draw: Details of Japan's task force are drawn from Prange, *At Dawn We Slept*, pp. 483–84; Headquarters, Army Forces Far East, "Pearl Harbor Operations: General Outline of Orders and Plans," Japanese Monograph #97, 1958, p. 9; Ryunosuka Kusaka, "Rengto Kantai (Combined Fleet): Reminiscence of Kusaka ex-Chief of Staff," April 1952, Box 58, Series 5.2, GWPP, p. 17; Mitsuo Fuchida, "I Led the Air Attack on Pearl Harbor," in Paul Stillwell, ed., *Air Raid: Pearl Harbor! Recollections of a Day of Infamy* (Annapolis, Md.: Naval Institute Press, 1981), p. 4.

2 Shore batteries along with battleships: Joint Committee on the Investigation of the Pearl Harbor Attack, *Investigation of the Pearl Harbor Attack*, 79th Cong., 2nd sess., July 20, 1946 (Washington, D.C.: GPO, 1946), pp. 67–71.

2 "The fate of our empire": Matome Ugaki diary, Dec. 7, 1941, in Ugaki, *Fading Victory*, p. 38.

2 wooden torpedo fins: Joint Committee on the Investigation of the Pearl Harbor Attack, *Investigation of the Pearl Harbor Attack*, p. 59.

2 On the eve: "Japanese Study of the Pearl Harbor Operation," in Donald M. Goldstein and Katherine V. Dillon, eds., *The Pearl Harbor Papers: Inside the Japanese Plans* (Washington, D.C.: Brassey's, 1993), p. 285; Sadao Chigusa, "Conquer the Pacific Ocean aboard Destroyer *Akigumo*: War Diary of the Hawaiian Battle," ibid., p. 173.

2 To increase: "Japanese Study of the Pearl Harbor Operation," ibid., p. 285; Minoru Genda, "Analysis No. 2 of the Pearl Harbor Attack," ibid., p. 38.

2 Fuel conservation: Genda, "Analysis No. 2 of the Pearl Harbor Attack," p. 38; Chigusa, "Conquer the Pacific Ocean aboard Destroyer *Akigumo*," pp. 180, 205–6.

3 One by one: John Toland, *The Rising Sun: The Decline and Fall of the Japanese Empire, 1936–1945* (New York: Random House, 1970), pp. 169–70.

3 To throw off: "Japanese Study of the Pearl Harbor Operation," p. 282.

3 The chief communications: Walter Lord, *Day of Infamy* (New York: Henry Holt, 1957), p. 21.

3 The Japanese flooded: Kusaka, "Rengto Kantai (Combined Fleet)," p. 10; "Japanese Study of the Pearl Harbor Operation," p. 282.

3 This charade: Chigusa, "Conquer the Pacific Ocean aboard Destroyer *Akigumo*," p. 183.

3 War planners: Kusaka, "Rengto Kantai (Combined Fleet)," pp. 5–6; Shigeru Fukudome, "Hawaii Operation," in Stillwell, ed., *Air Raid: Pearl Harbor!*," p. 62; Agawa, *The Reluctant Admiral*, pp. 250–51.

3 "Sink anything": Toland, *The Rising Sun*, p. 171.

3 refusing to change: Prange, *At Dawn We Slept*, p. 415.

3 The graduate of Japan's: Toland, *The Rising Sun*, pp. 171–72; Agawa, *The Reluctant Admiral*, pp. 253–54.

3 To his chief of staff: Kusaka, "Rengto Kantai (Combined Fleet)," pp. 20–21.

3 "I wonder if": Toland, *The Rising Sun*, p. 171.

3 "*Daijobu*": Ibid.

4 "This despatch": CNO to CINCAF, CINPAC, Nov. 27, 1941, in *Hearings before the Joint Committee on the Investigation of the Pearl Harbor Attack*, pt. 14, *Joint Committee Exhibits Nos. 9 through 43*, 79th Cong., 1st sess. (Washington, D.C.: GPO, 1946), p. 1406.

4 His Army counterpart: Joint Committee on the Investigation of the Pearl Harbor Attack, *Investigation of the Pearl Harbor Attack*, p. 70.

4 "Japanese future": George Marshall to Walter Short, Nov. 27, 1941, in *Hearings before the Joint Committee on the Investigation of the Pearl Harbor Attack*, pt. 14, p. 1328.

4 That Saturday night: Lord, *Day of Infamy*, pp. 4–7; Edwin T. Layton, with Roger Pineau and John Costello, *"And I Was There": Pearl Harbor and Midway—Breaking the Secrets* (New York: William Morrow, 1985), p. 299.

4 Off-duty troops: Ibid., pp. 9–10.

4 The bustling port: "List of Ships Present at Pearl Harbor at the Time of the Japanese Attack, Dec. 7, 1941," in *Hearings before the Joint Committee on the Investigation of the Pearl Harbor Attack*, pt. 12, *Joint Committee Exhibits Nos. 1 through 6*, 79th Cong., 1st sess. (Washington, D.C.: GPO, 1946), pp. 348–49.

5 "Isn't that a beautiful sight": Lord, *Day of Infamy*, pp. 6–7.

5 Pacific Fleet intelligence officer: Layton, *"And I Was There,"* pp. 299–300.

5 "Wake up, America!": Ibid., p. 299.

5 Earlier that day: Ibid., p. 275.

5 The Japanese used: Ibid., pp. 226–30, 237–38.

5 "Unknown—home waters?": Ibid., pp. 18, 243–44.

5 "What?": This exchange is ibid., pp. 18, 243–44.

6 Now after months: Agawa, *The Reluctant Admiral*, p. 254.

6 The gentle Hawaiian: Lord, *Day of Infamy*, pp. 11, 26.

6 pilots would go: Thurston Clark, *Pearl Harbor Ghosts: The Legacy of December 7, 1941* (New York: Ballantine Books, 2001), p. 92.

6 Aircrews on the Japanese task force's: Toland, *The Rising Sun*, p. 203.

6 Many had spent: Prange, *At Dawn We Slept*, pp. 386, 415; Kusaka, "Rengto Kantai (Combined Fleet)," p. 13.

6 Fighter pilot Yoshi Shiuga: Toland, *The Rising Sun*, p. 188.

6 That same fear: Chigusa, "Conquer the Pacific Ocean aboard Destroyer *Akigumo*," pp. 188–89.

6 Many of the airmen: Toland, *The Rising Sun*, p. 203.

6 The airmen dressed: Ibid.

6 The thirty-nine-year-old: Mitsuo Fuchida interview, Dec. 10, 1963.

6 The aircrews paused: Lord, *Day of Infamy*, p. 35; Agawa, *The Reluctant Admiral*, p. 255.

7 "We await the day": Matome Ugaki diary, Dec. 6, 1941, in Ugaki, *Fading Victory*, p. 38.

7 Nagumo's carriers battled: Fuchida, "I Led the Air Attack on Pearl Harbor," p. 8; Kusaka, "Rengto Kantai (Combined Fleet)," pp. 32–33.

7 One hundred and eighty-three: "Japanese Study of the Pearl Harbor Operation," pp. 299–301.

7 "First bomb": Agawa, *The Reluctant Admiral*, p. 254.

CHAPTER 1

9 "Air raid on Pearl Harbor": CINCPAC to CINCLANT, CINCAF, OPNAV, Dec. 7, 1941, Box 36, Map Room Papers, Franklin D. Roosevelt Presidential Library and Museum (FDRL), Hyde Park, N.Y.

9 President Franklin Roosevelt: The President's Appointments, Sunday, Dec. 7, 1941, in *Hearings before the Joint Committee on the Investigation of the Pearl Harbor Attack*, pt. 15, *Joint Committee Exhibits Nos. 44 through 87*, 79th Cong., 1st sess. (Washington, D.C.: GPO, 1946), p. 1634. A copy can also be found in Box 1, Official File (OF) 4675, FDRL.

9 the parlor: details on Roosevelt's study are drawn from Grace Tully, *F.D.R.: My Boss* (New York: Charles Scribner's Sons, 1949), pp. 10, 370–71; Hanson Baldwin, "Our 'Sailor-President' Charts a Course," *New York Times*, April 3, 1938, p. 117; "The White House in Color," *Life*, Sept. 2, 1940, pp. 66–70; "The White House," ibid., July 5, 1968, p. 9; Steven M. Gillon, *Pearl Harbor: FDR Leads the Nation into War* (New York: Basic Books, 2011), pp. 2–3.

10 "He mixed": Robert E. Sherwood, *Roosevelt and Hopkins: An Intimate History* (New York: Harper & Brothers, 1948), p. 214.

10 Roosevelt's Sunday lunch: Eleanor Roosevelt, *This I Remember* (New York: Harper & Brothers, 1949), pp. 232–33; James Roosevelt and Sidney Shalett, *Affectionately, F.D.R.: A Son's Story of a Lonely Man* (New York: Harcourt, Brace, 1959), p. 328.

10 Despite the demands: "Roosevelt's Stamps on View," *New York Times*, Aug. 4, 1935, p. 3; "Roosevelt among His Stamps," ibid., Sept. 10, 1933, p.

SM17; Geoffrey Hellman, "Franklin Roosevelt," *Life*, Jan. 20, 1941, pp. 66–73.

10 "No man": "Fireside Chat on National Security," Dec. 29, 1940, in B. D. Zevin, ed., *Nothing to Fear: The Selected Addresses of Franklin Delano Roosevelt, 1932–1945* (Boston: Houghton Mifflin, 1946), pp. 252, 257.

11 The island nation: United States Strategic Bombing Survey (USSBS), Transportation Division, *The War against Japanese Transportation, 1941–1945* (Washington, D.C.: GPO, 1947), p. 13.

11 Japan could produce: USSBS, Oil and Chemical Division, *Oil in Japan's War* (Washington, D.C.: GPO, 1946), p. 11; Harold Callender, "Oil: Major Factor in Another War," *New York Times*, Aug. 13, 1939, p. E4.

11 "Napoleon's armies": Arno Dosch-Fleurot, "Oil to Dominate Next World War," *New York Times*, June 19, 1938, p. E5.

11 The hunger: USSBS, Over-all Economic Effects Division, *The Effects of Strategic Bombing on Japan's War Economy* (Washington, D.C.: GPO, 1946), pp. 6–10.

11 "unholy alliance": Turner Catledge, "Roosevelt Calls for Greater Aid to Britain," *New York Times*, Dec. 30, 1940, p. 1.

11 Japan invaded: USSBS, *The Effects of Strategic Bombing on Japan's War Economy*, p. 9.

11 He ordered: Ibid.; "British Empire Joins Our Action; Canada and Netherlands in Move," *New York Times*, July 26, 1941, p. 1; "Batavia Risks War," ibid., July 29, 1941, p. 1; "Japanese Trade with U.S. to End," ibid., July 26, 1941, p. 5; "Japan to Allow Americans to Go; Tokyo Trade Hit," ibid., Aug. 23, 1941, p. 1; "Oil Policy Changes," ibid., Aug. 2, 1941, p. 1; "U.S. Solidifies Far East Policy," ibid., Aug. 17, 1941, p. E5; "Vast Trade Curbed," ibid., July 26, 1941, p. 1; "Washington Retaliates," ibid., Aug. 3, 1941, p. E1.

11 Japan had stockpiled: USSBS, *The Effects of Strategic Bombing on Japan's War Economy*, pp. 13, 29, 52.

11 To stretch supplies: USSBS, *Oil in Japan's War*, p. 1.

11 Workers punched: USSBS, *The Effects of Strategic Bombing on Japan's War Economy*, p. 13; USSBS (Pacific), Military Analysis Division, *Japanese Air Power* (Washington, D.C.: GPO, 1946), pp. 4–5, 28–29; USSBS, Chairman's Office, *Summary Report (Pacific War)* (Washington, D.C.: GPO, 1946), p. 9.

12 Aggressive recruitment: USSBS, *Summary Report (Pacific War)*, p. 10–12; David M. Kennedy, ed., *Library of Congress World War II Companion* (New York: Simon and Schuster, 2007), p. 257.

12 The Japanese Navy not only: Samuel Eliot Morison, *The Two-Ocean War: A Short History of the United States Navy in the Second World War* (Boston: Atlantic Monthly Press Book/Little, Brown, 1963), p. 39.

12 "I cannot guarantee": John Morton Blum, *From the Morgenthau Diaries*, vol. 2, *Years of Urgency, 1938–1941* (Boston: Houghton Mifflin, 1965), p. 391.

12 "Only in situations": "The President Sends a Personal Appeal to Emperor Hirohito to Avoid War in the Pacific, December 6, 1941," in Samuel I.

Rosenman, comp., *The Public Papers and Addresses of Franklin D. Roosevelt*, 1941 vol., *The Call to Battle Stations* (New York: Harper & Brothers, 1950), pp. 511–13.

12 Roosevelt's closet adviser: Sherwood, *Roosevelt and Hopkins*, pp. 1–3; Charles Hurd, "Hopkins: Right-Hand Man," *New York Times*, Aug. 11, 1940, p. 85.

12 "a strange, gnomelike creature": Joseph Stilwell diary, Feb. 9, 1942, in Joseph W. Stilwell, ed., *The Stilwell Papers*, ed. Theodore H. White (New York: William Sloane Associates, 1948), p. 36.

12 "a cadaver": Grace Tully interview, Dec. 15, 1970, Box 78, Series 5.2, GWPP.

12 Dressed in an old gray sweater: Roosevelt, *Affectionately, F.D.R.*, p. 327.

12 "Mr. President": Forrest Davis and Ernest K. Lindley, *How War Came: An American White Paper: From the Fall of France to Pearl Harbor* (New York: Simon and Schuster, 1942), p. 5.

13 "It was just the kind": Harry Hopkins memo, Dec. 7, 1941, in Sherwood, *Roosevelt and Hopkins*, p. 431.

13 The seventy-four-year-old New York native: "Henry L. Stimson Dies at 83 in His Home on Long Island," *New York Times*, Oct. 21, 1950, p. 1.

13 "Have you heard the news?": This exchange comes from Henry Stimson diary, Dec. 7, 1941, in *Hearings before the Joint Committee on the Investigation of the Pearl Harbor Attack*, pt. 11, *April 9 and 11, and May 23 and 31, 1946*, 79th Cong., 1st sess. (Washington, D.C.: GPO, 1946), p. 5438.

13 "Claude": This exchange comes from John L. McCrea, "War Plans under My Mattress," in Stillwell, ed., *Air Raid: Pearl Harbor!*, p. 104.

14 Though the precise details: Joint Committee on the Investigation of the Pearl Harbor Attack, *Investigation of the Pearl Harbor Attack*, pp. 64–65.

14 Casualties among soldiers: Shigeru Fukudome, "Hawaii Operation," in Stillwell, ed., *Air Raid: Pearl Harbor!*, p. 69.

14 The president hung up the phone: Linda Levin, *The Making of FDR: The Story of Stephen T. Early, America's First Modern Press Secretary* (Amherst, N.Y.: Prometheus Books, 2008), pp. 251–52.

14 "I think the President": This exchange comes from Mr. Early's Press Conference, Dec. 6, 1941, transcript, Box 41, Stephen T. Early Papers, FDRL.

14 "Have you got a pencil handy?": This exchange comes from Levin, *The Making of FDR*, p. 251.

14 Within minutes Early placed: Press Statement, Dec. 7, 1941, 2:25 p.m., Box 41, Stephen T. Early Papers, FDRL.

15 "All on?": Lyle C. Wilson, "World War II," in Cabell Phillips, ed., *Dateline: Washington: The Story of National Affairs Journalism in the Life and Times of the National Press Club* (New York: Green Press, 1968), p. 184; Correspondents of *Time, Life*, and *Fortune*, *December 7: The First Thirty Hours* (New York: Alfred A. Knopf, 1942), p. 10.

15 Secret Service agent Mike Reilly: Michael F. Reilly as told to William J. Slocum, *Reilly of the White House* (New York: Simon and Schuster, 1947), pp. 3–7.

15 "Start calling in": Ibid., p. 4.

15 "Why don't they": This exchange comes from Frank J. Wilson and Beth Day, *Special Agent: Twenty-Five Years with the U.S. Treasury Department and Secret Service* (London: Frederick Muller, 1965), pp. 141–42.

15 Reilly phoned Washington police chief: Reilly, *Reilly of the White House*, p. 4.

15 His trusted personal secretary: Grace Tully interview, Dec. 15, 1970.

15 "The president wants you right away": Tully, *F.D.R.*, p. 254.

16 "jumped to like a fireman": Grace Tully interview, Dec. 15, 1970.

16 "Crown Prince": Roosevelt, *Affectionately, F.D.R.*, p. 290.

16 "Hi, Old Man": This exchange comes from Doris Kearns Goodwin, *No Ordinary Time: Franklin and Eleanor Roosevelt: The Home Front in World War II* (New York: Touchstone Book/Simon and Schuster, 1994), p. 290.

16 "I became aware": Roosevelt, *Affectionately, F.D.R.*, p. 327.

16 "Hello, Jimmy": Ibid., p. 328.

16 Roosevelt's advisers crowded: The President's Appointments, Sunday, Dec. 7, 1941.

16 "Many of the moves": Harry Hopkins memo, Dec. 7, 1941, in Sherwood, *Roosevelt and Hopkins*, p. 432.

17 "The news was shattering": Tully, *F.D.R.*, pp. 254–55.

17 Poindexter told the president: Charles M. Hite, diary, Dec. 7, 1941, Box 126, John Toland Papers, FDRL.

17 "My God": Tully, *F.D.R.*, p. 255.

17 Roosevelt took another call: Harry Hopkins memo, Dec. 7, 1941, in Sherwood, *Roosevelt and Hopkins*, p. 432.

17 "We shall declare war on Japan!": This exchange comes from John Gilbert Winant, *Letter from Grosvenor Square: An Account of a Stewardship* (Boston: Houghton Mifflin, 1947), p. 277.

17 "Mr. President": This exchange comes from Winston S. Churchill, *The Grand Alliance* (Boston: Houghton Mifflin, 1950), p. 605.

18 "To have the United States": Ibid., pp. 606–7.

18 "The *Oklahoma* has capsized": "Memorandum for the President," 3:50 p.m., Dec. 7, 1941, Box 1, OF 4675, FDRL.

18 "Three battleships sunk": CINPAC to OPNAV, Dec. 7, 1941, Box 36, Map Room Papers, FDRL.

18 "Heavy losses sustained": OPNAV to All Naval Air Stations and Air Groups, Dec. 7, 1941, ibid.

18 "My God, how did it happen": Alonzo Fields, "Churchill Visit Leaves Lasting Mark," *Washington Post*, Sept. 20, 1961, p. D4.

18 Still unaware of the war's outbreak: Shirley Povich, "War's Outbreak Is Deep Secret to 27,102 Redskin Game Fans," *Washington Post*, Dec. 8, 1941, p. 24; Thomas R. Henry, "Capital Retains Outward Calm Despite Shock of War News," *Evening Star*, Dec. 8, 1941, p. A-6.

18 "Keep it short": Edward T. Folliard, "The Remembrance of That Fatal Day," *Washington Post*, Dec. 7, 1965, p. A18.

18 "The Japanese have kicked off": Ibid.

18 "Admiral W. H. P. Bland": Povich, "War's Outbreak Is Deep Secret to 27,102 Redskin Game Fans," p. 24.

18 "The Resident Commissioner": Ibid.

18 Fans began to buzz: Thomas R. Henry, "Capital Retains Outward Calm Despite Shock of War News," p. A-6; David Braaten, "A Quiet Washington Sunday . . . And a New Era Began," *Evening Star*, Dec. 7, 1966, p. 1.

18 Crowds in Times Square: "That Day the City Changed to the Way of War," *New York Times*, Dec. 7, 1966, p. 22.

19 "The Star Spangled Banner": Ibid.

19 "I want to beat them Japs": "What the People Said," *Time*, Dec. 15, 1941, p. 17.

19 "We'll stamp their front teeth": Ibid.

19 "Sit down, Grace": Tully, *F.D.R.*, p. 256.

19 Roosevelt normally depended: Samuel I. Rosenman, *Working with Roosevelt* (New York: Harper & Brothers, 1952), pp. 1–12, 305–6.

19 "Yesterday, December seventh": Tully, *F.D.R.*, p. 256; Rosenman, *Working with Roosevelt*, p. 307; "December 7, 1941—A Date Which Will Live in Infamy—Address to the Congress Asking That a State of War Be Declared between the United States and Japan," Dec. 8, 1941, in Rosenman, comp., *The Public Papers and Addresses of Franklin D. Roosevelt*, 1941 vol., pp. 514–16.

19 "eloquent defiance": Sherwood, *Roosevelt and Hopkins*, p. 437.

19 "represented Roosevelt": Ibid., p. 436.

20 "world history": Rosenman, *Working with Roosevelt*, p. 307.

20 "would forever describe": Ruth Dean, "When Roosevelt Gave a Tragic Date a Name," *Evening Star*, Dec. 8, 1964, p. B-9.

20 "With confidence": Tully, *F.D.R.*, p. 256; Rosenman, *Working with Roosevelt*, p. 307.

20 "No story at the White House": A. Merriman Smith, *Thank You, Mr. President: A White House Notebook* (New York: Harper & Brothers, 1946), pp. 113–14.

20 bulletins: This is based on a review of press releases and press conference transcripts from Dec. 7 that are on file in Box 41, Stephen T. Early Papers, FDRL; "War Brings a Tense Day to White House Press Room," *Washington Post*, Dec. 8, 1941, p. 4.

20 "I want to ask you": Mr. Early's Press Conference, 4:50 p.m., Dec. 7, 1941, transcript, Box 41, Stephen T. Early Papers, FDRL.

20 People poured out: Henry, "Capital Retains Outward Calm Despite Shock of War News," p. A-6; Braaten, "A Quiet Washington Sunday," p. 1.

21 "Folks wanted to be together": Henry, "Capital Retains Outward Calm Despite Shock of War News," p. A-6.

21 Vice President Henry Wallace: The President's Appointments, Sunday, Dec. 7, 1941; Harry Hopkins memo, Dec. 7, 1941, in Sherwood, *Roosevelt and Hopkins*, p. 432; "Remarks of the President on the Occasion of the Meeting of His Cabinet at 8:30 and Continuing at 9:00 with Legislative Leaders," Dec. 7, 1941, transcript, Box 1, OF 4675, FDRL.

21 Maps dangled from easels: Frances Perkins, "The President Faces War," in Stillwell, ed., *Air Raid: Pearl Harbor!*, p. 117.

21 "There was none": Frances Perkins, *The Roosevelt I Knew* (New York: Viking Press, 1947), p. 379.

21 "I'm thankful": Perkins, "The President Faces War," p. 117.

21 "Mr. President": Perkins, *The Roosevelt I Knew*, p. 379.

21 "The Secretary of the Navy": Claude Wickard diary, Dec. 7, 1941, Box 13, Cabinet Meetings, 1941–1942, Claude R. Wickard Papers, FDRL.

21 "His pride in the Navy": Perkins, "The President Faces War," p. 118.

22 "Find out, for God's sake": Ibid.

22 "That's the way they berth them": Ibid.

22 "The President disagreed": Claude Wickard diary, Dec. 7, 1941.

22 "The effect on the Congressmen": Henry Stimson diary, Dec. 7, 1941.

22 "How did it happen": Richard M. Ketchum, *The Borrowed Years, 1938–1941: America on the Way to War* (New York: Random House, 1989), p. 788. See also Harold L. Ickes diary, Dec. 14, 1941, in Harold L. Ickes, *The Secret Diary of Harold L. Ickes*, vol. 3, *The Lowering Clouds, 1939–1941* (New York: Simon and Schuster, 1954), pp. 661–66; Tom Connally as told to Alfred Steinberg, *My Name Is Tom Connally* (New York: Thomas Y. Crowell, 1954), pp. 248–50.

22 "I am amazed": "Remarks of the President on the Occasion of the Meeting of His Cabinet at 8:30 and Continuing at 9:00 with Legislative Leaders," Dec. 7, 1941, transcript.

22 "I don't know, Tom": Francis Biddle, *In Brief Authority* (Garden City, N.Y.: Doubleday, 1962), p. 206.

CHAPTER 2

23 "To the enemy we answer": *Congressional Record*, 77th Cong., 1st sess., Dec. 8, 1941, p. 9505.

23 Sixty-two million: Kenneth G. Bartlett, "Social Impact of the Radio," *Annals of the American Academy of Political and Social Science*, March 1947, pp. 89–97; Alan Barth to R. Keith Kane, Dec. 15, 1941, Intelligence Report No. 1, Microfilm Roll #23, President Franklin D. Roosevelt's Office Files, 1933–1944, pt. 4: Subject Files.

23 "We are now": "We Are Going to Win the War and We Are Going to Win the Peace That Follows"—Fireside Chat to the Nation Following the Declaration of War with Japan, Dec. 9, 1941, in Rosenman, comp., *The Public Papers and Addresses of Franklin D. Roosevelt*, 1941 vol., pp. 522–31.

23 Only days earlier: Report by the Secretary of the Navy to the President, Dec. 14, 1941, Microfilm Roll #7, President Franklin D. Roosevelt's Office Files, 1933–1944, pt. 3: Departmental Correspondence Files. A copy of this report is also on file in Box 59, President's Secretary's Files, 1933–1945, FDRL. For a modern analysis of Pearl Harbor damage, see Naval History and Heritage Command (NHHC), "Pearl Harbor Raid, 7 December 1941, Overview and Special Image Selection," which is available online.

24 "The *Arizona*": Report by the Secretary of the Navy to the President, Dec. 14, 1941.

24 "The battle is on": "To a Victorious End," editorial, *New York Herald Tribune*, Dec. 8, 1941, in *Congressional Record*, 77th Cong., 1st sess., Dec. 8, 1941, p. 9509.

24 "act of a mad dog": "Death Sentence of a Mad Dog," editorial, *Los Angeles Times*, Dec. 8, 1941, p. 1A.

24 "Japan has asked for it": Ibid.

24 "Do the war-mad": "War: Let Japan Have It!," editorial, *Philadelphia Inquirer*, Dec. 8, 1941, p. 14.

24 "If we have": "So It's War," editorial, *Palm Beach Post*, Dec. 8, 1941, p. 4.

24 "the nation is one": "Says But One Can Survive," editorial, *Chicago Sun*, Dec. 8, 1941, in *Congressional Record*, 77th Cong., 1st sess., Dec. 8, 1941, p. 9511.

24 "'Politics is adjourned'": "America at War!," editorial, *San Francisco Chronicle*, Dec. 8, 1941, p. 1.

24 Thousands of telegrams and letters: See Box 5, OF 4675, Public Sentiment after Pearl Harbor, FDRL, which includes telegrams and letters from many of the nation's governors.

24 "This is the home": John E. Miles to Franklin Roosevelt, Dec. 8, 1941, Box 5, OF 4675, Public Sentiment after Pearl Harbor, FDRL.

24 "Please command me": Alf M. Landon to Franklin Roosevelt, Dec. 7, 1941, ibid.

24 Dozens of mayors: See Box 5, OF 4675, FDRL.

25 Diverse groups: "Resolution by the Crow Indians to the President," Jan. 6, 1942, Box 8, OF 4675, FDRL; Capp Jefferson to Franklin Roosevelt, Dec. 8, 1941, Box 9, ibid.; Resolution Passed by the Realm of Washington, Knights of the Ku Klux Klan, Inc., Sept. 24, 1942, Box 18, ibid.

25 including a taxicab driver: Mr. Early's Press Conference, Dec. 8, 1941, transcript, Box 41, Stephen T. Early Papers, FDRL.

25 Others offered up: Helen M. Johnson to Franklin Roosevelt, Jan. 20, 1942, Box 12, OF 4675, FDRL; Mrs. Peace Junguito to Franklin Roosevelt, undated (ca. Dec. 1941), Box 12, ibid.; Mrs. Leroy Drury to Franklin Roosevelt, Jan. 30, 1942, Box 9, ibid.

25 "I would like to kick": E. E. Crane to Franklin Roosevelt, Dec. 19, 1942, Box 8, OF 4675, FDRL.

25 "I never wanted": Eleanor Roosevelt oral history, "The Roosevelt Years," Jan. 3, 1962, Session 11, Robert Graff Papers, FDRL.

25 sandbags crowded: Lawrence Davies, "San Francisco Puts Up Sand Bags, Starts Its Air Raid Precautions," *New York Times*, Dec. 12, 1941, p. 29; Tully, *F.D.R.*, pp. 258–59.

25 Polls showed: George H. Gallup, ed., *The Gallup Poll: Public Opinion 1935–1971*, vol. 1, *1935–1948* (New York: Random House, 1972), p. 311.

25 "You are": Harold Stark to Franklin Roosevelt, Dec. 12, 1941, Microfilm Roll #7, President Franklin D. Roosevelt's Office Files, 1933–1944, pt. 3: Departmental Correspondence Files.

25 The Secret Service: Reilly, *Reilly of the White House*, pp. 36–39; Tully, *F.D.R.*, p. 259.

26 "Henry": Roosevelt, *This I Remember*, p. 237.

26 "The shock": Alan Barth to R. Keith Kane, Dec. 15, 1941, Intelligence Report No. 1.

26 "Sick at heart": Breckinridge Long diary, Dec. 8, 1941, in Fred L. Israel, ed., *The War Diary of Breckinridge Long: Selections from the Years 1939–1944* (Lincoln: University of Nebraska Press, 1966), pp. 227–28.

26 These challenges confronted: Franklin Roosevelt appointment calendar, Dec. 21, 1941, which is available online through the FDRL.

26 Eleanor had hopped: Eleanor Roosevelt, "My Day," Dec. 20, 22, 23, 1941. This was a newspaper column she wrote that is widely available online. Charles Schwartz, *Cole Porter: A Biography* (New York: Da Capo Press, 1977), pp. 208–9.

26 "I wish": Eleanor Roosevelt, "My Day," Dec. 23, 1941.

26 Roosevelt opened: Conference in White House, Dec. 21, 1941, Microfilm Roll #205, Henry H. Arnold Papers (HHAP), LOC.

27 He planned: Notes of Meeting at the White House with the President and the British Prime Minister Presiding, Dec. 23, 1941, Microfilm Roll #205, HHAP.

27 "almost unanimous": Alan Barth to R. Keith Kane, Dec. 15, 1941, Intelligence Report No. 1.

27 Roosevelt had witnessed: Kenneth Campbell, "Army Is Inspected by the President," *New York Times*, Aug. 18, 1940, p. 3; Hanson W. Baldwin, "Units in 'War' Led by Green Officers," ibid., Aug. 7, 1940, p. 3.

27 Of America's three thousand: H. H. Arnold, *Global Mission* (New York: Harper & Brothers, 1949), p. 267.

27 So desperate: "Navy Standards Altered," *New York Times*, May 27, 1941, p. 10; "Navy Is Planning Use of Selectees," ibid., Nov. 27, 1941, p. 5; "Navy Announces Modified Physical Requirements," *Mt. Adams Sun*, Dec. 19, 1941, p. 1.

27 "The whole organization": Arthur Bryant, *The Turn of the Tide: A History of the War Years Based on the Diaries of Field-Marshal Lord Alanbrooke, Chief of the Imperial General Staff* (Garden City, N.Y.: Doubleday, 1957), p. 234.

28 a former fighter instructor: Claire Lee Chennault, *The Way of a Fighter: The Memoirs of Claire Lee Chennault*, ed. Robert Hotz (New York: G. P. Putnam's Sons, 1949), pp. 3–31.

28 The morning papers: "U.S. Fliers in China Down 4 Japanese," *New York Times*, Dec. 21, 1941, p. 27.

28 "The president": Arnold, *Global Mission*, p. 298.

28 Admiral Ernest King retired: Quentin Reynolds, *The Amazing Mr. Doolittle: A Biography of Lieutenant General James H. Doolittle* (New York: Appleton-Century-Crofts, 1953), pp. 170–72.

28 The admiral had: Chiefs of Staff Conference, Jan. 10, 1942, Microfilm Roll #205, HHAP. For a complete list of records related to the Arcadia Confer-

ence, see "Proceedings of the American-British Joint Chiefs of Staff Conferences Held in Washington, D.C., on Twelve Occasions between December 24, 1941 and January 14, 1942."

28 His flagship, the *Vixen*: James L. Mooney, ed., *Dictionary of American Naval Fighting Ships*, vol. 7 (Washington D.C.: GPO, 1981), pp. 552–53.

29 The six-foot-tall: Ernest King Navy Bio, July 21, 1965, Navy Department Library (NDL), Washington, D.C.; Thomas B. Buell, *Master of Sea Power: A Biography of Fleet Admiral Ernest J. King* (Boston: Little, Brown, 1980), pp. 10, 12, 36, 65, 88–89, 128–29.

29 "He is the most": W. J. Holmes, *Double-Edged Secrets: U.S. Naval Intelligence Operations in the Pacific War during World War II* (Annapolis, Md.: Naval Institute Press, 1979), p. 141.

29 A crossword puzzle: Buell, *Master of Sea Power*, pp. 9, 34–35.

29 His appreciation: Ibid., p. 161.

29 "No fighter": Ibid., p. 193.

29 Captain Francis Low: Francis Low Navy Bio, July 23, 1956, NDL; *The Lucky Bag*, vol. 22 (Annapolis, Md.: U.S. Naval Academy, 1915), p. 125.

30 "rather cruel": Francis S. Low, "A Personal Narrative of Association with Fleet Admiral Ernest, J. King, U.S. Navy," 1961, Box 10, Ernest J. King Papers, Naval War College Library, Newport, R.I., p. 19.

30 "little understood": Ibid., p. i.

30 "He was difficult": Ibid.

30 "Who made": Ibid., p. 15.

30 "What is it": Reynolds, *The Amazing Mr. Doolittle*, pp. 170–71.

30 "foolish idea": F. S. Low memorandum for F. H. Schneider, Nov. 16, 1951, Box 35, Ernest J. King Papers, LOC.

31 King's air operation: Donald Duncan Navy Bio, May 16, 1962, NDL.

31 "One thing": "The Reminiscences of Admiral Donald Duncan" (Columbia University Oral History Office, 1969), p. 349.

31 "This better": Reynolds, *The Amazing Mr. Doolittle*, pp. 171–73.

31 "As I see it": James H. "Jimmy" Doolittle, with Carroll V. Glines, *I Could Never Be So Lucky Again: An Autobiography* (New York: Bantam Books, 1991), pp. 234–35.

31 Duncan started: "The Reminiscences of Admiral Donald Duncan," pp. 324–26; D. B. Duncan to Ernest King, June 8, 1949, Box 18, Ernest J. King Papers, LOC; F. S. Low memorandum for F. H. Schneider, Nov. 16, 1951.

32 The Martin B-26: J. H. Doolittle, Report on the Aerial Bombing of Japan, June 5, 1942, Box 516, Record Group (RG) 18, Central Decimal Files, Oct. 1942–1944, National Archives and Records Administration (NARA), College Park, Md.

32 Lastly, a check: Aerology and Naval Warfare, "The First Raid on Japan," Feb. 1947, Chief of Naval Operations, Aerology Section, NDL.

32 "Go see General Arnold": Doolittle, *I Could Never Be So Lucky Again*, p. 235.

32 Few people: Arnold, *Global Mission*, pp. 1–29.

33 in just ten days: A. L. Welch, "Flying Report: Summary of Lt. Hen. H. Arnold's Training," May 3–13, 1911, Microfilm Roll #3, HHAP; Arnold, *Global Mission*, pp. 19–20, 29.

33 An avid: Thomas M. Coffey, *Hap: The Story of the U.S. Air Force and the Man Who Built It, General Henry H. "Hap" Arnold* (New York: Viking Press, 1982), p. 21; "Breaks Army Altitude Flight," *New York Times*, June 2, 1912, p. 4; "Gen. Arnold Heart Victim," *Milwaukee Journal*, Jan. 16, 1950, p. 1; Richard G. Davis, *Hap: Henry H. Arnold Military Aviator* (Washington, D.C.: Air Force History and Museums Program/GPO, 1997), pp. 3–5.

33 "to adjourn": Arnold letter to his mother, July 20, 1912, in John W. Huston, ed., *American Airpower Comes of Age: General Henry H. "Hap" Arnold's World War II Diaries*, vol. 1 (Maxwell Air Force Base, Ala.: Air University Press, 2002), p. 5.

33 two-time recipient: "General Arnold Wins Mackay Trophy Again," *New York Times*, March 16, 1935, p. 32.

33 Arnold's plane: Arnold, *Global Mission*, pp. 40–41.

33 "At the present time": H. H. Arnold to Commanding Officer, Signal Corps Aviation School, Washington, D.C., "Report upon Test of Aeroplane in Connection with Artillery Fires," Nov. 6, 1912, Microfilm Roll #3, HHAP. See also H. H. Arnold to Charles De F. Chandler, Nov. 7, 1912, ibid.

33 "That's it": Round Table Discussion on Early Aviation with Generals Benjamin Foulois, Frank Lahm, and Thomas Milling hosted by General Carl Spaatz, June 29, 1954, Air Force Historical Research Agency (AFHRA), Montgomery, Ala.

33 A sense of failure: Coffey, *Hap*, pp. 86–87.

33 The maverick spirit: Ibid., pp. 1–11.

33 Arnold even clashed: Arnold, *Global Mission*, pp. 184–86, 194.

33 "The best defense": Ibid., p. 290.

34 "Once the President": Ibid., p. 278.

34 Of the 231: Wesley Frank Craven and James Lea Cate, eds., *The Army Air Forces in World War II*, vol. 1, *Plans and Early Operations, January 1939 to August 1942* (1948; reprint, Washington, D.C.: Office of Air Force History, 1983), pp. 200, 213.

34 "Every commanding": Arnold, *Global Mission*, p. 271.

34 a California tire: "Tire Dealer Gives $1,000 Bond for First Tokyo Bomb," *Evening Independent*, April 18, 1942, p. 11.

34 "convince the mass": John Franklin Carter, Report on Suggestion for Bombing Japanese Volcanoes, May 21, 1942, Box 114, HHAP.

34 "It could": Amon G. Carter to E. M. Watson, Dec. 18, 1941, ibid.

34 "In his opinion": Arnold, *Global Mission*, pp. 276.

35 Arnold dismissed: Carroll V. Glines, *Doolittle's Tokyo Raiders* (Princeton, N.J.: D. Van Nostrand, 1964), p. 7.

35 "I always thought": Arnold, *Global Mission*, pp. 276–77.

35 "The minimum": Chiefs of Staff Conference minutes, Dec. 24, 1941, Microfilm Roll #205, HHAP.

35 "By transporting": Conference in White House minutes, Jan. 4, 1942, ibid.

35 An informal agreement: C. E. Duncan to A-3, Jan. 5, 1942, with E. L. Naiden memorandum for the record, Microfilm Roll #206, HHAP.

35 In response: John B. Cooley to Chief of the Air Corps, "Data Required on Army Airplanes for Carrier Operation," Jan. 17, 1942, Microfilm Roll #115, HHAP.

35 Analysts ruled out: H. H. Arnold to E. J. King, Jan. 22, 1942, ibid.

36 "It is not believed": Earl L. Naiden to Chief of the Army Air Forces, "Proposed Test of Cargo Planes Operating from Aircraft Carriers," Jan. 13, 1942, ibid.

36 Arnold enthusiastically: D. B. Duncan to Ernest King, June 8, 1949.

36 "Jim, what airplane": Doolittle, *I Could Never Be So Lucky Again*, p. 229.

36 Arnold picked up: Ibid, p. 236.

37 "Jim, I need": Ibid.

CHAPTER 3

38 "Doolittle is as gifted": Russell Owen, "Daring Doolittle Makes Pilots Gasp," *New York Times*, Sept. 23, 1927, p. 3.

38 "Jimmy Doolittle is the smallest": Doolittle, *I Could Never Be So Lucky Again*, p. 22.

39 "One of my punches": Ibid., p. 21.

39 "Since my size": Ibid., p. 22.

39 "The sights and sounds": Ibid., p. 24.

39 "You're going to get hurt": Ibid., p. 28.

40 "She wants you": Ibid., p. 30.

40 "Being incarcerated": Ibid.

40 "She was a very good": Ibid.

40 "There's no doubt": Ibid., p. 31.

40 "You must think": Ibid., p. 32.

41 "Alaska was not": Ibid., p. 33.

41 "He made a monkey": James H. Doolittle oral history with Robert S. Gallagher, March 4–6, 1973, Oral History Research Office, Columbia University, New York, N.Y.

41 "Luckiest thing": James Doolittle to Joe Doolittle, April 4, 1943, Box 64, Series IX, James H. Doolittle Papers (DPUT), University of Texas at Dallas; "Cadet Doolittle Scores Knockout As Eastern College Boxing Starts," *New York Times*, March 6, 1943, p. 17; "Syracuse Boxers Set Record to Win," ibid., March 7, 1943, p. S1.

42 "You all right?": Reynolds, *The Amazing Mr. Doolittle*, p. 28.

42 "My love for flying": Doolittle, *I Could Never Be So Lucky Again*, p. 42.

42 "I naturally went into fighters": Doolittle oral history with Gallagher, March 4–6, 1973.

43 "I was pretty upset": Steve Wilstein, "The Man Who Tweaked Japan's Nose," *Los Angeles Times*, Dec. 14, 1986, p. A3.

43 "Who's next?": Reynolds, *The Amazing Mr. Doolittle*, pp. 48–49.

43 "I was making about $140": Doolittle, *I Could Never Be So Lucky Again*, p. 47.

44 "What future is there": Reynolds, *The Amazing Mr. Doolittle*, p. 51.

44 "So close to one": Doolittle, *I Could Never Be So Lucky Again*, p. 49.

44 "I tried to invent": Ibid., p. 50.

44 "He is energetic": James H. Doolittle, Efficiency Report, Feb. 28, 1920, Doolittle Official Military Personnel File (DOMPF), National Personnel Records Center, Saint Louis, Mo.

45 "Gee, Lieutenant": Doolittle, *I Could Never Be So Lucky Again*, p. 50.

45 "It has to be Doolittle": Ibid., p. 51.

45 "Colonel": Coffey, *Hap*, p. 100.

45 "The only really dangerous": Doolittle oral history with Gallagher, March 4–6, 1973.

45 "Doolittle is more valuable": James H. Doolittle, Efficiency Report, May 18, 1922, DOMPF.

45 "Dynamic personality": James H. Doolittle, Efficiency Report, Feb. 6, 1932, DOMPF.

45 "One of the most daring": James H. Doolittle, Special Efficiency Report for Emergency Officers, April 29, 1920, DOMPF.

46 "The preparations for this flight": J. H. Doolittle, "Report of Cross Country Flight," Sept. 19, 1922, DOMPF.

46 On the evening of August 6: Ibid.; "Cross-Country Plane Plunges into Sea" *New York Times*, Aug. 7, 1922, p. 13.

46 "I was shocked": Doolittle, *I Could Never Be So Lucky Again*, p. 73.

46 "No": Ibid.

46 He oversaw the plane's repairs: J. H. Doolittle, "Report of Cross Country Flight," Sept. 19, 1922; "Flies with One Stop across Continent," *New York Times*, Sept. 6, 1922, p. 14.

46 "I realized the storm": Doolittle, *I Could Never Be So Lucky Again*, pp. 74–75.

47 "I have read": Mason M. Patrick to J. H. Doolittle, Oct. 16, 1922, DOMPF.

47 "I was glad I wore": Doolittle, *I Could Never Be So Lucky Again*, p. 91.

48 "We would often study": Ibid., p. 89.

48 To drum up interest: "Speed Fliers Ready for Pulitzer Race," *New York Times*, Oct. 12, 1925, p. 8.

48 "We performed aerobatics": Doolittle, *I Could Never Be So Lucky Again*, p. 102.

48 Doolittle cheered Bettis: Ibid., p. 103; "Pulitzer Race Won at 249-Mile Speed; Disappoints Fliers," *New York Times*, Oct. 13, 1925, p. 1.

48 "The flying of Doolittle": "American Seaplane Wins Schneider Race at 232-Mile Speed," *New York Times*, Oct. 27, 1925, p. 1.

49 "This was one": Mason M. Patrick to J. H. Doolittle, Nov. 6, 1925, DOMPF.

49 "Your splendid accomplishment": Doolittle, *I Could Never Be So lucky Again*, p. 108.

49 "I believe it very desirable": Mason M. Patrick memo for Chief of Staff, April 9, 1926, DOMPF.

49 "It was a dream": Doolittle, *I Could Never Be So Lucky Again*, p. 114.

49 At a May 23 cocktail party: Ibid., pp. 115–16; Board Proceedings, Jan. 17, 1927, Exhibit A, DOMPF.

50 "Embarrassment overcame": Doolittle, *I Could Never Be So Lucky Again*, p. 116.

50 His tenaciousness: "Doolittle's Courage Wins Big Plane Order," *New York Times*, Jan. 13, 1927, p. 18.

50 "These flights": James Hanson to Chief of Air Service, July 19, 1926, DOMPF.

50 "His injury may result": Testimony of Tom S. Mebane, Board Proceedings, Jan. 17, 1927, DOMPF.

51 When his treatment: G. C. Young to the Adjutant General, "Board Proceedings re: 1st Lieut. James H. Doolittle, A.C.," April 14, 1927, DOMPF.

51 He and other pilots at Walter Reed: Doolittle, *I Could Never Be So Lucky Again*, pp. 119–20.

51 He climbed up: "Doolittle Performs Outside Loop," *New York Times*, May 26, 1927, p. 5.

51 "Nothing to it": "Jimmy Doolittle Tells How an Outside Loop Is Made," *Milwaukee Journal*, March 10, 1931, p. 2.

51 "What would I do?": Doolittle, *I Could Never Be So Lucky Again*, p. 127.

51 "Fog is one of the greatest": Charles A. Lindbergh, "Lindbergh on Flying," *New York Times*, Jan. 20, 1929, p. XX12.

52 Doolittle throttled up: "'Blind' Plane Flies 15 Miles and Lands, Fog Peril Overcome," *New York Times*, Sept. 25, 1929, p. 1.

52 "This entire flight": James Doolittle, "Early Blind Flying: An Historical Review of Early Experiments in Flying," transcript of lecture at the Massachusetts Institute of Technology, April 28, 1961, AFHRA.

53 News of Doolittle's achievement: "Air Experts Acclaim 'Blind Flying' Tests," *New York Times*, Sept. 26, 1929, p. 9.

53 "On Tuesday": "Blind Flying Demonstrated," editorial, *New York Times*, Sept. 26, 1929, p. 28.

53 "That took real courage": H. H. Arnold to Lester D. Gardner, May 28, 1941, DOMPF.

53 "Over the years": Doolittle, *I Could Never Be So Lucky Again*, p. 150.

53 "I left the Air Force": James Doolittle oral history with Edgar F. Puryear Jr., Feb. 7, 1977, AFHRA.

53 Doolittle had not only: "Doolittle Hits 296-Mile Pace; Breaks the Land Plane Record," *New York Times*, Sept. 1, 1932, p. 1.

53 "Air racing is like hay fever": "Speed Crown to Doolittle," *Toledo News-Bee*, Sept. 6, 1932, p. 1.

54 "I have yet to hear": Jimmy Doolittle, "Testing Racing Planes," *Popular Aviation*, Nov. 1933, p. 339.

54 "Aviation has become a necessity": Bert Stoll, "Doolittle Hits Races," *New York Times*, Oct. 21, 1934, p. XX6.

55 "Shell had taken": Doolittle, *I Could Never Be So Lucky Again*, p. 192.

55 "On the streets": Ibid., p. 210.

55 "This thing is very close": J. H. Doolittle to Henry Arnold, Aug. 15, 1941, Microfilm Roll #13, HHAP.

55 his muscle worked: Prentiss Brown letter to Henry Arnold, Feb. 13, 1942, ibid.

55 "Don't think": Prentiss Brown letter to Henry Arnold, March 4, 1942, ibid.

55 "General Arnold supported me": James Doolittle oral history interview with Murray Green, Dec. 22, 1977, AFHRA.

56 "I am entirely": J. H. Doolittle to Ira C. Eaker, June 7, 1940, DOMPF.

56 "When he resigned": H. H. Arnold to Lester D. Gardner, May 28, 1941, DOMPF.

56 "My job was to marry": Doolittle oral history interview with Green, Dec. 22, 1977.

56 "I respectfully request": J. H. Doolittle to H. H. Arnold (Thru Channels), Dec. 8, 1941, DOMPF.

56 "How quickly": James H. Doolittle oral history interview with Lt. Col. Burch, Maj. Fogelman, and Capt. Tate, Sept. 26, 1971, AFHRA.

56 an unforgiving: James Doolittle oral history interview with Reuben Fleet, Aug. 14, 1970, Robert F. McDermott Library, U.S. Air Force Academy, Colorado Springs, Colo. A copy of this oral history is also on file at AFHRA.

56 Pilots quipped: Coffey, *Hap*, p. 247.

57 "The B-26 was a good airplane": James Doolittle oral history interview with Paul Ryan, Feb. 15, 1983, AFHRA. A copy of this oral history is also on file with the U.S. Naval Institute.

57 "There wasn't anything": Doolittle, *I Could Never Be So Lucky Again*, p. 228.

57 "the most important": Ibid., p. 229.

CHAPTER 4

58 "If you have one plane": Allan J. Johnson to Franklin Roosevelt, June 7, 1941, Box 12, OF 4675, FDRL.

58 "Special Aviation Project No. 1": Doolittle, *I Could Never Be So Lucky Again*, p. 238.

58 "Anything that I wanted": Jimmy Doolittle, Tokyo Raid Dinner, Monterey, Calif., April 19, 1988, press conference, cassette recording, Box 2, Series XIV, DPUT.

58 The veteran aviator envisioned: Doolittle handwritten draft plan, undated, Box 516, RG 18, Central Decimal Files, Oct. 1942–1944, NARA; Doolittle, *I Could Never Be So Lucky Again*, pp. 236–43.

58 It was developed: Background on the B-25 comes from N. L. Avery, *B-25 Mitchell: The Magnificent Medium* (St. Paul, Minn.: Phalanx Publishing, 1992), pp. 27–38; Tom Lilley et al., "Conversion to Wartime Production Techniques," in G. R. Simonson, ed., *The History of the American Aircraft Industry: An Anthology* (Cambridge, Mass.: MIT Press, 1968), p. 131; Irving Brinton Holley Jr., *Buying Aircraft: Matériel Procurement for the Army Air Forces* (Washington, D.C.: Center of Military History, U.S. Army, 1989), p. 550.

59 "It is a good": Hanson W. Baldwin, "Bombers Thrill War Game Troops," *New York Times*, Sept. 23, 1941, p. 7.

59 "The B-26 was a Lincoln": Forrest K. Poling, *From Farm Fields to Airfields* (Superior Township, Mich.: Zorado Press, 2006), p. 120.

60 "It is so much more": Ted W. Lawson, *Thirty Seconds over Tokyo*, ed. Bob Considine (New York: Random House, 1953), p. 16.

60 Opened in 1927: "Army Dedicates New Flying Center," *New York Times*, Oct. 13, 1927, p. 3; Charles J. Bauer, "New Test Equipment," ibid., April 6, 1941, p. XX5; Sidney M. Shalett, "Air Magic Show at Wright Field," ibid., Dec. 30, 1942, p. 8; Hanson W. Baldwin, "Wright Field Holds Great Air Secrets," ibid., Nov. 4, 1943, p. 12; Russell Owen, "Where the Impossible Is Done," ibid., March 18, 1945, p. SM8.

60 "Wright Field is the place": William A. Norris, "Wright Field Air Center of the World," *Milwaukee Sentinel*, June 4, 1944, p. 1.

60 "It is requested": J. H. Doolittle memo for the Chief of the Air Staff, Jan. 22, 1942, Iris #02053123, AFHRA.

60 Doolittle upped his request: Memo to Chief of the Air Corp, "Special B-25B Project," Jan. 29, 1942, ibid.; Doolittle, *I Could Never Be So Lucky Again*, p. 242.

60 Orders called for the bombers: John Y. York Jr., memo for A-3, Jan. 30, 1942, Wm. W. Dick to Commanding General, Air Force Combat Command, Bolling Field, D.C., Jan. 31, 1942, both in Iris #02053123, AFHRA.

60 The B-25 boasted: J. H. Doolittle, Report on the Aerial Bombing of Japan, June 5, 1942; "General Doolittle's Remarks at the Wings Club Dinner," Oct. 1, 1945, transcript, Box 7, Series IV, DPUT; Charles R. Greening, "The First Joint Action," Monograph Submitted to the Faculty of the Armed Forces Staff College, Norfolk, Virginia, Fourth Class, Dec. 21, 1948, AFHRA, pp. 1–6. Copies of Greening's report can also be found in Doolittle's personal papers at the LOC and the University of Texas.

62 "The purpose": Doolittle handwritten draft plan, undated, Box 516, RG 18, Central Decimal Files, Oct. 1942–1944, NARA.

62 Doolittle ordered: Doolittle, *I Could Never Be So Lucky Again*, p. 241.

62 "It is desired": Henry Arnold to Carl Spaatz, "Objective in Japan Most Desirable for Attack," Jan. 22, 1942, Microfilm Roll #114, HHAP.

62 "The above aircraft factories": AAF C/AS to Henry Arnold, "Objective in Japan Most Desirable for Attack," Jan. 31, 1942, ibid.

63 "Many of these objectives": Ibid.

63 "An initial study": Doolittle handwritten draft plan.

64 "Premature notification": Ibid.

64 On the frigid Sunday: *Hornet* deck log, Feb. 1, 1942, Box 4439, RG 24, Records of the Bureau of Naval Personnel, Deck Logs, 1941–1950, NARA.

64 $32 million new flattop: "Knox Praises Men Lost on the Kearny," *New York Times*, Oct. 21, 1941, p. 5.

64 had returned to Virginia: Lisle A. Rose, *The Ship That Held the Line* (Annapolis, Md.: Naval Institute Press, 1995), pp. 19–34.

64 The wiry officer: Marc Mitscher Navy Bio, Jan. 23, 1964, NDL; "Admiral

Mitscher, War Hero, 60, Dies," *New York Times*, Feb. 4, 1947, p. 5; Theodore Taylor, *The Magnificent Mitscher* (New York: W. W. Norton, 1954), pp. 14–27.

64 "I was a 2.5 man": Elmont Waite, "He Opened the Airway to Tokyo," *Saturday Evening Post*, Dec. 2, 1944, p. 88.

64 This unlikely leader: Marc Mitscher Navy Bio, Jan. 23, 1964.

65 The humble skipper: Waite, "He Opened the Airway to Tokyo," p. 20; Henry Suydan interview with George Murray, Feb. 1947, Box 1, Marc Andrew Mitscher Papers, LOC.

65 Long cruises: Taylor, *The Magnificent Mitscher*, p. 8; *The Reminiscences of Captain Stephen Jurika, Jr., U.S. Navy—Retired*, vol. 1 (Annapolis, Md.: U.S. Naval Institute, 1979), p. 493.

65 "I'm an old man now": "Admiral Mitscher," editorial, *New York Times*, Feb. 4, 1947, p. 24.

65 "In being selected": Marc Mitscher to Frederick Sherman, Feb. 24, 1942, Box 1, Marc Andrew Mitscher Papers, LOC.

65 "He wasted": Suydan interview with Murray, Feb. 1947.

65 "Even when": Waite, "He Opened the Airway to Tokyo," p. 20.

65 "Can you put": Taylor, *The Magnificent Mitscher*, p. 112.

66 "best combat crews": John B. Colley to the Commanding General, Air Force Combat Command, "Carrier Operation Test," Jan. 16, 1942, Microfilm Roll #115, HHAP.

66 "Airplanes will have combat": Ibid.

66 "Successive take-offs": C. E. Duncan to A-3, "Carrier Type of B-25's," Jan. 13, 1942, Microfilm Roll #115, HHAP.

66 Mitscher ordered: Taylor, *The Magnificent Mitscher*, p. 112.

66 Sailors lit: *Hornet* deck log, Feb. 2, 1942.

66 "Since flying": "Fitzgerald Paved Way for Tokyo Raid," *News and Courier*, April 16, 1967, p. 12-B.

67 "If we go into the water": Oscar H. Dodson, "The Doolittle Raid," *Bridge* 3, no. 3 (Spring 1987): 8.

67 During the more: Doolittle, *I Could Never Be So Lucky Again*, pp. 238–39.

67 "When I got": "Fitzgerald Paved Way for Tokyo Raid," p. 12-B.

67 Mitscher flashed: Taylor, *The Magnificent Mitscher*, p. 113.

67 Lieutenant James McCarthy: Doolittle, *I Could Never Be So Lucky Again*, pp. 238–39.

67 The Army aviator: D. B. Duncan memorandum to Ernest King, Feb. 4, 1942, Box 1, Ernest J. King Papers, NHHC.

67 The *Hornet*'s air patrol: Ibid.

67 "Frank": Alexander T. Griffin, *A Ship to Remember: The Saga of the Hornet* (New York: Howell, Soskin, 1943), p. 48.

68 "Very realistic drill": Taylor, *The Magnificent Mitscher*, p. 113.

68 "There was a six foot": D. B. Duncan memorandum to Ernest King, Feb. 4, 1942.

68 "Excellent": Ibid.

68 "The less you know": Taylor, *The Magnificent Mitscher*, p. 113.

68 Doolittle had asked: Doolittle, *I Could Never Be So Lucky Again*, p. 242; J. H. Doolittle, Report on the Aerial Bombing of Japan, June 5, 1942.

69 "When I saw it": Edgar McElroy, "When We Were One: A Doolittle Raider Remembers," *Trinity*, July 2010, p. 24.

69 "I couldn't eat": Lawson, *Thirty Seconds over Tokyo*, p. 7.

69 "rocket plane": McElroy, "When We Were One," p. 24.

69 "Not only did": Robert G. Emmens oral history interview with James C. Hasdorff, July 8–9, 1992, AFHRA.

69 The bombardment group: Lawson, *Thirty Seconds over Tokyo*, pp. 7–8.

69 "It was the first time": Jack A. Sims with A. B. Cook, *First over Japan: An Autobiography of a Doolittle-Tokyo Raider* (Fort Myers, Fla.: Southpointe Press, 2002), p. 10.

69 "The maneuvers were close": Lawson, *Thirty Seconds over Tokyo*, p. 9.

69 The men of the Seventeenth: This is based on a review of the oral histories with various Raiders on file at AFHRA.

70 "It was the greatest": William Bower oral history interview with Dave Edwards, Oct. 27, 1971, AFHRA.

70 "There was no tangible": Lawson, *Thirty Seconds over Tokyo*, pp. 12–13.

70 "Everybody was interested": Bower oral history interview with Edwards, Oct. 27, 1971.

70 "I sure would give anything": Robert Bourgeois to Ross Greening, Individual Histories questionnaire, undated (ca. 1950), Iris #01010162, AFHRA.

70 "We played poker": Joseph Manske diary, Feb. 10, 1942, Box 4, Series II, Doolittle Tokyo Raiders Association Papers (DTRAP), University of Texas at Dallas.

71 "We lived in tents": Billy Farrow undated letter to his mother, in Margaret Meadows Stem, *Tall and Free as Meant by God* (New York: Hearthstone Book/Carlton Press, 1969), pp. 33–34.

71 "Damn it": Reynolds, *The Amazing Mr. Doolittle*, p. 179; C. Ross Greening, *Not As Briefed: From the Doolittle Raid to a German Stalag*, comp. and ed. Dorothy Greening and Karen Morgan Driscoll (Pullman: Washington State University Press, 2001), p. 11.

71 "That's about all": Reynolds, *The Amazing Mr. Doolittle*, p. 180.

71 "The group commander was a colonel": James H. Doolittle oral history interview with Edward F. Puryear Jr., Feb. 7, 1977.

72 "Some of you fellows": Jacob D. DeShazer oral history interview with James C. Hasdorff, Oct. 10, 1989, AFHRA.

72 "Boy": Ibid.

72 "I was too big": Jeff Wilkinson, "'The Lord Told Me to Go Back,'" *State*, April 12, 2002, p. 1.

72 "The entire group stood": Emmens oral history interview with Hasdorff, July 8–9, 1992.

72 "Hands just kept": Charles J. Ozuk Jr. oral history interview with James C. Hasdorff, July 1989, AFHRA.

72 "The name 'Doolittle' meant": Robert L. Hite oral history interview with James C. Hasdorff, Dec. 16–17, 1982, AFHRA.

72 "You can't volunteer, Mac!": This exchange comes from McElroy, "When We Were One," p. 26.

73 "What are you holding": Bert M. Jordan oral history interview with James C. Hasdorff, June 15, 1988, AFHRA.

73 "I just wanted": Ibid.

73 "It was disgusting": Gary A. Warner, "Vets Recall Historic US Raid on Tokyo," *Orange County Register*, April 16, 1992, p. E02.

73 "Herb, what do you want?": James "Herb" Macia oral history interview with Floyd Cox, July 21, 2000, National Museum of the Pacific War, Fredericksburg, Tex.

73 "Doolittle has been": David M. Jones oral history interview with James C. Hasdorff, Jan. 13–14, 1987, AFHRA.

73 "There's been a change": This exchange comes from Lawson, *Thirty Seconds over Tokyo*, p. 17–18.

74 "Don't go denuding": Edward J. York oral history interview with James C. Hasdorff, July 23, 1984, AFHRA.

74 "We had so many": Ibid.

74 "You have to stay behind": Emmens oral history interview with Hasdorff, July 8–9, 1992.

74 "Knobby, you should": This exchange comes from Richard A. Knobloch oral history interview with James C. Hasdorff, July 13–14, 1987, AFHRA.

74 Japan's rampage: "Axis Fever," *Time*, Feb. 23, 1942, p. 16; Breckinridge Long diary, Jan. 28, 1942, and Feb. 5, 1942, in Israel, ed., *The War Diary of Breckinridge Long*, pp. 245–50.

74 The news: Breckinridge Long diary, Jan. 13 and Feb. 5, 1942, in Israel, ed., *The War Diary of Breckinridge Long*, pp. 242–43; David L. Roll, *The Hopkins Touch: Harry Hopkins and the Forging of the Alliance to Defeat Hitler* (New York: Oxford University Press, 2013), p. 180.

74 Isolationist newspapers: Bureau of Intelligence to the Director, Office of Facts and Figures, Survey of Intelligence Materials No. 9, Feb. 9, 1942, Microfilm Roll #23, President Franklin D. Roosevelt's Office Files, 1933–1944, pt. 4: Subject Files.

75 "There is a prevailing desire": Ibid.

75 America's efforts: Samuel Eliot Morison, *History of the United States Naval Operations in World War II*, vol. 3, *The Rising Sun in the Pacific, 1931–April 1942* (1948; reprint, Boston: Little, Brown, 1988), pp. 223–54.

75 "The enemy is on the island": Ibid., p. 248.

75 "Everyone seems to feel": Gordon W. Prange, with Donald M. Goldstein and Katherine V. Dillon, *Miracle at Midway* (New York: McGraw-Hill, 1982), p. 6.

75 "a worse blow": Ibid.

75 Constructed atop: "Singapore Stormed," *New York Times*, Feb. 15, 1942, p. E1.

75 "Christ": Joseph Stilwell diary, Feb. 18, 1942, in White, ed., *The Stilwell Papers*, p. 40.

75 For the first time: Survey of Intelligence Materials No. 10, Feb. 16, 1942,

Microfilm Roll #23, President Franklin D. Roosevelt's Office Files, 1933–1944, pt. 4: Subject Files.

75 "There can be": Hanson W. Baldwin, "10 Weeks of Pacific War Show Japan Unchecked," *New York Times*, Feb. 15, 1942, p. E4.

76 "If you will": Press Conference #807, Feb. 24, 1942, in *Complete Presidential Press Conferences of Franklin D. Roosevelt*, vol. 19, *1942* (New York: Da Capo Press, 1972), pp. 155–56.

76 "In the name": Survey of Intelligence Materials No. 10, Feb. 16, 1942.

76 The unity: Survey of Intelligence Materials No. 11, Feb. 23, 1942, Microfilm Roll #30, President Franklin D. Roosevelt's Office Files, 1933–1944, pt. 4: Subject Files; Goodwin, *No Ordinary Time*, pp. 321–23; Francis Biddle memo to Franklin Roosevelt, Feb. 17, 1942, Box 7, OF 18, FDRL; Kyle Palmer, "Speedy Moving of Japs Urged," *Los Angles Times*, Jan. 31, 1942, p. 1.

76 "A viper": W. H. Anderson, "The Question of Japanese-Americans," *Los Angeles Times*, Feb. 2, 1942, p. A4.

76 "Herd 'em up": Henry McLemore, "Why Treat the Japs Well Here?," *San Francisco Examiner*, Jan. 29, 1942, p. 9.

76 "A Jap's a Jap": Headquarters Western Defense Command and Fourth Army, Office of the Commanding General, "Transcript of Telephone Conversation between General DeWitt and Mr. McCloy, Asst. Secretary of War, Washington, D.C.," April 14, 1943, NARA.

76 "It looks to me": James Rowe Jr. to Grace Tully, Feb. 2, 1942, Box 33, James H. Rowe Jr. Papers, FDRL.

76 He signed Executive Order 9066: Greg Robinson, *By Order of the President: FDR and the Internment of Japanese Americans* (Cambridge, Mass.: Harvard University Press, 2001), pp. 3–4.

76 "I do not think": Biddle, *In Brief Authority*, p. 219.

77 "These people were not convicted": Eleanor Roosevelt, "A Challenge to American Sportsmanship," *Collier's*, Oct. 16, 1943, p. 71. A draft copy of this article is on file in Box 1414, Eleanor Roosevelt Papers, FDRL.

77 "deep undercurrent of bitterness": Survey of Intelligence Materials No. 14, Office of Facts and Figures, Bureau of Intelligence, March 16, 1942, Microfilm Roll #30, President Franklin D. Roosevelt's Office Files, 1933–1944, pt. 4: Subject Files.

77 "The Navy has": Marjorie McKenzie, "Pursuit of Democracy," *Bags and Baggage*, Jan. 1942, p. 5.

77 Another flashpoint: Albert Deutsch and Tom O'Connor, "Red Cross Blood Bias Called Hindrance to War Effort—Luxury We Can't Afford," *Afro-American*, Jan. 17, 1942, p. 9; "Red Cross to Use Blood of Negroes," *New York Times*, Jan. 29, 1942, p. 13.

77 "It is a matter": Survey of Intelligence Materials No. 14, March 16, 1942.

77 "The president stated that": Conference at the White House minutes, Jan. 28, 1942, Microfilm Roll #205, HHAP.

77 "For this reason I feel": Memorandum for the President, Jan. 28, 1942, Microfilm Roll #170, HHAP.

78 "Perhaps it is good": Eleanor Roosevelt, "My Day," Feb. 17, 1942.

78 "Let me say": "We Must Keep on Striking Our Enemies Wherever and Whenever We Can Meet Them"—Fireside Chat on Progress of the War, Feb. 23, 1942, in Samuel I. Rosenman, comp., *The Public Papers and Addresses of Franklin D. Roosevelt*, 1942 vol., *Humanity on the Defensive* (New York: Harper & Brothers, 1950), p. 112.

CHAPTER 5

79 "For a while": Agawa, *The Reluctant Admiral*, p. 292.

79 "Britain and America": Ibid., p. 286.

79 The son of a former samurai warrior: Ibid., pp. 1–3, 17–18, 64–65.

80 "Whenever I go": Ibid., p. 65.

80 Yamamoto twice lived: Ibid., 70–76, 84–85.

80 "A man who claims": Ibid., p. 74.

80 Yamamoto opposed: Ibid., pp. 161–67, 186–87, 385.

80 "If we are ordered": Ibid., p.189.

81 "My present situation": Goldstein and Dillon, *The Pearl Harbor Papers*, p. 124.

81 In past war games: Ibid., p. 116.

81 "The most important": Ibid.

81 The success of the attack: Agawa, *The Reluctant Admiral*, pp. 284–90.

81 "As I see it": Ibid., p. 287.

81 Likewise, he rejected: Ibid., p. 288.

81 "I could never wear them": Ibid., p. 297.

81 "I wonder how": Ibid., pp. 297–98.

81 In his first wartime: "The Militarists of Berlin and Tokyo Started This War. But the Massed, Angered Force of Common Humanity Will Finish It"— Address to the Congress on the State of the Union, Jan. 6, 1942, in Rosenman, comp., *The Public Papers and Addresses of Franklin D. Roosevelt*, 1942 vol., pp. 32–42.

82 "A military man can scarcely pride": Agawa, *The Reluctant Admiral*, p. 285.

82 In the weeks after the attack: "Triumphant Record of Battle of Hawaii Recounted," *Osaka Mainichi*, Jan. 3, 1942, p. 1; "Nippon Naval Planes Blast Hickam Field, Hawaii," ibid., Jan. 2, 1942, p. 1; "Start of Death-Defying Attack on Hawaii," ibid., Jan. 2, 1942, p. 1; "Smoke Covers Pearl Harbor after Bombing," ibid., Jan. 3, 1942, p. 4.

82 "the brilliant curtain": "Cinema and Account of Battle of Hawaii," editorial, *Osaka Mainichi*, Jan. 6, 1942, p. 4.

82 Other papers published poems: "Pearl Harbor," *Japan Times & Advertiser*, Jan. 11, 1942, p. 4; "Cinema and Account of Battle of Hawaii," editorial, *Osaka Mainichi*, Jan. 6, 1942, p. 4; "Movie and Theater Notes of Interest," *Japan Times & Advertiser*, March 5, 1942, p. 4.

82 "superhuman": Staff Naval Writer, "USA to Shift Strategy," *Osaka Mainichi*, March 24, 1942, p. 1.

82 celebrated them as gods: "Nine Naval Heroes Looked to as Gods," *Japan Times & Advertiser*, April 5, 1942, p. 3.

82 One newspaper article: "Japan's Conquest of Indies Predicted Many Years Ago by Prophet Boyo Moyo," *Japan Times & Advertiser*, Jan. 14, 1942, p. 1.

82 "As our country was founded": "Victory for Japan Seen as Certain," *Japan Times & Advertiser*, Jan. 8, 1942, p. 1.

82 Members of the House: "Representatives Cheer Singapore Fall," *Japan Times & Advertiser*, Feb. 17, 1942, p. 2.

82 Schools suspended class: "Tokyo Celebrates Singapore Victory," *Japan Times & Advertiser*, Feb. 17, 1942, p. 1. See *Japan Times & Advertiser*'s special twelve-page "Victory Supplement," published Feb. 17, 1942.

82 Despite rationing: "Singapore Surrender to Be Celebrated with Special Allocations of Beer, Rubber," *Japan Times & Advertiser*, Feb. 17, 1942, p. 3.

82 Even Emperor Hirohito: "Foe Celebrates Singapore's Fall," *New York Times*, Feb. 19, 1942, p. 4.

82 "The downfall of Singapore": "Singapore's Doom and Its Worldwide Effect," editorial, *Osaka Mainichi*, Feb. 15, 1942, p. 4.

83 "Our men": "A Unique Kigensetsu," editorial, *Japan Times & Advertiser*, Feb. 13, 1942, p. 6.

83 "Once a landing is made": "Can the United States Be Invaded?," editorial, *Japan Times & Advertiser*, Jan. 9, 1942, p. 6.

83 "Japan Raid by U.S.": "Japan Raid by U.S. Is Out of Question," *Japan Times & Advertiser*, Jan. 12, 1942, p. 1.

83 "No Fear of America": "No Fear of America Attacking Empire," *Japan Times & Advertiser*, Jan. 16, 1942, p. 2.

83 Most pointed out: "Japan Raid by U.S. Is Out of Question," *Japan Times & Advertiser*, Jan. 12, 1942, p. 1.

83 "As for aerial attacks": "U.S. Air Attacks Held Improbable," *Japan Times & Advertiser*, Feb. 22, 1942, p. 4.

83 Most of the nation's fighters: Headquarters, USAFFE and Eighth U.S. Army (Rear), "Homeland Air Defense Operations Record," Japanese Monograph #157, 1958, pp. 2, 11–12, 33; idem, "Homeland Operations Record," Japanese Monograph #17, 1958, pp. 6–7.

83 "Compared with": Headquarters, USAFFE and Eighth U.S. Army (Rear), "Homeland Operations Record," Japanese Monograph #17, 1958, p. 6.

84 "I do not think": Headquarters, USAFFE and Eighth U.S. Army (Rear), "Homeland Air Defense Operations Record," Japanese Monograph #157, 1958, p. 2.

84 That same confidence: Benjamin Franklin Cooling, ed., *Case Studies in the Achievement of Air Superiority* (Washington, D.C.: Center for Air Force History, 1994), p. 393.

84 The veteran admiral: Mitsuo Fuchida and Masatake Okumiya, *Midway: The Battle That Doomed Japan* (Annapolis, Md.: Naval Institute Press, 1955), pp. 64–65.

84 "He never failed": Ibid., p. 65.

84 Yamamoto ordered daily: Ibid., p. 66; USSBS, Civilian Defense Division,

Field Report Covering Air Raid Protection and Allied Subjects, Tokyo, Japan (Washington, D.C.: GPO, 1947), pp. 14–15.

84 "A lot of people are feeling": Agawa, *The Reluctant Admiral*, p. 298–99.

85 twenty-nine-year-old: Background on Henry Miller is drawn from Henry Miller Navy Bio, Jan. 5, 1972, NDL; *The Reminiscences of Rear Admiral Henry L. Miller, U.S. Navy (Retired)*, vol. 1 (Annapolis, Md.: U.S. Naval Institute, 1973), pp. 1–37.

85 "Is that the Great": *The Reminiscences of Rear Admiral Henry L. Miller*, vol. 1, p. 31.

85 Doolittle had requested: Doolittle, *I Could Never Be So Lucky Again*, p. 243.

85 founded in 1933: Historical Branch, Army Air Forces Proving Ground Command, Eglin Field, Fla., "History of the Army Air Forces Proving Ground Command" pt. 1, "Historical Outline," pp. iii–vii, 32–72, AFHRA.

85 "It was out in the boonies": Everett W. "Brick" Holstrom oral history interview with James C. Hasdorff, April 14–15, 1988, AFHRA.

86 "Inasmuch as this is": John B. Cooley to Commanding Officer, Eglin Field, "Accommodations," Feb. 17, 1942, Iris #2053039, AFHRA. Even though the Feb. 17 orders specified twenty combat crews, a total of twenty-four ultimately would participate in the training.

86 "It is requested": William W. Dick to Chief of the Bureau of Aeronautics, Feb. 17, 1942, ibid.

86 "Do you know": This exchange comes from *The Reminiscences of Rear Admiral Henry L. Miller*, vol. 1, p. 31.

86 "Have you ever flown": Ibid., p. 32.

86 "Well, that's all right": Henry A. Potter oral history interview with James C. Hasdorff, June 8–10, 1979, AFHRA.

87 "That is impossible": This exchange comes from Henry L. Miller, "Training the Doolittle Fliers," in John T. Mason Jr., ed., *The Pacific War Remembered: An Oral History Collection* (Annapolis: Md.: Naval Institute Press, 1986), p. 71.

87 The two dozen aircrews: Doolittle, *I Could Never Be So Lucky Again*, pp. 244–46; Merian C. Cooper to Commanding General, American Army Forces in China, Burma and India, Chungking, China, "The Doolittle Air Raid on Japan: Known as First Special Aviation Project," June 22, 1942, Box 46, RG 407, Military Reference Microfilm, NARA.

88 "I was a little awestruck": Bower oral history interview with Edwards, Oct. 27, 1971.

88 "He was a legend": James H. Macia oral history interview with James C. Hasdorff, July 15–16, 1987, AFHRA.

88 "I'd built him up": Harry C. McCool oral history interview with James C. Hasdorff, July 21, 1989, AFHRA.

88 "We were immediately captivated": Jones oral history interview with Hasdorff, Jan. 13–14, 1987.

88 "As soon as we heard": Charles McClure, "How We Bombed Tokyo: Thrilling Epic," *Chicago Daily Tribune*, April 27, 1943, p. 1.

88 "My name's Doolittle": Lowell Thomas and Edward Jablonski, *Doolittle: A Biography* (Garden City, N.Y.: Doubleday, 1976), p. 162.

88 "If you men": Lawson, *Thirty Seconds over Tokyo*, p. 20.

88 "Sir": Glines, *Doolittle's Tokyo Raiders*, p. 46.

88 "No, I can't": Lawson, *Thirty Seconds over Tokyo*, p. 20.

89 "The lives of many men": Glines, *Doolittle's Tokyo Raiders*, p. 46.

89 "Our training": Ibid.

89 "We've got about three weeks": Ibid.

89 Miller started work immediately: Henry L. Miller to D. B. Duncan, May 7, 1942, Report on Temporary Additional Duty Assignment, Box 6, Series II, DTRAP. A copy of this report is also attached to Miller's 1973 oral history with the U.S. Naval Institute.

90 "We can't do that": Travis Hoover oral history interview with James C. Hasdorff, June 20–21, 1988, AFHRA.

90 During preliminary training: Henry L. Miller to D. B. Duncan, May 7, 1942.

90 "Excellent": Ibid.

90 "After a little practice": Cooper, "The Doolittle Air Raid on Japan," June 22, 1942.

90 For the final rounds: Henry L. Miller to D. B. Duncan, May 7, 1942; Horace E. Crouch oral history interview with James C. Hasdorff, April 19, 1989, AFHRA.

90 "It became an intense competition": Bower oral history interview with Edwards, Oct. 27, 1971.

91 "Bates, you have to try it again": *The Reminiscences of Rear Admiral Henry L. Miller*, vol. 1, p. 35.

91 The lieutenant throttled up: Technical Report of Aircraft Accident Classification Committee Plus Enclosures, May 1, 1942, AFHRA.

91 "Sit down": *The Reminiscences of Rear Admiral Henry L. Miller*, vol. 1, p. 36.

91 "No one was hurt": James P. Bates, statement, included with Technical Report of Aircraft Accident Classification Committee Plus Enclosures, May 1, 1942.

91 "We just lost": This exchange comes from Emmens's oral history interview with Hasdorff, July 8–9, 1982.

92 Maintenance problems: Doolittle, *I Could Never Be So Lucky Again*, pp. 246–47; Greening, "The First Joint Action," pp. 3–6; J. H. Doolittle, Report on the Aerial Bombing of Japan, June 5, 1942.

92 "woefully deficient": Greening, "The First Joint Action," p. 3.

92 "A man could learn to play": Doolittle, *I Could Never Be So Lucky Again*, p. 246.

93 Greening zeroed in as well: Details on the Norden bombsight come from the following sources: Wayne Whittaker, "The Bombsight That Thinks," *Popular Mechanics*, Feb. 1945, pp. 7–10, 160–62; Volta Torrey, "The War's Most Closely Guarded Secret Revealed: How the Norden Bombsight Does Its Job," ibid., June 1945, pp. 70–73, 220–24, 228, 232; "Norden Bomb Sight Is Revealed as Almost Self Sufficient Device," *New York Times*, Nov. 25, 1944,

p. 11; C. Brooks Peters, "Japan Bombed with 20-Cent Sight," ibid., June 28, 1942, p. 1; Greening, *Not As Briefed*, pp. 14–15.

93 Mark Twain: Greening, *Not As Briefed*, p. 15.

93 "It was fine for the things": Lawson, *Thirty Seconds over Tokyo*, p. 24.

93 North American developed: Greening, "The First Joint Action," pp. 12–13.

93 "I understand you want": This exchange is ibid., p. 53.

94 Pilots flew under simulated: Ibid., pp. 12–13.

94 "This did not do the trick": Kenneth Reddy diary, March 20, 1942, Box 5, Series II, DTRAP.

94 Doolittle likewise demanded: J. H. Doolittle, Report on the Aerial Bombing of Japan, June 5, 1942; Greening, "The First Joint Action," pp. 13–16.

94 "Many Florida coast towns": Greening, "The First Joint Action," p. 16.

94 A Maui native: T. R. White to Jack J. Levand, Feb. 28, 1962, Box 5a, Series II, DTRAP; Thomas Robert White, family bio, Nov. 21, 1996, ibid.; Thomas R. White, Personal Data Sheet, 1958, ibid.

94 "To his great credit": Doolittle, *I Could Never Be So Lucky Again*, p. 248.

95 Mindful of weight limits: T. R. White to Air Surgeon, "Report of Activities Covering the Period from March 1, 1942, to June 16, 1942," June 23, 1942, Box 22, James H. Doolittle Papers (DPLOC), LOC.

95 "Difficulty was experienced": Ibid.

95 "No marked reactions": Ibid.

95 In addition to teaching: Thomas White, "Memoirs of 'Doc' White," unpublished memoir, p. 2.

95 taking in a performance: Joseph Manske diary, March 14, 1942.

95 "We caught a good mess of fish": Kenneth Reddy diary, March 23, 1942.

95 "Our commanding officer": Richard Cole to his mother, early 1942, Richard E. Cole Collection, Vernon R. Alden Library, Ohio University, Athens, Ohio.

95 "You're helping in national defense": William Farrow to Jesse Farrow, March 7, 1942, quoted in Jesse Farrow to James Doolittle, May 24, 1942, Box 22, DPLOC.

96 Lawson came out: Lawson, *Thirty Seconds over Tokyo*, p. 23.

96 "Doolittle has got some": Richard E. Cole oral history interview with James C. Hasdorff, Dec. 12–13, 1988, AFHRA.

96 "It was sort of obvious": Knobloch oral history interview with Hasdorff, July 13–14, 1987.

96 "We could do": Bower oral history interview with Edwards, Oct. 27, 1971.

96 "The first pilots were all": J. H. Doolittle, Report on the Aerial Bombing of Japan, June 5, 1942.

97 "General, it occurred to me": This exchange comes from Doolittle, *I Could Never Be So Lucky Again*, pp. 248–49.

CHAPTER 6

98 "These brutal and inexcusable attacks": "Japan's Atrocities in China," Feb. 3, 1942, Box 138, RG 226, Office of Strategic Services, NARA.

98 Donald Duncan stepped off: *The Reminiscences of Admiral Donald Duncan*, pp. 331–34.

98 "Well": This exchange is ibid., pp. 332–33.

99 the entire bay rimmed: Frederick Mears, *Carrier Combat* (Garden City, N.Y.: Doubleday, Doran, 1944), pp. 33–34.

99 The burned-out: Homer N. Wallin, *Pearl Harbor: Why, How, Fleet Salvage and Final Appraisal* (Washington, D.C.: GPO, 1968), pp. 253–80; "Report on Infamy," *Time*, Dec. 14, 1942, pp. 75–80; Robert Trumbull, "'Dead' Ships Rise at Pearl Harbor; Miracle in Salvage Cuts Loss to 3," *New York Times*, May 23, 1943, p. 1.

99 Workers only the month before: "Salvage Pearl Harbor Greetings," *New York Times*, Feb. 4, 1942, p. 5; Salvage Officer to the Commandant, Navy Yard, Pearl Harbor, Report of the Salvage of the USS *West Virginia*, June 15, 1942, in Wallin, *Pearl Harbor*, p. 349.

99 A fifty-seven-year-old: Chester Nimitz Navy Bio, June 21, 1948, NDL.

99 "May the good Lord": Nimitz Diary, Dec. 31, 1941, Papers of Fleet Admiral Chester W. Nimitz, 1901–1967, NHHC. Some entries in Nimitz's diary are written as traditional entries; others are written to his wife. For the purposes of consistency, all entries are referred to simply as his diary.

100 The deteriorating situation: Chester Nimitz diary, Jan. 29, 1942.

100 The Pacific Fleet had so far executed: E. B. Potter, *Nimitz* (Annapolis, Md.: Naval Institute Press, 1976), pp. 37–57.

100 "The Japs didn't mind": Potter, *Nimitz*, p. 52.

100 "I will be lucky": Chester Nimitz diary, March 22, 1942.

100 "arrived for conference": Nimitz Gray Book, vol. 1, March 19, 1942, p. 296.

100 The audacious operation: *The Reminiscences of Admiral Donald Duncan*, pp. 330–32.

100 "I had been told": Donald B. Duncan, "Secret Planning for the Tokyo Raid," in Mason Jr., ed., *The Pacific War Remembered*, p. 68.

100 "Pacific Fleet markedly inferior": CINCPAC to COMINCH msg. 080239, Box 4, Safe Files, FDRL.

100 "Pacific Fleet not": COMINCH to CINPAC msg. 092245, ibid.

101 The Pacific Fleet commander: Layton, *"And I Was There,"* pp. 380–81.

101 his own staff: Nimitz Gray Book, vol. 1, Feb. 10, 1942, p. 212.

101 "Tell Jimmy": *The Reminiscences of Admiral Donald Duncan*, pp. 334–35.

102 "Do you believe": William F. Halsey and J. Bryan III, *Admiral Halsey's Story* (New York: Whittlesey House/McGraw-Hill, 1947), pp. 100–101.

102 "crackpot": Phillip S. Meilinger, *Airmen and Air Theory* (Maxwell Air Force Base, Ala.: Air University Press, 2001), p. 27.

102 Few military leaders had as much: Barbara W. Tuchman, *Stilwell and the American Experience in China, 1911–1945* (New York: Macmillan, 1971), pp. xi–xiii, 9–89, 123–63.

102 "Dour, belligerent": Lewis Brereton diary, May 28, 1942, in Lewis H. Brereton, *The Brereton Diaries: The War in the Air in the Pacific, Middle East and Europe, 3 October 1941—8 May 1945* (New York: William Morrow, 1946), pp. 126–27.

102 "unreasonable, impatient": Tuchman, *Stilwell and the American Experience in China, 1911–1945*, p. 126.

102 "niggers": Ibid., p. 127.

102 "When I think": Joseph Stilwell diary, March 1, 1942, in White, ed., *The Stilwell Papers*, p. 49.

102 "rank amateur": Joseph Stilwell diary, Dec. 29, 1941, ibid., p. 16.

103 "Very unimpressive": Joseph Stilwell diary, Feb. 9, 1942, ibid., p. 36.

103 Spread across: "China's War Potential: Estimate," in U.S. Department of State, *Foreign Relations of the United States: Diplomatic Papers, 1942, China* (Washington, D.C.: GPO, 1956), pp. 71–82.

103 "Our ally, China": Frank Dorn, *Walkout: With Stilwell in Burma* (New York: Thomas Y. Crowell, 1971), p. 20.

103 The bespectacled Chinese leader: Ibid., pp. 17–20.

103 Stilwell viewed him: Joseph Stilwell diary, April 1, 1942, in White, ed., *The Stilwell Papers*, p. 80.

103 "He thinks he knows psychology": Joseph Stilwell diary, April 1, 1942, ibid., p. 77.

103 "a peanut perched": Dorn, *Walkout*, p. 23.

103 "The trouble in China": Theodore H. White, *In Search of History: A Personal Adventure* (New York: Harper & Row, 1978), p. 140.

103 "He's a vacillating": Chennault, *Way of a Fighter*, p. 226.

103 Stilwell's views stood: Tuchman, *Stilwell and the American Experience in China, 1911–1945*, pp. 187–88.

104 "Man & Wife of the Year": "Man & Wife of the Year," *Time*, Jan. 3, 1938, pp. cover, 12–16.

104 The Chinese leader's image: Alan Brinkley, *The Publisher: Henry Luce and His American Century* (New York: Alfred A. Knopf, 2010), p. 131.

104 The press proved equally adoring: For a few examples see "Modern Joan of Arc," *Portsmouth Times*, Dec. 10, 1937, p. 11; Clare Boothe, "What One Woman Can Do," *This Week* magazine section of the *Milwaukee Journal*, July 26, 1942, p. 10; Vanya Oakes, "Madame Chiang Kai-shek," *Toledo Blade*, March 13, 1943, p. 6.

104 "Each night it was like": Dorn, *Walkout*, p. 74.

104 "If St. Francis of Assissi": John Fischer, "Vinegar Joe's Problem," *Harper's Magazine*, Dec. 1944, p. 91.

104 "The true explanation": Research and Analysis Branch, "American Aid to China," Far Eastern Study No. 21, undated, Microfilm Roll #1, in Paul Kesaris, ed., *O.S.S./State Department Intelligence and Research Reports*, pt. 3, *China and India* (Washington, D.C.: University Publications of America, 1977).

105 "The probabilities": Joseph Stilwell memo to Lauchlin Currie, Aug. 1, 1942, Box 51, RG 165, Records of the War Department General and Special Staffs, NARA.

105 "With relation": George Marshall to H. H. Arnold, Feb. 11, 1942, Microfilm Roll #173, HHAP.

105 "Despite my request": John Magruder to Adjutant General (For AMMISCA), msg. No. 258, Feb. 9, 1942, ibid.

105 "Inhuman acts": "Japan's Atrocities in China," Feb. 3, 1942, Box 138, RG 226, Office of Strategic Services, NARA.

106 "There came a day": Ibid. The sword contest remains a controversial flashpoint in the history of the Rape of Nanking. Some Japanese historians have alleged that the contest, though published in the press at the time, was fabricated or at least exaggerated. The two officers were executed after the war.

106 The Japanese coaxed: Details are drawn from the report "Japan's Atrocities in China" and Iris Chang, *The Rape of Nanking: The Forgotten Holocaust of World War II* (New York: Penguin Books, 1998), pp. 3–7, 35–59.

106 "Perhaps when we were raping her": Azuma Shiro undated letter to Iris Chang, in Chang, *The Rape of Nanking*, p. 50.

106 The war crimes tribunal: Chang, *The Rape of Nanking*, p. 4.

106 "The actions of the Japanese soldiery": "Japan's Atrocities in China," Feb. 3, 1942.

107 "What progress": Cablegram to AMMISCA, Chungking, China, AAF RC 49, March 16, 1942, Microfilm Roll #A1250, AFHRA.

107 "Time is getting short": Cablegram to AMMISCA, Chungking, China, AAF RC 88, March 18, 1942, ibid.

107 Stilwell had only recently arrived: Dorn, *Walkout*, p. 31.

107 The capital and principal seaport: "Foe Gains in Burma," *New York Times*, March 9, 1942, p. 1; Raymond Daniell, "Rangoon Capture Confirmed in India," ibid., March 10, 1942, p. 5.

107 Although China boasted: Tuchman, *Stilwell and the American Experience in China, 1911–1945*, pp. 264–66.

107 "You will know long before": Joseph Stilwell diary, March 26, 1942, in White, ed., *The Stilwell Papers*, p. 70.

107 Because he was not briefed: Doolittle, *I Could Never Be So Lucky Again*, pp. 259–60.

107 "Please advise": Radiogram to AGWAR for AMMISCA, No. 391, March 22, 1942, Microfilm Roll #A1250, AFHRA.

107 Arnold ordered the fuel: Cablegram to AMMISCA, Chungking, China, AAF RC 279, March 25, 1942, ibid.

107 He further ordered: Cablegram to AMMISCA, Chungking, China, AAF RC 359, March 26, 1942, ibid.

108 "The success of a vital project": Cablegram to AMMISCA, Chungking, China, AAF RC 279, March 25, 1942, ibid.

108 Rather than import fuel: Cablegram to AGWAR for AMMISCA, No. 416, March 29, 1942, ibid.

108 "Other than fuel": Cablegram to AMMISCA, Chungking, China, AAF RC 467, March 30, 1942, ibid.

108 "On April 20th": Cablegram to AMMISCA, Chungking, China, AAF RC 505, March 31, 1942, ibid.

108 Doolittle had gotten: Doolittle, *I Could Never Be So Lucky Again*, pp. 249–50.

108 "Hey, come on": Holstrom oral history interview with Hasdorff, April 14–15, 1988.

108 "Get your financial affairs": McClure, "How We Bombed Tokyo: Thrilling Epic," p. 1.

109 Thomas White: T. R. White to Air Surgeon, "Report of Activities Covering the Period from March 1, 1942, to June 16, 1942," June 23, 1942; Richard Cole oral history interview with William J. Alexander, Aug. 8, 2000, University of North Texas, Denton, Tex.

109 "Rather than bump": Potter oral history interview with Hasdorff, June 8–10, 1979.

109 "Operations was like a mad house": Kenneth Reddy diary, March 24, 1942.

109 "I hear you had an accident": This exchange comes from *The Reminiscences of Rear Admiral Henry L. Miller*, vol. 1, p. 35.

109 "Newt, old boy": York oral history interview with Hasdorff, July 23, 1984.

109 "Where is everybody?": This exchange comes from Emmens oral history interview with Hasdorff, July 8–9, 1982.

110 "We kept so low": Lawson, *Thirty Seconds over Tokyo*, pp. 27–28.

110 "When we departed Eglin": Charles McClure to Ross Greening, Individual Histories questionnaire, undated (ca. 1950), Iris # 01010162, AFHRA.

110 "The trip to the West Coast": Aden Jones to Ross Greening, Individual Histories questionnaire, May 8, 1950, ibid.

110 "I pulled some sagebrush": DeShazer oral history interview with Hasdorff, Oct. 10, 1989.

110 Bad weather forced: Kenneth Reddy diary, March 24, 1942.

110 Doolittle, however: Lawson, *Thirty Seconds over Tokyo*, p. 28.

110 "I am going on a special mission": "Tokyo Lists 4 as Captive U.S. Airmen," *Sun*, Oct. 25, 1942, p. 3.

110 "We flew to Sacramento non-stop": Kenneth Reddy diary, March 25, 1942.

111 "Can you see": This exchange comes from Macia oral history interview with Hasdorff, July 15–16, 1987.

111 "Over Texas": McClure to Greening, Individual Histories questionnaire, undated (ca. 1950).

111 "I would like to have": This exchange comes from "Meeting of Doolittle Project B-25B's," transcript, March 25, 1942, Iris #00142923, AFHRA.

111 "Services and supplies": Vanaman to CO SAD, March 24, 1942, ibid.

112 "Under no circumstances": Edmund J. Borowski to C. G. Williamson, "Work to Be Accomplished on B-25B Doolittle Project," March 26, 1942, ibid.

112 "Stick close to the field": Lawson, *Thirty Seconds over Tokyo*, p. 29.

112 "You won't need it": Ibid., p. 29.

112 "Mind your own business": Reynolds, *The Amazing Mr. Doolittle*, p. 191.

112 "I had to stand by": Lawson, *Thirty Seconds over Tokyo*, p. 29.

112 "Things are going": Doolittle, *I Could Never Be So Lucky Again*, p. 253.

112 "What's going on here?": This exchange comes from *Reminiscences of General James H. Doolittle, U.S. Air Force (Retired)* (Annapolis, Md.: U.S. Naval Institute, 1987), p. 32.

112 "I was madder": Ibid.

114 The crews ran into a similar headache: York oral history interview with Hasdorff, July 23, 1984.

114 "In several instances": T. R. White to Air Surgeon, "Report of Activities Covering the Period from March 1, 1942, to June 16, 1942," June 23, 1942.

114 Ken Reddy went bowling: Kenneth Reddy diary, March 27–30, 1942.

114 "We lowered Dean Hallmark": Everett W. "Brick" Holstrom, "General Recollections," unpublished memoir, p. 30.

114 "Let's give him a hot foot": This exchange comes from Greening, "The First Joint Action," p. 55. See also Greening, *Not As Briefed*, p. 17.

114 "This will be": Jacob Eierman to J. George Eierman, March 9, 1942, in "Baltimore Airman Wins Valor Award," *Sun*, May 21, 1942, p. 24.

115 "Please don't worry": Melvin Gardner to parents, April 1, 1942, in "SSG Melvin J. Gardner," unpublished family narrative, Box 2, Series II, DTRAP.

115 The officers met: Details of the meeting are drawn from *Reminiscences of General James H. Doolittle*, pp. 15–17; Doolittle, *I Could Never Be So Lucky Again*, pp. 256–57; Halsey, *Admiral Halsey's Story*, p. 101.

115 "It immediately occurred": Halsey oral history, quoted in *Reminiscences of General James H. Doolittle*, p. 17.

115 "We discussed the operation": *Reminiscences of General James H. Doolittle*, pp. 15–16.

116 "This was understandable": Doolittle, *I Could Never Be So Lucky Again*, p. 256.

116 "We just happened to find out": "Interview with B-25 Crew That Bombed Tokyo and Was Interned by the Russians," transcript, June 3, 1943, Iris #00115694, AFHRA.

116 "We had to change": This exchange comes from York oral history interview with Hasdorff, July 23, 1984.

116 "How do you think": This exchange comes from *The Reminiscences of Rear Admiral Henry L. Miller*, vol. 1, pp. 36–37.

117 "I haven't got time": Reynolds, *The Amazing Mr. Doolittle*, pp. 192–93. This anecdote is recounted in several sources. I have depended largely on Greening's report, since it was written closet to the time.

117 "LOUSY": Greening, "The First Joint Action," p. 53; Doolittle, *I Could Never Be So Lucky Again*, p. 254.

117 "Just a minute, Colonel": Greening, "The First Joint Action," p. 53.

117 "If that's the case": Ibid.

117 "Who is that guy?": Ibid., p. 54.

117 "At less than 24 hours": John M. Clark to Assistant Chief, Air Service Command, April 2, 1942, Iris #00142923, AFHRA.

CHAPTER 7

119 "We believe the hand of God": Russell Ihrig, "A War Message to All Hands," included with *Cimarron* war diary, April 3, 1942, Box 731, RG 38, Records of the Office of the Chief of Naval Operations, World War II War Diaries, NARA.

119 The *Hornet* towered: *Hornet* deck log, April 1, 1942.

119 The 19,800-ton carrier: Background on the *Hornet* is drawn from Clayton

F. Johnson et al., eds., *Dictionary of American Naval Fighting Ships*, vol. 3 (Washington D.C.: GPO, 1968), pp. 367–69; Francis E. McMurtrie, ed., *Jane's Fighting Ships: 1941* (London: Sampson Low, Marston and Co., 1942) p. 460; Chief of the Bureau of Ships to the Secretary of the Navy, April 12, 1943, USS *Hornet* (CV-8) – Final Settlement under Navy Department Contract Nod-1126 dated April 10, 1939, with Newport News Shipbuilding and Dry Dock Company, Newport News, Va., Box 738, RG 19, Bureau of Ships, General Correspondence, 1940–1945, NARA.

120 Sailors slept sixty: Rose, *The Ship That Held the Line*, pp. 4–5, 24–27.

120 "The food on carriers": Mears, *Carrier Combat*, p. 22.

120 "There was always noise": Ibid., p. 21.

121 "Remember Pearl Harbor": Taylor, *The Magnificent Mitscher*, p. 109.

121 Doolittle arrived first: Doolittle, *I Could Never Be So Lucky Again*, p. 254.

121 "Lieutenant Colonel Doolittle, Captain": Griffin, *A Ship to Remember*, pp. 52–53.

121 "You'll be holding": Doolittle, *I Could Never Be So Lucky Again*, pp. 260–61.

121 "All right with me, Jim": Ibid., p. 255.

121 By the afternoon of April 1: John M. Clark to Assistant Chief, Air Service Command, April 2, 1942, Iris #00142923, AFHRA.

121 He had instructed his pilots: Doolittle, *I Could Never Be So Lucky Again*, p. 254.

122 "What do you think?": This exchange comes from Emmens oral history interview with Hasdorff, July 8–9, 1982.

122 "How much time": Ibid.

122 "The moment York introduced me": Robert G. Emmens, *Guests of the Kremlin* (New York: Macmillan, 1949), p. 2.

122 "What about flying": Lawson, *Thirty Seconds over Tokyo*, p. 30.

123 "As I put the flaps down": Ibid.

123 "Damn!": Ted W. Lawson, "Thirty Seconds over Tokyo," pt. 1, *Collier's*, May 22, 1943, p. 80.

123 "Is everything okay?": This exchange comes from Lawson, *Thirty Seconds over Tokyo*, p. 30.

123 "It was an eye-opener": Sims, *First over Japan*, p. 18.

123 "I don't think any of us": Bower oral history interview with Edwards, Oct. 27, 1971.

123 "My heavens": Ibid.

124 "postage stamp": Greening, *Not As Briefed*, p. 19.

124 "We knew we were going": Hoover oral history interview with Hasdorff, June 20–21, 1988.

124 "She was a great sight": Lawson, *Thirty Seconds over Tokyo*, p. 31.

124 "Don't tell the Navy boys": Ibid.

124 "You know, I talked": This exchange comes from *The Reminiscences of Rear Admiral Henry L. Miller*, vol. 1, p. 37.

124 "My, don't those fellows": John F. Sutherland oral history interview with the Navy, May 14, 1943, Box 26, RG 38, Records of the Office of the Chief of

Naval Operations, World War II Oral Histories and Interviews, 1942–1946, NARA.

124 "I think *our* initial reaction": *The Reminiscences of Captain Stephen Jurika, Jr.*, vol. 1, pp. 456–57.

124 "I've done everything I can": Ibid., pp. 461–62.

125 four thousand people: "Knox Praises Men Lost on the Kearny," *New York Times*, Oct. 21, 1941, p. 5.

125 "I never saw such a small": Hoover oral history interview with Hasdorff, June 20–21, 1988.

125 The Army's enlisted men: Jacob Eierman, "I Helped Bomb Japan," *Popular Mechanics*, July 1943, p. 65; AFHRA oral histories with Holstrom, Emmens, Macia, and McCool.

125 "I was a First Lieutenant": Lawson, *Thirty Seconds over Tokyo*, p. 32.

125 "You had to go down the hall": Cole oral history interview with Hasdorff, Dec. 12–13, 1988.

125 In addition to the *Hornet*: The compilation of ships present is drawn from the April 1–2, 1942, deck logs of the *Hornet*, *Cimarron* (Box 2044), *Vincennes* (Box 9371) and *Nashville* (Box 6158), all found in RG 24, Records of the Bureau of Naval Personnel, Deck Logs, 1941–1950, NARA.

125 A high-pressure area: "Aerology and Naval Warfare: The First Raid on Japan," Chief of Naval Operations, Aerology Section, Feb. 1947.

125 With the bombers: *Hornet* deck log, April 1, 1942.

125 "All right, everyone is free": Emmens oral history interview with Hasdorff, July 8–9, 1982.

126 "Understand you're moving": Doolittle, *I Could Never Be So Lucky Again*, p. 257.

126 "His remark proved": Ibid.

126 "We had enough time": Knobloch oral history interview with Hasdorff, July 13–14, 1987.

126 "It was a beautiful night": Charles L. McClure, tape transcription, Dec. 1987, Box 4, Series II, DTRAP.

126 the bombers silhouetted: "A Trip to Japan," *Time*, May 3, 1943, p. 30.

126 The Navy had put out the story: Doolittle, *I Could Never Be So Lucky Again*, p. 261.

126 "Just putting the aircraft": Macia oral history interview with Hasdorff, July 15–16, 1987.

126 "We had some concerns": Potter oral history interview with Hasdorff, June 8–10, 1979.

126 The *Hornet* swayed: *Hornet* deck log, April 2, 1942.

127 "Hear sundry rumors": James Doolittle Jr. to James Doolittle, April 4, 1942, Box 64, Series IX, DPUT.

127 "I'll be out of the country": Doolittle, *I Could Never Be So Lucky Again*, p. 257.

127 "We had many separations": Ibid., p. 258.

127 Doolittle returned to the carrier: Ibid., pp. 260–61.

127 "You will be constantly": George Marshall to James Doolittle, March 31, 1942, Microfilm Roll #169, HHAP.

127 "When I learned": Ernest King handwritten memo to James Doolittle, in Doolittle, *I Could Never Be So Lucky Again*, p. 261.

128 "Doolittle?": This exchange is ibid., pp. 261–62.

128 The light cruiser *Nashville*: *Hornet* and *Nashville* deck logs, April 2, 1942; *Nashville* war diary, April 2, 1942 (Box 1249), *Gwin* war diary (Box 914), and *Cimarron* war diary (Box 731), all found in RG 38, Records of the Office of the Chief of Naval Operations, World War II War Diaries, NARA.

128 The *Hornet* with its guests: *Hornet*, *Vincennes*, and *Cimarron* deck logs, April 2, 1942; Report of Major Harry Johnson Jr., Adjutant, B25B Project, undated, Box 516, RG 18, Army Air Forces, Central Decimal Files, Oct. 1942–1944, NARA. The *Hornet* action report states that 70 Army officers and 130 enlisted men boarded the carrier, a figure higher than the 70 officers and 64 enlisted men cited in Johnson's report. Given Johnson's position as the mission's adjutant, I considered his report more accurate.

128 The ships steamed: *Vincennes* deck log, April 2, 1942.

128 The mission had finally begun: Rose, *The Ship That Held the Line*, pp. 52–53.

128 "It was quite a thrill": William Bower diary, April 18, 1942, Box 1, Series II, DTRAP.

128 "Our send off": Kenneth Reddy diary, April 2, 1942.

128 "As we passed": George Larkin diary, April 2, 1942, Papers of George Elmer Larkin Jr., 1918–1942, Filson Historical Society, Louisville, Ky. A copy of Larkin's diary is also on file in Box 4, Series II, DTRAP.

129 "For the benefit": Lawson, *Thirty Seconds over Tokyo*, p. 33.

129 "We all had a whoopee": Jeff Wilkinson, "Spied by Japanese, Raiders Take Off Early," *State*, April 8, 2002, p. 1.

129 "I can't tell you": Lawson, *Thirty Seconds over Tokyo*, p. 33.

129 "All of the training": Holstrom, "General Recollections," p. 31.

129 "Douglas MacArthur was having": Emmens oral history interview with Hasdorff, July 8–9, 1982.

129 "Now, we're going": Lawson, *Thirty Seconds over Tokyo*, p. 33.

129 "Now hear this": Griffin, *A Ship to Remember*, p. 54.

129 "This ship will carry": Taylor, *The Magnificent Mitscher*, p. 117.

129 "Cheers from every section": Marc Mitscher to Chester Nimitz, April 28, 1942, Report of Action, April 18, 1942, with Notable Events Prior and Subsequent Thereto," Box 1038, RG 38, Records of the Office of the Chief of Naval Operations, World War II Action and Operational Reports, NARA.

129 "It was the biggest thrill": "A Tokyo Raider Tells Just Part of That Great Story," *San Francisco Chronicle*, April 21, 1943, p. 11.

130 "I don't know who was more excited": Robert Bourgeois to Ross Greening, Individual Histories questionnaire, undated (ca. 1950).

130 "It froze everybody": Field, "With the Task Force," *Life*, May 3, 1943, p. 90.

130 "Carry me back": Ibid.

130 "Hi-ho, hi-ho": Ibid.

130 War planners had mapped: Griffin, *A Ship to Remember*, p. 56.

130 The task force would follow: "Aerology and Naval Warfare: The First Raid on Japan," Chief of Naval Operations, Aerology Section, Feb. 1947.

130 "We went north": Sutherland oral history interview with the Navy, May 14, 1943.

130 Shore-based planes: Marc Mitscher to Chester Nimitz, April 28, 1942, "Report of Action, April 18, 1942, with Notable Events Prior and Subsequent Thereto"; *Hornet* deck log, April 2, 1942.

131 "Our new assignment": R. M. Ihrig, "A War Message to All Hands," included with *Cimarron* war diary, April 3, 1942.

131 To prepare for such threats: "Battle Instructions No. 1," included with *Cimarron* war diary, April 3, 1942, and "Battle Instructions No. 2," April 4, 1942.

131 "Don't think of the Japs": Ihrig, "A War Message to All Hands."

131 "I have served six years": Ibid.

131 Lawson passed out: Lawson, *Thirty Seconds over Tokyo*, p. 34.

131 "Well, Hank": This exchange comes from *The Reminiscences of Rear Admiral Henry L. Miller*, vol. 1, p. 38.

132 He told the skipper: Doolittle, *I Could Never Be So Lucky Again*, p. 263.

132 "Well, Miller": The exchange comes from *The Reminiscences of Rear Admiral Henry L. Miller*, vol. 1, p. 38.

132 "I'm a Lieutenant now": Henry Miller, "Doolittle Tokyo Raid," unpublished narrative, Box 2, Series IX, DTRAP.

132 "The hell with them": Ibid.

133 The lightning successes: John J. Stephan, *Hawaii under the Rising Sun: Japan's Plans for Conquest after Pearl Harbor* (Honolulu: University of Hawaii Press, 1984), pp. 95–96; Yasuji Watanabe interview, Jan. 7, 1965, Box 6, Series 7, GWPP.

133 "We shall be able to finish": Matome Ugaki diary Jan. 5, 1942, in Ugaki, *Fading Victory*, p. 68.

133 War planners debated: Background on the planning of the Midway operation, unless otherwise noted, is drawn from the following sources: Agawa, *The Reluctant Admiral*, pp. 293–98; Fuchida and Okumiya, *Midway*, pp. 48–63; Stephan, *Hawaii under the Rising Sun*, pp. 89–121; H. P. Willmott, *The Barrier and the Javelin: Japanese and Allied Pacific Strategies, February to June 1942* (Annapolis, Md.: Naval Institute Press, 1983), pp. 31–80; Prange, Goldstein, and Dillon, *Miracle at Midway*, pp. 1–29; Jonathan Parshall and Anthony Tully, *Shattered Sword: The Untold Story of the Battle of Midway* (Washington, D.C.: Potomac Books, 2005), pp. 19–38.

133 "We want to invade Ceylon": Willmott, *The Barrier and the Javelin*, p. 79.

133 "It's annoying to be passive": Matome Ugaki diary, March 11, 1942, in Ugaki, *Fading Victory*, p. 103.

133 Japan had anticipated: Interrogation of Captain Mitsuo Fuchida, Oct. 10, 1945, in USSBS, *Interrogations of Japanese Officials*, vol. 1, pp. 122–31; Agawa, *The Reluctant Admiral*, p. 264; Joint Committee on the Investiga-

tion of the Pearl Harbor Attack, *Investigation of the Pearl Harbor Attack,* pp. 65, 166.

133 Vice Admiral Chuichi Nagumo should have: Chester Nimitz, "Pearl Harbor Attack," undated observations, Naval War College Library, Newport, R.I.

134 That threat had first: Publication Section, Combat Intelligence Branch, Office of Naval Intelligence, *Early Raids in the Pacific Ocean, February 1 to March 10, 1942: Marshall and Gilbert Islands, Rabaul, Wake and Marcus, Lae and Salamaua* (Washington, D.C.: GPO, 1943), pp. 1–34, found in Box 5, RG 38, Records of the Chief of Naval Operations, Records of the Office of Naval Intelligence, Security-Classified Publications of the Office of Naval Intelligence, Combat Narratives, 1942–1944, NARA; Morison, *History of the United States Naval Operations in World War II,* vol. 3, pp. 261–65; Matome Ugaki diary, Feb. 1, 1942, in Ugaki, *Fading Victory,* pp. 81–83.

134 "They have come": Matome Ugaki diary, Feb. 1, 1942, in Ugaki, *Fading Victory,* p. 81.

134 "guerrilla warfare": "Japanese Press Comments," *Japan Times & Advertiser,* March 6, 1942, p. 2; Stephan, *Hawaii under the Rising Sun,* p. 101.

134 "This attack was Heaven's": Layton, *"And I Was There,"* p. 363.

134 "ridiculous": Matome Ugaki diary, Feb. 2, 1942, in Ugaki, *Fading Victory,* p. 83.

134 "Pearl Harbor was a complete": Matome Ugaki diary, Feb. 1, 1942, ibid., p. 82.

134 "It was fortunate": Matome Ugaki diary, Feb. 2, 1942, ibid., p. 84.

134 "Whatever happens": Layton, *"And I Was There,"* p. 363.

135 The United States followed up: Publication Section, Combat Intelligence Branch, Office of Naval Intelligence, *Early Raids in the Pacific Ocean, February 1 to March 10, 1942,* pp. 35–68; Morison, *History of the United States Naval Operations in World War II,* vol. 3, pp. 265–68, 387–89; John B. Lundstrom, *The First Team: Pacific Naval Air Combat from Pearl Harbor to Midway* (Annapolis, Md.: Naval Institute Press, 1984), pp. 85–107, 111–35; Matome Ugaki diary, Feb. 20, 1942, in Ugaki, *Fading Victory,* pp. 92–93.

135 "The failure to destroy": Statement of Minoru Genda, Nov. 6, 1950, Box 19, Series 5.2, GWPP.

135 "Don't swing such a long": Mitsuo Fuchida interview, March 1, 1964.

135 Halsey's attack: Matome Ugaki diary, March 4, 1942, in Ugaki, *Fading Victory,* p. 101.

135 "If real enemy planes": Matome Ugaki diary, March 12, 1942, ibid. p. 104.

135 "How shall we defend": Yoshitake Miwa diary, Feb. 1, 1942, Box 3, Series 7, GWPP.

136 "the sentry for Hawaii": Stephan, *Hawaii under the Rising Sun,* p. 109.

137 "One wonders whether": Agawa, *The Reluctant Admiral,* p. 296.

137 "The success or failure": Fuchida and Okumiya, *Midway,* p. 60.

137 "If the C. in C.'s so set": Agawa, *The Reluctant Admiral,* p. 297.

CHAPTER 8

138 "We shall not begrudge": "The Battle off the Coast of Java," editorial, *Japan Times & Advertiser*, Feb. 8, 1942, p. 6.

138 Few in the Navy: Background on Stephen Jurika Jr., is drawn from the following sources: Stephen Jurika Jr., Navy Bio, June 4, 1957, NDL; "Stephen Jurika Jr., 82, Officer and a Scholar," *New York Times*, July 24, 1993, p. 27; *The Reminiscences of Captain Stephen Jurika, Jr.*, vol. 1, pp. 1–55, 205–7, 304–425.

139 employed a wartime peak: USSBS, Military Supplies Division, *Japanese Naval Shipbuilding* (Washington, D.C.: GPO, 1946), p. 7.

139 Military police interrogated: *The Reminiscences of Captain Henri Smith-Hutton U.S. Navy (Retired)*, vol. 1 (Annapolis, Md.: U.S. Naval Institute, 1976), pp. 282–83, 321–22.

140 "Tokyo is really a city": Stephen Jurika letter to Harry Smith, Oct. 27, 1940.

140 "As an aviator": *The Reminiscences of Captain Stephen Jurika, Jr.*, vol. 1, p. 387.

140 "Each time I drove": Ibid., p. 389.

140 "We started to fill": Ibid.

141 "When he went": Ibid., p. 392.

141 "By the time": Ibid., p. 343.

141 "We know that you": This exchange is ibid., p. 393.

142 Tokyo served: USSBS, *Field Report Covering Air Raid Protection and Allied Subjects, Tokyo, Japan*, pp. 1–2.

142 According to the 1940 census: Sekijiro Takagaki, ed. *The Japan Yearbook, 1941–1942* (Tokyo: Foreign Affairs Association of Japan, 1941), p. 833.

142 the density in some wards: Warren Moscow, "51 Square Miles Burned Out in Six B-29 Attacks on Tokyo," *New York Times*, May 30, 1945, p. 1.

142 Areas classified industrial: USSBS, *Field Report Covering Air Raid Protection and Allied Subjects, Tokyo, Japan*, p. 3.

142 Visitors complained: *The Reminiscences of Captain Stephen Jurika, Jr.*, vol. 1, p. 317; John Morris, *Traveler from Tokyo* (New York: Sheridan House, 1944), pp. 24–26.

142 These quirks: Background on Tokyo is drawn from Takagaki, ed., *The Japan Yearbook, 1941–1942*, pp. 833–38.

143 Wealthy patrons strolled: "Notes for the Traveler," *New York Times*, Nov. 3, 1935, p. XX2.

143 Broadway of Tokyo: Hugh Byas, "Martial Law Rules City," *New York Times*, Feb. 27, 1936, p. 1.

143 Others flocked: Elmer Rice, "On the Modern Theatre of Japan," *New York Times*, Nov. 1, 1936, p. X1.

143 The Imperial Palace: Background on the Imperial Palace is drawn from Otto D. Tolischus, "The Riddle of the Japanese," *New York Times*, Sept. 7, 1941, p. 123; Takagaki, ed., *The Japan Yearbook, 1941–1942*, p. 7; USSBS,

Field Report Covering Air Raid Protection and Allied Subjects, Tokyo, Japan, p. 3.

143 "a piece of heaven": Otto D. Tolischus, "The Riddle of the Japanese," *New York Times*, Sept. 7, 1941, p. 123.

143 A few blocks south: Hugh Byas, "New $8,500,000 Diet Will Open in Tokyo," *New York Times*, Nov. 1, 1936, p. N12.

143 New arrivals accustomed: Otto Tolischus diary, Feb. 7, 1941, in Otto D. Tolischus, *Tokyo Record* (New York: Reynal & Hitchcock, 1943), p. 5.

143 How could a nation: Takagaki, ed., *The Japan Yearbook, 1941–1942*, pp. 837–38.

143 "It is a city old and new": Henry C. Wolfe, "Gloomy Heart of an Embattled Japan," *New York Times*, Feb. 8, 1942, p. SM12.

143 nauseating odor: Otto Tolischus diary, Feb. 9, 1941, in Tolischus, *Tokyo Record*, p. 9.

143 "Both sides of the road": Ibid., p. 6.

144 More than four years of war with China: Background on wartime life in Tokyo is drawn from Wolfe, "Gloomy Heart of an Embattled Japan," p. SM12; Henry C. Wolfe, "Tokyo, Capital of Shadows," *New York Times*, Oct. 26, 1941, p. SM6; Ray Cromley, "Japan's War Economy," *Wall Street Journal*, Aug. 31, 1942, p. 1; *The Reminiscences of Captain Stephen Jurika, Jr.*, vol. 1, p. 321.

144 "I've seen housewives": Cromley, "Japan's War Economy," p. 1.

144 Tokyo was cursed: Details on the earthquake are drawn from the following sources: "Tokio Collapsed with First Shock," *New York Times*, Sept. 7, 1923, p. 1; Roderick Matheson," Scenes of Terror as Tokio Toppled," ibid., Sept. 9, 1923, p. 3; "Yokohama Is Wiped Out; Tokio in Ruins," ibid., Sept. 4, 1923, p. 1; "Americans Saved Tell of Horrors," ibid., Sept. 10, 1923, p. 1; "More Food in Tokio But New Tremors Keep People in Fear," ibid., Sept. 11, 1923, p. 1; "Eyewitness Tells of Quake Horrors." ibid., Sept. 23, 1923, p. 3; Henry C. Wolfe, "What the Japanese Fear Most," ibid., April 26, 1942, p. SM6; Joshua Hammer, *Yokohama Burning: The Deadly 1923 Earthquake and Fire That Helped Forge the Path to World War II* (New York: Free Press, 2006), pp. 87–148.

145 "Yokohama, the city": Henry W. Kinney, "Earthquake Days," *Atlantic Monthly*, Jan. 1924, p. 23.

145 Though an earthquake: Hugh Byas, "Most of All Japan Fears an Air Attack," *New York Times*, Aug. 4, 1935, p. SM6.

145 To limit the spread of fire: USSBS, *Field Report Covering Air Raid Protection and Allied Subjects Tokyo, Japan*, pp. 71–72.

145 "If you can start": Lawson, *Thirty Seconds over Tokyo*, p. 37.

146 Doolittle debated: Background on raid planning is drawn from J. H. Doolittle, Report on the Aerial Bombing of Japan, June 5, 1942; Doolittle, *I Could Never Be So Lucky Again*, pp. 264–65.

146 "I spent more time": Jack Hilger, undated questionnaire, Box 3, Series II, DTRAP.

147 The fliers pored over: Chase Nielsen testimony in the case of *United States of America vs. Shigeru Sawada, Yusei Wako, Ryuhei Okada, and Sotojiro Tatsuta*, Box 1728, RG 331, Supreme Commander for the Allied Powers, Legal Section, Prosecution Division, NARA; *The Reminiscences of Captain Stephen Jurika, Jr.*, vol. 1, pp. 458–60.

147 "Every outline of the coast": Charles L. McClure as told to William Shinnick, "How We Bombed Tokio: Flyers aboard *Hornet*," *Chicago Daily Tribune*, April 28, 1943, p. 4.

147 "We went over": James Doolittle testimony in the case of *United States of America vs. Shigeru Sawada et al.*

147 "A briefing": *The Reminiscences of Captain Stephen Jurika, Jr.*, vol. 1, p. 457.

147 "If they were captured": Ibid., p. 473.

147 "We all wanted it": Chase Nielsen testimony in the case of *United States of America vs. Shigeru Sawada et al.*

147 "You are to bomb": Doolittle, *I Could Never Be So Lucky Again*, pp. 265–66.

148 "Even though I could have": Ibid., p. 266.

148 Most would carry: Charles R. Greening to James H. Doolittle, Report on Bombs Used in Tokyo-Osaka Raid, May 2, 1942, included with Merian C. Cooper, "The Doolittle Air Raid on Japan," June 22, 1942.

148 "You will drop the demolition": This exchange comes from Doolittle, *I Could Never Be So Lucky Again*, pp. 266–67.

148 "Each pilot must decide": Ibid., p. 270.

149 "We figured": Ralph Wakley, "Fliers Risked Lives in Daring Raid," *Standard-Examiner*, April 5, 1992, p. 1.

149 Each combat crew member: Report of Major Harry Johnson Jr., Adjutant, B25B Project, undated.

149 "I went through": McElroy, "When We Were One," p. 28.

149 "*Lusau hoo metwa fugi*": Stephen Jurika Jr., "Prepare to Launch," in *Carrier Warfare in the Pacific: An Oral History Collection*, ed. E.T. Wooldridge (Washington, D.C.: Smithsonian Institution Press, 1993), p. 27.

149 "The Japanese wore *tabi*": *The Reminiscences of Captain Stephen Jurika, Jr.*, vol. 1, pp. 488–89.

149 Greening continued: J. H. Doolittle, Report on the Aerial Bombing of Japan, June 5, 1942; Report of Major Harry Johnson Jr., Adjutant, B25B Project, undated.

149 "Know anything about a tail gun?": "Tokyo Flyer," *Los Angeles Times*, April 25, 1943, p. G2.

149 "Pilots plotted": Report of Major Harry Johnson Jr., Adjutant, B25B Project, undated.

149 "I don't want you": Lawson, *Thirty Seconds over Tokyo*, pp. 42–43.

150 Mission doctor Thomas White administered: T. R. White to Air Surgeon, "Report of Activities Covering the Period from March 1, 1942, to June 16, 1942," June 23, 1942.

150 "One chap swore": Thomas White, "Memoirs of 'Doc' White," p. 2.

150 "The way the Doc talked": Joseph Manske diary, April 15, 1942.

150 "Are there snakes": This exchange comes from Richard Tedesco, "Thirty Seconds over Tokyo," *San Antonio Light*, March 4, 1989, p. H1.

CHAPTER 9

151 "Four months today": Breckinridge Long diary, April 7, 1942, in Israel, ed., *The War Diary of Breckinridge Long*, p. 255.

151 Japan had seized: USSBS, *The Campaigns of the Pacific War*, pp. 26–32; Raymond Daniell, "Rangoon Capture Confirmed in India," *New York Times*, March 10, 1942, p. 5; "Darwin Is Raided," ibid., Feb. 19, 1942, p. 1; "Darwin Raids Rank with London Blitz," ibid., Feb. 22, 1942, p. 3; "Java Seen Most Involved," ibid., Feb. 21, 1942, p. 3.

151 who sulked for weeks: Winston Churchill to Franklin Roosevelt, April 1, 1942, in Francis L. Loewenheim, Harold D. Langley, and Manfred Jonas, eds., *Roosevelt and Churchill: Their Secret Wartime Correspondence* (New York: Saturday Review Press/E. P. Dutton, 1975), p. 200.

151 "I do not like": Winston Churchill to Franklin Roosevelt, Feb. 19, 1942, ibid., p. 181.

151 "The weight of the war": Winston Churchill to Franklin Roosevelt, March 7, 1942, ibid., p. 187.

151 "No matter how serious": Franklin Roosevelt to Winston Churchill, Feb. 18, 1942, ibid., p. 179.

151 "There is no use": Franklin Roosevelt to Winston Churchill, March 18, 1942, ibid., p. 195.

151 "Once a month": Ibid., p. 196.

152 "You wax positively": Franklin Roosevelt to Fred I. Kent, March 12, 1942, in Elliott Roosevelt, ed., *F.D.R.: His Personal Letters, 1928–1945*, vol. 2 (New York: Duell, Sloan and Pearce, 1950), pp. 1294–95.

152 Under orders from Roosevelt: Joseph T. McNarney memo to Franklin Roosevelt, Food Situation in the Philippines, April 8, 1942, Box 55, RG 165, Records of the War Department General and Special Staffs, Office of the Director of Plans and Operations, NARA; Jonathan Wainwright, "Wainwright's Story," pt. 9, "Japs Struck Bataan like Silent Snakes," *Evening Citizen*, Oct. 15, 1945, p. 3.

152 "Our troops have been subsisted": Jonathan Wainwright radiogram to George Marshall, April 8, 1942, quoted in Joseph T. McNarney memo to Franklin Roosevelt, Situation in Bataan, April 8, 1942, Box 55, RG 165, Records of the War Department General and Special Staffs, Office of the Director of Plans and Operations, NARA.

152 "In view of my intimate": Douglas MacArthur radiogram to George Marshall, April 8, 1942, quoted ibid.

152 "I have nothing": Franklin Roosevelt proposed dispatch to Jonathan Wainwright, undated, ibid.

153 "terrible silence": Jonathan Wainwright, "Wainwright's Story," pt. 13, "Half-Starved Troops Ordered to Attack," *Evening Citizen*, Oct. 19, 1945, p. 3.

153 "If there is anything": Ibid.

153 "Our flag still flies": Jonathan Wainwright to Franklin Roosevelt, April 10, 1942, quoted in Joseph T. McNarney memo to Franklin Roosevelt, undated, Box 55, RG 165, Records of the War Department General and Special Staffs, Office of the Director of Plans and Operations, NARA.

153 "Bataan is a bugle call": *San Francisco Chronicle*, as quoted in Bureau of Intelligence, Office of Facts and Figures, Survey of Intelligence Materials No. 19, April 15, 1942, Microfilm Roll #30, President Franklin D. Roosevelt's Office Files, 1933–1944, pt. 4: Subject Files.

153 "Attack is not only suited": "From Lease-Lend to Attack," editorial, *New York Times*, March 12, 1942, p. 18.

153 "Deck lashings": Sims, *First over Japan*, p. 23.

154 "Can you fix it?": This exchange comes from Edward Saylor, "Doolittle Tokyo Raid," personal narrative, Jan. 14, 1989, Box 5, Series II, DTRAP.

154 "There was nobody around": Ibid.

154 "Ran it up": Ibid.

155 "All right, sir": Lawson, *Thirty Seconds over Tokyo*, p. 38.

155 "I've been training": This exchange comes from Hite oral history interview with Hasdorff, Dec. 16–17, 1982.

155 "I would have gone": Ibid.

155 The airmen used: Greening, "The First Joint Action," p. 18.

155 With a background: Jack Hilger, undated questionnaire, Box 3, Series II, DTRAP.

155 Doolittle's navigator: Potter oral history interview with Hasdorff, June 8–10, 1979.

155 Richard Cole likewise: Cole oral history interview with Hasdorff, Dec. 12–13, 1988.

155 Joseph Manske visited: Joseph Manske diary, April 10, 12, 1942.

155 "Hey, has Bill been here?": This exchange comes from Macia oral history interview with Hasdorff, July 15–16, 1987.

155 "The meals in the Navy": Kenneth Reddy diary, April 2, 1942.

155 "The Navy fattened": Lawson, *Thirty Seconds over Tokyo*, p. 38.

155 "I had never eaten": Robert Bourgeois to Ross Greening, Individual Histories questionnaire, undated (ca. 1950).

156 "What in the world": Jones oral history interview with Hasdorff, Jan. 13–14, 1987.

156 "I fear the dice games": McClure as told to Shinnick, "How We Bombed Tokio: Flyers Aboard *Hornet*," p. 4.

156 "Since I've been aboard": Kenneth Reddy diary, April 7–15, 1942.

156 Davy Jones shared: Jones oral history interview with Hasdorff, Jan. 13–14, 1987; Greening, *Not As Briefed*, p. 20.

156 "When you brag": Barrett Tillman, *Clash of the Carriers: The True Story of the Marianas Turkey Shoot of World War II* (New York: NAL Caliber, 2006), p. 77.

156 "Deep in the Heart of Texas": Edward B. Harp Jr., "God Stood beside Us," in *This Is It!*, ed. Harry Davis (New York: Vanguard Press, 1944), p. 22.

156 "He forgot one thing": Greening, "The First Joint Action," p. 54.

157 The Navy's senior officers: *Balch* deck log, April 15, 1942, Box 688, RG 24, Records of the Bureau of Naval Personnel, Deck Logs, 1941–1950, NARA.

157 "How are you doing?": This exchange comes from Sutherland oral history interview with the Navy, May 14, 1943.

157 "Most of them slept in": *The Reminiscences of Captain Stephen Jurika, Jr.*, vol. 1, p. 462.

157 "Being so flush": McClure as told to Shinnick, "How We Bombed Tokio: Flyers Aboard *Hornet*," p. 4.

157 "If you didn't play poker": Richard Cole, undated questionnaire, Box 1, Series II, DTRAP.

157 The airmen spied whales: Joseph Manske diary, April 6, 1942. Details of the tuna are drawn from NARA photos #330696-97.

157 "I began to wonder": C. Hoyt Watson, *DeShazer* (Winona Lake, Ind.: Light and Life Press, 1972), p. 22.

158 "Looking down": Harp Jr., "God Stood beside Us," p. 12.

158 "The service was nice": Kenneth Reddy diary, April 5, 1942.

158 "Easter Sunday": Joseph Manske diary, April 5, 1942.

159 "When I boarded the plane": Halsey, *Admiral Halsey's Story*, p. 102.

159 Halsey spent April 7: E. B. Potter, *Bull Halsey* (Annapolis, Md.: Naval Institute Press, 1985), pp. 57–58.

159 The *Enterprise* sortied: *Enterprise* deck log, April 8, 1942, Box 3150, RG 24, Records of the Bureau of Naval Personnel, Deck Logs, 1941–1950, NARA; G. D. Murray to Chester Nimitz, "Report of Action in Connection with the Bombing of Tokyo on April 18, 1942," April 23, 1942, Box 966, RG 38, Records of the Office of the Chief of Naval Operations, World War II Action and Operational Reports, NARA.

159 "same old Punch and Judy show": Robert Casey diary, April 8, 1942, in Robert J. Casey, *Torpedo Junction: With the Pacific Fleet from Pearl Harbor to Midway* (Garden City, N.Y.: Halcyon House, 1944), p. 290.

159 "Maybe things": Ibid.

159 "All we know": Robert Casey diary, April 9, 1942, ibid., p. 291.

159 "Cold as all Alaska": Walter Karig and Welbourn Kelley, *Battle Report: Pearl Harbor to Coral Sea* (New York: Rinehart, 1944), p. 295.

159 "The ships ahead": Robert Casey diary, April 12, 1942, in Casey, *Torpedo Junction*, p. 300.

160 The *Hornet* had received news: Marc Mitscher to Chester Nimitz, April 28, 1942, "Report of Action, April 18, 1942, with Notable Events Prior and Subsequent Thereto"; *Hornet* deck log, April 12–13, 1942.

160 "As I flew": Ronald W. Russell, *No Right to Win: A Continuing Dialogue with Veterans of the Battle of Midway* (New York: iUniverse, 2006), p. 15.

160 "They're B-25s!": This exchange comes from Potter, *Bull Halsey*, pp. 58–59.

160 *Hornet* took over: *Hornet* deck log, April 13, 1942; G. D. Murray to Chester Nimitz, Report of Action in Connection with the Bombing of Tokyo on April 18, 1942, April 23, 1942.

160 "This force": Halsey, *Admiral Halsey's Story*, p. 102.

161 "Never have I heard": Ibid.

161 "Intention fuel heavy ships": *Ellet* war diary, April 13–14, 1942, Box 832, RG 38, Records of the Office of the Chief of Naval Operations, World War II War Diaries, NARA.

161 "This is a big force": Robert Casey diary, April 13, 1942, in Casey, *Torpedo Junction*, p. 423.

161 "You are about to take part": Ibid., p. 425.

161 The same day the task force: *Hornet* deck log, April 13–15, 1942.

161 "Here lies": Robert Casey diary, April 14, 1942, in Casey, *Torpedo Junction*, p. 302.

161 Each new day: Details are drawn from a review of *Hornet* deck log, April 1–18, 1942; *Hornet* war diary, April 7, 1942, Box 953, RG 38, Records of the Office of the Chief of Naval Operations, World War II War Diaries, NARA.

162 "It seemed to me": Robert Bourgeois to Ross Greening, Individual Histories questionnaire, undated (ca. 1950).

162 The danger was reflected: R. M. Ihrig, "Battle Instructions No. 2," April 4, 1942, and "Battle Instructions No. 3," April 6, 1942, included with *Cimarron* war diary.

162 "Throw overboard": R. M. Ihrig, "Battle Instructions No. 3," April 6, 1942.

162 "Keep all unnecessary lights": Ibid.

162 Bad weather continued: Marc Mitscher to Chester Nimitz, April 28, 1942, "Report of Action, April 18, 1942, with Notable Events Prior and Subsequent Thereto"; *Cimarron* war diary, April 7, 1942.

162 The *Vincennes* lost: *Vincennes* deck log, April 6, 1942; *Cimarron* deck log, April 9, 1942.

162 Heavy seas one night: *Vincennes* deck log, April 7, 1942; Joseph W. Manske oral history interview with James C. Hasdorff, June 22, 1988, AFHRA; Lawson, *Thirty Seconds over Tokyo*, p. 39.

162 "We ran into the God damnedest weather": Robin Merton Lindsey oral history interview with the Navy, Sept. 17, 1943 Box 17, RG 38, Records of the Office of the Chief of Naval Operations, World War II Oral Histories and Interviews, 1942–1946, NARA.

163 "You could feel it": Field, "With the Task Force," p. 90.

163 "Anybody seen the Staten Island ferry": Ibid.

163 "How are we going": This exchange comes from Taylor, *The Magnificent Mitscher*, p. 119.

163 "In the dusk I saw": Harp Jr., "God Stood beside Us," p. 16.

163 Doolittle held a final inspection: "Preparation for Flight," undated (ca. April 1942), included with Cooper, "The Doolittle Air Raid on Japan," June 22, 1942.

163 "It sure didn't sound": Joseph Manske diary, April 14, 1942.

163 Shorty Manch packed: Greening, "The First Joint Action," p. 54; Kenneth Reddy diary, April 7–17, 1942.

163 "It may be quite": Robert Emmens to Mrs. J. J. Emmens, April 14, 1942, Box 8, Series II, DTRAP.

164 "Reuters, British news agency": Field, "With the Task Force," p. 90.

164 The news alarmed Halsey: Potter, *Bull Halsey*, p. 59; Lawson, *Thirty Seconds over Tokyo*, p. 40; E. B. Mott oral history interview with the Navy, March 22, 1944, Box 20, RG 38, Records of the Office of the Chief of Naval Operations, World War II Oral Histories and Interviews, 1942–1946, NARA.

164 "The Japanese radio": "A Denial on Previous Day," *New York Times*, April 18, 1942, p. 3.

164 The *Cimarron* came along: Information is drawn from the *Cimarron, Hornet, Northampton, Salt Lake City, Sabine, Nashville, Enterprise*, and *Vincennes* deck logs, April 17, 1942; Task Force Sixteen war diary, April 17, 1942, Box 61, *Cimarron* war diary, April 17, 1942, Box 731, and *Sabine* war diary, April 17, 1942, Box 1394, all in RG 38, Records of the Office of the Chief of Naval Operations, World War II War Diaries, NARA.

164 "I had left the destroyers": "Halsey Remembers Day Doolittle Struck Tokyo," *Arizona Daily Star*, April 18, 1959, p. B1.

165 Sailors brought the incendiary bombs: A. Soucek, "Air Department Plan for Friday, 17 April, 1942," Box 1, Series XI, DTRAP.

165 Others helped load: Doolittle, *I Could Never Be So Lucky Again*, p. 273; Travis Hoover, Personal Report, May 15, 1942. All personal reports of the mission are included with Cooper, "The Doolittle Air Raid on Japan," June 22, 1942.

165 Two freshly painted: Doolittle, *I Could Never Be So Lucky Again*, p. 271.

165 Airplane handlers spotted: Marc Mitscher to Chester Nimitz, April 28, 1942, "Report of Action, April 18, 1942, with Notable Events Prior and Subsequent Thereto."

165 "Jim, we're in the enemy's backyard": Doolittle, *I Could Never Be So Lucky Again*, p. 271.

165 Two Brooklyn Navy Yard employees: H. Vormstein to Frank Knox, Jan. 26, 1942, and E. J. Marquart to Frank Knox, Jan. 31, 1942, Box 1731, RG 38, Records of the Office of the Chief of Naval Operations, World War II Action and Operational Reports, NARA; "Japanese Medals Dropped on Tokyo," *New York Times*, June 16, 1942, p. 5.

165 "May we request": H. Vormstein to Frank Knox, Jan. 26, 1942.

165 "Following the lead": Daniel J. Quigley to Frank Knox, March 2, 1942, Box 1731, RG 38, Records of the Office of the Chief of Naval Operations, World War II Action and Operational Reports, NARA.

165 Jurika contributed: *The Reminiscences of Captain Stephen Jurika, Jr.*, vol. 1, pp. 467–69.

165 The reserved Mitscher: Doolittle, *I Could Never Be So Lucky Again*, pp. 272–73.

165 Thatcher grinned: McClure, "How We Bombed Tokio: Flyers aboard *Hornet*," p. 4.

165 "I don't want to set": M. A. Mitscher to W. F. Halsey, April 23, 1942, Box 1731, RG 38, Records of the Office of the Chief of Naval Operations, World War II Action and Operational Reports, NARA.

166 "You'll get a BANG": Greening, "The First Joint Action," p. 54.

166 "Bombs Made in America": Floyd Arnold to Jimmy Doolittle, Dec. 8, 1977, Box 2, Series I, DPUT.

166 "This one is from Peggy": Griffin, *A Ship to Remember*, p. 66.

166 "We painted them all up": "Tokyo Bombs Carried Plenty of Jap Medals," *Los Angeles Times*, April 22, 1943, p. 4.

166 "One of the most vivid": Thad Blanton, "We Bombed Japan," Army Air Forces School of Applied Tactics, *Intelligence Reports*, no. 17 (Oct. 1943): 8.

166 "It would take more": Kenneth Reddy diary, April 18, 1942.

166 He kept his instructions brief: Greening, "The First Joint Action," p. 26.

166 "If all goes well": Doolittle, *I Could Never Be So Lucky Again*, p. 272.

166 "When we get to Chungking": Ibid., p. 273.

166 Across the task force: Field, "With the Task Force," p. 90.

166 "Listen, you fellows": Lawson, *Thirty Seconds over Tokyo*, p. 45.

166 Lieutenant Colonel Edward Alexander: Details of Alexander's mission, unless otherwise noted, are drawn from the following sources: E. H. Alexander to Briefing Officer, First Special Aviation Project, June 17, 1942, Report of Flight Operations in Support of First Special Aviation Project, Microfilm Box 3200, Box 46, RG 407, Classified Decimal File, 1940–42, NARA; S. L. A. Marshall, "Tokyo Raid," undated (ca. 1944), Box 1, RG 319, Records of the Army Staff, Historical Branch, Background Files to the Study "Tokyo Raid," 1942–1944, NARA, pp. 62–64. A copy of Marshall's report is also on file with the U.S. Army Center of Military History.

167 "My instructions": E. H. Alexander to Briefing Officer, First Special Aviation Project, June 17, 1942.

167 "Signal transmitted": Chungking msg. to AGWAR for AMMISCA, No. 524, April 16, 1942, Microfilm Roll #A1250, AFHRA.

168 "Neither Lieut. Spurrier": Clayton L. Bissell, Note for Record, Instructions Issued to Lieut. Spurrier, April 3, 1942, Microfilm Box 3200, Box 46, RG 407, Classified Decimal File, 1940–42, NARA.

168 Spurrier's plane crashed: Chungking msg. to AGWAR for AMMISCA, No. 524, April 16, 1942.

168 Japanese bombers: Ibid., No. 446, April 2, 1942, and Chungking msg. to Adjutant General, No. 459, April 4, 1942, both in Microfilm Roll #A1250, AFHRA.

168 Tokyo claimed: "China Offers Closest Belligerent Bases for an Aerial Assault on Japanese Capital," *New York Times*, April 18, 1942, p. 3.

168 "Three essential fields": Joseph Stilwell diary, April 4, 1942, in White, ed., *The Stilwell Papers*, p. 81.

168 "The surface weather": E. H. Alexander to Briefing Officer, First Special Aviation Project, June 17, 1942.

169 "It is to be particularly noted": Ibid.

169 Chiang Kai-shek had initially agreed: "Contributory Material Submitted to Lt. Col. Sam Marshall for His Story on Tokyo Raid," undated (ca. 1943), p.

7, included in Doolittle Raid, Misc. Special Study, Iris #00116402, AFHRA. Pages 6–11 of this document include a detailed synopsis of the message traffic related to preparations for the raid that I depended on to construct this scene.

169 prompting Chiang to urge: Ibid., p. 9.

169 "Execution of first special mission": George Marshall to AMMISCA, War Dept. No. 449, April 12, 1942, Box 51, RG 165, Records of the War Department General and Special Staffs, Office of the Director of Plans and Operations, NARA.

169 "First project cannot": Arnold msg. to AMMISCA, No. 461, April 13, 1942, Iris #00116401, AFHRA.

169 Stilwell met with Chiang: Stilwell msg. to Adj. Gen., No. 522, April 15, 1942, ibid.; "Contributory Material Submitted to Lt. Col. Sam Marshall for His Story on Tokyo Raid," undated (ca. 1943), p. 10.

170 "We regret the apparent misunderstanding": George Marshall to AMMISCA, War Dept. No. 479, April 15, 1942, Box 51, RG 165, Records of the War Department General and Special Staffs, Office of the Director of Plans and Operations, NARA.

170 "The project is now": Ibid.

170 "Please report": Ibid.

170 Chiang's repeated objections: Memorandum for the President, First Special Bombing Mission (China), April 16, 1942, Box 55, RG 165, Records of the War Department General and Special Staffs, Office of the Director of Plans and Operations, NARA.

170 "I want personally": Dwight D. Eisenhower, Memorandum to the War Department Classified Message Center, Far Eastern Situation, April 17, 1942, Box 51, ibid.; Chief of Staff (Marshall) to Generalissimo Chiang Kai-shek, April 17, 1942, in U.S. Department of State, *Foreign Relations of the United States: Diplomatic Papers, 1942, China*, p. 32.

171 "Desire that there be no": Dwight D. Eisenhower, Memorandum to the War Department Classified Message Center, Far Eastern Situation, April 18, 1942, Box 51, RG 165, Records of the War Department General and Special Staffs, Office of the Director of Plans and Operations, NARA.

CHAPTER 10

172 "Measures now in hand": Franklin Roosevelt to Winston Churchill, April 16, 1942, in Warren F. Kimball, ed., *Churchill & Roosevelt: The Complete Correspondence*, vol. 1, *Alliance Emerging, October 1933–November 1942* (Princeton, N.J.: Princeton University Press, 1984), p. 455.

172 The darkened task force: *Enterprise* and *Hornet* deck logs, April 18, 1942; *Enterprise* war diary, April 18, 1942; Task Force Sixteen war diary, April 18, 1942, Box 61.

172 throughout the carrier: Field, "With the Task Force," p. 90.

172 "Two enemy surface": Ibid.

173 Halsey ordered: Task Force Sixteen war diary, April 18, 1942.

173 The contacts faded: *Enterprise* deck log, April 18, 1942; *Enterprise* war diary, April 18, 1942.

173 Low broken clouds: M. F. Leslie to Commanding Officer, U.S.S. *Enterprise*, Reports of Action, April 19, 1942, Box 386, RG 38 Records of the Office of the Chief of Naval Operations, World War II Action and Operational Reports, NARA.

173 "Went on deck": Robert Casey diary, April 18, 1942, in Casey, *Torpedo Junction*, p. 426.

173 "The sea was rough": Kenneth Reddy diary, April 18, 1942.

173 Lieutenant j.g. Osborne Wiseman: Excerpts of War Diary, VB-3, for April 1942, included with "The Navy's Share of the Tokyo Raid," Box 118, RG 38, NHHC, WWII Command Files, NARA.

173 Halsey again: Task Force Sixteen war diary, April 18, 1942; *Hornet* deck log, April 18, 1942.

173 "Three enemy carriers": Military History Section, Headquarters, Army Forces Far East, "Homeland Defense Naval Operations: December 1941–March 1943," Japanese Monograph #109, pt. 1, 1953, p. 8.

173 The *Nashville* sounded: Details on the *Nashville*'s engagement are drawn from *Nashville* war diary, April 18, 1942, Box 1249, RG 38, Records of the Chief of Naval Operations, World War II War Diaries, NARA; F. S. Craven to Chester Nimitz, "Report of Sinking of Two Enemy Patrol Boats on 18 April, 1942," April 21, 1942, Box 1264, RG 38, Records of the Office of the Chief of Naval Operations, World War II Action and Operational Reports, NARA; W. Kirten Jr., "Report by Gunnery Officer on Firing at Japanese Patrol Boats on 18 April, 1942," April 19, 1942, ibid.

174 "Terrific barrage": Robert Casey diary, April 18, 1942, in Casey, *Torpedo Junction*, p. 426.

174 "Her guns blazed": Field, "With the Task Force," p. 91.

174 "I remember thinking": Sutherland oral history interview with the Navy, May 14, 1943.

174 "Well, if it's all": Ibid.

174 "I could see the salvos": *The Reminiscences of Captain Stephen Jurika, Jr.*, vol. 1, p. 466.

175 "What's going on?": Holstrom, "General Recollections," p. 32.

175 The *Nashville*'s thunderclap: Thomas White, "Memoirs of 'Doc' White," p. 7.

175 "The whole side": DeShazer oral history interview with Hasdorff, Oct. 10, 1989.

175 Eight *Enterprise* fighters: Lundstrom, *The First Team*, pp. 149–50.

175 *Enterprise* bomber pilot: Report of U.S. Aircraft Action with Enemy by Ensign J. Q. Roberts, A-V(N), USNR, included with M. F. Leslie to Commander in Chief, United States Fleet, Report of Action, April 18, 1942, Box 386, RG 38, Records of the Office of the Chief of Naval Operations, World War II Action and Operational Reports, NARA; Bombing Squadron Three war diary, April 18, 1942.

175 "Liquidation of enemy": R. W. Mehle, "U.S. Aircraft—Action with Enemy," April 18, 1942, Box 436, RG 38, Records of the Office of the Chief of Naval Operations, World War II Action and Operational Reports, NARA.

175 "a bloodthirsty": Lundstrom, *The First Team*, p. 150.

175 The *Nitto Maru* erupted: *Nashville* war diary, April 18, 1942; F. S. Craven to Chester Nimitz, "Report of Sinking of Two Enemy Patrol Boats on 18 April, 1942," April 21, 1942.

176 "Expenditure of 915 rounds": F. S. Craven to Chester Nimitz, "Report of Sinking of Two Enemy Patrol Boats on 18 April, 1942," April 21, 1942.

176 "It looks like": Doolittle, *I Could Never Be So Lucky Again*, p. 4.

176 "Launch planes": Ibid.

176 "Now hear this!": Ibid.

176 Ross Greening had just: Greening, *Not As Briefed*, p. 22; McElroy, "When We Were One," p. 28.

176 "I happened to be": Sims, *First over Japan*, p. 26.

176 "Would you help": *The Reminiscences of Rear Admiral Henry L. Miller*, vol. 1, p. 40.

176 "We had spent months": C. Jay Nielsen, "Doolittle Fliers' Saga of Living Death: First Day Was Bad But the Worst Was Yet to Come," *News and Courier*, Sept. 16, 1945, p. 3.

177 Davy Jones had suffered: David M. Jones, Narrative Report, May 15, 1942; Jones oral history interview with Hasdorff, Jan. 13–14, 1987.

177 Ross Greening ordered: Greening, *Not As Briefed*, p. 23.

177 "When the alarm sounded": Carrol V. Glines, *The Doolittle Raid: America's Daring First Strike against Japan* (Atglen, Pa.: Schiffer Military/Aviation History, 1991), p. 114.

177 "Hey": Lawson, *Thirty Seconds over Tokyo*, p. 48.

177 "I wish to hell": Ted W. Lawson, "Thirty Seconds over Tokyo," pt. 2, *Collier's*, May 29, 1943, p. 82.

177 Crews knew: Doolittle, *I Could Never Be So Lucky Again*, p. 5.

177 "Captain Greening": Greening, *Not As Briefed*, p. 23.

177 "I wasn't concerned": Potter oral history interview with Hasdorff, June 8–10, 1979.

177 "The way things are now": Eierman, "I Helped Bomb Japan," p. 66.

178 "This couldn't have": Macia oral history interview with Hasdorff, July 15–16, 1987.

178 "Not a man withdrew": Eierman, "I Helped Bomb Japan," p. 66.

178 "What the hell": Holstrom, "General Recollections," p. 32.

178 "We just got one chance": Watson, *DeShazer*, p. 26.

178 "We knew that the pilots": *The Reminiscences of Rear Admiral Henry L. Miller*, vol. 1, p. 41.

178 "I was scared": Carl R. Wildner, "The First of Many," *American Man* 1, no. 2 (Jan. 1966): 9.

179 "It's the only time": "Halsey Remembers Day Doolittle Struck Tokyo," *Arizona Daily Star*, April 18, 1959, p. B1.

179 "It sure was windy!": Russell, *No Right to Win*, p. 18.

179 "Look at me": Doolittle, *I Could Never Be So Lucky Again*, p. 275.

179 "We all stood around": Eierman, "I Helped Bomb Japan," p. 66.

179 "*Hornet* preparing": Field, "With the Task Force," p. 91.

179 "Sailors, like stockbrokers": Alvin B. Kernan, *Crossing the Line: A Blue-jacket's Odyssey in World War II* (New Haven, Conn.: Yale University Press, 2007), p. 47.

180 "Everything all right": This exchange comes from Reynolds, *The Amazing Mr. Doolittle*, pp. 203–4.

180 The time required: *The Reminiscences of Captain Stephen Jurika, Jr.*, vol. 1, pp. 471–72.

180 The bomber roared: All bomber takeoff times come from J. H. Doolittle, Report on the Aerial Bombing of Japan, June 5, 1942.

180 "The scream of those two engines": Greening, *Not As Briefed*, p. 24.

180 "He'll never make it": Field, "With the Task Force," p. 91.

180 "Doolittle's gone": Chas. L. McClure as told to William Shinnick, "How We Bombed Tokio: Flyers Locate Targets," *Chicago Daily Tribune*, April 29, 1943, p. 2.

180 "Yes!": McElroy, "When We Were One," p. 29.

180 "The shout that went up": Thomas White, "Memoirs of 'Doc' White," p. 8.

181 "First bomber off": Robert Casey diary, April 18, 1942, in Casey, *Torpedo Junction*, p. 426.

181 In the skies overhead: Doolittle, *I Could Never Be So Lucky Again*, p. 7; Potter oral history interview with Hasdorff, June 8–10, 1979.

181 "I was running out of deck": Hoover oral history interview with Hasdorff, June 20–21, 1988.

181 "Up! Up!": McElroy, "When We Were One," p. 29.

181 "I felt wonderful": Hoover oral history interview with Hasdorff, June 20–21, 1988.

181 "kangaroo": Sutherland oral history interview with the Navy, May 14, 1943.

181 "They are the most comfortable": "Details of Individual Adventures in China: For Possible Use of Bureau of Public Relations," included with Cooper, "The Doolittle Air Raid on Japan," June 22, 1942.

181 "We watched his plane": Greening, *Not As Briefed*, p. 24.

182 "He got away with it": Henry L. Miller to D. B. Duncan, May 7, 1942, Report on Temporary Additional Duty Assignment.

182 "Nice take-off, Ski": This exchange comes from Emmens, *Guests of the Kremlin*, p. 3. Despite York's claim, Miller's records show he made at least one practice takeoff at Eglin.

182 "It seemed like": William R. Pound, "We Bombed 'The Land of the Dwarfs,'" in Glines, *Doolittle's Tokyo Raiders*, pp. 240–41.

182 "I could see many faces": Greening, *Not As Briefed*, p. 24.

182 "Sailors, slipping": Robert "Bobby" L. Hite, "Doolittle Raider and Japanese POW," in Jonna Doolittle Hoppes, comp., *Just Doing My Job: Stories from Service in World War II* (Santa Monica, Calif.: Santa Monica Press, 2009), p. 43.

182 "Give them hell": DeShazer oral history interview with Hasdorff, Oct. 10, 1989; David Thatcher undated letter to author.

182 "Help me get him": Ibid.

183 "The seaman's arm": George Barr, "Destination: Forty Months of Hell," in Glines, *Doolittle's Tokyo Raiders*, p. 307.

183 "Should I tell": DeShazer oral history interview with Hasdorff, Oct. 10, 1989.

183 "When the last plane": Press Release, Seventh Naval District, Public Relations Office, undated, Box 148, RG 428, General Records of the Department of the Navy, Office of Information Subject Files, 1940–1958, NARA.

183 "We all cheered loudly": Kernan, *Crossing the Line*, p. 48.

183 "For a few minutes": Field, "With the Task Force," p. 91.

183 "Quiet on the horizon": Robert Casey diary, April 18, 1942, in Casey, *Torpedo Junction*, p. 426.

183 The veteran aviator had tensed up: Taylor, *The Magnificent Mitscher*, p. 120.

183 "With only one exception": Marc Mitscher to Chester Nimitz, April 28, 1942, "Report of Action, April 18, 1942, with Notable Events Prior and Subsequent Thereto."

184 "The job that was done": Frederick L. Riefkohl oral history interview with the Navy, Jan. 26, 1945, Box 24, RG 38, Records of the Office of the Chief of Naval Operations, World War II Oral Histories and Interviews, 1942–1946, NARA.

184 "Without a doubt": *The Reminiscences of Rear Admiral Henry L. Miller*, vol. 1, p. 44.

184 "Take-off was easy": James H. Doolittle, Personal Report, May 4, 1942, included as Appendix 1 to J. H. Doolittle, Report on the Aerial Bombing of Japan, June 5, 1942.

184 He reviewed plans: Doolittle, *I Could Never Be So Lucky Again*, pp. 7–8.

184 "It never once occurred": Richard Cole undated questionnaire, Box 1, Series II, DTRAP.

184 "One time": Ibid.

184 Hoover spotted: Travis Hoover, Personal Report, May 15, 1942.

185 "Why am I here": Wildner, "The First of Many," p. 10.

185 "There was no rendezvous": Lawson, *Thirty Seconds over Tokyo*, p. 54.

185 some buzzing so low: McElroy, "When We Were One," p. 30; Hite oral history interview with Hasdorff, Dec. 16–17, 1982.

185 pilot Davy Jones: Joseph W. Manske, "Doolittle Raider Had Close Calls," *Sunday Express-News*, Aug. 11, 1985, p. 2L.

185 "Well, boys": Tedesco, "Thirty Seconds over Tokyo," p. H1.

185 "What in the world": J. Michael Parker, "Doolittle Raid Changed Course of War for U.S.," *San Antonio Express-News*, Dec. 1, 1991, p. 8W.

185 "Being brought up": Joseph Manske to Duane Schultz, Nov. 4, 1987, Box 4, Series II, DTRAP.

185 The harried takeoff: Bert M. Jordan, Personal Report, May 5, 1942.

185 Davy Jones realized his bomber: David M. Jones, Narrative Report, May 15, 1942; Eldred V. Scott, Personal Report, May 14, 1942.

186 "We've got a hole": This exchange comes from DeShazer oral history interview with Hasdorff, Oct. 10, 1989.

186 "We're entering the danger zone": This exchange comes from Gene Casey, "Conversation over Kobe," *Collier's*, Sept. 5, 1942, p. 23.

186 "A twin-engined land plane": David M. Jones, Narrative Report, May 15, 1942.

186 "It immediately dove": Richard O. Joyce, Report of Tokyo Raid, undated (ca. May 1942).

186 "Damn, boy": Lawson, "Thirty Seconds over Tokyo," pt. 2, *Collier's*, May 29, p. 84.

186 "Let's drop one": This exchange comes from Lawson, *Thirty Seconds over Tokyo*, p. 56.

187 "A normal program": Donald G. Smith, Personal Report, May 14, 1942.

187 "That's what you've": Chase Nielsen oral history interview with Rick Randle, Feb. 22, 2005.

187 "We kept going in": Lawson, *Thirty Seconds over Tokyo*, p. 57.

187 "We were too busy": Nielsen, "Doolittle Fliers' Saga of Living Death: First Day Was Bad," p. 3.

187 "Conversations were short": Emmens, *Guests of the Kremlin*, p. 4.

187 "I thought about the stack": Ibid.

188 "Forty precious gallons": Lawson, *Thirty Seconds over Tokyo*, p. 55.

188 "Navy got jittery": David Jones diary, April 18, 1942, Box 3, Series II, DTRAP.

188 "Hey, Bob": This exchange comes from Emmens, *Guests of the Kremlin*, pp. 5–7.

188 "Great": David Pohl as told to Don Dwiggins, "We Crash Landed in Russia—and Escaped," *Cavalier*, p. 12, in Box 5, Series II, DTRAP.

188 The crew had few options: Emmens, *Guests of the Kremlin*, p. 6.

188 "Have you got a course": This exchange is ibid.

189 "Russia's neutral": Pohl as told to Dwiggins, "We Crash Landed in Russia—and Escaped," p. 12.

189 "Doolittle didn't exactly": This exchange comes from Emmens, *Guests of the Kremlin*, pp. 6–7.

189 "There's the coast": Pohl as told to Dwiggins, "We Crash Landed in Russia—and Escaped," p. 12.

189 The *Nitto Maru*'s report: Background on Japan's preparations for the raid, unless otherwise noted, is drawn from the following sources: Matome Ugaki diary, April 18, 1942, in Ugaki, *Fading Victory*, pp. 111–13; Fuchida and Okumiya, *Midway*, pp. 66–68; Military History Section, Headquarters, Army Forces Far East, "Homeland Defense Naval Operations: December 1941–March 1943," Japanese Monograph #109, pt. 1, 1953, pp. 8–10.

189 "Enemy task force": Layton, *"And I Was There,"* p. 386.

190 "Well": Fuchida and Okumiya, *Midway*, p. 67.

191 The Japanese public: Wolfe, "Gloomy Heart of an Embattled Japan," p. SM12; USSBS, *Field Report Covering Air Raid Protection and Allied Subjects, Tokyo, Japan*, pp. 5–13, 145; USSBS, Civilian Defense Division, *Final*

Report Covering Air Raid Protection and Allied Subjects, Japan (Washington, D.C.: GPO, 1947), pp. 1–3, 16–17, 30–31.

191 Just two weeks earlier: "Cherry Blossoms Attract Thousands," *Japan Times & Advertiser*, April 3, 1942, p. 1.

191 Music lovers still chatted: "Piano Soloist Stars in Concert at Hibya," *Japan Times & Advertiser*, April 18, 1942, p. 2.

191 while gadflies buzzed: "Tokyo Candidates Hotly Contesting Seats in House," *Japan Times & Advertiser*, April 21, 1942, p. 1.

191 No fewer than 230 campaign: Ibid.

191 The Tokyo university baseball: "Today's Sports," *Japan Times & Advertiser*, April 18, 1942, p. 3; "'Big 6' Ball Games," *Osaka Mainichi*, April 18, 1942, p. 2.

191 Articles in the press: "Japanese Readers Are Best Sellers in Hongkong City," *Japan Times & Advertiser*, April 19, 1942, p. 2.

191 Other accounts: "Southern Regions Returning Rapidly to Normal Status," *Japan Times & Advertiser*, April 18, 1942, p. 1.

192 Closer to home: "Bereaved from Taiwan First of 30,000 Here for Special Yasukuni Shrine Rites," *Japan Times & Advertiser*, April 19, 1942, p. 3; "3,000 Relatives of War Dead Come to Tokyo to Attend Special Yasukuni Shrine Festival," ibid., April 22, 1942, p. 1; "Enshrinement Service for War Dead at Yasukuni Shrine Set for Tomorrow," ibid., April 22, 1942, p. 1; "Impressive Rituals for 15,017 War Dead Will Open Festival," ibid., April 23, 1942, p. 1; "Solemn Rites Held for 15,017 Spirits of Fallen Heroes," ibid., April 24, 1942, p. 1.

192 "I am overwhelmed with awe": "3,000 Relatives of War Dead Come to Tokyo to Attend Special Yasukuni Shrine Festival," p. 1.

192 "With the imminent fall": "The Projected Offensive against Japan," editorial, *Japan Times & Advertiser*, April 18, 1942, p. 6.

192 "Without any base": Ibid.

192 Newspapers two days earlier: S. L. A. Marshall, "Tokyo Raid," undated (ca. 1944), pp. 33–35; *The Reminiscences of Captain Henri Smith-Hutton*, vol. 1, p. 344.

192 Tokyo residents enjoyed: "500 Army Planes Road over Tokyo Skies in Tribute to Yasukuni Shrine War Dead," *Japan Times & Advertiser*, April 27, 1942, p. 1.

CHAPTER 11

194 "Once off the carrier": McClure to Greening, Individual Histories questionnaire, undated (ca. 1950).

194 Doolittle closed in on Japan: Unless otherwise noted, details of Doolittle's attack on Japan are drawn from the following sources: James H. Doolittle, Personal Report, May 4, 1942; Doolittle, *I Could Never Be So Lucky Again*, pp. 8–9; Fred A. Braemer, Personal Report, May 5, 1942; Henry A. Potter, Report of Navigator, May 5, 1942; Paul J. Leonard, Personal Report, undated (ca. May 1942); Reynolds, *The Amazing Mr. Doolittle*, pp. 204–6; Interview

with Lt. H. A. Potter, Navigator of Airplane No. 40-2344 Commanded by General Doolittle, undated (ca. 1942), in Summary of Targets in Japanese Raid and Memoranda of Personal Interviews with Major J. F. Pinkney, Microfilm Roll #A1250, AFHRA; Interview with Staff Sergeant Leonard, Gunner, Plane No. 40-2344 (Gen. Doolittle), undated (ca. 1942), ibid.; Marshall, "Tokyo Raid," undated (ca. 1944), pp. 40–43; Takehiko Shibata and Katsuhiro Hara, *Dōrittoru Kūshū Hiroku: Nichibei Zenchōsa* [Doolittle's Tokyo Raid, 18 April 1942] (Tokyo: Ariadone Kikaku, 2003), pp. 46–53, 211; Affidavit of Hitoshi Hiraoka, Naohiko Tsuda, and Shoei Kokubu, March 13, 1946, in the case of *United States of America vs. Shigeru Sawada et al.*

194 "We're either fifty miles": This exchange comes from Reynolds, *The Amazing Mr. Doolittle*, p. 204.

194 "Was somewhat north": James H. Doolittle, Personal Report, May 4, 1942.

195 "We've got company": Reynolds, *The Amazing Mr. Doolittle*, pp. 204–5.

195 "Japan looked green": Richard Cole questionnaire, undated, Box 1, Series II, DTRAP.

195 "We looked down": Grace Wing, "Five Who Bombed Tokio Surprised They're Heroes," *Miami Daily News*, July 16, 1943, p. 1.

195 "on the water": Interview with Staff Sergeant Leonard, Gunner, Plane No. 40-2344 (Gen. Doolittle), undated (ca. 1942).

196 "Approaching target": This exchange comes from Reynolds, *The Amazing Mr. Doolittle*, p. 205.

196 "Bomb-like objects fell": Affidavit of Hitoshi Hiraoka, Naohiko Tsuda, and Shoei Kokubu, March 13, 1946.

197 "Everything okay back there": This exchange comes from Reynolds, *The Amazing Mr. Doolittle*, p. 206.

197 "Colonel, can't we burn up": This exchange is ibid.

197 "Relax, Fred": Ibid.

198 First Lieutenant Travis Hoover reached: Unless otherwise noted, details of Hoover's attack on Japan are drawn from the following sources: Travis Hoover, Mission Report of Doolittle Project on April 18, 1942, May 16, 1942; Travis Hoover, Personal Report, May 15, 1942; William N. Fitzhugh, Personal Report, May 15, 1942; Carl R. Wildner, Personal Report, May 14, 1942; Richard E. Miller, Personal Report, May 14, 1942; Douglas V. Radney, Personal Report, May 14, 1942; Report of Interview with Lt. Hoover and Lt. Miller-Airplane No. 2292, in Summary of Targets in Japanese Raid and Memoranda of Personal Interviews with Major J. F. Pinkney; Marshall, "Tokyo Raid," pp. 41–43; Shibata and Hara, *Dōrittoru Kūshū Hiroku*, pp. 53–58, 211; Legal Section, 1st Demobilization Ministry, "Damages Sustained in the Air Attack of 18 April 1942," in case of *United States of America vs. Shigeru Sawada et al.*

198 "What'll I do?": Carl Wildner, "Navigator Recalls Doolittle's Tokyo Raid," *Press-Enterprise*, Aug. 9, 1985, pp. 8–9.

198 "In all my life": Wildner, "The First of Many," p. 10.

198 "There were no pursuit planes": Carl R. Wildner, Personal Report, May 14, 1942.

198 "The people that I observed": Richard E. Miller, Personal Report, May 14, 1942.

199 "Nothing of military importance": Travis Hoover, Personal Report, May 15, 1942.

199 "There's our target": Richard E. Miller, Personal Report, May 14, 1942.

199 "I spotted a large factory": Ibid.

199 "Bombs away": Ibid.

199 "The concussion": Carl R. Wildner, Personal Report, May 14, 1942.

199 Even Richard Cole: Richard Cole questionnaire, undated; Douglas V. Radney to Ross Greening, Individual Histories questionnaire, undated (ca. 1950), Iris #01010162, AFHRA.

200 "I looked back": Douglas V. Radney, Personal Report, May 14, 1942.

200 "Yes, sir": Wildner, "The First of Many," p. 11.

200 "OK, gang": Ibid.

200 "I glanced": Ibid., p. 73.

200 "Over or under it?": This exchange comes from Wildner, "Navigator Recalls Doolittle's Tokyo Raid," p. 9.

200 "I want to get out": Ibid.

200 First Lieutenant Gray tore: Unless otherwise noted, details of Gray's attack on Japan are drawn from the following sources: Robert M. Gray, Mission Report on Project April 18, 1942, May 2, 1942; Charles J. Ozuk Jr., Personal Report, May 15, 1942; Charles J. Ozuk Jr., Addition to Report of Lt. Charles J. Ozuk Jr., May 18, 1942; Memorandum of Interview with Lt. C. J. Ozuk, Navigator of Crew of Airplane No. 40-2270 Piloted by Lt. R. M. Gray, Summary of Targets in Japanese Raid and Memoranda of Personal Interviews with Major J. F. Pinkney; Aden Jones to Ross Greening, Individual Histories questionnaire, May 8, 1950; Marshall, "Tokyo Raid," pp. 43–45; Shibata and Hara, Dōrittoru Kūshū Hiroku, pp. 59–64, 211; Legal Section, 1st Demobilization Ministry, "Damages Sustained in the Air Attack of 18 April 1942"; Affidavit of School Teachers Furusawa and Okamura, March 11, 1946, in the case of United States of America vs. Shigeru Sawada et al.

201 "They're shooting at us": Aden Jones to Ross Greening, Individual Histories questionnaire, May 8, 1950.

201 "Dropped our bombs": Ibid.

201 "Observed heavy smoke": Charles J. Ozuk Jr., Personal Report, May 15, 1942.

202 "I saw fifteen to twenty bodies": Addition to Report of Lt. Charles J. Ozuk Jr., May 18, 1942.

202 "This student was immediately": Affidavit of School Teachers Furusawa and Okamura, March 11, 1946.

202 First Lieutenant Everett Holstrom: Unless otherwise noted, details of Holstrom's attack on Japan are drawn from the following sources: Everett M. Holstrom, Mission Report of Doolittle Project on April 18, 1942, May 14, 1942; E. W. Holstrom, Personal Report, May 14, 1942; Lucian N. Youngblood, Personal Report, May 3, 1942; Harry C. McCool, Personal Report,

May 5, 1942; Robert J. Stephens, Personal Report, May 5, 1942; Bert M. Jordan, Personal Report, May 5, 1942; Report of Interview with Lt. H. C. McCool, Member of Crew in Airplane No. 40-2282 Commanded by Lt. Holstrom on Mission to Attack Tokyo April 18, 1942, Aug. 23, 1942, Summary of Targets in Japanese Raid and Memoranda of Personal Interviews with Major J. F. Pinkney; Marshall, "Tokyo Raid," pp. 45–46; Shibata and Hara, *Dōrittoru Kūshū Hiroku*, pp. 65–67, 211.

203 "The red dots": Lucian Youngblood diary, April 18, 1942, Box 6, Series II, DTRAP.
203 "When I saw": Holstrom oral history interview with Hasdorff, April 14–15, 1988.
203 "I made up my mind": Holstrom, "General Recollections," p. 33.
204 "It's kind of a sickening": McCool oral history interview with Hasdorff, July 21, 1989.
204 Captain Davy Jones: Unless otherwise noted, details of Jones's attack on Japan are drawn from the following sources: David M. Jones, Mission Report of Doolittle Project, May 14, 1942; David M. Jones, Narrative Report, May 15, 1942; David M. Jones, Addition to Narrative Report of Capt. David M. Jones, May 18, 1942; Report of Interview with Captain Jones and Lt. Wilder, Members of Crew in Airplane No. 40-2283 Which Attacked Tokyo April 18, 1942, undated (ca. 1942), Summary of Targets in Japanese Raid and Memoranda of Personal Interviews with Major J. F. Pinkney; Marshall, "Tokyo Raid," pp. 46–48; Shibata and Hara, *Dōrittoru Kūshū Hiroku*, pp. 67–72, 211; Legal Section, 1st Demobilization Ministry, "Damages Sustained in the Air Attack of 18 April 1942."
204 "We didn't know": Jones oral history interview with Hasdorff, Jan. 13–14, 1987.
204 "Well": Ibid.
205 "The building assumed": Peters, "Japan Bombed with 20-Cent Sight," p. 1.
205 "It was easy to hit": David M. Jones, Narrative Report, May 15, 1942.
205 "When I saw": Joseph Manske transcript of speech, Box 2, Series IV, DTRAP.
205 Second Lieutenant Hallmark: Unless otherwise noted, details of Hallmark's attack on Japan are drawn from the following sources: Nielsen, "Doolittle Fliers' Saga of Living Death: First Day Was Bad," p. 3; Chase J. Nielsen testimony in the case of *United States of America vs. Shigeru Sawada et al.*; Nielsen oral history interview with Randle, Feb. 22, 2005; Marshall, "Tokyo Raid," pp. 46–47; Shibata and Hara, *Dōrittoru Kūshū Hiroku*, pp. 73–77, 211.
205 "It was so pleasant": Nielsen, "Doolittle Fliers' Saga of Living Death: First Day Was Bad," p. 3.
206 "The Japs sure did": Dean Hallmark to parents, Dec. 11, 1941.
206 "I'll figure that out": This exchange comes from Chase Nielsen oral history interview with Rick Randle, Feb. 22, 2005.
206 "We couldn't miss": Nielsen, "Doolittle Fliers' Saga of Living Death: First Day Was Bad," p. 3.
207 "I didn't feel": Ibid.

207 "That's a bulls-eye!": Ibid.

207 "We Don't Want": Ibid. The actual title of the song is "I Don't Want to Set the World on Fire."

207 "We felt good": Ibid.

207 First Lieutenant Ted Lawson: Unless otherwise noted, details of Lawson's attack on Japan are drawn from the following sources: Lawson, *Thirty Seconds over Tokyo*, pp. 56–65; McClure as told to Shinnick, "How We Bombed Tokio: Flyers Locate Targets," p. 2; Chas. L. McClure as told to William Shinnick, "How We Bombed Tokio: Hit, Run, Crash in Sea!," *Chicago Daily Tribune*, April 30, 1943, p. 4; David J. Thatcher, Personal Report, May 15, 1942; David J. Thatcher, Personal Report (Continued) (To be added to the other report), May 18, 1942; Memorandum of Interview with Lieutenant Davenport, Co-Pilot of Airplane No. 40-2261 (Pilot Lawson) Which Attacked South Central area of Tokyo April 18, 1942, undated (ca. 1942), Summary of Targets in Japanese Raid and Memoranda of Personal Interviews with Major J. F. Pinkney; Memorandum of Interview with Lieutenant Clever, Bombardier on Lt. Lawson's Plane, No. 40-2261, undated (ca. 1942), ibid.; Marshall, "Tokyo Raid," pp. 49–50; Shibata and Hara, *Dōrittoru Kūshū Hiroku*, pp. 77–84, 211.

207 "I had an ingrained": Lawson, *Thirty Seconds over Tokyo*, p. 57.

208 "The fresh spring grass": Ibid., p. 58.

208 "I saw quite a few": David J. Thatcher, Personal Report (Continued), May 18, 1942.

208 "It was like getting hit": Lawson, *Thirty Seconds over Tokyo*, p. 58.

208 "Keep your eyes open": This exchange is ibid., pp. 58–60.

208 "Nowhere was there": McClure as told to Shinnick, "How We Bombed Tokio: Flyers Locate Targets," p. 2.

209 "In days and nights": Lawson, *Thirty Seconds over Tokyo*, p. 61.

209 "I became disgusted": McClure as told to Shinnick, "How We Bombed Tokio: Hit, Run, Crash in Sea!," p. 4.

210 "That's flak": Ibid.

210 "There was not the slightest sign": Morris, *Traveler from Tokyo*, p. 196.

210 "Most of the people": Assistant Chief of Air Staff—Intelligence, Headquarters Army Air Forces, *Mission Accomplished: Interrogations of Japanese Industrial, Military and Civil Leaders of World War II* (Washington, D.C.: GPO, 1946), p. 100.

210 "Bombs?": Robert Guillain, *I Saw Tokyo Burning: An Eyewitness Narrative from Pearl Harbor to Hiroshima*, trans. William Byron (Garden City, N.Y.: Doubleday, 1981), p. 59.

211 "Still": Ibid.

211 "A raid at high noon!": Ibid.

211 "Everyone was out of doors": Ibid., pp. 59–60.

211 "The sirens did not even go off": Assistant Chief of Air Staff—Intelligence, Headquarters Army Air Forces, *Mission Accomplished*, p. 27.

211 "As for military weapons": USSBS, Morale Division, *The Effects of Strategic Bombing on Japanese Morale* (Washington, D.C.: GPO, 1947), p. 212.

211 "Wonderful!": Toland, *The Rising Sun*, p. 309.

212 "My goodness": Current Intelligence Section, A-2, Interview with Joseph E. Grew, Ambassador to Japan, Sept. 8, 1942, AFHRA.

212 "All this was very exciting": Joseph Grew diary, April 18, 1942, in Joseph C. Grew, *Ten Years in Japan: A Contemporary Record Drawn from the Diaries and Private and Official Papers of Joseph C. Grew* (New York: Simon and Schuster, 1944), p. 527. See also "U.S. Air Raid on Tokyo Witnessed by Grew," *New York Times*, Sept. 1, 1942, p. 3.

212 "Half of our group": *The Reminiscences of Captain Henri Smith-Hutton*, vol. 1, p. 346.

212 "We saw three bombers": Current Intelligence Section, A-2, Interview with Joseph E. Grew, Ambassador to Japan, Sept. 8, 1942.

213 "Well": This exchange is ibid.

213 "Our fondest wish": Tom Bernard, "Japs Were Jumpy after Tokyo Raid, *Stars and Stripes*, April 27, 1943, p. 2.

213 "I ran into a building": Ibid.

213 "It is so unfair": Ibid.

213 Danish Minister to Japan, Lars Tillitse: Lars Tillitse, "When Bombs Rained on Us in Tokyo," *Saturday Evening Post*, Jan. 12, 1946, p. 34.

213 "I looked down the streets": "'Worst' Feared for Tokyo Fliers by Neutral Diplomats in Japan," *New York Times*, April 25, 1943, p. 26.

213 "If these raids go on": Ibid.

214 "It is true": Office of Strategic Services, Research and Analysis Branch, Far Eastern Section, "Information Gathered on the S.S. *Gripsholm*," Report No. 77, Aug. 27, 1942, Microfilm Roll #A1250, AFHRA.

214 "an American air armada": Otto Tolischus diary, April 18, 1942, in Tolischus, *Tokyo Record*, p. 369.

214 "My friendly floor guard": Ibid., pp. 368–69.

214 "the thrill of a lifetime": Joseph Dynan, "Interned Americans Were Thrilled by Raid on Japs," *Tuscaloosa News*, July 28, 1942, p. 2.

214 "We were having coffee": Joseph Dynan, "Americans Saw Doolittle's Attack on Japan," *New York Times*, July 29, 1942, p. 4.

CHAPTER 12

215 "Tokyo is our capital": Yoshitake Miwa diary, Feb. 8, 1942.

215 Ski York roared: Unless otherwise noted, details of York's attack on Japan are drawn from the following sources: Emmens, *Guests of the Kremlin*, pp. 8–12; "Interview with B-25 Crew That Bombed Tokyo and Was Interned by the Russians," transcript, June 3, 1943, Iris #00115694, AFHRA; David Pohl as told to Don Dwiggins, "We Crash Landed in Russia—and Escaped," *Cavalier*, pp. 12, 55, in Box 5, Series II, DTRAP; Marshall, "Tokyo Raid," pp. 53–54; Shibata and Hara, *Dōrittoru Kūshū Hiroku*, pp. 85–89, 211.

215 "Kee-rist": Emmens, *Guests of the Kremlin*, p. 8.

215 "Where in the hell": Ibid., p. 9.

216 "Course from Tokyo": Ibid.

216 "Damn it, Bob": Ibid.

216 "Maybe a ray of hope": Ibid., p. 10.

216 "After flying for about 30 minutes": "Interview with B-25 Crew That Bombed Tokyo and Was Interned by the Russians," transcript, June 3, 1943.

216 "Open your bomb bay doors": Emmens, *Guests of the Kremlin*, p. 11.

216 "Though I walk": Jeff Wilkinson, "Crew Became 'Guests of the Kremlin," *State*, April 11, 2002, p. 1.

217 "Bombs away!": Emmens, *Guests of the Kremlin*, p. 11.

217 "Keep your eyes peeled": Ibid., p. 12.

217 "I'll bet we're the first B-25 crew": Ibid.

217 First Lieutenant Harold Watson piloted: Unless otherwise noted, details of Watson's attack on Japan are drawn from the following sources: Harold F. Watson, Mission Report of Doolittle Project on April 18, 1942, May 14, 1942; James M. Parker Jr., Personal Report, May 14, 1942; Thomas C. Griffin, May 15, 1942; Eldred V. Scott, Personal Report, May 15, 1942; Wayne M. Bissell, Personal Report, May 14, 1942; Interview with Lt. J. M. Parker, Co-pilot of Airplane No. 40-2303 Piloted by Lt. H. F. Watson, in Summary of Targets in Japanese Raid and Memoranda of Personal Interviews with Major J. F. Pinkney; Memorandum of Interview with Sergeant Scott (Gunner), Member of Airplane Crew in No. 40-2303 Piloted by Lt. Watson, ibid.; Marshall, "Tokyo Raid," pp. 50–51; Shibata and Hara, *Dōrittoru Kushū Hiroku*, pp. 90–96, 211.

218 "A nice, sunshiny": Peters, "Japan Bombed with 20-Cent Sight," p. 1.

218 "I expected to see holes": Ibid.

218 "majestic deliberation": Marshall, "Tokyo Raid," p. 51.

218 "I dropped two demolition": Wayne M. Bissell, Personal Report, May 14, 1942.

219 "Tracers were looping up": Eldred V. Scott, "A Bridge between Free Peoples," in Glines, *Doolittle's Tokyo Raiders*, p. 221.

219 First Lieutenant Richard Joyce piloted: Unless otherwise noted, details of Joyce's attack on Japan are drawn from the following sources: Richard O. Joyce, Mission Report of Doolittle Project on April 18, 1942, May 5, 1942; Richard O. Joyce, Report of Tokyo Raid, undated (ca. May 1942); Horace E. Crouch, May 5, 1942; Marshall, "Tokyo Raid," pp. 52–53; Shibata and Hara, *Dōrittoru Kūshū Hiroku*, pp. 97–99, 211.

219 "When we were a short way": Horace Crouch undated questionnaire, Box 1, Series II, DTRAP.

219 "The targets were so thick": J. Reilly O'Sullivan and Preston Grover, "'Thanks for the Ride,' and Raider Bails Out," *Spokane Daily Chronicle*, April 24, 1943, p. 2.

220 "I remember looking down": Crouch oral history interview with Hasdorff, April 19, 1989.

221 "I turned south": Richard O. Joyce, Report of Tokyo Raid, undated (ca. May 1942).

221 "It seemed that": George Larkin diary, April 18.

221 Captain Ross Greening: Unless otherwise noted, details of Greening's attack on Japan are drawn from the following sources: Charles R. Greening, Mission Report on Doolittle Project, April 18, 1942, May 2, 1942; Interview with Major Greening–Airplane No. 40-2249–Pilot, undated (ca. 1942), in Summary of Targets in Japanese Raid and Memoranda of Personal Interviews with Major J. F. Pinkney; Greening, *Not As Briefed*, pp. 27–33; Marshall, "Tokyo Raid," pp. 54–55; Shibata and Hara, *Dōrittoru Kūshū Hiroku*, pp. 99–103, 211.

221 "Let's be nonchalant": Greening, *Not As Briefed*, p. 29.

221 "I don't think I'd ever flown": Ibid.

221 "Two of these were shot down": Interview with Major Greening–Airplane No. 40-2249–Pilot, undated (ca. 1942).

221 "We hugged the ground": Peters, "Japan Bombed with 20-Cent Sight," p. 1.

221 "I flew so low": Greening, *Not As Briefed*, p. 31.

222 "I could see a concentration": Ibid., pp. 31–32.

222 "Oh, if my wife": Peters, "Japan Bombed with 20-Cent Sight," p. 1.

222 "There were great sheets": Ibid.

222 "When we turned": Kenneth Reddy diary, April 18, 1942.

223 First Lieutenant Bill Bower: Unless otherwise noted, details of Bower's attack on Japan are drawn from the following sources: William J. Bower, Mission report of Doolittle Project on April 18, 1942, May 2, 1942; Report of Interview with Lt. Bowers and Lt. Pound–Airplane No. 40-2278, undated (ca. 1942), in Summary of Targets in Japanese Raid and Memoranda of Personal Interviews with Major J. F. Pinkney; Report of Interview with Sergeant W. J. Bither, Bombardier in Plane No. 40-2278, Commanded by Lt. Bower, Aug. 23, 1942, Ibid.; Marshall, "Tokyo Raid," pp. 55–56; Shibata and Hara, *Dōrittoru Kūshū Hiroku*, pp. 103–6, 211.

223 "I became a busy boy": William Bower diary, April 18, 1942, Box 1, Series II, DTRAP.

223 "Why on earth": Bower oral history interview with Edwards, Oct. 27, 1971.

223 "Ahead was the bay": William Bower diary, April 18, 1942.

223 "About that time": Ibid.

223 "Bombs away": Ibid.

223 The total time: A post-raid report stated that the distance between the four targets was about a half-mile. In all likelihood, it was closer to a quarter-mile.

223 "I was watching": Pound, "We Bombed 'The Land of the Dwarfs,'" p. 242.

224 "Our bombs": Blanton, "We Bombed Japan," p. 10.

224 "Because we were not allowed": Pound, "We Bombed 'The Land of the Dwarfs,'" p. 243.

224 First Lieutenant Edgar McElroy: Unless otherwise noted, details of McElroy's attack on Japan are drawn from the following sources: Edgar E. McElroy, Mission Report of Doolittle Project on April 18, 1942; Edgar E. McElroy, Personal Report, May 4, 1942; Richard A. Knobloch, Personal Report, May 5, 1942; Robert C. Bourgeois, Personal Report, May 5, 1942; Clayton J. Campbell, Report of Navigator on #40-2247–Yokosuka Naval St., May 5, 1942; Marshall, "Tokyo Raid," pp. 56–57; Shibata and Hara, *Dōrittoru Kūshū Hiroku*, pp. 107–8, 211.

224 "Mac, I think we're going": McElroy, "When We Were One," p. 30.

225 "It was a thrilling sensation": Robert Bourgeois, "Road Back from Tokyo," *Barksdale Bark*, Christmas Edition, 1943, p. 5.

225 "I had looked at the pictures": Robert Bourgeois to Ross Greening, Individual Histories questionnaire, undated (ca. 1950).

225 "There were furious": McElroy, "When We Were One," p. 30.

225 "Get ready!": Ibid.

225 "A blind man": Wing, "Five Who Bombed Tokio Surprised They're Heroes," p. 1.

225 "Bombs away!": McElroy, "When We Were One," p. 30.

225 "We got an aircraft carrier!": Ibid.

225 "The large crane": Edgar E. McElroy, Personal Report, May 4, 1942.

226 "I looked out the window": Frank Gibney, ed., *Sensō: The Japanese Remember the Pacific War*, trans. Beth Cary (Armonk, N.Y.: M. E. Sharpe, 1995), p. 203.

226 "The enemy": Ibid.

226 Major Jack Hilger: Unless otherwise noted, details of Hilger's attack on Japan are drawn from the following sources: John A. Hilger, Report on Doolittle Project, May 5, 1942; John A. Hilger, Report of Airplane No. 40-2297, undated (ca. May 1942); Jack O. Sims, Personal Report, May 5, 1942; James H. Macia Jr., Personal Report, May 5, 1942; J. Eierman, Personal Report, undated (ca. May 1942); Edwin V. Bain, Personal Report, May 5, 1942; Interview with Lieutenant J. H. Macia, Navigator and Bombardier of Airplane No. 40-2297 Which Attacked Nagoya on April 18, 1942, undated (ca. 1942), in Summary of Targets in Japanese Raid and Memoranda of Personal Interviews with Major J. F. Pinkney; Interview with Lt. Sims–Airplane No. 40-2297 Which Attacked Nagoya April 18, 1942, undated (ca. 1942), ibid.; Marshall, "Tokyo Raid," pp. 57–58; Shibata and Hara, *Dōrittoru Kūshū Hiroku*, pp. 108–16, 211; Sims, *First over Japan*, pp. 29–30.

226 "Where are those fighters?": Cindy Hayostek, "Exploits of a Doolittle Raider," *Military History*, March 1996, p. 61.

226 "It was a beautiful spring day": John Hilger diary, April 18, 1942, in John Hilger, "On the Raid," *Life*, May 3, 1943, p. 92.

226 "We climbed over": Macia oral history interview with Hasdorff, July 15–16, 1987.

227 "Look, they've got a ball game": Eierman, "I Helped Bomb Japan," p. 67.

227 "While over Japan": John A. Hilger, Report of Airplane No. 40-2297, undated (ca. May 1942).

227 "Major Hilger, sir": Eierman, "I Helped Bomb Japan," p. 67.

227 "Some of the stuff": Ibid.

227 "No": This exchange comes from Jack Hilger, undated questionnaire, Box 3, Series II, DTRAP.

228 "I saw some ten to fifteen fires": Edwin V. Bain, Personal Report, May 5, 1942.

228 "A tremendous building": John Hilger diary, April 18, 1942, in Hilger, "On the Raid," p. 92.

228 "All I had to do": James "Herb" Macia oral history with Floyd Cox, July 21, 2000, National Museum of the Pacific War, Fredericksburg, Tex.

228 "Our fourth and last target": John Hilger diary, April 18, 1942, in Hilger, "On the Raid," p. 92.

228 "That was a beautiful hit": Eierman, "I Helped Bomb Japan," p. 67.

228 "As we passed over": Ibid.

228 "I fired a burst": Edwin V. Bain, Personal Report, May 5, 1942.

228 "His left fist": Eierman, "I Helped Bomb Japan," p. 68.

229 "Boy": Jack Hilger, undated questionnaire, Box 3, Series II, DTRAP.

229 First Lieutenant Donald Smith: Unless otherwise noted, details of Smith's attack on Japan are drawn from the following sources: Donald G. Smith, Mission Report of Doolittle Project on April 18, 1942, May 14, 1942; Donald G. Smith, Personal Report, May 14, 1942; Griffith P. Williams, Personal Report, undated (ca. May 1942); Howard A. Sessler, Personal Report, May 14, 1942; Edward J. Saylor, Personal Report, May 15, 1942; Gene Casey, "Conversation over Kobe," p. 23; Memorandum of Interview with Lt. D. G. Smith, Pilot of Airplane No. 40-2267, and Lt. T. R. White, Medical Officer on the Same Ship, Which Attacked Kobe April 18, 1942, undated (ca. 1942), in Summary of Targets in Japanese Raid and Memoranda of Personal Interviews with Major J. F. Pinkney; Notes Taken during an Interview with the Flyers Who Bombed Kobe April 18, 1942, June 17, 1942, ibid.; Marshall, "Tokyo Raid," pp. 57–58; Shibata and Hara, *Dōrittoru Kūshū Hiroku*, pp. 116–21, 211.

229 "This took place": Donald G. Smith, Personal Report, May 14, 1942.

229 "Oh-oh!": Casey, "Conversation over Kobe," p. 23.

229 "We ought to be seeing": Ibid.

229 "Here's a good chance": This exchange is ibid.

229 "The only person we bothered": Thomas White diary, April 18, 1942, in Thomas Robert White, "The *Hornet* Stings Japan," *Atlantic Monthly*, June 1943, p. 41.

229 "We had our first opposition": Thomas White, "Memoirs of 'Doc' White," p. 10.

230 "Say, Saylor, start pushing": Casey, "Conversation over Kobe,", p. 23.

230 "Very pretty and interesting": Thomas White diary, April 18, 1942, in White, "The *Hornet* Stings Japan," p. 42.

230 "Trains, streetcars and busses": Thomas White, "Memoirs of 'Doc' White," p. 10.

230 The airmen spotted: William W. Kelly, "Sense and Sensibility at the Ballpark: What Fans Make of Professional Baseball in Modern Japan," in William W. Kelly, ed., *Fanning the Flames: Fans and Consumer Culture in Contemporary Japan* (Albany: State University of New York Press, 2004), p. 80.

230 "Everything looked very much": Donald G. Smith, Personal Report, May 14, 1942.

231 "There's the steel foundries": This exchange comes from Casey, "Conversation over Kobe," p. 23.

231 "Bomb bay doors open": Ibid.

231 "Hey, when you going": Ibid.

232 "Nobody realized": Peters, "Japan Bombed with 20-Cent Sight," p. 1.

232 "It was like the old sleeper play": "Don Smith Relates Story of Raid on Japan for Home Folk," *Daily Belle Fourche Post*, July 3, 1942, p. 1.

232 Second Lieutenant Billy Farrow: Unless otherwise noted, details of Farrow's attack on Japan are drawn from the following sources: George Barr, Robert Hite, and Jacob DeShazer testimonies in the case of *United States of America vs. Shigeru Sawada et al.*; Robert "Bobby" L. Hite, "Doolittle Raider and Japanese POW," in Hoppes, comp., *Just Doing My Job*, pp. 43–45; DeShazer oral history interview with Hasdorff, Oct. 10, 1989; Hite oral history interview with Hasdorff, Dec. 16–17, 1982; Shibata and Hara, *Dōrittoru Kūshū Hiroku*, pp. 122–25, 211.

232 "We came in over": Jim Arpy, "You Are to Bomb the Japanese Homeland," *Sunday Times-Democrat*, April 12, 1964, p. 1D–2D.

232 "Get set to drop bombs": Watson, *DeShazer*, p. 30.

232 "See that gasoline tank?": DeShazer oral history interview with Hasdorff, Oct. 10, 1989.

232 "To the left of us": Watson, *DeShazer*, p. 31.

233 "Let your bombs go": DeShazer oral history interview with Hasdorff, Oct. 10, 1989.

233 "We didn't miss": Robert L. Hite and Jacob DeShazer, "Doolittle Fliers' Saga of Living Death: Men Pretty Low As They Face Japs in Courtroom," *News and Courier*, Sept. 22, 1945, p. 5.

CHAPTER 13

234 "Saturday's experience": "First Enemy Air Raid," *Nichi Nichi*, in "Today's Press Comments," *Japan Times & Advertiser*, April 19, 1942, p. 2.

234 Three minutes after: Task Force Sixteen war diary, April 18, 1942; *Hornet* and *Enterprise* deck logs, April 18, 1942.

234 Sailors hustled to ready: Rose, *The Ship That Held the Line*, p. 72.

234 The *Nitto Maru*'s contact report: *The Reminiscences of Captain Stephen Jurika, Jr.*, vol. 1, pp. 479–80.

234 Doctors and corpsmen: Jerry L. Strickland oral history with Jan K. Herman, Nov. 9, 2001, Bureau of Medicine and Surgery, Falls Church, Va.

235 "It will have to come off": This exchange comes from Harp Jr., "God Stood beside Us," pp. 19–20.

235 The *Enterprise* turned: *Enterprise* and *Hornet* deck logs, April 18, 1942; *Enterprise*, *Hornet*, and Task Force Sixteen war diaries, April 18, 1942.

236 At 11:50 a.m.: Report of U.S. Aircraft Action with Enemy by Ensign R. K. Campbell, A-V(N), USNR, included with M. F. Leslie to Commander in Chief, United States Fleet, Report of Action, April 18, 1942, Box 386, RG 38, Records of the Office of the Chief of Naval Operations, World War II Action and Operational Reports, NARA.

236 "The enemy maneuvered": M. F. Leslie to Commanding Officer, U.S.S. *Enterprise*, Reports of Action, April 19, 1942, ibid.

236 Lieutenant Ralph Arndt: Report of U.S. Aircraft Action with Enemy by Lieutenant R. W. Arndt, U.S. Navy, included with M. F. Leslie to Commander in Chief, United States Fleet, Report of Action, April 18, 1942; M. F. Leslie to Commanding Officer, U.S.S. *Enterprise*, Reports of Action, April 19, 1942.

236 Ensign John Butler: Report of U.S. Aircraft Action with Enemy by Ensign J. C. Butler, A-V(N), USNR, included with M. F. Leslie to Commander in Chief, United States Fleet, Report of Action, April 18, 1942; M. F. Leslie to Commanding Officer, U.S.S. *Enterprise*, Reports of Action, April 19, 1942.

236 Radar at one point: Task Force Sixteen war diary, April 18, 1942.

236 Lookouts on the *Enterprise*: Ibid.; *Enterprise* deck log, April 18, 1942; R. J. Hoyle, "U.S. Aircraft—Action with Enemy," April 18, 1942, Box 436, RG 38, Records of the Office of the Chief of Naval Operations, World War II Action and Operational Reports, NARA.

236 The *Nashville* charged: *Nashville* war diary, April 18, 1942; F. S. Craven to Chester Nimitz, "Report of Sinking of Two Enemy Patrol Boats on 18 April, 1942," April 21, 1942, Box 1264, RG 38, Records of the Office of the Chief of Naval Operations, World War II Action and Operational Reports, NARA; W. Kirten Jr., "Report by Gunnery Officer on Firing at Japanese Patrol Boats on 18 April, 1942," April 19, 1942, ibid.

236 "Her whole starboard side": W. Kirten Jr., "Report by Gunnery Officer on Firing at Japanese Patrol Boats on 18 April, 1942," April 19, 1942.

237 "One was wounded": F. S. Craven to Chester Nimitz, "Report of Sinking of Two Enemy Patrol Boats on 18 April, 1942," April 21, 1942.

237 "Two of our beautiful": This exchange comes from J. Bryan III, "Four-Star Sea Dog," *Saturday Evening Post*, Jan. 1, 1944, p. 52; Halsey, *Admiral Halsey's Story*, p. 103.

237 One of the *Enterprises*'s bombers: *Enterprise* war diary, April 18, 1942.

237 The task force: Robert J. Cressman, *The Official Chronology of the U.S. Navy in World War II* (Annapolis, Md.: Naval Institute Press, 2000), pp. 88–89; War History Office, National Institute for Defense Studies, *Hondo Hōmen Kaigun Sakusen* [Naval Operations in Home Waters], *Senshi Sōsho* [War History Series], vol. 85 (Tokyo: Asagumo Shinbunsha, 1975), pp. 82–85.

237 "She had a grand day": Robin Merton Lindsey oral history interview with the Navy, Sept. 17, 1943.

238 At Mitscher's request: *The Reminiscences of Captain Stephen Jurika, Jr.*, vol. 1, pp. 477–78.

238 Others scanned: Griffin, *A Ship to Remember*, pp. 68–69; "Pilots Who Were on *Hornet* Tell How Raid Upset Tokyo," *Milwaukee Journal*, April 24, 1943, p. 2.

238 "All the ship's radios": Harp Jr., "God Stood beside Us," pp. 20–21.

238 "Boy, oh boy": Ibid., p. 21.

238 "There was nothing": *The Reminiscences of Captain Stephen Jurika, Jr.*, vol. 1, p. 478.

238 "We began to worry": Harp Jr., "God Stood beside Us," p. 21.

238 "Lady Haw Haw": Griffin, *A Ship to Remember*, pp. 64, 69; "Lady Haw-Haw," *Time*, Jan. 19, 1942, p. 32.

238 "A moment before": Harp Jr., "God Stood beside Us," p. 21.

238 "Enemy bombers appeared": *Hornet* deck log, April 18, 1942.

239 "A large fleet": Ibid.

239 "They made it": Bryan III, "Four-Star Sea Dog," p. 52.

239 "It doesn't take much": E. B. Mott oral history interview with the Navy, March 22, 1944.

239 One bulletin claimed: Robert Casey diary, April 18, 1942, in Casey, *Torpedo Junction*, p. 427.

239 "Even if she had": Robert Casey diary, April 19, 1942, ibid., p. 429.

239 "The woman's had a shock": Ibid., pp. 307–8.

239 "Give your blood": Ibid., p. 429.

239 "An interesting moment": Ibid., p. 430.

240 "There has been no damage": Ibid., p. 309.

240 "You notice that nobody": Ibid.

240 "More evidence": Ibid., p. 310.

240 On board the *Hornet*: Harp Jr., "God Stood beside Us," p. 13.

240 "REMEMBER PEARL HARBOR!!": *News Digest*, April 19, 1942, Box 1, Series XI, DTRAP.

240 "rowdy": Harp Jr., "God Stood beside Us," p. 14.

240 "How does it feel": *News Digest*, April 19, 1942.

241 "Twas the eighteenth": Griffin, *A Ship to Remember*, pp. 70–71.

241 "It gives me great pleasure": *The Big E*, pp. 66–67.

241 "No one could": Harp Jr., "God Stood beside Us," pp. 23–24.

CHAPTER 14

242 "There have been thousands": Jones oral history interview with Hasdorff, Jan. 13–14, 1987.

242 Doolittle settled: Marshall, "Tokyo Raid," undated (ca. 1944), pp. 53, 61, 74–78.

243 "The sky was just purple": Peters, "Japan Bombed with 20-Cent Sight," p. 1.

243 "The most opposition": Ibid.

243 "I was amazed": W. H. Lawrence, "Airman Decorated," *New York Times*, May 20, 1942, p. 1.

243 "The over-all picture": Headquarters, Army Air Forces, Director of Intelligence Service, Informational Intelligence Summary (Special) No. 20, "The Tokyo Raid, April 18, 1942: Objectives, Preparation, the Action, Enemy Resistance, Mechanical Equipment, Conclusions," Iris #00114966, AFHRA.

243 "As we paralleled": Wildner, "The First of Many," p. 73.

243 "We sang songs": Hite and DeShazer, "Doolittle Fliers' Saga of Living Death: Men Pretty Low," p. 5.

244 "Wow!": Lawson, *Thirty Seconds over Tokyo*, p. 65.

244 "About this time": Thomas White, "Memoirs of 'Doc' White," p. 11.

244 "Just as Birch": Kenneth Reddy diary, April 18, 1942.

244 "It soon stopped": Ibid.

244 "One of the shells": Peters, "Japan Bombed with 20-Cent Sight," p. 1.

244 Saylor uncapped: Edward Saylor, "Doolittle Tokyo Raid," Jan. 14, 1989; Charles L. McClure, tape transcription, Dec. 1987, Box 4, Series II, DTRAP.

244 "Up until now": McElroy, "When We Were One," p. 30.

244 "My feelings of exhilaration": Sims, First over Japan, p. 30.

245 "By stretching": Bourgeois, "Road Back from Tokyo," p. 6.

245 "I saw sharks": Doolittle, I Could Never Be So Lucky Again, p. 9.

245 "We've got a tail wind": Cole oral history interview with Hasdorff, Dec. 12–13, 1988.

245 "For the first time": John Hilger diary, April 18, 1942, in Hilger, "On the Raid," p. 94.

245 "Chances of reaching land": Edward Oxford, "Against All Odds," American History Illustrated, April 1992, p. 60.

245 "See that the raft": Reynolds, The Amazing Mr. Doolittle, p. 207.

245 Copilot Dick Cole: Richard Cole interview with author, Aug. 24, 2011; Cole oral history interview with Hasdorff, Dec. 12–13, 1988.

246 "There it is": Reynolds, The Amazing Mr. Doolittle, p. 207.

246 The charts showed: Doolittle, I Could Never Be So Lucky Again, pp. 9–10; James H. Doolittle, Personal Report, May 4, 1942; Marshall, "Tokyo Raid," undated (ca. 1944), p. 64.

246 "Without a ground radio": Doolittle, I Could Never Be So Lucky Again, p. 10.

246 "We'll have to bail out": This exchange comes from Reynolds, The Amazing Mr. Doolittle, p. 209.

246 "When we get as close": Potter oral history interview with Hasdorff, June 8–10, 1979.

246 Potter folded up: Thomas M. Hatfield, "The Doolittle Raid: An Early Inspiration," American-Statesman, April 28, 1990, p. A23.

246 "Get going": Reynolds, The Amazing Mr. Doolittle, p. 209.

246 Leonard and Braemer: Fred A. Braemer, Personal Report, May 5, 1942; Paul J. Leonard, Personal Report, undated (ca. May 1942).

246 "Be seeing you": Reynolds, The Amazing Mr. Doolittle, p. 209.

246 "I was one scared turkey": Richard Cole letter, Jan. 2, 2004.

246 He had flown: James H. Doolittle, Personal Report, May 4, 1942; Doolittle, I Could Never Be So Lucky Again, p. 10.

247 Doolittle's jump marked: Doolittle, I Could Never Be So Lucky Again, p. 10.

247 "I heard movement inside": Ibid., p. 11.

247 "First you hear": Cole oral history interview with Hasdorff, Dec. 12–13, 1988.

247 "I tried using my flashlight": Richard E. Cole oral history interview with William J. Alexander, Aug. 8, 2011, University of North Texas, Denton, Tex.

247 Cole drifted down: Richard E. Cole, Personal Report, May 5, 1942.

247 "I was in all one 'scared piece'": Richard Cole, undated questionnaire.

247 Leonard landed: Paul J. Leonard, Personal Report, undated (ca. May 1942).

247 Potter likewise landed: Potter oral history interview with Hasdorff, June 8–10, 1979; Henry Potter, Personal Report, May 5, 1942.

248 "Couldn't see": Fred A Braemer, Personal Report, May 5, 1942.

248 Dean Hallmark roared: Unless otherwise noted, details of Hallmark's arrival in China are drawn from the following sources: Chase J. Nielsen testimony in the case of *United States of America vs. Shigeru Sawada et al.*; Nielsen, "Doolittle Fliers' Saga of Living Death: First Day Was Bad," p. 3; Chase Nielsen oral history interview with Winston P. Erickson, July 11, 2000, Marriott Library, Special Collections Department, University of Utah, Salt Lake City, Utah; Nielsen oral history interview with Randle, Feb. 22, 2005; Glines, *The Doolittle Raid*, pp. 100–103.

248 "Three minutes": Chase Nielsen oral history interview with Rick Randle, Feb. 22, 2005.

248 "No": Nielsen oral history interview with Erickson, July 11, 2000.

248 "Prepare for crashing landing": Nielsen, "Doolittle Fliers' Saga of Living Death: First Day Was Bad," p. 3.

248 "Well": Ibid.

248 "All went black": Chase Nielsen undated manuscript, in Glines, *The Doolittle Raid*, p. 101.

249 "The gunner was crawling": Nielsen oral history interview with Erickson, July 11, 2000.

249 "I thought about": Chase Nielsen undated manuscript, in Glines, *The Doolittle Raid*, p. 102.

249 "I figured": Nielsen oral history interview with Erickson, July 11, 2000.

250 "I crawled until": Nielsen, "Doolittle Fliers' Saga of Living Death: First Day Was Bad," p. 3.

250 The *Ruptured Duck* closed: Unless otherwise noted, details of Lawson's arrival in China are drawn from the following sources: Lawson, *Thirty Seconds over Tokyo*, pp. 66–87; McClure as told to Shinnick, "How We Bombed Tokio: Hit, Run, Crash in Sea!," p. 4; Charles L. McClure as told to William Shinnick, "How We Bombed Tokio: Chinese Rescue Flyers!," *Chicago Daily Tribune*, May 1, 1943, p. 5; Charles L. McClure, tape transcription, Dec. 1987; David J. Thatcher, Personal Report, May 15, 1942; David J. Thatcher, Personal Report (Continued), May 18, 1942; David Thatcher interview with author, Aug. 27, 2011; David Thatcher oral history memoir, Aug. 10, 1999, National Museum of the Pacific War, Fredericksburg, Tex.; McClure to Greening, Individual Histories questionnaire, undated (ca. 1950).

250 "I think we ought to go": Lawson, *Thirty Seconds over Tokyo*, p. 68.

250 "I don't think": Ibid.

250 "It was by all means": Ibid., p. 69.

251 "We're crashing": McClure as told to Shinnick, "How We Bombed Tokio: Hit, Run, Crash in Sea!," *Chicago Daily Tribune*, April 30, 1943, p. 4.

251 "I'm dead": Lawson, *Thirty Seconds over Tokyo*, p. 71.

251 "The bottom lip": Ibid., p. 73.

252 "Good God!": This exchange is ibid.

252 "I must go up": McClure as told to Shinnick, "How We Bombed Tokio: Hit, Run, Crash in Sea!," p. 4.

252 "I reached out": McClure as told to Shinnick, "How We Bombed Tokio: Chinese Rescue Flyers!," p. 5.

252 "Help me in": This exchange is ibid.

252 "Come on, you son": Charles L. McClure, tape transcription, Dec. 1987.

252 "He called me fighting names": McClure as told to Shinnick, "How We Bombed Tokio: Chinese Rescue Flyers!," p. 5.

252 "Should I shoot 'em?": This exchange comes from Charles L. McClure, tape transcription, Dec. 1987.

253 "Chinga": Lawson, *Thirty Seconds over Tokyo*, p. 76.

253 "Under other circumstances": McClure as told to Shinnick, "How We Bombed Tokio: Chinese Rescue Flyers!," p. 5.

253 "The top of his head": David J. Thatcher, Personal Report (Continued), May 18, 1942.

254 "If he'd only had": Ibid.

254 "My shoulder pains": McClure as told to Shinnick, "How We Bombed Tokio: Chinese Rescue Flyers!," p. 5.

254 "I felt that my body": Ibid.

254 "Hospital—soon": Ibid.

255 "I had no idea": Lawson, *Thirty Seconds over Tokyo*, p. 78.

255 "No": "For Public Relations Branch: When, As, and If War Department Thinks Proper," June 12, 1942, included with Cooper, "The Doolittle Air Raid on Japan," June 22, 1942.

255 "Me—Charlie": This exchange comes from Lawson, *Thirty Seconds over Tokyo*, pp. 80–81.

256 "The nose was just": David J. Thatcher, Personal Report, May 15, 1942.

256 "It was only": David J. Thatcher, Personal Report (Continued), May 18, 1942.

CHAPTER 15

257 "We must always give": Billy Farrow to Jessie Farrow, undated, in Jessie Farrow to James Doolittle, May 24, 1942, Box 22, DPLOC.

257 Ski York's bomber closed: Unless otherwise noted, details of York's arrival in Russia are drawn from the following sources: Emmens, *Guests of the Kremlin*, pp. 13–32; Emmens oral history interview with Hasdorff, July 8–9, 1982; York oral history interview with Hasdorff, July 23, 1984; "Interview with B-25 Crew That Bombed Tokyo and Was Interned by the Russians," transcript, June 3, 1943; Pohl as told to Dwiggins, "We Crash Landed in Russia—and Escaped," p. 55.

257 "What do you think": This exchange comes from Emmens, *Guests of the Kremlin*, p. 14.

257 "Lord": Ibid., p. 15.

258 "You can't fly around": Ibid., p. 16.

258 "For Christ's sake": Ibid., p. 17.

258 "Now, at last": Ibid.

258 "Leave fifteen degrees": Ibid.

258 "You guys stay": This exchange is ibid., p. 19.

259 "Americansky": Ibid., p. 20.

259 "Good-will flight": Emmens oral history interview with Hasdorff, July 8–9, 1982.

259 "This guy's no dummy": Emmens, *Guests of the Kremlin*, p. 25.

259 "Not sneeringly": Ibid., p. 26.

259 "I guess that guy wasn't fooled": Ibid.

260 "Colonel, we would like": This exchange is ibid., p. 27.

260 "It was like the Three Bears": Emmens oral history interview with Hasdorff, July 8–9, 1982.

260 "A Russian always begins": Emmens, *Guests of the Kremlin*, p. 29.

260 "someone had drawn": Ibid.

260 "I think we should": Ibid., p. 30.

260 "In behalf of my government": Ibid., p. 31.

260 "When we went to bed": "Interview with B-25 Crew That Bombed Tokyo and Was Interned by the Russians," transcript, June 3, 1943.

261 "I thought about home": Emmens, *Guests of the Kremlin*, p. 32.

261 Pilot Donald Smith: Unless otherwise noted, details of Smith's arrival in China are drawn from the following sources: Donald G. Smith, Mission Report of Doolittle Project on April 18, 1942, May 14, 1942; Donald G. Smith, Personal Report, May 14, 1942; D. G. Smith, "Pilots Report on Water Landing of B-25-B," May 15, 1942; Griffith P. Williams, Personal Report, undated (ca. May 1942); Griffith P. Williams, Co-Pilot's Report on Water Landing of B-25, May 18, 1942; Howard A. Sessler, Personal Report, May 14, 1942; H. A. Sessler, Addition to Report of Lt. H. A. Sessler (Bombing–Water Landing), May 18, 1942; Edward J. Saylor, Personal Report, May 15, 1942; E. J. Saylor, Notes on a Water Landing in a B 25 B, undated (ca. May 1942); Thomas White diary, April 18, 1942, in White, "The *Hornet* Stings Japan," pp. 41–42; Thomas White, "Memoirs of 'Doc' White," pp. 11–14; Edward Saylor, "Doolittle Tokyo Raid," Jan. 14, 1989; "For Public Relations Branch: When, As, and If War Department Thinks Proper," June 12, 1942.

261 "Brace yourselves": Thomas White, "Memoirs of 'Doc' White," p. 12.

262 "The sea was so rough": Edward Saylor, "Doolittle Tokyo Raid," Jan. 14, 1989.

263 "Turned over three times": Thomas White diary, April 18, 1942, in White, "The *Hornet* Stings Japan," p. 42.

263 "Current nearly swept": Ibid.

263 "There was a cold": Thomas White, "Memoirs of 'Doc' White," p. 13.

263 "We had one waterlogged": Ibid.

263 "We decided to curl up": Ibid.

263 "We warmed our chilled": Ibid.

264 "For most of these people": Ibid.

264 "We told them": Ibid., p. 14.

264 "No springs": Ibid.

264 The sixteenth bomber roared: Unless otherwise noted, details of Farrow's arrival in China are drawn from the following sources: Watson, *DeShazer*, pp. 31–35; DeShazer oral history interview with Hasdorff, Oct. 10, 1989; Hite oral history interview with Hasdorff, Dec. 16–17, 1982; George Barr testimony in the case of *United States of America vs. Shigeru Sawada et al.*; George Barr, "Destination: Forty Months of Hell," in Glines, *Doolittle's Tokyo Raiders*, pp. 305–12; Jim Arpy, "You are to Bomb the Japanese Homeland," *Sunday Times-Democrat*, April 12, 1964, p. 1D.

265 "The weather was bad": George Barr testimony in the case of *United States of America vs. Shigeru Sawada et al.*

265 "We're out of gas": This exchange comes from DeShazer oral history interview with Hasdorff, Oct. 10, 1989.

265 "That's Nanchang": Carroll V. Glines, *Four Came Home* (Princeton, N.J.: D. Van Nostrand, 1966), p. 66.

265 "Jake, you're first": DeShazer oral history interview with Hasdorff, Oct. 10, 1989.

265 "Boy": Ibid.

266 "I'll go towards the west": Ibid.

266 "As soon as I went through": Arpy, "You are to Bomb the Japanese Homeland," p. 1D.

266 "My heart stood still": Barr, "Destination," p. 310.

266 "I was still hoping": Ibid., pp. 311–12.

267 "I was standing there": Hite oral history interview with Hasdorff, Dec. 16–17, 1982.

267 "I could see inside": Watson, *DeShazer*, p. 33.

267 "China?": This exchange comes from DeShazer oral history interview with Hasdorff, Oct. 10, 1989.

268 "Their guns were all": Ibid.

268 "How did you get here?": This exchange is ibid.

268 "You're in the hands": Ibid.

268 "Aren't you afraid?": Watson, *DeShazer*, p. 35.

268 "I had a pocketful": Hite oral history interview with Hasdorff, Dec. 16–17, 1982.

269 "Well": Ibid.

269 Private First Class Tatsuo Kumano: Tatsuo Kumano testimony in the case of *United States of America vs. Shigeru Sawada et al.*

269 "I am not saying anything": Ibid.

269 "I am under oath": Ibid.

CHAPTER 16

270 "When we hit": Wing, "Five Who Bombed Tokio Surprised They're Heroes," p. 1.

270 Doolittle had suffered: Unless otherwise noted, details of Doolittle and

his crew's escape through China are drawn from the following sources: Doolittle, *I Could Never Be So Lucky Again*, pp. 11–13, 275–79; Reynolds, *The Amazing Mr. Doolittle*, pp. 209–14; James H. Doolittle, Personal Report, May 4, 1942; Richard E. Cole, Personal Report, May 5, 1942; Henry A. Potter, Report of Navigator, May 5, 1942; Fred A. Braemer, Personal Report, May 5, 1942; Paul J. Leonard, Personal Report, undated (ca. May 1942).

270 Shorty Manch seized: Jacob E. Manch, "The Last Flight of 'Whiskey Pete,'" in Glines, *Doolittle's Tokyo Raiders*, p. 158.

271 "It was the blackest hole": William Steponkus, "A Raider Recalls 'Blackest Hole,'" *Journal Herald*, in Box 3, Series II, DTRAP.

271 Eight of the bombers: S. L. A. Marshall, "Tokyo Raid," undated (ca. 1944), pp. 64–65.

271 The forced bailout: John M. Birch, Report on Death and Burial of Corporal Leland D. Faktor, United States Army Air Corps, included with Cooper, "The Doolittle Air Raid on Japan," June 22, 1942.

271 The jump and subsequent: Harold F. Watson, Mission Report of Doolittle Project on April 18, 1942, May 14, 1942; T. R. White to Air Surgeon, "Report of Activities Covering the Period from March 1, 1942, to June 16, 1942," June 23, 1942.

271 Navigator Charles Ozuk: Charles J. Ozuk Jr., Personal Report, May 15, 1942.

271 Shorty Manch realized: Greening, "The First Joint Action," p. 51.

271 Other airmen: Eldred V. Scott, Personal Report, May 15, 1942.

271 "I lit a cigarette": Waldo J. Bither, Personal Report, undated (ca. May 1942).

271 "I had landed in the China": John Hilger diary, April 19, 1942, in Hilger, "On the Raid," p. 98.

272 "I had the idea": Kerry Gunnels, "Austinite Recalls Role in Doolittle Raid of '42," *American-Statesman*, April 18, 1983, in Box 5, Series, II, DTRAP.

272 "I'll lead you": Reynolds, *The Amazing Mr. Doolittle*, p. 211.

272 "They say they heard": Doolittle, *I Could Never Be So Lucky Again*, p. 11.

272 "The major smiled": Ibid.

273 "He showed me a picture": Cole oral history interview with Hasdorff, Dec. 12–13, 1988.

273 Chinese soldiers escorted: Cole oral history interview with Alexander, Aug. 8, 2011.

273 "When I saw him": Potter oral history interview with Hasdorff, June 8–10, 1979.

273 "Let's get out of here": Fred A. Braemer, Personal Report, May 5, 1942.

273 "Well": Potter oral history interview with Hasdorff, June 8–10, 1979.

273 "Me China boy": Fred A. Braemer, Personal Report, May 5, 1942.

273 "Well": Potter oral history interview with Hasdorff, June 8–10, 1979.

274 "Hey": Ibid.

274 "We go": Ibid.

274 "One motioned to me": Paul J. Leonard, Personal Report, undated (ca. May 1942).

274 "I didn't know": Potter oral history interview with Hasdorff, June 8–10, 1979.

274 "There is no worse sight": Doolittle, *I Could Never Be So Lucky Again*, p. 12.

275 "This was my first": Ibid.

275 "disconsolate": "Diary Reveals Doolittle Believed Raid Failed," *Reading Eagle*, April 23, 1943, p 15.

275 "What do you think will happen": This exchange comes from Doolittle, *I Could Never Be So Lucky Again*, pp. 12–13.

275 "It was the supreme compliment": Ibid.

276 "Tokyo successfully bombed": James H. Doolittle, Personal Report, May 4, 1942.

276 "Now you guys": Potter oral history interview with Hasdorff, June 8–10, 1979.

276 Missionary John Birch had fled: John M. Birch oral history interview with 14th Air Force Historical Office Staff, March 20, 1945, AFHRA; "Who Was John Birch," *Time*, April 14, 1941, p. 29.

276 "Have you any Americans": This exchange comes from Birch oral history interview with 14th Air Force Historical Office Staff, March 20, 1945.

277 "Well, Jesus Christ": This exchange comes from Potter oral history interview with Hasdorff, June 8–10, 1979.

277 "Come in here!": Birch oral history interview with 14th Air Force Historical Office Staff, March 20, 1945.

277 "Of course, I was glad to": Ibid.

277 "I will see": This exchange comes from Greening, "The First Joint Action," p. 54.

277 Chase Nielsen awoke: Unless otherwise noted, details of the *Green Hornet*'s survival are drawn from the following sources: Chase J. Nielsen testimony in the case of *United States of America vs. Shigeru Sawada et al.*; Nielsen, "Doolittle Fliers' Saga of Living Death: First Day Was Bad," p. 3; C. Jay Nielsen, "Doolittle Fliers' Saga of Living Death: Raider Tortured in Effort to Learn Point of Takeoff," *News and Courier*, Sept. 17, 1945, p. 9; Nielsen oral history interview with Erickson, July 11, 2000; Nielsen oral history interview with Randle, Feb. 22, 2005; Glines, *Four Came Home*, pp. 46–59; Glines, *The Doolittle Raid*, pp. 102–6.

278 "Good Lord": Nielsen, "Doolittle Fliers' Saga of Living Death: First Day Was Bad," p. 3.

278 "Why": Chase Nielsen oral history interview with Rick Randle, Feb. 22, 2005.

278 "Boy, this is a fine pickle": Ibid.

278 "The next thing I saw": Nielsen oral history interview with Erickson, July 11, 2000.

278 "Stand up or me shoot!": Glines, *The Doolittle Raid*, p. 103.

278 "I might be able": Glines, *Four Came Home*, p. 50.

278 "You Japanese": This exchange comes from Nielsen oral history interview with Erickson, July 11, 2000.

278 "They dead": Chase Nielsen, undated manuscript, in Glines, *The Doolittle Raid*, p. 103.

279 "Japanese come": Chase Nielsen oral history interview with Winston P. Erickson, July 11, 2000.

279 "It was a welcome sight": Glines, *Four Came Home*, p. 51.

279 The men returned: Earl L. Dieter letter to Jesse and May, Sept. 6, 1945, Box 2, Series II, DTRAP.

279 "Hallmark, Meder and myself": Chase Nielsen letter to Mrs. Dieter, Sept. 18, 1945, ibid.

279 "Hurry, hurry, hurry": Nielsen, "Doolittle Fliers' Saga of Living Death: First Day Was Bad," p. 3.

279 "Soon": Nielsen, "Doolittle Fliers' Saga of Living Death: Raider Tortured," p. 9.

279 "We felt we had": Ibid. In later interviews and oral histories, Nielsen stated that the airmen were smuggled aboard a sampan and taken to Wenchow, where the Japanese captured them. However, both his sworn testimony before the war crimes tribunal and a detailed newspaper account he authored in 1945 contradict that account.

280 "Japanese come": Ibid.

280 "We talked briefly": Ibid.

280 "The Chinese led": Ibid.

280 "You now Japanese prisoner": Ibid.

280 David Thatcher returned: Unless otherwise noted, details of the *Ruptured Duck* crew's escape through China are drawn from the following sources: Lawson, *Thirty Seconds over Tokyo*, pp. 87–106; McClure as told to Shinnick, "How We Bombed Tokio: Chinese Rescue Flyers!," p. 5; McClure as told to Shinnick, "How We Bombed Tokio: Flyers Trek to Safety," p. 6; Charles L. McClure, tape transcription, Dec. 1987; David J. Thatcher, Personal Report, May 15, 1942; David J. Thatcher, Personal Report (Continued), May 18, 1942; David Thatcher interview with author, Aug. 27, 2011; David Thatcher oral history memoir, Aug. 10, 1999; McClure to Greening, Individual Histories questionnaire, undated (ca. 1950).

280 "I got to the plane": Lawson, *Thirty Seconds over Tokyo*, p. 87.

280 "It was no comfortable sedan chair": McClure as told to Shinnick, "How We Bombed Tokio: Chinese Rescue Flyers!," p. 5.

281 "They slipped in the mud": Ibid.

281 "As we rose": Lawson, *Thirty Seconds over Tokyo*, p. 91.

281 "One of the toughest-looking": Ibid., p. 92.

281 "It was hard not to moan": Ibid., p. 96.

282 "With sick, mingled fears": Ibid., p. 97.

282 "We moved along like a snail": Ibid., p. 98.

283 "Only after getting tired": David J. Thatcher, Personal Report (Continued), May 18, 1942.

283 "With this injury": Ibid.

283 "He tried to sleep": Ibid.

283 "Don't let them cut": This exchange comes from Lawson, *Thirty Seconds over Tokyo*, p. 99.

283 "I was pretty darned hungry": David J. Thatcher, Personal Report (Continued), May 18, 1942.

283 "It was like raw": Lawson, *Thirty Seconds over Tokyo*, p. 100.

283 "the blackest night": McClure to Greening, Individual Histories questionnaire, undated (ca. 1950).

283 "Lawson was wanting water": David J. Thatcher, Personal Report, May 18, 1942.

284 "I was carried": McClure to Greening, Individual Histories questionnaire, undated (ca. 1950).

284 "Anything we got is yours": Lawson, *Thirty Seconds over Tokyo*, p. 102.

284 "They had nothing": Ibid.

284 "Sitting in one of the anterooms": McClure to Greening, Individual Histories questionnaire, undated (ca. 1950).

284 "man-eating bug": McClure as told to Shinnick, "How We Bombed Tokio: Flyers Trek to Safety," p. 6.

285 "I didn't get much rest": Ibid.

285 "I tried to go to sleep": Lawson, *Thirty Seconds over Tokyo*, p. 102.

285 Dr. Chen Shenyan arrived: Statement by Dr. Shen-Yen, Co-Direction, En-Tse Hosptial, Ling Hai, undated (ca. May 1942), included with Cooper, "The Doolittle Air Raid on Japan," June 22, 1942.

285 "There was a compound fracture": Ibid.

285 "He also had multiple": Ibid.

285 "We were given": David J. Thatcher, Personal Report (Continued), May 18, 1942.

286 "It brought a lump": Lawson, *Thirty Seconds over Tokyo*, p. 104.

286 "At the top of a ridge": McClure as told to Shinnick, "How We Bombed Tokio: Flyers Trek to Safety," p. 6.

286 "There were times": Lawson, *Thirty Seconds over Tokyo*, pp. 104–5.

286 "You're safe here": This exchange is ibid., p. 106.

286 "It was a hospital now": McClure as told to Shinnick, "How We Bombed Tokio: Flyers Trek to Safety," p. 6.

286 "It was forty miles": David J. Thatcher, Personal Report (Continued), May 18, 1942.

CHAPTER 17

287 "I had many things": Kenneth Reddy diary, April 18, 1942.

287 The Russians woke York: Unless otherwise noted, details of York's arrival in Russia are drawn from the following sources: Emmens, *Guests of the Kremlin*, pp. 32–58; Emmens oral history interview with Hasdorff, July 8–9, 1982; York oral history interview with Hasdorff, July 23, 1984; "Interview with B-25 Crew That Bombed Tokyo and Was Interned by the Russians," transcript, June 3, 1943; Pohl as told to Dwiggins, "We Crash Landed in Russia—and Escaped," pp. 55–56.

287 "Business must never": Emmens, *Guests of the Kremlin*, p. 33.

287 "During this time": Emmens oral history interview with Hasdorff, July 8–9, 1982.

288 "Tell you what": Pohl as told to Dwiggins, "We Crash Landed in Russia—and Escaped," p. 55.

288 "Are you sure": Emmens, *Guests of the Kremlin*, p. 35.

288 "You must hurry": Ibid., p. 36.

288 "My God": Emmens oral history interview with Hasdorff, July 8–9, 1982.

288 "I finally had to pull York": Ibid.

288 "Roosky Dooglas": Ibid.

288 "Where are we going": This exchange comes from Emmens, *Guests of the Kremlin*, p. 37.

288 "Khabarovsk": Ibid., p. 38.

288 "May I introduce to you": Ibid., p. 39.

289 "General Stern was the nearest": Emmens oral history interview with Hasdorff, July 8–9, 1982.

289 "The General has asked": Emmens, *Guests of the Kremlin*, p. 40.

289 "Well, here we are": Ibid., p. 44.

289 "There wasn't anything": Ibid.

290 "I speak a little English": Ibid.

290 "My God": Ibid., p. 47.

290 "Anything that resembled": "Interview with B-25 Crew That Bombed Tokyo and Was Interned by the Russians," transcript, June 3, 1943.

290 "Every day had been": Emmens, *Guests of the Kremlin*, p. 55.

291 "Leaving!": Emmens oral history interview with Hasdorff, July 8–9, 1982.

291 "Where are we going?": Ibid.

291 An influx of visitors: Unless otherwise noted, details of Smith's crew's time in China are drawn from the following sources: Donald G. Smith, Mission Report of Doolittle Project on April 18, 1942, May 14, 1942; Donald G. Smith, Personal Report, May 14, 1942, Griffith P. Williams, Personal Report, undated (ca. May 1942); Howard A. Sessler, Personal Report, May 14, 1942; Edward J. Saylor, Personal Report, May 15, 1942; Thomas White diary, April 19–24, 1942, in White, "The *Hornet* Stings Japan," pp. 42–45; Thomas White, "Memoirs of 'Doc' White," pp. 14–29.

291 "He was still intact": Thomas White diary, April 19, 1942, in White, "The *Hornet* Stings Japan," p. 42.

291 "Several times other boats": Thomas White, "Memoirs of 'Doc' White," p. 15.

292 "The only sound": Ibid.

292 "Damn and fuck": Ibid., p. 16.

293 "I noticed the extreme age": Thomas White diary, April 20, 1942, in White, "The *Hornet* Stings Japan," p. 43.

293 "The old priest": Ibid.

293 "We felt trapped": Thomas White diary, April 21, 1942, in White, "The *Hornet* Stings Japan," p. 43.

293 "Several times we heard": Thomas White, "Memoirs of 'Doc' White," p. 19.

294 "I don't know whether": Edward Saylor, "Doolittle Tokyo Raid," Jan. 14, 1989.

294 "The air in the cave": Thomas White, "Memoirs of 'Doc' White," p. 19.

294 "Clattering noises": "For Public Relations Branch: When, As, and If War Department Thinks Proper," June 12, 1942.

294 "Everyone relaxed": Thomas White diary, April 21, 1942, in White, "The *Hornet* Stings Japan," p. 43.

294 "They had evidently": Thomas White, "Memoirs of 'Doc' White," p. 19.

294 "Fascinating countryside": Thomas White diary, April 21, 1942, in White, "The *Hornet* Stings Japan," p. 43.

295 "Glad to get": Ibid., p. 44.

295 "We replied": Thomas White, "Memoirs of 'Doc' White," p. 22.

295 "Had a gorgeous night's sleep": Thomas White diary, April 23, 1942, in White, "The *Hornet* Stings Japan," p. 44.

295 "Safe and well": Ibid.

295 "a triumphal procession": Ibid.

295 "We went up a long valley": Ibid.

296 "Everywhere we went": Ibid.

296 Lawson's conditioned had worsened: T. R. White to Department Surgeon, Far Eastern Dept., "Report of Injuries Received in Aircraft Accident," April 26, 1942, included with Cooper, "The Doolittle Air Raid on Japan," June 22, 1942. For description of his wounds, see also T. R. White to Air Surgeon, "Report of Activities Covering the Period from March 1, 1942, to June 16, 1942," June 23, 1942.

296 "All of the wounds": Thomas White, "Memoirs of 'Doc' White," p. 27.

296 "The area of gangrene": Ibid.

297 "The fact that Ted": Ibid., p. 26.

297 The Japanese loaded: Tatsuo Kumano and George Barr testimonies in the case of *United States of America vs. Shigeru Sawada et al.*

297 Guards ushered the raiders: Glines, *Four Came Home*, p. 67.

297 Guards tossed: George Barr testimony in the case of *United States of America vs. Shigeru Sawada et al.*; Watson, *DeShazer*, p. 36.

297 The Japanese pulled DeShazer: Watson, *DeShazer*, pp. 36–37; DeShazer oral history interview with Hasdorff, Oct. 10, 1989.

297 "I'm the kindest judge": This exchange comes from DeShazer oral history interview with Hasdorff, Oct. 10, 1989.

298 "When you speak": Watson, *DeShazer*, p. 37.

298 "Tomorrow morning": This exchange comes from DeShazer oral history interview with Hasdorff, Oct. 10, 1989.

298 "You will please to sit down": This exchange comes from Glines, *Four Came Home*, pp. 68, 70.

299 "You couldn't fly that far": This exchange comes from Hite oral history interview with Hasdorff, Dec. 16–17, 1982.

299 George Barr suffered: George Barr testimony in the case of *United States of America vs. Shigeru Sawada et al.*

299 "The water was going": Ibid.

299 "My hands were tied": DeShazer oral history interview with Hasdorff, Oct. 10, 1989.

300 The Japanese loaded: This scene is based on Nielsen's testimony in the 1946 war crimes trial and the series of newspaper articles he authored after the war in 1945.

300 "Nobody said anything": Nielsen, "Doolittle Fliers' Saga of Living Death: Raider Tortured," p. 9.

301 "We have methods": Ibid.

301 "That crack about my folks": Ibid.

301 "There was absolutely": Ibid.

301 "A man has to breathe": Ibid.

301 "I felt more or less": Chase Nielsen testimony in the case of *United States of America vs. Shigeru Sawada et al.*

301 "With the water trickling": C. Jay Nielsen, "Doolittle Fliers' Saga of Living Death: Raider Tortured in Effort to Learn Point of Takeoff," *News and Courier*, Sept. 17, 1945, p. 9.

301 "Talk": Ibid.

302 "I can't stand this": C. Jay Nielsen, "Doolittle Fliers' Saga of Living Death: Sadistic Delight Taken in Torturing Captured Yanks," *News and Courier*, Sept. 18, 1945, p. 7.

302 "The sweat was pouring": Ibid.

302 "With each blow": Ibid.

302 "I've given you": Ibid.

302 "I could feel the edges": Ibid.

302 "Well": Ibid.

302 "We'll see about that": Ibid.

303 "Tell it to me": Ibid.

303 "How do you like that?": Ibid.

303 "If you insist on not telling": Ibid.

303 "My mind was in a whirl": C. Jay Nielsen, "Doolittle Fliers' Saga of Living Death: Japs Change Pace in Their Methods of Torturing Yank," *News and Courier*, Sept. 19, 1945, p. 5.

303 "The sweat was pouring": Ibid.

303 "My whole life flashed": Ibid.

304 "Well, well, well": Ibid.

304 "If you boys don't": Ibid.

304 "Panic seized me": Ibid.

304 "There were periods of consciousness": Ibid.

304 "When I let my arms down": Chase Nielsen testimony in the case of *United States of America vs. Shigeru Sawada et al.*

304 "I could see a little bit": Nielsen, "Doolittle Fliers' Saga of Living Death: Japs Change Pace," p. 5.

CHAPTER 18

305 "Far from winning": "Remember Tokyo," editorial, *Pittsburgh Press*, April 20, 1942, p. 10.

305 "As the enemy position": Yoshitake Miwa diary, April 18, 1942.

305 The lack of widespread damage: Toland, *The Rising Sun*, p. 309.
306 "Helped in my hard-labored": Goldstein and Dillon, eds., *The Pearl Harbor Papers*, p. 129.
306 Early reports: Matome Ugaki diary, April 18, 1942, in Ugaki, *Fading Victory*, pp. 111–13.
306 "We have missed": Ibid., p. 113.
306 Erroneous reports of new attacks: War History Office, National Institute for Defense Studies, *Hondo Hōmen Kaigun Sakusen*, pp. 92–95; Military History Section, Headquarters, Army Forces Far East, "Homeland Defense Naval Operations: December 1941–March 1943," Japanese Monograph #109, pt. 1, 1953, pp. 10–11.
307 Reports indicated: Matome Ugaki diary, April 19, 1942, in Ugaki, *Fading Victory*, pp. 113–14.
307 "The reason": Ibid., p. 113.
307 "What relation there was": Yoshitake Miwa diary, April 19, 1942.
307 The Japanese captured: War Department, Office of Assistant Chief of Staff, G-2, Magic Summary, "Bombing of Tokyo," April 22, 1942, in *The Magic Documents: Summaries and Transcripts of the Top Secret Diplomatic Communications of Japan, 1938–1945* (Washington, D.C.: University Publications of America, 1980), Microfilm Roll #1; Matome Ugaki diary, April 19, 1942, in Ugaki, *Fading Victory*, pp. 113–14.
307 "They never told": Matome Ugaki diary, April 19, 1942, in Ugaki, *Fading Victory*, p. 113.
307 "What the enemy intended": Ibid., p. 114.
308 By the following evening: Matome Ugaki diary, April 20, 1942, in Ugaki, *Fading Victory*, pp. 114–15.
308 "The enemy, already withdrawn": Ibid., p. 115.
308 "One has the embarrassing feeling": Agawa, *The Reluctant Admiral*, p. 300.
308 Ugaki knew by April 21: Matome Ugaki diary, April 21–22, 1942, in Ugaki, *Fading Victory*, pp. 115–16.
308 "How the sixteen planes": Matome Ugaki diary, April 22, 1942, in Ugaki, *Fading Victory*, p. 116.
308 A final tally: Shibata and Hara, *Dōrittoru Kūshū Hiroku*, p. 211.
309 In Tokyo: Legal Section, 1st Demobilization Ministry, "Damages Sustained in the Air Attack of 18 April 1942."
309 A postwar analysis: Shibata and Hara, *Dōrittoru Kūshū Hiroku*, p. 211.
309 including a woman: Hayakawa Fuyo affidavit, March 11, 1946, in case of *United States of American vs. Shigeru Sawada et al.*
309 "One father wrote": Allied Translator and Interpreter Section, South West Pacific Area, Research Report, "Psychological Effect of Allied Bombing on the Japanese," Sept. 21, 1944, Australian War Memorial, Canberra, Australia.
310 "Today, April 18": "Enemy Planes Raid Tokyo-Y'hama; Defense Units Shoot Down 9 Craft," *Osaka Mainichi*, April 19, 1942, p. 1.
310 That was followed: "Warnings Sounded," *Japan Times & Advertiser*, April 19, 1942, p. 1.

310 "The time has come": "Enemy Planes Fly over Nagoya, Kobe," *Osaka Mainichi*, April 19, 1942, p. 1.

310 "Incendiary bombs were dropped": "Fires Extinguished," *Osaka Mainichi*, April 19, 1942, p. 1.

310 "The corps guarding the air": "Warnings Sounded," *Japan Times & Advertiser*, April 19, 1942, p. 1.

310 "The Army announced": Yoshitake Miwa diary, April 19, 1942.

311 "In connection": War Department, Office of Assistant Chief of Staff, G-2, Magic Summary, "Tokyo Bombing," May 6, 1942, in *The Magic Documents*, Microfilm Roll #1.

311 "This afternoon a few spots": "International Law Grossly Violated by Enemy Air Units," *Japan Times & Advertiser*, April 20, 1942, p. 1.

311 Newspaper headlines: "9 Enemy Raiders Downed," *Japan Times & Advertiser*, April 19, 1942, p. 1; "Damage by Incendiary Bombs Small; Planes Repulsed," ibid., April 19, 1942, p. 1; "Dog-Fights Staged in Air over Capital," ibid., April 19, 1942, p. 1; "Nearly All Planes in Saturday Attack Were Brought Down," ibid., April 21, 1942, p. 1; "Shot Down or Crashed in Sea Is Fate of All Enemy Planes Which Raided Tokyo, Yokohama," ibid., April 22, 1942, p. 1.

311 "The few enemy planes": "That Air Raid Last Saturday," editorial, *Japan Times & Advertiser*, April 22, 1942, p. 6.

311 Even Emperor Hirohito: "Imperial Family Absolutely Safe in First Air Raid over Capital," *Japan Times & Advertiser*, April 19, 1942, p. 1.

311 Others noted that motion picture: "Shows Go on Despite Raid," *Japan Times & Advertiser*, April 20, 1942, p. 2.

311 Financial markets: "All Markets Calm in Face of Air-Raid," *Japan Times & Advertiser*, April 21, 1942, p. 5; "Stocks Unaffected by Initial Air Raid," ibid., April 21, 1942, p. 5.

312 "valuable experience": "Yuzawa Commends People's Conduct during Air Attack," *Japan Times & Advertiser*, April 20, 1942, p. 1.

312 "Air raids are nothing to be feared": Ibid.

312 "The truth is": "Air-Raid Is Desperate American Move to Cover Up Own Successive Debacles," *Osaka Mainichi*, April 23, 1942, p. 2.

312 "Air raids alone": "Lt.-Gen. Kobayashi Highly Praises Nation's Defense against Air-Raid," *Osaka Mainichi*, April 21, 1942, p. 1.

312 "I pursued this plane": "2 Enemy Raiders Are Forced Down after Being Chased by Nippon Planes," *Osaka Mainichi*, April 22, 1942, p. 1; Shibata and Hara, *Dōrittoru Kūshū Hiroku*, pp. 99–101.

312 "We saw her right engine": "2 Enemy Raiders Are Forced Down after Being Chased by Nippon Planes," *Osaka Mainichi*, April 22, 1942, p. 1.

312 "The enemy's daring enterprise": "First Enemy Air Raid," *Nichi Nichi*, in "Today's Press Comments," *Japan Times & Advertiser*, April 19, 1942, p. 2.

312 "The manner in which": "Visit of Enemy Planes," *Miyako*, in "Today's Press Comments," *Japan Times & Advertiser*, April 19, 1942, p. 2.

312 "Their weak attacking": "Brace Up!," *Hochi*, in "Today's Press Comments," *Japan Times & Advertiser*, April 19, 1942, p. 2.

312 "The most important thing": "Enemy's Feeble Raid on Japan," *Chugai Shogyo*, in "Press Comments," *Japan Times & Advertiser*, April 20, 1942, p. 3.

313 "It was a mere gesture": "That Air Raid Last Saturday," editorial, *Japan Times & Advertiser*, April 22, 1942, p. 6.

313 Reports revealed: "All Markets Calm in Face of Air-Raid," *Japan Times & Advertiser*, April 21, 1942, p. 5; "More Benefit Is Due for Air-Raid Victims," *Osaka Mainichi*, April 24, 1942, p. 3.

313 "The law provides": "Sufferers Protection Law to Apply to Those Affected by Recent Raid," *Osaka Mainichi*, April 22, 1942, p. 1.

313 "It is sometimes so poor": Current Intelligence Section, A-2, Interview with Joseph E. Grew, Ambassador to Japan, Sept. 8, 1942.

313 Not until April 26: "Miserable Remains of Wrecked Enemy Raider," *Japan Times & Advertiser*, April 26, 1942, p. 3.

314 To maintain the charade: Stilwell msg. to AGO for AMMISCA, No. 699, May 18, 1942, Iris #00116401, AFHRA.

314 "We expected photographs": Tom Bernard, "Japs Were Jumpy after Tokyo Raid," *Stars and Stripes*, April 27, 1943, p. 2.

314 "For two weeks after the raid": Ibid.

314 "The raid by Doolittle": "'Worst' Feared for Tokyo Fliers by Neutral Diplomats in Japan," *New York Times*, April 25, 1943, p. 26.

314 "The raid did the Japanese": Guillain, *I Saw Tokyo Burning*, p. 63.

315 "The Doolittle raid produced": Office of Strategic Services, Research and Analysis Branch, Far Eastern Section, "Information Gathered on the S.S. *Gripsholm*," Report No. 77, Aug. 27, 1942.

315 "It could hardly be called": Agawa, *The Reluctant Admiral*, p. 300.

315 "The bombing of Tokyo": Togo Shigenori, *The Cause of Japan*, trans. and ed. Togo Fumihiko and Ben Bruce Blakeney (New York: Simon and Schuster, 1956), pp. 235.

315 "In point of physical damage": Fuchida and Okumiya, *Midway*, pp. 70–71.

315 "The attack unnerved": Saburo Sakai with Martin Caidin and Fred Saito, *Samurai!* (Garden City, N.Y.: Doubleday, 1978), p. 128.

316 "The bombing of Tokyo": Ibid.

316 Just six days before: Stephan, *Hawaii under the Rising Sun*, pp. 112–13.

316 "It was just as if a shiver": Kameto Kuroshima interview, Nov. 28, 1964, Box 2, Series 7, GWPP.

316 "The Doolittle raid": Yasuji Watanabe interview, Sept. 26, 1964, Box 6, Series 7, GWPP.

316 "With the Doolittle raid": Yasuji Watanabe interview, Sept. 25, 1964, ibid.

316 "Even the most vociferous": Fuchida and Okumiya, *Midway*, pp. 71–72.

317 "Why, everybody wants": Carlyle Holt, "Raid Infuriates Japan," *Daily Boston Globe*, April 21, 1942, p. 1.

317 "For the best news": Edward T. Folliard, "Enemy Only Source of News in American Raids on Japan," *Washington Post*, April 19, 1942, p. 2.

317 "I wonder why": Yoshitake Miwa diary, April 22, 1942.

317 "The American papers": "Information Please! Says Anxious Tokyo," *Washington Post*, April 24, 1942, p. 1.

318 "This will prove TNT": "Washington Hails Report of Bombing," *New York Times*, April 19, 1942, p. 38.

318 "hardly a token": "Congress Leaders Hail Raids on Jap Centers as Opening Offensive," *Evening Star*, April 18, 1942, p. 1.

318 "This is the only way": "Washington Hails Report of Bombing," *New York Times*, April 19, 1942, p. 38.

318 who had left two days: William Hassett diary, April 16, 1942, in William D. Hassett, *Off the Record with F.D.R., 1942–1945* (New Brunswick, N.J.: Rutgers University Press, 1958), p. 36.

318 "Until twenty-four hours": King, *Fleet Admiral King*, p. 376.

318 "President Roosevelt": Ernest King to D. B. Duncan, June 2, 1949, Box 18, Ernest J. King Papers, LOC.

318 "Hell's a-poppin": Margaret Suckley diary, April 17, 1942, in Geoffrey C. Ward, ed., *Closest Companion: The Unknown Story of the Intimate Friendship between Franklin Roosevelt and Margaret Suckley* (Boston: Houghton Mifflin, 1995), p. 156.

318 "bad humor": Margaret Suckley diary, April 17, 1942, in Ward, ed., *Closest Companion*, p. 156.

318 "So many things": Eleanor Roosevelt, "My Day," April 20, 1942.

318 That evening the president: William Hassett diary, April 17, 1942, in Hassett, *Off the Record with F.D.R., 1942–1945*, p. 36.

318 Roosevelt had settled: Rosenman, comp., *The Public Papers and Addresses of Franklin D. Roosevelt*, 1942 vol., pp. 215–16.

318 "The President was": Ibid., p. 216.

319 "Mr. President": Ibid.

319 "What's the news?": William Hassett diary, April 19, 1942, in Hassett, *Off the Record with F.D.R., 1942–1945*, pp. 40–41.

319 "You know": Ibid.

319 "That seemed to me": Ibid.

319 "The base": Ibid.

319 "I was unfamiliar": Ibid.

319 He liked it so much: Margaret Suckley diary, April 21, 1942, in Ward, ed., *Closest Companion*, p. 156.

320 "I think the time has come": Press Conference no. 820, April 21, 1942, in *Complete Presidential Press Conferences of Franklin D. Roosevelt*, vol. 19, pp. 291–92.

320 though as Daisy recorded: Margaret Suckley diary, April 21, 1942, in Ward, ed., *Closest Companion*, p. 156.

320 "Would you care": This exchange comes from Press Conference no. 820, April 21, 1942, in *Complete Presidential Press Conferences of Franklin D. Roosevelt*, vol. 19, pp. 292–93.

320 "Is there any news today": Press Conference no. 821, April 24, 1942, ibid., vol. 19, pp. 298–99.

320 "A southern newspaper editor": This exchange comes from Press Conference no. 828, May 26, 1942, ibid., pp. 349–50.

320 Roosevelt would later go: Rosenman, comp., *The Public Papers and Addresses of Franklin D. Roosevelt*, 1942 vol., p. 216.

320 The Navy followed: James L. Mooney, ed., *Dictionary of American Naval Fighting Ships*, vol. 6 (Washington, D.C.: GPO, 1976), pp. 463–64.

320 "Shangri-La to Shangri-La": J. H. Doolittle, Pilot's Book, April 18, 1942, Box 1, Series XVI, DPUT.

321 "Mr. President, there are complaints": This exchange comes from Press Conference no. 821, April 24, 1942, in *Complete Presidential Press Conferences of Franklin D. Roosevelt*, vol. 19, pp. 299–300.

321 "As you will have seen": Franklin Roosevelt to Winston Churchill, April 21, 1943, in Kimball, ed., *Churchill & Roosevelt*, p. 466.

321 "The number of airplanes": H. H. Arnold to Franklin Roosevelt, "Recent Attack on Japan," April 21, 1942, Microfilm Roll #A1250, AFHRA.

321 "From the viewpoint": Ibid.

321 The general had finally received: T. V. Soong to Henry H. Arnold, April 21, 1942, Microfilm Roll #A1250, AFHRA.

322 "Everything points to Doolittle": H. H. Arnold to Franklin Roosevelt, "Recent Attack on Japan," April 22, 1942, ibid.

322 "The Soviet military authorities": William Standley, msg. No. 121, April 22, 1942, ibid.

322 "The crew": George Marshall to Franklin Roosevelt, "Interning of American Plane in Vladivostok," April 23, 1942, Box 55, RG 165, Records of the War Department General and Special Staffs, Office of the Director of Plans and Operations, NARA.

322 "It would appear desirable": George Marshall to U.S. Military Attaché, Moscow, April 23, 1942, Box 41, ibid.

322 "This might have been": William D. Leahy, *I Was There: The Personal Story of the Chief of Staff to Presidents Roosevelt and Truman Based on His Notes and Diaries Made at the Time* (New York: Whittlesey House/McGraw-Hill, 1950), p. 86.

322 "I have always been": Henry Stimson diary, April 18, 1942, Box 75, Series 5.2, GWPP.

323 "few earnest words": Henry Stimson diary, April 21, 1942, ibid.

323 "The United States government": "Stimson Warns of Raids on U.S.," *New York Times*, May 29, 1942, p. 1.

323 "Don't forget the payoff": "24-Hour Air Alert by Police Ordered," *New York Times*, April 20, 1942, p. 1.

323 Brooklyn held a massive: "Second Blackout Darkens Brooklyn," *New York Times*, April 22, 1942, p. 14.

323 Similar fears triggered: "3-Hour Alert on Coast," *New York Times*, April 20, 1942, p. 3.

323 "We drank a bottle": Lewis Brereton diary, April 18, 1942, in Brereton, *The Brereton Diaries*, p. 119.

323 "Tokyo bombed!": "At Our Enemy's Heart," editorial, *Washington Post*, April 19, 1942, p. B6.

323 "If we can do it once": "Remember Tokyo," editorial, *Pittsburgh Press*, April 20, 1942, p. 10.

323 "blow at the heart": "A Blow at Japan's Heart," editorial, *New York Times*, April 20, 1942, p. 20.

323 "For 2,600 years": Ibid.

324 "balm for the wounds": "Omens of Victory Seen in Attack; Output of Tanks Is Leading Axis," *Washington Post*, April 19, 1942, p. 1.

324 "consider this another installment": "The Voice of Vengeance over Japan," editorial, *Los Angeles Times*, April 19, 1942, p. A4.

324 "Encouraging as the news is": "Bombs on Tokyo," editorial, *Chicago Daily Tribune*, April 24, 1942, p. 12.

324 "Satisfaction felt": "Japan in the Jitters," editorial, *Daily Boston Globe*, April 20, 1942, p. 14.

CHAPER 19

325 "Don't forget, America": "Threat to Fliers," *New York Times*, April 23, 1943, p. 1.

325 Davy Jones and his men: David Jones diary, April 19–21, 1942, Box 3, Series II, DTRAP; Kenneth Reddy diary, April 20, 1942.

325 By the time Doolittle: John Hilger diary, April 18, 1942, in Hilger, "On the Raid," p. 100.

325 "It was like a homecoming": Ibid.

325 "Everywhere we went": Wildner, "The First of Many," p. 74.

326 "I am Danny Wang": Alan Burgess, *The Longest Tunnel: The True Story of World War II's Great Escape* (Annapolis, Md.: Naval Institute Press, 1990), p. 91.

326 "It was the kind": John Hilger diary, April 19, 1942, in Hilger, "On the Raid," p. 98.

326 "Signs of every known": Eugene McGurl diary, April 18, 1942, Box 3, Series XVI, DPUT.

326 "The Chinese pluck": George W. Cooper, "Capt. Clayton Campbell, Orofino Hero of Doolittle Raid on Tokyo, Tells of Varied Chinese Culture," *Lewiston Morning Tribune*, June 21, 1943, p. 2.

326 At Chuchow the Chinese: Greening, *Not As Briefed*, p. 43.

326 One of the pilots: "A Trip to Japan," *Time*, May 3, 1943, p. 30.

326 "These people are the most sincere": David Jones diary, April 25, 1942.

326 The Chinese had stripped: James Doolittle, "My Raid over Tokyo, April 1942," transcript of 1965 speech, Box 4, Series IV, DPUT.

327 "He had the worst cut": Joseph Manske diary, April 24, 1942.

327 Some of the fliers blamed: David Jones diary, April 25, 1942.

327 Fu Man Jones: Greening, *Not As Briefed*, p. 42.

327 lost seven dollars: David Jones diary, April 22, 1942.

327 "When we met up": Edward Kennedy, "Groceries Fall As U.S. Pilot Pulls Ripcord," *Calgary Herald*, April 22, 1943, p. 8.

327 "He was so tired": "Details of Individual Adventures in China: For Possible Use of Bureau of Public Relations," undated.

327 "We called our home": Kenneth Reddy diary, April 21, 1942.

327 "It's a crime": William Bower diary, April 21, 1942.

327 "Frequently, bodies": Greening, *Not As Briefed*, p. 43.

328 "The rails don't click": William Bower diary, April 26, 1942.

328 "Ham and eggs": Ibid.

328 "The courtyard outside": John Hilger diary, April 29, 1942, in Glines, *Doolittle's Tokyo Raiders*, pp. 274–75.

328 "I got my first Chinese shave": Kenneth Reddy diary, April 26, 1942.

328 "I rode a Japanese horse": Ibid., April 29, 1942.

328 "When it flew over": Ibid.

329 Perched atop a promontory: Details on life in Chungking come from the following sources: Dorn, *Walkout*, p. 32; Diana Lary, *The Chinese People at War: Human Suffering and Social Transformation, 1937–1945* (New York: Cambridge University Press, 2010), p. 87.

329 "There was no escape": LaVonne Telshaw Camp, *Lingering Fever: A World War II Nurse's Memoir* (Jefferson, N.C.: McFarland, 1997), p. 99.

329 "distinguish between": Henry R. Luce, "China to the Mountains," *Life*, June 30, 1941, p. 84.

329 The Japanese had launched: Lloyd E. Eastman, "Nationalist China during the Sino-Japanese War, 1937–1945," in Denis Twitchett and John K. Fairbank, eds., *The Cambridge History of China*, vol. 13, *Republican China, 1912–1949*, pt. 2 (Cambridge: Cambridge University Press, 1986), p. 567; Lary, *The Chinese People at War*, p. 87.

329 The single most savage: Lary, *The Chinese People at War*, p. 87.

329 "The city of Chungking boiled": Robert B. Ekvall, "The Bombing of Chungking," *Asia*, Aug. 1939, p. 472.

329 named the most bombed: "Chungking: Free China's Much-Bombed Capital Fights On," *Life*, March 31, 1942, p. 93; "Chungking," *Daily News*, Aug. 18, 1941, p. 5.

329 Bombs and fires: Dorn, *Walkout*, p. 32; "Chungking: Bravest City in the World," *Saturday Evening Post*, April 8, 1942, pp. 50–51.

329 Air-raid sirens screamed: "Chungking: Free China's Much-Bombed Capital Fights On," p. 93; "City of Caves," *Life*, March 31, 1942, p. 99.

329 "Downtown Chungking": Dorn, *Walkout*, pp. 35–36.

330 The raid against Tokyo: Harrison Forman, "Chinese Elated at Word of Raids on Japan," *New York Times*, April 19, 1942, p. 39; "Chinese Cheer News of Yanks' Raid on Jap Cities," *Washington Post*, April 19, 1942, p. 1; "Heard in Chungking," editorial, ibid., April 26, 1942, p. B6.

330 "The nightmare": Forman, "Chinese Elated at Word of Raids on Japan," p. 39.

330 "We have been waiting": "Chinese Cheer News of Yanks' Raid on Jap Cities," p. 1.

330 Doolittle's men disembarked: Greening, *Not As Briefed*, p. 44; Kenneth Reddy diary, April 29, 1942.

330 "We were all astounded": Kenneth Reddy diary, April 30, 1942.

330 "For a minute": William Bower diary, April 30, 1942.

330 "I couldn't breathe": Greening, *Not As Briefed*, p. 44.

330 The Chungking-based officers: Kenneth Reddy diary, April 30, 1942.

330 Engineer George Larkin: George Larkin diary, April 30, 1942.

331 "Started drinking wine": Eugene McGurl diary, April 30, 1942.

331 "His home was very lovely": Kenneth Reddy diary, May 1, 1942.

331 "I'll bet": William Bower diary, May 1, 1942.

331 Born in Shanghai: Hannah Pakula, *The Last Empress: Madame Chiang Kai-shek and the Birth of Modern China* (New York: Simon and Schuster, 2009), pp. 16–26; Seth Faison, "Madame Chiang Kai-shek, a Power in Husband's China and Abroad, Dies at 105," *New York Times*, Oct. 24, 2003, p. A15.

331 "Scarlett O'Hara accent": Pakula, *The Last Empress*, p. 24.

331 "a clever, brainy woman": Joseph Stilwell diary, April 1, 1942, in White, ed., *The Stilwell Papers*, p. 80.

331 "Direct, forceful, energetic": Ibid.

331 "The Madame": Kenneth Reddy diary, May 1, 1942.

332 "It was": Ibid.

332 "He entered the room": Greening, *Not As Briefed*, p. 45.

332 After lunch the raiders: Kenneth Reddy diary, May 1, 1942.

332 "In order to get": Ibid.

332 "I had a bit": Greening, *Not As Briefed*, p. 44.

332 "in a conspicuous place": Kenneth Reddy diary, May 1, 1942.

332 "This should make my girl": Ibid.

332 "The entire Chinese people": Madame Chiang Kai-shek to the Valiant American Airmen Who Bombed Japan, May 4, 1942, in Jim Dustin, "Bombardier on Doolittle's Plane Tells of Historic Flight over Tokio," *St. Petersburg Times*, June 4, 1944, p. 25.

333 "Praise be it": William Bower diary, May 1, 1942.

333 "almost as bad": Ibid., April 30, 1942.

333 Joseph Manske spent: Joseph Manske diary, April 30–May 2, 1942; Kenneth Reddy diary, April 30, 1942.

333 The first group of twenty: Greening, *Not As Briefed*, p. 45; David Jones diary, April 26, 1942; Chungking to AGWAR, May 4, 1942, Microfilm Roll #A1250, AFHRA.

333 Birch held a memorial: John M. Birch, Report on Death and Burial of Corporal Leland D. Faktor, United States Army Air Corps, included with Cooper, "The Doolittle Air Raid on Japan," June 22, 1942.

333 "Shall accept": John M. Birch, Report on Activities in Ch'u Hsien (Also Called Chuchow), Chekiang, undated, included ibid.

333 "On your truly wonderful": Henry Arnold to AMMISCA, Chungking, China, April 22, 1942, Microfilm Roll #173, HHAP.

333 "The President sends": George Marshall to Joseph Stilwell, No. 527, April

22, 1942, Box 51, RG 165, Records of the War Department General and Special Staffs, Office of the Director of Plans and Operations, NARA.

334 Doolittle had learned: Doolittle, *I Could Never Be So Lucky Again*, pp. 280–81.

334 "He offered me a swig": Ibid., p. 281.

334 "We're all as happy": John Hilger diary, May 3, 1942, in Hilger, "On the Raid," p. 100.

334 Doolittle later: J. H. Doolittle to Clayton L. Bissell, July 25, 1942, Box 5, Merian C. Cooper Papers, Harold B. Lee Library, Brigham Young University, Provo, Utah.

334 "My second in command": Doolittle, *I Could Never Be So Lucky Again*, p. 281.

334 "I realize you are": Richard Cole to his parents, May 4, 1942, Richard E. Cole Collection, Vernon R. Alden Library, Ohio University.

335 A forty-eight-year-old: Merian C. Cooper, State of Service and Bio, Official Military Personnel File, Iris #01155636, AFHRA; Merian Cooper to James Doolittle, April 7, 1971, Box 5, Merian C. Cooper Papers, Harold B. Lee Library, Brigham Young University; Dinitia Smith, "Getting That Monkey off His Creator's Back," *New York Times*, Aug. 13, 2005, p. B9.

335 "T. E. Lawrence of the movies": Smith, "Getting That Monkey off His Creator's Back," p. B9.

335 "I can remember you well": Merian Cooper to James Doolittle, April 7, 1971.

335 "It seems that I have done": John Hilger diary, May 5, 1942, in Glines, *Doolittle's Tokyo Raiders*, p. 278.

335 "Had it not been": J. H. Doolittle to Mrs. Merian C. Cooper, May 21, 1942, Box 5, Merian C. Cooper Papers, Harold B. Lee Library, Brigham Young University.

335 "I told you": Merian Cooper to James Doolittle, April 7, 1971.

336 "I had used gold coins": Ibid.

336 "I told him": Ibid.

336 "I was pretty broken up": Ibid.

336 Ted Lawson's condition: Unless otherwise noted, this scene is based on Lawson, *Thirty Seconds over Tokyo*, pp. 107–67; Ted Lawson, "Thirty Seconds over Tokyo," pt. 4, *Collier's*, June 12, 1943, pp. 40–44; Thomas White, "Memoirs of 'Doc' White," pp. 29–51; Thomas White diary, April 25–May 17, 1942, in White, "The *Hornet* Stings Japan," pp. 45–46; T. R. White to Air Surgeon, "Report of Activities Covering the Period from March 1, 1942, to June 16, 1942," June 23, 1942.

336 "I had no means": Thomas White, "Memoirs of 'Doc' White," p. 29.

337 "Installing the splint": Ibid.

337 The magistrate brought: Thomas White diary, April 26, 1942, in White, "The *Hornet* Stings Japan," p. 45; Charles L. McClure as told to William Shinnick, "How We Bombed Tokyo: Enemy Perils Flyers," *Chicago Daily Tribune*, May 5, 1943, p. 2.

337 "We all sent letters": Thomas White, "Memoirs of 'Doc' White," p. 30.

337 "Ted stopped breathing": Ibid.

337 White dressed his wounds: Thomas White diary, April 29, 1942, in White, "The *Hornet* Stings Japan," p. 45.

337 "Lawson no better": Thomas White diary, May 3, 1942, ibid.

337 White wired Chunking: Thomas White, "Memoirs of 'Doc' White," p. 31.

337 "By Monday Lawson": Ibid.

338 "Yeah": Lawson, *Thirty Seconds over Tokyo*, p. 113.

338 "Doc didn't ask me": Ibid.

338 "That's all I wanted to know": Ibid.

338 "Above the knee": Ibid., p. 114.

338 "If I did that": Ibid.

338 "We had to make our skin incision": Thomas White, "Memoirs of 'Doc' White," p. 31.

338 "I couldn't see any blood": Lawson, *Thirty Seconds over Tokyo*, p. 115.

339 "Doc stepped away": Ted Lawson, "Thirty Seconds over Tokyo," pt. 4, p. 41.

339 "Just a few more now": Lawson, *Thirty Seconds over Tokyo*, p. 116.

339 "Just one more": Ibid.

339 "The next day": Thomas White, "Memoirs of 'Doc' White," p. 32.

340 "It was screwy": Lawson, *Thirty Seconds over Tokyo*, p. 117.

340 "He is very sick": Charles L. McClure as told to William Shinnick, "How We Bombed Tokyo: Raiders Turn to Bible," *Chicago Daily Tribune*, May 3, 1943, p. 3.

340 "We were all solemn": Ibid.

340 "Lawson's temperature normal": Thomas White diary, May 11, 1942, in White, "The *Hornet* Stings Japan," p. 46.

340 "Had three more dentistry patients": Thomas White diary, May 9, 1942, ibid.

340 "A keepsake to the officers": Thomas White, "Memoirs of 'Doc' White," p. 35.

340 "Whatever people can say": Thomas White diary, May 17, 1942, in White, "The *Hornet* Stings Japan," p. 46.

341 "We whooped and yelled": Charles L. McClure as told to William Shinnick, "How We Bombed Tokyo: Fliers Cheer for Navy," *Chicago Daily Tribune*, May 4, 1943, p. 3.

341 "It looked like white rubber": McClure as told to Shinnick, "How We Bombed Tokyo: Enemy Perils Flyers," p. 2.

341 "News not so good": Thomas White diary, May 17, 1942, in White, "The *Hornet* Stings Japan," p. 46.

341 "I want to show you": Lawson, *Thirty Seconds over Tokyo*, p. 125.

341 "It was a new one": Ibid.

341 "We crossed the pontoon bridge": Thomas White, "Memoirs of 'Doc' White," pp. 36–37.

341 "Many of the hills": Ibid., p. 37.

342 "En route Chushien": Ibid.

342 "The spirit and pluck": Ibid., p. 38.

342 "See you in Chungking": Lawson, *Thirty Seconds over Tokyo*, pp. 127–28.

342 "It seemed to me": Ibid., p. 128.

342 "Welcome to American Air Heroes": Thomas White, "Memoirs of 'Doc' White," p. 39.

342 "Shift him into high-blower!": Ibid., pp. 39–40.

342 "It's no use": Ibid.

342 "One had evidently": Thomas White, "Memoirs of 'Doc' White," pp. 40–41.

342 "Every time we'd hit a bump": Lawson, *Thirty Seconds over Tokyo*, p. 132.

342 "It was a real luxury": Thomas White, "Memoirs of 'Doc' White," p. 41.

343 "Japanese too close": Lawson, *Thirty Seconds over Tokyo*, p. 132.

343 "The bus's brakes": Ibid., p. 133.

343 "It must be some sort": Ibid., p. 135.

343 "It was my leg": Ibid., p. 136.

343 "We had talked of little else": Ibid., p. 137.

343 "All of us were welted": Ibid.

343 "It was his first crack": Thomas White, "Memoirs of 'Doc' White," pp. 43–44.

344 "There was no plane": Lawson, *Thirty Seconds over Tokyo*, p. 140.

344 "It was a battle": Thomas White, "Memoirs of 'Doc' White," p. 148.

344 "I knew I'd start crying": Lawson, *Thirty Seconds over Tokyo*, p. 146.

CHAPTER 20

345 "I was beaten": George Barr, "Badger 'Doolittle' Flier Tortured by Japs Pleads for Foe," *Milwaukee Sentinel*, May 12, 1946, p. 13.

345 The plane carrying: Unless otherwise noted this scene is drawn from the following sources: C. Jay Nielsen, "Doolittle Fliers' Saga of Living Death: Japanese Vainly Attempt to Gain More Information," *News and Courier*, Sept. 20, 1945, p. 9; Chase J. Nielsen, Robert L. Hite, and Jacob D. DeShazer testimonies in the case of *United States of America vs. Shigeru Sawada et al.* All dialogue is from the *News and Courier* article.

345 "The gendarmerie is the worst": Intelligence Report, Sept. 12, 1942, "Description of Conditions at Bridge House, Shanghai; Character Sketch of the Japanese Gendarmie," Box 9, RG 24, Records of the Bureau of Naval Personnel, Casualty Branch, NARA.

347 "We didn't get the brutal treatment": Nielsen, "Doolittle Fliers' Saga of Living Death: Japanese Vainly Attempt," p. 9.

347 "The first two weeks": Hite oral history interview with Hasdorff, Dec. 16–17, 1982.

347 "Japanese method scientee-fic": George Barr, "Rough Draft of a Story by Capt. George Barr, Pertinent to the Trials in Shanghai of Those Japanese Officials Held Responsible for Execution of Three Doolittle Fliers Who Participated in the Raid on Tokyo," March 30, 1946, Box 20, DPLOC.

347 one such hit: Barr, "Badger 'Doolittle' Flier Tortured by Japs Pleads for Foe," p. 13.

347 "Hose don't make marks": Nielsen oral history interview with Erickson, July 11, 2000.

347 "Well": Ibid.

347 "Is it chance": Barr, "Rough Draft of a Story by Capt. George Barr."

347 "You were the bombardier": DeShazer's exchanges with the Japanese interrogators come from DeShazer oral history interview with Hasdorff, Oct. 10, 1989.

348 "Sanitation facilities": Nielsen, "Doolittle Fliers' Saga of Living Death: Japanese Vainly Attempt," p. 9.

348 "Nothing is the hardest": Ibid.

348 "We had just come": Hite oral history interview with Hasdorff, Dec. 16–17, 1982.

348 "You can't smoke": Nielsen, "Doolittle Fliers' Saga of Living Death: Japanese Vainly Attempt," p. 9.

348 "What's a *Hornet?*": Chase Nielsen oral history interview with Winston P. Erickson, July 11, 2000.

349 "We confessed": Chase J. Nielsen testimony in the case of *United States of America vs. Shigeru Sawada et al.*

350 "What were your feelings": All excerpts, with the exception of some of Farrow's, are from Nakamura Akihito, Commander of Gendarmerie, to Gen. Hajime Sugiyama, C of S, Gendarmerie 3, Special Secret Service Report #352, May 26 1942, in the case of *United States of America vs. Shigeru Sawada et al.* Portions of Farrow's excerpts, because of the deterioration of the original document on file in the NARA, are drawn from Glines, *Four Came Home*, p. 88.

351 ambassador to Russia: William H. Standley and Arthur A. Ageton, *Admiral Ambassador to Russia* (Chicago: Henry Regnery, 1955), pp. 221–24.

352 A four-star admiral: "Adm. William H. Standley Dies," *New York Times*, Oct. 26, 1963, p. 27.

352 "Of course, Mr. Ambassador": Standley and Ageton, *Admiral Ambassador to Russia*, p. 222.

352 "no annoyance": William Standley to Cordell Hull, April 24, 1942, in U.S. Department of State, *Foreign Relations of the United States: Diplomatic Papers, 1942*, vol. 3, *Europe* (Washington, D.C.: GPO, 1961), p. 548.

352 "regretted": Ibid.

352 "What would happen": This exchange comes from Standley and Ageton, *Admiral Ambassador to Russia*, pp. 222–23.

352 "Look, fellows": Ibid., p. 223.

353 "wholly unintentional": William Standley to Cordell Hull, April 26, 1942, in U.S. Department of State, *Foreign Relations of the United States: Diplomatic Papers, 1942*, vol. 3, p. 548.

353 "After thanking me": Ibid., pp. 548–49.

353 Standley followed up: U.S. Department of State, *Foreign Relations of the United States: Diplomatic Papers, 1942*, vol. 3, p. 550.

353 "stating in effect": Ibid.

353 "Of course, information": Cordell Hull to William Standley, May 2, 1942, in U.S. Department of State, *Foreign Relations of the United States: Diplomatic Papers, 1942*, vol. 3, pp. 550–51.

353 "If the Soviet merely intern": War Department, Office of Assistant Chief of Staff, G-2, May 3, 1942, "Magic Summary," in *The Magic Documents*, Microfilm Roll #1.

354 "merely intern the planes": War Department, Office of Assistant Chief of Staff, G-2, May 13, 1942, ibid.

354 "endeavor to avoid": War Department, Office of Assistant Chief of Staff, G-2, May 3, 1942, ibid.

354 "Whatever steps": War Department, Office of Assistant Chief of Staff, G-2, May 16, 1942, ibid.

354 "If the United States sees": War Department, Office of Assistant Chief of Staff, G-2, May 19, 1942, ibid.

354 "Since the other planes": Ibid.

354 "I advise that we discard": War Department, Office of Assistant Chief of Staff, G-2, May 20, 1942, ibid.

354 Guards at the dacha: Background on York and his crew comes from Emmens, *Guests of the Kremlin*, pp. 59–72; Emmens oral history interview with Hasdorff, July 8–9, 1982; York oral history interview with Hasdorff, July 23, 1984; "Interview with B-25 Crew That Bombed Tokyo and Was Interned by the Russians," transcript, June 3, 1943; Pohl as told to Dwiggins, "We Crash Landed in Russia—and Escaped," pp. 56–57.

355 "It didn't take us long": Emmens oral history interview with Hasdorff, July 8–9, 1982.

355 "The children": Emmens, *Guests of the Kremlin*, p. 63.

355 "One of the children": Ibid., pp. 63–64.

355 "I think your people": Ibid., p. 66.

356 "We shined our brass": Ibid., p. 67.

356 "Not one word": Emmens oral history interview with Hasdorff, July 8–9, 1982.

356 "The same sad": Emmens, *Guests of the Kremlin*, p. 70.

356 "Well, here we are!" This exchange is ibid., p. 72.

CHAPTER 21

357 "As parents of one":, Mr. and Mrs. E. H. Miller telegram to James H. Doolittle, May 20, 1942, Box 22, DPLOC.

357 Doolittle arrived back: Doolittle, *I Could Never Be So Lucky Again*, pp. 283–88.

358 "With the 15 planes": H. H. Arnold to Franklin Roosevelt, Raid on Tokyo, May 3, 1942, Microfilm Roll #A1250, AFHRA.

358 "Jim": This exchange comes from Doolittle, *I Could Never Be So Lucky Again*, p. 287.

358 "was successful far beyond": George Marshall to William Harm, Nov. 4,

1942, in Larry I. Bland, ed., *The Papers of George Catlett Marshall*, vol. 3, *"The Right Man for the Job," December 7, 1941–May 31, 1943* (Baltimore, Md.: Johns Hopkins University Press, 1991), p. 425.

358 "It will be necessary": Memorandum for General Arnold, May 12, 1942, ibid. p. 197.

358 "General, that award": This exchange comes from Doolittle, *I Could Never Be So Lucky Again*, p. 287.

358 "This was the only time": Ibid.

359 The officers arrived: Details of the Medal of Honor ceremony are drawn from the following sources: Doolittle, *I Could Never Be So Lucky Again*, pp. 287–88; W. H. Lawrence, "Airman Decorated," *New York Times*, May 20, 1942, p. 1; "Tells How U.S. Bombed Japan without a Loss," *Chicago Daily Tribune*, May 20, 1942, p. 1; "Raid Leader's Success No Surprise to His Wife," *New York Times*, May 22, 1942, p. 25.

359 "Brigadier General James H. Doolittle": W. H. Lawrence, "Airman Decorated," *New York Times*, May 20, 1942, p. 1.

359 The War Department handed: Press Release, "Congressional Medal of Honor Awarded to Leader of Tokyo Raid," May 19, 1942, Box 22, DPLOC; Press Release, "Statement by Brigadier General James H. Doolittle Regarding Bombing Raid Led by Him on Japan," May 19, 1942, Box 23, DPLOC.

359 "No group of men": Press Release, "Radio Talk by Brigadier General James H. Doolittle," May 20, 1942, Box 1, Series XI, DTRAP.

360 "We flew low enough": This exchange comes from Lawrence, "Airman Decorated," p. 1.

360 "I was able to run away": Ibid.

360 "Are you going": This exchange comes from "N.E. Men in Tokio Raid," *Daily Boston Globe*, May 20, 1942, p. 1.

360 "Why": "Shock from Tokyo," *Newsweek*, May 3, 1943, p. 22.

360 "No planes were left in Japan": John G. Norris, "Bombs Dropped within Sight of Imperial Palace, Hero Discloses," *Washington Post*, May 20, 1942, p. 1.

360 "The Japanese do not have": Richard L. Turner, "Leader of Recent Air Raid on Japan Revealed at White House Medal Presentation," *Schenectady Gazette*, May 20, 1942, p. 1.

360 "I'm too thrilled to speak": Ibid.

360 "Doolittle emphasized": "Tells How U.S. Bombed Japan without a Loss," *Chicago Daily Tribune*, May 20, 1942, p. 1.

361 "His Life Story": Bob Considine, "His Life Story Reads like a Thriller, but with Perfect Timing," *Washington Post*, May 20, 1942, p. 1.

361 "Jimmy Doolittle is a man": "Much Done by Doolittle," *Sun*, May 20, 1942, p. 4.

361 "He should be named": This is quoted in "Jimmy Did It," *Time*, June 1, 1942, p. 17.

361 "Jimmy did it": Ibid.

361 "This was a test": "The Raid on Japan," editorial, *New York Times*, May 20, 1942, p. 18.

361 "The bombing of Tokio": "The Man from Nowhere," editorial, *Chicago Daily Tribune*, May 21, 1942, p. 12.

362 "I'm pretty cocky": "Jimmy Did It," *Time*, June 1, 1942, p. 17.

362 "Yippee!": Ibid.

362 "I think you should have gone": Mrs. T. J. Dykema to Franklin Roosevelt, May 29, 1942, OF 5510, FDRL.

362 "Give us more Doolittles": James N. Jordan to Franklin Roosevelt, May 29, 1942, ibid.

362 "We only know": Marty Moore to James Doolittle, May 21, 1942, Box 64, Series IX, DPUT.

362 "It is glorious news": Herb Maxson to Joe Doolittle, May 19, 1942, ibid.

362 "*So* your Jimmie": Maude T. Howell to Joe Doolittle, May 21, 1942, ibid.

362 "Among the scores": Mrs. Archie R. Potter to Joe Doolittle, May 25, 1942, ibid.

362 "I hated to dump": William Halsey to James Doolittle, April 24, 1942, in "Official Papers of Fleet Admiral Ernest J. King" (Wilmington, Del.: Scholarly Resources, 1991), Microfilm Roll #2.

362 "You have struck": Ibid.

363 "Congratulations, you dog!": Roscoe Turner telegram to James Doolittle, in Doolittle, *I Could Never Be So Lucky Again*, p. 292.

363 "The day the bombs fell": Roscoe Turner to Joe Doolittle, June 2, 1942, Box 64, Series IX, DPUT.

363 Doolittle sat down: This scene is based on a review of all the letters Doolittle sent to the families of the raiders in May 1942, which are on file with his papers at the LOC. Only those I quote from are cited below.

363 "I am pleased to report": J. H. Doolittle to Mrs. Fred Cole, May 20, 1942, Box 21, DPLOC.

364 "Under separate cover": J. H. Doolittle to Virginia Hilger, May 20, 1942, ibid.

364 "It is with the deepest regret": J. H. Doolittle to Mr. Edward Ginkle, May 21, 1942, ibid.

364 "The latest news": J. H. Doolittle to Jessie Farrow, May 22, 1942, ibid.

365 "I am extremely sorry": J. H. Doolittle to Ollie D. Hallmark, May 21, 1942, ibid.

365 "All of the plane's crew": J. H. Doolittle to Mrs. Joseph H. Thatcher, May 21, 1942, ibid.

365 "I doubt if the rules": H. D. Watson to Ray Tucker, Nov. 2, 1942, Box 22, DPLOC.

365 "I can't express in words": Thelma Bourgeois to James Doolittle, May 27, 1942, ibid.

365 "I am hoping to get married": Virginia Harmon to James Doolittle, May 30, 1942, ibid.

366 "Robert is mighty proud": Marvin and Della Gray to James Doolittle, June 4, 1942, ibid.

366 "Your leadership inspired": Florence Fisk White telegram to James Doolittle, June 28, 1942, ibid.

366 "My heart grieves": Mrs. Floyd Nielsen to Franklin Roosevelt, June 1, 1942, ibid.

366 "I just pray God": Mrs. R. P. Hite to James Doolittle, May 27, 1942, ibid.

366 "Your kindness": J. H. Doolittle to Mrs. J. T. Dieter, July 3, 1942, ibid.

367 "If it is His purpose": Jessie Farrow to James Doolittle, May 24, 1942, ibid.

367 "To All Officers and Men: J. H. Doolittle to All Officers and Men with me at Shangri-La, June 15, 1942, Box 23, DPLOC.

367 "You will grant": Ibid.

367 Army Air Forces officials initially: Sherman Atlick to A. D. Surles, Reception for General Doolittle Crewmen, June 15, 1942, ibid.

367 More than two dozen raiders: Peters, "Japan Bombed with 20-Cent Sight," p. 1.

367 "These officers and enlisted men": Citation for Distinguished Flying Cross, undated but with handwritten notes about presentation, Box 22, DPLOC; Scott Hart, "Airmen Tell Reactions in Daring Raid," *Washington Post*, June 28, 1942, p. 1.

368 "Don't cry, honey": "Tokyo Raiders' Wives Thrilled," *Los Angeles Times*, June 28, 1942, p. 5.

368 "When I heard": Ibid.

368 "Something like a picnic": Hart, "Airmen Tell Reactions in Daring Raid," p. 1.

368 "No information should": Edgar F. G. Swasey to Major Weeks, Security Policy in Connection with the Handling of Publicity on Returning Tokyo Bombers, June 12, 1942, Box 1, Series XI, DTRAP.

368 "You fellows use": H. H. Arnold to Colonels Cabell and Norstad, May 18, 1942, "Additional Bombing Raids over Japan," Microfilm Roll #201, HHAP.

368 He recommended that Hilger: J. H. Doolittle letters to Commanding General, Army Air Forces, Distinguished Service Crosses, or Distinguished Service Medals, May 19, 1942 (this citation includes four letters, one each for Hilger, Greening, Hoover, and Jones), Box 22, DPLOC.

368 The Army ultimately: J. A. Ulio letters to James H. Doolittle, July 6, 1942 (this citation includes four letters, one each for Hilger, Greening, Hoover, and Jones), Box 22, DPLOC; Max B. Boyd letters to David J. Thatcher, T. R. White, and Dean Davenport, July 1, 1942, ibid.

369 "Beyond the limits": "For Public Relations Branch: When, As, and If War Department Thinks Proper," June 12, 1942.

369 Doolittle likewise recommended: J. H. Doolittle to Commanding General, Army Air Forces, Promotions, May 19, 1942, and J. H. Doolittle to Commanding General, Army Air Forces, Promotions, May 20, 1942, both in Box 23, DPLOC.

369 "The crew of the airplane": J. H. Doolittle to Commanding General, Army Air Forces, Promotions, May 19, 1942, ibid.

369 The plane carrying Ted Lawson: This scene is based on Lawson, *Thirty Seconds over Tokyo*, pp. 167–72.

369 "I tried to stand up": Ibid., p. 168.

369 "How about the family situation": This exchange is ibid., pp. 168–69.

370 "Well, what do you think": Roger H. Aylworth, "No Secrets: Chico Pilot's Wife Knew about 1942 Doolittle Raid," *Enterprise Record*, April 14, 2002, p. 1.

370 "He is in good health": James Doolittle to Ellen Lawson, June 17, 1942, Box 22, DPLOC.

370 "I'm glad to know": Lawson, *Thirty Seconds over Tokyo*, p. 170.

370 "I jumped up": Ibid., p. 172.

371 "He's still got some of that beach": Ibid., p. 173.

371 McClure likewise: Charles L. McClure as told to William Shinnick, "How We Bombed Tokio: Heroic Odyssey Ended," *Chicago Daily Tribune*, May 6, 1943, p. 7; "Lt. C.L. McClure, Doolittle Tokyo Flier, Weds Miss Jean Buchanan after Hospital Romance," *New York Times*, Feb. 2, 1943, p. 24.

371 chief of the Army: "6 Army Fliers Decorated," *New York Times*, July 7, 1942, p. 5.

371 "were injured in an airplane crash": "3 Raiders of Tokyo Get Chinese Honor," *New York Times*, July 26, 1942, p. 9.

371 "You have exploded the myth": Ibid.

371 shipping a box of cigars: "File Gen. Doolittle under 'Gifts' with cross-file on J. H. Patton," Aug. 30, 1942, with Parachute Inspection and Drop Test Card, Box 21, DPLOC.

371 He requested that: J. H. Doolittle to Officers and Men Who Raided Japan and Are Now in U.S., Request for Information Regarding Chinese Who Gave You Assistance, July 30, 1942, Box 22, DPLOC.

371 Harold Watson suggested: Harold F. Watson, undated statement, and David J. Thatcher to J. H. Doolittle, Aug. 12, 1942, both ibid.

371 "Neither man would take": Thomas R. White statement in Charles W. Glanz to Assistant Chief of Staff, A-1, Dec. 3, 1942, "Recommendations for Decoration of Chinese Nationals Who Aided Special Project No. 1," ibid.

372 Pilot Bill Bower: H. W. Maxson to William Bower, July 24, 1942, ibid.

372 navigator Tom Griffin: F. M. Young to James H. Doolittle, July 23, 1942, ibid.

372 Pilots Griffith Williams and Ken Reddy: Steadham Acker to Henry H. Arnold, Aug. 10, 1942, ibid.

372 engineer Jacob Eierman on his tour: Alex Smith to James H. Doolittle, Aug. 3, 1942, ibid.

372 "Even though Ross": Will J. Conner to J. H. Doolittle, July 21, 1942, ibid.

372 "Jap planes couldn't": "Doolittle Praises Men Who Built Wright Engines," *Wall Street Journal*, May 23, 1942, p. 4.

372 "Through those radios": James H. Doolittle telegram to the Employees of Western Electric Co., May 21, 1942, Box 22, DPLOC.

372 Doolittle stopped by: "Doolittle Reveals Shangri-La Location," *Reading Eagle*, June 2, 1942, p. 20; "Doolittle Hails B-25," *New York Times*, June 2, 1942, p. 2.

372 "Don't tell a soul": James Doolittle, transcript of speech, June 1, 1942, Box 23, DPLOC.

372 "He not only made": J. H. Kindelberger to Mrs. J. H. Doolittle, June 4, 1942, Box 64, Series IX, DPUT.

373 a mission so dramatic: Howard Hawks to H. H. Arnold, March 22, 1943, and Jack L. Warner to H. H. Arnold, April 23, 1943, both on Microfilm Roll #165, HHAP.

373 "the plain, honest American face": "The Man from Nowhere," editorial, *Chicago Daily Tribune*, May 21, 1942, p. 12.

373 The Rotary Club: J. H. Doolittle to Louis L. Roth, March 15, 1943, Box 19, DPLOC.

373 San Diego Consistory: James K. Remick to Josephine Doolittle, July 30, 1943, and J. H. Doolittle to James K. Remick, Aug. 31, 1943, both ibid.

373 The Dayton district commissioner: Al Kolleda to James Doolittle, Nov. 6, 1943, and James Doolittle to Al Kolleda, Dec. 3, 1943, both ibid.

373 Fan mail arrived: Samples of the mail Doolittle received are on file in Box 19 of his papers at the Library of Congress and in Box 64, Series IX, of his papers at the University of Texas.

373 An Oklahoma woman: Mrs. Homer L. Piper to James Doolittle, Oct. 11, 1943, Box 2, Series I, DPUT.

373 Total strangers wrote: John Mitseff to James Doolittle, Aug. 19, 1943, with "The World Will Be Free," Box 19, DPLOC.

373 "There is a man": Patsy Browning, May 1942, untitled poem, Box 3, Series VII, DPUT.

373 "Doolittle did plenty": Tony Mele, undated poem, Box 19, DPLOC.

374 "My son gets in a fight": Everett Hastings to James Doolittle, June 28, 1943, ibid.

374 Doolittle's fame grew so much: George A. Schneider to James Doolittle, Sept. 18, 1943, ibid.

374 A newly incorporated: "Doolittle Honors General Doolittle," *Windsor Daily Star*, Oct. 12, 1946, p. 2.

374 "We may not be big": James Doolittle, transcript of speech, Oct. 11, 1946, Box 7, Series IV, DPUT.

374 "I deeply appreciate": Ibid.

CHAPTER 22

375 "One cannot imagine": Louis Bereswill to sister and niece, Jan. 29, 1943, Box 1, Louis Bereswill Personnel Files, DeAndreis-Rosati Memorial Archives (DRMA), Special Collections and Archives Department, DePaul University Library, Chicago, Ill.

375 Japanese leaders fumed: Headquarters, USAFFE and Eighth U.S. Army (Rear), "Army Operations in China: December 1941–December 1943," Japanese Monograph #71, pp. 78–127.

375 "The primary mission": Ibid., p. 85.

376 "The captured areas": Ibid., p. 86.

376 "When the Japs come": "Fr. Vandenberg, C.M., Tells Story of Journey," *De Andrein* 13, no. 7 (April 1943): 3.

376 American priest: "Priest Here Saw Japs Ravage, Burn, Kill after Doolittle's Raid," *Milwaukee Journal*, May 26, 1943, p. 1L; "The March of Time," May 27, 1943, NBC, recorded from the broadcast of KDKA, Pittsburgh, J. David Goldin Collection; Affidavit of Wendelin Dunker, Dec. 1, 1966, Box 2, Vincentian Foreign Mission Society Files, DRMA.

376 "They came to us on foot": "The March of Time," May 27, 1943.

376 The arrival of the raiders: "Priest Here Saw Japs Ravage, Burn, Kill after Doolittle's Raid," p. 1L; "The March of Time," May 27, 1943; Wendelin J. Dunker, "The Life of Wendelin Joseph Dunker, C.M. and the Continuation of Life Experiences While Stationed in China," unpublished memoir, pp. 21–22; "Fr. Vandenberg, C.M., Tells Story of Journey," p. 3.

377 "Where are the Americans?": "Priest Here Saw Japs Ravage, Burn, Kill after Doolittle's Raid," p. 1L.

377 "Come on!": "The March of Time," May 27, 1943.

377 "It was a mad screaming": Ibid.

377 "Ihwang was in the mountains": Dunker, "The Life of Wendelin Joseph Dunker," p. 21.

378 "The Japs are here": Ibid., p. 24.

378 "Was out the back gate": Wendelin Dunker to parents, Aug. 18, 1942, Box 2, Wendelin Dunker Personnel Files, DRMA.

378 "We thought we were fast": Ibid.

378 "Believe me": Wendelin Dunker to John O'Shea, July 23, 1942, Box 1a, Wendelin Dunker Personnel Files, DRMA.

378 "Bullets whistled over": "The March of Time," May 27, 1943.

378 "When we stopped": Wendelin Dunker to John O'Shea, July 23, 1942.

378 "The more I thought": Dunker, "The Life of Wendelin Joseph Dunker," p. 27.

378 "The Lord was with us": Wendelin Dunker to John O'Shea, July 23, 1942.

378 "When I entered": Dunker, "The Life of Wendelin Joseph Dunker," p. 28.

379 "in body if not in mind": Wendelin Dunker to John O'Shea, July 23, 1942.

379 "I had to ride": Wendelin Dunker to parents, Aug. 18, 1942.

379 "It was half way up": Dunker, "The Life of Wendelin Joseph Dunker," p. 30.

379 "We found a package": "Bishop Tells of Jap Torture in Wake of Doolittle Raid," *Chicago Sun*, Sept. 26, 1943, in Box 1, Charles Quinn Personnel Files, DRMA.

380 "With haste we moved": William C. Stein photo commentary, May 3, 1995, Box 1, William Stein Personnel Files, DRMA.

380 "Bill, what are we to do?": Ibid.

380 "Under the tutorage": Ibid.

380 "All of us lost": Ibid.

380 "What a scene": Dunker, "The Life of Wendelin Joseph Dunker," pp. 32–33.

381 "They shot any man": Ibid., pp. 31–32.

381 "Things were dumped": Wendelin Dunker to John O'Shea, July 23, 1942.

381 "If you are unfortunate": Ibid.

381 "The sight": "Bishop Tells of Jap Torture in Wake of Doolittle Raid."

381 "Death came in horrible": Clancy M'Quigg, "Japs Execute 250,000 Chinese over Tokyo Raid," *Chicago Herald-American*, in Box 1, Vincent Smith Personnel Files, DRMA.

381 "Jap soldiers": William Charles Quinn, "Bishop Tells More Japanese Atrocities," *Chicago Herald-American*, in Box 1, Charles Quinn Personnel Files, DRMA.

382 Quinn returned: William C. Quinn, "Damage in the Vicariate of Yukiang during the Japanese Occupation in 1942," March 31, 1947, Box 2, Vincentian Foreign Mission Society Files, DRMA; Affidavit of Wendelin Dunker, Dec. 1, 1966, ibid.; Hazel MacDonald, "China Bishop Here Tells Jap Horrors," *Chicago Times*, Sept. 26, 1943, in Box 1, Charles Quinn Personnel Files, DRMA.

382 "In a pond": M'Quigg, "Japs Execute 250,000 Chinese over Tokyo Raid."

382 The Japanese had bayoneted: MacDonald, "China Bishop Here Tells Jap Horrors."

382 "human candles": Charles L. Meeus, "'God Will Punish Them': Aftermath of Doolittle's Tokio Raid—II," *China at War* 12, no. 3 (March 1944): 33.

382 "The total number": Quinn, "Damage in the Vicariate of Yukiang during the Japanese Occupation in 1942."

382 The walled city of Nancheng: "Japan's Chekiang-Kiangsi Campaign in 1942, as Reported in the Chinese Press," Sept. 6, 1943, Box 495, RG 226, Office of Strategic Services, Intelligence Reports, 1941–45, NARA.

382 "the Rape of Nancheng": Frederick A. McGuire, "Fire and Sword in Eastern Kiangsi: Aftermath of Doolittle's Tokyo Raid—I," *China at War* 12, no. 2 (Feb. 1944): 27.

382 "For one month": Ibid., p. 28.

382 At the end: Charles H. Corbett, "A Case Study in Japanese Devastation: Chekiang and Kiangsi in August, 1942," Sept. 1943, United States Preparatory Studies on United Nations Relief and Rehabilitation Administration, Box 960, RG 169, Records of the Economic Intelligence Division, NARA; "Japan's Chekiang-Kiangsi Campaign in 1942, as Reported in the Chinese Press," Sept. 6, 1943; McGuire, "Fire and Sword in Eastern Kiangsi," pp. 27–29; Wilfred G. Burchett, *Democracy with a Tommygun* (Melbourne, Australia: F. W. Cheshire, 1946), pp. 66–67.

383 "Broken doors": "Japan's Chekiang-Kiangsi Campaign in 1942, as Reported in the Chinese Press," Sept. 6, 1943.

383 "bloody spear": Chennault, *Way of a Fighter*, p. 169.

383 Enemy forces looted: "Japan's Chekiang-Kiangsi Campaign in 1942, as Reported in the Chinese Press," Sept. 6, 1943; Corbett, "A Case Study in Japanese Devastation"; Burchett, *Democracy with a Tommygun*, pp. 63–64; Chennault, *Way of a Fighter*, p. 169.

383 "The thoroughness": "Japanese Invasion of China: Reminiscences," Box 1, China and Taiwan Missions Files, DRMA.

383 "Like a swarm": Dunker, "The Life of Wendelin Joseph Dunker," p. 32.

383 Outside of this punitive: "Japan's Chekiang-Kiangsi Campaign in 1942, as Reported in the Chinese Press," Sept. 6, 1943.

383 In Yintang: Meeus, "'God Will Punish Them,'" p. 32.

383 "They killed": Charles L. Meeus, "A Bridge between Free Peoples," *Reader's Digest*, May 1944, back cover.

383 In the town of Kweiyee: Meeus, "'God Will Punish Them,'" pp. 32–33.

384 "I cannot tell": M'Quigg, "Japs Execute 250,000 Chinese over Tokyo Raid."

384 "The whole countryside": "Japanese Vengeance Described by Priest," *New York Times*, May 26, 1943, p. 3.

384 Troops beat and starved: MacDonald, "China Bishop Here Tells Jap Horrors"; "Two Friends from Orient Meet in Chicago," *New World*, Oct. 1, 1943, in Box 1, Charles Quinn Personnel Files, DRMA.

384 "You want to go": "Two Friends from Orient Meet in Chicago."

384 The Japanese looted: Quinn, "Damage in the Vicariate of Yukiang during the Japanese Occupation in 1942."

384 "Christ is defeated": Meeus, "'God Will Punish Them,'" p. 33.

384 "It was a fearful sight": "The March of Time," May 27, 1943.

384 "bullet contest": Meeus, "'God Will Punish Them,'" p. 31.

384 The Japanese found: Ibid.

384 "Little did": Ibid.

385 The Japanese flew: Corbett, "A Case Study in Japanese Devastation."

385 "Out of twenty-eight": Ibid.

385 "Yushan was once": William Stein letter to family, Aug. 15, 1943, Box 1, William Stein Personnel File, DRMA.

385 A clandestine outfit: Background on Unit 731 comes from Peter Williams and David Wallace, *Unit 731: Japan's Secret Biological Warfare in World War II* (New York: Free Press, 1989), pp. 5–20; Sheldon H. Harris, *Factories of Death: Japanese Biological Warfare, 1932–45, and the American Cover-Up* (London: Routledge, 1994), pp. 13–48; Indictment and Speech by the State Prosecutor L. N. Smirnov, in *Materials on the Trial of Former Servicemen of the Japanese Army Charged with Manufacturing and Employing Bacteriological Weapons* (Moscow: Foreign Languages Publishing House, 1950), pp. 7–37, 405–66.

386 At full capacity: Testimonies of Kiyoshi Kawashima and Tomio Karasawa, in *Materials on the Trial of Former Servicemen of the Japanese Army*, pp. 56, 254, 267.

386 To test these awful germs: Testimonies of Takeo Tachibana and Satoru Kurakazu and the Speech by the State Prosecutor L. N. Smirnov, ibid, pp. 360–68, 426–37.

386 The Japanese often kept: Harris, *Factories of Death*, p. 50.

386 At Pingfan: Ibid., p. 48; Testimony of Kiyoshi Kawashima, in *Materials on the Trial of Former Servicemen of the Japanese Army*, pp. 56–57, 256–58.

386 As a macabre souvenir: Nicholas D. Kristof, "Japan Confronting Gruesome War Atrocity," *New York Times*, March 17, 1995, p. A1.

386 "No one": Testimony of Kiyoshi Kawashima, in *Materials on the Trial of Former Servicemen of the Japanese Army*, p. 116.

386 Experiments ran the gamut: Testimonies of Toshihide Nishi, Yoshio Furuichi,

Satoru Kurakazu, and the Speech by the State Prosecutor L. N. Smirnov, ibid., pp. 289–90, 357–58, 367–68, 426–37; Williams and Wallace, *Unit 731*, p. 49.

386 Researchers fed prisoners: Testimonies of Toshihide Nishi and Yoshio Furuichi, in *Materials on the Trial of Former Servicemen of the Japanese Army*, pp. 286, 356; Harris, *Factories of Death*, p. 62.

386 At other times: Testimonies of Tomio Karasawa and Toshihide Nishi, in *Materials on the Trial of Former Servicemen of the Japanese Army*, pp. 268–69, 289–90.

386 "The fellow knew": Kristof, "Japan Confronting Gruesome War Atrocity," p. A1.

386 Researchers struggled: Testimonies of Toshihide Nishi and Ryuji Kajitsuka, in *Materials on the Trial of Former Servicemen of the Japanese Army*, pp. 290, 298–99; Williams and Wallace, *Unit 731*, pp. 20–25.

386 Researchers at Unit 731: Testimony of Kiyoshi Kawashima and Finding of the Experts, in *Materials on the Trial of Former Servicemen of the Japanese Army*, pp. 255–56, 400–401.

387 Ishii tested those theories: Testimonies of Tomio Karasawa and Toshihide Nishi and the Speech by the State Prosecutor L. N. Smirnov, ibid., pp. 269–70, 287–88, 437–40; Chen Wen-Kuei, "Memorandum on Certain Aspects of Japanese Bacterial Warfare," in "Report of the International Scientific Commission for the Investigation of the Facts concerning Bacterial Warfare in Korea and China," Peking, 1952, p. 213.

387 After returning from Tokyo: Speech by the State Prosecutor L. N. Smirnov in *Materials on the Trial of Former Servicemen of the Japanese Army*, p. 441.

387 The plan was to target: Testimonies of Kiyoshi Kawashima, Tomio Karasawa, Yoshio Furuichi, Takayuki Mishina, and Speech by the State Prosecutor L. N. Smirnov, ibid., pp. 260–62, 270–71, 353–55, 386–89, 441–44.

388 "Those who returned": "Japan's Chekiang-Kiangsi Campaign in 1942, as Reported in the Chinese Press," Sept. 6, 1943.

388 "Everybody is sick": Ibid.

388 "She was perfectly right": Ibid.

388 "Belly ache": Ibid.

388 "We avoided staying": Burchett, *Democracy with a Tommygun*, p. 64.

388 In December 1942 Tokyo radio: "Chinese Cholera Epidemic Now Mammoth," Dec. 14, 1942, Document #JWC 42/11a, Box 2, RG 9999, IWG Reference Collection, Select Documents on Japanese War Crimes and Japanese Biological Warfare, 1934–2006, NARA; FCC Transcript, April 8, 1943, Document #JWC 42/11e, ibid.

388 "As a note": "Chinese Cholera Epidemic Now Mammoth."

388 "The losses suffered": Chen Wen-Kuei, "Memorandum on Certain Aspects of Japanese Bacterial Warfare," p. 215.

389 "Diseases were particularly": Headquarters, United States Army Forces, China Theater, Office of the A.C. of S, G-2, "Japanese Preparations for Bacteriological Warfare in China," Dec. 12, 1944, Document #JWC

314/12b, Box 12, RG 9999, IWG Reference Collection, Select Documents on Japanese War Crimes and Japanese Biological Warfare, 1934–2006, NARA.

389 "it being common practice": Ibid.

389 The three-month campaign: Burchett, *Democracy with a Tommygun*, pp. 71–72.

389 "After they had been caught": "Chiang Reveals Massacres as Tokyo Raid Reprisals," *New York Times*, April 29, 1943, p. 1.

389 "It was even worse": Joseph Stilwell diary, Oct. 6, 1942, in White, ed., *The Stilwell Papers*, p. 158.

389 "Entire villages": Chennault, *Way of a Fighter*, p. 169.

390 "The Japanese have chosen": "The Japanese in China," editorial, *New York Times*, May 28, 1943, p. 20.

390 "To say that these slayings": "New Japanese Outrages Call for Vengeance," editorial, *Los Angeles Times*, April 30, 1943, p. A4.

CHAPTER 23

391 "I went through ninety-two days": W. N. Dickson, statement, Aug. 31, 1945, Box 57, RG 226, Records of the Office of Strategic Services, Washington/ Pacific Coast/Field Station Files, NARA.

391 Ski York and his crew: Unless otherwise noted, details of York's crew's time in Russia are drawn from the following sources: Emmens, *Guests of the Kremlin*, pp. 73–114; Emmens oral history interview with Hasdorff, July 8–9, 1982; York oral history interview with Hasdorff, July 23, 1984; "Interview with B-25 Crew That Bombed Tokyo and Was Interned by the Russians," transcript, June 3, 1943; Pohl as told to Dwiggins, "We Crash Landed in Russia—and Escaped," p. 57.

391 "Most important of all": Emmens, *Guests of the Kremlin*, p. 74.

391 "We later learned": Ibid., p. 75.

392 "Always the thought": Ibid., p. 76.

392 "Now we would find": Ibid., p. 85.

392 "How long have you": This exchange is ibid., pp. 86–88.

393 "In the meantime": Emmens oral history interview with Hasdorff, July 8–9, 1982.

393 "Athletic facilities": William Standley to Cordell Hull, May 25, 1942, in U.S. Department of State, *Foreign Relations of the United States: Diplomatic Papers, 1942*, vol. 3, p. 563.

393 "We were completely shut": "Interview with B-25 Crew That Bombed Tokyo and Was Interned by the Russians," transcript, June 3, 1943.

394 "Food and cigarette": Emmens, *Guests of the Kremlin*, p. 104.

394 "Were there only": Ibid., p. 105.

394 "What do you think": This exchange is ibid.

394 "We are leaving": This exchange is ibid., pp. 113–14.

394 The Japanese pulled: C. Jay Nielsen, "Doolittle Fliers' Saga of Living Death: Meet Darlington Man on Train Ride to Prison," *News and Courier*, Sept.

21, 1945, p. 6; Chase J. Nielsen testimony in the case of *United States of America vs. Shigeru Sawada et al.*

395 "The coal soot": Watson, *DeShazer*, p. 42.

395 "dreaded 'Hell Hole'": James Brown, undated statement, Box 101, RG 153, Records of the Office of the Judge Advocate General (Army), War Crimes Branch, NARA.

395 the cream-colored Bridge House: Details of the Bridge House are drawn from the following sources: Tillman Durdin, "Shanghai Reveals Torture Secrets," *New York Times*, Sept. 18, 1945, p. 2; Lewis. S. Bishop, "Bridge House Jail, Shanghai," undated, Box 2121, RG 389, Records of the Office of the Provost Marshall General, American POW Information Bureau Records Branch, General Subject File, 1942–46, NARA; James L. Norwood and Emily L. Shek, "Prisoner of War Camps in Areas Other Than the Four Principal Islands of Japan," July 31, 1946, Box 33, RG 389, Office of the Provost Marshall General, Historical File, 1941–1958, NARA.

395 "the walls": Raymond C. Phillips, undated statement, "Mistreatment of Prisoners in Shanghai," Box 101, RG 153, Records of the Office of the Judge Advocate General (Army), War Crimes Branch, NARA.

395 "We all slept": Alfred P. Pattison, statement, Aug. 31, 1945, Box 57, RG 226, Records of the Office of Strategic Services, Washington/Pacific Coast/Field Station Files, NARA.

396 Prisoners broiled: Details of prisoner experiences are drawn in part of from a review of more than 100 pages of written statements of former Bridge House prisoners on file in Box 57, RG 226, Records of the Office of Strategic Services, Washington/Pacific Coast/Field Station Files, NARA. The statements I found particularly helpful included those of Henry Forsyth Pringle (Aug. 28, 1945), James Edgar (undated), William Slade Bungey (Aug. 28, 1945), Geoffrey Gordon Forestier (Aug. 31, 1945), Erskine Muton (Aug. 31, 1945), Kenneth William Johnstone (Aug. 30, 1945), and J. M. Watson (undated). Two additional folders containing another 200 pages of Bridge House prisoner statements and reports can be found in Box 101, RG 153, Records of the Office of the Judge Advocate General (Army), War Crimes Branch, NARA. Statements and reports of particular interest included those of Lewis Sherman Bishop (Aug. 7, 1945); Raymond C. Phillips (undated); War Department General Staff G-2, Military Intelligence Service, Ex-Report No. 669, July 12, 1945, Bishop, Lewis S.; Edwin Arthur Thompson (undated); Hazel N. Montilla (Oct. 20, 1945); Frederick George Jones (Oct. 7, 1945); Robert J. Reed (May 28, 1945); C.D. Smith (Feb. 26, 1945); Henry H. Comen (undated); and James Brown (undated). Other sources included the folder Bridge House Jail, Shanghai, China, in Box 2121, RG 389, Records of the Office of Provost Marshal General, American POW Information Bureau Records Branch, General Subject File, 1942–46, NARA; J. B. Powell, "Prisoner of the Japanese," *Nation*, Oct. 10, 1942, pp. 335–37; M. C. Ford, "Slow Death in a Jap Cage," *Collier's*, Sept. 5, 1942, pp. 14–15, 32.

396 "I had no idea": Henry H. Comen, undated statement, Box 101, RG 153,

Records of the Office of the Judge Advocate General (Army), War Crimes Branch, NARA.

396 "it is truly a hell on earth": Intelligence Report, "Description of Conditions at Bridge House, Shanghai; Character Sketch of the Japanese Gendarmie," Sept. 12, 1942, Box 9, RG 24, Records of the Bureau of Naval Personnel, Casualty Branch, NARA.

396 "The guards": S. W. Harris, statement, Aug. 30, 1945, Box 57, RG 226, Records of the Office of Strategic Services, Washington/Pacific Coast/Field Station Files, NARA.

396 "It isn't so bad": Tillman Durdin, "Shanghai Reveals Torture Secrets," *New York Times*, Sept. 18, 1945, p. 2.

396 "The torture chambers": William Slade Bungey, statement, Aug. 28, 1945.

396 "The screams": Henry H. Comen, undated statement.

396 "Are you a Christian?": Durdin, "Shanghai Reveals Torture Secrets," p. 2.

397 "I was seized": Henry Forsyth Pringle, statement, Aug. 28, 1945.

397 American journalist John Powell: Powell, "Prisoner of the Japanese," pp. 335–37; "Jap's Enemy No. 1," *Time*, Sept. 7, 1942, p. 65; "Jap's Victim Walks Again," *Time*, April 30, 1945, p. 69; John B. Powell, *My Twenty-Five Years in China* (New York: Macmillan, 1945), pp. 370–422.

397 "I wouldn't say": "Americans Return from Jap Prison Camps," *Life*, Sept. 7, 1942, p. 23.

397 "He was in a pitiable condition": J. M. Watson, undated statement.

397 He died two days later: "Protests concerning British Officials William Hutton Interned in Shanghai," Reference Code # B02032502500, Japan Center for Asian Historical Records, Tokyo, Japan. See also Greg Leck, *Captives of Empire: The Japanese Internment of Allied Civilians in China, 1941–1945* (Bangor, Pa.: Shandy Press, 2006), pp. 115–17.

397 The Japanese forced: Details of the airmen's experiences in Bridge House are drawn from the following sources: Chase J. Nielsen testimony in the case of *United States of America vs. Shigeru Sawada et al.*; Nielsen, "Doolittle Fliers' Saga of Living Death: Meet Darlington Man," p. 6.

397 "A Jap and a Chinese": Nielsen, "Doolittle Fliers' Saga of Living Death: Meet Darlington Man," p. 6.

398 Allied prisoners: "Summary of Interviews with Frederick B. Opper, Associate Editor of the *Shanghai Evening Post and Mercury* in New York City, February 23, 26, & March 4," Box 1, Series XI, DTRAP; Frederick B. Opper, "Opper Recalls Imprisonment of U.S. Pilots," *Shanghai Evening Post and Mercury*, April 30, 1943, p. 1.

398 "What's Shanghai like?" Opper, "Opper Recalls Imprisonment of U.S. Pilots," p. 1.

398 "Tokyo": Ibid.

398 "We grinned cheerfully": Ibid.

398 "The building was infested": Chase J. Nielsen testimony in the case of *United States of America vs. Shigeru Sawada et al.*

398 "We maintained a guard": Nielsen, "Doolittle Fliers' Saga of Living Death: Meet Darlington Man," p. 6.

398 "It was the first time": Watson, *DeShazer*, p. 45.

399 "It was hard to take": Hite oral history interview with Hasdorff, Dec. 16–17, 1982.

399 "Bill, I don't know": Doug Clarke, "The Raid: Long Ago 'n' Bombs Away," *Fort Worth Star-Telegram*, April 18, 1982, p. 1.

399 "We would have gone stark": Nielsen, "Doolittle Fliers' Saga of Living Death: Meet Darlington Man," p. 6.

399 "We talked a lot": Ibid.

399 seventeen days without: Raymond C. Phillips, "Mistreatment of Prisoners in Shanghai," undated.

399 "He had no control": Chase J. Nielsen testimony in the case of *United States of America vs. Shigeru Sawada et al.*

399 "He wanted me to sing": Hite oral history interview with Hasdorff, Dec. 16–17, 1982.

400 "Notify Chief of Army Air Corps": Arthur Vincent Toovey Dean, statement, Aug. 28, 1945, Box 57, RG 226, Records of the Office of Strategic Services, Washington/Pacific Coast/Field Station Files, NARA.

400 The Japanese came: The trial of the raiders is covered in great detail in the war crimes records found in Box 1728, RG 331, Supreme Commander for the Allied Powers, Legal Section, Prosecution Division, NARA. To re-create this scene I relied on the testimonies of Chase Nielsen, George Barr, Robert Hite and Jacob Deshazer, Ryuhei Okada, Yusei Wako, and Sotojiro Tatsuta, as well as Itsuro Hata, "Particulars Relating to the Punishment of the American Airmen Who Raided the Japanese Homeland on 18 April 1942," and the Record of Trial, Aug. 28, 1942.

400 "The flies buzzed": Nielsen, "Doolittle Fliers' Saga of Living Death: Meet Darlington Man," p. 6.

400 "As a matter of fact": Chase J. Nielsen testimony in the case of *United States of America vs. Shigeru Sawada et al.*

401 "It is evident": Ryuhei Okada testimony in the case of *United States of America vs. Shigeru Sawada et al.*

401 "What is it?": This exchange comes from Nielsen, "Doolittle Fliers' Saga of Living Death: Meet Darlington Man," p. 6.

401 Dysentery had reduced: Descriptions of Hallmark are drawn from the testimonies of Alexander Hindrava, Alexander John Sterelny, and Teh Ling Chung in the case of *United States of America vs. Shigeru Sawada et al.*

401 "His bowels": Testimony of Alexander Hindrava, ibid.

401 "only as much as his bones": Ibid.

401 The seven other raiders: Details on Kiangwan are drawn from Chase Nielsen's testimony in the case of *United States of America vs. Shigeru Sawada et al.*

401 "We had nothing to read": Robert L. Hite and Jacob DeShazer, "Doolittle Fliers' Saga of Living Death: Confinement in Filthy Cell Can Be Horrible," *News and Courier*, Sept. 23, 1945, p. 12.

401 Ten days after the attack: Testimony of Ryukichi Tanaka, in R. John

Pritchard and Sonia Magbanua Zaide, eds., *The Tokyo War Crimes Trial*, 22 vols. (New York: Garland, 1981), vol. 6, pp. 14,353–63, 14,379–84.

402 "This shouldn't happen": Stephan, *Hawaii under the Rising Sun*, pp. 113–14.

402 "Should they deserve to be Japanese": Yoshitake Miwa diary, April 27, 1942.

402 "North American Aircraft, Banzai!": Edward J. Drea, *The 1942 Japanese General Election: Political Mobilization in Wartime Japan* ([Lawrence]: Center for East Asian Studies, University of Kansas, 1979), p. 133.

402 General Hajime Sugiyama: Edwin P. Hoyt, *Japan's War: The Great Pacific Conflict* (New York: Cooper Square Press, 2001), p. 277.

402 He made that demand: Testimony of Koichi Kido, in Pritchard and Zaide, eds., *The Tokyo War Crimes Trial*, vol. 13, p. 31,062.

402 Sugiyama likewise pressed: Testimony of Hideki Tojo, ibid., vol. 6, pp. 14,601–2.

402 "It was not against": Ibid., p. 14,600.

402 "This was the first time": Ibid., p. 14,601.

402 Others shared Tojo's reluctance: Testimony of Ryukichi Tanaka, ibid., vol. 12, pp. 29,048–49.

402 the vice minister of war: Ibid., vol. 6, pp. 14,401–2.

402 Top commanders on the ground: Testimony of Shigeru Sawada, ibid., vol. 11, p. 27,454; testimony of Masatoshi Miyano, ibid., vol. 12, pp. 28,870–71.

402 "I believe it was due": Testimony of Ryukichi Tanaka, ibid., vol. 6, p. 14,420.

403 Tojo's meeting that Tuesday: Ibid., pp. 14,401–2.

403 General Hata not only: Testimony of Masatoshi Miyano, ibid., vol. 12, pp. 28,870–74.

403 "Arisue was sent": Testimony of Ryukichi Tanaka, ibid., vol. 12, p. 29,044.

403 "At no time": Testimony of Masatoshi Miyano, ibid., vol. 12, p. 28,879.

403 Japan had failed: Affidavit of Hideki Tojo, pp. 191–95, in Box 35, Series 5.2, GWPP.

403 Military Law Concerning the Punishment of Enemy Airmen: A copy of this law can be found in the war crimes files in Box 1728, RG 331, Supreme Commander for the Allied Powers, Legal Section, Prosecution Division, NARA.

403 Sugiyama's staff: Saibu Tanabe to Jun Ushiromiya, "Memo Pertaining to the Disposition of Enemy Airmen," July 28, 1942, ibid.

403 As soon as the judges: Testimony of Hideki Tojo, in Pritchard and Zaide, eds., *The Tokyo War Crimes Trial*, vol. 6, p. 14,602.

403 "At 11:30 Premier Tojo": Koichi Kido diary, Oct. 3, 1942, ibid., p. 14,608.

404 "Being fully aware": Affidavit of Hideki Tojo, p. 195.

404 "The five whose death sentences": Hajime Sugiyama to Shunroku Hata, Oct. 10, 1942, "Disposition of Convicted American Airmen," in Box 1728, RG 331, Supreme Commander for the Allied Powers, Legal Section, Prosecution Division, NARA.

404 The job of carrying out: Sotojiro Tatsuta testimony in the case of *United States of America vs. Shigeru Sawada et al.*

404 By that point: Testimonies of Alexander Hindrava, Alexander John Sterelny,

and Teh Ling Chung, ibid.; War Department General Staff G-2, Military Intelligence Service, Ex-Report No. 669, July 12, 1945, Bishop, Lewis S.

404 That evening: Caesar Luiz Dos Remedios testimony in the case of *United States of America vs. Shigeru Sawada et al.*

405 "I hardly know": Dean Hallmark to Mr. and Mrs. O. D. Hallmark, Oct. 1942, in the case of *United States of America vs. Shigeru Sawada et al.*

405 "All that I am": Dean Hallmark to Mrs. O. D. Hallmark, undated.

405 "I want you to know": Harold Spatz to Robert Spatz, undated (ca. Oct. 1942), in the case of *United States of America vs. Shigeru Sawada et al.*

405 "a cold, hard cruel world": Daddy to William Farrow, undated, William G. Farrow Collection, South Carolina Military Museum, Columbia, S.C.

405 "We've both been cheated": William Farrow to Margie Wilson, Jan. 25, 1939 (envelope date), ibid.

405 "Here's wishing you": William Farrow to Jessie Farrow, Oct. 1942, in the case of *United States of America vs. Shigeru Sawada et al.*

405 "I know, Mom": Ibid.

406 "Well, here we've come": William Farrow to Margaret Stem, undated (ca. Oct. 1942), Box 2, Series II, DTRAP.

406 "Do you remember": William Farrow to Ivan Ferguson, undated (ca. Oct. 1942), ibid.

406 "full of pep": William Farrow to Margie Wilson, Feb. 28, 1940, William G. Farrow Collection, South Carolina Military Museum.

406 "You are to me": William Farrow to Elizabeth Sims, undated (ca. Oct. 1942), in "Letters of the Late Lt. William G. Farrow to Relatives and Friends," *News and Press*, March 14, 1946, p. 1.

407 "Find yourself the good man": Ibid.

407 Farrow entrusted Remedios: Caesar Luiz Dos Remedios testimony in the case of *United States of America vs. Shigeru Sawada et al.*

407 Around 10 a.m. on October 15: Details of the execution are drawn from the testimonies of Sotojiro Tatsuta, Shigeji Mayama, Yoneya Tomoichi, Yusei Wako, Yutaka Minezaki, and Yoneda Isamu, ibid.

407 The record of the execution: "Record of Execution," Oct. 15, 1942, ibid.

408 "I do not know": Sotojiro Tatsuta testimony, ibid.

408 "Please tell the folks": Ibid.

408 "Christ was born": Ibid.

408 "Attention": Yoneda Isamu testimony, ibid.

408 "The men who fired": Sotojiro Tatsuta testimony, ibid.

409 "capture, trial, and severe punishment": Robert A. Kinney Memorandum for Colonel Booth, June 16, 1944, Box 2215, RG 165, Records of the War Department General and Special Staffs, Military Intelligence Division, "Regional File," 1922–44, NARA.

409 "I saw school kids": "Tokyo (Domei) in English at 7:30 AM to the World," transcript, Box 18, RG 24, Records of the Bureau of Naval Personnel, Casualty Branch, NARA.

409 Rumors that at least a few: David Anderson, "Japan Is Punishing Seized U.S. Fliers," *New York Times*, Oct. 20, 1942, p. 1.

409 "The American public": "Tokyo in English at 7:00 PM to North America," transcript, Box 18, RG 24, Records of the Bureau of Naval Personnel, Casualty Branch, NARA.

410 "For those who are skeptical": "Tokyo in English at 4:00 AM to Europe," transcript, ibid.

410 The press initially questioned: "Wild Stories Told to Japs," *Warsaw Daily Union*, Oct. 21, 1942, p. 2.

410 At an October 22 press conference: "Stimson Lists Men Japan May Hold," *New York Times*, Oct. 23, 1942, p. 5.

410 "sly propaganda campaign.": "Japs Release Names of More Yanks Captured," *Victoria Advocate*, Oct. 23, 1942, p. 2.

410 "The news is released": Raymond Clapper, "Delayed News Worries Nation," *Schenectady Gazette*, Oct. 26, 1942, p. 10.

410 who had once meticulously: Billy Farrow, College Algebra, notebook, Box 1, William G. Farrow Collection, South Carolina Military Museum, Columbia, S.C.

410 "The time has come": David Lawrence, "Today in Washington," *Pittsburgh Post-Gazette*, Oct. 23, 1942, p. 12.

411 "Stay close to God": Ibid.

411 "He was neither a poet": David Lawrence, "A Pilot's Memorandum to Himself," *Evening Independent*, Jan. 1, 1964, p. 6-A.

411 Letters of support: Howard Suttle, "Farrow's Code for Living Talk of U.S. Armed Forces," *News and Courier*, Nov. 8, 1942, p. 9II.

411 Churches across the country: Stem, *Tall and Free As Meant by God*, pp. 58–59.

411 "An American's Creed for Victory": "An American's Creed for Victory," Northwestern National Life Insurance Company, pamphlet, Box 1, Series XI, DTRAP.

411 "No matter what has happened": "Mrs. Doolittle Sends Mother's Day Message," *Schenectady Gazette*, May 10, 1943, p. 2.

411 The United States meanwhile scrambled: Robert A. Kinney Memorandum for Colonel Booth, June 16, 1944.

411 "What may be more stigmatized": Leland Harrison to Cordell Hull, Feb. 23, 1943, Microfilm Roll #A1250, AFHRA. See also U.S. Department of State, *Foreign Relations of the United States: Diplomatic Papers, 1943*, vol. 3, *The British Commonwealth, Eastern Europe, the Far East* (Washington, D.C.: GPO, 1963), pp. 965–66.

412 "The American Government": Ibid.

412 "The full texts": Breckinridge Long, March 20, 1943, in U.S. Department of State, *Foreign Relations of the United States: Diplomatic Papers, 1943*, vol. 3, p. 972.

412 "proceed immediately": Ibid.

412 "I am not unmindful": Ibid., p. 973.

412 "Any deterioration": Ibid.

412 "statement to the effect": Ibid.

413 "Until we know": Ibid., p. 974.

413 "bestial methods": Cordell Hull draft message to Leland Harrison, April 5, 1943, Box 5, OF 4675, FDRL.

413 "If, as would appear": Ibid. A final copy of this note dated April 12 can be found in U.S. Department of State, *Foreign Relations of the United States: Diplomatic Papers, 1943*, vol. 3, pp. 980–82.

413 "Questions of retaliation": Cordell Hull to Franklin Roosevelt, April 7, 1943, Box 5, OF 4675, FDRL.

413 "OK, FDR:" Cordell Hull draft message to Leland Harrison, April 5, 1943, ibid.

413 "I am deeply stirred": F.D.R. to Cordell Hull, April 8, 1943, ibid.

414 "Our note to Japan": April 9, 1943, memo, ibid.

414 "Please let me have": F.D.R. to Cordell Hull, April 8, 1943, ibid.

414 "Will we be told": "Story of Tokyo Raid to Be Revealed Soon," *New York Times*, April 15, 1943, p. 1.

414 "After consultation": "Delays Tokyo Raid Story," *New York Times*, April 17, 1943, p. 2.

414 "The Japanese captured": "The Bombing of Tokyo," editorial, *New York Times*, April 20, 1943, p. 22.

414 The Japanese seized: Official Japanese Broadcasts, More Details of U.S. Raid Revealed, April 21, 1943, Box 2215, RG 165, Records of the War Department General and Special Staffs, Military Intelligence Division, "Regional File," 1922–1944, NARA; "Tokyo Air Raid Details Are Given Out by Yahagi When U.S. Army Demurs," *Nippon Times*, April 21, 1943, p. 1.

414 "I take pleasure": "Japanese Tell Their Version of Shangri-La to Give People of U.S. 'the Full Story,'" *New York Times*, April 21, 1943, p. 4.

415 "We have the pleasure": "Tokyo Air Raid Details Are Given Out by Yahagi When U.S. Army Demurs," p. 1.

415 America had no choice: Press Release, "The Raid on Japan, April 18, 1942," April 20, 1943, Box 23, DPLOC; "Text of War Department's Account of Raid on Tokyo April 18, 1942," *New York Times*, April 21, 1943, p. 4; Edwin D. Gritz, "Raid Story Was Told in Effort to Head Off Japanese Version," *Washington Post*, April 22, 1943, p. 1.

415 "patched-up production": "U.S. Bares 'Flop Raid' Details," *Nippon Times*, April 23, 1943, p. 1.

415 "The American people": "Anger Sweeps U.S. on Tokyo Raid Lies," *Nippon Times*, April 25, 1943, p. 4. See also "The Report on the Raid," editorial, *New York Times*, April 22, 1943, p. 22; "Murder in Tokyo," *Time*, May 3, 1943, p. 20.

415 "I believe that any government": *Congressional Record*, 78th Cong., 1st sess., April 22, 1943, p. 3716.

416 "It is with a feeling": "Texts of the Statements on Japan," *New York Times*, April 22, 1943, p. 4; Bertram D. Hulen, "President Aghast," ibid., April 22, 1943, p. 1.

416 "President Roosevelt has issued": Navy Department, Office of Public Relations, Analysis Section, Daily Digest, April 22, 1943, No. 553, Box 19, RG 24, Records of the Bureau of Naval Personnel, Casualty Branch, NARA.

416 The reaction from members of Congress: "Congress Aroused by Japanese News," *New York Times*, April 22, 1943, p. 3.

416 "We are fighting a bunch of beasts": *Congressional Record*, 78th Cong., 1st sess., April 22, 1943, p. 3704.

416 "So gruesome it defies comment": "Congress Aroused by Japanese News," *New York Times*, April 22, 1943, p. 3.

416 "yellow devils": *Congressional Record*, 78th Cong., 1st sess., April 22, 1943, p. 3702.

416 "Where there is a drop": "U.S. Bars Reprisals against Prisoners," *New York Times*, April 23, 1943, p. 5.

416 "Those boys were not killed": "What to Do with Japs—in U.S. and Tokio," *Chicago Daily Tribune*, April 27, 1943, p. 1.

417 Rollie Toles of Pasadena: Rollie Toles to Franklin Roosevelt, May 2, 1943, Box 4, OF 4675, FDRL.

417 "In the face of your report: Ira R. Seltzer to Franklin Roosevelt, April 22, 1943, ibid.

417 "With horror, we hear": W. A. McMahon to Franklin Roosevelt, April 21, 1943, ibid.

417 North American Aviation announced: "Name Planes for Tokyo Raiders," *New York Times*, May 30, 1943, p. 22; "Made-in-Japan for the Air Raid on Tokyo," ibid., April 18, 1943, p. 33.

417 Bond sales soared: "Bond Sales Soar after Executions; City over Quota," *New York Times*, April 23, 1943, p. 1; "Bond Drive Nears 4-Billion City Goal," ibid., April 25, 1943, p. 3.

417 "Japanese Beasts": "Japanese Beasts," editorial, *Chicago Daily Tribune*, April 22, 1943, p. 1.

417 "The Savages of Tokyo": "The Savages of Tokyo," editorial, *New York Times*, April 22, 1943, p. 22.

417 "Those Jap Murderers": "Those Jap Murders," editorial, *Independent-Tribune*, May 1, 1943, in Box 2215, RG 165, Records of the War Department General and Special Staffs, Military Intelligence Division, "Regional File" 1922–44, NARA.

417 "Never before has Japan": Navy Department, Office of Public Relations, Analysis Section, Daily Digest, April 22, 1943, No. 553, Box 19, RG 24, Records of the Bureau of Naval Personnel, Casualty Branch, NARA.

417 "Civilization": "Murder in Tokyo," *Time*, May 3, 1943, p. 20.

417 "The Japs are even lower": "Those Jap Murders," editorial, *Independent-Tribune*, May 1, 1943, in Box 2215, RG 165, Records of the War Department General and Special Staffs, Military Intelligence Division, "Regional File" 1922–44, NARA.

418 "Horror breeds a demand:" "Japanese Barbarity," editorial, *Washington Post*, April 23, 1943, p. 10.

418 "The raid on Tokyo": David Lawrence, "Was Doolittle's Raid on Japan Worth Men and Planes It Cost?," *Spokane Daily Chronicle*, April 24, 1943, p. 4. See also "Shangri-la," editorial, *Christian Science Monitor*, April 21, 1943, p. 20.

418 "We must not rest": "Arnold Pledges Men to Revenge," *New York Times*, April 22, 1943, p. 4.

418 "We'll make the bastards pay!": Halsey, *Admiral Halsey's Story*, p. 104.

418 "We will drop each bomb": "Doolittle Pledges New Blows to Make Japan Beg Mercy," *New York Times*, April 23, 1943, p. 1.

418 "The day will come": Ibid.

419 "We won't forget!": Joseph W. Manskc, "We'll Return, Vow of Tokio Raider," *New York Journal-American*, April 23, 1943, p. 5.

419 "She was very upset": Sid Gross to Stephen Early, June 28, 1943, Box 4, OF 4675, FDRL.

419 "The Japanese just can't be": "Mothers Pray Japs Spared Captured Men," *Chicago Daily Tribune*, April 23, 1943, p. 6.

419 "I don't see how": Ibid.

419 "What the Japs are dealing out": "Mother of Flier Captured by Japs says Nation Must Be Humane to Prisoners," *St. Petersburg Times*, April 22, 1943, p. 6.

CHAPTER 24

420 "For victory": "They Must Be Avenged!," editorial, *Philadelphia Inquirer*, April 22, 1943, p. 12.

420 Ski York and his crew: Unless otherwise noted, details of York's crew's time in Russia are drawn from the following sources: Emmens, *Guests of the Kremlin*, pp. 114–291; Emmens oral history interview with Hasdorff, July 8–9, 1982; York oral history interview with Hasdorff, July 23, 1984; "Interview with B-25 Crew That Bombed Tokyo and Was Interned by the Russians," transcript, June 3, 1943; Pohl as told to Dwiggins, "We Crash Landed in Russia—and Escaped," pp. 57–59.

420 "There was no pavement": Emmens oral history interview with Hasdorff, July 8–9, 1982.

420 "The odor": Emmens, *Guests of the Kremlin*, p. 131.

420 "I will never forget": Ibid., p. 137.

421 "I wonder how old": This exchange is ibid.

421 "The countryside": Standley, *Admiral Ambassador to Russia*, p. 227.

421 "Boy": Emmens, *Guests of the Kremlin*, p. 141.

421 "I saw a little group": Standley, *Admiral Ambassador to Russia*, p. 227.

421 "Wonderful country": This exchange comes from Emmens, *Guests of the Kremlin*, p. 143. Standley recounts this exchange as well in his book, on pp. 227–28.

421 "log cabin": Standley, *Admiral Ambassador to Russia*, p. 227.

421 "Not cxactly like home": Emmens, *Guests of the Kremlin*, p. 143.

421 "What news do you have": This exchange is ibid., pp. 144–48.

422 "I felt a tremendous letdown": Ibid., p. 148.

422 "I felt terribly sorry": Standley, *Admiral Ambassador to Russia*, p. 229.

422 "General, we are having": This exchange comes from Emmens, *Guests of the Kremlin*, pp. 148–50.

423 "I felt as if": Ibid., p. 150.

423 "good health": William Standley to Cordell Hull, Sept. 13, 1942, in U.S. Department of State, *Foreign Relations of the United States: Diplomatic Papers, 1942*, vol. 3, p. 637.

423 "I knew how": Standley, *Admiral Ambassador to Russia*, p. 230.

424 "Our morale": Emmens, *Guests of the Kremlin*, p. 158.

424 "yes, sir": York oral history interview with Hasdorff, July 23, 1984.

424 "I knew we had": Ibid.

424 "In America": Emmens, *Guests of the Kremlin*, p. 175.

424 "I spent about ten hours": York oral history interview with Hasdorff, July 23, 1984.

424 "The heaviest loser": Emmens, *Guests of the Kremlin*, p. 158.

424 "Well, what are": This exchange is ibid., p. 163.

425 "I see some indications": Ibid., p. 168.

425 "Based on Soviet standards": Loy Henderson to Cordell Hull, Nov. 30, 1942, in U.S. Department of State, *Foreign Relations of the United States: Diplomatic Papers, 1942*, vol. 3, p. 665.

425 "It would be desirable": Ibid.

425 "Looks like we're here": This exchange comes from Emmens, *Guests of the Kremlin*, pp. 172–73.

426 "We turned down": Emmens oral history interview with Hasdorff, July 8–9, 1982.

426 "We would stake": Ibid.

426 "Our spirits": Emmens, *Guests of the Kremlin*, p. 206.

426 "On one of the trips": Ibid., pp. 206–7.

426 "Our gums were bleeding": Ibid., p. 211.

427 "Are you serious?": This exchange is ibid.

427 "You don't know about us": York oral history interview with Hasdorff, July 23, 1984.

427 "I will mail it at once": This exchange comes from Emmens, *Guests of the Kremlin*, p. 213.

427 "We never stopped": Ibid.

427 "God, won't it be a day": This exchange is ibid., p. 216.

428 "This letter was received": This exchange is ibid., pp. 220–21.

428 "I couldn't believe": York oral history interview with Hasdorff, July 23, 1984.

428 "Where are we going?": This exchange comes from Emmens, *Guests of the Kremlin*, pp. 222–23.

428 "We had to walk up": Emmens oral history interview with Hasdorff, July 8–9, 1982.

429 "At the end": Emmens, *Guests of the Kremlin*, p. 229.

429 "Chkolov presented": Ibid., p. 232.

429 "Well worn": Ibid., p. 234.

429 "Where are you going?": This exchange comes from Emmens oral history interview with Hasdorff, July 8–9, 1982.

429 "You must be patient": Emmens, *Guests of the Kremlin*, p. 237.

430 "I had nothing to do": This exchange is ibid., p. 243.

430 "This news was a shock": Ibid., p. 248.

430 "Very well": Ibid., p. 252.

430 "The border is manned": Ibid.

431 "Our spirits rose": Emmens oral history interview with Hasdorff, July 8–9, 1982.

431 "Sergeant, why don't": Emmens, *Guests of the Kremlin*, p. 254.

431 "You and that goddamn": This exchange comes from Emmens oral history interview with Hasdorff, July 8–9, 1982.

432 "I can't be seen": Ibid.

432 "You're Abdul Arram": This exchange comes from Emmens, *Guests of the Kremlin*, pp. 258–61.

432 "It seemed like a dream": Ibid., p. 264.

433 "There was only silence": Ibid., p. 270.

433 "Suddenly we all heard": Ibid.

433 "More—Mashhad": Ibid., p. 271.

433 "It ground over": Emmens oral history interview with Hasdorff, July 8–9, 1982.

433 "The bottom of that truck": Emmens, *Guests of the Kremlin*, p. 273.

433 "We could tell": Emmens oral history interview with Hasdorff, July 8–9, 1982.

434 "Out": Ibid.

434 "Pssst": Ibid.

434 "You would take one step": Ibid.

434 "I don't think": Ibid.

434 "The guy who had been": Ibid.

435 "I was staring directly": Emmens, *Guests of the Kremlin*, p. 278.

435 "Oh, my God": Emmens oral history interview with Hasdorff, July 8–9, 1982.

435 "Slowly the guardrail": Emmens, *Guests of the Kremlin*, pp. 278–79.

435 "It was desolate country": Emmens oral history interview with Hasdorff, July 8–9, 1982.

435 "Out": This exchange is ibid.

435 "Impossible": Emmens, *Guests of the Kremlin*, p. 280.

435 "Well, here we are!": This exchange is ibid., p. 282.

436 "Now's our chance!": Ibid., p. 284.

436 "It wasn't more than": Ibid.

436 "We took a deep breath": Emmens oral history interview with Hasdorff, July 8–9, 1982.

436 "American! American!": This exchange is ibid.

436 "Did you ever see anything": This exchange comes from Emmens, *Guests of the Kremlin*, p. 287.

437 "My God": Ibid., p. 288.

437 "Where in the hell": Emmens oral history interview with Hasdorff, July 8–9, 1982.

437 "Would you like": Ibid.

CHAPTER 25

438 "In war as it is fought today": Ernest Lindley, "New Japanese Horror," *Washington Post*, April 23, 1943, p. 11.

438 "Though we were in separate cells": Hite and DeShazer, "Doolittle Fliers' Saga of Living Death: Confinement," p. 12.

439 "We lined up": Ibid.

439 "For bombing and strafing": Ibid.

439 "But through the gracious": Ibid.

439 "I could not help": Watson, *DeShazer*, p. 50.

439 "Notify U.S. Army": Irene Kuhn, "Tea and Ashes," in Overseas Press Club of America, *Deadline Delayed* (New York: E. P. Dutton, 1947), p. 275.

439 Other raiders likewise used: Caesar Luis Dos Remedios testimony in the case of *United States of America vs. Shigeru Sawada et al.*

439 "Lt. G. Barr, USAAC": Kuhn, "Tea and Ashes," p. 274.

439 The airmen struggled: Chase J. Nielsen testimony in the case of *United States of America vs. Shigeru Sawada et al.*

440 "We were so thrilled": Hite oral history interview with Hasdorff, Dec. 16–17, 1982.

440 DeShazer shimmied up: Watson, *DeShazer*, p. 53.

440 Hite set a goal: Hite oral history interview with Hasdorff, Dec. 16–17, 1982.

440 "These are things": Ibid.

440 "It was flat country": Robert L. Hite and Jacob DeShazer, "Doolittle Fliers' Saga of Living Death: Single Prisoner Battles Jap Guards over Foot-Washing," *News and Courier*, Sept. 24, 1945, p. 3.

440 The men arrived: Details drawn from the testimony of Chase Nielsen in the case of *United States of America vs. Shigeru Sawada et al.*; Robert L. Hite and Jacob DeShazer, "Doolittle Fliers' Saga of Living Death: Single Prisoner Battles," p. 3.

440 "The furnishings consisted": Hite and DeShazer, "Doolittle Fliers' Saga of Living Death: Single Prisoner Battles," p. 3.

441 "The rest of the time": Ibid.

441 "Day in and day out": Robert L. Hite and Jacob DeShazer, "Doolittle Fliers' Saga of Living Death: 'Tin Cup' News Service Outwitted Japs for Time," *News and Courier*, Sept. 25, 1945, p. 5.

441 "Some guards would torment": Barr, "Rough Draft of a Story by Capt. George Barr."

441 "Connie G. Battles": Hite and DeShazer, "Doolittle Fliers' Saga of Living Death: 'Tin Cup' News Service," p. 5.

441 "tincup news service": Ibid.

441 "Russians on German border": Ibid.

442 "That way we learned": Ibid.

442 "He could see something funny": Robert L. Hite and Jacob DeShazer, "Doolittle Fliers' Saga of Living Death: Death of American Prisoner Bitter Experience," *News and Courier*, Sept. 26, 1945, p. 9.

442 "He was certain": Hite and DeShazer, "Doolittle Fliers' Saga of Living Death: 'Tin Cup' News Service," p. 5.

442 "toothpick": Hite and DeShazer, "Doolittle Fliers' Saga of Living Death: Death of American Prisoner," p. 9.

442 "We begged to go": Barr, "Rough Draft of a Story by Capt. George Barr."

442 "Listen": Hite and DeShazer, "Doolittle Fliers' Saga of Living Death: Death of American Prisoner," p. 9.

442 "It was sort of sad": Hite oral history interview with Hasdorff, Dec. 16–17, 1982.

442 "Just pray": Ibid.

443 "Immediately artificial": "Medical Report on the Death of Lt. Meder," Dec. 1, 1943, Box 2179, RG 389, Records of the Office of the Provost Marshal General, American POW Information Bureau Records Branch, General Subject File, 1942–46, NARA.

443 Unaware that his friend: Watson, *DeShazer*, p. 57.

443 The Japanese had stuffed: Hite oral history interview with Hasdorff, Dec. 16–17, 1982.

443 "The body was": Hite and DeShazer, "Doolittle Fliers' Saga of Living Death: Death of American Prisoner," p. 9.

443 "For several days": Ibid.

443 "To be opened": Bob Meder to Family, undated, Box 21, DPLOC.

443 "I am writing this letter": Ibid.

444 "His mission was accomplished": Address of Lt. Gen. J. H. Doolittle, Cleveland Aviation Club, Cleveland, Oct. 18, 1945, transcript, Box 7, Series IV, DPUT.

444 "Any of us can die": Hite oral history interview with Hasdorff, Dec. 16–17, 1982.

444 "We had to fight": Robert L. Hite and Jacob DeShazer, "Doolittle Fliers' Saga of Living Death: Men Want Peace and Quiet and Love Now," *News and Courier*, Sept. 27, 1945, p. 3.

444 Nielsen envisioned: Watson, *DeShazer*, p. 58.

444 "I would think": Jim Arpy," You're to Bomb the Japanese Homeland," *Sunday Times-Democrat*, April 12, 1964, p. 1D.

445 "I saw red": Barr, "Badger 'Doolittle' Flier Tortured by Japs Pleads for Foe," p. 13.

445 "Panic comes quick": Ibid.

445 "We could hear him": Hite and DeShazer, "Doolittle Fliers' Saga of Living Death: Single Prisoner Battles," p. 3.

445 "My lungs, heart, liver": Barr, "Rough Draft of a Story by Capt. George Barr."

445 "The perspiration poured": Barr, "Badger 'Doolittle' Flier Tortured by Japs Pleads for Foe," p. 13.

445 "Misake was among": Barr, "Rough Draft of a Story by Capt. George Barr."

445 "He took a frightful": Barr, "Badger 'Doolittle' Flier Tortured by Japs Pleads for Foe," p. 13.

446 "After awhile": George Barr, "Jap Brutality Dazed Badger Flier," *Milwaukee Sentinel*, May 13, 1946, p. 4.

446 "At times the swelling": Chase J. Nielsen to J. H. Doolittle, Jan. 5, 1968, Box 38, Series IX, DPUT.

446 "We began to think": Hite and DeShazer, "Doolittle Fliers' Saga of Living Death: Death of American Prisoner," p. 9.

446 "We thought a lot": Arpy," You're to Bomb the Japanese Homeland," p. 1D.

446 "Faith kept me alive": Edward Oxford, "Against All Odds," *American History Illustrated*, April 1992, p. 67.

446 stamped with a $1.97: Jeff Wilkinson, " 'The Lord Told Me to Go Back,' " *State*, April 12, 2002, p. 1.

446 "It was sort of like a man": Hite oral history interview with Hasdorff, Dec. 16–17, 1982.

446 "I lived on hate": Ibid.

446 DeShazer echoed Hite: Jacob DeShazer as told to Don. R. Falkenberg, "I Was a Prisoner of Japan," Bible Mediation League, 1950, Asbury Theological Seminary, Wilmore, Ky.

446 "The way the Japanese treated me": Oxford, "Against All Odds," p. 69.

446 "We decided that we had": Hite and DeShazer, "Doolittle Fliers' Saga of Living Death: Death of American Prisoner," p. 9.

447 "One day in my cell": Ibid.

447 "Hunger, starvation": Watson, *DeShazer*, p. 65.

447 "How are you?": This exchange comes from Wilkinson, " 'The Lord Told Me to Go Back,' " p. 1.

447 "I was so sick": Doug Clarke, "The Raid: Long Ago 'n' Bombs Away," *Fort Worth Star-Telegram*, April 18, 1982, p. 1.

447 "Hite won't be here": Robert L. Hite, "Veteran's Day Remembrances," speech transcript, Box 3, Series II, DTRAP.

447 "I thought I was": Clarke, "The Raid: Long Ago 'n' Bombs Away," p. 1.

448 "It was the best food": Hite and DeShazer, "Doolittle Fliers' Saga of Living Death: Men Want Peace," p. 3.

448 There raiders landed: "North China 1407 Prison Camp," Aug. 6, 1945, Box 57, RG 226, Records of the Office of Strategic Services, Washington/Pacific Coast/Field Stations Files, NARA; "Prison #1407, in Which Doolittle Raiders Were Confined," Oct. 3, 1945, Box 2179, RG 389, Records of the Office of Provost Marshall, American POW Information Bureau Records Branch, NARA.

448 "hell": Charles Albert Stewart Jr., undated statement, Box 2121, RG 389, Records of the Office of the Provost Marshall General, American POW Information Bureau Records Branch, General Subject File, 1942–46, NARA.

448 "We were placed": Hite and DeShazer, "Doolittle Fliers' Saga of Living Death: Men Want Peace," p. 3.

448 "Hell is on us": Interrogation of Fleet Admiral Osami Nagano, Nov. 20, 1946, in USSBS, Naval Analysis Division, *Interrogations of Japanese Officials*, vol. 2 (Washington, D.C.: GPO, 1946), p. 356.

448 "staggers the imagination": Statement by Lieutenant General James H. Doolittle, July 23, 1945, Box 38, DPLOC.

448 The four-engine bomber: Foster Hailey, "Superfortress Is Largest and Swiftest Bomber in the World," *New York Times*, June 16, 1944, p. 4; "The Mighty B-29," ibid., Aug. 5, 1945, p. 67.

449 America demonstrated: Bruce Rae, "Record Air Attack," *New York Times*, March 10, 1945, p. 1; Martin Sheridan, "Giant Tokyo Fires Blackened B-29's," ibid., March 11, 1945, p. 14; Warren Moscow, "City's Heart Gone," ibid., March 11, 1945, p. 1; "Tokyo in Flames," editorial, ibid., March 12, 1945, p. 18; USSBS, *Summary Report (Pacific War)*, pp. 16–17; Wesley Frank Craven and James Lea Cate, eds., *The Army Air Forces in World War II*, vol. 5, *The Pacific: Matterhorn to Nagasaki, June 1944 to August 1945* (Washington, D.C.: GPO, 1983), pp. 614–17.

449 "I have never seen": Sheridan, "Giant Tokyo Fires Blackened B-29's," p. 14.

449 In the war's final months: "Air Might Clinched Battle of Japan," *New York Times*, Aug. 15, 1945, p. 11; "B-29's List Gains in Year's Attacks," ibid., July 17, 1945, p. 2; Craven and Cate, eds., *The Army Air Forces in World War II*, vol. 5, pp. 751–55.

449 "Japan eventually will be": "Doolittle Pledges Devastated Japan," *New York Times*, July 27, 1945, p. 6.

449 These attacks built up: Paul W. Tibbets Jr., *Return of the Enola Gay* (Columbus, Ohio: Mid Coast Marketing, 1998), pp. 196–244; W. H. Lawrence, "5 Plants Vanish," *New York Times*, Aug. 8, 1945, p. 1; USSBS, Chairman's Office, *The Effects of the Atomic Bombs on Hiroshima and Nagasaki* (Washington, D.C.: GPO, 1946), pp. 3–10, 25; USSBS, *Summary Report (Pacific War)*, pp. 22–25.

449 American investigators: Exact casualties in the attacks on Hiroshima and Nagasaki are difficult to determine; figures vary even within reports prepared by the USSBS. The figures used here come from the following sources: USSBS, Medical Division, *The Effects of the Atomic Bombs on Health and Medical Services in Hiroshima and Nagasaki* (Washington, D.C.: GPO, 1947), p. 57; USSBS, *The Effects of the Atomic Bombs on Hiroshima and Nagasaki*, p. 15.

449 Three days later: Tibbets Jr., *Return of the Enola Gay*, pp. 241–44; USSBS, *The Effects of the Atomic Bombs on Health and Medical Services in Hiroshima and Nagasaki*, p. 57; USSBS, *The Effects of the Atomic Bombs on Hiroshima and Nagasaki*, pp. 3–5.

450 DeShazer awoke: Watson, *DeShazer*, p. 82; DeShazer oral history interview with Hasdorff, Oct. 10, 1989.

450 Beriberi had stricken: Aug. 25, 1945, message, and Medical Report, Aug. 29, 1945, both in Box 187, RG 226, Records of the Office of Strategic Services, Field Station Files, NARA.

450 "What shall I pray about?": Watson, *DeShazer*, p. 82.

450 "You don't need": Ibid., p. 83; DeShazer oral history interview with Hasdorff, Oct. 10, 1989.

CHAPTER 26

451 "The recent uninvited": "Fuehrer Hitler Speaks," editorial, *Osaka Maini-chi*, April 29, 1942, p. 4.

451 Ray Nichols looked down: Melvin Richter and Ray N. Nichols to Strategic Services Officer OSS/CT, "Informal Report on Magpie Mission," Box 49, RG 226, Records of the Office of Strategic Services, NARA; "The Men of the Magpie Mission," undated, Box 187, ibid.

451 The team's mission: Headquarters, Office of Strategic Services, China Theater, APO 627, "Operation Magpie," Aug. 13, 1945, ibid.

451 Magpie was just one: Ronald H. Spector, *In the Ruins of Empire: The Japanese Surrender and the Battle for Postwar Asia* (New York: Random House, 2007), pp. 6–15.

452 The B-24 had lifted off: Airdrop Manifest, Magpie, Aug. 13, 1945, Box 218, RG 226, Records of the Office of Strategic Services, NARA.

452 "The weather was perfect": F. G. Jarman Jr. to Carroll Glines, April 19, 1965, in Glines, *The Doolittle Raid*, p. 191.

452 To prepare officials: Dick Hamada, "Japanese-American Soldier for the Office of Strategic Services (OSS)," in Hoppes, comp., *Just Doing My Job*, pp. 320–21.

452 "the nuns found": Melvin Richter and Ray N. Nichols to Strategic Services Officer OSS/CT, "Informal Report on Magpie Mission."

452 In addition, team members: F. G. Jarman Jr. to Carroll Glines, April 19, 1965, in Glines, *The Doolittle Raid*, p. 192.

452 "We were low enough": Ibid., p. 191.

452 "Happy hunting!": Hamada, "Japanese-American Soldier for the Office of Strategic Services (OSS)," in Hoppes, comp., *Just Doing My Job*, p. 321.

452 "The plane circled once more": F. G. Jarman Jr. to Carroll Glines, April 19, 1965, in Glines, *The Doolittle Raid*, p. 191.

452 "A long shot rang out": Melvin Richter and Ray N. Nichols to Strategic Services Officer OSS/CT, "Informal Report on Magpie Mission."

453 "What is going on here?": This exchange comes from Hamada, "Japanese-American Soldier for the Office of Strategic Services (OSS)," in Hoppes, comp., *Just Doing My Job*, p. 322.

453 "with much flourish": Melvin Richter and Ray N. Nichols to Strategic Services Officer OSS/CT, "Informal Report on Magpie Mission."

453 "The General": Ibid.

453 "Relations were courteous": Ibid.

453 "During all this day": Ibid.

453 "We are anxious": This exchange is ibid.

454 Nichols messaged: Aug. 19, 1945, message, and Aug. 20, 1945, message, Box 187, RG 226, Records of the Office of Strategic Services, Shanghai Intelligence Files, NARA.

454 "It was much like calling": Melvin Richter and Ray N. Nichols to Strategic Services Officer OSS/CT, "Informal Report on Magpie Mission."

454 "Give it to 'em, lads": Ibid.

454 "While all this discussion": Ibid.

455 "We watched them": Hite and DeShazer, "Doolittle Fliers' Saga of Living Death: Men Want," p. 3.

455 "Ima amata watachi tomoduce": Ibid.

455 "We had to stand up": Ibid.

455 "You can go": Ibid.

455 "We were so happy": Ibid.

455 "He looks like an American": This exchange comes from Nielsen oral history interview with Erickson, July 11, 2000.

456 "A smiling little Chinese": Hite and DeShazer, "Doolittle Fliers' Saga of Living Death: Men Want Peace," p. 3.

456 "Lord, that was so good!": Hite oral history interview with Hasdorff, Dec. 16–17, 1982.

456 "To us": Nielsen oral history interview with Erickson, July 11, 2000.

456 "From now on": This exchange comes from DeShazer oral history interview with Hasdorff, Oct. 10, 1989.

456 "Have secured release": Aug. 21, 1945, message, Box 187, RG 226, Records of the Office of Strategic Services, Field Station Files, NARA.

457 "Theater desires": Aug. 23, 1945, message, ibid.

457 "Hallmark, Farrow and Spatz": Aug. 25, 1945, message, ibid.

457 "There is nothing": H. H. Arnold to Ollie D. Hallmark, Sept. 26, 1945.

457 The navigator's weight: "George Barr, 50; in Raid on Tokyo," *New York Times*, July 13, 1967, p. 37.

457 "He arrived in a state": Medical Report, Aug. 29, 1945, Box 187, RG 226, Records of the Office of Strategic Services, Field Station Files, NARA.

457 "Present condition": Ibid.

457 "I would then gently": Karel Frederik Mulder to James Doolittle, April 21, 1964, Box 1, Series IX, DTRAP.

458 "Brought back a load": Jack Van Norman diary, Aug. 25, 1945, Box 2, Series XII, DTRAP.

458 News of the rescue: "4 Doolittle Fliers Saved," *New York Times*, Aug. 22, 1945, p. 1.

458 "The three men": "3 Doolittle Fliers Weak But Happy," *New York Times*, Aug. 26, 1945, p. 5.

458 "They looked at first glance": "Doolittle Men Tell of Dark Prison Years," *Chicago Daily Tribune*, Aug. 26, 1945, p. 1.

458 "It's good to get": Ibid.

458 "I feel that I'm": Ibid.

458 "He was a different": Ibid.

458 "Three members": Albert Wedemeyer to General Doolittle, Aug. 25, 1945, Box 21, DPLOC.

458 Hite, Nielsen, and DeShazer: Press Release, "First Three 'Doolittle' Fliers Return from Jap Prison Camp," Sept. 5, 1945, Iris #01010163, AFHRA.

459 "Their gaunt": Sidney Shalett, "Doolittle Fliers Describe 'Hell' of 40 Months as War Prisoners," *New York Times*, Sept. 6, 1945, p. 17.

459 "I was convinced": George Barr, "Jap Brutality Dazed Badger Flier," *Milwaukee Sentinel*, May 13, 1946, p. 4.

459 "I was a bed patient": Ibid.

459 "Awoke suddenly": Nurses' Report, in Glines, *Four Came Home*, p. 189.

459 "All my past suspicions": Glines, *The Doolittle Raid*, p. 198.

459 Barr saw his chance: Ibid., pp. 198–99.

460 "I was regaining": Barr, "Jap Brutality Dazed Badger Flier," p. 4.

460 "Why don't I see": Ibid.

460 "This is a trick": Ibid.

460 Barr arrived: Glines, *Four Came Home*, pp. 197–98; Glines, *The Doolittle Raid*, p. 199.

460 "Show the lieutenant": Glines, *Four Came Home*, p. 198.

460 "Take your clothes off": Ibid.

460 Barr did as told: Ibid., pp. 198–200.

460 "The administrative failure": S. H. Green medical report, Oct. 17, 1945, ibid., p. 200.

460 "He will require": Ibid., p. 202.

461 Orphaned at a young age: Doolittle, *I Could Never Be So Lucky Again*, pp. 459–60.

461 "I knew then": Barr, "Jap Brutality Dazed Badger Flier," p. 4.

461 "He tried to tell me": Doolittle, *I Could Never Be So Lucky Again*, p. 462.

461 "The last of my": Ibid.

461 "I unloaded": Ibid.

461 "I have instructed": Malcolm C. Grow to James H. Doolittle, Feb. 4, 1946, Box 20, DPLOC.

462 "Yes, sir": This exchange comes from Doolittle, *I Could Never Be So Lucky Again*, pp. 462–63.

CHAPTER 27

463 "I don't want revenge": Barr, "Jap Brutality Dazed Badger Flier," p. 4.

463 "Lord, I was nervous": Hite oral history interview with Hasdorff, Dec. 16–17, 1982.

463 "We have memories": Hite and DeShazer, "Doolittle Fliers' Saga of Living Death: Men Want Peace," p. 3.

463 Despite his own struggles: Hite oral history interview with Hasdorff, Dec. 16–17, 1982.

464 "We never saw": Robert L. Hite to Mr. and Mrs. Hallmark, Oct. 10, 1945 (envelope date), Box 3, Series II, DTRAP.

464 "Dean was a splendid": Ibid.

464 "Why are you here": Hite oral history interview with Hasdorff, Dec. 16–17, 1982.

464 "Those were answers": Ibid.

464 "I want to extend": Robert L. Hite to Mr. and Mrs. Robert A. Spatz, Oct. 1945, Box 5, Series II, DTRAP.

465 "I know they are": Ibid.

465 "Bill and Fitz": Chase Nielsen to May Dieter, Sept. 18, 1945, Box 2, Series II, DTRAP.

465 "In each coffin": Chase Nielsen to May Dieter, April 30, 1946, ibid.

465 May Dieter had grown: May Dieter to J. II. Doolittle, Sept. 16, 1946, Box 20, DPLOC.

465 "Do you think": Ibid.

465 Despite Tatsuta's promise: Sotojiro Tatsuta testimony in the case of *United States of America vs. Shigeru Sawada et al.*

466 A fellow prisoner: Glines, *Four Came Home*, pp. 164–65.

466 Captain Jason Bailey: Kuhn, "Tea and Ashes," pp. 268–77.

466 "These are Captain Meder's": This exchange is ibid. pp. 277–79.

466 "None of us": Ibid., p. 277.

466 "Give the box": Ibid.

466 "I put out my hands": Ibid., pp. 277–78.

467 "A book of traveller's": Ibid., p. 278.

467 "A personal check book": Ibid.

467 "There was a picture": Ibid., p. 279.

467 "Dean is buried": James Macia Jr. to Mrs. O. D. Hallmark, April 2, 1957.

467 The four defendants: Proceedings of the trial, totaling some 750 pages of testimony and exhibits, can be found in Box 1728, RG 331, Supreme Commander for the Allied Powers, Legal Section, Prosecution Division, NARA.

468 "open and shut": "Last of Fliers' Slayers Arrested," *Deseret News*, Jan. 18, 1946, p. 7.

468 "I sit here": J. H. Doolittle to Mrs. G. E. Larkin, March 4, 1946, Box 20, DPLOC. Doolittle quotes Nielsen's letter in this correspondence.

468 "Crews were repeatedly": James H. Doolittle testimony in the case of *United States of America vs. Shigeru Sawada et al.*

469 "It is quite impossible": Ibid.

469 "In all my life": Robert Dwyer closing argument, ibid.

469 "We have charged": Ibid.

469 "Every detail": Shinji Somiya closing argument, ibid.

469 "I say unto you": Ibid.

469 "The offenses of each": Conclusions, ibid.

470 "The Commission by awarding": "Review of the Record of Trial by a Military Commission of Sawada, Shigeru, Lieutenant General, Imperial Japanese Army, et al," Aug. 1946, Box 1659, RG 331, Supreme Commander for the Allied Powers, Legal Section, Prosecution Division, USA Versus Japanese War Criminals, Case File, 1945–59, NARA.

470 Reporters who covered: "4 Get Jail Terms in Doolittle Case," *New York Times*, April 16, 1946, p. 3; "Japs Sentenced for Executions," *Miami Daily News*, April 15, 1946, p. 2-A.

470 "On behalf": Sentence in the case of *United States of America vs. Shigeru Sawada et al.*

470 "Have you any": D. R. McCollugh to parents of Lieut. Dean Hallmark, April 16, 1946.

470 "In my estimation": Raleigh Hallmark, undated comments.

471 "I thought if I went": C. Jay Nielsen to Mrs. Hallmark, April 19, 1946.

471 "I am sorry justice": Chase Nielsen to May Dieter, April 30, 1946, Box 2, Series II, DTRAP.

471 "heart day and night": Shigeru Sawada to Major Lacey, May 5, 1949, Box 1194, RG 331, Supreme Commander for the Allied Powers, Legal Section, Prosecution Division, POW 201 File, NARA.

471 "Since this was": Ibid.

471 Sawada, Okada, and Tatsuta: "Japanese General Free after Serving Sentence," *Stars & Stripes*, Jan. 11, 1950, p. 2.

471 Yusei Wako was found: General Headquarters, Far East Command, July 9, 1950, Document No. 2-b, Box 23, RG 84, Records of the Foreign Service Posts of the Department of State, Japanese War Crime Cases, NARA; General Headquarters, Supreme Commander for the Allied Powers, July 9, 1950, ibid.; Yusei Wako, "Application for Clemency," Aug. 1952, ibid; Yutaka Tsuchida, "A Decision on Recommendation Re Reduction of Sentence," Oct. 9, 1953, ibid.

471 Even then he would: Matsusuke Shirane, "Decision on Recommendation for Parole," Feb. 6, 1956, ibid.

471 Wako's prison record: Takeshi Kumon, "Opinion of the Governor of Prison on Clemency," undated, ibid.

471 "I intend": Yusei Wako, "Application for Parole," Sept. 22, 1955, ibid.

472 War crime investigators: C. A. Willoughby memorandum for the Chief of Staff, Feb. 18, 1947, Box 719, RG 319, Office of the Assistant Chief of Staff for Intelligence, G-2, NARA.

472 In December 1945: Ibid.; C. A. Willoughby to the Chief of Staff, "Disposition of Shimomura, Sadamu, Interned at Sugamo Prison as Suspected War Criminal," Feb. 18, 1947, ibid.

472 "It is common knowledge": Ralph Teatsorth, "McCloy Visits General Mac in Jap Capital," *Bend Bulletin*, Oct. 23, 1945, p. 1.

472 "It is believed": John H. Hendren Jr. to Col. Abe McGregor Goff, International Prosecution Section, Jan. 3, 1946, Box 719, RG 319, Office of the Assistant Chief of Staff for Intelligence, G-2, NARA.

472 War crimes investigators filed: C. A. Willoughby memorandum for the Chief of Staff, Feb. 18, 1947, ibid.

472 "international standpoint": Ibid.

472 Rather than hand: Ibid.; this document includes fifteen supporting attachments, ranging from statements to a copy of the Imperial Hotel register.

473 "As the final decision": C. A. Willoughby to the Chief of Staff, "Disposition of Shimomura, Sadamu, Interned at Sugamo Prison as Suspected War Criminal," Feb. 18, 1947, ibid.

473 "The War Crimes mission": Ralph E. Hinner to General Headquarters, Supreme Commander for the Allied Powers, APO 500, Sept. 27, 1946, ibid.

473 Willoughby personally oversaw: Bratton to Willoughby, "Release of Shimomura Sadamu," March 17, March 13, and March 6, 1947, ibid.

473 "to a quiet place": Memo to Colonel Davis, March 12, 1947, ibid.

473 "It is directed": John B. Cooley to Commanding General, Eighth Army, APO 343, "Release of Shimomura Sadamu from Internment," Feb. 12, 1947, ibid.

EPILOGUE

474 "Immortality will always": Los Angeles Office of Information Services, Public Information Division Office, Secretary of the Air Force, Press Release, April 21, 1955, Iris #1010174, AFHRA.

474 "When we get to Chungking": Doolittle, *I Could Never Be So Lucky Again*, p. 273.

474 "Now seems to be": J. H. Doolittle to William M. Bower, Nov. 27, 1945, Box 21, DPLOC.

475 "I will be there": David M. Jones to James H. Doolittle, Nov. 26, 1945, ibid.

475 "General, I want": J. E. Manch to James H. Doolittle, Nov. 30, 1945, ibid.

475 "You may count": C. Ross Greening to J. H. Doolittle, Nov. 26, 1945, ibid.

475 "When I realize": Chase J. Nielsen to J. H. Doolittle, Dec. 1, 1945, ibid.

475 Of the eighty: J. H. Doolittle to William M. Bower, Nov. 27, 1945, ibid.

475 "The softening point": J. H. Doolittle to Mrs. Paul J. Leonard, Jan. 10, 1943, Box 4, Series II, DTRAP.

475 "the saddest letter": Colin D. Heaton, "Jimmy Doolittle and the Emergence of American Air Power," *World War II*, May 2003, p. 49.

475 "If he had to go": J. H. Doolittle to Mrs. Paul J. Leonard, Jan. 10, 1943.

475 "I found what was left": Doolittle, *I Could Never Be So Lucky Again*, p. 335.

476 "hand of Heaven": George Kennedy, "Connecticut Pilot in Doolittle's Party Says 'We Couldn't Miss,'" *Daily Boston Globe*, April 22, 1943, p. 5.

476 "The carrier action": USSBS (Pacific), Naval Analysis Division, *The Campaigns of the Pacific War* (Washington, D.C.: GPO, 1946), p. 60.

476 "My bitterness": Chennault, *Way of a Fighter*, p. 168.

476 "The invaders made": "Madness as a War Weapon," editorial, *New York Times*, Sept. 16, 1942, p. 22.

476 Nielsen asked Doolittle: Chase J. Nielsen to J. H. Doolittle, May 9, 1946, Box 20, DPLOC.

476 "The Doolittle boys": Tom Willemstyn to Mr. Freeman, April 19, 1947, Iris #1010167, AFHRA.

476 They had such a great time: Bob Morrison, "The Last Hurrah?," *Sarasota Herald-Tribune*, April 14, 1998, p. 1E.

477 "Bill is here": "Fliers Remember Lt. W. G. Farrow at Reunion," *State*, Jan. 23, 1946, in William G. Farrow Papers, Darlington Historical Commission, Darlington, S.C.

477 "When this is done": US Military Mission Moscow, Russia to War Department, Oct. 12, 1944, Iris #2053795, AFHRA.

477 Jacob DeShazer followed: Bob Dotson and Al Roker, "Jake DeShazer Describes Being Held Prisoner in World War II and Returning to Japan as a Preacher," NBC News transcript, April 18, 2002; Donald M. Goldstein and Carol Aiko DeShazer Dixon, *The Return of the Raider* (Lake Mary, Fla.: Creation House, 2010), pp. 123–31; Jacob DeShazer to Robert G. Emmens, June 23, 1949, Iris #1010169, AFHRA.

478 "I was very lost": Dotson and Roker, "Jake DeShazer Describes Being Held Prisoner in World War II and Returning to Japan as a Preacher."

478 "He appears to have": Eleanor Towns to James Doolittle, Feb. 13, 1946, Box 1, Series II, DTRAP.

478 "The nightmares": Barr, "Jap Brutality Dazed Badger Flier," p. 4.

478 A heart attack: "George Barr, 50; in Raid on Tokyo," *New York Times*, July 13, 1967, p. 37.

478 "I do not believe": J. H. Doolittle to Marcine Barr, Jan. 19, 1968, Box 3, Series IX, DPUT.

478 "He would awake": Mrs. Robert Lowell Hite, Statement in Support of Claim, Aug. 28, 1971, Box 21, ibid.

478 "It's not that I love": Los Angeles Office of Information Services, Public Information Division Office, Secretary of the Air Force, Press Release, April 21, 1955, Iris #1010174, AFHRA.

479 "Young guys like us": Jeff Wilkinson, "Buffeted by the Sea—and Waves of Fear—Raiders Flew into History," *State*, April 18, 2002, p. A11.

479 "It wasn't only": Sidney Shalett, "Only Military Targets Hit, Tokyo Raid Fliers Declare," *New York Times*, April 23, 1943, p. 1.

479 "I flew 40 missions": Elizabeth Mullener, "Robert Bourgeois, 84, Doolittle Raider," *Times Picayune*, Nov. 15, 2001, p. A-22.

479 "I think we're all": Douglas V. Radney to Ross Greening, Individual Histories questionnaire, undated (ca. 1950).

479 At the raiders' seventeenth: Carroll Glines, Speech at the Final Toast, Nov. 9, 2013.

480 "Gentleman, I propose": Richard Cole, Final Toast, Nov. 9, 2013.

SELECT BIBLIOGRAPHY

Agawa, Hiroyuki. *The Reluctant Admiral: Yamamoto and the Imperial Navy.* Translated by John Bester. New York: Kodansha International, 1979.

Arnold, H. H. *Global Mission.* New York: Harper & Brothers, 1949.

Assistant Chief of Air Staff—Intelligence, Headquarters Army Air Forces. *Mission Accomplished: Interrogations of Japanese Industrial, Military and Civil Leaders of World War II.* Washington, D.C.: GPO, 1946.

Avery, N. L. *B-25 Mitchell: The Magnificent Medium.* St. Paul, Minn.: Phalanx Publishing, 1992.

Behre, Edward. *Hirohito: Behind the Myth.* New York: Villard Books, 1989.

Bergamini, David. *Japan's Imperial Conspiracy.* New York: William Morrow, 1971.

Biddle, Francis. *In Brief Authority.* Garden City, N.Y.: Doubleday, 1962.

Bland, Larry I., ed. *The Papers of George Catlett Marshall.* Vol. 3, *"The Right Man for the Job," December 7, 1941–May 31, 1943.* Baltimore, Md.: Johns Hopkins University Press, 1991.

Blum, John Morton. *From the Morgenthau Diaries.* Vol. 2, *Years of Urgency, 1938–1941.* Boston: Houghton Mifflin, 1965.

Brereton, Lewis H. *The Brereton Diaries: The War in the Air in the Pacific, Middle East and Europe, 3 October 1941–8 May 1945.* New York: William Morrow, 1946.

Brinkley, Alan. *The Publisher: Henry Luce and His American Century.* New York: Alfred A. Knopf, 2010.

Browne, Courtney. *Tojo: The Last Banzai.* New York: Holt, Rinehart and Winston, 1967.

Bryant, Arthur. *The Turn of the Tide: A History of the War Years Based on the Diaries of Field-Marshal Lord Alanbrooke, Chief of the Imperial General Staff.* Garden City, N.Y.: Doubleday, 1957.

Buell, Thomas B. *Master of Sea Power: A Biography of Fleet Admiral Ernest J. King.* Boston: Little, Brown, 1980.

Burchett, Wilfred G. *Democracy with a Tommygun.* Melbourne, Australia: F. W. Cheshire, 1946.

Burgess, Alan. *The Longest Tunnel: The True Story of World War II's Great Escape.* Annapolis, Md.: Naval Institute Press, 1990.

Butow, Robert J. C. *Tojo and the Coming of War.* Stanford, Calif.: Stanford University Press, 1962.

Byas, Hugh. *The Japanese Enemy: His Power and His Vulnerability.* New York: Alfred A. Knopf, 1942.

Camp, LaVonne Telshaw. *Lingering Fever: A World War II Nurse's Memoir.* Jefferson, N.C.: McFarland, 1997.

Casey, Robert J. *Torpedo Junction: With the Pacific Fleet from Pearl Harbor to Midway.* Garden City, N.Y.: Halcyon House, 1944.

Chang, Iris. *The Rape of Nanking: The Forgotten Holocaust of World War II.* New York: Penguin Books, 1998.

Chennault, Claire Lee. *The Way of a Fighter: The Memoirs of Claire Lee Chennault.* Edited by Robert Hotz. New York: G. P. Putnam's Sons, 1949.

Chun, Clayton K. S. *The Doolittle Raid 1942: America's First Strike Back at Japan.* Oxford, U.K.: Osprey Publishing, 2006.

Churchill, Winston S. *The Grand Alliance.* Boston: Houghton Mifflin, 1950.

———. *The Hinge of Fate.* Boston: Houghton Mifflin, 1950.

Clark, Thurston. *Pearl Harbor Ghosts: The Legacy of December 7, 1941.* New York: Ballantine Books, 2001.

Coffey, Thomas M. *Hap: The Story of the U.S. Air Force and the Man Who Built It, General Henry H. "Hap" Arnold.* New York: Viking Press, 1982.

Cohen, Stan. *Destination: Tokyo: A Pictorial History of Doolittle's Tokyo Raid, April 18, 1942.* Missoula, Mont.: Pictorial Histories Publishing Company, 1983.

Complete Presidential Press Conferences of Franklin D. Roosevelt. Vols. 19–20, *1942.* New York: Da Capo Press, 1972.

Connally, Tom, as told to Alfred Steinberg. *My Name Is Tom Connally.* New York: Thomas Y. Crowell, 1954.

Cook, Haruko, and Theodore F. Cook. *Japan at War: An Oral History.* New York: New Press, 1992.

Cooling, Benjamin Franklin, ed. *Case Studies in the Achievement of Air Superiority.* Washington, D.C.: Center for Air Force History, 1994.

Craven, Wesley Frank, and James Lea Cate, eds. *The Army Air Forces in World War II.* Vol. 1, *Plans and Early Operations, January 1939 to August 1942.* 1948; reprint, Washington, D.C.: Office of Air Force History, 1983.

———. *The Army Air Forces in World War II.* Vol. 5, *The Pacific: Matterhorn to Nagasaki, June 1944 to August 1945.* Washington, D.C.: GPO, 1983.

Cressman, Robert J. *The Official Chronology of the U.S. Navy in World War II.* Annapolis, Md.: Naval Institute Press, 2000.

Dallek, Robert. *Franklin D. Roosevelt and American Foreign Policy, 1932–1945.* New York: Oxford University Press, 1979.

Daso, Dik Alan. *Doolittle: Aerospace Visionary.* Washington, D.C: Brassey's, 2003.

Davis, Forrest, and Ernest K. Lindley. *How War Came: An American White Paper: From the Fall of France to Pearl Harbor.* New York: Simon and Schuster, 1942.

Davis, Harry. *This Is It!* New York: Vanguard Press, 1944.

Doolittle, James H. "Jimmy," with Carroll V. Glines. *I Could Never Be So Lucky Again: An Autobiography.* New York; Bantam Books, 1991

Dorn, Frank. *Walkout: With Stilwell in Burma.* New York: Thomas Y. Crowell, 1971.

Drea, Edward J. *The 1942 Japanese General Election: Political Mobilization in Wartime Japan.* [Lawrence]: Center for East Asian Studies, University of Kansas, 1979.

Emmens, Robert G. *Guests of the Kremlin.* New York: Macmillan, 1949.

Fairbank, John King. *Chinabound: A Fifty-Year Memoir.* New York: Harper & Row, 1982.

Farmer, Rhodes. *Shanghai Harvest: A Diary of Three Years in the China War.* London: Museum Press, 1945.

Fields, Alonzo. *My 21 Years in the White House.* New York: Coward-McCann, 1961.

Fleisher, Wilfrid. *Volcanic Isle.* Garden City, N.Y.: Doubleday, Doran, 1941.

Fuchida, Mitsuo, and Masatake Okumiya. *Midway: The Battle That Doomed Japan.* Annapolis, Md.: Naval Institute Press, 1955.

Gallup, George H., ed. *The Gallup Poll: Public Opinion 1935–1971.* Vol. 1, *1935–1948.* New York: Random House, 1972.

Gibney, Frank, ed. *Sensō: The Japanese Remember the Pacific War.* Translated by Beth Cary. Armonk, N.Y.: M. E. Sharpe, 1995.

Gillon, Steven M. *Pearl Harbor: FDR Leads the Nation into War.* New York: Basic Books, 2011.

Glines, Carroll V. *The Doolittle Raid: America's Daring First Strike against Japan.* Atglen, Pa.: Schiffer Military/Aviation History, 1991.

———. *Doolittle's Tokyo Raiders.* Princeton, N.J.: D. Van Nostrand, 1964.

———. *Four Came Home.* Princeton, N.J.: D. Van Nostrand, 1966.

Goldstein, Donald M., and Carol Aiko DeShazer Dixon. *The Return of the Raider.* Lake Mary, Fla.: Creation House, 2010.

Goldstein, Donald M., and Katherine V. Dillon, eds. *The Pearl Harbor Papers: Inside the Japanese Plans.* Washington, D.C.: Brassey's, 1993.

Goodwin, Doris Kearns. *No Ordinary Time: Franklin and Eleanor Roosevelt:*

The Home Front in World War II. New York: Touchstone Book/Simon and Schuster, 1994.

Greening, C. Ross. *Not As Briefed: From the Doolittle Raid to a German Stalag.* Compiled and edited by Dorothy Greening and Karen Morgan Driscoll. Pullman: Washington State University Press, 2001.

Grew, Joseph C. *Ten Years in Japan: A Contemporary Record Drawn from the Diaries and Private and Official Papers of Joseph C. Grew.* New York: Simon and Schuster, 1944.

Griffin, Alexander T. *A Ship to Remember: The Saga of the* Hornet. New York: Howell, Soskin, 1943.

Guillain, Robert. *I Saw Tokyo Burning: An Eyewitness Narrative from Pearl Harbor to Hiroshima.* Translated by William Byron. Garden City, N.Y.: Doubleday, 1981.

Halsey, William F., and J. Bryan III. *Admiral Halsey's Story.* New York: Whittlesey House/McGraw-Hill, 1947.

Hammer, Joshua. *Yokohama Burning: The Deadly 1923 Earthquake and Fire That Helped Forge the Path to World War II.* New York: Free Press, 2006.

Harriman, W. Averell, and Elie Abel. *Special Envoy: to Churchill and Stalin, 1941–1946.* New York: Random House, 1975.

Harris, Mark Jonathan, Franklin D. Mitchell, and Steven J. Schechter, *The Homefront: America during World War II.* New York: G. P. Putnam's Sons, 1984.

Harris, Sheldon H. *Factories of Death: Japanese Biological Warfare, 1932–45, and the American Cover-Up.* London: Routledge, 1994.

Hassett, William D. *Off the Record with F.D.R., 1942–1945.* New Brunswick, N.J.: Rutgers University Press, 1958.

Havens, Thomas R. H. *Valley of Darkness: The Japanese People and World War II.* New York: W. W. Norton, 1978.

Holley, Irving Brinton, Jr. *Buying Aircraft: Matériel Procurement for the Army Air Forces*, in *Special Studies*. Washington, D.C.: Center of Military History, United States Army, 1989.

Holmes, W. J. *Double-Edged Secrets: U.S. Naval Intelligence Operations in the Pacific War during World War II.* Annapolis, Md.: Naval Institute Press, 1979.

Hoppes, Jonna Doolittle. *Calculated Risk: The Extraordinary Life of Jimmy Doolittle—Aviation Pioneer and World War II Hero.* Santa Monica, Calif.: Santa Monica Press, 2005.

———, comp. *Just Doing My Job: Stories from Service in World War II.* Santa Monica, Calif.: Santa Monica Press, 2009.

Hoyt, Edwin P. *Japan's War: The Great Pacific Conflict.* New York: Cooper Square Press, 2001.

———. *Warlord: Tojo against the World.* Lanham, Md.: Scarborough House, 1993.

Hull, Cordell. *The Memoirs of Cordell Hull.* Vol. 2. New York: Macmillan, 1948.

Huston, John W., ed. *American Airpower Comes of Age: General Henry H. "Hap" Arnold's World War II Diaries.* Vol. 1. Maxwell Air Force Base, Ala.: Air University Press, 2002.

Ickes, Harold L. *The Secret Diary of Harold L. Ickes.* Vol. 3, *The Lowering Clouds, 1939–1941.* New York: Simon and Schuster, 1954.

Israel, Fred L., ed. *The War Diary of Breckinridge Long: Selections from the Years 1939–1944.* Lincoln: University of Nebraska Press, 1966.

Johnson, Clayton F., et al., eds. *Dictionary of American Naval Fighting Ships.* Vol. 3. Washington, D.C.: GPO, 1968.

Karig, Walter, and Welbourn Kelley, *Battle Report: Pearl Harbor to Coral Sea* New York: Rinehart, 1944.

Kelly, William W., ed. *Fanning the Flames: Fans and Consumer Culture in Contemporary Japan.* Albany: State University of New York Press, 2004.

Kennedy, David M., ed. *Library of Congress World War II Companion.* New York: Simon and Schuster, 2007.

Kernan, Alvin B. *Crossing the Line: A Bluejacket's Odyssey in World War II.* New Haven, Conn.: Yale University Press, 2007.

Ketchum, Richard M. *The Borrowed Years, 1938–1941: America on the Way to War.* New York: Random House, 1989.

Kimball, Warren F., ed. *Churchill & Roosevelt: The Complete Correspondence.* Vol. 1, *Alliance Emerging, October 1933–November* 1942. Princeton, N.J.: Princeton University Press, 1984.

King, Ernest J., and Walter Muir Whitehill. *Fleet Admiral King: A Naval Record.* New York: W. W. Norton, 1952.

Laird, Nathan. "We Only Want Volunteers: An Examination of the Doolittle Raid, April 18, 1942." M.A. thesis, University of New Brunswick, 1998.

Large, Stephen S. *Emperor Hirohito and Shōwa Japan: A Political Biography.* London: Routledge, 1992.

Larrabee, Eric. *Commander in Chief: Franklin Delano Roosevelt, His Lieutenants, and Their War.* New York: Harper & Row, 1987.

Lary, Diana. *The Chinese People at War: Human Suffering and Social Transformation, 1937–1945.* New York: Cambridge University Press, 2010.

Lash, Joseph P. *Eleanor and Franklin: The Story of Their Relationship, Based on Eleanor Roosevelt's Private Papers.* New York: W. W. Norton, 1971.

Lawson, Ted. W. *Thirty Seconds over Tokyo.* Edited by Bob Considine. New York: Random House, 1953.

Layton, Edwin T., with Roger Pineau and John Costello. *"And I Was There": Pearl Harbor and Midway—Breaking the Secrets.* New York: William Morrow, 1985.

Leahy, William D. *I Was There: The Personal Story of the Chief of Staff to Presi-*

dents Roosevelt and Truman Based on His Notes and Diaries Made at the Time. New York: Whittlesey House/McGraw-Hill, 1950.

Leck, Greg. *Captives of Empire: The Japanese Internment of Allied Civilians in China, 1941–1945,* Bangor, Pa.: Shandy Press, 2006.

Levin, Linda Lotridge. *The Making of FDR: The Story of Stephen T. Early, America's First Modern Press Secretary.* Amherst, N.Y.: Prometheus Books, 2008.

Loewenheim, Francis L., Harold D. Langley, and Manfred Jonas, eds. *Roosevelt and Churchill: Their Secret Wartime Correspondence.* New York: Saturday Review Press/E. P. Dutton, 1975.

Lord, Walter. *Day of Infamy.* New York: Henry Holt, 1957.

Lundstrom, John B. *The First Team: Pacific Naval Air Combat from Pearl Harbor to Midway.* Annapolis, Md.: Naval Institute Press, 1984.

Mason, John T., Jr., ed. *The Pacific War Remembered: An Oral History Collection.* Annapolis, Md.: Naval Institute Press, 1986.

Materials on the Trial of Former Servicemen of the Japanese Army Charged with Manufacturing and Employing Bacteriological Weapons. Moscow: Foreign Languages Publishing House, 1950.

McIntire, Ross T., in collaboration with George Creel. *White House Physician.* New York: G. P. Putnam's Sons, 1946.

McMurtrie, Francis E., ed. *Jane's Fighting Ships: 1941.* London: Sampson Low, Marston and Co., 1942.

Mears, Frederick. *Carrier Combat.* Garden City, N.Y.: Doubleday, Doran, 1944.

Meilinger, Phillip S. *Airmen and Air Theory.* Maxwell Air Force Base, Ala.: Air University Press, 2001.

Merrill, James M. *Target Tokyo: The Halsey-Doolittle Raid.* Chicago: Rand McNally, 1964.

Mooney, James L., ed. *Dictionary of American Naval Fighting Ships.* Vol. 6 (Washington D.C.: GPO, 1976.

———. *Dictionary of American Naval Fighting Ships.* Vol. 7. Washington D.C.: GPO, 1981.

Morison, Samuel Eliot. *History of the United States Naval Operations in World War II.* Vol. 3, *The Rising Sun in the Pacific, 1931–April 1942.* 1948; reprint, Boston: Little, Brown, 1988.

———. *The Two-Ocean War: A Short History of the United States Navy in the Second World War.* Boston: Atlantic Monthly Press Book/Little, Brown, 1963.

Morris, John. *Traveler from Tokyo.* New York: Sheridan House, 1944.

Nelson, Craig. *The First Heroes: The Extraordinary Story of the Doolittle Raid—America's First World War II Victory.* New York: Viking Press, 2002.

Overseas Press Club of America. *Deadline Delayed.* New York: E. P. Dutton, 1947.

Pakula, Hannah. *The Last Empress: Madame Chiang Kai-shek and the Birth of Modern China*. New York: Simon and Schuster, 2009.

Parshall, Jonathan, and Anthony Tully. *Shattered Sword: The Untold Story of the Battle of Midway*. Washington, D.C.: Potomac Books, 2005.

Perkins, Frances. *The Roosevelt I Knew*. New York: Viking Press, 1947.

Phillips, Cabell, *Dateline: Washington: The Story of National Affairs Journalism in the Life and Times of the National Press Club*. New York: Greenwood Press, 1968.

Poling, Forrest K. *From Farm Fields to Airfields*. Superior Township, Mich.: Zorado Press, 2006.

Potter, E. B. *Bull Halsey*. Annapolis, Md.: Naval Institute Press, 1985.

———. *Nimitz*. Annapolis, Md.: Naval Institute Press, 1976.

Powell. John B. *My Twenty-Five Years in China*. New York: Macmillan, 1945.

Prados, John. *Combined Fleet Decoded: The Secret History of American Intelligence and the Japanese Navy in World War II*. New York: Random House, 1995.

Prange, Gordon W., with Donald M. Goldstein and Katherine V. Dillon. *At Dawn We Slept: The Untold Story of Pearl Harbor*. New York: McGraw-Hill, 1981.

———. *God's Samurai: Lead Pilot at Pearl Harbor*. Washington, D.C.: Brassy's, 1990.

———. *Miracle at Midway*. New York: McGraw-Hill, 1982.

Pritchard, R. John, and Sonia Magbanua Zaide, eds. *The Tokyo War Crimes Trial*. 22 vols. New York: Garland Publishing, 1981.

Reilly, Michael F., as told to William J. Slocum. *Reilly of the White House*. New York: Simon and Schuster, 1947.

Reynolds, Quentin. *The Amazing Mr. Doolittle: A Biography of Lieutenant General James H. Doolittle*. New York: Appleton-Century-Crofts, 1953.

Robinson, Greg. *By Order of the President: FDR and the Internment of Japanese Americans*. Cambridge, Mass.: Harvard University Press, 2001.

Roll, David L. *The Hopkins Touch: Harry Hopkins and the Forging of the Alliance to Defeat Hitler*. New York: Oxford University Press, 2013.

Roosevelt, Eleanor. *This I Remember*. New York: Harper & Brothers, 1949.

Roosevelt, Elliott, ed., *F.D.R.: His Personal Letters, 1928–1945*. Vol. 2. New York: Duell, Sloan and Pearce, 1950.

Roosevelt, James, and Sidney Shalett. *Affectionately, F.D.R.: A Son's Story of a Lonely Man*. New York: Harcourt, Brace, 1959.

Rose, Lisle A. *The Ship That Held the Line*. Annapolis, Md.: Naval Institute Press, 1995.

Rosenman, Samuel I. *Working with Roosevelt*. New York: Harper & Brothers, 1952.

————, comp. *The Public Papers and Addresses of Franklin D. Roosevelt*. 1941 volume, *The Call to Battle Stations*. New York: Harper & Brothers, 1950.

————. *The Public Papers and Addresses of Franklin D. Roosevelt*. 1942 volume, *Humanity on the Defensive*. New York: Harper & Brothers, 1950.

Russell, Ronald W. *No Right to Win: A Continuing Dialogue with Veterans of the Battle of Midway*. New York: iUniverse, 2006.

Sakai, Saburo, with Martin Caidin and Fred Saito. *Samurai!* Garden City, N.Y.: Nelson Doubleday, 1978.

Schultz, Duane. *The Doolittle Raid*. New York: St. Martin's Press, 1988.

Simonson, G. R., ed. *The History of the American Aircraft Industry: An Anthology*. Cambridge, Mass.: MIT Press, 1968.

Symonds, Craig L. *The Battle of Midway*. New York: Oxford University Press, 2011.

Sherwood, Robert E. *Roosevelt and Hopkins: An Intimate History*. New York: Harper & Brothers, 1948.

Shibata, Takehiko, and Katsuhiro Hara. *Dōrittoru Kūshū Hiroku: Nichibei Zenchōsa* [Doolittle's Tokyo Raid, 18 April 1942]. Tokyo: Ariadone Kikaku, 2003.

Shigenori, Togo. *The Cause of Japan*. Translated and edited by Togo Fumihiko and Ben Bruce Blakeney. New York: Simon and Schuster, 1956.

Sims, Jack A., with A. B. Cook. *First over Japan: An Autobiography of a Doolittle-Tokyo Raider*. Fort Myers, Fla.: Southpointe Press, 2002.

Smith, A. Merriman. *Thank You, Mr. President: A White House Notebook*. New York: Harper & Brothers, 1946.

Spector, Ronald H. *In the Ruins of Empire: The Japanese Surrender and the Battle for Postwar Asia*. New York: Random House, 2007.

Stafford, Edward P. *The Big E: The Story of the USS Enterprise*. New York: Random House, 1962.

Standley, William H., and Arthur A. Ageton. *Admiral Ambassador to Russia*. Chicago: Henry Regnery, 1955.

Steele, Richard W. *The First Offensive 1942: Roosevelt, Marshall and the Making of American Strategy*. Bloomington: Indiana University Press, 1973.

Stem, Margaret Meadows. *Tall and Free as Meant by God*. New York: Hearthstone Book/Carlton Press, 1969.

Stephan, John J. *Hawaii under the Rising Sun: Japan's Plans for Conquest after Pearl Harbor*. Honolulu: University of Hawaii Press, 1984.

Stillwell, Paul, ed. *Air Raid: Pearl Harbor! Recollections of a Day of Infamy*. Annapolis, Md.: Naval Institute Press, 1981.

Stilwell, Joseph W. *The Stilwell Papers*. Edited by Theodore H. White. New York: William Sloane, 1948.

Stimson, Henry L., and McGeorge Bundy. *On Active Service in Peace and War*. New York: Octagon Books, 1971.

Takagaki, Sekijiro, ed. *The Japan Yearbook, 1941–1942*. Tokyo: Foreign Affairs Association of Japan, 1941.

Taylor, Theodore. *The Magnificent Mitscher*. New York: W. W. Norton, 1954.

Thomas, Lowell, and Edward Jablonski. *Doolittle: A Biography*. Garden City, N.Y.: Doubleday, 1976.

Tibbets, Paul W., Jr. *Return of the Enola Gay*. Columbus, Ohio: Mid Coast Marketing, 1998.

Tillman, Barrett. *Clash of the Carriers: The True Story of the Marianas Turkey Shoot of World War II*. New York: NAL Calider, 2006.

Time, Life, and *Fortune*, correspondents of. *December 7: The First Thirty Hours*. New York: Alfred A. Knopf, 1942.

Toland, John. *But Not in Shame: The Six Months after Pearl Harbor*. New York: Random House, 1961.

———. *Infamy: Pearl Harbor and Its Aftermath*. Garden City, N.Y.: Doubleday, 1982.

———. *The Rising Sun: The Decline and Fall of the Japanese Empire, 1936–1945*. New York: Random House, 1970.

Tolischus, Otto D. *Tokyo Record*. New York: Reynal & Hitchcock, 1943.

Toll, Ian W. *Pacific Crucible: War at Sea in the Pacific, 1941–1942*. New York: W. W. Norton, 2012.

Tuchman, Barbara W. *Stilwell and the American Experience in China, 1911–1945*. New York: Macmillan, 1971.

Twitchett, Denis, and John K. Fairbank, eds. *The Cambridge History of China*. Vol. 13, *Republican China, 1912–1949*. Pt. 2. Cambridge: Cambridge University Press, 1986.

Tully, Grace. *F.D.R.: My Boss*. New York: Charles Scribner's Sons, 1949.

Ugaki, Matome. *Fading Victory: The Diary of Admiral Matome Ugaki, 1941–1945*, Edited by Donald M. Goldstein and Katherine V. Dillon. Translated by Masataka Chihaya. Pittsburgh, Pa.: University of Pittsburgh Press, 1991.

U.S. Department of State. *Foreign Relations of the United States: Diplomatic Papers, 1942, China*. Washington, D.C.: GPO, 1956.

U.S. Department of State. *Foreign Relations of the United States: Diplomatic Papers, 1942*. Vol. 3, *Europe*. Washington, D.C.: GPO, 1961.

U.S. Department of State. *Foreign Relations of the United States: Diplomatic Papers, 1943*. Vol. 3, *The British Commonwealth, Eastern Europe, The Far East*. Washington, D.C.: GPO, 1963.

Wallin, Homer N. *Pearl Harbor: Why, How, Fleet Salvage and Final Appraisal*. Washington, D.C.: GPO, 1968.

War History Office, National Institute for Defense Studies. *Hokutō Hōmen Kaigun Sakusen* [Northeastern Naval Operations]. *Senshi Sōsho* [War History Series], vol. 29. Tokyo: Asagumo Shinbunsha, 1968.

———. *Hondo Hōmen Kaigun Sakusen* [Naval Operations in Home Waters]. *Senshi Sōsho* [War History Series], vol. 85. Tokyo: Asagumo Shinbunsha, 1975.

Ward, Geoffrey C., ed. *Closest Companion: The Unknown Story of the Intimate Friendship between Franklin Roosevelt and Margaret Suckley*. Boston: Houghton Mifflin, 1995.

Watson, C. Hoyt. *DeShazer*. Winona Lake, Ind.: Light and Life Press, 1972.

Welles, Sumner. *The Time for Decision*. New York: Harper & Brothers, 1944.

White, Theodore H. *In Search of History: A Personal Adventure*. New York: Harper & Row, 1978.

Williams, Peter, and David Wallace. *Unit 731: Japan's Secret Biological Warfare in World War II*. New York: Free Press, 1989.

Willmott, H. P. *The Barrier and the Javelin: Japanese and Allied Pacific Strategies, February to June 1942*. Annapolis, Md.: Naval Institute Press, 1983.

Wilson, Frank J., and Beth Day. *Special Agent: Twenty-Five Years with the U.S. Treasury Department and Secret Service*. London: Frederick Muller, 1965.

Winant, John Gilbert. *Letter from Grosvenor Square: An Account of a Stewardship*. Boston: Houghton Mifflin, 1947.

Winfield, Betty Houchin. *FDR and the News Media*. Urbana: University of Illinois Press, 1990.

Winton, John. *Ultra in the Pacific: How Breaking Japanese Codes & Cyphers Affected Naval Operations against Japan, 1941–1945*. Annapolis, Md.: Naval Institute Press, 1993.

Wooldridge, E. T., ed. *Carrier Warfare in the Pacific: An Oral History Collection*. Washington, D.C.: Smithsonian Institution Press, 1993.

Yoshimura, Akira. *Zero Fighter*. Translated by Retsu Kaiho and Michael Gregson. Westport, Conn.: Praeger, 1996.

Zevin, B. D., ed. *Nothing to Fear: The Selected Addresses of Franklin Delano Roosevelt, 1932–1945*. Boston: Houghton Mifflin, 1946.

INDEX